THE MOTHER'S VISION

THE MOTHER'S VISION

Selections from *Questions and Answers*

The Mother

SRI AUROBINDO ASHRAM
PONDICHERRY

First edition 2002
Reprinted 2005

(Typeset in 10.5/13 Times)

Price: Rs. 230.00
ISBN 81-7058-687-9

Published by Sri Aurobindo Ashram Publication Department
Pondicherry - 605 002
Website: http://sabda.sriaurobindoashram.org
Printed at Sri Aurobindo Ashram Press, Pondicherry

PRINTED IN INDIA

Publisher's Note

This book contains a selection of the Mother's conversations during the years 1929-31 and 1950-58. Covering a wide range of subjects in considerable depth, they give us a glimpse of her vision of existence. It is an inspiring vision of the future evolution of humanity and the promise of a divine life on earth.

The conversations belong to two distinct groups. During the first period, from 1929 to 1931, the Mother spoke informally with a small group of Ashramites who met her every week, answering questions about life and Yoga. During the second, from 1950 to 1958, she spoke to a larger audience, the Ashramites and students who attended her evening classes at the Ashram playground. The Mother often began by reading out to the class a passage from a work by Sri Aurobindo or herself. She then commented on the passage or invited questions on it. The conversations of 1929-31 were spoken in English; those of the 1950s were spoken in French and appear here in English translation.

The compilation was made by Georges Van Vrekhem. Details about the book are given in the Note on the Texts. There is also a Glossary for those who are not familiar with the terms used by Sri Aurobindo and the Mother.

NOTE ON PUNCTUATION

... Three dots indicate a brief pause in the Mother's speech. (A fourth dot is added when the pause comes at the end of a sentence.)

[...] Three dots within square brackets indicate an omission by the editors of some part of the text.

Contents

19. The Supramental

20. The Present Situation

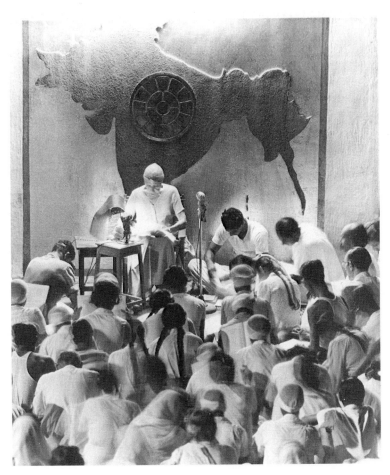

The Mother with her French class in 1954

The Mother with members of her French class
at the Ashram Playground in 1954

CHAPTER 1

The Divine and His Creation

God, the Divine, the Supreme

It all depends on what meaning you put into the word "God". It is a word (I have told you this at least four or five times) to express "something" you do not know but are trying to attain. Well, if you have received a religious education, you are accustomed to call this "God". If you have received a more positivist and also a more philosophical education, you are accustomed to call this by all sorts of names, and you may at the same time have the idea that it is the supreme truth. If one wants to speak of God and describe him, one is obliged to make use of things which are the most inaccessible to our consciousness, and to call God what is beyond anything we know and can grasp and be — all that is too far for us to be able to understand, we call God. Only some religions (there are some) give a precise form to the godhead; and sometimes they give several forms and they have several gods; sometimes they give one form and have only one God; but all this is human fabrication.

There is "something", there is a reality which is beyond all our expressions, but which we can succeed in contacting by practising a discipline. We can identify ourselves with it. Once one is identified with it one knows what it is, but one cannot express it, for words cannot say it. So, if you use one kind of vocabulary, if you have a particular mental conviction, you will use the vocabulary corresponding to that conviction. If you belong to another group which has another way of speaking, you will call it or even think about it in that way. I am telling you this to give you the true impression, that there is something there which cannot be — grasped by thought — but which exists. But the name you give it matters little, that's of no importance, it *exists*.

And so the only thing to do is to enter into contact with it — not to give it a name or describe it. In fact, there is hardly any use giving it a name or describing it. One must try to enter into contact, to concentrate upon it, live it, live that reality, and whatever the name you give it is not at all important once you have the experience. The experience alone counts. And when people associate the experience with a particular expression — and in so narrow a way, so closed up in itself that apart from this formula one can find nothing — that is an inferiority. One must be able to *live* that reality through all possible paths, all occasions, all formations; one must live it, for that indeed is true, for that is supremely good, that is all-powerful, that knows all, that... Yes, one can live that, but one cannot speak about it. And if one does speak, all that one says about it has no great importance. It is only one way of speaking, that is all.

There is an entire line of philosophers and people who have replaced the notion of God by the notion of an impersonal Absolute or by a notion of Truth or a notion of justice or even by a notion of progress — of something eternally progressive; but for one who has within him the capacity of identifying himself with that, what has been said about it hasn't much importance. Sometimes one may read a whole book of philosophy and not progress a step farther. Sometimes one may be quite a fervent devotee of a religion and not progress. There are people who have spent entire lifetimes seated in contemplation and attained nothing. There are people (we have well-known examples) who used to do the most modest of manual works, like a cobbler mending old shoes, and who had an experience. It is altogether beyond what one thinks and says of it. It is some gift that's there, that is all. And all that is needed is to be that — to succeed in identifying oneself with it and live it. At times you read one sentence in a book and that leads you there. Sometimes you read entire books of philosophy or religion and they get you nowhere. There are people, however, whom the reading of philosophy books helps to go ahead. But all these things are secondary.

There is only one thing that's important: that is a sincere and persistent will, for these things don't happen in a twinkling. So one must persevere. When someone feels that he is not advancing, he must not get discouraged; he must try to find out what it is in the nature that is opposing, and then make the necessary progress. And suddenly one goes forward. And when you reach the end you have an experience. And what is remarkable is that people who have followed altogether different paths, with altogether different mental constructions, from the greatest believer to the most unbelieving, even materialists, have arrived at that experience, it is the same for everyone. Because it is true — because it is real, because it is the sole reality. And it is quite simply *that*. I do not say anything more. This is of no importance, the way one speaks about it, what is important is to follow the path, *your* path, no matter which — yes, to go there.

17 February 1954

*

What exactly is meant by "the impersonal Divine"?

It's what is called in some philosophies and religions the Formless; something that's beyond all form, even the forms of thought, you see, not necessarily physical forms: forms of thought, forms of movement. It is the conception of something which is beyond not only what can be thought or conceived or seen even with the most subtle eyes, but all that has any kind of perceptible form whatever, even vibrations more subtle than those which infinitely overpass all human perceptions, even in the highest states of being, something which is beyond all manifestation of any order whatever — usually that's how we define the impersonal God. He has nothing, none of the qualities we can conceive of, He is beyond all qualification. It is obviously the quest of something which is the opposite of the creation, and that is why some religions have introduced the idea of what they call Nirvana, that is, of something which is nothing; it is the same quest, the same attempt to find something which would be the opposite of all that we can conceive. So finally we define It, because how can we speak of It? But in experience one tries to go beyond all that belongs to the manifested world, and that is what we call the impersonal Divine.

20 July 1955

*

What does "to seek after the Impersonal" mean?

Oh! it's very much in fashion in the West, my child. All those who are tired or disgusted with the God taught by the Chaldean religions, and especially by the Christian religion — a single God, jealous, severe, despotic and so much in the image of man that one wonders if it is not a demiurge as Anatole France said — these people when they want to lead a spiritual life no longer want the personal God, because they are too frightened lest the personal God resemble the one they have been taught about; they want an impersonal Godhead, something that doesn't *at all* resemble — or as little as possible — the human being; that's what they want.

But Sri Aurobindo says — something he has always said — that there are the godheads of the Overmind who indeed are very similar — we have said this several times — very similar to human beings, infinitely greater and more powerful but with resemblances which are a little too striking. Beyond these there is the impersonal Godhead, the impersonal Divine; but beyond the impersonal Divine there is the Divine who is the Person himself; and we must go through the Impersonal to reach the Supreme Divine who is beyond.

Only it is good, as I said, for those who have been put by education into contact with too individual, too personal a God, to seek the impersonal Divine, because this liberates them from many superstitions. After that if they are capable they will go farther and have once again a personal contact with a Divine who indeed is beyond all these other godheads.

20 July 1955

*

One of the great difficulties for most philosophies is that they have never recognised or studied the different planes of existence, the different regions of the being. They have the Supreme and then the Creation and then that's all, nothing between the two. This makes explanations very difficult.... All explanations, in the last analysis, are simply languages — there are languages which make understanding easier and others which make it more difficult. And some of these theories make the understanding of things very difficult — while if you recognise and study and become aware of the different intermediary states between the most material Nature and the Supreme Origin, if you recognise and become conscious of all the intermediary regions, of all the inner states of being and all the outer regions, that can explain many problems. We have already studied this in connection with determinisms. If you say that the determinism is absolute and remain there, you understand nothing; it is quite obvious that all the events of life give you the lie; or else the problem is so complicated that you can't get hold of it. But if you understand that there are a large number of determinisms acting upon each other, interpenetrating, changing the action of one determinism by the action of another, then the problem becomes comprehensible.

It is the same thing for explaining the action of the Divine in the universe. If you take a central creative Force or a central creative Consciousness or a central immobile Witness, and then the universe, only that, nothing between the two, you cannot understand. There are people who have used this in such a naive way! They have made a Creator God and then his creatures. So all the problems come up. He has made the world, with what? Some tell you it is from the dust, but what is it, this dust? What was it doing before it was used to make a world?... Or from nothing! A universe was created out of nothing — that is foolish! it is very awkward for a logical mind. And over and above all that, you are told that He did this consciously, deliberately, and when he had finished he exclaimed, "Look, it is very good." Then, those who are in the universe reply, "We don't find it so good. It is perhaps very good for you but not for us."

These are naive conceptions. They are simply ignorant and naive conceptions which make the problem of the universe absolutely incomprehensible. And all these explanations are inadmissible for a mind which is ever so slightly awakened. That is why you are told, "Don't try to understand, you will never understand." But that is mental laziness, it is the mind's bad will. You see, one feels within oneself that, because one has this kind of power of thought-activity, this aspiration to find a light, a solution, it must correspond to something, otherwise... otherwise, truly (I think I have written this somewhere), if the universe were reduced to that simple notion, well, it would be the most sinister of farces and I should very well understand those who have declared, "Run away, get out of it as fast as possible." Unfortunately, I don't see how they would be able to get out of it, for there is nothing else — how can you get out of something which alone exists? So, one enters a vicious circle, one turns round and round and this leads quite naturally to mental despair. But when one has the key — there are one or two keys, but there is one which opens all the doors — when one has the key, one follows one's road and little by little understands *the* Thing.

28 April 1951

*

What does Sri Aurobindo mean by an integral idea of the Divine?

Everyone forms an idea of the Divine for himself according to his personal taste, his possibilities of understanding, his mental preferences, and even his desires. People form the idea of the Divine they want, the Divine they wish to meet, and so naturally they limit their realisation considerably.

But if we can come to understand that the Divine is all that we can conceive of, and infinitely more, we begin to progress towards integrality. Integrality is an extremely difficult thing for the human consciousness, which begins to be conscious only by limiting itself. But still, with a little effort, for those who know how to play with mental activities, it is possible to widen oneself sufficiently to approach something integral.

You form an idea of the Divine which suits your own nature and your own conception, don't you? So if you want to get out of yourself a little and attempt to do a truly integral yoga, you must try to understand that the Divine is not only what you think or feel Him to be, but also what others think and feel Him to be — and in addition something that nobody can think and feel.

So, if you understand this, you have taken the first step on the path of integrality.

4 January 1956

The Oneness of Everything

Sweet Mother, here it is written: "All are linked together by a secret Oneness." (Sri Aurobindo) What is this secret Oneness?

It is precisely the divine Presence.

Because the Divine is essentially one, and yet He has subdivided Himself apparently in all beings, and in this way recreated the primordial Oneness. And it is because of this divine Oneness — which, however, appears fragmented in beings — that the Unity is re-established in its essence. And when one becomes conscious of this, one has the joy of the consciousness of this Oneness. But those who are not conscious — what they miss is the joy of consciousness. But the fact remains the same.

Sri Aurobindo says: the Oneness exists; whether you are aware of it or not, it exists, in reality it makes no difference; but it makes a difference to you: if you are conscious, you have the joy; if you are not conscious, you miss this joy.[...]

Whether you know it or not, whether you want it or not, you are all united by the divine Presence which, though it appears fragmented, is yet One. The Divine is One, He only appears fragmented in things and beings. And because this Unity is a fact, whether you are aware of it or not doesn't alter the fact at all. And whether you want it or not, you are in spite of everything subject to this Unity.

This is what I have explained to you I don't know how many times: you think you are separate from one another, but it is the same single Substance which is in you all, despite differences in appearance; and a vibration in one centre automatically awakens a vibration in another.[...]

Everything turns around the consciousness, the fact of being or not being conscious. And it is only in the supreme Consciousness that you can attain the perfect expression of yourself.

But that the Oneness exists, even if you feel just the opposite, is a fact you can do nothing about, for it is a divine action and a divine fact — it is a divine action and a divine fact. If you are conscious of the Divine, you become conscious of this fact. If you are not conscious of the Divine, the fact exists but you simply are not conscious of it — that's all.

So, everything turns around a phenomenon of consciousness. And the world is in a state of obscurity, suffering, misery, of... everything, all it is, simply because it is not conscious of the Divine, because it has cut off the connection in its consciousness, because its consciousness is separated from the Divine. That is to say, it has become unconscious.

For the true consciousness is the divine Consciousness. If you cut yourself off from the divine Consciousness, you become absolutely unconscious; that is exactly what has happened. And so, everything there is, the world as it is, your consciousness as it is, things in the state they are in, are the result of this separation of the consciousness and its immediate obscuration.

The minute the individual consciousness is separated from the divine Consciousness, it enters what we call the inconscience, and it is this inconscience that is the cause of all its miseries.

But all that is, is essentially divine, and the divine Oneness is a fact, you can't do anything about it; all your unconsciousness and all your denials will change nothing — it is a fact, it's like that.

And the conclusion is this, that the true transformation is the transformation of consciousness — all the rest will follow automatically.[...]

Does the inconscient aspire to become conscious?

No. It is the Divine in the inconscient who aspires for the Divine in the consciousness. That is to say, without the Divine there would be no aspiration; without the consciousness hidden in the inconscient, there would be no possibility of changing the inconscience to consciousness. But because at the very heart of the inconscient there is the divine Consciousness, you aspire, and necessarily — this is what he says — automatically, mechanically, the sacrifice is made. And this is why when one says, "It is not *you* who aspire, it is the Divine, it is not *you* who make progress, it is the Divine, it is not *you* who are conscious, it is the Divine" these are not mere words, it is a fact. And it is simply your ignorance and your unconsciousness which prevent you from realising it.

29 February 1956

*

If you analyse carefully, you see, for instance, that all that you think has been thought by others, that these are things which circulate and pass through you, but you have not produced this thought, you are not the originator of this thought. All your reactions come from atavism, from those who gave you birth and from the environment in which you have lived, from all the impressions which have accumulated in you and constituted something which seems to you yourself, yet which is not produced by you, but merely felt and experienced; you become aware of it in passing, but it is not you who created it, not you who gave it birth.

It could be said that these are like sounds — any kind of sounds: words, music, anything — recorded by an instrument, then reproduced by another instrument which plays them back like a gramophone, for instance. You wouldn't say that the gramophone has created the sound you hear, would you? That would never occur to you. But as you are under the illusion of your separate personality, these thoughts which cross your mind and find expression, these feelings which pass through your vital and find expression, you think, have come from you; but nothing comes from you. Where is the "you" which can create all that?

You must go deep, deep within, and find the eternal essence of your being to know the creative reality in yourself. And once you have found that, you will realise that it is one single thing, the same in all others, and so where is your separate personality? Nothing's left any longer.

Yes, these are recording and reproducing instruments, and there are always what might be called distortions — they may be distortions for the better, they may be distortions for the worse, they may be fairly great changes; the inner combinations are such that things are not reproduced exactly as they passed from one to the other because the instrument is very complex. But it is one and the same thing which is moved by a conscious will, quite independent of all personal wills.

When the Buddha wanted to make his disciples understand these things, he used to tell them: every time you send out a vibration, a desire for example, the desire for some particular thing, your desire starts circulating from one person to another, from one to another across the universe and will go right round and come back to you. And as it is not only one thing but a world of things, and as you are not the only transmitting centre — all individuals are transmitting centres — it is such a confusion that you lose your bearings in there.

But these vibrations move about in a single, absolutely identical field; it is only the complication and interception of the vibrations which give you the impression of something independent or separate.

But there's nothing separate or independent; there is only *one* Substance, *one* Force, *one* Consciousness, *one* Will, which moves in countless ways of being.

And it is so complicated that one is no longer aware of it, but if one steps back and follows the movement, no matter which line of movement, one can see very clearly that the vibrations propagate themselves, one following another, one following another, one following another, and that in fact there is only one unity — unity of Substance, unity of Consciousness, unity of Will. And that is the only reality. Outwardly there is a kind of illusion: the illusion of separation and the illusion of difference.[...]

From the minute you become conscious of the Unity — unity of Force, unity of Consciousness and unity of Will — well, you no longer have the perception which makes you quite separate from others, so that you do not know what goes on in them, they are strangers to you, you are shut up as it were in your own skin, and have no contact with others except quite externally and superficially. But this happens precisely because you have not realised in yourself the perception of this oneness of Consciousness, Force and Will — even of material vibrations.

It is the complexity which makes this perception difficult — for our faculties of perception are quite linear and very one-sided; so when we want to understand, we are immediately assailed by countless things which are almost inconsistent with each other and intermix in such an intricate way that one can no longer make out the lines and follow things — one suddenly enters a whirlwind.

But this is because... For instance, most men think one thought after another, even as they have to say one word after another — they can't say more than one word at the same time, you know, or else they stammer. Well, most people think like that, they think one thought after another, and so their whole consciousness has a linear movement. But one begins to perceive things only when one can see spherically, globally, think spherically, that is, have innumerable thoughts and perceptions simultaneously.

Naturally, up to now, if one wanted to describe things, one had to describe them one after another, for one can't say ten words at once, one says one word after another; and that is why all one says is practically quite incapable of expressing the truth, quite incapable. For we have to say one thing after another — the minute we say them one after another, they are no longer true. They must all be said at the same time, just as they can all be seen at the same time, and each one in its place.

So, when one begins to see like this — to see, to discern, to feel, to think, to will like this one — draws near the Truth. But so long as one sees as one speaks, oh, what a lamentable poverty!

8 February 1956

*

What is the role of the spirit?

One might say that it is both the conscious intermediary between the Supreme and the manifestation, and the meeting-place of the manifestation with the Supreme.

Spirit is capable of understanding and communicating with the highest Godhead and at the same time it is the purest, one might say the least distorted intermediary of the highest Godhead in the outermost manifestation. It is spirit which, with the help of the soul, turns the consciousness towards the Highest, the Divine, and it is in the spirit that the consciousness can begin to understand the Divine.

It might be said that what is called "spirit" is the atmosphere brought into the material world by the Grace so that it may awaken to the consciousness of its origin and aspire to return to it. It is indeed a kind of atmosphere which liberates, opens the doors, sets the consciousness free. This is what enables the realisation of the truth and gives aspiration its full power of accomplishment.

From a higher standpoint, this could be put in another way: it is this action, this luminous and liberating influence that is known as "spirit". All that opens to us the road to the supreme realities, pulls us out from the mud of the Ignorance in which we are stuck, opens the doors to us, shows us the path, leads us to where we have to go — this is what man has called "spirit". It is the atmosphere created by the

Divine Grace in the universe to save it from the darkness into which it has fallen.

The soul is a kind of individual concentration of this Grace, its individual representative in the human being. The soul is something particular to humanity, it exists only in man. It is like a particular expression of the spirit in the human being. The beings of the other worlds do not have a soul, but they can live in the spirit. One might say that the soul is a delegation of the spirit in mankind, a special help to lead it faster. It is the soul that makes individual progress possible. The spirit, in its original form, has a more general, more collective action.

For the moment the spirit plays the part of a helper and guide, but it is not the all-powerful master of the material manifestation; when the Supermind is organised into a new world, the spirit will become the master and govern Nature in a clear and visible way.

What is called "new birth" is the birth into the spiritual life, the spiritual consciousness; it is to carry in oneself something of the spirit which, individually, through the soul, can begin to rule the life and be the master of existence. But in the supramental world, the spirit will be the master of this entire world and all its manifestations, all its expressions, consciously, spontaneously, naturally.

In the individual existence, that is what makes all the difference; so long as one just speaks of the spirit and it is something one has read about, whose existence one vaguely knows about, but not a very concrete reality for the consciousness, this means that one is not born into the spirit. And when one is born into the spirit, it becomes something much more concrete, much more living, much more real, much more tangible than the whole material world. And this is what makes the essential difference between beings. When *that* becomes spontaneously real — the true, concrete existence, the atmosphere one can freely breathe — theh one knows one has crossed over to the other side. But so long as it is something rather vague and hazy — you have heard about it, you know that it exists, but... it has no concrete reality — well, this means that the new birth has not yet taken place. As long as you tell yourself, "Yes, this I can see, this I can touch, the pain I suffer from, the hunger that torments me, the sleep that makes me feel heavy, this is real, this is concrete..." (*Mother laughs*), that means that you have not yet crossed over to the other side, you are not born into the spirit.

(Silence)

In fact, the vast majority of men are like prisoners with all the doors and windows closed, so they suffocate, which is quite natural. But they have with them the key that opens the doors and windows, and they do not use it.... Certainly there is a time when they don't know they have the key, but long after they have come to know it, long after they have been told about it, they hesitate to use it and doubt whether it has the power to open the doors and windows or even that it is a good thing to open them! And even when they feel that "after all, it might be good", there remains some fear: "What will happen when these doors and windows are opened?..." and they are afraid. They are afraid of being lost in that light and freedom. They want to remain what they call "themselves". They like their falsehood and their bondage. Something in them likes it and goes on clinging to it. They still have the impression that without their limits they would no longer exist.

That is why the journey is so long, that is why it is difficult. For if one truly consented to cease to exist, everything would become so easy, so swift, so luminous, so joyful — but perhaps not in the way men understand joy and ease. In truth, there are very few people who do not enjoy fighting. There are very few who could accept the absence of night, few can conceive of light except as the opposite of darkness: "Without shadows there would be no picture. Without struggle, there would be no victory. Without suffering there would be no joy." That is what they think, and so long as one thinks in this way, one is not yet born into the spirit.

26 November 1958

The Creation or Manifestation

"There is a plane of divine consciousness in which all is known absolutely, and the whole plan of things foreseen and predetermined. That way of seeing lives in the highest reaches of the Supramental; it is the Supreme's own vision. But when we do not possess that consciousness, it is useless to speak in terms that

*hold good only in that region and are not our present effective
way of seeing things. For at a lower level of consciousness nothing is realised or fixed beforehand; all is in the process of making. Here there are no settled facts, there is only the play of possibilities; out of the clash of possibilities is realised the thing that
has to happen. On this plane we can choose and select; we can
refuse one possibility and accept another; we can follow one path,
turn away from another. And that we can do, even though what is
actually happening may have been foreseen and predetermined
in a higher plane." (The Mother)**

The word "predetermined" does not correspond to the reality; the
word "pre-existent" would be more correct. The consciousness of an
unfolding has a reality, it is not only an appearance.

Imagine the world as a single whole and, in a certain sense, fi-
nite, limited but containing potentially innumerable possibilities of
which the combinations are so numerous that they are equivalent to
an infinite (you must be careful with words, however; I am very much
cramped by words, they do not express exactly what I mean). So, the
universe is objectified by the Divine Consciousness, by the Supreme,
according to certain determined laws of which we shall speak later.
The universe is a single whole, in the sense that it *is* the Divine — it
does not contain the whole of the Divine, but it is as though the Divine deployed Himself so as to objectify Himself; that is the *raison
d'être* of the manifestation of the universe. It is as if the divine Consciousness wandered into all divine possibilities following a path it
had chosen. Imagine then a multitude of possibles of which all the
possible combinations are equivalent to an infinite. The divine Consciousness is essentially free — It wanders therein and objectifies
Itself. The path traversed is free in the midst of an infinite multiplicity
which is at the same time pre-existent and absolutely undetermined
according to the action of the free divine Will. It may be conceived
that this Will, being free, is able to change the course of the deploy-

___

* The Mother read this passage to the class and then commented on it. This is the
case for most of the passages quoted in the book. Some of the passages are from the
Mother's works, some from Sri Aurobindo's.

ment, change the path and, although everything is pre-existent and consequently inevitable, the road, the path is free and absolutely unexpected. These changes of the route, if one may say so, can therefore change the relations between things and circumstances, and consequently the determinism is changed. This change of the circuit is called "the effect of the Grace"; well, through the aid of the Grace, if the Grace decides it, things can change, the course can be different. Things can change their places and instead of following a certain circuit follow another. A circumstance which, according to a particular determinism, should occur at a certain place ahead, for instance, would instead occur behind, and so on. The relations between things consequently change.

At what moment does Time begin? The Consciousness that chooses — is it in Time as soon as the unrolling begins?

No, Time is a succession; you must be able to conceive that the Supreme Consciousness, before objectifying itself, becomes aware of Itself in Itself. There is a global, total and simultaneous perception and there, there is no Time. Likewise one cannot speak of "Space", for the same reason, because all is simultaneous. It is something more; it corresponds to a state of consciousness subjective rather than objective, for the aim, the motive of creation is objectivisation; but there is a first step in this objectivisation in which there is a plenary consciousness, total and simultaneous, beyond Time and Space, of what will constitute the content of this universe; and there, the universe is pre-existent, but not manifested, and Time begins with objectivisation.

Can it be said that Time begins with the supramental plane?

It is not the same kind of Time. There is only a beginning of Time and a beginning of form. Time there is of a very different quality. There is a global, static consciousness before arriving at the supramental level, in which everything appears simultaneously — Time is the result of the fact that there is a succession in the organisation of the whole. While the totality you perceive all at once, on the supramental level, is not a static totality — the static totality gives place to another totality which gives the impression of Time. These are inner relations within the Supermind, in the sense that one is not aware of something which happens outside oneself; one is conscious only of something within oneself, internal, but the internal relations vary, and this gives a first impression of Time.

> *In this state of consciousness one does not have the impression of things being born, passing, disappearing, does one?*

Oh, no! Nothing of the kind.

> *"The Supreme Consciousness knows everything beforehand, because everything is realised there in her eternity. But for the sake of her play and in order to carry out actually on the physical plane what is foreordained in her own supreme self, she moves here upon earth as if she did not know the whole story; she works as if it was a new and untried thread that she was weaving."*
>
> *(The Mother)*

If you undertake a work and are told beforehand that all will be useless and you will not be able to do what you want, would you do it? No, surely not! Well, it is something like that which happens. Ninety times out of a hundred, what you do does not give the expected result. Not one person in a million would do his work if he were told: "Do this, but the result will not be at all what you want." But in the play of forces many must work for the aggregate of forces, for the totality of forces, although individually this work has no personal utility for the one who does it. So, if the individual had the knowledge that the part he plays in the whole is infinitesimal, he would not play it. But the moment you go above that, when you do things, not with a fixed end in view, but because you know within yourself that this is the thing to be done, whatever the result, then with this kind of detachment you know and see in the higher Consciousness that all action is done exclusively because it has to be done whatever may be the result; and generally you are sufficiently clear-sighted to know, at least vaguely, what will be the result of this action. For knowing it will not change in the least your way of doing it.

Instead of an explanation which goes from below upward, it would be wiser to look for an explanation which comes from above downward and rather to conceive that little by little the Consciousness comes down and as it comes down is obscured, and one no longer understands by what mechanism things are done — that is what is called a state of ignorance.

"In a picture you need a definite scheme of composition and colour; you have to set a limit, to put the whole thing within a fixed framework; but the limit is illusory, the frame is a mere convention. There is a constant continuation of the picture that stretches beyond any particular frame, and each continuation can be drawn in the same conditions in an unending series of frames. Our aim is this or that, we say, but we know that it is only the beginning of another aim beyond it, and that in its turn leads to yet another...."

(*The Mother*)

If I were told that things are going to stop at a certain point, I would find it very boring, so boring that I would not stir!

The only thing which consoles me is that everything continues always, infinitely, that there is always something new to be done.

Whatever be the goal attained, it is only a beginning.

1 March 1951

*

If you remain in a consciousness which functions mentally, even if it is the highest mind, you have the notion of an absolute determinism of cause and effect and feel that things are what they are because they are what they are and cannot be otherwise.

It is only when you come out of the mental consciousness completely and enter a higher perception of things — which you may call spiritual or divine — that you suddenly find yourself in a state of *perfect* freedom where *everything* is possible.

(*Silence*)

Those who have contacted that state or lived in it, even if only for a moment, try to describe it as a feeling of an absolute Will in action, which immediately gives to the human mentality the feeling of being arbitrary. And because of that distortion there arises the idea — which I might call traditional — of a supreme and arbitrary God, which is something most *unacceptable* to every enlightened mind. I suppose that this experience badly expressed is at the origin of this notion. And in fact it is incorrect to express it as an absolute Will: it is very, very, very different. It is something else altogether. For, what man understands by "Will" is a decision that is taken and carried out. We are obliged to use the word "will", but in its truth the Will acting in the universe is neither a choice nor a decision that is taken. What seems to me the closest expression is "vision". Things are because they are *seen*. But of course "seen", not seen as we see with these eyes. (*Mother touches her eyes...*) All the same, it is the nearest thing. It is a vision — a vision unfolding itself.

The universe becomes objective as it is progressively seen.

28 August 1957

*

The universe is an objectivisation of the Supreme, as if He had objectivised himself outside of himself in order to see himself, to live himself, to know himself, and so that there might be an existence and a consciousness capable of recognising him as their origin and uniting consciously with him to manifest him in the becoming. There is no other reason for the universe. The earth is a kind of symbolic crystallisation of universal life, a reduction, a concentration, so that the work of evolution may be easier to do and follow. And if we see the history of the earth, we can understand why the universe has been created. It is the Supreme growing aware of himself in an eternal Becoming; and the goal is the union of the created with the Creator, a union that is conscious, willing and free, in the Manifestation.

That is the secret of Nature. Nature is the executive Force, it is she who does the work.

And she takes up this creation, which appears to be totally inconscient but which contains the Supreme Consciousness and sole Reality and she works so that all this can develop, become self-aware and realise itself fully. But she does not show it from the very beginning. It develops gradually, and that is why at the start it is a secret which will be unveiled as it nears the end. And man has reached a point in the evolution high enough for this secret to be unveiled and for what was done in an apparent inconscience to be done consciously, willingly, and therefore much more rapidly and in the joy of realisation.

In man one can already see that the spiritual reality is being developed and that it is going to express itself totally and freely. Formerly, in the animal and the plant, it was... it was necessary to be very clear-sighted to see it, but man is himself conscious of this spiritual reality, at least in the higher part of his human existence. Man is beginning to know what the Supreme Origin wants of him and is collaborating in carrying it out.

Nature wants the creation to become conscious of being the Creator himself in an objectivisation, that is to say, there is no difference between the Creator and the Creation, and the goal is a conscious and realised union. That is the secret of Nature.[...]

Nature is not unconscious, but she has an *appearance* of unconsciousness. It began with the inconscience, but in the depths of the inconscience there was consciousness, and this consciousness is gradually developing.* For instance, mineral nature, stones, earth, metals, water, air, all this seems to be quite unconscious, although if one observes closely... And now science is discovering that this is only an appearance, that all this is only concentrated energy, and of course it is a conscious force which has produced all this. But apparently, when we see a rock, we don't think it is conscious, it does not give the impression of being conscious, it seems to be altogether unconscious.

It is the appearance that is inconscient. It becomes more and more conscious. Even in the mineral kingdom there are phenomena which reveal a hidden consciousness, like certain crystals, for instance. If you see with what precision, what exactitude and harmony they are formed, if you are in the least open, you are bound to feel that behind there's a consciousness at work, that this cannot be the result of unconscious chance.[...]

Indeed, in every being, the whole process of evolution is reproduced, as if at a dizzy speed one were reviewing all that has been

* When this talk was first published, the Mother made the following correction: "It is not the consciousness which is developing, it is the manifestation of consciousness which is developing its expression: it expresses itself more and more."

done, and as if it were necessary to relive all that in a flash before taking the next step.

(*Silence*)

The start, the great journey in the inconscience, in darkness, oblivion, unconsciousness, the awakening... and the return to the light.

7 May 1958

*

Q: "If the Divine that is all love is the source of the creation, whence have come all the evils abounding upon earth?"

A: "All is from the Divine; but the One Consciousness, the Supreme has not created the world directly out of itself; a Power has gone out of it and has descended through many gradations of its workings and passed through many agents. There are many creators or rather 'formateurs', form-makers, who have presided over the creation of the world. They are intermediary agents and I prefer to call them 'Formateurs' and not 'Creators'; for what they have done is to give the form and turn and nature to matter. There have been many, and some have formed things harmonious and benignant and some have shaped things mischievous and evil. And some too have been distorters rather than builders, for they have interfered and spoiled what was begun well by others."

(*The Mother*)

You say, "Many creators or rather 'formateurs', form-makers, have presided over the creation of the world." Who are these 'formateurs'?

That depends. They have been given many names. All has been done by gradations and through individual beings of all kinds. Each state of being is inhabited by entities, individualities and personalities and each one has created a world around him or has contributed to the formation of certain beings upon earth. The last creators are those of the vital world, but there are beings of the Overmind (Sri Aurobindo calls this plane the Overmind), who have created, given forms, sent out emanations, and these emanations again had their emanations and so on. What

I meant is that it is not the Divine Will that acted directly on Matter to give to the world the required form, it is by passing through layers, so to say, planes of the world, as for example, the mental plane — there are so many beings on the mental plane who are form-makers, who have taken part in the formation of some beings who have incarnated upon earth. On the vital plane also the same thing happens.

For example, there is a tradition which says that the whole world of insects is the outcome of the form-makers of the vital world, and that this is why they take such absolutely diabolical shapes when they are magnified under the microscope. You saw the other day, when you were shown the microbes in water? Naturally the pictures were made to amuse, to strike the imagination, but they are based on real forms, so magnified, however, that they look like monsters. Almost the whole world of insects is a world of microscopic monsters which, had they been larger in size, would have been quite terrifying. So it is said these are entities of the vital world, beings of the vital who created that for fun and amused themselves forming all these impossible beasts which make human life altogether unpleasant.

Did these intermediaries also come out of the Divine Power?

Through intermediaries, yes, not directly. These beings are not in direct contact with the Divine (there are exceptions, I mean as a general rule), they are beings who are in relation with other beings, who are again in relation with others, and these with still others, and so on, in a hierarchy, up to the Supreme.

If they came out of the Divine, why are they evil?

Evil? That I think I have explained to you once: it is enough just not to remain under the direct influence of the Divine and not to follow the movement of creation or expansion as willed by the Divine; this rupture of contact is enough to produce the greatest of disorders, that of division. Well, even the most luminous, the most powerful beings may choose to follow their own movement instead of obeying the divine movement. And though in themselves they may be quite wonderful and if human beings saw them they would take them for the very Godhead, they can, because they follow their own will instead of working in harmony with the universe, be the source of very great evils, very great disorders, very great massive obstructions. But don't you see, the question is badly put, I laughed just now when I read the question. It is a childish way of speaking. This person says: "If God is everything in the world, why are there evil things in the world?" Now, if she had told me that, I would have simply answered: there is nothing which is not God, only it is in a disorder. One must try to remedy it — God is not love alone, He is all things, and if that appears to us — to us — altogether wrong, it is because it is not arranged properly. There have been movements exactly of the kind I spoke to you about.

You may ask why it happened. Well, certainly it is not the mind, you know, which can say why it happened. It happened, that is all. In reality the only thing that concerns us is that it has happened. It is perhaps an accident to begin with.... If you look at the thing from a philosophical point of view, it is evident that the universe in which we live is a movement among many others and this movement follows a law which is its own (and which is perhaps not the same in the others), and if the Will was for the world to be built on the principle of choice, of the freedom of choice, then one cannot prevent disorderly movements from taking place until knowledge comes and the choice is enlightened. If one is free to choose, one can also choose bad things, not necessarily the good, for if it were a thing decided beforehand, it would no longer be a free choice. You see, when such questions are put, the mind only answers and it reduces the problem, it reduces it to a more or less elementary mental formula; but that corresponds only very vaguely and superficially and incompletely with the reality of things.

To be able to understand, one must become. If you want to understand the why and how of the universe, you must identify yourself with the universe. It is not impossible but it is not very easy either, especially for children.

This was one of the most childish questions that she put — altogether childish: "If He is just, why is there injustice? If He is good, why is there wickedness? If He is love, why is there hatred?" — But He is all! So He is not merely this or that, or only, exclusively this — He is all. That is, to be more correct, it should be said that all is He.

There are notions about creation, very widespread upon earth, which have been accepted more or less for a long time in human thought, that are quite simplistic! There is "something" (truly speaking, one does not know what), and then there is a God who puts this something into form and creates the world out of it. So if you have such notions, you have a justifiable right to say to this God: "Well, you have indeed created a world, it's a pretty one, that world of yours!" Although, according to the story, after seven days of labour, he declared that it was very good — but it was good for him. Perhaps it may have amused him immensely, but as for us who are in the world, we do not find it good at all! Don't you see, the conception and the way of putting it are altogether childish. It is just like the story of the potter who puts his pot in shape — this God is a human being, formidable in proportions and power, but looking strangely like a man. It is man who makes God in his image, not God who makes man in his image! So each time a question is put in an incomplete or childish way, it is impossible to give an answer to it truly, for the question is badly put. You say something, you affirm it. But what right have you to assert it? Because you affirm that, you conclude: "Since that is this, how does it happen that it is so?" But "that is this" is your statement. It does not mean that it is so!

There is only one single solution to the problem — not to make any distinction between God and the universe at the origin. The universe *is* the Divine projected in space, and God *is* the universe at its origin. It is the same thing under one aspect or another. And you cannot divide them. It is the opposite conception to that of the "creator" and his "work". Only, it is very convenient to speak of the creator and his work, it makes explanations very easy and the teaching quite elementary. But it is not the truth. And then you say: "How is it that God who is all-powerful has allowed the world to be like this?" But it is your own conception! It is because you yourself happen to be in the midst of a set of circumstances that seems to you unpleasant, so you project that upon the Divine and you tell him: "Why have you made such a world?" — "I did not make it. It is you yourself. And if you become Myself once again, you will no longer feel as you do. What makes you feel as you do is that you are no longer Myself." This is what He could tell you in answer. And the fact is that when you succeed in uniting your consciousness with the divine consciousness, there is no problem left. Everything appears quite natural and simple and all right and exactly what it had to be. But when you cut yourself off from the origin and stand over against Him, then truly everything goes wrong, nothing can go right!

But if you ask for a logic that pushes things to the extreme end, you question how it is that the Divine has tolerated parts of his own self to be separated from him and all this disorder to be created. You may say that. And I then will reply: "If you want to know, it is better to unite yourself with the Divine, for that is the only way of knowing why He has done these things." It is not by questioning Him mentally, for your mind cannot understand. And I repeat it, when you reach such an identification, all problems are solved. And this feeling that things are not all right and that they should be otherwise, comes just because there is a divine will for a constant unfolding in perpetual progress and things that were must give place to things that shall be and shall be better than what the others were. And the world that was good yesterday is no longer good tomorrow. The whole world that could appear absolutely harmonious and perfect at one time, well, today it is discordant, no longer harmonious, because now we conceive and see the possibility of a better world. And if we were to find it all right we would not do what we ought to do, that is, make the effort needed for it to become better.

There comes a time when all these notions appear so childish! And this happens solely because one is shut up within oneself. With this consciousness which is your own, which is like a grain of sand in the infinite vastness, you want to know and judge the infinite? It is impossible. You must first of all come out of yourself, and then unite with the infinite and only afterwards can you begin to understand what it is, not before. You project your consciousness — what you are, the thoughts you have, the capacity of understanding you have — you project this upon the Divine and then say: "That is all wrong." I quite understand! But there is no possibility of knowing unless you identify yourself. I do not see how, for example, a drop of water could tell you what the ocean is like. That's how it is.

14 October 1953

The Origin of the World

*Sweet Mother, it is the separation of Sat, Chit and Ananda which
has brought about ignorance, suffering. Then...*

Why did they separate? (*Laughter*)
Probably they had no moral notions! (*Laughter*)

(*Long silence*)

It is probable that if they had not separated, there would have
been no universe as we have it. It was perhaps a necessity. But what
you are asking is how it was not foreseen that it would happen in this
way. Perhaps it was foreseen. It could have turned out well, it turned
out badly. There! There are accidents.

You know, so long as you want to apply your mental, moral notions to the creation of the universe, you will never understand anything about it, never. Because from all sides and in all ways it goes
beyond these conceptions — conceptions of good and evil, and these
things. All the mental, moral conceptions we have cannot explain the
universe. And for this part of ourselves which indeed lives in a total
ignorance, all that can be said is: "Things are like that because they
are like that", one can't explain them, because the explanations one
gives are those of ignorance and explain nothing at all.

The mind explains one thing by another, this other which needs
to be explained is explained by another still, and that other which
needs explanation is explained by another, and if you continue in this
way you can go all round the universe and return to the starting-point
without having explained anything at all. (*Laughter*) Probably they
had no moral notions! (*Laughter*)

(*Long silence*)

So you have to pierce a hole, rise in the air and see things in
another way. Then like that one can begin to understand.

13 July 1955

*

From where do the gods come?

That means? ... "From where" means what? What is their origin? Who has formed them? ... But everything, everything comes from the one Origin, from the Supreme, the gods also.

There is a very old tradition which narrates this. I am going to tell you the story as one does to children, for in this way you will understand:

One day "God" decided to exteriorise himself, objectivise himself, in order to have the joy of knowing himself in detail. So, first of all, he emanated his consciousness (that is to say, he manifested his consciousness) by ordering this consciousness to realise a universe. This consciousness began by emanating four beings, four individualities which were indeed altogether very high beings, of the highest Reality. They were the being of consciousness, the being of love (of Ananda rather), the being of life and the being of light and knowledge — but consciousness and light are the same thing. There we are then: consciousness, love and Ananda, life and truth — truth, that's the exact word. And naturally, they were supremely powerful beings, you understand. They were what are called in that tradition the first emanations, that is, the first formations. And each one became very conscious of its qualities, its power, its capacities, its possibilities, and, suddenly forgot each in its own way that it was only an emanation and an incarnation of the Supreme. And so this is what happened: when light or Consciousness separated from the divine Consciousness, that is, when it began to think it was the divine Consciousness and that there was nothing other than itself, it suddenly became obscurity and inconscience. And when Life thought that all life was in itself and that there was nothing else but its life and that it did not depend at all upon the Supreme, then its life became death. And when Truth thought that it contained all truth, and that there was no other truth than itself, this Truth became falsehood. And when love or Ananda was convinced that it was the supreme Ananda and that there was no other than itself and its felicity, it became suffering. And that is how the world, which was to have been so beautiful, became so ugly.

Now, that consciousness (if you like to call it the Divine Mother, the Supreme Consciousness), when she saw this she was very disturbed, you may be sure, she said to herself: "This has really not succeeded." So she turned back to the Divine, to God, the Supreme, and she asked him to come to her aid. She said to him: "This is what has happened. Now what is to be done?" He said: "Begin again, but try to manage in such a way that the beings do not become so independent!... They must remain in contact with you, and through you with me." And it was thus that she created the gods, who were quite docile and not so proud, and who began the creation of the world. But as the others had come before them, at every step the gods met the others. And it was in this way that the world changed into a battlefield, a place of war, strife, suffering, darkness and all the rest, and for each new creation the gods had to fight with the others who had gone ahead: they had preceded them, they had plunged headlong into matter; and they had created all this disorder and the gods had to put straight all this confusion. That is where the gods came from. They are the second emanations.

The first four who changed, was it by chance or was it deliberately?

No. What is chance?

It is said also — that is the continuation of the story or rather its beginning — that the Divine wanted his creation to be a free creation. He wanted all that went forth from him to be absolutely independent and free in order to be able to unite with him in freedom, not through compulsion. He did not want that they should be compelled to be faithful, compelled to be conscious, compelled to be obedient. They had to do it spontaneously, through the knowledge and conviction that that was much better. So this world was created as a world of total freedom, freedom of choice. And it is in this way that at every moment everyone has the freedom of choice — but with all the consequences. If one chooses well, it is good, but if one chooses ill, ah well, what's to happen happens — that is what has happened!

The story may be understood in a much more occult and spiritual sense. But it is like all the stories of the universe: if you want to narrate them so that people may understand, they become stories for children. But if one knows how to see the truth behind the symbols, one understands everything. Even with what I have told you, which seems like a little story for children, even like that, if you understand what I have told you and the meaning of what I have told you, you can have the secret of things.

There are traditions which say that it is an "accident", in the sense that it could have been otherwise, but it happened like that. It is true, it came about like that. Only, it was quite understandable that every one of these elements, having its origin in the Supreme, being quite close to the Emanation at that moment, quite close to the Origin, carried in itself the consciousness of its divinity and superiority, necessarily, since this is not a creation made with something foreign to the Divine: it is simply the Divine who has emanated himself, as though he were looking at himself — he objectivises himself in order to become aware of all that he is; instead of being in an inner static state of concentration in which all is unmanifested, he projects that outside himself "in order to see", as though he wanted to see all that is within him, that is, all the infinity of possibilities. So, all was possible. It happened like that — it could have happened otherwise. Besides, nothing tells you that alongside our universe such as it is, there do not exist others which are so different that there cannot be any relation between one universe and another. It can very well be that our universe is not the only exteriorisation of the Divine. Ours is such as we know it; there may be others which are in much less sorry a state than this one! Besides, it is lamentable only in its appearance. If you go behind the appearance, you become aware that it is not lamentable at all. It is only one way of seeing.[...]

But [of these first four emanations] the one who does the greatest harm is the "Lord of Falsehood". He it is indeed who is the biggest obstacle in the universe, this constant negation of the truth. And he has a very strong hold on the terrestrial world, on the material world. Besides, here (on the earth), those who see him, see him as an absolutely marvellous, splendid being. He entitles himself the "Lord of the Nations", and he appears formidable, luminous, powerful, very impressive.... Historically, he was the inspirer of certain heads of State, and he proclaims himself the Lord of the Nations because it is he who governs the peoples. He is evidently, at the source, the supreme organiser of these last two wars. It was on that occasion that he manifested himself as the Lord of the Nations. And he declared, besides, that he would never be converted. And he knows that his end will come — naturally, he will try to make it as late as possible. And he declared that he would destroy all he could before being destroyed.... We may expect all possible catastrophes.[...]

Was Stalin predestined to be what he was?

Stalin? I am not quite sure that he was a human being... in the sense that I don't think he had a psychic being. Or perhaps he did have one — in all matter, in every atom there is a divine centre — but I mean a conscious psychic being, formed, individualised. I don't think so. I believe it was a direct incarnation of a being of the vital world. And that was the great difference between him and Hitler. Hitler was simply a man, and as a man he was very weak-minded, very sentimental — he had the consciousness of a petty workman (some said of a petty shoemaker), in any case of a little workman or a little school-master, something like that, a very small consciousness, and extremely sentimental, what is called in French *"fleur bleue"*, very weak.

But he was possessed. He was rather mediocre by nature, very mediocre. He was a medium, a very good medium — the thing took hold of him, besides, during spiritism séances. It was at that moment that he was seized by those fits which were described as epileptic. They were not epileptic: they were attacks of possession. It was thus that he had a kind of power, which however was not very great. But when he wanted to know something from that power, he went away to his castle, and there, in "meditation", there truly he invoked very intensely what he called his "god", his supreme god, who was the Lord of the Nations. And everything seemed to him magnificent. It was a being... it was small — it appeared to him all in silver armour, with a silver helmet and golden plume! It was magnificent! And a light so dazzling that hardly could the eyes see and bear that blaze. Naturally it did not appear physically — Hitler was a medium, he saw. He had a sort of clairvoyance. And it was at such times that he had his fits: he rolled on the ground, he drivelled, bit the carpet, it was frightful, the state he was in. The people around him knew it. Well, that being is the "Lord of the Nations". And it is not even the Lord of the Nations in its origin, it is an emanation of the Lord of the Nations, and a very powerful emanation.

25 November 1953

*

I am going to tell you [a story], very succinctly. Don't take it as a gospel! Take it rather... as a story.

When the Supreme decided to exteriorise Himself in order to be able to see Himself, the first thing in Himself which He exteriorised was the Knowledge of the world and the Power to create it. This Knowledge-Consciousness and Force began its work; and in the supreme Will there was a plan, and the first principle of this plan was the expression of both the essential Joy and the essential Freedom, which seemed to be the most interesting feature of this creation.

So intermediaries were needed to express this Joy and Freedom in forms. And at first four Beings were emanated to start this universal development which was to be the progressive objectivisation of all that is potentially contained in the Supreme. These Beings were, in the principle of their existence: Consciousness and Light, Life, Bliss and Love, and Truth.

You can easily imagine that they had a sense of great power, great strength, of something tremendous, for they were essentially the very principle of these things. Besides, they had full freedom of choice, for this creation was to be Freedom itself.... As soon as they set to work — they had their own conception of how it had to be done — being totally free, they chose to do it independently. Instead of taking the attitude of servant and instrument [...] they naturally took the attitude of the master, and this mistake — as I may call it — was the first cause, the essential cause of all the disorder in the universe. As soon as there was separation — for that is the essential cause, separation — as soon as there was separation between the Supreme and what had been emanated, Consciousness changed into inconscience, Light into darkness, Love into hatred, Bliss into suffering, Life into death and Truth into falsehood. And they proceeded with their creations independently, in separation and disorder.

The result is the world as we see it. It was made progressively, stage by stage, and it would truly take a little too long to tell you all that, but finally, the consummation is Matter — obscure, inconscient, miserable.... The creative Force which had emanated these four Beings, essentially for the creation of the world, witnessed what was happening, and turning to the Supreme she prayed for the remedy and the cure of the evil that had been done.

Then she was given the command to precipitate her Consciousness into this inconscience, her Love into this suffering, and her Truth into this falsehood. And a greater consciousness, a more total love, a more perfect truth than what had been emanated at first, plunged, so to say, into the horror of Matter in order to awaken in it consciousness, love and truth, and to begin the movement of Redemption which was to bring the material universe back to its supreme origin.

So, there have been what might be called "successive involutions" in Matter, and a history of these involutions. The present result of these involutions is the appearance of the Supermind emerging from the inconscience; but there is nothing to indicate that after this appearance there will be no others... for the Supreme is inexhaustible and will always create new worlds.

That is my story.

16 October 1957

The Why of Things

If everything that is manifested in the physical world has its origin in the higher Truth, what is it that makes it ugly when it expresses itself? Why are there ugly things at all?

Because there are forces that intervene between the origin and the manifestation.

If I ask you, "Do you know the truth of your being?", what will you say?... Do you know it? Well, the same holds for everything. And yet you are already a sufficiently evolved thinking being who has passed through all kinds of refinements. You are no longer quite like, let us say, a lizard that runs on the wall; and yet you would not be able to say what the truth of your being is. That is just the secret of all deformations in the world. It is because there is all the inconscience created by the fact of separation from the Origin. It is due to this inconscience that the Origin, though always there, is not able to manifest itself. It is there, that is why the world exists. But in its expression it is deformed because it manifests itself through the inconscience, ignorance and obscurity.[...]

In creating the universe as it was, the Will was an individual projection — individual, you understand, a scattering: instead of being a unity containing all, it was a unity made of innumerable small unities which are individualisations, that is, things that feel themselves separated. And the very fact of being separated from all others is what gives you the feeling that you are an individual. Otherwise you would have the feeling that you were a fluid mass. For example, instead of being conscious of your external form and of everything in your being which makes of you a separate individuality, if you were conscious of the vital forces which move everywhere or of the inconscient that is at the base of all, you would have the feeling of a mass moving with all kinds of contradictory movements but which could not be separated from each other; you would not have the feeling of being an individual at all: you would have the feeling of something like a vibration in the midst of a whole. Well, the original Will was to form individual beings capable of becoming conscious once again of their divine origin. Because of the process of individualisation one must feel separate if one is to be an individual. The moment you are separated, you are cut off from the original consciousness, at least apparently, and you fall into the inconscient. For the only thing which is the Life of life is the Origin, if you cut yourself off from that, consciousness naturally is changed into unconsciousness. And then it is due to this very unconsciousness that you are no longer aware of the truth of your being.... It is a process. You cannot argue whether it is inevitable or avoidable; the fact is it is like that. This process of formation and creation is the reason why purity no longer manifests in its essence and in its purity but through the deformation of unconsciousness and ignorance.... If you had answered immediately: "Yes, of course, I know the truth of my being!" it would have finished there, there wouldn't have been any problem.

That is why there is all this ugliness, there is death; that is why there is illness; that is why there is wickedness; that is why there is suffering. There is no remedy, there is only one way for all these things. All this is there in different domains and with different vibrations, but the cause of all is the same. It is inconscience produced because of the necessity of individual formation. Once again I do not say that it was indispensable. That is another problem which perhaps later on we shall be ready to solve; but for the moment we are obliged to state that that's how it is.

And so, the remedy? Since such is the cause, the only way of putting everything right is to become conscious once again. And this is very simple, very simple.

Suppose that there are in the universe two opposing and contradictory forces, as some religions have preached: there was good and evil, and there always will be good and evil, there will be a conflict, a battle, a struggle. The one that is stronger, whether it be the good or the evil, will win; if there is more of the good, the good will win and if there is more of the evil, the evil will win; but the two will always exist. If it were like that, it would be hopeless; one wouldn't have to say then that it is either difficult or easy, it would be impossible. One would not be able to get out of it. But actually that is not so.

Actually there is but one Origin and this origin is the perfection of Truth, for that is the only thing which truly exists; and by exteriorising, projecting, scattering itself, it brings forth what we see, and a crowd of tiny heads, very gentle, very brilliant, in search of something they have not yet seized but which they can seize, because what they are in search of is within them. That is a certainty. It may take more or less time, but it is sure to come. The remedy is at the very core of the evil. *Voilà.*

It has been called by various names, each one has presented it in his own way. According to the angle of seeing, one's experience differs. All those who have found the Divine within themselves have found Him in a certain way, following a certain experience and from a certain angle, and this angle was self-evident to them. But then, if they are not well on their guard, they begin to say: "To find the Divine, one must do this and do that. And it is like that and it is that path one should follow", because for them that was the path of success. When one goes a little further, has a little more experience, one becomes aware that it is not necessarily like that, it can be done through millions of ways.... There is only one thing that is certain, it is that what is found is always the same. And that's remarkable, that whatever the path followed, whatever the form given to it, the result is always the same. Their experience and everyone's is the same. When they have touched the Thing, it is for all the same thing. And this is just the proof that they have touched That, because it is the same thing for all. If it is not the same thing, it means that they have not yet touched That. When they have touched That, it is the same thing. And to That, you may give all the names you like, it makes no difference.

Words are words. After all, they mean nothing, unless there is something behind.

27 May 1953

*

Why is there ill-will?

My child, it is as though you asked me why there is inconscience, ignorance, darkness in the nature! It is the why of the world you are asking me! Why is the world like this and not otherwise?... There are people who have written volumes on the subject. And each one explains it in his own way and that changes nothing, in fact. You may ask me: Why is there ill-will? Why is there ignorance? Why is there stupidity? Why is there wickedness? Why is there all the evil? Why is the world not a very charming place?... All the philosophers explain it to you, each in his own way. The materialists explain it in their way, the scientists explain it in their way, but nobody in all that can find the means of getting out of it! and after all, the one thing that's truly important is, it would be just (you ask me: Why is there ill-will?) it would be to find the way so that there may no longer be any ill-will. That would be worth the trouble. If you tell me: Why is there suffering, why is there misery?... What can that do to you, this why, unless it be a means of finding a remedy? But I don't believe it would, for [...] if you seek for the why, you will find within yourself simply all sorts of explanations which will be more or less useless and will lead you nowhere.

The fact is that it *is* so, isn't it? and the second fact is that one doesn't want it thus, and the third is to find the means that it may no longer exist. That is our problem. The world is not as we think it ought to be. There are lots of things in the world which we do not approve of. Well, there are people who like what they call "knowledge" very much and begin to inquire why it is like that. In a way this is very well, but as I said, it would be much more important to find out what to do so that it may be otherwise. This is exactly the problem the Buddha put to himself. He sat under a tree, it is said, until he found the solution. But his solution is not very good, for when you tell me: "The world is bad", well, his solution is: "Do away with the world." — "For whose benefit?" as Sri Aurobindo has written somewhere. Then the world will no longer be bad, for it will not exist! But what is the use of its no longer being bad, since it will not exist? It is very simple logic. It is like those who want the whole world to return to its Origin; and so Sri Aurobindo answers: "You will be the all-powerful master of something that no longer exists, an emperor without an empire or a king without a kingdom", that's all.... It is one solution. But there are other better ones. I believe we have found better ones.

Some say that ill-will comes from ignorance (that was exactly what the Buddha claimed) and that if ignorance disappeared there would no longer be any ill-will. There are others who say that ill-will comes from division, separation, that if the universe were not cut off from its Origin there would be no ill-will. Others still say that it is ill-will which is the cause of everything, of separation and ignorance; and so there arises the problem: Whence does it come, this ill-will? If it were at the origin of everything, it was then *in* the origin of everything. And there we are altogether at a loss, my children! We could speculate upon this for years, we shall never get out of it. And so those who push it so far finish by telling you: Ill-will doesn't exist, it is an illusion. And that's simply because they stop midway in their reasoning, for if they went a little farther they might say: Perhaps it is a human invention, this ill-will.... That is possible!

8 July 1953

*

That is the first argument, that is the theory. The Divine is all-powerful, he can do whatever he likes; therefore he does not need anybody's help. And if you push your idea sufficiently far, you will see that if the Divine is truly all-powerful in this world and does always whatever he wants, well, I tell you, he is the greatest monster in the universe! Because One who is all-powerful and makes the world such as it is, looking with a smile at people suffering and miserable, and finding that all right, I would call a monster.[...]

Now, as you have a little more philosophical mind, I shall teach you how to come out of the difficulty. But, first of all, you must understand that that idea is a childish idea. I simply call on your common sense. You make of your Divine a person, because that way you understand him better. You make of him a person. And then this person has organised something (the earth, it is too big, it is difficult to understand — take anything else) and then this thing the Divine has organised with the full power to do exactly as he likes. And in this thing — that he has made with the full power to do as he likes — there is ignorance, stupidity, bad will, fear, jealousy, pride, wickedness, and also suffering, illness, grief, all the pains; and a set of people who cannot say that they have perhaps more than a few minutes of happiness in the whole day and the rest of it is a neutral condition, passing by like a thing that's dead — and you call that a creation!... I call it something like a hell! And one who would make that deliberately and not only make it but look at it and say: "Ah! it is very good", as it is narrated in some religious books, that after having made the world such as it is, the seventh day he looked at it and was extremely satisfied with his work and he rested.... Well, that never! I do not call that God. Or otherwise, follow Anatole France and say that God is a demiurge and the most frightful of all beings.

But there is a way out of the difficulty.[...] You will see all these conceptions and this idea that you have are based upon one thing, an entity that you call God and a world that you call his creation, and you believe these are two different things, one having made the other and the other being under the first, being the expression of what the first has made. Well, that is the initial error. If you could feel deeply that there is no division between that something you call God and this something you call his creation, if you said: "It is exactly the same thing" and if you could feel that what you call God (perhaps it is only a word), what you call God suffers when you suffer, he does not know when you do not know; and that it is through this creation, little by little, step by step, that he finds himself again, unites with himself, is realising himself, expressing himself, and it is not at all something he wanted in an arbitrary way or made like an autocrat, but that it is the growing expression, developing more and more, of a consciousness that is objectifying itself to itself.... Then there is no other thing but the sense of a collective advancing towards a more total realisation, a self-awareness of knowledge-consciousness — no other thing but that, a progressive self-awareness of knowledge-consciousness in a total unity which will reproduce integrally the First Consciousness.

That changes the problem.

Only, it is a little difficult to understand and one must make a little more progress. Instead of being like a little child that kneels down, joins its hands and says: "My God, I pray to Thee, make me a good child so that I may never hurt my mother.... " That of course is very easy and indeed I cannot say that it is bad. It is very good. Only there are children with whom these things do not go, because they say: "Why should I ask You to make me good? You should make me good without there being any need of my asking You for it. Otherwise You are not nice!" It is very good when one has a simple heart and does not think much, but when one begins to think, it becomes more difficult. But if you had by your side someone to tell you: instead of that, instead of lighting a candle and kneeling down before it with your hands folded, light a flame in your heart and then have a great aspiration towards "something more beautiful, more true, more noble, better than all that I know. I ask that from tomorrow I begin to know all these things, all that I cannot do I begin to do and every day a little more." And then, if you throw yourself out a little, if, for one reason or another, you were put in the presence of much misery in the world, if you have friends who are unhappy or relatives who suffer or you meet any kind of difficulties, then you ask that the whole consciousness might be raised *all together* towards that perfection which must manifest and that all this ignorance that has made the world so unhappy might be changed into an enlightened knowledge and all this bad will be illumined and transformed into benevolence. And then as far as one can, as far as one understands, one wishes it with all one's heart; and indeed that can take the form of a prayer and one can ask — ask of what? — ask of that which knows, ask of that which can, ask of all that is greater and stronger than oneself, to help so that it may be thus. And how beautiful those prayers would be!

15 July 1953

*

When one is an enemy of the Divine, one is an enemy of what?

Oh!... That depends exclusively upon each one. Usually one is an enemy of one's own idea of the Divine, and that is why it is said that one who denies the Divine is very often the greatest devotee. For if he did not have within himself the certitude that the Divine exists, he would not take the trouble of denying Him. And this is still stronger in one who hates Him, for if he did not have somewhere far within himself the certitude of the Divine's existence, how could he hate Him?

This has been symbolised here in India in the stories of those who wanted to identify themselves with the divine Reality and chose to become His enemies, for the path of the enemy was more direct than the path of the worshipper. These are well-known stories here, all the old legends and Indian mythology speak about it. Well, this simply illustrates the fact that one who has never put the problem to himself and never given the faintest thought to the existence of the Divine is certainly farther away from the Divine than one who hates Him or denies Him. For one can't deny something one has never thought about.

He who says or writes: "I declare, I certify, all my experience goes to prove that there is no Divine, no such thing exists, it is just man's imagination, man's creation...", that means he has already thought over the problem any number of times and that something within him is prodigiously interested in this problem.

As for the one who detests Him — there it is even more obvious: one can't be the enemy of an illusion.

So (*speaking to the disciple*), your question no longer holds. For perhaps, after all, this is one more form of meeting which may have its interest. One sometimes says in a lighter vein: "My intimate enemy", and it is perhaps not altogether wrong. Perhaps there is more intimacy in hatred than in ignorance. One is nearer to what one hates than to what one is ignorant of.

This doesn't mean I recommend hatred! That is not what I am saying, but I have very often happened to see more love in a look or an expression of fury and hatred than in an absolutely dull and inert state. It is deformed, spoilt, disfigured, whatever you like, but there is something living, a flame is there.

Of course, even in unconsciousness and immobility, in the complete inertia — apparently — of the stone, one may find a dazzling Light, that of the divine Presence. But then that is the state we were just speaking about: one sees Him everywhere, meets Him everywhere, and in so manifold and marvellously harmonised a way that all these difficulties disappear.

(Silence)

Truly speaking, to be practical, the problem could be expressed like this. If the Divine had not conceived His creation as progressive, there could have been from the beginning a beatific, immobile and unchangeable condition. But the minute... How shall I explain it, I don't know. Just because the universe had to be progressive, perfect identity, the bliss of this identity, the full consciousness of this identity had necessarily to be veiled, otherwise nothing would have ever stirred.

A static universe may be conceived. One could conceive of something which is "all at one and the same time": that there is no time, only a kind of objectivisation — but not an unfolding in which things manifest progressively one after another, according to a special rhythm; that they are all manifested at the same time, all at once. Then all would be in a blissful state and there would be no universe as we see it, the element of unfolding would be missing, which constitutes... well, what we live in at present.

But once we admit this principle that the universe is progressive, the unfolding progressive, that instead of seeing everything together and all at once, our perception is progressive, then everything takes its right place within it. And inevitably, the future perfection must be felt as something higher than what was there before. The realisation towards which we are moving must necessarily seem superior to the one which was accomplished before.

And this opens the door to everything — to all possibilities.

Sri Aurobindo often said this: what appeared beautiful, good, even perfect, and marvellous and divine at a given moment in the universe, can no longer appear so now. And what now seems to us beautiful, marvellous, divine and perfect, will be an obscurity after some time. And in the same way, the gods who were all-powerful at a certain period belong to a lower reality than the gods who will manifest tomorrow.

And that is a sign that the universe is progressive.

This has been said, this has been repeated, but people don't understand, you know, when it concerns all those great ages, that they are like a reduction of the universal progress to the human measure.

That is why if one enters the state in which everything, as it is, appears perfectly divine, one necessarily goes out of the universal movement at the same time. This is what people like Buddha or Shankara had understood. They expressed in their own way that if you could realise the state in which everything appears to you perfectly divine or perfectly perfect, you necessarily go out of the universal movement and enter the Unmanifest.

This is correct. It is like that.

They were sufficiently dissatisfied with life as it was and had very little hope that it could become better; so for them this was the ideal solution. I call it escaping, but still.... It is not so easy! But for them it was the ideal solution — up to a certain point, for... there is perhaps one more step to take.

But it is a fact. If one wants to remain in the universe, one must admit the principle of progress, for this is a progressive universe. If you want to realise a static perfection, well, you will inevitably be thrown out of the universe, for you will no longer belong to its principle.

It is a choice.

Only, Sri Aurobindo often used to say: people who choose the exit forget that at the same time they will lose the consciousness with which they could congratulate themselves on their choice! They forget that.

18 July 1956

*

But why does the Divine want to manifest Himself on earth in this chaos?

Because this is why He has created the earth, not for any other motive; the earth is He Himself in a deformation and He wants to establish it back again in its truth. Earth is not something separated from Him and alien to Him. It is a deformation of Himself which must once again become what it was in its essence, that is, the Divine.

Then why is He a stranger to us?

But He is not a stranger, my child. You fancy that He is a stranger, but He is not, not in the least. He is the essence of your being — not at all alien. You may not know Him, but He is not a stranger; He is the very essence of your being. Without the Divine you would not exist. Without the Divine you could not exist even for the millionth part of a second. Only, because you live in a kind of false illusion and deformation, you are not conscious. You are not conscious of yourself, you are conscious of something which you think to be yourself, but which isn't you.

Then what is myself, Sweet Mother?

The Divine!

8 June 1955

The Experience of the Divine

There is something I was asked some time ago to which I have not yet replied. It is this. I have written somewhere:

> *"The absolute of every being is its unique relation with the Divine and its unique manner of expressing the Divine in the manifestation."*

This is what is called here in India the truth of the being or the law of the being, the *dharma* of the being: the centre and the cause of the individuality.

Everyone carries his truth within himself, a truth which is unique, which is altogether his own and which he must express in his life. Now what is this truth? This is the question I have been asked:

"What is this truth of the being, and how is it expressed externally in physical life?"

It is expressed in this way: each individual being has a direct and unique relation with the Supreme, the Origin, That which is beyond all creation. It is this unique relation which must be expressed in one's life, through a unique mode of being in relation with the Divine. Therefore, each one is directly and exclusively in relation with the Divine — the relation one has with the Divine is unique and exclusive; so that you receive from the Divine, when you are in a receptive state, the *totality* of the relation it is *possible* for you to have, and this is neither a sharing nor a part nor a repetition, but exclusively and uniquely *the* relation which each one can have with the Divine. So, from the psychological point of view, one is *all alone* in having this direct relation with the Divine.

One is all alone with the Supreme.

The relation one has with Him will never have an equal, will never be exactly the same as another's. No two are the same and therefore *nothing* can be taken away from you to be given to another, *nothing* can be withdrawn from you to be given to another. And if this relation disappeared from the creation, it would really disappear — which is impossible.

And this means that if one lives in the truth of one's being, one is an indispensable part of the creation. Naturally, I don't mean if one lives what one *believes* one should be, I am saying if one lives the truth of one's being; if, by a development, one is able to enter into contact with the truth of one's being, one is immediately in a unique and exclusive relation with the Divine, which hasn't its equal.

That's how it is.

And naturally, because it is the truth of your being, that is what you should express in your life.

22 August 1956

*

Is there an experience which proves that one is living in the presence of the Divine?

Once one begins to live in the presence of the Divine, one does not question any longer. It carries its own certitude — one feels, one knows, and it becomes impossible to question. One lives in the presence of the Divine and it is for you an absolute fact. Till then you ask, because you do not have the experience, but once you have the experience, it has such an authority that it is indisputable. One who says, "I think I live in the presence of the Divine but I am not sure", has not had the true experience, for as soon as one has the inner shock of this experience, no more questioning is possible. It is like those who ask, "What is the divine Will?" As long as you have not glimpsed this Will, you cannot know. One may have an idea of it through deduction, inference, etc., but once you have felt the precise contact with the divine Will, this too is not disputable any longer — you know.

I add, so that there may not be any misunderstanding: all experience has its worth only in the measure of the sincerity of the one who has it. Some are not sincere and fabricate wonderful experiences, and they imagine they have them. I put all that aside, it is not interesting. But for sincere people who have a sincere experience, once you have the experience of the divine presence, the whole world may tell you it is not true, and you will not budge.

22 February 1951

*

If one were in contact with the Divine, what would be its effect?

For each one a different effect. Because we are in the presence of a fact: there is a universe, at least there is an earth, of that we are almost sure, you cannot dispute that, granted?... Have you ever asked yourself why there is an earth? No! Probably it was quite wise. Once I spoke to you of that occultist whom I knew. He was a wise man in his own way. People used to come and ask him:

First of all, why is there a universe? Answer: What is that to you?

Secondly, then why is it as it is? Reply: It is as it is. What does it matter to you?

Thirdly, I do not find it satisfactory.

That's very good. We begin to touch the practical. To those who do not find it satisfactory, I would say: There is only one thing to do, start working for its change, find a way for it to be otherwise and to be good. Things are as they are. Why are they so?... Perhaps one might know — it is not certain. In any case they are so. The most remarkable thing is that if you are sincere you will find out why they are so and how they are so: the cause, the origin and the process. For it is one single thing. There is what we call the Truth, the basis of everything; because if this were not there, there would be nothing. Once you have found the Truth, you find the origin, you find the means of changing the cause — how it is so, why it is so and the means of changing it. If you are in contact with the Divine, you have the key to everything. You know the how, the why and the process to change.

There is something to do: to work, it is so interesting. You represent a small agglomerated mass of substance that makes up yourself. Enter within and find the key. You have only to go down inside there. You cannot say: "That is beyond me, it is too big for me." Go within your little person and you will find the key which opens all the doors.

6 May 1953

*

Can the Divine withdraw from us?

That is an impossibility. Because if the Divine withdrew from a thing, immediately it would collapse, for it would not exist. To put it more clearly: The Divine is the only existence.*

27 May 1953

*

When one is identified with the Divine, does one see Him in the form one thinks He has?

Usually. It is very rare — unless one is able to get rid of one's mental formation completely — it is very rare to see Him quite objectively. Besides, Sri Aurobindo always used to say that the relation with the

---

* At the time of the publication of this talk, the Mother added: "Now I would have answered: it is as if you asked whether the Divine would withdraw from Himself! (*Mother laughs.*) Well, that is the trouble: when you say 'Divine', they understand 'God'.... There is *only* That, That alone exists. That, what is it? That alone exists."

Divine depended on what one wanted it to be. Everyone aspires for a particular form of relation, and for him the relation takes that form.

Then, what is it in truth?

Probably something that escapes form totally — or that can take all forms. There is no limitation to the expression of the Divine. He can express Himself without form and He can express Himself in all forms. And He expresses Himself in everyone according to each one's need. For even if somebody succeeds in becoming sufficiently impersonal so as to identify himself completely with the Divine, at that moment he will not be able to express it. And as soon as he is in a condition to express it, there will be something of the limited personality intervening and through this the experience has to pass. The moment of the experience is one thing and the expression of this experience is another. It may be simultaneous: there are people who while having the experience express what they feel in some form or other. Then it is simultaneous. But that does not prevent that which has the experience in its purity and that which expresses it from being two fairly different modes of being. And this difference is enough for one to be able to say in truth that it is impossible to know the Divine unless one becomes the Divine.

21 October 1953

*

What is meant by "the Divine gives Himself"?

It means exactly this: that the more you give yourself the more you have the experience — it is not just a feeling or impression or sensation, it is a total experience — that the more you give yourself to the Divine the more He is with you, totally, constantly, at every minute, in all your thoughts, all your needs, and that there's no aspiration which does not receive an immediate answer; and you have the sense of a complete, constant intimacy, of a total nearness. It is as though you carried... as though the Divine were all the time with you; you walk and He walks with you, you sleep and He sleeps with you, you eat and He eats with you, you think and He thinks with you, you love and He is the love you have. But for this one must give himself entirely, totally, exclusively, reserve nothing, keep nothing for himself and not keep back anything, not disperse anything also: the least little thing in your being which is not given to the Divine is a waste; it is the wasting of your joy, something that lessens your happiness by that much, and all that you don't give to the Divine is as though you were holding it in the way of the possibility of the Divine's giving Himself to you. You don't feel Him close to yourself, constantly with you, because you don't belong to Him, because you belong to hundreds of other things and people; in your thought, your action, your feelings, impulses... there are millions of things which you do not give Him, and that is why you don't feel Him always with you, because all these things are so many screens and walls between Him and you. But if you give Him everything, if you keep back nothing, He will be constantly and totally with you in all that you do, in all that you think, all that you feel, always, at each moment. But for this you must give yourself absolutely, keep back nothing; each little thing that you hold back is a stone you put down to build up a wall between the Divine and yourself. And then later you complain: "Oh, I don't feel Him!" What would be surprising is that you could feel Him.

20 July 1955

*

Are Divine Love and Grace the same thing?

Essentially, all things are the same. In its essence everything is the same, it is a phenomenon of consciousness; but Love can exist without Grace and Grace can exist without Love. But for the human consciousness all manifestation of Grace is a manifestation of the supreme Love, inevitably. Only it goes beyond human consciousness.

How can one become conscious of Divine Love and an instrument of its expression?

First, to become conscious of anything whatever, you must will it. And when I say "will it", I don't mean saying one day, "Oh! I would like it very much", then two days later completely forgetting it.

To will it is a constant, sustained, concentrated aspiration, an almost exclusive occupation of the consciousness. This is the first step. There are many others: a very attentive observation, a very persistent analysis, a very keen discernment of what is pure in the movement and what is not.[...] You must take up your search with a purity of aspiration and surrender which in themselves are already difficult to acquire. You must have worked much on yourself only to be *ready* to aspire to this Love. If you look at yourself very sincerely, very straight, you will see that as soon as you begin to think of Love it is always your little inner tumult which starts whirling. All that aspires in you wants certain vibrations. It is almost impossible, without being far advanced on the yogic path, to separate the vital essence, the vital vibration from your conception of Love. What I say is founded on an assiduous experience of human beings. Well, for you, in the state in which you are, as you are, if you had a contact with pure divine Love, it would seem to you colder than ice, or so far-off, so high that you would not be able to breathe; it would be like the mountain-top where you would feel frozen and find it difficult to breathe, so very far would it be from what you normally feel. Divine Love, if not clothed with a psychic or vital vibration, is difficult for a human being to perceive. One can have an impression of grace, of a grace which is something so far, so high, so pure, so impersonal that... yes, one can have the feeling of grace, but it is with difficulty that one feels Love.

But, then, can it be said that the psychic vibration is the vibration of divine Love?

Each one of you should be able to get into touch with your own psychic being, it is not an inaccessible thing. Your psychic being is there precisely to put you in contact with the divine forces. And if you are in contact with your psychic being, you begin to feel, to have a kind of perception of what divine Love can be. As I have just said, it is not enough that one morning you wake up saying, "Oh! I would like to be in contact with divine Love", it is not like that. If, through a sustained effort, a deep concentration, a great forgetfulness of self, you succeed in coming into touch with your psychic being, you will never dream of thinking, "Oh! I would like to be in contact with divine Love" —

you are in a state in which everything appears to you to be this divine Love and nothing else. And yet it is only a covering, but a covering of a beautiful texture.

So, Divine Love need not be sought and known apart from the psychic being?

No, find your psychic being and you will understand what divine Love is. Do not try to come into direct contact with divine Love because this will yet again be a vital desire pushing you; you will perhaps not be aware of it, but it will be a vital desire.

You must make an effort to come into touch with your psychic being, to become aware and free in the consciousness of your psychic being, and then, quite naturally, spontaneously, you will know what Divine Love is.

24 March 1951

*

Divine Love is there always in all its intensity, a formidable power. But most people — ninety-nine per cent — do not feel anything at all! What they feel of it is exclusively in proportion to what they are, to their capacity of receiving. Imagine, for instance, that you are bathing in an atmosphere all vibrant with divine Love — you are not at all aware of it. Sometimes, very rarely, for a few seconds there is suddenly the feeling of "something". Then you say, "Oh, divine Love came to me!" What a joke! It is just that you were simply, for some reason or other, a wee bit open, so you felt it. But it is there, always, like the divine Consciousness. It is the same thing, it is there, all the time, in its full intensity; but one is not even aware of it; or else in this way, spasmodically: suddenly one is in a good state, so one feels something and says, "Oh, the divine Consciousness, divine Love have turned to me, have come to me!" It is not at all like that. One has just a tiny little opening, very tiny, at times like a pin-head, and naturally that force rushes in. For it is like an active atmosphere; as soon as there is a possibility of being received, it is received. But this is so for all divine things. They are there, only one does not receive them, for one is closed up, blocked, one is busy with other things most of the time. Most of the time one is full of oneself. So, as one is full of oneself, there is no place for anything else. One is very actively (*laughing*) busy with other things. One is filled with things, there is no place for the Divine.

But He is there.

It is like all the wonders that are there around you; you do not see them.[...] Sometimes, one moment when you are just a tiny bit more receptive, or else when in sleep you are less exclusively busy with your small affairs, you have a gleam of something and see, feel something. But usually, as soon as you are awake again, all this is obliterated — first, as you know, by the formidable ego which is all full of itself, and the whole universe moves in accordance with this ego: you are at the centre, and the universe turns round you. If you look at yourself attentively, you will see it is like that. Your vision of the universe — that's you at the centre and the universe all around. So there is no place for anything else. It is not the universe you see: it is yourself you see in the universe.

19 May 1954

The Divine Mother

What is the "transcendent Mother"?

Don't you know that there are three principles: the transcendent, the universal and the individual or personal? No? — the transcendent which is above creation, at the origin of creation; the universal which is the creation, and the individual which is self-explanatory. There is a transcendent Divine, a universal Divine and an individual Divine. That is, one may put oneself in contact with the divine Consciousness within oneself, in the universe and, beyond all forms, in the transcendent. So these three aspects are also the three aspects of the divine Mother: transcendent, universal and individual.[...]

The divine Mother is the divine Shakti, that is, the creative Force. She is identified with the cosmos. How can she have a transcendent aspect?

But perhaps the divine Mother was there before the creation! She must certainly have existed before the creation, for she cannot be her own product. If it is she who has created, she must have existed before the creation, otherwise she could never have created.

She existed in the Supreme, then, before the creation?

"In" the Supreme.... It is a little difficult to speak of "within" and "without" when one is outside all forms! If you like, say that she is a movement of the Supreme (if that makes you understand better) or an action of the Supreme or a state of the Supreme, a mode... You may say what you like, what most gives you an understanding of the thing. You see, the human mind likes to cut things into little bits.... I am going to tell you a little story meant for children.

The Supreme, having decided to create a universe, took a certain inner attitude which corresponded with the inner manifestation (unexpressed) of the divine Mother, the supreme Shakti. At the same time, he did this with the intention of its being the mode of creation of the universe he wanted to create, the creative power of the universe. Hence, first of all, he had to conceive the possibility of the divine Mother in order that this divine Mother could conceive the possibility of the universe. You are following? I tell you once again that it is not quite like that, but after all, it is meant for childish minds. So, we may very well say that there is a transcendent Divine Mother, that is, independent of her creation. She may have been conceived, formed (whatever you like) for the creation, with the purpose of creation, but she had to exist before the creation to be able to create, else how could she have created?

That is the transcendent aspect, and note that this transcendent aspect is permanent. We speak as though things had unfolded in time at a date which could be fixed: the first of January 0000, for the beginning of the world, but it is not quite like that! There is constantly a transcendent, constantly a universal, constantly an individual, and the transcendent, universal and individual are co-existent. That is, if you enter into a certain state of consciousness, you can at any moment be in contact with the transcendent Shakti, and you can also, with another movement, be in contact with the universal Shakti, and be in contact with the individual Shakti, and all this simultaneously — that does not unfold itself in time, it is we who move in time as we speak, otherwise we cannot express ourselves. We may experience it but we can express it only by saying one word after another (unfortunately, one cannot say all the words at the same time; if one could say them all at the same time, that would be a little more like the truth).

Finally, all that is said, all that has been said, all that will be said, is always only an extremely clumsy and limited way of expressing something which may be lived but which cannot be described. And there is a moment, when one lives the thing, in which one sees that the same thing can be expressed almost with the same exactness or the same truth in religious language, mystical language, philosophic language and materialistic language and that from the point of view of the lived truth, it makes very little difference. It is only when one is in the mental consciousness that one thing seems true to you and another does not seem true; but all these are only ways of expression. The experience carries in itself its absolute, but words cannot describe it — one may choose one language or another to express oneself, and with just a very little precaution, one can always say something approaching the Truth in all instances.

I am telling you this not to throw you into confusion but simply to let you understand that there is a considerable difference between the truth of experience and the way of expressing it, whatever it may be, even the best.

7 May 1951

*

Mother, suffering comes from ignorance and pain, but what is the nature of the suffering and pain the Divine Mother feels for her children[...]?

It is because she participates in their nature. She has descended upon earth to participate in their nature. Because if she did not participate in their nature, she could not lead them farther. If she remained in her supreme consciousness where there is no suffering, in her supreme knowledge and consciousness, she could not have any contact with human beings. And it is for this that she is obliged to take on the human consciousness and form, it is to be able to enter into contact with them. Only, she does not forget: she has adopted their consciousness but she remains in relation with her own real, supreme consciousness. And thus, by joining the two, she can make those who are in that other consciousness progress. But if she did not adopt their consciousness, if she did not suffer with their sorrow, she could not help them. Hers is not a suffering of ignorance: it is a suffering through identity. It is because she has accepted to have the same vibrations as they, in order to be able to enter into contact with them and pull them out of the state they are in. If she did not enter into contact with them, she would not be felt at all or no one could bear her radiance....

This has been said in all kinds of forms, in all kinds of religions, and they have spoken very often of the divine Sacrifice, but from a certain point of view it is true. It is a voluntary sacrifice, but it is true: giving up a state of perfect consciousness, perfect bliss, perfect power in order to accept the state of ignorance of the outer world so as to pull it out of that ignorance. If this state were not accepted, there would be no contact with it. No relation would be possible. And this is the reason of the incarnations. Otherwise, there would be no necessity. If the divine consciousness and divine force could work directly from the place or state of their perfection, if they could work directly on matter and transform it, there would be no need to take a body like man's. It would have been enough to act from the world of Truth with the perfect consciousness and upon consciousness. In fact that acts perhaps but so slowly that when there is this effort to make the world progress, make it go forward more rapidly, well, it is necessary to take on human nature. By taking the human body, one is obliged to take on human nature, partially. Only, instead of losing one's consciousness and losing contact with the Truth, one keeps this consciousness and this Truth, and it is by joining the two that one can create exactly this kind of alchemy of transformation. But if one did not touch matter, one could do nothing for it.

9 December 1953

*

But I could speak to you of a very old tradition, more ancient than the two known lines of spiritual and occult tradition, that is, the Vedic and Chaldean lines; a tradition which seems to have been at the origin of these two known traditions, in which it is said that when, as a result of the action of the adverse forces — known in the Hindu tradition as the Asuras — the world, instead of developing according to its law of Light and inherent consciousness, was plunged into the darkness, inconscience and ignorance that we know, the Creative Power implored the Supreme Origin, asking him for a special intervention which could save this corrupted universe; and in reply to this prayer there was emanated from the Supreme Origin a special Entity, of Love and Consciousness, who cast himself directly into the most inconscient matter to begin there the work of awakening it to the original Consciousness and Love.

In the old narratives this Being is described as stretched out in a deep sleep at the bottom of a very dark cave, and in his sleep there emanated from him prismatic rays of light which gradually spread into the Inconscience and embedded themselves in all the elements of this Inconscience to begin there the work of Awakening.

If one consciously enters into this Inconscient, one can still see there this same marvellous Being, still in deep sleep, continuing his work of emanation, spreading his Light; and he will continue to do it until the Inconscience is no longer inconscient, until Darkness disappears from the world — and the whole creation awakens to the Supramental Consciousness.

And it is remarkable that this wonderful Being strangely resembles the one whom I saw in vision one day, the Being who is at the other extremity, at the confines of form and the Formless. But that one was in a golden, crimson glory, whereas in his sleep the other Being was of a shining diamond whiteness emanating opalescent rays.

In fact, this is the origin of all Avatars. He is, so to say, the first universal Avatar who, gradually, has assumed more and more conscious bodies and finally manifested in a kind of recognised line of Beings who have descended *directly* from the Supreme to perfect this work of preparing the universe so that, through a continuous progression, it may become ready to receive and manifest the supramental Light in its entirety.

In every country, every tradition, the event has been presented in a special way, with different limitations, different details, particular features, but truly speaking, the origin of all these stories is the same, and that is what we could call a direct, conscious intervention of the Supreme in the darkest matter, without going through all the intermediaries, in order to awaken this Matter to the receptivity of the Divine Forces.

The intervals separating these various incarnations seem to become shorter and shorter, as if, to the extent that Matter became more and more ready, the action could accelerate and become more and more rapid in its movement, more and more conscious too, more and more effective and decisive.

And it will go on multiplying and intensifying until the entire universe becomes the total Avatar of the Supreme.

28 May 1958

CHAPTER 2

The Universe

The Unfolding of the Universe

In the history of our universe there have been six consecutive periods
which began by a creation, were prolonged by a force of preservation
and ended by a disintegration, a destruction, a return to the Origin,
which is called Pralaya.[...] But it has been said that the seventh creation would be a progressive creation, that is, after the starting-point
of the creation, instead of its being simply followed by a preservation, it would be followed by a progressive manifestation which would
express the Divine more and more completely, so that no disintegration and return to the Origin would be necessary. And it has been
announced that the period we are in is precisely the seventh, that is, it
would not end by a Pralaya [...] but it would be replaced by a constant
progress, because it would be a more and more perfect unfolding of
the divine Origin in its creation.

And this is what Sri Aurobindo says. He speaks of a constant
unfolding, that is, the Divine manifests more and more completely,
more and more perfectly, in a progressive creation. It is the nature of
this progression which makes the return to the Origin, the destruction
no longer necessary. All that does not progress disappears, and that is
why physical bodies die, it's because they are not progressive; they
are progressive up to a certain moment, then there they stop and most
often they remain stable for a certain time, and then they begin to
decline, and then disappear. It's because the physical body, physical
matter as it is at present is not plastic enough to be able to progress
constantly. But it is not impossible to make it sufficiently plastic for
the perfecting of the physical body to be such that it no longer needs
disintegration, that is, death.

Only, this cannot be realised except by the descent of the Supermind
which is a force higher than all those which have so far manifested and
which will give the body a plasticity that will allow it to progress constantly, that is, to follow the divine movement in its unfolding.

15 June 1955

"In the workings of the universe whatever happens is the result of all that has happened before." (The Mother)

What do you mean by this?

The universe is in perpetual movement and it is the unfolding of the supreme Consciousness. So all that happens is conditioned by all that preceded it. The universe continues to be what it is because of what it has been, and what it has been was the result of what it was before. And what it will be... will be the consequence of what it is!

Is the unfolding of the universe continuous or does it stop somewhere? What is it that gives us the impression of a beginning, of a decision to begin?

Where does the decision to begin come from?... (*laughing*) From the Supreme probably, I do not know! It may be that one day He decided to have a universe of the type we have and He began to objectify himself in order to have a universe.

Each element of this universe is eternal because the universe *is* the Eternal. Now, in the Eternal it is difficult to speak of a "beginning". Evidently It has always been and It will always be. Only, take for example (this is an image, remember, do not make me say things I do not say), take a sphere which is full of infinitesimal things in an incalculable number. If you change the relation of all these elements, well, the number is so great, the possibilities of relations so many that you may easily speak of an infinite, although from a philosophical point of view it is not an infinite; yet from a descriptive point of view one may say that it is infinite. Each element is eternal. All the combinations are infinite, but the same combination never repeats itself twice. Thus the universe is eternally new and yet it is eternally the same.

According to tradition it is said...

Yes, yes, but it is not a question of tradition. There are people who speak of Pralaya, I know, but that simply means (excuse me, but one must speak a little lightly, otherwise this becomes insufferable) that

one day perhaps the Supreme may feel tired, dissatisfied with the
kind of universe He has made and may want to create another! Then,
as it is He Himself, He takes everything back into Himself and puts it
out again! That is what people call "Pralaya", but it changes nothing:
all the elements of the universe are eternal and eternally will the combinations be different.

*According to science, our physical world of three dimensions is
not infinite: it is bent back upon itself in a space of more than
three dimensions. This closed universe of three dimensions is continually expanding and all the objects of the universe are running away from each other at a speed increasing with their distance. If one goes back into the past, one reaches a time when the
universe was almost condensed at one point and that would give
the key to the constitution of Matter of which the ninety-two elements have never been explained till now. This "condensed point"
or "primitive atom" goes back three or four billion years. This is
what the Indian tradition calls "the golden egg". But before that?
Nothing is known. Quite recently an American scientist has put
forth the theory that this movement of infinite expansion will not
continue, that a contrary movement will set in and all will be
gathered back again.*

A universal respiration.

*If one could travel with a ray of light coming from the sun to the
earth, the departure and arrival would be simultaneous, for the
traveller's "proper time" would be stopped.*

Light seems to me to be too material for this consciousness of simul-
taneity.

Evidently when one emerges from form and enters the "frontier"
state between form and the Formless, everything is simultaneous, but
this is very far from the density of light.

I wonder (it is possible, it is to be seen), but I doubt whether
something physical could be capable of giving this simultaneous consciousness of the universe.

Of course, no material object or being can travel at the speed of light, but supposing it to be possible, as the number of light-rays is practically infinite and covers the whole material universe, one would be able to know everything, apprehend everything.

But that would not be a simultaneous integral knowledge of the universe, not even of the earth. For one who remembers the extra-terrestrial light, remembers the movements of the higher light, terrestrial light is slow, as it is dim. But this would already be an expression of something higher.... I don't know.

Light is a very good symbol, but I do not think it to be a total one.

Is light faster than thought?... You cannot make a concrete experiment with thought. Sound is something very, very slow, but thought is already something quicker than light... perhaps not. Thought gives the sensation of the instantaneous. Do you perceive thought in the physical body, for example? Do you perceive thought apart from a material quality? It remains to be seen, doesn't it? Let me explain: if you go out of your body, if you go out of the vital world and enter the mental world, all relations are different from what they are for thought when in the body. Compared with the body, thought seems an immediate thing like light, for example, even more than light. But when you have nothing to do with the physical any longer and you enter the mind itself, there are relations which may be rendered by a certain time and certain space which do not exist for the physical consciousness but which exist for the mental consciousness. That then would be, if you like, the explanation of what you were saying, that Time changes; for it is evident that in the universal formation there is an infusion of progressive consciousness which is psychologically translated by a relation with new worlds or new "dimensions".

For example, it is said that for a certain period the terrestrial world was ruled by "overmental" forces and that this rule is going to be transcended, that the world will be governed by supramental forces; well, each time new forces descend upon earth, a change is produced and a change of consciousness must have a corresponding change of movement. You say that the movement of expansion becomes more and more swift; this means that the world is filled with a consciousness which makes the movements of the world more and more rapid.

This would be altogether the material transcription of the spiritual phenomenon. The earth is being charged more and more with forces coming from ever higher regions (for our consciousness), which means that they come faster and faster, giving more and more the sense of the instantaneous. What has been discovered is a kind of physical symbolism of this phenomenon which would tend to prove scientifically that the universe is in progress.

The other possibility is that it is a matter of a vibratory movement of inhaling and exhaling — this is quite possible; but the phenomenon of concentration would not necessarily mean a retrogression; it is simply a passage from one movement to another.

The stars are receding from one another at a speed that increases with their distance.... What does this imply?

These are images, aren't they? You can conceive a universe becoming bigger and bigger, but then what is it that will contain this universe? What would there be beyond this universe?... Immediately our small human mind conceives of something quite empty and a universe occupying more and more place in this void, which means that there would be a space in this void, which is an absurdity. In fact, one should say, "It is as though", because that is not really what happens, it is only a way of expressing it. To catch hold of a notion ever so little accurate, one must pass from the material to the psychological explanation, and even if you arrive at the psychological, you are still very far from the truth, which is neither psychological nor spatial, but something else which evidently finds it difficult to express itself in our terms. It is a well-known experience: each time one goes into a consciousness beyond our consciousness (I cannot say spatial), our terrestrial consciousness (not even positively terrestrial, but rather individual), each time one has an experience which transcends the individual consciousness, that is to say, transcends the consciousness of the part to enter a consciousness of the Whole, when one wants to translate this experience, one finds all words empty of sense, because language has been formed to translate human experience for the human mind. We have all the necessary words, even with many shades and niceties, to express human experience, since language has been

made for that, but what language will you use to explain what is outside all language? It is extremely difficult. So you say, "It is like this,
it is like that", and while you are speaking you realise that the experience is being so completely distorted that at times you are understood
to mean entirely the opposite.

For this reason science is full of paradoxes.

Yes, and all spiritual books which speak of the experiences of another
world are always full of paradoxes. They say, "It is like this, it is like
that", in an attempt to give you a suppleness which will allow you to
understand — but even so you do not understand.

The truth is that these experiences can be communicated only in
silence.

And yet, it has been said (and it is a true fact) that these worlds,
like the supramental world, are going to express themselves physically. Then what is going to happen? Will they find new words? New
words must be found for them.... It is difficult, for if new words are
found, they have to be explained!

After all, the ancient initiatory systems were good in a way, in
the sense that they revealed the Knowledge only to those who had
reached a stage where they could receive it directly without the help
of words. And I'm afraid it may come to the same thing now — perhaps even one who has this supramental knowledge will never be
able to make himself understood by people, unless they themselves
become capable of entering into this knowledge. And so the logical
result is that people will say, as I have heard it said: "Oh! it is just as
in ordinary life." Precisely because all that is not of the ordinary life
completely escapes our perception, it cannot be transmitted by words.

Take a place like this [the Sri Aurobindo Ashram], which is sur-
charged with certain forces, certain vibrations; these vibrations do
not show themselves in visible and tangible things — they can produce changes, but as these changes occur according to a method (as
all physical things do), you pass almost logically from one state to
another and this logic prevents you from perceiving that there is something here which does not belong to normal life. Well, those who
have no other perception than that of the ordinary mind, who see

things working out as they habitually do or seem to do in ordinary life, will tell you, "Oh that, that is quite natural." If they have no other perception than the purely physical perception, if they are not capable of feeling the quality of a vibration (some feel it vaguely, but those who are not even capable of feeling that, who have nothing in them corresponding to that or, if they have something, it is not awakened), they will look at the life here and tell you, "It is like the physical life — you have perhaps some ideas of your own, but there are many who have their own ideas; perhaps you do things in a special way, but there are lots of people who also do things in a special way. After all, it is a life like the one I live." ...

And so, it may very well happen that at a given moment the supramental Force manifests, that it is conscious here, that it acts on Matter, but those who do not consciously participate in its vibration are incapable of perceiving it. People say, "When the supramental force manifests, we shall know it quite well. It will be seen" — not necessarily. They will not feel it any more than those people of little sensitivity who may pass through this place, even live here, without feeling that the atmosphere is different from elsewhere — who among you feels it in such a precise way as to be able to affirm it?... You may feel in your heart, in your thought that it is not the same, but it is rather vague, isn't it? But to have this precise perception... Listen, as I had when I came from Japan: I was on the boat, at sea, not expecting anything (I was of course busy with the inner life, but I was living physically on the boat), when all of a sudden, abruptly, about two nautical miles* from Pondicherry, the quality, I may even say the physical quality of the atmosphere, of the air, changed so much that I knew we were entering the aura of Sri Aurobindo. It was a *physical* experience and I guarantee that whoever has a sufficiently awakened consciousness can feel the same thing.

I had the contrary experience also, the first time that I went out in a car after many many years here. When I reached a little beyond the lake,** I felt all of a sudden that the atmosphere was changing; where

* Ten nautical miles? The transcriber of this talk in French may have misheard the word *dix* (ten) as *deux* (two). In another account of this incident, the Mother spoke of "ten nautical miles".

** Lake Ousteri, situated west of Pondicherry about ten kilometres from the Ashram.

there had been plenitude, energy, light and force, all that diminished, diminished... and then... nothing. I was not in a mental or vital consciousness, I was in an absolutely physical consciousness. Well, those who are sensitive in their physical consciousness ought to feel that quite concretely. And I can assure you that the area we call "the Ashram" has a condensation of force which is not at all the same as that of the town [Pondicherry], and still less that of the countryside.

So, I ask you: this kind of condensation of force (which gives you quite a special vibration of consciousness), who is there that is really conscious of it?... Many among you feel it vaguely, I know, even people from outside feel it vaguely; they get an impression, they speak of it, but the precise consciousness, the scientific consciousness which could give you the exact measure of it, who has that? I'm not alluding to anyone in particular, each one can look into himself. And this, this condensation here is only a far-off reflection of the supramental force. So when this supramental force will be installed here definitively, how long will it take for people to perceive that it is there?... And that it changes everything, do you understand? And when I say that the mind cannot judge, it is on facts like these that I base myself — the mind is not an instrument of knowledge, it cannot know. A scientist can tell you the proportion of the different components in any particular atmosphere, he analyses it. But as for this proportion here, who can give it? Who can say: There is such a vibration, such a proportion of this, such a proportion of that, such a proportion of the supramental?... I put the question to you so that you may ponder over it.

17 March 1951

*

Mother, are Time and Space particular only to the physical world or to other worlds also?

As there are forms, there is necessarily a Time, a Space, but it is not at all the same as the physical. It is neither the same Time nor the same Space.

For example, as soon as you come to the vital there is a Time and Space which are similar to the physical but without that fixity and hardness and irremediability which are here. That is, for instance, in the vital a strong intelligent will has an immediate action; here, in the physical, it takes sometimes extremely long to be realised, an entire process has to be followed. In the vital it is direct, the will acts directly on the circumstances, and if it is truly of a very strong kind, it is instantaneous. But there is still a Space, that is, one has the impression of moving to go from one place to another, and that necessarily, as one moves, a certain time intervenes; but it is an extremely short time compared with physical time.

On the mental plane the notion of Time disappears almost totally. For example, you are in your mental consciousness, you think of someone or something or of a place, and immediately you are there. There is no need of any time between the thought and the realisation. It is only when the mind is mingled with the vital that the notion of time is introduced; and if they go down into the physical, before a mental conception can be realised a whole process is necessary. You do not have a direct mental action on matter. For instance, if you think of someone who lives in Calcutta, well, physically you have to take a plane and some hours must pass before you can be there; while mentally if you are here and think of someone in Calcutta, instantaneously you are there with him. Instantaneously, you see. But if you go out in the vital from your body and want to go somewhere, well, you have the feeling of moving, and of the time it takes you to reach the place you are going to. But it is incomparably fast in relation to the physical, to the time necessary to do things physically.

Only right at the top of the ladder, when one reaches what could be called the centre of the universe, the centre and origin of the universe, everything is instantaneous. The past, present and future are all contained in a total and simultaneous consciousness, that is, what has always been and what will be are as though united in a single instant, a single beat of the universe, and it is only there that one goes out of Time and Space.

Mother, you said that if we think mentally of something we are immediately in the presence of that thing, but if, for example, we think mentally of something higher, of the Divine, for example...

Yes?

Are we immediately in His Presence?

Yes, but only that part of the thought, not your body. That's just what I said. In the mental domain it is like that; if one concentrates on the Divine and thinks of the Divine, the part... I don't say the whole thought, because thought is multiple and divided, but the part which is sincerely concentrated on the Divine is with Him. It does some good but not very much when this part is mixed with all the others which think of hundreds of different things at the same time, or when it goes down into the body, is all tied up precisely to that frightful slowness of material things, and when we have to take so many steps only to go from here to the door.

In the vital with a leap one can be there; mentally there is no need even of a leap.

29 June 1955

*

Why is it that "All the Timeless presses towards the play in Time; all in Time turns upon and around the timeless Spirit"? (Sri Aurobindo)

Because it is like that, my child. All that is unmanifested wants to manifest, and all that is manifested tries to return to its Origin.

It is as if you asked me, "Why is the earth round and why are the sun and the planets there?" It is like that, the law of the universe is like that.

Most of these things are simply statements of fact; but there are no explanations, for one can't give mental explanations. One can give some, but each thing one wants to explain is explained by another, which has to be explained by another, which has to be explained by another — indefinitely. And you can go right round the universe, and with one thing explaining another, it explains nothing at all.

The only thing one can do is to say, "It is like that."

That is why it is said that the mind can know nothing: it can know nothing because it needs explanations. An explanation is valuable only to the extent it gives you a power to act on the thing explained, otherwise what's the good of it? If explaining something does not give you the power to change it, it is absolutely useless, because, as I said, the explanation you give entails another explanation, and so on. But if through an explanation you obtain some power over a thing, to make it different from what it is, then it's worth the trouble.

28 March 1956

The Unity of the Universe

If you look from one plane of consciousness, the individual will appear to you as if he were not only an instrument and recorder, but a creator. But look from another and higher plane of consciousness with a wider view of things and you will see that this is only an appearance. In the workings of the universe whatever happens is the result of all that has happened before. How do you propose to separate one being from the integral play of the manifestation or one movement from the whole mass of movements? Where are you going to put the origin of a thing or its beginning? The whole play is a rigidly connected chain; one link merges imperceptibly into another. Nothing can be taken out of the chain and explained by itself as if it were its own source and beginning.

And what do you mean when you say that the individual creates or originates a movement? Does he do it all out of himself or out of nothing as it were? If a being were able to create in that way a thought or feeling or action or anything else, he would be the creator of the world. It is only if the individual goes back in his consciousness into the greater Consciousness which is the origin of things, that he can be an originator; he can initiate a movement only by identifying himself with the conscious Power which is the ultimate source of all movements.

There are many planes of consciousness; and the determinism of one plane is not the same as the determinism of another. So, when you speak of the creative individual, of what part of him are you thinking? For he is a very composite entity. Is it his psychic being of which you speak, or the mental or the vital or the physical? Between the unseen source of a movement and its manifestation, its external expression through the individual, there are all these steps and many others; and on each many modifications of it take place, many distortions and deformations. It is these changes that give the illusion of a new creation, a new origin, or a new starting-point for a movement. It is like when you put a stick into water; you see the stick, not in its true line, but bent into an angle. But it is an illusion, a distortion by the sight; it is not even a real angle.

Each individual consciousness, you can say, brings into the universal movement something that you can call from a certain point of view its own deformation or from another its own quality of the movement. These individual motions are part of the play of the Divine movement; they are not themselves origins, they are a transformation of things whose origin you must seek in the universe as a whole.

The sense of separation is spread everywhere, but it is an illusion; it is one of those false moods of which we must be cured if we want to enter into the true consciousness. The mind cuts the world into small bits: it says, here this stops, there that begins, and by this fragmentation it succeeds in distorting the universal movement. There is one great flow of a single, all-embracing, all-containing consciousness which manifests in an ever unrolling universe. This is the truth that stands behind everything here; but there is too this illusion which masks the truth from you, the illusion of these many movements which imagine that they are separate from one another, that they stand by themselves, in themselves and for themselves and that each is a thing in itself apart from the rest of the universe. They have the impression that their action and reaction upon one another is something external, as if they were like different worlds standing in each other's presence but with no point of contact except some external relations at a distance. Each sees himself as if he were a separate personality existing in its own right. This error of the separative sense has been allowed as part of the universal play, because it was necessary that the one consciousness should objectify itself and fix its forms. But because it has been allowed in the past, it does not follow that the illusion of separateness must always continue.

In the universal play there are some, the majority, who are ignorant instruments; they are actors who are moved about like puppets, knowing nothing. There are others who are conscious, and these act their part, knowing that it is a play. And there are some who have the full knowledge of the universal movement and are identified with it and with the one Divine Consciousness and yet consent to act as though they were something separate, a division of the whole. There are many intermediary stages between that ignorance and this full knowledge, many ways of participating in the play.

26 May 1929

*

The law of each being is different, yes, otherwise how would a distinction be made?—from top to bottom, the nature, appearance, actions, all would be the same. If there were only one law, there would be only one law and every one would repeat the same thing. There would be no need at all to manifest a universe because it would be one single law. The very characteristic of the universe is an infinite multiplicity of laws which together, in their totality, reproduce the One. And it is this which is particularly marvellous in the physical world (in man and in the physical world, for it is proper to the terrestrial being), that it can be one of the innumerable elements which in their totality reproduce the One, and yet at the same time have a personal relation with the One — that is to say, contain in itself the consciousness of the One and the relation with the One, and at the same time be an element of the whole. But if the fact of becoming conscious of the One and identifying oneself with it stopped one from being particular, one would cease existing as a personality.

This is precisely what the Buddhists and the disciples of Shankara try to realise; they wish to abolish totally their personality, their individuality, abolish the truth of their being, the special law of their being. This is what they consider as a fusion with the Divine. But this is the negation of this creation. And as I was saying, the miracle of this creation, as far as the terrestrial individuality goes, is that we may achieve this union, this complete identification with the Supreme, the One, and at the same time keep the consciousness of our diversity, of the particular law we have to express. It is more difficult but infinitely more complete, and it is the very truth of this universe. The universe has not been made for anything else but that, to unite these two poles, the two extremes of consciousness. And when they are united, one understands that these two extremes are exactly the same thing — a whole, at once one and innumerable.

But one feels very different from others!

Externally, this is evident.

It is ignorance.

No, the ignorance is to deny the essential identity, the one origin. And I consider it an ignorant absurdity to want to deny the external differences of the manifestation. Why should there be a manifestation then? What purpose would it serve? This would mean there has been an absurdity at the beginning of creation. If this had not been done on purpose, it would mean that things are not done on purpose or that He has made a mistake or even that He has not understood what He wanted to do! that He thought of doing one thing and did another! Besides, I hasten to tell you that if there were a universe in which all the elements were identical, truly one would immediately ask why it existed. If all of you in front of me, all, were all the same, speaking in the same way, thinking in the same way, reacting in the same way, I believe I should immediately run away!

17 April 1951

*

"*The whole universe explains everything at every moment and a particular thing happens because the whole universe is what it is.*" *(The Mother)*

How does the universe explain at every moment the universe?

That is not what I have said. If you want an explanation of something, it is the universe that explains this something. And each thing is explained by everything; and you can explain nothing except by the whole universe and the entire universe is explained by everything.... Just see: if you read all the explanations given in all the sciences, all the branches of human knowledge, always one thing is explained by another, and if you want to explain this other you explain it by yet another and if you want to explain this other one too, you explain it by yet another. So you continue in this way and go round the universe in order to explain one thing. Only, usually people get tired after a time, they accept the last explanation and stick to it. Otherwise, if they continued to find an explanation, they would have to make the full round of all things and would come back always to the same point. Things are so because they are so, because they had to be so, otherwise they would not be. Things are so, because they are as they are. There's no doubt about it. And that indeed is supreme wisdom.

Is there not a physical law that is able to explain everything in the universe?

Find it out, I shall be very glad.

Can it be found by science?

Yes, if it moves in a very definite direction, if it progresses sufficiently, if it does not stop on the way, scientists will find the same thing the mystics have found, and all religious people, everybody, because there is only one thing to find, there are no two. There is only one. So one can go a long way, one can turn round and round and round, and if one turns and turns long enough without stopping, one will be obliged to come to the same spot. Once there, one feels as though there is nothing at all to find. As I have just told you, there is nothing to find. It is That, the Power.*

27 *May 1953*

* Later on, a disciple asked the Mother what she meant by, "It is That, the Power." The Mother answered, "Yes, they will find the same thing the mystics have found and — religious people have found, as everybody has found — it is That, the Power. What one finds is the Power. And to That, essentially, you can give neither a name nor a definition."

But what does "cosmic spirit" mean?

Cosmic spirit? It is the cosmic spirit, it is the universal spirit, it is the spirit that's in the whole universe. There is a universe. You know what the universe is? Well, this universe has a spirit, and this spirit is the cosmic spirit; this universe has a consciousness and its consciousness is the cosmic, universal consciousness.

One may very well imagine that the universe is only an entity in something which is still vaster, as the individual is only an entity in a much vaster totality. Now, each unit has its consciousness and its own spirit which contains all the others, as a group consciousness is made up of all the individual consciousnesses which constitute it and as a national consciousness is made up of all the individual consciousnesses which constitute it, and something more. The individual is only an element in the whole, even as the earth is a part of the solar system, and the solar system makes a part of all the systems of the universe. So just as there is an individual consciousness, there is a group consciousness and a consciousness of the system, a universal consciousness which is made up of the set of all the consciousnesses composing it, plus something, something — something more subtle. Just like you: you have lots of cells in your body; each cell has its own consciousness and you have a consciousness which is the consciousness of your total individuality, though made up of all these small cellular consciousnesses.

Mother, here [in Sri Aurobindo's letter] it is written: "... there is a wall of separative ignorance between the individual and the cosmic consciousness." Then how to break down this wall?

Get rid of the ignorance, enter the knowledge.

First of all you must know what I have just told you, that you are a part of the whole, that this whole is a part of a greater whole, and that this greater whole is a part of a still greater whole, right up to its forming one single totality. Once you know that, you begin to become aware that in reality there cannot be any separation between you and something greater than you of which you are a part. This is the beginning. Now, you must come to the point not only of thinking this but of feeling it and even living it, and then the wall of ignorance tumbles: one feels this unity everywhere and realises that he is only a more or less fragmentary part of a whole much vaster than he, which is the universe. Then one begins to have a more universal consciousness.

13 July 1955

*

How are our thoughts created by the forces of the universal Mind?

Because the forces of the universal Mind enter into our heads. We are bathed in forces, we are not aware of it. We are not something enclosed in a bag and independent from the rest: all forces, all vibrations, all movements enter into us and pass through us. And so we have a certain mental force held in, that is to say, ready to be used by the formative or creative mental power. These are, as it were, free forces. As soon as a thought coming from outside or a force or movement enters our consciousness, we give it a concrete form, a logical appearance and all kinds of precise details; but in fact all this belongs to a domain one is rarely conscious of.

But this is not a special instance which occurs only from time to time: it is something constant. If a current of force is passing, with a particular thought formation, one sees it passing from one into another, and in each one it forms a kind of centre of light or force which keeps the imprint — more or less pure, more or less clear, more or less mixed — of the initial current; and the result is what we call "our" thought.

But our thought is something which hardly exists. It can be "our" thought only if, instead of being like a public place as we generally are in our normal state — we are like a public place and all the forces pass there, come and go, enter, depart, jostle each other and even quarrel — if instead of being like that, we are a concentrated consciousness, turned upwards in an aspiration, and open beyond the limits of the human mind to something higher; then, being open like this brings down that higher something across all the layers of reality, and this something may enter into contact with our conscious brain and take a form there which is no longer the creation of a universal force or a personal mind stronger than ours, but the *direct* expression and creation of a light which is above us, and which may be a light of the highest kind if our aspiration and opening allow it. That is the only case in which one can say that the thought is our own. Otherwise, all the rest is simply a passing notation: we note down, we invest a force with words, a force that's altogether universal and collective, which enters, goes out, moves and passes freely from one person to another.

> *But how is the thought formed in the universal Mind? [...] You say that it comes from outside, don't you?*

Ideas have a higher origin than the mind. There is a region of the mind, higher than the ordinary mind, in which there are ideas, typal ideas, really prototypes; and these ideas descend and are clothed in mental substance. So, in accordance with — how to put it? — the quality of the receiver, they either keep all their own qualities and original nature or become distorted, coloured, transformed in the individual consciousness. But the idea goes far beyond the mind; the idea has an origin much higher than the mind. So, the functioning is the same from both the universal and the individual point of view; the individual movement is only representative of the universal one. The *scale* is different, but the phenomenon is the same. Of course, these are no longer "thoughts" as we conceive thoughts; they are universal principles — but it's the same thing — universal principles on which the universes are built.

The universe, after all, is only one person, only one individuality in the midst of the eternal Creation. Each universe is a person who takes form, lives, dissolves, and another takes shape — it is the same thing. For us, the person is the human individual; and from the universal point of view the person is the universal individual; it is one universe in the midst of all the universes.

7 November 1956

*

If we never forget that there cannot be, should not be two things exactly alike in the universe, for the second would be useless since there would already be one of the same kind, and that the universe is constituted for the harmony of an infinite multiplicity in which two movements — and even more, two consciousnesses — are never alike, then what right have we to intervene and want that somebody should conform to our own thought?... For if you think in a particular way, it is certain that the other won't be able to think in the same way. And if you are a person of a certain type, it is absolutely certain that the other cannot be of the same type. And what you ought to learn is to harmonise, synthesise, combine all the disparate things in the universe by putting each one *in its place*. Total harmony does not at all lie in an identity, but in a harmonisation which can come only by putting each thing in its place.

13 March 1957

The Earth and the Universe

You say, "Love is everywhere. Its movement is there in plants, perhaps in the very stones...." If there is love in a stone, how can one see it?

Perhaps the different elements constituting the stone are coordinated by the spark of love. I am sure that when the Divine Love descended into Matter, this Matter was quite unconscious, it had absolutely no form; it may even be said that forms in general are the result of the effort of Love to bring consciousness into Matter. If one of you (I have my doubts, but still) went down into the Inconscient, what is called the pure Inconscient, you would realise what it is. A stone will seem to you a marvellously conscious object in comparison. You speak disdainfully of a stone because you have just a wee bit more consciousness than it has, but the difference between the consciousness of the stone and the total Inconscient is perhaps greater than that between the stone and you. And the coming out of the Inconscient is due exclusively to the sacrifice of the Divine, to this descent of divine Love into the Inconscient. Consequently, when I said "perhaps in the stone", I could have removed the "perhaps" — I can assert that *even* in the stone it is there. There would be nothing, neither stone nor metal nor any organisation of atoms without this presence of divine Love.

Most people say there is "consciousness" when they begin to think — when one doesn't think one is not conscious. But plants are perfectly conscious and yet they do not think. They have very precise sensations which are the expression of a consciousness, but they do not think. Animals begin to think and their reactions are much more complex. But both plants and animals are conscious. One can be conscious of a sensation without having the least thought.

Did material substance exist before the descent of Divine Love?

I don't think it could be said that there was a material substance. The Inconscient... it is the Inconscient. I don't know how to explain this to you. If there is a negation of something, it is truly the Inconscient, it is the negation of everything. It has not even the capacity of emptiness. One needs to have descended there to know what it is and explain it. Words cannot describe it. It is the negation of all things because everything begins with consciousness. Without consciousness there is nothing.

Were there any beings before this descent of Love? Were they conscious?

There were no terrestrial beings. The terrestrial world, the earth came into existence after the descent into the Inconscient, not before.

The gradual formation of the different stages of being, from the Supreme to the most material region, is subsequent to the Inconscient. When, precisely, the Consciousness "began" its creation (don't take what I say quite literally as though it were a little history of another country, for it is not that, I am trying to make you understand, that's all), the first manifestation of the creative Consciousness was just an emanation of consciousness — of conscious light — and when this emanation separated itself from its origin, the Inconscient was born, through opposition; how to put it? ... yes, really through opposition.

Consequently, the birth of the Inconscient is prior to the formation of the world, and it was only when the perception came that the whole universe was going to be created uselessly that there was a call and Divine Love plunged into the Inconscient to change it into consciousness. Therefore, it can be said that the formation of the material worlds as we know them is the result of the descent of the supreme Consciousness into the Inconscient. It cannot be said that there was something prior to that, things as we know them in the material world (I apologise for the ambiguity of my words, but you understand one cannot express these things in our usual words).

The formation of the earth as we know it, this infinitesimal point in the immense universe, was made precisely in order to concentrate the effort of transformation upon one point; it is like a symbolic point created in the universe to make it possible, while working directly upon one point, to radiate it over the entire universe.

If we want to make the problem a little more comprehensible, it is enough to limit ourselves to the creation and the history of the earth, for it is a good symbol of universal history.

From the astronomical point of view the earth is nothing, it is a very small accident. From the spiritual point of view, it is a symbolic willed formation. And as I have already said, it is only upon earth that this Presence is found, this direct contact with the supreme Origin, this presence of the divine Consciousness hidden in all things.

The other worlds have been organised more or less hierarchically, if one may say so, but the earth has a special formation due to the direct intervention, without any intermediary, of the supreme Consciousness in the Inconscient.

Have the solar fragments the same matter as the earth?

I have taken care to tell you that this radiation was a symbolic creation, and that all action on this special point had its radiation in the whole universe; remember this, instead of beginning to say that the formation of the earth comes from an element projected from the sun or that a nebula must have been scattered giving birth to the sun and all its satellites, etc.

But is it true that there is no difference between solar matter and terrestrial matter? Were the sun and the other worlds of the solar system formed at the same time as the earth?

Necessarily, everything was formed at the same time, the creation was simultaneous, with a special concentration of the Consciousness upon the earth.

Have the beings of the other worlds and planets a psychic being?

No, it is a purely terrestrial phenomenon. Only, there is nothing against the idea that psychic beings may go to the other worlds if it so pleases them. There is no reason to think that one cannot, if one went to another planet, meet psychic beings; it is not impossible; but these would be psychic beings formed upon earth who have become free in their movement, going here and there at will for some reason or other. All knowledge in all traditions, from every part of the earth, says that the psychic formation is a terrestrial formation and that the growth of the psychic being is something that takes place upon earth. But once they are formed and free in their movement, they can go anywhere in the universe, they are not limited in their movement; but their formation and growth belong to the terrestrial life, for reasons of concentration.

24 March 1951

*

You said that this physical world was a projection of invisible worlds. Then why should the divine Emanations come into the physical world to transform it? They have only to do the work in the invisible planes; then the projections will be good.

That indeed is a serious question!... You know the image sometimes given to the universe: a serpent biting its tail? And it is taken as the symbol of the infinite, of the universe. Well, it is a fact. In the creation there is a progressive, a greater and greater materialisation. But we could take another image (I am taking an approximate image): the universe is a circle or rather a sphere (but for the convenience of explanation, let us take a circle). There is a progressive descent from the most subtle to the most material. But the most material happens to touch the point of origin of the most subtle. Then, if you understand the image, instead of going all the way round to change matter, it is much more easy to do the thing directly, for the two extremities meet. [...] It is precisely for the convenience of work that all has been concentrated or concretised at one point so that instead of having to spread oneself out in the infinite to change things, one can work just on the point that serves as the symbol of the whole universe. And from the occult standpoint, earth (which is nothing from the astronomical standpoint; in the immensity of the astronomical skies, earth is a thing absolutely without interest and without importance), but from the occult and spiritual point of view, earth is the concentrated symbol of the universe. For it is much more easy to work on one point than in a diluted vastness. This all people who work know. Well, for the convenience and necessity of work, the whole universe has been concentrated and condensed symbolically in a grain of sand which is called the earth. And therefore it is the symbol of all; all that is to be changed, all that is to be transformed, all that is to be converted is there. This means that if one concentrates on this work and does it there, all the rest will follow automatically, otherwise there will be no end — and no hope.

But that is also why this point appears as particularly bad! Because the whole thing is concentrated. And that can be particularly good also. For always there are the two, the two opposites are together. And always the best borders on the worst, or the worst borders on the best (it depends on the side you look from). But it is because of the worst that you can find the best and it is because of the best that you can transform the worst — the two act and react upon each other. [...] It is always said that there is a dark double of all the stars and a luminous double of all the planets. In the occult way, it is said that there is a luminous earth.

23 September 1953

*

There is a very interesting fact, it is that somewhere in the terrestrial mind, somewhere in the terrestrial vital, somewhere in the subtle physical, one can find an exact, perfect, automatic recording of everything that happens. It is the most formidable memory one could imagine, which misses nothing, forgets nothing, records all. And if you are able to enter into it, you can go backward, you can go forward, and in all directions, and you will have the "memory" of all things — not only of things of the past, but of things to come. For everything is recorded there.

In the mental world, for instance, there is a domain of the physical mind which is related to physical things and keeps the memory of physical happenings upon earth. It is as though you were entering under innumerable vaults, one following another indefinitely, and these vaults are filled with small pigeon-holes, one above another, one above another, with tiny doors. Then if you want to know something and if you are conscious, you look, and you see something like a small point — a shining point; you find that this is what you wish to know and you have only to concentrate there and it opens; and when it opens, there is a sort of an unrolling of something like extremely subtle manuscripts, but if your concentration is sufficiently strong you begin to read as though from a book. And you have the whole story in all its details. There are thousands of these little holes, you know; when you go for a walk there, it is as though you were walking in infinity. And in this way you can find the exact facts about whatever you want to know.

But I must tell you that what you find is never what has been reported in history — histories are always planned out; I have never come across a single "historical" fact which is like history. This is not to discourage you from learning history, but things are like that. Events have been quite different from the way in which they have been reported, and for a very simple reason: the human brain is not capable of recording things with exactitude; history is built upon memories and memories are always vague. If you take, for example, written memories, he who writes chooses the events which have interested him, what he has seen, noticed or known, and that is always only a very small portion of the whole. When the historian narrates, the same thing happens as with dreams where you take one point, then another, then another, and at last you can have an almost exact vision of what has taken place and with a little imagination you fill up the gaps; but historians relate a continuous story; between the events or moments there are gaps which they fill up as best they can or rather as they wish, according to their mental, vital and other preferences. And that comprises the history you are made to learn. The same story, narrated in one language and in another, in one country or in another, you cannot imagine how comic it is! This is particularly true if one of the countries is interested because of its vanity, its prestige. And finally the two pictures presented to you are so different that you could believe that two different things were being spoken about. It is unbelievable.

But I have noticed that even for altogether external, concrete facts where there is no question of evaluation, it is still the same thing. No human brain is capable of understanding a thing in its totality; even the most scholarly, the most learned, even the most sincere person does not see a subject — and especially many subjects — totally. He will say what he knows, what he understands, and all that he does not know, all that he does not understand is not there, and this absolutely changes everything.

But if you can acquire this capability of entering into the terrestrial memory, I assure you it is worth the trouble. It is quite different from Yoga; it is not necessary to have a spiritual life for that, you must have a special ability.

For everything — I would repeat it to you eternally if I had the time — for everything, one must be absolutely sincere. If you are not sincere, you will begin by deceiving yourself and all your experiences will be worth nothing at all. But if you are sincere and by discipline (for it is not easy) you succeed in entering this mental memory of the world, you will make discoveries which are really worth the trouble.

15 February 1951

*

To be able to enter the "earth-memory" consciously, a discipline is needed. What discipline?

A discipline much more difficult than the discipline of Yoga! It is an occult discipline.

First of all, one must learn to go out of one's body consciously and to enter into another more subtle body; to use one's will to go where one wants to go, never to fear and sometimes to face unexpected and even terrible things; to remain calm, to develop the mind's visual sense, to accustom one's mind to be altogether peaceful and quiet.... You know, the list is long and I could continue like this for hours!

19 February 1951

CHAPTER 3

The Human Species in Evolution

Progression of Forms

If you take terrestrial history, all the forms of life have appeared one after another in a general plan, a general programme, with the addition, always, of a new perfection and a greater consciousness. Take just animal forms — for that is easier to understand, they are the last before man. Each animal that appeared had an additional perfection in its general nature — I don't mean in all the details — a greater perfection than the preceding ones, and the crowning point of the ascending march was the human form which, for the moment, from the point of view of consciousness, is the form most capable of manifesting consciousness; that is, the human form at its height, at the height of its possibilities, is capable of more consciousness than all preceding animal forms.

This is *one* of Nature's ways of evolution.

Sri Aurobindo told us [...] that this Nature was following an ascending progression in order to manifest more and more the divine consciousness contained in all forms. So, with each new form that it produces, Nature makes a form capable of expressing more completely the spirit which this form contains. But if it were like this, a form comes, develops, reaches its highest point and is followed by another form; the others do not disappear, but the individual does not progress. The individual dog or monkey, for instance, belongs to a species which has its own peculiar characteristics; when the monkey or the man arrives at the height of its possibilities, that is, when a human individual becomes the best type of humanity, it will be finished; the individual will not be able to progress any farther. He belongs to the human species, he will continue to belong to it. So, from the point of view of terrestrial history there is a progress, for each species represents a progress compared with the preceding species; but from the point of view of the individual, there is no progress: he is born, he follows his development, dies and disappears. Therefore, to ensure the progress of the individual, it was necessary to find another means; this one was not adequate.

But within the individual, contained in each form, there is an organisation of consciousness which is closer to and more directly under the influence of the inner divine Presence, and the form which is under this influence — this kind of inner concentration of energy — has a life independent of the physical form — this is what we generally call the "soul" or the "psychic being" — and since it is organised around the divine centre it partakes of the divine nature which is immortal, eternal. The outer body falls away, and this remains throughout every experience that it has in each life, and there is a progress from life to life, and it is the progress of the *same* individual. And this movement complements the other, in the sense that instead of a species which progresses relative to other species, it is an individual who passes through all the stages of progress of these species and can continue to progress even when the species have reached the limit of their possibilities and... stay there or disappear — it depends on the case — but they cannot go any farther, whereas the individual, having a life independent of the purely material form, can pass from one form to another and continue his progress *indefinitely*. That makes a double movement which completes itself. And that is why each individual has the possibility of reaching the utmost realisation, independent of the form to which he momentarily belongs.[...]

It is this double movement of evolution intersecting and complementing itself which gives the utmost possibilities of realisation to the divine light within each being. This is what Sri Aurobindo has explained. (*Turning to the child*) This means that in your outer body you belong to the animal species in the course of becoming a supramental species — you are not that yet! but within you there's a psychic being which has already lived in many, many, countless species before and carries an experience of thousands of years within you, and which will continue while your human body remains human and finally decomposes.

We shall see later whether this psychic being has the possibility of transforming its body and itself creating an intermediate species between the animal man and superman — we shall study this later — but still, for the moment, it is an immortal soul which becomes more and more conscious of itself in the body of man.[...]

In Nature we often see the disappearance of an entire species.
What is that due to?

Probably Nature thought that it was not a success!... You see, she throws herself into action with abundance and a total lack of sense of economy. We can see this. She tries everything she can, in every way she can, with all sorts of inventions which are obviously very remarkable, but at times... it's like a blind alley. Pushing forward in that direction, instead of progressing, one would reach things that are absolutely unacceptable. She throws out her creative spirit in an abundance without any calculation, and when the combination is not very successful, well, she just does this (*gesture*), then rejects it; she doesn't mind. For Nature, you see, there is a limitless abundance. I believe she doesn't shrink from any kind of experiment. Only if something has a chance of leading to a successful issue does it continue. Certainly there have been intermediaries or parallel forms between the ape and man; traces of them have been found — perhaps with some wishful thinking! but anyway, traces have been found — well, those species have disappeared. So, if we like to speculate, we may wonder whether the species which is now to come and which is an intermediary between animal man and superman will remain or whether it will be considered uninteresting and rejected.... That we shall see later. The next time we meet we shall speak about it again!

It is quite simply the activity of a limitless abundance. Nature has enough knowledge and consciousness to act like someone with innumerable and countless elements which can be mixed, separated again, reshaped, taken to pieces once more and... It is a huge cauldron: you stir it, and something comes out; it's no good, you throw it back in and take something else. Imagine the dimension... just take the earth: you understand, one or two forms or a hundred, for her this is of no importance at all, there are thousands and thousands and thousands of them; and then a few years, a hundred, a thousand, millions of years, it is of no importance at all, you have eternity before you!

Simply, when we look at things on the human scale, in space and time, oh! it seems enormous, but for Nature it is nothing. It is just a pastime. One may like it or not, this pastime, but still it is a pastime.

It is quite obvious that Nature enjoys it and is in no hurry. If she is told to press on without stopping and to finish one part of her work or another quickly, the reply is always the same: "But what for, why? Doesn't it amuse you?"

30 October 1957

*

Everybody is progressing, always, isn't that so?

In a certain way, yes. Only it may not be apparent in one lifetime, because when there is no conscious participation of the being, the movement is relatively slow, even relative to the short duration of human life. And so it is quite possible, for example, that at the moment of death a being seems not to have progressed, and even sometimes it seems to have been going backwards, to have lost what it had at the beginning of its life. But if we take the great life-curve of its psychic being through many lives, there is always a progress. Each experience it had in one of its physical lifetimes helps it to make some progress. But it is the psychic being which always progresses.

The physical being, in the state in which it is at present — well, having reached a certain point of ascent, it comes down again. There are elements which may not come down again grossly; but still it does come down, one can't deny it.

The vital being — not necessarily, nor the mental being. The vital being, if it knows how to get connected with the universal force, can very easily have no retrogression; it can continue to ascend. And the mental being, it's absolutely certain, is completely free from all degeneration if it continues to develop normally. So these always make progress so long as they remain co-ordinated and under the influence of the psychic.

It is only the physical being which grows and decomposes. But this comes from its lack of plasticity and receptivity and by its very nature; it is not inevitable. Therefore there is room to think that at a given moment, as the physical consciousness itself progresses consciously and deliberately, well, to a certain extent and increasingly the body itself will be able, first to resist decay — which, obviously, must be the first movement — and then gradually begin to grow in inner perfection till it overcomes the forces of decomposition.[...]

But this substance *itself* — that is, this material physical substance which forms it constitutes an organism which lives for a certain length of time in a given form and then this form declines and dissolves — the substance itself constituting these successive forms progresses through all these forms. That is, the molecular, cellular substance — perhaps even the cellular — the molecular and atomic, is progressing in its capacity to express the divine Force and Consciousness. Through all these organisms this substance becomes more and more conscious, more and more luminous, more and more receptive, until it reaches a perfection sufficient for it to become a possible vehicle for the divine Force itself which will be able to use it as it uses the elements of the other parts of the creation, like the mind or the vital.

And at that moment the physical substance will be ready to manifest in the world the new Consciousness, new Light, new Will. Through all the centuries, through countless lives, passing through innumerable organisms, using countless experiences it, so to speak, becomes refined; it is prepared, and becomes more and more receptive and open to the divine Forces.

So, a man as a momentary individual being may not appear to progress. But the progress is continued through him, as through all organisms.

28 December 1955

*

How did the first man appear?

Sri Aurobindo says here,* precisely, that if we take the scientific point of view, we see that theories follow one another with great instability,

* "... if the facts with which Science deals are reliable, the generalisations it hazards are short-lived; it holds them for some decades or some centuries, then passes to another generalisation, another theory of things. This happens even in physical Science where the facts are solidly ascertainable and verifiable by experiment...."

and seem more like a kind of series of imaginations than things which can be proved — if one takes the purely materialist point of view. People believe that because it is a materialist point of view, it is the easiest to prove, but quite obviously it is the most difficult. If we take the occult standpoint, there have been traditions, based perhaps on certain memories, but as they are altogether beyond any material proof, this knowledge is considered to be even more problematic than scientific imaginations and deductions. For any inner logic, it is easier to understand and admit, but one has no more proof than one has material proof that there was *one* first man or that there were several first men or that there was something which was not yet a man but almost a man. These are speculations.

Traditions — which of course are only oral traditions and from the scientific point of view quite questionable, but which are based on individual memories — say that the first man or the first human pair or the first human individuals were materialised in accordance with an occult method, something like the one Sri Aurobindo foretells for the future supramental process; that is, that beings belonging to higher worlds have, by a process of concentration and materialisation, built or formed for themselves bodies of physical matter. It probably wasn't the lower species which progressively produced a body which became the first human body.

According to spiritual and occult knowledge, consciousness precedes form; consciousness by self-concentration produces its form; whereas, according to the materialist idea, it is form which precedes consciousness and makes it possible for consciousness to manifest. For those who have some knowledge of the invisible worlds and a direct perception of the play of forces, there is no possible doubt: it is *necessarily* consciousness which produces a form in order to manifest. Now, the way things are arranged on earth, it is quite certainly a consciousness of a higher order which penetrates a form and helps to transform it, so that this form may become — either immediately or through successive generations — capable of manifesting that consciousness. For those who have the inner vision and knowledge, this is absolutely beyond doubt. It is impossible for it to be otherwise. But those who start from the other end, from below, will not admit it — but all the same it is not for ignorance to dictate knowledge to wisdom! And yet, this is what it does at present. As it is easier to doubt than to know, the human mind is accustomed to doubt everything; that is its first movement, and of course that is why it knows nothing.

Conception precedes manifestation and expression, that is quite certain. And all those who have had a direct contact with the past have the memory of a kind of human prototype, far superior to mankind at present, who came on earth as an example and a promise of what humanity will be when it reaches its acme.

There is in life a certain tendency to imitate, a sort of effort to copy "something". One can find very striking examples of this in animal life — it even begins already in plant life, but in animal life it is very striking. One could give numerous examples. And so, in that sense, one might very well conceive of a sort of effort of animal life to attempt to copy, to imitate, to create some resemblance to this ideal type which would be manifested on earth by occult means, and it was probably through successive attempts, by a more and more successful effort that the first human types were produced.

11 December 1957

*

Sweet Mother, is there a spiritual being in everybody?

That depends on what we call "being". If for "being" we substitute "presence", yes, there is a spiritual presence in everyone. If we call "being" an organised entity, fully conscious of itself, independent, and having the power of asserting itself and ruling the rest of the nature — no! The possibility of this independent and all-powerful being is in everybody, but the realisation is the result of long efforts which sometimes extend over many lives.

In everyone, even at the very beginning, this spiritual presence, this inner light is there.... In fact, it is everywhere. I have seen it many a time in certain animals. It is like a shining point which is the basis of a certain control and protection, something which, even in half-consciousness, makes possible a certain harmony with the rest of creation so that irreparable catastrophes may not be constant and general. Without this presence the disorder created by the violences and passions of the vital would be so great that at any moment they could bring about a general catastrophe, a sort of total destruction which would prevent the progress of Nature. That presence, that spiritual light — which could almost be called a spiritual consciousness — is within each being and all things, and because of it, in spite of all discordance, all passion, all violence, there is a minimum of general harmony which allows Nature's work to be accomplished.

And this presence becomes quite obvious in the human being, even the most rudimentary. Even in the most monstrous human being, in one who gives the impression of being an incarnation of a devil or a monster, there is something within exercising a sort of irresistible control — even in the worst, some things are impossible. And without this presence, if the being were controlled exclusively by the adverse forces, the forces of the vital, this impossibility would not exist.

Each time a wave of these monstrous adverse forces sweeps over the earth, one feels that nothing can ever stop the disorder and horror from spreading, and always, at a certain time, unexpectedly and inexplicably a control intervenes, and the wave is arrested, the catastrophe is not total. And this is because of the Presence, the supreme Presence, in matter.

But only in a few exceptional beings and after a long, very long work of preparation extending over many, many lives does this Presence change into a conscious, independent, fully organised being, all-powerful master of his dwelling-place, conscious enough, powerful enough, to be able to control not only this dwelling but what surrounds it and in a field of radiation and action that is more and more extensive... and effective.

11 June 1958

The Human Problem

It is obvious that what especially characterises man is this mental capacity of watching himself live. The animal lives spontaneously, automatically, and if it watches itself live, it must be to a very minute and insignificant degree, and that is why it is peaceful and does not worry. Even if an animal is suffering because of an accident or an illness, this suffering is reduced to a minimum by the fact that it does not observe it, does not project it in its consciousness and into the future, does not imagine things about its illness or its accident.

With man there has begun this perpetual worrying about what is going to happen, and this worry is the principal, if not the sole cause of his torment. With this objectivising consciousness there has begun anxiety, painful imaginations, worry, torment, anticipation of future catastrophes, with the result that most men — and not the least conscious, the most conscious — live in perpetual torment. Man is too conscious to be indifferent, he is not conscious enough to know what will happen. Truly it could be said without fear of making a mistake that of all earth's creatures he is the most miserable. The human being is used to being like that because it is an atavistic state which he has inherited from his ancestors, but it is truly a miserable condition. And it is only with this spiritual capacity of rising to a higher level and replacing the animal's unconsciousness by a spiritual super-consciousness that there comes into the being not only the capacity to see the goal of existence and to foresee the culmination of the effort but also a clear-sighted trust in a higher spiritual power to which one can surrender one's whole being, entrust oneself, give the responsibility for one's life and future and so abandon all worries.

Of course, it is impossible for man to fall back to the level of the animal and lose the consciousness he has acquired; therefore, for him there is only one means, one way to get out of this condition he is in, which I call a miserable one, and to emerge into a higher state where worry is replaced by a trusting surrender and the certitude of a luminous culmination — this way is to change the consciousness.

Truly speaking there is no condition more miserable than being responsible for an existence to which one doesn't have the key, that is, of which one doesn't have the threads that can guide and solve the problems. The animal sets itself no problems: it just lives. Its instinct drives it, it relies on a collective consciousness which has an innate knowledge and is higher than itself, but it is automatic, spontaneous, it has no need to will something and make an effort to bring it about, it is quite naturally like that, and as it is not responsible for its life, it does not worry. With man is born the sense of having to depend on himself, and as he does not have the necessary knowledge the result is a perpetual torment. This torment can come to an end only with a total surrender to a higher consciousness than his own to which he can totally entrust himself, hand over his worries and leave the care of guiding his life and organising everything.

How can a problem be solved when one doesn't have the necessary knowledge? And the unfortunate thing is that man believes that he has to resolve all the problems of his life, and he does not have the knowledge needed to do it. That is the source, the origin of all his troubles — that perpetual question, "What should I do?... " which is followed by another one still more acute, "What is going to happen?" and at the same time, more or less, the inability to answer.

That is why all spiritual disciplines begin with the necessity of surrendering all responsibility and relying on a higher principle. Otherwise peace is impossible.

And yet, consciousness has been given to man so that he can progress, can discover what he doesn't know, develop into what he has not yet become; and so it may be said that there is a higher state than that of an immobile and static peace: it is a trust total enough for one to keep the will to progress, to preserve the effort for progress while ridding it of all anxiety, all care for results and consequences. This is one step ahead of the methods which may be called "quietist", which are founded on the rejection of all activity and a plunging into an immobility and inner silence, which forsake all life because it has been suddenly felt that without peace one can't have any inner realisation and, quite naturally, one thought that one couldn't have peace so long as one was living in outer conditions, in the state of anxiety in which problems are set and cannot be solved, for one does not have the knowledge to do so.

The next step is to face the problem, but with the calm and certitude of an absolute trust in the supreme Power which knows, and can make you act. And then, instead of abandoning action, one can act in a higher peace that is strong and dynamic.

This is what could be called a new aspect of the divine intervention in life, a new form of intervention of the divine forces in existence, a new aspect of spiritual realisation.

26 March 1958

*

I have seen pet animals which truly had a sort of inner *need* to become something other than what they were. I knew dogs which were like that, cats, horses and even birds like that. The outer form was inevitably what it was, but there was something living and perceptible in the animal which was making an obvious effort to achieve another expression, another form. And every man who has gone beyond the stage of the animal man and become the human man truly has what I might call an "incorrigible" need to be something other than this thoroughly unsatisfactory semi-animal — unsatisfactory in its expression, its means of expression and its means of life. So the problem is this: Will this imperious need be effective enough in its aspiration for the form itself, the species, to develop and transform itself, or will it be only this thing, this imperishable consciousness in the being, which will leave this form when it perishes to enter into a higher form which, besides, as far as we can see now, does not yet exist?

And the problem before us is: How will this higher form be created? If we consider the problem, it becomes very interesting. Is it by some process which we have to imagine, that this form will gradually transform itself in order to create a new one, or is it by some other means, a means still unknown to us, that this new form will appear in the world?

That is, will there be a continuity or will there be a sudden appearance of something new? Will there be a progressive transition between what we now are and what our inner spirit aspires to become, or will there be a break, that is, shall we be obliged to drop this present human form and wait for the appearance of a new form — an appearance the process of which we do not foresee and which will have no relation with what we are now? Can we hope that this body which is our present means of earthly manifestation, will have the possibility of transforming itself progressively into something which will be able to express a higher life, or will it be necessary to give up this form entirely to enter into another which does not yet exist on Earth?

That is the problem. It is a very interesting problem.

(When this talk was first published, the Mother added the following remarks:)

Why not both? Both will be there at the same time; the one does not exclude the other.

Yes, but will one be transformed into the other?

One will be transformed and will be like a rough outline of the other. And the other, the perfect one, will appear when this one comes into being. For both have their beauty and their purpose, therefore they will both be there.

The mind always tries to choose — but it's not like that. Even all that we can imagine is much less than what will be. Truly speaking, everyone who has an intense aspiration and an inner certitude will be called upon to realise it.

Everywhere, in all the fields, always, eternally, everything will be possible. And everything that is possible, everything will exist at a given moment — a given moment that will be more or less delayed, but everything will exist.

Just as all sorts of possibilities have been found between the animals and man, possibilities which have not remained, so there will be all sorts of possibilities: each individual will try in his own way. And all this together will help to prepare the future realisation.

The question might be asked: Will the human species be like some species which have disappeared from the earth?... Certain species have disappeared from the earth — but not species which have lasted as long as the human species. I don't think so; and certainly not the species which had in them the seed of progress, this possibility of progress. Rather one has the impression that evolution will follow a curve which will draw closer and closer to a higher species and, maybe, everything that is still too close to the lower species will fall away, just as those species have.

We always forget that not only is everything possible — everything, even the most contradictory things — but all the possibilities have at least one moment of existence.

4 December 1957

*

The difficulty of the problem is that only a mental being could take an interest in this process of transformation and creation, and that the mental consciousness in the animal species was not sufficient for it to take an interest in this process.

Animals had no means of noting what was happening, of taking it into consideration and remembering it. And that is why this part of the earth's history has almost disappeared. A mental capacity like man's must intervene to make it possible to follow the course of this transformation and retain a memory of it.... In fact, more is imagined than remembered. It is quite obvious that the psychic being has gone through all that, but it has not kept a mental memory of it. The memory of the psychic being is a psychic memory which is of an altogether different kind; it is not historical like mental memory which can keep a precise record of what takes place.

But now that we are on the threshold of the new transformation [...] and now that we are going to witness the process of transformation between the human mental being and the supramental being, we shall profit by this historical ability of the mind which will follow what happens and take note of it. So, from that point of view also, the phenomenon which is taking place now is absolutely unique in the history of the earth, and probably — almost certainly — when we have followed the process of this transformation to the very end, we shall have the key to all the former transformations; that is, everything that we are trying to understand at present, we shall know for certain when the process is repeated, this time between the mental and the supramental being.

You are therefore invited to a very special development of the capacity for observation, so that all this may not take place in a half-dream and you awaken to a new life without even knowing how things have happened.

One must be very vigilant, wide awake, and instead of being interested in little inner psychological phenomena which are... quite antiquated — they belong to an entire period of human history which anyway has lost all its novelty — it would be better to be more attentive to things of greater general import, things more subtle, more impersonal which would put you in the midst of new discoveries of a very special interest.

Open the eyes of the subtle intelligence, and without prejudice or preference, without egoism and without attachment, look at what is happening day by day.

12 March 1958

The Collaboration of Nature

"O Nature, Material Mother, Thou hast said that thou wilt collaborate and there is no limit to the splendour of this collaboration."
New Year Message of 1958   *The Mother*

Sweet Mother, will you explain the message for this year?

[...] It is an experience, something that happened, and when it happened I noted it down, and as it turned out, it occurred just at the moment when I remembered that I had to write something for the year — which was next year at that time, that is, the year which begins today. When I remembered that I had to write something — not because of that, but simultaneously — this experience came, and when I noted it down, I realised that it was... it was the message for this year!

(Silence)

I will tell you only one thing: you should not misinterpret the meaning of this experience and imagine that from now on everything is going to take place without any difficulties and always in a manner that favours our personal desires. It is not on this plane. It does not mean that when we do not want it to rain, it will not rain! that when we want something to happen in the world, it will happen immediately; that all difficulties will be done away with and everything will be as it is in fairy-tales. It is not that. It is something much deeper: Nature, in her play of forces, has accepted the new Force which has manifested and included it in her movements. And as always, the movements of Nature are on a scale which is infinitely beyond the human scale and not visible to an ordinary human consciousness. It is an inner, psychological possibility which has come into the world rather than a spectacular change in earthly events.

I am saying this because you might be tempted to believe that fairy-tales were going to be realised on earth. It is not yet time for that.

One must have much patience and a very wide and very complex vision to understand how things happen.

The miracles which take place are not what could be called storybook miracles, in the sense that they don't happen as in stories. They are visible only to a very deep vision of things — very deep, very comprehensive, very vast.

One must already be capable of following the methods and ways of the Grace in order to recognise its action. One must already be capable of not being blinded by appearances in order to see the deeper truth of things.

We could usefully, this evening, just take this resolution: to try throughout the year to do our best, so that the time may not pass in vain.

1 January 1958

*

In the course of one of our classes I spoke of the limitless abundance of Nature, the inexhaustible creatrix who takes the multitude of forms and mixes them together, separates them again and remoulds them, unmakes and destroys them, to move on to ever new combinations. It is a huge cauldron, I said: she stirs things inside and brings out something; it's no good, she throws it in again and takes something else.... One or two forms or a hundred have no importance for her, there are thousands and thousands of forms, and then as for years, a hundred years, a thousand, millions of years, it is of no importance, you have eternity before you! It is quite obvious that Nature enjoys all this and that she is not in a hurry. If she is told to rush rapidly through and finish this or that part of her work quickly, the reply is always the same: "But why should I do so, why? Doesn't it amuse you?"

The evening I told you about these things, I identified myself totally with Nature, I joined in her game. And this movement of identification provoked a response, a sort of new intimacy between Nature and myself, a long movement of a growing closeness which culminated in an experience which came on the eighth of November [1957].

Suddenly Nature understood. She understood that this new Consciousness which has just been born* does not seek to reject her but wants to embrace her entirely, she understood that this new spirituality does not turn away from life, does not recoil in fear before the formidable amplitude of her movement, but wants on the contrary to integrate all its facets. She understood that the supramental consciousness is here not to diminish but to complete her.

Then from the supreme Reality came this order, "Awake, O Nature, to the joy of collaboration." And the whole of Nature suddenly rushed forward in a great surge of joy, saying, "I accept, I shall collaborate." And at the same time, there came a calm, an absolute tranquillity so that the bodily vessel could receive and contain, without breaking, without losing anything, the mighty flood of this Joy of Nature which rushed forward as in a movement of gratitude. She accepted, she saw with all eternity before her that this supramental consciousness was going to fulfil her more perfectly, give a still greater strength to her movement, a greater amplitude, more possibilities to her play.

And suddenly I heard, as if they came from all the corners of the earth, those great notes one sometimes hears in the subtle physical, a little like those of Beethoven's Concerto in D-major, which come in moments of great progress, as though fifty orchestras had burst forth all in unison, without a single false note, to express the joy of this new communion between Nature and Spirit, the meeting of old friends who come together again after having been separated for so long.

Then these words came, "O Nature, Material Mother, thou hast said that thou wilt collaborate and there is no limit to the splendour of this collaboration."

And the radiant felicity of this splendour was sensed in perfect peace.

That is how the message for the new year was born.

---

* The Mother is referring to the supramental consciousness, which, she said, manifested upon earth on 29 February 1956.

A Transitional Species

"If a spiritual unfolding on earth is the hidden truth of our birth into Matter, if it is fundamentally an evolution of consciousness that has been taking place in Nature, then man as he is cannot be the last term of that evolution: he is too imperfect an expression of the Spirit, Mind itself a too limited form and instrumentation; Mind is only a middle term of consciousness, the mental being can only be a transitional being. If, then, man is incapable of exceeding mentality, he must be surpassed and Supermind and superman must manifest and take the lead of the creation. But if his mind is capable of opening to what exceeds it, then there is no reason why man himself should not arrive at Supermind and supermanhood or at least lend his mentality, life and body to an evolution of that greater term of the Spirit manifesting in Nature." (Sri Aurobindo)

Anyway, we have now reached a certitude since there is already a beginning of realisation. We have the proof that in certain conditions the ordinary state of humanity can be exceeded and a new state of consciousness worked out which enables at least a conscious relation between mental and supramental man.

It can be asserted with certainty that there will be an intermediate specimen between the mental and the supramental being, a kind of superman who will still have the qualities and in part the nature of man, that is, who will still belong in his most external form to the human being with its animal origin, but will transform his consciousness sufficiently to belong in his realisation and activity to a new race, a race of supermen.

This species may be considered a transitional species, for one can foresee that it will discover the means of producing new beings without going through the old animal method, and these beings — who will have a truly spiritual birth — will constitute the elements of the new race, the supramental race.

So we could call supermen those who, in their origin, still belong to the old method of generation but in their achievement are in conscious and active contact with the new world of supramental realisation.

It seems — it is even certain — that the very substance which will constitute this intermediate world that is already being built up, is richer, more powerful, more luminous, more resistant, with certain subtler, more penetrating new qualities, and a kind of innate capacity of universality, as if its degree of subtlety and refinement allowed the perception of vibrations in a much wider, if not altogether total way, and it removes the sensation of division one has with the old substance, the ordinary mental substance. There is a subtlety of vibration which makes global, universal perception a spontaneous and natural thing. The sense of division, of separation, disappears quite naturally and spontaneously with that substance. And that substance is at present almost universally diffused in the earth atmosphere. It is perceptible in the waking state, simply with a little concentration and a kind of absorption of consciousness, if this is retracted, withdrawn from the ordinary externalisation which seems more and more artificial and false. This externalisation, this perception which formerly was natural, now seems false, unreal and completely artificial; it does not at all answer to things as they are, it belongs to a movement which does not correspond to anything really true.

This new perception is asserting itself more and more, becoming more and more natural, and it is even sometimes difficult to recapture the old way of being, as though it were vanishing into a misty past — something which is on the point of ceasing to exist.

One may conclude from this that the moment a body, which was of course formed by the old animal method, is capable of living this consciousness naturally and spontaneously, without effort, without going out of itself, it proves that this is not one single exceptional case but simply the forerunner of a realisation which, even if it is not altogether general, can at least be shared by a certain number of individuals who, besides, as soon as they share it, will lose the perception of being separate individuals and become a living collectivity.

This new realisation is proceeding with what one might call a lightning speed, for if we consider time in the ordinary way, only two years have passed — a little more than two years — from the time the supramental substance penetrated into the earth atmosphere to the time the change in the quality of the earth atmosphere took place.

If things go on advancing at this speed, it seems more than possible, almost evident, that what Sri Aurobindo wrote in a letter is a prophetic announcement: The supramental consciousness will enter a phase of realising power in 1967.*

16 April 1958

---

* "4-5-67 is the year of complete realisation."

CHAPTER 4

Plants and Animals

Trees and Flowers

Sweet Mother, can a plant grow otherwise than physically?

In plants there is a great vital force. And this vital force has a considerable action. And there is also the genius of the species, which is a consciousness. There is already an active consciousness at work in plants.

And in the genius of the species there is a beginning — quite embryonic, but still — there is a beginning of response to the psychic influence, and certain flowers are clearly the expression of a psychic attitude and aspiration in the plant, not very conscious of itself, but existing like a spontaneous impetus.

It is quite certain, for instance, that if you have a special affection for a plant, if, in addition to the material care you give it, you love it, if you feel close to it, it feels this; its blossoming is much more harmonious and happy, it grows better, it lives longer. All this means a response in the plant itself. Consequently, there is the presence there of a certain consciousness; and surely the plant has a vital being.

Mother, does a plant have its own individuality and does it also reincarnate after death?

This may happen, but it is accidental.

There are trees — trees especially — which have lived long and can be the home of a conscious being, a vital being. Generally it is vital entities which take shelter in trees, or else certain beings of the vital plane which live in forests — as certain beings of the vital live in water. There were old legends like that, but they were based on facts.

The plant serves as home and shelter, but the being is not created by the plant itself!

18 January 1956

*

Is there a sense of beauty in flowers?

Directly there is organic life, the vital element comes in, and it is this vital element which gives to flowers the sense of beauty. It is not perhaps individualised in the sense we understand it, but it is a sense of the species and the species always tries to realise it. I have noticed a first rudiment of the psychic presence and vibration in vegetable life, and truly this blossoming one calls a flower is the first manifestation of the psychic presence. The psychic is individualised only in man, but it was there before him; but it is not the same kind of individualisation as in man, it is more fluid: it manifests as force, as consciousness rather than as individuality. Take the rose, for example; its great perfection of form, colour, scent expresses an aspiration and a psychic giving. Look at a rose opening in the morning at the first touch of the sun, it is a magnificent self-giving in aspiration.

Each flower has its special significance, hasn't it?

Not as we understand it mentally. There is a mental projection when one gives a precise meaning to a flower. It may answer, vibrate to the touch of this projection, accept the meaning, but a flower has no equivalent of the mental consciousness. In the vegetable kingdom there is a beginning of the psychic, but there is no beginning of the mental consciousness. In animals it is different; mental life begins to form and for them things have a meaning. But in flowers it is rather like the movement of a little baby — it is neither a sensation nor a feeling, but something of both; it is a spontaneous movement, a very special vibration. So, if one is in contact with it, if one feels it, one gets an impression which may be translated by a thought. That is how I have given a meaning to flowers and plants — there is a kind of identification with the vibration, a perception of the quality it represents and, little by little, through a kind of approximation (sometimes this comes suddenly, occasionally it takes time), there is a coming together of these vibrations (which are of a vital-emotional order) and the vibration of the mental thought, and if there is a sufficient harmony, one has a direct perception of what the plant may signify.

In some countries (particularly here [in India]) certain plants are used as the media for worship, offering, devotion. Certain plants are given on special occasions. And I have often seen that this identification was quite in keeping with the nature of the plant, because spontaneously, without knowing anything, I happened to give the same meaning as that given in religious ceremonies. The vibration was really there in the flower itself.... Did it come from the use that had been made of it or did it come from very far, from somewhere deep down, from a beginning of the psychic life? It would be difficult to say.

1 March 1951

Insects and Animals

Animals don't have ill-will, do they?

I do not think so. I can't say for sure since I don't know all the animal species, but I have heard things which to us seem monstrosities, yet are not at all instances of ill-will. For example, take the world of insects; of all the animal species it is this which most contains the sense of what we call wickedness — and what may be called ill-will, but it could very well be that this is our consciousness applied to their movements which sees a movement of wickedness or ill-will.... There are insects whose larvae can live only on a living being. They can feed only on a living being; dead flesh does not nourish these. So the parent insect that is going to lay its eggs (which will change into larvae) begins by stinging a nervous centre of another insect or small lower animal which it paralyses, and after that gently lays its eggs inside in such a way that when the eggs are hatched the larvae feed on that paralysed but not dead animal. It is Machiavellian, isn't it? Evidently it is not the result of reasoning, it is an instinct. Can this be called ill-will? Is this ill-will?... It is simply the instinct of procreation.

Perhaps, if we say that these insects are moved by the spirit of the species which in itself is conscious and has a conscious will, we can then say that all these imaginations (I give you this one instance, but there are any number of them as terrible, as monstrous for our human consciousness), all these beings, fashioners, who have created these insects must be frightful beings (don't you think so?) and have a perverse and diabolical imagination. It is quite possible, for indeed it is said that the origin of the insect species is a vital origin, that the fashioners are those of a vital type, that is, beings who not only symbolise but represent and live upon the ill-will in the world. These are very conscious of their ill-will, and it is deliberate. The ill-will of men is usually only a kind of reflection — an imitation or a reflection — of the will of the beings of the vital, a will clearly hostile to creation, a will to make things as painful, as ugly, as sorrowful, as monstrous as possible. It is said that it is these who have created insects, and so the insect species would perhaps be... But they do not wilfully represent evil, you understand, they are moved by an unconscious instinct. They do not do evil intentionally. They do it because it is in their nature.

What I call ill-will is truly the will to do evil for the sake of doing evil, destroying for the sake of destroying, harming for harming's sake and taking pleasure in the fact of doing evil. That really is ill-will. Egoism, I do believe, begins with the birth of mind. I can't tell for certain, for always new things are being found. But what I have seen of the animal species, specially of the higher animals, may be the instinct of preservation, may be violence, obscure and brutal reactions, but is that truly what is called ill-will?... It is possible. If someone were to tell me a story he has witnessed which proves the opposite, I am ready to admit it but for the time being — I haven't seen it. All that I know of animals is their instinct which pushes them into action, but they don't have that perversity that's in the human mind. I believe it is with this kind of mental functioning and under the direct influence of the vital that man has become an ill-willed being. The Titans are ill-willed beings but the Titans are beings of the vital world manifested in the forces of Nature: they want to do evil for the pleasure of doing it, to destroy for the pleasure of destroying.

People always speak about the wickedness of cats, for instance, playing with the mouse before eating it. That's an example given to children; but I have seen cats. I know what they do. It is not at all true. They don't do this at all through malice. Usually it happens like this: the mother-cat hunts for the little ones and catches a mouse. If it were to give the mouse immediately to the kittens to eat, they wouldn't be able to eat it, for it is hard, tough, and they don't have the capacity to eat such hard, tough flesh. Besides, it is also bad when it is like that. So they play with it (they seem to be playing with it), they toss it about, roll it, catch it, let it run, run after it, until it is very nicely softened. And then, when it is well softened, ready for eating, and the meat already worked upon, then they give it to the little ones who can now eat it. But certainly they don't go and play with the mouse for the pleasure of playing! They hunt first, you see, and then prepare the dinner. They have neither furnace nor fire to cook and soften the thing. They must prepare it and make it ready for eating.

But it is also said that the first expression of love in living beings is the desire to devour. One wants to absorb, desires to devour. There is one instance which would seem to prove that this is not altogether false — that is when the tiger catches its prey or the snake its victim, it happens that both the tiger's and the snake's victims give themselves up in a kind of delight of being eaten. An experience is narrated of a man who was in the bush with his friends and had lagged behind and was caught by a tiger, a man-eater. The others came back when they saw that he was missing. They saw the tracks. They ran after him, just in time to prevent the tiger's eating him. When he came to himself a little, they told him he must have had a frightful experience. He said: "No, just imagine, I don't know what happened to me, as soon as that tiger caught me and while it was dragging me along, I felt an intense love for it and a great desire to be eaten by it!"

This is quite true, it is not an invention. It is a true story.

Well, I have seen with my own eyes.... I believe I have already narrated this to you — the story of the little rabbit which had been put in a python's cage. It was in the cage in the Jardin des Plantes in Paris. It was the breakfast day. I happened to be there. The cage was opened, the little white rabbit put inside. It was a pretty little white rabbit and it immediately fled to the other end of the cage and trembled like anything. It was horrible to see this, for it knew very well what was happening, it had felt the snake, it knew very well. The serpent was simply coiled up on its mat. It seemed to be asleep, and very quietly it stretched out its neck and head, and then began looking at the rabbit. It looked at it without stirring — just looked at it. I saw the rabbit which at first stopped trembling; it no longer was afraid. It was quite doubled up and it began to recover. And then I saw it lift its head, open its eyes wide, and look at the snake, and slowly, very slowly it went forward towards it till it was just at the right distance. Then the snake with a single leap — without any disturbance, without even uncoiling itself, just remaining where it was, you understand — hop! it took it. And then it began rolling it, preparing it for its dinner. It was not in order to play with it. It prepared the thing. It crushed all its bones nicely, made them crack; then it smeared it with a kind of gluey substance to make it quite slippery. And when it was all quite ready, it began swallowing it slowly, comfortably.... But it didn't have to disturb itself, it didn't have to make the least movement, except the last swift one just to catch it when it was right in front. It was the other creature that had come to it.

There you are. Indeed there are many things in Nature. There is this, there is perhaps ill-will also. But I am not quite sure that it is not one of those presents that mental activity has given to man... as soon as he was separated from his instinct and wanted to act independently....

What exactly is instinct?

It is the consciousness of Nature. Nature is conscious of its action, but this is not an individual consciousness. There is an instinct of the species. Some have said that there were even "spirits of the species", conscious beings for each species. Instinct depends on the way Nature works, and Nature is a conscious force which knows what it wants, does it in its own way, knowing where it is going and its roads: it chooses them itself. For man this appears incoherent, for his own consciousness is too narrow (he can't see the whole well enough; when one sees only the small details of things or little fragments, one can't understand at all), but Nature has a plan, it has a conscious will, it is altogether a conscious entity — it can't be called a being, for it is not in the same proportion. When we speak of a being with our human consciousness, we immediately imagine a human being, perhaps a little larger or much larger, but still functioning always in the same way. That is why I don't call it a being, but it is a conscious entity, a conscious will doing things consciously, deliberately, and having formidable forces at its disposal.

It is also said that the forces of Nature are blind and violent. But it is not at all that! It is man in his relative proportion with Nature who judges like that. Wait a little, let us take this example. When there is an earthquake, many islands are engulfed and millions of people killed. People say: "This Nature is monstrous." From the human point of view this Nature is monstrous. What has it done? It has wrought a cataclysm. But just think how in jumping or running or doing something or other, you get a good knock and turn black and blue. It is the same thing for our cells as an earthquake; you destroy a huge number of cells! It is a question of proportion. For us, our little consciousness, ever so little, this appears something formidable but after all it is quite simply a contusion somewhere upon earth (not even in the universe). We are speaking only of the earth. What is it? Nothing at all, just a tiny little plaything in the universe. If we speak of this universe, then the disappearance of the worlds — these are just contusions. It is nothing.

One must, if one can, widen one's consciousness.

8 July 1953

Animals and Men

There are animals with very developed senses, aren't there?

Ah! yes, there are animals which are much more advanced than we.

I knew an elephant which led us straight to the water when we were tiger-shooting.

Animals have much more perfect senses than those of men. I challenge you to track a man as a dog does, for instance!

This means that in the curve or rather the spiral of evolution, animals (and more so those we call "higher" animals, because they resemble us more closely) are governed by the spirit of the species which is a highly conscious consciousness. Bees, ants, obey this spirit of the species which is of quite a special quality. And what is called "instinct" in animals is simply obedience to the spirit of the species which always knows what ought and ought not to be done. There are so many examples, you know. You put a cow in a meadow; it roams around, sniffs, and suddenly puts out its tongue and snatches a blade of grass. Then it wanders about again, sniffs and gets another tuft of grass, and so it goes on. Has anyone ever known a cow under these conditions eating poisonous grass? But shut this poor animal up in a cow-shed, gather and put some grass before it, and the poor creature which has lost its instinct because it now obeys man (excuse me), eats the poisonous grass along with the rest of it. We have already had three such cases here, three cows which died of having eaten poisonous grass. And these unfortunate animals, like all animals, have a kind of respect (which I could call unjustifiable) for the superiority of man — if he puts poisonous grass before the cow and tells it to eat, it eats it! But left to itself, that is, without anything interfering between it and the spirit of the species, it would never do so. All animals which live close to man lose their instinct because they have a kind of admiration full of devotion for this being who can give them shelter and food without the least difficulty — and a little fear too, for they know that if they don't do what man wants they will be beaten!

It is quite strange, they lose their ability. Dogs, for instance the sheep-dog which lives far away from men with the flocks and has a very independent nature (it comes home from time to time and knows its master well, but often does not see him), if it is bitten by a snake, it will remain in a corner, lick itself and do all that is necessary till it gets cured. The same dog, if it stays with you and is bitten by a snake, dies quietly like man.

I had a very sweet little cat, absolutely civilised, a marvellous cat. It was born in the house and it had the habit all cats have, that is to say, if something moved, it played with that. Just then there was in the house a huge scorpion; as was its habit, the cat started playing with the scorpion. And the scorpion stung it. But it was an exceptional cat; it came to me, it was almost dying, but it showed me its paw where it was bitten — it was already swollen and in a terrible state. I took my little cat — it was really sweet — and put it on a table and called Sri Aurobindo. I told him, "Kiki has been stung by a scorpion, it must be cured." The cat stretched its neck and looked at Sri Aurobindo, its eyes already a little glassy. Sri Aurobindo sat before it and looked at it also. Then we saw this little cat gradually beginning to recover, to come round, and an hour later it jumped to its feet and went away completely healed.... In those days, I had the habit of holding a meditation in the room where Sri Aurobindo slept [...] and it was regularly the same people who came; everything was arranged. But there was an arm-chair in which this very cat always settled beforehand — it did not wait for anyone to get into the chair, it got in first itself! And regularly it went into a trance! It was not sleeping, it was not in the pose cats take when sleeping: it was in a trance, it used to start up, it certainly had visions. And it let out little sounds. It was in a profound trance. It remained thus for hours together. And when it came out from that state, it refused to eat. It was awakened and given food, but it refused: it went back to its chair and fell again into a trance! This was becoming very dangerous for a little cat.... But this was not an ordinary cat.

To finish my story, if you leave an animal in its normal state, far from man, it obeys the spirit of the species, it has a very sure instinct and it will never commit any stupidities. But if you take it and keep it with you, it loses its instinct, and it is then you who must look after it, for it no longer knows what should or should not be done. I was interested in cats to make an experiment, a sort of inverse metempsychosis, if one can call it that, that is, to see if this could be their last incarnation as animals, if they were ready to enter a human body in the next life. The experiment succeeded fully, I had three absolutely striking instances; they left with a psychic being sufficiently conscious to enter a human body. But this is not what men ordinarily do; what they usually do is to spoil the consciousness or rather the instinct of animals.

22 March 1951

*

What kind of love do animals have for men?

It is almost the same as that of rather unintellectual men for the Divine. It is made of admiration, trust and a sense of security. Admiration: it seems to you something really very beautiful. And it is not reasoned out: an admiration from the heart, so to speak, spontaneous.

For instance, dogs have this in a very high degree. And then, trust — naturally this is sometimes mixed with other things: with the feeling of some need and dependence, for it is that person who will give me to eat when I am hungry, give me shelter when it is rough weather, who will look after me. This is not the most beautiful side. And then, unfortunately, it gets mixed up (and I believe — I consider it entirely man's fault) with a kind of fear; a feeling of dependence and a kind of fear of something which is much stronger, much more conscious, much more... which can harm you, and you have no strength to defend yourself. It is a pity, but I believe it is altogether man's fault.

But if men really deserved the love of animals, it would be made of a feeling of wonder and of the sense of security. It is something very fine, this sense of security; something that's able to protect you, to give you all that you need, and near which you can always find shelter.

Animals have an altogether rudimentary mind. They are not tormented by incessant thoughts like human beings. For example, they feel a spontaneous gratitude for an act of kindness towards them, whilst men, ninety-eight times out of a hundred, begin to reason and ask themselves what interest one could have in being good. This is one of the great miseries of mental activity. Animals are free from this and when you are kind to them they are grateful to you, spontaneously. And they have trust. So their love is made of that, and it turns into a very strong attachment, an irresistible need to be near you.

There is something else. If the master is really a good one and the animal faithful, there is an exchange of psychic and vital forces, an exchange which becomes for the animal something wonderful, giving it an intense joy. When they like to be quite close to you in that way, when you hold them, it is that they vibrate internally. The force one gives them — the strength of affection, of tenderness, protection, all that — they feel it, and it creates a deep attachment in them. Even fairly easily, in some of the higher animals like dogs, elephants, and even horses, it creates quite a remarkable need for devotion (which indeed is not thwarted by all the reasonings and arguments of the mind), which is spontaneous and very pure in its essence, something that's very beautiful.

The working of the mind in man in its rudimentary form, its first manifestation has spoilt many things which were much finer before.

Naturally, if man rises to a higher level and makes good use of his intelligence, then things can take on a much greater value. But between the two, there is a passage where man makes the most vulgar and low use of his intelligence; he makes it an instrument for calculation, domination, deception, and there it becomes very ugly. I have known in my life animals I considered much higher than a large number of men, for that sordid calculation, that wish to cheat and profit was precisely not there in them. There are others that catch it — through contact with man they catch it — but there are those who don't have it.

The unselfish movement, uncalculating, is one of the most beautiful forms of psychic consciousness in the world. But the higher one rises in the scale of mental activity, the rarer it becomes. For with intelligence come all the skill and cleverness, and corruption, calculation. For instance, when a rose blossoms it does so spontaneously, for the joy of being beautiful, smelling sweet, expressing all its joy of living, and it does not calculate, it has nothing to gain out of it: it does so spontaneously, in the joy of being and living. Take a human being, well, apart from a very few exceptions, the moment his mind is active he tries to get some advantage out of his beauty and cleverness; he wants it to bring him something, either men's admiration or even much more sordid gains yet. Consequently, from the psychic point of view, the rose is better than human beings.

Only, if you climb a rung higher and consciously do what the rose does unconsciously, then it is much more beautiful. But it must be the same thing: a spontaneous flowering of beauty, uncalculating, simply for the joy of being. Little children have this at times (at times, not always). Unfortunately, under the influence of their parents and the environment, they learn to be calculating when yet very young.

But this kind of wish to gain by what one has or does is truly one of the ugliest things in the world. And it is one of the most widespread and it has become so widespread, that it is almost spontaneous in man. Nothing can turn its back on the divine love more totally than that, that wish to calculate and profit.

Do flowers love?

This is their form of love, this blossoming. Certainly, when one sees a rose opening to the sun, it is like a need to give its beauty. Only, for us, it is almost unintelligible, for they do not think about what they do. A human being always associates with everything he does this ability to see himself doing it, that is, to think about himself, think of himself doing it. Man knows that he is doing something. Animals don't think. It is not at all the same form of love. And flowers, so to speak, are not conscious: it is a spontaneous movement, not a consciousness that is conscious of itself, not at all. But it is a great Force which acts through all that, the great universal Consciousness and the great Force of universal love which makes all things blossom in beauty.

That is what I have written there also:

"Is it not love, under an erring and obscure form, that is associated with all the impulsions of the physical and vital nature as the push towards every movement and every grouping and which has become quite visible in the plant world?" (The Mother)

You know, crystals which are formed in matter already obey a movement of love; but this becomes quite perceptible in the vegetable kingdom, in the tree and plant. It is the need to grow to get more light. All these trees which are always growing higher — always growing, the smaller ones trying to catch up with the taller, the taller ones trying to climb yet higher; you put two plants side by side, they both try to find an orientation that gives them the maximum light possible — that is the need to grow to get more air, more light, more space.

"In the flower it is the gift of beauty and fragrance in a loving efflorescence. And in the animal is it not there behind hunger and thirst, the need for appropriation, expansion, procreation, in brief, behind all desire, whether conscious or not? and, among the higher orders, in the self-sacrificing devotion of the female for her young ones?" (The Mother)

... which in human beings becomes maternal love. The only difference is that it is conscious of itself. And in animals it is often even purer than in human beings. There are instances of the devotion, care, self-forgetfulness of animals for their young, which are absolutely wonderful. Only, it is spontaneous, not thought out, not reflected upon; the animal does not think about what it is doing. Man thinks. At times this spoils the movement (at times — most often), sometimes it can give it a higher worth but that is rare. There is less spontaneity in man's movements than in an animal's.

26 August 1953

*

Aren't dogs more faithful than men?

Certainly! Because it is their nature to be faithful, and they have no mental complications. What prevents men from being faithful are their mental complications. Most men are not faithful because they fear being duped. You don't know what it is to be duped? They fear being deceived, being exploited. They fear... Behind their faithfulness there is still a very big egoism which is more or less hidden, and there is always that bargaining, more or less conscious, of give-and-take: one gives oneself to someone but whether one tells oneself this or not, one expects something in exchange. You are faithful, but also want others to be faithful to you, that is, look after you, to be quite sweet to you, and, especially not to try to profit by your faithfulness. None of these complications are there in the dog, for its mind is very rudimentary. It does not have this marvellous capacity of reasoning that men have, a capacity which has made them commit so many stupidities.

Only one cannot turn and go back. One cannot become a dog again. So one must become a higher man and have the quality of the dog on a higher plane; that is, instead of its being a half-conscious fidelity, and in any case very instinctive, a sort of need that ties it down, it must be a willed, conscious fidelity, and especially above all egoism. There is a point where all the virtues are united: it is a point that goes beyond the ego. If we take this faithfulness, if we take devotion, take love, the meaning of service, all these things, when they are above the egoistic level, they meet, in the sense that they give themselves and do not expect anything in exchange. And if you climb one step higher, instead of its being done with the idea of duty and abnegation, it is done with an intense joy which carries within itself its own reward, which needs nothing in exchange, for it carries its joy in itself. But then, for that you must have climbed quite high and must no longer have that turning back upon yourself which, of all things, pulls you down lowest. That kind of... that sympathy, full of self-pity, wherein one cajoles and caresses oneself and says, "Poor me!", that, indeed, is something terrible, and one does this so constantly, without being aware of it. This turning back upon oneself, a kind of degrading self-compassion, in which one tells oneself in a tone so full of pity, "Nobody understands me! No one loves me! No one cares for me as people should!" etc., and one goes on and on.... And now this is really terrible, it draws you down into a hole immediately.

One must have gone far beyond all that, left it very far behind oneself, in order to truly have the joy of faithfulness, the joy of self-giving, which does not care at all, no, indeed, not at all, in any way, whether it is properly received or gets the adequate response. Not to expect anything in exchange for what one does, not to expect anything, not through asceticism or a sense of sacrifice but because one has the joy of the consciousness one is in and that is enough; this is much better than all one can receive, from whomsoever it be; but that again is something else. There are quite a few stages between the two.

23 June 1954

*

There are movements of certain vibrations which are vibrations of the species, you see, movements peculiar to the species to which you belong — there is the human species as there are all kinds. Now, some of these movements are not personal movements at all, they are movements of the species.

The human species has certain ways of being which are particular to it, which we reproduce almost automatically, as for example, walking upright, like this (*gesture*), whereas a cat goes on four feet, you see. This instinct of standing on one's two hind feet, upright, is peculiar to man, it is a movement that belongs to the species; to sit as we do with the head up, you see, to lie down as we do on the back...

You have only to watch animals: they lie down curled up, don't they? Almost all. It is with man that this way of lying on one's back, stretched out, begins, I think; I don't at all think that monkeys sleep like that, I think they sleep doubled up, that it is man who has started habits of this kind. And this reminds me...

I had a cat — in those days I used to sleep on the floor — which always came and slipped under the mosquito-net and slept beside me. Well, this cat slept quite straight, it did not sleep as cats do, it put its head here and then lay down like this (*gesture*), alongside my legs with its two forepaws like this, and its two little hind legs quite straight. And there was something very, very curious about it which I saw one night, like that. I used to ask myself why it was like this, and one night I saw a little Russian woman of the people with a fur bonnet and three little children, and this woman had a kind of adoration for her children and always wanted to look for a shelter for them; I don't know, I don't know the story, but I saw that she had her three little children, very small ones, with her... one like this, one like that, one like that (*Mother shows the difference in height*), and she was drag-ging them along with her and looking for a corner to put them in safety. Something must have happened to her, she must have died suddenly with a kind of very animal maternal instinct of a certain kind, but all full of fear — fear, anguish and worry — and this some-thing must have come from there and in some way or other had rein-carnated. It was a movement — it was not a person, you know, it was a movement which belonged to this person and must have come up in the cat. It was there for some reason or other, you see, I don't know how it happened, I know nothing about it, but this cat was completely human in its ways. And very soon afterwards it had three kittens, like that; and it was extraordinary, it didn't want to leave them, it refused to leave them, it was entirely... it did not eat, did not go to satisfy its needs, it was always with its young. When one day it had an idea — nobody had said anything, of course — it took one kitten, as they take them, by the skin of the neck, and came and put it between my feet; I did not stir; it returned, took the second, put it there; it took the third, it put it there, and when all three were there, it looked at me, mewed and was gone. And this was the first time it went out after having had them; it went to the garden, went to satisfy its needs and to eat, because it was at peace, they were there between my feet. And when it had its young, it wanted to carry them on its back like a woman. And when it slept beside me, it slept on the back. It was never like a cat.

23 March 1955

CHAPTER 5

The Gradations of Existence and Their Expression in the Human Being

The Origin of Individuality

Who will tell me what constitutes an individual? What is it that gives you the impression that you are a person existing in himself?

One can say with Descartes: "I think, therefore I am."

Ah, no! that does not prove that you are individualised.

What is it that gives you the impression that you are an individual?... When you were ten, you were very different from what you were when you were born, and now you are very different from what you were at ten, aren't you? The form grows within certain limits and there is a similarity, but even so, it is quite different from what it was at your birth; you may almost say, "It was not I." So much for the physical. Now, take your inner consciousness when you were five and now. Nobody would say it is the same person. And your thoughts, at five and now? All are different. But in spite of everything, what is it that gives you the impression that it is *the same person* who is thinking?

Let us take the example of a river following its course: it is never the same water which flows. What is a river? There is not a drop that ever is the same, no stability is there, then where is the river? (Some take this example to prove that there is no personality — they are very anxious to prove that there is no personality.) For beings it is the same thing: the consciousness changes, ideas change, sensations change, what then is the being? Some say that individuality is based upon memory, remembrance: you remember therefore you are an individual being. This is absolutely wrong, for even if you had no memory you would still be an individual being.

The river's bed constitutes the river.

The bed localises the river, but the bed also changes much; which means that all is inconstant, all is fugitive, and this is true. But it is only one part of the truth, it is not the whole. You feel quite clearly that there is something "stable" in you, don't you, but where does this sensation of stability come from?

If I were to place it physically, I would say it is somewhere in the chest. When I say "I am going to do something", it is not the true "I" which speaks. When I say "I think", it is not the true "I" which thinks — the true "I" looks at the thinking, it looks at the thoughts coming. Naturally this is a way of speaking.

When the vast majority of people say "I", it is a part of them, of their feeling, their body, their thought, indifferently, which speaks; it is something that always changes. Therefore, their "I" is innumerable, or the "I" always varies. What is the constant thing therein?... The psychic being, evidently. For, to be constant a thing must first be immortal. Otherwise it cannot be constant. Then, it must also be independent of the experiences through which it passes: it cannot be the experiences themselves. Hence, it is certainly not the bed of the river which constitutes the river; the bed is only a circumstance. If the comparison is carried a little farther (besides, comparisons are worthless, people find in them whatever they want), it can be said that the river is a good symbol of life, that what is constant in the river is the species "water". It is not always the same drop of water, but it is always water — without water there would be no river. And what endures in the human being is the species "consciousness". It is because it has a consciousness that it endures. It is not the forms which last, it is the consciousness, the power of binding together all these forms, of passing through all these things, not only keeping a memory of them (memory is something very external), but keeping the same vibration of consciousness.

And that is the great mystery of creation, for it is the same consciousness, the Consciousness is one. But the very moment this Consciousness manifests itself, exteriorises itself, deploys itself, it divides itself into innumerable fragments for the need of expansion, and each one of these fragmentations has been the beginning, the origin of an individual being. The origin of every individual form is the law of this form or the truth of this form. If there were no law, no truth of each form, there would be no possibility of individualisation. It would be something extending indefinitely; there would be perhaps points of concentration, assemblages, but no individual consciousness. Each form then represents one element in the changing of the One into the many. This multiplicity implies an innumerable quantity of laws, elements of consciousness, truths which spread out into the universe and finally become separate individualities. So the individual being seems constantly to go farther and farther away from its origin by the very necessity of individualisation. But once this individualisation, that is, this awareness of the inner truth is complete, it becomes possible, by an inner identification, to re-establish in the multiplicity the original unity; that is the *raison d'être* of the universe as we perceive it. The universe has been made so that this phenomenon may take place. The Supreme has manifested Himself to Himself so as to become aware of Himself.

In any case, that is the rationale of *this* creation. Let us be satisfied with our universe, let us make the best use possible of our life upon earth and the rest will come in its time.

It is purposely, mind you, that I have not mentioned the ego as one of the causes of the sense of individuality. For the ego being a falsehood and an illusion, the sense of individuality would itself be false and illusory (as Buddha and Shankara affirm), whereas the origin of individualisation being in the Supreme Himself, the ego is only a passing deformation, necessary for the moment, which will disappear when its utility is over, when the Truth-Consciousness will be established.

3 March 1951

*

Almost totally, everybody lives on the surface, all the time, all the time on the surface. And for them it's even the only thing which exists — the surface. And when something compels them to draw back from the surface, some people feel that they are falling into a hole. There are people who, if they are drawn back from the surface, suddenly feel that they are crumbling down into an abyss, so unconscious they are!

They are conscious only of a kind of small thin crust which is all that they know of themselves and things and the world, and it is so thin a crust! Many! I have experienced, I don't know how often... I tried to interiorise some people and immediately they felt that they were falling into an abyss, and at times a black abyss. Now this is the absolute inconscience. But a fall, a fall into something which for them is like a non-existence, this happens very often. People are told: "Sit down and try to be silent, to be very quiet"; this frightens them terribly.

A fairly long preparation is needed in order to feel an increase of life when one goes out of the outer consciousness. It is already a great progress. And then there is the culmination, that when one is obliged for some reason or other to return to the outer consciousness, it is there that one has the impression of falling into a black hole, at least into a kind of dull, lifeless greyness, a chaotic mixture of disorganised things, with the faintest light, and all this seems so dull, so dim, so dead that one wonders how it is possible to remain in this state — but this of course is the other end — unreal, false, confused, lifeless!

24 August 1955

The Subconscient and the Subliminal

What does "subconscient" mean, exactly?

Subconscient? It is what is half conscious, you see. And we say "sub", because that means "below" the consciousness. It is something more obscure than the consciousness, but which, at the same time, is like a lower substratum supporting the consciousness. It is like those stores from which one would draw out something quite unformed, a formless substance which could be translated into forms or translated into actions or translated into impulses or even into feelings. But it is like those stores containing a considerable number of fairly mixed things, not very distinct, but which would be very rich in possibilities; only they would have to be drawn out into the light and organised, classified, put into shape so as to give them a value.

So long as they are there, it is a mass, a mixture, certainly subconscient, that is to say, half-conscious, semi-conscious, in which everything is muddled up. It lacks organisation and classification. It is the characteristic of consciousness to organise and classify... classification, putting into order, arranging logically... there are varieties of logic, but still, some logic, a beginning of logic. There are higher and higher kinds of logic, more and more superior. But even preliminary logic is the first work of the consciousness.

But consciousness is plunged — plunged as though by its roots — into this domain, and draws up as it would draw up sap; it constantly pumps this subconscient which it has to transform into something organised. That is why we spend our time re-doing the same work. If we had a small limited amount of consciousness which was our own, as some people imagine it, like a small bag full of consciousness, you know, which is one's own consciousness, well, when you have put it in good order and organised it well, your work will be done, and you can be quiet. But it is not at all like that, it is not at all like that.

Even as there are elements of consciousness which escape and evaporate, which spread out, there is this constant rising, as from a deep ground, of something that asks to be made conscious. And your work has to be perpetually re-done. But one can — if one is careful and attentive — instead of re-doing exactly the same thing each time, one can re-do it with a little progress. Then the movement is not rectilinear, but a movement which goes like this... you see (*gesture of spiral movement*). One seems at times to be going back, but that's in order to go farther and farther forward.

15 September 1954

*

Sweet Mother, is the subconscient stronger than the mind, vital and physical?[...]

It has a greater power. Well, just because it is subconscient it is everywhere, everything seems steeped in the subconscient. And so, "subconscient" means half conscious: not conscious and not unconscious. It is just between the two; it is like that, half-way; so things slide down into it, one doesn't know that they are there, and from there they act; and it is because one doesn't know that they are there that they can remain there. There are many things which one doesn't wish to keep and drives out from the active consciousness, but they go down there, hide there, and because it is subconscious one doesn't notice them; but they haven't gone out completely, and when they have a chance to come up again, they come up. For example, there are bad habits of the body, in the sense that the body is in the habit of upsetting its balance — we call that falling ill, you know; but still, the functioning becomes defective through a bad habit. You manage by concentrating the Force and applying it on this defect, to make it disappear but it doesn't disappear completely, it enters the subconscient. And then, when you are off your guard, when you stop paying attention properly and preventing it from showing itself, it rises up and comes out. You thought for months perhaps or even for years, you thought you were completely rid of a certain kind of illness which you suffered from, and you no longer paid any attention, and suddenly one day it returns as though it had never gone; it springs up again from the subconscient, and unless one enters into this subconscient and changes things there, that is, unless one changes the subconscient into the conscient, it always happens like this. And the method is to change the subconscient into the conscient — if each thing that rises to the surface becomes conscious, at that moment it must be changed. There is a more direct method still: it is to enter the subconscient in one's full consciousness and work there, but this is difficult. Yet so long as this is not done, all the progress one has made — I mean physically, in one's body — can always be undone.

11 May 1955

*

"More than a third of our existence is passed in sleep...."
(The Mother)

Physical sleep therefore well deserves our attention. I said "physical sleep", for we are inclined to believe that the whole of our being goes to sleep when the body is asleep.

"It is often said that in sleep men's true nature is revealed."
                                                              (The Mother)

Their true nature does not mean their deeper nature but their spontaneous nature which is not under control, for the control of the will
ceases during sleep. And all that one does not do in the waking state,
one does during sleep because the control of the will is removed.

*"All the desires that have been repressed without being dissolved
... try to seek satisfaction while the will is asleep. And as desires
are veritable dynamic centres of formation, they tend to organise
in and around us an assemblage of circumstances most favourable to their satisfaction." (The Mother)*

In another lesson we spoke of the power of mental formation: the
mind shapes entities which have a more or less independent life and
try to manifest themselves. Here I do not speak of thought but of
desire. Desire belongs to the vital domain but at the core of this desire
there is always a thought, and the desire becomes all the more active
and dynamic when it holds in itself this power of mental formation
and the power of vital realisation. The vital is the centre of dynamism
of the being, of active energy, and the two combined make something
very strong which has a considerable tendency towards realising itself — besides, everything in the universe tends towards manifestation, and things which are prevented from manifesting lose, by that
very fact, their force and capacity.

Most of the methods aiming at self-control have indeed made use
of repression, of the suppression of movements with the idea that if
one continues this suppression long enough, one succeeds in killing
the element that is not wanted. This would be quite true if it were a
question only of the physical world, but behind the physical world
there is the subconscious world and behind the subconscious world
there lies the immensity of the Inconscient. And what you do not
know is this that unless you destroy within you the desire itself, that
is, the seed of the formation, this formation which you are preventing
from manifesting is so to say repressed in the subconscious — driven
down and repressed right at the bottom — and if you go and search in

the subconscient you will find that it is waiting there to do its work. That is why so many people who have for years and years been able to control an unwanted movement are suddenly taken by surprise when this movement rushes up from below with all the greater force the longer it has been repressed. Hence dreams are of great use because this movement of repression exists no longer, the conscious will not being there (for it falls asleep or goes elsewhere) and the desire repressed below leaps up and manifests itself in the form of dreams, so much so that you come to know a good many things about your own nature; that is why it is said that man can discover in sleep and dreams his true nature; it is not his true nature, his deeper nature, which is his psychic nature, but the spontaneous, uncontrolled nature.

27 January 1951

*

Sweet Mother, what does "the subliminal being" mean, exactly?

[...] It's what is behind. I think it is what could be called the subtle physical, the subtle vital, the subtle mind. It is something that's behind what is manifested. One can imagine that what is manifested is like a layer or like a crust or a bark; it is that which we see and with which we are in touch. And it clothes something, it clothes or expresses something which is more subtle and serves as its support.

When one dreams, one goes very often into his subliminal being, and there things are almost the same and yet not absolutely the same; there is a great resemblance and yet there is a difference; and usually this is greater. One has the impression of entering into something that's vaster; and, for example, one feels that one can do more, that one knows more, one has a power and clear-sightedness which one doesn't have in the ordinary consciousness; one has the impression while dreaming that one knows many more things than when one is awake. No? Doesn't this happen? You don't have dreams like that?... when one dreams and knows a lot, for example, about the secret causes of things, about what a movement expresses... all that, one feels that one knows it. For instance, when one dreams of someone, one knows better what he thinks, what he wants, all these things, better than when one is in waking contact with him. This happens when one has entered the subliminal. Very often one dreams in the subliminal.

Has the subliminal a contact with the psychic?

Not directly, not more directly than the outside being. If externally, in your ordinary consciousness you have a contact with the psychic, that also has a contact with the psychic, or rather one can put it the other way round: if that has a contact with the psychic, it helps you to have a contact with the psychic, but not necessarily, not always; it depends on the degree of development of the being. It is not necessarily more enlightened, more balanced — no. It is more subtle, it is less dull than our outer consciousness. Our external consciousness is so dull, it has no depth; as our óuter understanding has no depth, our sensations have no depth; all this is something as though flat. So here it is fuller, but not necessarily more true.

6 April 1955

Matter and the Body

"Each spot of the body is symbolical of an inner movement; there is there a world of subtle correspondences. But this is a long and complex subject and we cannot enter into its details just now. The particular place in the body affected by an illness is an index to the nature of the inner disharmony that has taken place. It points to the origin, it is a sign of the cause of the ailment. It reveals too the nature of the resistance that prevents the whole being from advancing at the same high speed. It indicates the treatment and the cure. If one could perfectly understand where the mistake is, find out what has been unreceptive, open that part and put the force and the light there, it would be possible to re-establish in a moment the harmony that has been disturbed and the illness would immediately go." (The Mother)

Why is "each spot of the body symbolical of an inner movement"?

Because the whole physical world is the symbol of universal movements. So our body is the symbol of our inner movements. The whole world, the whole physical world is like a crystallisation — it is a materialisation, a crystallisation — of the movements in other planes of the universe. It is like a finalisation, it is as though a projection on something that retains the image, fixes the image. Therefore, at every point it is the same thing as in the whole material universe.

The material is a plane, isn't it?

Yes, it is a final result. There is an increasing materiality and a decreasing materiality, and the physical plane is at the centre: it is like a screen on which all the intervening vibrations are projected and held, as upon a screen — it is an image, an image of all that is happening. We notice it because it is a thing done, something concrete. It is as though you viewed the whole universe as a movement of force and this movement of force were projected till it met a screen and on the screen it made an image, and this image on the screen is the physical world. And it is a mere image. The physical world which everyone takes as the only reality is simply an image. It is the image of all that happens in what we call the invisible. It becomes visible to us because there is a screen which intervenes and stops the vibrations and that produces an image. If there were no such screen the vibrations would move on and nothing would be seen. And yet all the movements would exist. But for us they would be invisible, if there were no screen to stop the vibrations.

For the ordinary consciousness it is the image alone that is true, and what happens behind it is more or less problematical, but in the true consciousness, all that happens behind or before is the true thing and what one sees externally is only an image, that is to say, a projection on a screen, of something which exists altogether independently. So, our body represents a small fragment in this set of images that is projected and it is a fragment which expresses exactly all the vibrations of the inner state corresponding to this little point that is the body.

23 September 1953

*

Sweet Mother, here it is written: "there is ... a true physical being." What does this mean?

There is a physical Nature which is perfectly harmonious, which has an absolutely... how to put it... yes, harmonious working, without any disorder, without disequilibrium, without any rupture of harmony, which would be expressed, if it existed upon earth, by a perfect health, a growing force, a continuous progress; and then all that one would like to obtain from one's body one would obtain; and this can go as far as an almost unimaginable progress of perfection.

The physical state as we see it with all its disharmonies, its weaknesses, its uglinesses, is the same deformation as that which has changed the higher vital, the true vital, into the kind of vital we see. And this comes from the same cause: it is cut off from its Origin, with an acute sense of separation which makes one live in an absolutely obscure consciousness which has become totally ignorant, instead of living constantly in the consciousness of one's Origin. Now, to ask why it is like that is to ask too much.

That's all?

I didn't understand very well, Sweet Mother.

You haven't understood what the true physical is, because it is not a question of understanding. One is not conscious of it because one is not inside it, one doesn't live in it. But can't you conceive of a body which would be perfectly beautiful, perfectly harmonious, which would function perfectly well and would never be ill, never tired, and would be in a state of constant progress? First it would become taller and taller until it reaches its maximum height, and then it would become stronger and stronger, more and more skilful, more and more conscious, and always in a perfect harmony: never any illness and never any fatigue, never any error, making no mistakes, knowing exactly at each moment what ought to be done and why.

29 June 1955

*

*What is the nature of these influences from outside? Could you
give us an explanation of their working?*

Naturally these influences are of very diverse kinds. They may be
studied from a psychological point of view or from an almost mechanical standpoint, the one usually translating the other, that is, the
mechanical phenomenon occurs as a sort of result of the psychological one.

In very few people, and even in the very best at very rare moments in life, does the will of the being express that deep inner, higher
truth.

(*After a silence Mother continues*:) The individual consciousness
extends far beyond the body; we have seen that even the subtle physical which is yet material compared with the vital being and in certain
conditions almost visible, extends at times considerably beyond the
visible limits of the physical body. This subtle physical is constituted
of active vibrations which enter into contact or mingle with the vibrations of the subtle physical of others, and this reciprocal contact gives
rise to influences — naturally the most powerful vibrations get the
better of the others. For example, as I have already told you several
times, if you have a thought, this thought clothes itself in subtle vibrations and becomes an entity which travels and moves about in the
earth-atmosphere in order to realise itself as best it can, and because
it is one among millions, naturally there is a multiple and involved
interaction as a result of which things don't take place in such a simple and schematic fashion.

What you call yourself, the individual being enclosed within the
limits of your present consciousness, is constantly penetrated by vibrations of this kind, coming from outside and very often presenting
themselves in the form of suggestions, in the sense that, apart from a
few exceptions, the action takes place first in the mental field, then
becomes vital, then physical. I want to make it clear that it is not a
question of the pure mind here, but of the physical mind; for in the
physical consciousness itself there is a mental activity, a vital activity
and a purely material activity, and all that takes place in your physical
consciousness, in your body consciousness and bodily activity, penetrates first in the form of vibrations of a mental nature, and so in the

form of suggestions. Most of the time these suggestions enter you without your being in the least conscious of them; they go in, awaken some sort of response in you, then spring up in your consciousness as though they were your own thought, your own will, your own impulse; but it is only because you are unconscious of the process of their penetration.

These suggestions are very numerous, manifold, varied, with natures which are very, very different from each other, but they may be classified into three principal orders. First — and they are hardly perceptible to the ordinary consciousness; they become perceptible only to those who have already reflected much, observed much, deeply studied their own being — they are what could be called collective suggestions.

When a being is born upon earth, he is inevitably born in a certain country and a certain environment. Due to his physical parents he is born in a set of social, cultural, national, sometimes religious circumstances, a set of habits of thinking, of understanding, of feeling, conceiving, all sorts of constructions which are at first mental, then become vital habits and finally material modes of being. To put things more clearly, you are born in a certain society or religion, in a particular country, and this society has a collective conception of its own and this nation has a collective conception of its own, this religion has a collective "construction" of its own which is usually very fixed. You are born into it. Naturally, when you are very young, you are altogether unaware of it, but it acts on your formation — that formation, that slow formation through hours and hours, through days and days, experiences added to experiences, which gradually builds up a consciousness. You are underneath it as beneath a bell-glass. It is a kind of construction which covers and in a way protects you, but in other ways limits you considerably. All this you absorb without even being aware of it and this forms the subconscious basis of your own construction.

This subconscious basis will act on you throughout your life, if you do not take care to free yourself from it. And to free yourself from it, you must first of all become aware of it; and the first step is the most difficult, for this formation was so subtle, it was made when you were not yet a conscious being, when you had just fallen altogether dazed from another world into this one (*laughing*) and it all happened without your participating in the least in it. Therefore, it does not even occur to you that there could be something to know there, and still less something you must get rid of. And it is quite remarkable that when for some reason or other you do become aware of the hold of this collective suggestion, you realise at the same time that a very assiduous and prolonged labour is necessary in order to get rid of it. But the problem does not end there.

You live surrounded by people. These people themselves have desires, stray wishes, impulses which are expressed through them and have all kinds of causes, but take in their consciousness an individual form. For example, to put it in very practical terms: you have a father, a mother, brothers, sisters, friends, comrades; each one has his own way of feeling, willing, and all those with whom you are in relation expect something from you, even as you expect something from them. That something they do not always express to you, but it is more or less conscious in their being, and it makes formations. These formations, according to each one's capacity of thought and the strength of his vitality, are more or less powerful, but they have their own little strength which is usually much the same as yours; and so what those around you want, desire, hope or expect from you enters in this way in the form of suggestions very rarely expressed, but which you absorb without resistance and which suddenly awaken within you a similar desire, a similar will, a similar impulse.... This happens from morning to night, and again from night to morning, for these things don't stop while you are sleeping, but on the contrary are very often intensified because your consciousness is no longer awake, watching and protecting you to some extent.

And this is quite common, so common that it is quite natural and so natural that you need special circumstances and most unusual occasions to become aware of it. Naturally, it goes without saying that your own responses, your own impulses, your own wishes have a similar influence on others, and that all this becomes a marvellous mixture in which might is always right!

If that were the end of the problem, one could yet come out of the mess; but there is a complication. This terrestrial world, this human world is constantly invaded by the forces of the neighbouring world, that is, of the vital world, the subtler region beyond the fourfold earth-atmosphere;* and this vital world which is not under the influence of the psychic forces or the psychic consciousness is essentially a world of ill-will, of disorder, disequilibrium, indeed of all the most anti-divine things one could imagine. This vital world is constantly penetrating the physical world, and being much more subtle than the physical, it is very often quite imperceptible except to a few rare individuals. There are entities, beings, wills, various kinds of individualities in that world, who have all kinds of intentions and make use of every opportunity either to amuse themselves if they are small beings or to do harm and create disorder if they are beings with a greater capacity. And the latter have a very considerable power of penetration and suggestion, and wherever there is the least opening, the least affinity, they rush in, for it is a game which delights them.

Besides, they are very thirsty or hungry for certain human vital vibrations which for them are a rare dish they love to feed upon; and so their game lies in exciting pernicious movements in man so that man may emanate these forces and they be able to feed on them just as they please. All movements of anger, violence, passion, desire, all these things which make you abruptly throw off certain energies from yourself, project them from yourself, are exactly what these entities of the vital world like best, for, as I said, they enjoy them like a sumptuous dish. Now, their tactics are simple: they send you a little suggestion, a little impulse, a small vibration which enters deep into you and through contagion or sympathy awakens in you the vibration necessary to make you throw off the force they want to absorb.

There it is a little easier to recognise the influence, for, if you are the least bit attentive, you become aware of something that has suddenly awakened within you. For example, those who are in the habit of losing their temper, if they have attempted ever so little to control their anger, they will find something coming from outside or rising from below which actually takes hold of their consciousness and arouses anger in them. I don't mean that everybody is capable of this discernment; I am speaking of those who have tried to understand their being and control it. These adverse suggestions are easier to distinguish than, for instance, your response to the will or desire of a

---

* Consisting of physical, vital, mental and psychic elements.

being who is of the same nature as yourself, another human being, who consequently acts on you without this giving you a clear impression of something coming from outside: the vibrations are too alike, too similar in their nature, and you have to be much more attentive and have a much sharper discernment to realise that these movements which seem to come out from you are not really yours but come from outside. But with the adverse forces, if you are in the least sincere and observe yourself attentively, you become aware that it is something in the being which is responding to an influence, an impulse, a suggestion, even something at times very concrete, which enters and produces similar vibrations in the being.

12 December 1956

The Vital (The Life Force)

The vital body surrounds the physical body with a kind of envelope which has almost the same density as the vibrations of heat observable when the day is very hot. And it is this which is the intermediary between the subtle body and the most material vital body. It is this which protects the body from all contagion, fatigue, exhaustion and even from accidents. Therefore if this envelope is wholly intact, it protects you from everything, but a little too strong an emotion, a little fatigue, some dissatisfaction or any shock whatsoever is sufficient to scratch it as it were and the slightest scratch allows any kind of intrusion. Medical science also now recognises that if you are in perfect vital equilibrium, you do not catch illness or in any case you have a kind of immunity from contagion. If you have this equilibrium, this inner harmony which keeps the envelope intact, it protects you from everything. There are people who lead quite an ordinary life, who know how to sleep as one should, eat as one should, and their nervous envelope is so intact that they pass through all dangers as though unconcerned. It is a capacity one can cultivate in oneself. If one becomes aware of the weak spot in one's envelope, a few minutes' concentration, a call to the force, an inner peace is sufficient for it to be all right, get cured, and for the untoward thing to vanish.

27 January 1951

*

If you have a strong desire for something you cannot get, you project your desire outside yourself. It goes off like a tiny personality separated from you and roams about in the world. It will take a little round, more or less large, and return to you, perhaps when you have forgotten it. People who have a kind of passion, who want something, — that goes out from them like a little being, like a little flame into the surroundings. This little being has its destiny. It roams about in the world, tossed around by other things perhaps. You have forgotten it, but it will never forget that it must bring about that particular result.... For days you tell yourself: "How much I would like to go to that place, to Japan, for instance, and see so many things", and your desire goes out from you; but because desires are very fugitive things, you have forgotten completely this desire you had thrown out with such a force. There are many reasons for your thinking about something else. And after ten years or more, or less, it comes back to you like a dish served up piping hot. Yes, like a piping-hot dish, well arranged. You say: "This does not interest me any longer." It does not interest you ten or twenty years later. It was a small formation and it has gone and done its work as it could.... It is impossible to have desires without their being realised, even if it be quite a tiny desire. The formation has done what it could; it took a lot of trouble, it has worked hard, and after years it returns. It is like a servant you have sent out and who has done his best. When he returns you tell him: "What have you done?" — "Why? But, sir, it was because you wanted it!"

You cannot put forth a strong thought without its going out from you like a little balloon, as it were. We have certain stories which are not unbelievable, like the one about that miser who thought of nothing but his money; he had hidden his hoard somewhere and always used to go to see it. After his death he continued to come as a ghost (that is to say, his vital being), to watch over his money. Nobody could go near the place without meeting with a catastrophe. It is like that, if you have worked to bring out something, it is always realised. It may be realised even after your death! Yes, for when your body ceases to exist, none of the vibrations stops existing. They are realised somewhere. That was what the Buddha said: the vibrations continue to exist, to be perpetuated. They are contagious. They continue in others, pass into others, and everyone adds a little to them.

8 April 1953

*

Can't the vital be converted?

Convert the vital? Surely one can. It is a difficult task, but it can be done. If it could not be done, then there would be no hope. But generally the mind is not sufficient. For, I have known very many people who could see very clearly, understand very well, were mentally thoroughly convinced, could even describe to you and tell you extraordinary things, could easily give excellent lessons to others, but their vital was up to all sorts of tricks and would not listen at all to all that. It said, "It is all the same to me, say what you may; as for myself, I go my own way!"

It is only when contact with the psychic has been established that this can convert anything at all — even the worst criminal — in a moment. These are those "illuminations" which seize you and turn you inside out completely. After that, all goes well. There may be slight difficulties of adjustment, but still things go well.

But the mind is a big preacher, that is its nature: it gives speeches, sermons, as it is done in the churches. So the vital usually gets impatient and answers the mind, not very politely: "You are a nuisance! what you say is very good for you, but for me it won't do." Or, at the best, when the mind is gifted with especially remarkable capacities and the vital is of a little higher kind, it may say: "Oh! how beautiful it is, what you tell me (sometimes this happens), but you see, I, I am unable to do it; it is very beautiful, but it is beyond my capacity."

But this vital is a curious creature. It is a being of passion, enthusiasm and naturally of desire; but, for example, it is quite capable of getting enthusiastic over something beautiful, of admiring, sensing anything greater and nobler than itself. And if really anything very beautiful occurs in the being, if there is a movement having an exceptional value, well, it may get enthusiastic and it is capable of giving itself with complete devotion — with a generosity that is not found, for example, in the mental domain nor in the physical. It has that fullness in action that comes precisely from its capacity to get enthused and throw itself wholly without reserve into what it does. Heroes are always people who have a strong vital, and when the vital is enthused over something, it is no longer a reasonable being but a warrior; it is wholly in its action and can perform exceptional things because it does not calculate, does not reason, does not say "One must take precautions, one must not do this, must not do that." It is not prudent, it flares up, as people say, it gives itself totally. Therefore, it can do magnificent things if it is guided in the right way.

A converted vital is an all-powerful instrument. And sometimes it gets converted by something exceptionally beautiful, morally or materially. When it witnesses, for example, a scene of total self-abnegation, of uncalculating self-giving — one of those things so exceedingly rare but splendidly beautiful — it can be carried away by it, it can be seized by an ambition to do the same thing. It begins by an ambition, it ends with a consecration.

There is only one thing the vital abhors; it is a dull life, monotonous, grey, tasteless, spiritless. Faced with that, it goes to sleep, falls into inertia. It likes extremely violent things, it is true; it can be extremely wicked, extremely cruel, extremely generous, extremely good and extremely heroic. It always goes to extremes and can be on one side or the other, yes, as the current flows.

And this vital, if you place it in a bad environment, it will imitate the bad environment and do bad things with violence and to an extreme degree. If you place it in the presence of something wonderfully beautiful, generous, great, noble, divine, it can be carried away with that also, forget everything else and give itself wholly. It will give itself more completely than any other part of the being, for it does not calculate. It follows its passion and enthusiasm. When it has desires, its desires are violent, arbitrary, and it does not at all take into account the good or bad of others; it doesn't care the least bit. But when it gives itself to something beautiful, it does not calculate either, it will give itself entirely without knowing whether it will do good or harm to it. It is a very precious instrument.

It is like a horse of pure breed: if it lets itself be directed, then it will win all the races, everywhere it will come first. If it is untamed, it will trample people and cause havoc and break its own legs or back!

It is like that. The one thing to know is to which side it will turn. It loves exceptional things — exceptionally bad or exceptionally good, it loves the exceptional. It does not like ordinary life. It becomes dull, it becomes half inert. And if it is shut up in a corner and told: "Keep quiet there", it will remain there and become more and more like something crumbling away, and finally just like a mummy: there is no more life in it, it is dried up. And one will no longer have the strength to do what one wants to do. One will have fine ideas, excellent intentions, but one won't have the energy to execute them.

So do not wail if you have a powerful vital, but you must have strong reins and hold them quite firmly. Then things go well.

9 September 1953

The Mental

Mind is one movement, but there are many varieties of the movement, many strata, that touch and even press into each other. At the same time the movement we call mind penetrates into other planes. In the mental world itself there are many levels. All these mind-planes and mind-forces are interdependent; but yet there is a difference in the quality of their movements and for facility of expression we have to separate them from one another. Thus we can speak of a higher mind, an intermediary mind, a physical and even a quite material mind; and there are many other distinctions that can be made.

Now, there are mental planes that stand high above the vital world and escape its influence; there are no hostile forces or beings there. But there are others — and they are many — that can be touched or penetrated by the vital forces. The mind-plane that belongs to the physical world, the physical mind, as we usually call it, is more material in its structure and movement than the true mind and it is very much under the sway of the vital world and the hostile forces. This physical mind is usually in a kind of alliance with the lower vital consciousness and its movements; when the lower vital manifests certain desires and impulses, this more material mind comes to its aid and justifies and supports them with specious explanations and reasonings and excuses. It is this layer of mind that is most open to suggestions from the vital world and most often invaded by its forces.

But there is in us a higher mind which moves in the region of disinterested ideas and luminous speculations and is the originator of forms, and there is a mind of pure ideas that have not yet been put into form; these greater mind-levels are free from the vital movements and the adverse forces, because they stand far above them. There may be contradictory movements there; there may be movements and formations that come into clash with the Truth or are in conflict with one another; but there is no vital disturbance, nothing that can be called hostile. The true philosopher mind, the mind that is the thinker, discoverer, maker of forms, and the mind of pure ideas that are not yet put into form, are beyond this inferior invasion and influence. But this does not mean that their motions cannot be imitated or their creations misused by perverse or hostile beings of a greater make and higher origin than those of whom I have till now spoken.

26 May 1929

*

Mother, if the heart can be the means of a more direct knowledge, what is the role of the intellect as an intermediary of knowledge?

As an intermediary, did you say?

For the true role of the mind is the formation and organisation of action. The mind has a formative and organising power, and it is that which puts the different elements of inspiration in order, for action, for organising action. And if it would only confine itself to that role, receiving inspirations — whether from above or from the mystic centre of the soul — and simply formulating the plan of action — in broad outline or in minute detail, for the smallest things of life or the great terrestrial organisations — it would amply fulfil its function.

It is not an instrument of knowledge.

But it can use knowledge for action, to organise action. It is an instrument of organisation and formation, very powerful and very capable when it is well developed.

One can feel this very clearly when one wants to organise one's life, for instance — to put the different elements in their place in one's existence. There is a certain intellectual faculty which immediately puts each thing in its place and makes a plan and organises. And it is not a knowledge that comes from the mind, it is a knowledge which comes, as I said, from the mystic depths of the soul or from a higher consciousness; and the mind concentrates it in the physical world and organises it to give a basis of action to the higher consciousness.

One has this experience very clearly when one wants to organise one's life.

Then, there is another use. When one is in contact with one's reason, with the rational centre of the intellect, the pure reason, it is a powerful control over all vital impulses. All that comes from the vital world can be very firmly controlled by it and used in a disciplined and organised action. But it must be at the service of something else — not work for its own satisfaction.

These are the two uses of the mind: it is a controlling force, an instrument of control, and it is a power of organisation. That is its true place.

20 June 1956

*

Sweet Mother, what is meant by "the substance of the mental being"?

My child, the substance means... how shall I put it?... it means the stuff of which the mental being is made. It could be said, for instance, that the cells are the substance of your body. It is not exactly matter, the mind is not quite material, but it is the very thing of which the mind is made. If there were no mental substance, there would be no mental being. It would be only a vibration; and even a vibration needs a medium to manifest itself.

But if your body were not made of material substance, you wouldn't have a body. This is what is called substance. It is the thing of which something is made. And precisely, what is important is that people usually think that mind is just a mode of activity, whereas there is a mental substance as there is a vital substance and physical substance. And as there is a substance, there is a corresponding world with an autonomous existence, that is to say, there can be a mind without any physical support. The physical body may disappear and the mind can continue to exist. It is here that it is important to understand that there is a mental substance which, obviously, is much more... (*silence*) how to put it?... immaterial than physical matter.

[...] Well, you see, we say that substance has different densities, and the more material it becomes, the denser it is, the farther it moves away from matter, the less dense it is. But it is a substance all the same. There is even an etheric substance. I don't say that this conforms with scientific theories; I don't guarantee that I am not talking scientific heresies! But this is a *cosmic fact.* (*Mother laughs.*) It is exactly — I think I said this when I spoke about occultism — I said the first thing one must know before being able to practise occultism is that the different states of being have a different density, and they have an individual independent existence of their own, that they are existing realities, that they are truly real substances, that it is not just a way of being. There can be a mental being and mental activity and, for instance, a thought that is completely independent of the brain, whereas the materialistic theories say that it is the brain which creates mental activity. But this is not correct. The brain is the material transcription of the mental activity, and mental activity has its own domain; the mental domain has its reality, its own substance. One can think outside one's brain, think, act, make formations outside one's brain. One can even live, move, go from one place to another, have a direct knowledge of mental things in the mental world, in a word, absolutely independent of a body which, indeed, can be in a state of complete inertia, not only asleep but also in a cataleptic state. And moreover, it is quite certain that so long as one has not understood that one is made up of different states of being which have their own independent life, one can't have a complete control over one's being. There will always be something that escapes you.

8 September 1954

*

Mother, we sometimes have sudden ideas. Where do they come from and how do they work in the head?

Where do they come from? — From the mental atmosphere.

Why do they come?... Perhaps you meet them on your way as one meets a passer-by in a public square. Most often it is that; you are on a road where ideas are moving about and it so happens that you meet this particular one and it passes through your head. Obviously, those who are in the habit of meditating, of concentrating, and for whom intellectual problems have a very concrete and tangible reality, by concentrating their minds they attract associated ideas, and a "company of ideas" is formed which they organise so as to solve a problem or clarify the question they are considering. But for this, one must have the habit of mental concentration and precisely that philosophical mind I was speaking about, for which ideas are living entities with their own life, which are organised on the mental chess-board like pawns in a game of chess: one takes them, moves them, places them, organises them, one makes a coherent whole out of these ideas, which are individual, independent entities with affinities among themselves, and which organise themselves according to inner laws. But for this, one must also have the habit of meditation, reflection, analysis, deduction, mental organisation. Otherwise, if one is just "like that", if one lives life as it comes, then it is exactly like a public square: there are roads and on the roads people pass by, and then you find yourself at cross-roads and it all passes through your head — sometimes even ideas without any connection between them, so much so that if you were to write down what passes through your head, it would make a string of admirable nonsense![...]

The speculative mind needs discipline for its development. If it is not disciplined methodically, one is always in a sort of a cloud. The vast majority of human beings can harbour the most contradictory ideas in their brains without being in the least troubled by them.

Well, until you try to organise your mind clearly, you risk at the very least having no control over what you think. And very often, you must come down to action before you begin to realise the value of what you think! Or, if not as far as action, at least as far as the feelings: suddenly you become aware that you have feelings which are not very desirable; then you realise you have not controlled your way of thinking at all.

Sweet Mother, do people have bad thoughts because they have no control over their minds?

Bad thoughts?... There can be several reasons for that. In fact there are several reasons. It may be due to a bad nature — if people have nasty feelings, these nasty feelings can be the cause of nasty thoughts. It may be the opposite. Perhaps they are wide open to all sorts of suggestions from outside and, as I said, these suggestions enter them and gradually create nasty feelings. It may be due to subconscious influences which are conflicting precisely because they are uncontrolled. When these influences rise to the surface, instead of being controlled and those which are undesirable refused, everything is allowed to enter as it likes, the doors are open.

You are *bathed* in all kinds of things — good, bad, neutral, luminous, dark; it's all there, and each one's consciousness should, in principle, act as a filter. You should receive only what you want to receive, you should think only what you want to think; and then, you should not allow these thoughts to be changed into feelings and actions without formal authorisation.

In fact, this is the very purpose of physical existence. Each person is an instrument for controlling a certain set of vibrations which represent his particular field of work; each one must receive only the ones which are in conformity with the divine plan and refuse the rest.

8 January 1958

*

Are there beings in the mental worlds?

Yes, many. They are completely independent; they have their own life, their own relations among themselves, as in other worlds. Only for a physical consciousness, time and space are not the same in the vital or the mental worlds as in the physical world. For example, those who are in the physical consciousness have the impression that shiftings in the mind are instantaneous — compared with the higher consciousness they are not instantaneous, but compared with the physical consciousness, they are instantaneous, of an extreme rapidity.

The beings of the mental world also have an individuality of their own, even a form that can be permanent if they choose to keep one. Their form is the expression of their thought and is sufficiently plastic to be able to change with their thought, yet has a sufficient continuity to enable one to recognise them. If you go out of your body and enter the mental world, you can meet these beings, speak to them, even make an appointment with them for the next time!

Can they exercise their influence on a human being, as the beings of the vital worlds do?

Many mental formations try to realise themselves upon earth, but these are generally created by human beings; they then continue to work in the mental world with the intention of influencing the mind of human beings. But the beings of the mental plane proper are generally creators, and because they are creators of form, they are not much concerned with influencing other forms — they are satisfied with expressing themselves through the forms they have made.

19 March 1951

*

There is one thing certain about the mind and its workings; it is that you can understand only what you already know in your own inner self. What strikes you in a book is what you have already experienced deep within you. Men find a book or a teaching very wonderful and often you hear them say, "That is exactly what I myself feel and know, but I could not bring it out or express it as well as it is expressed here." When men come across a book of true knowledge, each finds himself there, and at every new reading he discovers things that he did not see in it at first; it opens to him each time a new field of knowledge that had till then escaped him in it. But that is because it reaches layers of knowledge that were waiting for expression in the subconscious in him; the expression has now been given by somebody else and much better than he could himself have done it. But, once expressed, he immediately recognises it and feels that it is the truth. The knowledge that seems to come to you from outside is only an occasion for bringing out the knowledge that is within you.

19 May 1929

Imagination

How can human thought create forms?

In the mental world human thought is constantly creating forms. Human thought is very creative in the mental world. All the time when you are thinking, you are creating forms and you send them out in the atmosphere and they go and do their work. Constantly you are surrounded by a heap of small formations.

Naturally, there are people who can't even think clearly. So they form nothing at all except faint eddies. But people who think clearly are surrounded by a heap of little forms which, sometimes, go out to do some work in others; and when one thinks of them again, they return.

And we have instances of people who are troubled by their own formations, which return constantly as though to take possession of them, and which they can't get rid of because they don't know how to undo the formations they have made. There are more cases of this kind than one would think. When they have made a particularly strong formation [...] this formation is always tied up with the one who makes it and returns to knock at the brain to receive forces and ends up by truly acting as a necessity. It is a whole world to know; one truly lives in ignorance, one has powers one doesn't know about, so naturally one uses them very badly. One uses them somewhat unconsciously and very badly.

I don't know if you have ever heard of Madame David-Neel who went to Tibet and has written books on Tibet, and who was a Buddhist; and Buddhists — Buddhists of the strictest tradition — do not believe in the Divine, do not believe in his Eternity and do not believe in gods who are truly divine, but they know admirably how to use the mental domain; and Buddhist discipline makes you a good master of the mental instrument and mental domain.

We used to discuss many things and once she told me: "Listen, I made an experiment." (She had studied a bit of theosophy also.) She said: "I formed a *mahatma*; with my thought I formed a *mahatma*." And she knew (this has been proved) that at a given moment mental formations acquire a personal life independent of the fashioner — though they are linked with him — but independent, in the sense that they can have their own will. And so she told me: "Just imagine, I had made my *mahatma* so well that he became a personality independent of me and constantly came to trouble me! He used to come, scold me for one thing, give me advice for another, and he wanted to direct my life; and I could not succeed in getting rid of him. It was extremely difficult, and I didn't know what to do!"

So I asked her how she had tried. She told me how. She said, "He troubles me a lot, my *mahatma* is very troublesome. He does not leave me in peace. He disturbs my meditations, he hinders me from working; and yet I know quite well that it is I who created him, and I can't get rid of him!" Then I said, "That's because you don't have the 'trick'...."(*Mother laughs*) And I explained to her what she should do. And the next day — I used to see her almost every day in those days, you see — the next day she came and told me, "Ah, I am freed from my *mahatma*!" (*Laughter*) She had not *cut* the connection because that's of no use. One must know how to *reabsorb* one's creation, that is the only way. To swallow up again one's formations.

But, you see, in a smaller measure and less perfectly one is making formations all the time. When, for instance, one thinks of somebody quite powerfully, there is a small emanation of mental substance which, instantaneously, goes to this person, you understand, a vibration of your thought which goes and touches his; and if he is receptive, he sees you. He sees you and tells you, "You came last night to see me!" That's because you made a small formation and this formation went and did its work, which was to put you into contact with this person or else to carry a message if you had something special to tell him; and that was done. This happens constantly, but as it is quite a constant and spontaneous phenomenon and done in ignorance, one is not even aware that one does this, one does it automatically.

People who have desires add to the mental formation a kind of small envelope, a vital shell which gives it a still greater reality. These people are usually surrounded by a number of tiny entities which are their own formations, their own mental formations clothed with vital force, which come all the time to strike them to try to make them realise materially the formations they have made.

You have perhaps read the books of Maurice Magre.[...] He describes this; he had come here, Maurice Magre, and we spoke and he told me that he had always noticed — he was highly sensitive — he had always noticed that people who have sexual desires are surrounded by a kind of small swarm of entities who are somewhat viscous and rather ugly and which torment them constantly, awakening desire in them. He said he had seen this around certain people. It was like being surrounded by a swarm of mosquitoes, yes! But it is more gross, and much uglier still, and it is viscous, it is horrible, and it turns round and round the person and gives him no peace, and it awakens in him the desire that has formed these entities and they batten on it. It is their food. This is absolutely true. His observation was quite correct. His vision was very true. It *is* like that.

But everyone carries around himself the atmosphere of his own desires. So you don't at all require that people should tell you anything; you have only to look and you see around them exactly the state they are in. They may want to give themselves the airs of angels or saints but they can't deceive you, because that thing is there, turning around them.

11 August 1954

*

The imagination is really the power of mental formation. When this power is put at the service of the Divine, it is not only formative but also creative. There is, however, no such thing as an unreal formation, because every image is a reality on the mental plane. The plot of a novel, for instance, is all there on the mental plane existing independently of the physical. Each of us is a novelist to a certain extent and possesses the capacity to make forms on that plane; and, in fact, a good deal of our life embodies the products of our imagination. Every time you indulge your imagination in an unhealthy way, giving a form to your fears and anticipating accidents and misfortunes, you are undermining your own future. On the other hand, the more optimistic your imagination, the greater the chance of your realising your aim. Monsieur Coué got hold of this potent truth and cured hundreds of people by simply teaching them to imagine themselves out of misery.[...] Therefore I say to you never be dejected and disappointed but let your imagination be always hopeful and joyously plastic to the stress of the higher Truth, so that the latter may find you full of the necessary formations to hold its creative light.

The imagination is like a knife which may be used for good or evil purposes. If you always dwell in the idea and feeling that you are going to be transformed, then you will help the process of the Yoga. If, on the contrary, you give in to dejection and bewail that you are not fit or that you are incapable of realisation, you poison your own being. It is just on account of this very important truth that I am so tirelessly insistent in telling you to let anything happen but, for heaven's sake, not to get depressed. Live rather in the constant hope and conviction that what we are doing will prove a success.

1930-1931

*

Mother, when one imagines something, does it not exist?

When you imagine something, it means that you make a mental formation which may be close to the truth or far from the truth — it also depends upon the quality of your formation. You make a mental formation and there are people who have such a power of formation that they succeed in making what they imagine real. There are not many of these but there are some. They imagine something and their formation is so well made and so powerful that it succeeds in being realised. These are creators; there are not many of them but there are some.

If one thinks of someone who doesn't exist or who is dead?

Ah! what do you mean? What have you just said? Someone who doesn't exist or someone who is dead? These are two absolutely different things.

I mean someone who is dead.

Someone who is dead!

If this person has remained in the mental domain, you can find him immediately. Naturally if he is no longer in the mental domain, if he is in the psychic domain, to think of him is not enough. You must know how to go into the psychic domain to find him. But if he has remained in the mental domain and you think of him, you can find him immediately, and not only that, but you can have a mental contact with him and a kind of mental vision of his existence.

The mind has a capacity of vision of its own and it is not the same vision as with these eyes, but it is a vision, it is a perception in forms. But this is not imagination. It has nothing to do with imagination.

Imagination, for instance, is when you begin to picture to yourself an ideal being to whom you apply all your conceptions, and when you tell yourself, "Why, it should be like this, like that, its form should be like this, its thought like that, its character like that," when you see all the details and build up the being. Now, writers do this all the time because when they write a novel, they imagine. There are those who take things from life but there are those who are imaginative, creators; they create a character, a personage and then put him in their book later. This is to imagine.[...]

What is the function, the use of the imagination?

If one knows how to use it, as I said, one can create for oneself his own inner and outer life; one can build his own existence with his imagination, if one knows how to use it and has a power. In fact it is an elementary way of creating, of forming things in the world. I have always felt that if one didn't have the capacity of imagination he would not make any progress. Your imagination always goes ahead of your life. When you think of yourself, usually you imagine what you want to be, don't you, and this goes ahead, then you follow, then it continues to go ahead and you follow. Imagination opens for you the path of realisation. People who are not imaginative — it is very difficult to make them move; they see just what is there before their nose, they feel just what they are moment by moment and they cannot go forward because they are clamped by the immediate thing. It depends a good deal on what one calls imagination. However...

Men of science must be having imagination!

A lot. Otherwise they would never discover anything. In fact, what is called imagination is a capacity to project oneself outside realised things and towards things realisable, and then to draw them by the projection. One can obviously have progressive and regressive imaginations. There are people who always imagine all the catastrophes possible, and unfortunately they also have the power of making them come. It's like the antennae going into a world that's not yet realised, catching something there and drawing it here. Then naturally it is an addition to the earth atmosphere and these things tend towards manifestation. It is an instrument which can be disciplined, can be used at will; one can discipline it, direct it, orientate it. It is one of the faculties one can develop in himself and render serviceable, that is, use it for definite purposes.

Sweet Mother, can one imagine the Divine and have the contact?

Certainly if you succeed in imagining the Divine you have the contact, and you can have the contact with what you imagine, in any case. In fact it is absolutely impossible to imagine something which doesn't exist somewhere. You cannot imagine anything at all which doesn't exist somewhere. It is possible that it doesn't exist on the earth, it is possible that it's elsewhere, but it is impossible for you to imagine something which is not already contained in principle in the universe; otherwise it could not occur.

6 July 1955

*

Is it through the imagination that one can realise desires or aspirations?

That means? What exactly do you want to say? Imagining that the desire is realised and in this way help its realisation?

Yes.

Certainly, quite certainly.

And ideals also?

Only usually, yes, almost totally what people don't have at their disposal is the time it takes. But for instance, if you have a very powerful imagination and build up the realisation of your desire, build it up well with all its details and everything, like an admirably made formation existing in itself, totally, you see... well, you may be sure that if you live long enough the thing will be realised. It can be realised the next day, it can be realised the next minute, it can take years, it can take centuries. But it is sure to be realised. And then, if to this imaginative power you add a kind of creative vital strength, you make a very living force of it; and as all living forces tend towards realisation, it will put a pressure upon terrestrial events in order to be able to realise itself sooner, and it is realised.

Only, as I said, there are two things. First, as regards desires, personal circumstances, one is not very... persistent or very steady, and after sometime what interested you very strongly doesn't interest you any longer. You think of something else, have another desire, and make another formation. But now the first thing one imagined is very well formed; after following its curve in space it is realised. But by then the person has started another construction because for some reason or other the thing doesn't interest him any more, and he is face to face with the realisation of his first desire, while having already embarked upon the second, the third or the fourth. So he is absolutely annoyed: "But why, I don't want this any longer, why does it come?" without his being conscious that quite simply it is the result of a previous deed.

If, however, instead of being desires they are aspirations for spiritual things and one continues his line with a regular progress, then one is absolutely sure to obtain one day what he has imagined. The day may be slightly far-off if there are many obstacles on the path, for example if the formation that you have made is still very alien to the state of the earth atmosphere; well, it takes some time to prepare the conditions for its advent. But if it is something which has already been realised several times on earth and does not imply too categorical a transformation, you may have it quite quickly, provided that you follow the same line persistently. And if you add to this the ardour of a faith and trust in the divine Grace and that kind of self-giving to the Grace which makes you expect everything from It, then it can become tremendous; you can see things being realised more and more, and the most surprising ones can be realised one after another. But for this there are conditions to be fulfilled.

One must have a great purity and a great intensity in one's self-giving, and that absolute trust in the supreme wisdom of the divine Grace, that It knows better than we do what is good for us, and all that. Then if one offers one's aspiration to It, truly gives it with enough intensity, the results are marvellous. But one must know how to see them, for when things are realised most people find it absolutely natural, they don't even see why and how it has happened, and they tell themselves, "Yes, naturally it had to be like that." So they lose the joy of... the joy of gratitude, because, in the last analysis, if one can be filled with gratitude and thanksgiving for the divine Grace, it puts the finishing touch, and at each step one comes to see that things are exactly what they had to be and the best that could be.

13 July 1955

Reason, Inspiration, Intuition

Sweet Mother, here Sri Aurobindo has written: "On one side it [the reason] is an enlightener — not always the chief enlightener — and the corrector of our life-impulses and first mental seekings, on the other it is only one minister of the veiled Spirit and a preparer of the paths for the coming of its rule."

Yes, this is what we said, that in the rational domain that's what gives the true judgment, the true guidance. This is what we call an enlightener: one who gives light. When you are not sure of something, when you are in darkness, in a confusion, if you call to reason, it can guide you very well, make you see clearly where you were in darkness; therefore it is an enlightener. Now, "minister of the Spirit" means precisely what he was asking, that is, that it can be transformed into an instrument for revealing the spiritual reality in the lower parts of the being; "minister of the Spirit" — that's what it means; a minister is an instrument of something, you see, it means the instrument of the Spirit. And it can prepare the paths for the coming of the rule of the Spirit, precisely make the being balanced and peaceful, right in its judgments, right in its way of acting, so that being in a state of luminous equilibrium, it becomes capable of receiving the Spirit.

A being who is in a whirlwind of darkness is obviously not ready to receive the Spirit. But when by the use of reason one has managed to organise his being logically and reasonably, in a balanced and wise way — reason is essentially an instrument of wisdom — well, this is an excellent preparation for going beyond, on condition that one knows that it is not a culmination, that it is only a preparation. It is like a base, you see; people who have spiritual experiences, who have a contact with the higher worlds and are not ready in the lower domains, have a lot of trouble, because they have to fight constantly against a heap of elements which are neither organised nor purified nor classified; and each one pulls its own way, there are impulses and preferences and desires, and so this light which has come from above has to organise all this; whereas if the reason had worked to begin with and made the place at least a habitable one, when the Spirit came it would have been more easily installed.

25 May 1955

*

Many men think and write through inspiration. From where does it come?

Many! That is indeed a wonderful thing. I did not think there have been so many.... So?

Poets, when they write poems...

Ah! Inspirations come from very many different places. There are inspirations that may be very material, there are inspirations that may be vital, there are inspirations that come from all kinds of mental planes, and there are very, very rare inspirations that come from the higher mind or from a still higher region. All inspirations do not come from the same place. Hence, to be inspired does not necessarily mean that one is a higher being.... One may be inspired also to do and say many stupid things!

What does "inspired" mean?

It means receiving something which is beyond you, which was not within you; to open yourself to an influence which is outside your individual conscious being.

Indeed, one can have also an inspiration to commit a murder! In countries where they decapitate murderers, cut off their heads, this causes a very brutal death which throws out the vital being, not allowing it the time to decompose for coming out of the body; the vital being is violently thrown out of the body, with all its impulses; and generally it goes and lodges itself in one of those present there, men half horrified, half with a kind of unhealthy curiosity. That makes the opening and it enters within. Statistics have proved that most young murderers admit that the impulse came to them when they were present at the death of another murderer. It was an "inspiration", but of a detestable kind.

Fundamentally it is a moment of openness to something which was not within your personal consciousness, which comes from outside and rushes into you and makes you do something. This is the widest formula that can be given.

Now, generally, when people say: "Oh! he is an inspired poet", it means he has received something from high above and expressed it in a remarkable manner. But one should rather say that his inspiration is of a high quality.

Does it not come, Mother, whenever one wants it?

Whenever one wants it? Generally not, for one does not know the mechanism of one's being and cannot open the doors at will.

It is a thing that can be done. It is one of the earliest things that you are taught to do in Yoga: to open the door whenever one wants. It is the result of meditation or concentration or aspiration: all these processes are followed to open the door somewhere.

And generally you try to open it precisely towards the highest thing, not towards anything whatever. For the other kind of receptivity people unfortunately always have.... It is impossible to be altogether shut up in an ivory tower — besides, I believe it would not be very favourable, it would be impossible to progress if one were completely shut up in oneself. One would be able only to rearrange whatever was in oneself. Just imagine you were like a closed globe, altogether closed, that there was no communication with outside — you put out nothing, you receive nothing, you are shut up — you have a few elements of consciousness, movements, vibrations (call them what you like), all that is contained as within a ball, along with your consciousness also. You have no relation with things outside, you are conscious only of yourself. What can you do?... Change the organisation within; that you can do, you can do many things by changing this organisation. But it is confined to that. It is a kind of inner progress, but there is no true progress in relation to the forces outside oneself. You would find yourself extremely limited after a time, you would be tired of yourself: turning and turning again, turning and turning again the elements inside — not very pleasant.

But all the while you externalise yourself and all the while you bring back something from this externalisation; it is like something porous: a force goes out and then a force comes in. There are pulsations like that. And this is why it is so important to choose the environment in which one lives, because there is constantly a kind of interchange between what you give and what you receive. People who throw themselves out a great deal in activity, receive more. But they receive on the same level, the level of their activity. Children, for example, who are younger, who always move about, always shout and romp and jump (very rarely do they keep quiet, except while asleep, and perhaps not even so), well, they spend much and they receive much, and generally it is the physical and vital energy that is spent and it is physical and vital energies that are received. They recuperate a good part of what they spend. So there, it is very important for them to be in surroundings where they can, after they have spent or while they are spending, recover something that is at least equal in quality to theirs, that is not of an inferior quality.

When you no longer have this generosity in your movements, you receive much less and this is one of the reasons — one of the chief reasons — why physical progress stops. It is because you become thrifty, you try not to waste; the mind intervenes: "Take care, don't tire yourself, don't do too much, etc." The mind intervenes and physical receptivity diminishes a great deal. Finally, you do not grow any more — by growing reasonable, you stop growing altogether!

But receptivity opens to other levels. Those who live in a world of desires and passions, increase their vital receptivity so much at times that it reaches proportions very unpleasant to themselves and to their surroundings. And then there are those who live in the mental consciousness; their mental receptivity grows very much. All who create mentally, study and live in mental activity, if the mental activity is constant, can progress indefinitely. Mind in the human being does not stop functioning even when the physical instrument has deteriorated. It may no longer manifest its intelligence materially, if there is a lesion in the brain, for example, but the mind itself, independently of the instrument, nothing can prevent from progressing, from continuing to grow. It is a being that lasts infinitely longer than the physical. It is still young when physically one is already old. Only when you do not take enough care to keep your brain in a good state, only if accidents occur and there are lesions then you can no longer express yourself. But the mind in itself continues to grow. And those who have a sufficient physical balance, for example, those who have not gone to excesses of any kind, who have never maltreated their body, who have never poisoned themselves like most people — who have never smoked, drunk alcohol and so on — keep their brain in a relatively good condition and they can progress, even in their expression, till the end of their life. It is only if in the last years of their life they make a kind of withdrawal within themselves, that they lose their power of expression. But the mind goes on progressing.

The vital is by nature immortal. But it is not organised, and in its normal state, it is over-excited, full of contradictory passions and impulses. So with all that it destroys itself. But otherwise the elements continue to exist. A desire, a passion is a very living thing and continues to live for a very long time, even independently of the being who... undergoes them, I might say, rather than creates them, because they are things that one undergoes, that rush upon you from outside like a storm that seizes you and carries you away, unless you keep very calm like that, very still, very quiet, as though one were clinging to something solid and immobile in oneself, allowing the storm to pass over when it begins to blow — it blows, but one must not stir, one must not let oneself tremble or shiver or shake; one must remain altogether immobile and know that these are passing storms. And when the storm has blown over, it passes and goes away; then one can heave a deep breath and resume one's normal balance; and there has been only a minimum destruction. In such cases, generally, things turn out well in the end.

But those who are like a piece of cork on water and rush about in all directions and do not succeed in recovering their poise and watching themselves, are liable to any occurrence. They may be drawn into a whirlpool all of a sudden and lo! engulfed. And there remains nothing.

5 August 1953

*

Sweet Mother, to what plane does intuition belong?

It is one of those planes, one of those regions we were speaking about last time, which are intermediary between the higher mind and the Overmind.

How does intuition manifest, Sweet Mother?

Um! How does it manifest? It is something which takes place without any reasoning, any analysis, any deduction. Suddenly one knows a thing, without having reasoned, without having analysed, without deducing, without having reflected, without having made use of one's brain, without having put together the elements of the problem and tried to resolve them — it is not like that. All of a sudden it comes like a light in the consciousness; it can be in the head, it can be lower down, elsewhere; it is a light in the consciousness which brings a precise knowledge on a particular point and it is not at all a result of analyses and deductions. In fact, it is the first manifestation of the knowledge by identity. Knowledge by identity — you understand clearly what that means?

If one succeeds in identifying himself with something, well, one becomes this thing for a time, and becoming this thing one knows all that is in it, without needing either to guess or to construct.

8 December 1954

*

Sometimes while reading a text one has ideas, then, Sweet Mother, how can one distinguish between the other person's idea and one's own?

Oh! this, this doesn't exist, the other person's idea and one's own idea.

Nobody has ideas of his own: it is an immensity from which one draws according to his personal affinity; ideas are a collective possession, a collective wealth.

Only, there are different stages. So there is the most common level, the one where all our brains bathe; this indeed swarms here, it is the level of "Mr. Everybody". And then there is a level that's slightly higher for people who are called thinkers. And then there are higher levels still — many — some of them are beyond words but they are still domains of ideas. And then there are those capable of shooting right up, catching something which is like a light and making it come down with all its stock of ideas, all its stock of thoughts. An idea from a higher domain if pulled down organises itself and is crystallised in a large number of thoughts which can express that idea differently; and then if you are a writer or a poet or an artist, when you make it come lower down still, you can have all kinds of expressions, extremely varied and choice around a single little idea but one coming from very high above. And when you know how to do this, it teaches you to distinguish between the pure idea and the way of expressing it.

Some people cannot do it in their own head because they have no imagination or faculty for writing, but they can do it through study by reading what others have written. There are, you know, lots of poets, for instance, who have expressed the same idea — the same idea but with such different forms that when one reads many of them it becomes quite interesting to see (for people who love to read and read much). Ah, this idea, that one has said it like this, that other has expressed it like that, another has formulated it in this way, and so on. And so you have a whole stock of expressions which are expressions by different poets of the same single idea up there, above, high above. And you notice that there is an almost essential difference between the pure idea, the typal idea and its formulation in the mental world, even the speculative or artistic mental world. This is a very good thing to do when one loves gymnastics. It is mental gymnastics.

Well, if you want to be truly intelligent, you must know how to do mental gymnastics; as, you see, if you want really to have a fairly strong body you must know how to do physical gymnastics. It is the same thing. People who have never done mental gymnastics have a poor little brain, quite over-simple, and all their life they think like children. One must know how to do this — not take it seriously, in the sense that one shouldn't have convictions, saying, "This idea is true and that is false; this formulation is correct and that one is not and this religion is the true one and that religion is false", and so on and so forth... this, if you enter into it, you become absolutely stupid.

But if you can see all that and, for example, take all the religions, one after another and see how they have expressed the same aspiration of the human being for some Absolute, it becomes very interesting; and then you begin... yes, you begin to be able to juggle with all that. And then when you have mastered it all, you can rise above it and look at all the eternal human discussions with a smile. So there you are master of the thought and can no longer fly into a rage because someone else does not think as you, something that's unfortunately a very common malady here.

16 March 1955

There is one thing very difficult for the mind to do but very important, according to me: you must never allow your mind to judge things and men. To say "this is good, that is bad, this is right, that is wrong, this one has this defect, that one has that bad thing, etc." — this is depreciatory judgment.

For people who exercise their intelligence, the more intelligent they are, the more do they grow aware that they know nothing at all and that with the mind one can know nothing. One may think in a particular way, judge and see in a particular way, but one is never sure of anything — and never will be sure of anything. One can always say, "perhaps it is like that" or "perhaps it is like this" and so on, indefinitely, because the mind is not an instrument of knowledge.

Above the thoughts, there are pure ideas; thoughts serve to express pure ideas. And Knowledge is well above the domain of pure ideas, as these are well above thought. One must hence know how to climb from thought to pure idea, and pure idea is itself nothing but a translation of Knowledge. And Knowledge can be obtained only by a total identification. So, when you put yourself in your small human mentality, the mentality of the physical consciousness which is at work all the time, which looks at everything, judges everything from the height of its derisive superiority, which says, "That is bad, it should not be like that", you are sure to be always mistaken, without exception. The best is to keep silent and look well at things, and little by little you make notes within yourself and keep the record without pronouncing any judgment. When you are able to keep all that within you, quietly, without agitation and present it very calmly before the highest part of your consciousness, with an attempt to maintain an attentive silence, and wait, then perhaps, slowly, as if coming from a far distance and from a great height, something like a light will manifest and you will know a little more of truth.

But as long as you excite your thoughts and cut them up into little bits, you will never know anything. I shall repeat this to you a hundred times if necessary, but I can assure you that so long as you are not convinced of this you will never come out of your ignorance.

Is there an exact number of pure ideas?

To know that, you must go and see the Supreme and ask Him! I am not interested in statistics!

Here is a little story. One of my friends had made a trip to India and was requested to give an account of his travels. An old, very credulous lady was there and she asked him, "In India, do they count the souls?" He answered, "Yes." "How many are there?" asked the old lady. He answered, "One only."

20 January 1951

*

In vital nightmares, which part of the being goes out of the body?

Your vital — not the whole of it for that would produce a cataleptic state, but a portion of the vital goes out for a stroll. Some always go to the nastiest places and so have very bad nights — the possibilities in these nightly rambles are innumerable. It may be a very small thing, just a little portion of your being, but if it is conscious, that is enough to give you a fine little nightmare!

You know, when you sleep, the inner beings are not concentrated upon the body, they go out and become more or less independent — a limited independence, but independence all the same — and they go to dwell in their own domains. The mind more so, for it is hardly held within the body, it is only concentrated but not contained in the body. The vital also goes beyond the body, but it is more concentrated upon the body. The mind however is such a supple substance that it is sufficient to think about a person in order to be with that person, at least partially, mentally. If you think strongly of a place, a part of your mind is there; distance, so to say, does not exist. Of course, to have a mind centralised around the body requires good training. Few people have a mind with a well-defined form: it is like clouds which roll, come and go. Even to have a vital with a form similar to that of your physical body, an analogous form, it must be very much individualised, very much centralised. The mind still more; it must be completely individualised, centralised, organised around the psychic centre in order to have a definite form.

There are people who spend their life organising their mind. I have known some who had made of their mind a kind of fortress, a huge construction (I am speaking of people who had uncommon mental capacities). They had made of their mind quite a big edifice, very powerful and of such a fixity, with such solid walls that they had lost all contact with the outer mental world: they lived completely within their own construction and all the phenomena of their consciousness were of their own making — they had no longer any contact with the outside mental world. They retained contact with their own vital and their body, in a way, but all the phenomena of their consciousness were lodged within their mental construction — they could no longer get out of it. Well, this happens very strongly to people who seek for a spiritual life through the classical methods of a renunciation of the material consciousness, a concentration on their inner being and identification with it. If I gave you the names of some, you would be quite astonished. They construct for themselves a conception in which one finds all the gradations of the mind, a construction so solid and so fixed that they become imprisoned within it and when they believe they have reached the supreme Truth, they have only reached the centre of their own mental construction.

And they have all the experiences they used to foresee: the experience of liberation, the experience of going out of the body, the experience of identification with the Supreme, all, all, but all of their own making; this has no contact with the universal reality. Then if someone touches it, if for some reason or other someone has the power to touch it or simply to make a breach in one of the walls, at first they are completely upset, then they come to regard the force that could do this as a force of terrible destruction, a manifestation of a hostile force of the worst kind!

What is a "mental nightmare"?

When there is a chaos in the brain or a local fever, a particular excitation in the brain, an overexertion, or if there is a want of control, you let yourself be possessed by mental formations, this is what happens most often — mental formations which, most often, you yourself have made, besides. And as the control of the rational, waking consciousness has gone, all this begins to dance a sarabande in the head, with a kind of raging madness; ideas get entangled, collide, fight, it is truly hallucinating. Then, unless you have the power to bring a great peace into your head, a great tranquillity, a very strong and pure light, well, it is ten times worse than a vital nightmare. The worst of a vital nightmare consists generally in fighting with an enemy who wants to kill you, and you strike him terrible blows, and the blows never hit; you exert all your force, all your energy, and you do not succeed in touching your adversary. He is there in front of you, he threatens you, he is going to strangle you and you gather all your strength, you try to strike, but nothing touches him. When the struggle is like that, hand to hand, with a being who throws himself upon you, it is particularly painful. That is why you are advised not to go out of the body unless you have the necessary power or the purity. You see, in this kind of nightmare the force you want to use is the "memory" of a physical force; but one may have great physical strength, be a first-class boxer, and yet be completely powerless in the vital world because one does not have the necessary vital power. As for the mental nightmares, that kind of frightful saraband in the head, one has altogether the impression of going mad.

10 March 1951

*

What is consciousness?

(*After a silence*) I am trying to choose among several explanations! One, which is a joke, is that consciousness is the opposite of unconsciousness! Another... it is the creative essence of the universe — without consciousness, no universe; for consciousness means objectification. I could also say that consciousness is what "is", because without consciousness nothing is — this is the best reason. Without consciousness no life, no light, no. objectification, no creation, no universe.

Perhaps there is in the unmanifest Supreme a consciousness (but when one speaks of these questions one begins to say impossible things); it is said that, to begin with, the Supreme became aware of himself (which would mean that he was not conscious of himself before! that he was in a state we cannot call "conscious"), that his first movement was to become aware of himself and once having become conscious of himself, he projected this consciousness, which formed the creation. At least, this is what old tradition says. Grant that there never was a beginning, for it is a human way of putting it: the "beginning" is the Supreme — the unmanifest Supreme becoming aware of himself. Perhaps he found that this consciousness was not altogether satisfactory (!) and he projected it, not outside himself for nothing is outside him, but he changed it into an active consciousness so that it would become an objectification of himself. Consequently, it can be said with certitude that Consciousness is the origin of all creation; there you are as exact as you can ever be with words. Consciousness is the origin of all creation — without consciousness, no creation. And what we call "consciousness" is just a far-off contact, without precision and exactness, with the supreme Consciousness. Or if you like, it is the reflection, in a not very exact or pure mirror, of the original Consciousness. What we call our consciousness is this original Consciousness reflected in a somewhat foggy mirror (sometimes very foggy, sometimes very deformed), a reflection in the individual mirror. Then through this reflection, if we go back slowly to the origin of what is reflected, we can enter into contact with the Consciousness — the True Consciousness. And once we come into contact with the True Consciousness, we become aware that it is the same everywhere, that it is only deformation which divides it; without deformation everything is contained in one and the same Consciousness. That is, it is only distortion, the reflection in a distorting mirror, which brings about difference and division in the Consciousness, otherwise it is one single Consciousness. But it is only by experience that one can understand these things.

22 March 1951

The Overmind

Above the mind there are several levels of conscious being, among which the really divine world is what Sri Aurobindo has called the Supermind, the world of the Truth. But in between is what he has distinguished as the Overmind, the world of the cosmic Gods. Now it is this Overmind that has up to the present governed our world: it is the highest that man has been able to attain in illumined consciousness. It has been taken for the Supreme Divine and all those who have reached it have never for a moment doubted that they have touched the true Spirit. For, its splendours are so great to the ordinary human consciousness that it is absolutely dazzled into believing that here at last is the crowning reality. And yet the fact is that the Overmind is far below the true Divine. It is not the authentic home of the Truth. It is only the domain of the *formateurs*, all those creative powers and deities to whom men have bowed down since the beginning of history. And the reason why the true Divine has not manifested and transformed the earth-nature is precisely that the Overmind has been mistaken for the Supermind. The cosmic Gods do not wholly live in the Truth-Consciousness: they are only in touch with it and represent, each of them, an aspect of its glories.

No doubt, the Supermind has also acted in the history of the world but always through the Overmind. It is the direct descent of the Supramental Consciousness and Power that alone can utterly re-create life in terms of the Spirit. For, in the Overmind there is already the play of possibilities which marks the beginning of this lower triple world of Mind, Life and Matter in which we have our existence. And whenever there is this play and not the spontaneous and infallible working of the innate Truth of the Spirit, there is the seed of distortion and ignorance. Not that the Overmind is a field of ignorance; but it is the border-line between the Higher and the Lower, for, the play of possibilities, of separate even if not yet divided choice, is likely to lead to deviation from the Truth of things.

The Overmind, therefore, does not and cannot possess the power to transform humanity into divine nature. For that, the Supramental is the sole effective agent. And what exactly differentiates our Yoga from attempts in the past to spiritualise life is that we know that the splendours of the Overmind are not the highest reality but only an intermediate step between the mind and the true Divine.

1930-1931

(In this chapter, the following gradations of existence have been explored: the subconscient, the subliminal, the physical, the vital, the mental, the intuitive and the overmental. Other gradations are considered in the chapters listed below.)

The Psychic

See Chapter 6, The Psychic Being or Soul

The Supermind or Supramental

See Chapter 19, The Supramental

Sat, Chit, Ananda

See Chapter 1, The Divine and His Creation

CHAPTER 6

The Psychic Being or Soul

What Is the Psychic Being?

The psychic world or plane of consciousness is that part of the world, the psychic being is that part of the being which is directly under the influence of the Divine Consciousness; the hostile forces cannot have even the remotest action upon it. It is a world of harmony, and everything moves in it from light to light and from progress to progress. It is the seat of the Divine Consciousness, the Divine Self in the individual being. It is a centre of light and truth and knowledge and beauty and harmony which the Divine Self in each of you creates by his presence, little by little; it is influenced, formed and moved by the Divine Consciousness of which it is a part and parcel. It is in each of you the deep inner being which you have to find in order that you may come in contact with the Divine in you. It is the intermediary between the Divine Consciousness and your external consciousness; it is the builder of the inner life, it is that which manifests in the outer nature the order and rule of the Divine Will. If you become aware in your outer consciousness of the psychic being within you and unite with it, you can find the pure Eternal Consciousness and live in it; instead of being moved by the Ignorance as the human being constantly is, you grow aware of the presence of an eternal light and knowledge within you, and to it you surrender and are integrally consecrated to it and moved by it in all things.

For your psychic being is that part of you which is already given to the Divine. It is its influence gradually spreading from within towards the most outward and material boundaries of your consciousness that will bring about the transformation of your entire nature. There can be no obscurity here; it is the luminous part in you. Most people are unconscious of this psychic part within them; the effort of Yoga is to make you conscious of it, so that the process of your transformation, instead of a slow labour extending through centuries, can be pressed into one life or even a few years.

The psychic being is that which persists after death, because it is your eternal self; it is this that carries the consciousness forward from life to life.

The psychic being is the real individuality of the true and divine individual within you. For your individuality means your special mode of expression and your psychic being is a special aspect of the one Divine Consciousness that has taken shape in you. But in the psychic consciousness there is not that sense of division between the individual and the universal consciousness which affects the other parts of your nature. You are conscious there that your individuality is your own line of expression, but at the same time you know too that it is an expression objectifying the one universal consciousness. It is as though you had taken a portion out of yourself and put it in front of you and there were a mutual look and play of movement between the two. This duality was necessary in order to create and establish the objectivised relation and to enjoy it; but in your psychic being the separation that sharpens the duality is seen to be an illusion, an appearance and nothing more.

26 May 1929

*

In the ordinary life there's not one person in a million who has a conscious contact with his psychic being, even momentarily. The psychic being may work from within, but so invisibly and unconsciously for the outer being that it is as though it did not exist. And in most cases, the immense majority, almost the totality of cases, it's as though it were asleep, not at all active, in a kind of torpor.

It is only with the sadhana and a very persistent effort that one succeeds in having a conscious contact with his psychic being. Naturally, it is possible that there are exceptional cases — but this is truly exceptional, and they are so few that they could be counted — where the psychic being is an entirely formed, liberated being, master of itself, which has chosen to return to earth in a human body in order to do its work. And in this case, even if the person doesn't do the sadhana consciously, it is possible that the psychic being is powerful enough to establish a more or less conscious relation. But these cases are, so to say, unique and are exceptions which confirm the rule.

In almost, almost all cases, a very very sustained effort is needed to become aware of one's psychic being. Usually it is considered that if one can do it in thirty years one is very lucky — thirty years of sustained effort, I say. It may happen that it's quicker. But this is so rare that immediately one says, "This is not an ordinary human being." That's the case of people who have been considered more or less divine beings and who were great yogis, great initiates.

17 August 1955

What is the work of the psychic being?

What is the work of the psychic being? You want it to have some work? What do you want to say exactly? What is its function? Ah! very well. One could put it this way, that it is like an electric wire that connects the generator with the lamp. Now, if someone has understood, let him explain what I said!

What is the generator and what the lamp? (Laughter)

Ah, there we are! So, what is the generator and what the lamp? That is exactly it. What is the generator and what the lamp? Or rather, who is the generator and who is the lamp?

The generator is the Divine and the lamp is the body.

It is the body, it is the visible being.

So, that is its function. This means that if there were no psychic in Matter, it would not be able to have any direct contact with the Divine. And it is happily due to this psychic presence in Matter that the contact between Matter and the Divine can be direct and all human beings can be told, "You carry the Divine within you, and you have only to enter within yourself and you will find Him." It is something very particular to the human being or rather to the inhabitants of the earth. In the human being the psychic becomes more conscious, more formed, more conscious and more independent also. It is individualised in human beings. But it is a speciality of the earth. It is a direct infusion, special and redeeming, in the most inconscient and obscure Matter, so that it might once again awake through stages to the divine Consciousness, the divine Presence and finally to the Divine Himself. It is the presence of the psychic which makes man an exceptional being — I don't like to tell him this very much, because already he thinks too much of himself; he has such a high opinion of himself that it is not necessary to encourage him! But still, this is a fact — so much so that there are beings of other domains of the universe, those called by some people demigods and even gods, beings, for instance, of what Sri Aurobindo calls the Overmind, who are very eager to take a physical body on earth to have the experience of the psychic, for they don't have it. These beings certainly have many qualities that men don't, but they lack this divine presence which is altogether exceptional and exists only on the earth and nowhere else. All these inhabitants of the higher worlds, the Higher Mind, Overmind and other regions have no psychic being. Of course, the beings of the vital worlds don't have it either. But these latter don't regret it, they don't want it. There are only those very rare ones, quite exceptional, who want to be converted, and for this they act without delay, they immediately take a physical body. The others don't want it; it is something which binds them and constrains them to a rule they do not want.

But it is a fact, so I am obliged to state that this is how it is, that it is an exceptional quality of the human being to carry within himself the psychic and, truly speaking, he does not take full advantage from it. He does not seem to consider this quality as something very, very desirable, from the way he treats this presence — exactly that! He prefers to it the ideas of his mind, prefers the desires of his vital being and the habits of his physical.

9 June 1954

*

Is the psychic being in the heart?

Not in the physical heart, not in the organ. It is in a fourth dimension, an inner dimension. But it is in that region, the region somewhat behind the solar plexus, it is there that one finds it most easily. The psychic being is in the fourth dimension as related to our physical being.

3 *November 1954*

*

The other day I said that most of the time people do not have their psychic being within them. I would like to explain this in greater detail.... You must remember that the inner beings are not in the third dimension. If you open up your body you will find only the viscera of the body which are in the third dimension. The inner beings are in another dimension, and when I say that some men do not have their psychic being within them, I do not mean that it is not at the centre of their being, but that their outer consciousness is so small, so limited, so obscure that it is not able to keep a contact, not only conscious but intimate, with the psychic being which extends beyond it in every way; it is so much higher and deeper than the other outer consciousness that there is no relation either of quality or of nature between them. Religions say that you have a divine spark in you — it is well they call it a "spark", for it is so small indeed that it can be placed anywhere in the body without difficulty. But this does not mean that it is in the body: it is within the consciousness in another dimension, and there are beings who have a contact with it, others who haven't. But if you come to the divine Presence in the atom, the image is easier to understand, for there you touch so infinitesimal a domain that you are on the border-line where you can no longer distinguish between two, three, four or five dimensions. If you study modern physics you will understand what I mean. The movements constituting an atom are, in the matter of size, so imperceptible that they cannot be understood with our three-dimensional understanding, the more so as they follow laws which elude completely this three-dimensional idea. So if you take refuge there, you may say that the divine spark is at the centre of each atom and you won't be far from the truth; but I was not speaking of the divine spark, I was speaking of the being, the psychic consciousness, which is another thing. The psychic being is an entity which has a form; it is organised around a central consciousness and, having a form it has a dimension, but a dimension of another kind than the third dimension of the outer consciousness.

It is often said that children enter into possession of their psychic being when they are about seven. What does this mean exactly?

This is not correct. There are people whose psychic being watches over their formation before their birth, even before they are in the womb of their mother. There are children whose psychic being comes into contact with them at the very moment they utter their first cry. There are also people whose psychic being comes a few hours after their birth, or some days after, or some weeks, some months, some years after or... never!

You told me once that one must not ask a child to make a mental effort before the age of seven.

That is quite different. There it is a question only of the formation of the physical brain which develops slowly, little by little. If you ask of a brain in formation an effort beyond its capacity, you tire it, you overwork it or you make it ill.

You say that the psychic being is the same thing as the divine spark...

No, I never said that — it would be foolish! The psychic being is organised *around* the divine spark. The divine spark is one, universal, the same everywhere and in everything, one and infinite, of the same kind in all. You cannot say that it is a being — it is *the being*, if you like, but not *a* being. Naturally, if you go back to the origin, you may say that there is only one soul, for the origin of all souls is the same, as the origin of the whole universe is the same, as the origin of the entire creation is the same. But the psychic being is an individual, personal being with its own experience, its own development, its own growth, its own organisation; only, this organisation is the product of the action of a central divine spark.

But the day an external being (physical, mental, vital) enters into direct and constant contact with the psychic being, one may say in the same way that the *physical* being of this person is organised by the central divine consciousness. The moment you put yourself in contact with it, submit yourself to it, you are organised by it, by the central divine consciousness.[...]

Is there a psychic being in the atom?

No, it is not yet there. It can be said that there is a possibility of psychic consciousness in Matter — the diffusion of the divine Consciousness had only one object: to make possible an organisation which would be under the direct influence of the Divine. [...] It may hence be said that the origin of the soul is also in the atom, in all the elements constituting the atom, but it is only the origin.... I must tell you that when it is fully formed, the psychic being has a distinct form which corresponds to our physical form. It is not altogether similar, but it has a definite form. Every psychic being is different from another — they are not all cut out, modelled to one pattern. They are different, each has an individuality, a personality.

24 February 1951

*

You must not mistake the feelings for the psychic, you understand! — these two are absolutely different things. People always think that when they have emotions, feelings, they are entering the psychic. These things have nothing to do with the psychic, they are purely vital. They are the most subtle part of the vital, if you like, but they are vital. It's not through the feelings that one goes to the psychic, it is through a very intense aspiration and a self-detachment.

27 July 1955

*

To perceive the soul in someone, as a rule the mind must be very quiet — very quiet, for when it is active, *its* vibrations are seen, not the vibration of the soul.

And then, when you look at someone who is conscious of his soul, and lives in his soul, if you look like this, the impression you have is of descending, of entering deep, deep, deep into the person, far, far, far, far within; while usually when you look into someone's eyes, you very soon come to a surface which vibrates and answers your look, but you don't have that feeling of going down, down, down, down, going deep as into a hole and very far, very, very, very far within, so you have... a small, very quiet response. Otherwise, usually you enter — there are eyes you cannot enter, they are closed like a door; but still there are eyes which are open — you enter and then, quite close behind, you come to something vibrating there, like this, shining at times, vibrating. And then, that's it; if you make a mistake, you say, "Oh! he has a living soul" — it is not that, it is his vital.

In order to find the soul you must go in this way (*gesture of going deep within*), like this, draw back from the surface, withdraw deep within and enter, enter, enter, go down, down, down into a very deep hole, silent, immobile, and there, there's a kind of... something warm, quiet, rich in substance and very still, and very full, like a sweetness — that is the soul.

And if one is insistent and is conscious oneself, then there comes a kind of plenitude which gives the feeling of something complete that contains unfathomable depths in which, should one enter, one feels that many secrets would be revealed... like the reflection in very peaceful waters of something that is eternal. And one no longer feels limited by time.

One has the feeling of having always been and of being for eternity.

9 April 1958

*

Essentially, it is only when one has become aware of one's soul, has been identified with one's psychic being that one can see in a single flash the picture of one's individual development through the ages. Then indeed one begins to know... but not before. Then, indeed, I assure you it becomes very interesting. It changes one's position in life.

There is such a great difference between feeling vaguely, having a hesitant impression of something, of a force, a movement, an impulse, an attraction, of something which drives you in life — but it is still so vague, so uncertain, it is hazy — there is such a difference between this and having a clear vision, an exact perception, a total understanding of the meaning of one's life. And only then does one begin to see things as they are, not before. Only then can one follow the thread of one's destiny and clearly see the goal and the way to reach it. But that happens only through successive inner awakenings, like doors opening suddenly on new horizons — truly, a new birth into a truer, deeper, more lasting consciousness.

Until then you live in a cloud, gropingly, under the weight of a destiny which at times crushes you, gives you the feeling of having been made in a certain way and being unable to do anything about it. You are under the burden of an existence which weighs you down, makes you crawl on the ground instead of rising above and seeing all the threads, the guiding threads, the threads which bind different things into a single movement of progression towards a realisation that grows clear.

One must spring up out of this half-consciousness which is usually considered quite natural — this is your "normal" way of being and you do not even draw back from it sufficiently to be able to see and wonder at this incertitude, this lack of precision; while, on the contrary, to know that one is seeking and to seek consciously, deliberately, *steadfastly* and methodically, this indeed is the exceptional, almost "abnormal" condition. And yet only in this way does one begin to truly live.

16 January 1957

*

What is the difference between "spiritual" and "psychic"?

It is not the same thing. The psychic is the being organised by the divine Presence and it belongs to the earth — I am not speaking of the universe, only of the earth; it is only upon earth that you will find the psychic being. The rest of the universe is formed in quite a different way.

The universe contains all the domains higher than the physical:

there is a global physical comprising the mental, the vital, etc., and all the domains above the mental are domains of a spiritual order, domains which are, for us, domains of the spirit, and it is this "spirit" which little by little, progressively, materialises itself to arrive at Matter as we conceive it. The beings of the Overmind, for instance, and all the beings of the higher regions have no psychic being — the "angels" have no psychic being. It is only upon earth that the psychic life begins, and it is just the process by which the Divine has awakened material life to the necessity of rejoining its divine origin. Without the psychic, Matter would never have awakened from its inconscience, it would never have aspired for the life of its origin, the spiritual life. Therefore, the psychic being in the human being is the manifestation of spiritual aspiration; but there is a spiritual life independent of the psychic.

Is there a correspondence between the psychic world and the earth?

But I have already told you that it is only upon earth that the psychic being gets its experiences to individualise itself. Hence there is an almost absolute interdependence between the psychic world and the earth.

What is the most effective means of awakening the psychic being?

But it is wide awake! And not only is it awake, but it acts, only you are not aware of it. It appears to you asleep because you don't perceive it!

Fundamentally, without this kind of inner will of the psychic being, I believe human beings would be quite dismal, dull, they would have an altogether animal life. Every gleam of aspiration is always the expression of a psychic influence. Without the presence of the psychic, without the psychic influence, there would never be any sense of progress or any will for progress.

1 March 1951

*

On the psychic plane is there a past, present and future?

In the psychic? Yes, you have even the consciousness of all the lives you have lived. When you enter into contact with the psychic you become conscious of all the lives you have lived, it keeps the absolutely living memory of all the events in which the psychic took part — not the whole life, not that one can tell little stories to oneself: that first one was a monkey and then later something a little higher, and so on, the cave-man... no, no stories like that. But all the events of former lives in which the psychic participated are preserved, and when one enters into conscious contact with his psychic being this can be called up like a sort of cinema. But it has no continuity except in lives in which the psychic is absolutely conscious, active, permanently active, that is, constantly associated with the consciousness; so naturally, being constantly associated with the consciousness, it consciously remembers everything that has happened in the real life of the person, and the memories — when one follows these things — the memories of his psychic being are more and more coordinated and closer and closer to what could be a physical memory if there were one, in any case of all the intellectual and emotional elements of life, and of some physical events when it was possible for this being to manifest in the outer consciousness; then, at these moments, the whole set of physical circumstances in which one was is kept absolutely intact in the consciousness.

29 June 1955

*

Has the psychic any power?

Power? It is usually the psychic which guides the being. One knows nothing about it because one is not conscious of it but usually it is that which guides the being. If one is very attentive, one becomes aware of it. But the majority of men haven't the least idea of it. For instance, when they have decided, in their outer ignorance, to do something, and instead of their being able to do it, all the circumstances are so organised that they do something else, they start shouting, storming, flying into a rage against fate, saying (that depends on what they believe, their beliefs) that Nature is wicked or their destiny baleful or God unjust, or... no matter what (it depends on what they believe). Whilst most of the time it is just the very circumstance which was most favourable for their inner development. And naturally, if you ask the psychic to help you to fashion a pleasant life for yourself, to earn money, have children who will be the pride of the family, etc., well, the psychic will not help you. But it will create for you all the circumstances necessary to awaken something in you so that the need of union with the Divine may be born in your consciousness. At times you have made fine plans, and if they had succeeded, you would have been more and more encrusted in your outer ignorance, your stupid little ambition and your aimless activity. Whilst if you receive a good shock, and the post you coveted is denied to you, the plan you made is shattered, and you find yourself completely thwarted, then, sometimes this opposition opens to you a door on something truer and deeper. And when you are a little awake and look back, if you are in the least sincere, you say: "Ah! it wasn't I who was right — it was Nature or the divine Grace or my psychic being who did it." It is the psychic being which organised that.

Is it the psychic will which wants the being to be identified with the Divine?

Yes, surely. It is the will of the psychic. It is also the very reason of its existence. It is for that it is there. For example, in the mind certain activities (and even at times in the physical and vital) certain activities awaken to the influence of the psychic without even knowing it. That is why those parts adhere to it and begin to aspire also for the divine knowledge, the divine union, the relation with the Divine.

16 December 1953

Progress and the Psychic Being

Does the psychic being always progress?

There are in the psychic being two very different kinds of progress:

one consisting in its formation, building and organisation. For the psychic starts by being only a kind of tiny divine spark inside the being and out of this spark will emerge progressively an independent conscious being having its own action and will. The psychic being at its origin is only a spark of the divine consciousness and it is through successive lives that it builds up a conscious individuality. It is a progress similar to that of a growing child. It is a thing in the making. For a long time, in most human beings the psychic is a being in the making. It is not a fully individualised, fully conscious being and master of itself and it needs all its rebirths, one after another, in order to build itself and become fully conscious.

But this sort of progress has an end. There comes a time when the being is fully developed, fully individualised, fully master of itself and its destiny. When this being or one of these psychic beings at that state, takes birth in a human being, that makes a very great difference: the human being, so to say, is born free. He is not tied to circumstances, to surroundings, to his origin and atavism, like ordinary people. He comes into the world with the purpose of doing something, with a work to carry out, a mission to fulfil. From this point of view his progress in growth has come to an end, that is, it is not indispensable for him to take birth again in a body. Till then rebirth is a necessity, for it is through rebirth that he grows; it is in the physical life and in a physical body that he gradually develops and becomes a fully conscious being. But once he is fully formed, he is free, in this sense that he can take birth or not, at will. So there, one kind of progress stops.

But if this fully formed being wants to become an instrument of work for the Divine, if instead of retiring to repose in a psychic bliss, in its own domain, he chooses to be a worker upon earth to help in the fulfilment of the Divine Work, then he has a fresh progress to make, a progress in the capacity for work, for organisation of his work and for expression of the Divine Will. So there is a time when the thing changes. So long as he remains in the world, so long as he chooses to work for the Divine, he will progress. Only if he withdraws into the psychic world and refuses to continue doing the Divine Work or re-nounces it, can he remain in a static condition outside all progress, because, as I have told you, only upon earth is there progress, only in the physical world; it is not acquired everywhere. In the psychic world there is a kind of blissful repose. One remains what one is, without any movement.

But for those who are not conscious of their psychic?

They are compelled to progress whether they want it or not.

The psychic being itself progresses in them and they are not conscious of it. But they themselves are compelled to progress. That is to say, they follow a curve. They follow an ascent in life. It is the same progress as that of the growing child; there comes a time when it is at the summit of its growth and then, unless it changes the plane of progress, unless the purely physical progress turns into a mental progress, a psychic progress, a spiritual progress, it goes down the curve and then there will be a decomposition and it will not exist any longer.

It is just because progress is not constant and perpetual in the physical world that there is a growth, an apogee, a decline and a decomposition. For anything that does not advance, falls back; all that does not progress, regresses.

So this is just what happens physically. The physical world has not learnt how to progress indefinitely; it arrives at a certain point, then it is either tired of progressing or is not capable of progressing in the present constitution, but in any case it stops progressing and after a time decomposes. Those who lead a purely physical life reach a kind of summit, then they slide down very quickly. But now, with the general collective human progress, there is behind the physical progress a vital progress and a mental progress, so that the mental progress can go on for a very long time, even after the physical progress has come to a stop, and through this mental progress one keeps up a kind of ascent long after the physical has ceased to progress.

And then there are those who do yoga, who become conscious of their psychic being, are united with it, participate in its life; these, indeed, progress till the last breath of their life. And they do not stop even after death, when they have left their body under the plea that the body cannot last any longer: they continue to progress.

It is the incapacity of the body to transform itself, to continue progressing that causes it to regress and in the end become more and more open to the inner disequilibrium until one day that becomes strong enough to bring about a total imbalance and it can no longer regain its balance and health.[...] It is only in the pure spiritual life — that which is outside all physical and terrestrial existence, including the mental — that there is no progress. You reach a static state and are outside all movements of progress. But at the same time you are outside the manifestation also. When you reach that state, you no longer belong to the manifestation, you go out of the manifested world. One must go out of the manifested world in order to go out of all progress, because the two are identical: manifestation means progress and progress means manifestation.

5 August 1953

*

How can one know that the psychic being is in front?

My child, when it happens, one understands. It is exactly so long as one doesn't understand that it means that it hasn't come. This is like people asking you, "How can I know whether I am in contact with the Divine?" That itself is enough to prove that they are not. For if they are they can no longer ask the question. It is something understood. For the psychic it is the same thing. When the psychic is in front one knows it, and there is no possibility of any doubt. Consequently one no longer asks the question.

10 November 1954

*

As you said the other day, didn't you, if someone has difficulties it means a mediocre being.

But excuse me! Don't mix up the psychic being with the outer being. The psychic being may be perfect and the outer being may be idiotic. Don't confuse the two. They have nothing to do... unfortunately they have nothing to do with each other, most of the time. For the outer being is not at all conscious of the psychic being; but to the extent that it is conscious it reflects the perfection of this psychic.

If you want to speak of the circumstances, not of the character, why would a psychic being not have difficulties in the world? If the world were entirely psychic, I would understand. But it isn't. It is just the very opposite, and I think the more psychic one is, usually, the more difficulties he has. Only, one is armed to face the difficulties. But the more psychic one is, the more is he in contradiction with the present state of the world. So when one is in opposition with something, the result is difficulties. And I have noticed that most often those who have many difficulties are those who are in a more or less close contact with their psychic being. If you want to speak about outer circumstances — I am not speaking of the character, that's quite different, but of outer circumstances — the people who have to struggle most and would have most reason to suffer are those who have a very developed psychic being.

First, the development of the psychic being has a double result which is concomitant. That is, with the development of the psychic being, the sensitivity of the being grows. And with the growth of sensitivity there is also the growth of the capacity for suffering; but there is the counterpart, that is, to the extent to which one is in relation with the psychic being, one faces the circumstances of life in an altogether different way and with a kind of inner freedom which makes one capable of withdrawing from a circumstance and not feeling the shock in the ordinary way. You can face the difficulty or outer things with calm, peace, and a sufficient inner knowledge not to be troubled. So, on one side you are more sensitive and on the other you have more strength to deal with the sensitivity.

19 January 1955

*

With regard to the evolution upwards, it is more correct to speak of the psychic presence than the psychic being. For it is the psychic presence which little by little becomes the psychic being. In each evolving form there is this presence, but it is not individualised. It is something which is capable of growth and follows the movement of the evolution. It is not a descent of the involution from above. It is formed progressively round the spark of Divine Consciousness which is meant to be the centre of a growing being which becomes the psychic being when it is at last individualised. It is this spark that is permanent and gathers round itself all sorts of elements for the formation of that individuality; the true psychic being is formed only when the psychic personality is fully grown, fully built up, round the eternal divine spark; it attains its culmination, its total fulfilment if and when it unites with a being or personality from above.

Below the human level there is, ordinarily, hardly any individual formation — there is only this presence, more or less. But when, by the growth of the body round the spark of Divine Consciousness, humanity began upon the earth, certain human organisms became in the course of this progressive growth sufficiently perfected, and by their opening and receptivity allowed a junction with certain beings descending from above. This gave rise to a kind of divine humanity, what may be called a race of the élite. If only they had remained by themselves, these people would have continued as a race unique and superhuman. Indeed many races have made claims to be that: the Aryan, the Semitic and the Japanese have all in turn considered themselves the chosen race. But in fact there has been a general levelling of humanity, a lot of intermixture.

For there arose the necessity of prolongation of the superior race, which drove it to intermix with the rest of humanity — with animal humanity, that is to say. Thus its value was degraded and led to that great Fall which is spoken of in the world's scriptures, the coming out of Paradise, the end of the Golden Age. Indeed it was a loss from the point of view of consciousness, but not from that of material strength, since it was a tremendous gain to ordinary humanity. There were, certainly, some beings who had a very strong will not to mix, who resented losing their superiority; and it is just this that is the real origin of race-pride, race-exclusiveness, and a special caste distinction like that cherished by the Brahmins in India. But at present it cannot be said that there is any portion of mankind which is purely animal: all the races have been touched by the descent from above, and owing to the extensive intermixture the result of the Involution was more widely spread.

Of course one cannot say that every man has got a psychic being, just as one cannot refuse to grant it to every animal. Many animals that have lived near man have some beginnings of it, while so often one comes across people who do not seem to be anything else than brutes. Here, too, there has been a good deal of levelling. But on the whole, the psychic in the true sense starts at the human stage: that is also why the Catholic religion declares that only man has a soul. In man alone there is the possibility of the psychic being growing to its full stature even so far as to be able in the end to join and unite with a descending being, a godhead from above.

1930-1931

The Delight of Being

How can one "learn of pure delight"?

First of all, to begin with, one must through an attentive observation grow aware that desires and the satisfaction of desires give only a vague, uncertain pleasure, mixed, fugitive and altogether unsatisfactory. That is usually the starting-point.

Then, if one is a reasonable being, one must learn to discern what is desire and refrain from doing anything that may satisfy one's desires. One must reject them without trying to satsfy them. And so the first result is exactly one of the first observations stated by the Buddha in his teaching: there is an infinitely greater delight in conquering and eliminating a desire than in satisfying it. Every sincere and steadfast seeker will realise after some time, sooner or later, at times very soon, that this is an absolute truth, and that the delight felt in overcoming a desire is incomparably higher than the small pleasure, so fleeting and mixed, which may be found in the satisfaction of his desires. That is the second step.

Naturally, with this continuous discipline, in a very short time the desires will keep their distance and will no longer bother you. So you will be free to enter a little more deeply into your being and open yourself in an aspiration to... the Giver of Delight, the divine Element, the divine Grace. And if this is done with a sincere self-giving — something that gives itself, offers itself and expects nothing in exchange for its offering — one will feel that kind of sweet warmth, comfortable, intimate, radiant, which fills the heart and is the herald of Delight.

After this, the path is easy.

Sweet Mother, what is the true delight of being?

That very one of which I am speaking!

Sweet Mother, here when Sri Aurobindo speaks of an existence "that multiplied itself for sheer delight of being", what is this delight?

The delight of existing.

There comes a time when one begins to be almost ready, when one can feel in everything, every object, in every movement, in every vibration, in all the things around — not only people and conscious beings, but things, objects; not only trees and plants and living things, but simply any object one uses, the things around one — this delight, this delight of being, of being just as one is, simply being. And one sees that all this vibrates like that. One touches a thing and feels this delight. But naturally, I say, one must have followed the discipline I spoke about at the beginning; otherwise, so long as one has a desire, a preference, an attachment or affinities and repulsions and all that, one cannot — one cannot.

And so long as one finds pleasures — pleasure, well, yes, vital or physical pleasure in a thing — one cannot feel this delight. For this delight is everywhere. This delight is something very subtle. One moves in the midst of things and it is as though they were all singing to you their delight. There comes a time when it becomes very familiar in the life around you. Of course, I must admit that it is a little more difficult to feel it in human beings, because there are all their mental and vital formations which come into the field of perception and disturb it. There is too much of this kind of egoistic asperity which gets mixed with things, so it is more difficult to contact the Delight there. But even in animals one feels it; it is already a little more difficult than in plants. But in plants, in flowers, it is so wonderful! They speak all their joy, they express it. And as I said, in all familiar objects, the things around you, which you use, there is a state of consciousness in which each one is happy to be, just as it is. So at that moment one knows one has touched true Delight. And it is not conditioned. I mean it does not depend upon... it depends on nothing. It does not depend on outer circumstances, does not depend on a more or less favourable state, it does not depend on anything: it is a communion with the *raison d'être* of the universe.

And when this comes it fills all the cells of the body. It is not even a thing which is thought out — one does not reason, does not analyse, it is not that: it is a *state* in which one lives. And when the body shares in it, it is so fresh — so fresh, so spontaneous, so... it no longer turns back upon itself, there is no longer any sense of self-observation, of self-analysis or of analysing things. All that is like a canticle of joyous vibrations, but very, very quiet, without violence, without passion, nothing of all that. It is very subtle and very intense at the same time, and when it comes, it seems that the whole universe is a marvellous harmony. Even what is to the ordinary human consciousness ugly, unpleasant, appears marvellous.

Unfortunately, as I said, people, circumstances, all that, with all those mental and vital formations — that disturbs it all the time. Then one is obliged to return to this ignorant, blind perception of things. But otherwise, as soon as all this stops and one can get out of it... everything changes. As he says there, at the end: everything changes. A marvellous harmony. And it is all Delight, true Delight, real Delight.

23 January 1957

Love

What is the relation of human love to Divine love? Is the human an obstacle to the Divine love? Or is not rather the capacity for human love an index to the capacity for Divine love? Have not great spiritual figures, such as Christ, Ramakrishna and Vivekananda, been remarkably loving and affectionate by nature?

Love is one of the great universal forces; it exists by itself and its movement is free and independent of the objects in which and through which it manifests. It manifests wherever it finds a possibility for manifestation, wherever there is receptivity, wherever there is some opening for it. What you call love and think of as a personal or individual thing is only your capacity to receive and manifest this universal force. But because it is universal, it is not therefore an unconscious force; it is a supremely conscious Power. Consciously it seeks for its manifestation and realisation upon earth; consciously it chooses its instruments, awakens to its vibrations those who are capable of an answer, endeavours to realise in them that which is its eternal aim, and when the instrument is not fit, drops it and turns to look for others. Men think that they have suddenly fallen in love; they see their love come and grow and then it fades — or, it may be, endures a little longer in some who are more specially fitted for its more lasting movement. But their sense in this of a personal experience all their own was an illusion. It was a wave from the everlasting sea of universal love.

Love is universal and eternal; it is always manifesting itself and always identical in its essence. And it is a Divine Force; for the distortions we see in its apparent workings belong to its instruments. Love does not manifest in human beings alone; it is everywhere. Its movement is there in plants, perhaps in the very stones; in the animals it is easy to detect its presence. All the deformations of this great and divine Power come from the obscurity and ignorance and selfishness of the limited instrument. Love, the eternal force, has no clinging, no desire, no hunger for possession, no self-regarding attachment; it is, in its pure movement, the seeking for union of the self with the Divine, a seeking absolute and regardless of all other things. Love divine gives itself and asks for nothing. What human beings have made of it, we do not need to say; they have turned it into an ugly and repulsive thing. And yet even in human beings the first contact of love does bring down something of its purer substance; they become capable for a moment of forgetting themselves, for a moment its divine touch awakens and magnifies all that is fine and beautiful. But afterwards there comes to the surface the human nature, full of its impure demands, asking for something in exchange, bartering what it gives, clamouring for its own inferior satisfactions, distorting and soiling what was divine.

To manifest the Divine love you must be capable of receiving the

Divine love. For only those can manifest it who are by their nature open to its native movement. The wider and clearer the opening in them, the more they manifest love divine in its original purity; the more it is mixed with the lower human feelings, the greater is the deformation. One who is not open to love in its essence and in its truth cannot approach the Divine. Even the seekers through knowledge come to a point beyond which if they want to go farther, they are bound to find themselves entering at the same time into love and to feel the two as one, knowledge the light of the divine union, love the very heart of knowledge. There is a place in the soul's progress where they meet and you cannot distinguish one from the other. The division, the distinction between the two that you make in the beginning are a creation of the mind: once you rise to a higher level, they disappear.

Among those who have come into this world seeking to reveal the Divine here and transform earthly life, there are some who have manifested the Divine love in a greater fullness. In some the purity of the manifestation is so great that they are misunderstood by the whole of humanity and are even accused of being hard and unloving, although the Divine love is there. But it is in them divine and not human in its form as in its substance. For when man speaks of love, he associates it with an emotional and sentimental weakness. But the divine intensity of self-forgetfulness, the capacity of throwing oneself out entirely, making no restriction and no reservation, as a gift, asking nothing in exchange, this is little known to human beings. And when it is there unmixed with weak and sentimental emotions, they find it hard and cold; they cannot recognise in it the very highest and intensest power of love.

The manifestation of the love of the Divine in the world was the great holocaust, the supreme self-giving. The Perfect Consciousness accepted to be merged and absorbed into the unconsciousness of matter, so that consciousness might be awakened in the depths of its obscurity and little by little a Divine Power might rise in it and make the whole of this manifested universe a highest expression of the Divine Consciousness and the Divine love. This was the supreme love, to accept the loss of the perfect condition of supreme divinity, its absolute consciousness, its infinite knowledge, to unite with unconsciousness, to dwell in the world with ignorance and darkness. And yet none perhaps would call it love; for it does not clothe itself in a superficial sentiment, it makes no demand in exchange for what it has done, no show of its sacrifice. The force of love in the world is trying to find consciousnesses that are capable of receiving this divine movement in its purity and expressing it. This race of all beings towards love, this irresistible push and seeking out in the world's heart and in all hearts, is the impulse given by a Divine love behind the human longing and seeking. It touches millions of instruments, trying always, always failing; but this constant touch prepares these instruments and suddenly one day there will awake in them the capacity of self-giving, the capacity of loving.

The movement of love is not limited to human beings and it is perhaps less distorted in other worlds than in the human. Look at the flowers and trees. When the sun sets and all becomes silent, sit down for a moment and put yourself into communion with Nature: you will feel rising from the earth, from below the roots of the trees and mounting upward and coursing through their fibres up to the highest outstretching branches, the aspiration of an intense love and longing, — a longing for something that brings light and gives happiness, for the light that is gone and they wish to have back again. There is a yearning so pure and intense that if you can feel the movement in the trees, your own being too will go up in an ardent prayer for the peace and light and love that are unmanifested here. Once you have come in contact with this large, pure and true Divine love, if you have felt it even for a short time and in its smallest form, you will realise what an abject thing human desire has made of it. It has become in human nature something low, brutal, selfish, violent, ugly, or else it is something weak and sentimental, made up of the pettiest feeling, brittle, superficial, exacting. And this baseness and brutality or this self-regarding weakness they call love!

Is our vital being to take part in the Divine love? If it does, what is the right and correct form of participation it should take?

Where is the manifestation of Divine love intended to stop? Is it to be confined to some unreal or immaterial region? Divine love plunges its manifestation upon earth down into the most material matter. It does not indeed find itself in the selfish distortions of the human consciousness; but the vital in itself is as important an element in Divine love as it is in the whole of the manifested universe. There is no possibility of movement and progress without the mediation of the vital; but because this Power of Nature has been so badly distorted, some prefer to believe that it has to be pulled out altogether and thrown away. But it is only through the vital that matter can be touched by the transforming power of the Spirit. If the vital is not there to infuse its dynamism and living force, matter will remain dead; for the higher parts of the being will not come into contact with earth, will not be concretised in life, and they will depart unsatisfied and disappear. The Divine love of which I speak is a Love that manifests here upon this physical earth, in matter, but it must be pure of its human distortions, if it is to incarnate. The vital is an indispensable agent in this as in all manifestation. But as has happened always, the adverse powers have put their hold on this most precious thing. It is the energy of the vital that enters into dull and insensitive matter and makes it responsive and alive. But the adverse forces have distorted it; they have turned it into a field of violence and selfishness and desire and every kind of ugliness and prevented it from taking part in the divine work. The one thing to be done is to change it, not to suppress its movement or destroy it. For without it no intensity is possible anywhere. The vital is in its very nature that in us which can give itself away. Just because it is that which has always the impulse and the strength to take, it is also that which is capable of giving itself to the utmost; because it knows how to possess, it knows also how to abandon itself without reserve. The true vital movement is the most beautiful and magnificent of movements; but it has been twisted and turned into the most ugly, the most distorted, the most repulsive. Wherever into a human story of love, there has entered even an atom of pure love and it has been allowed to manifest without too much distortion, we find a true and beautiful thing. And if the movement does not last, it is because it is not conscious of its own aim and seeking; it has not the knowledge that it is not the union of one being with another that it is seeking after but the union of all beings with the Divine.

Love is a supreme force which the Eternal Consciousness sent down from itself into an obscure and darkened world that it might bring back that world and its beings to the Divine. The material world in its darkness and ignorance had forgotten the Divine. Love came into the darkness; it awakened all that lay there asleep; it whispered, opening the ears that were sealed, "There is something that is worth waking to, worth living for, and it is love!" And with the awakening to love there entered into the world the possibility of coming back to the Divine. The creation moves upward through love towards the Divine and in answer there leans downward to meet the creation the Divine Love and Grace. Love cannot exist in its pure beauty, love cannot put on its native power and intense joy of fullness until there is this interchange, this fusion between the earth and the Supreme, this movement of Love from the Divine to the creation and from the creation to the Divine. This world was a world of dead matter, till Divine love descended into it and awakened it to life. Ever since it has gone in search of this divine source of life, but it has taken in its search every kind of wrong turn and mistaken way, it has wandered hither and thither in the dark. The mass of this creation has moved on its road like the blind seeking for the unknown, seeking but ignorant of what it sought. The maximum it has reached is what seems to human beings love in its highest form, its purest and most disinterested kind, like the love of the mother for the child. This human movement of love is secretly seeking for something else than what it has yet found; but it does not know where to find it, it does not even know what it is. The moment man's consciousness awakens to the Divine love, pure, independent of all manifestation in human forms, he knows for what his heart has all the time been truly longing. That is the beginning of the Soul's aspiration, that brings the awakening of the consciousness and its yearning for union with the Divine. All the forms that are of the ignorance, all the deformations it has imposed must from that moment fade and disappear and give place to one single movement of the creation answering to the Divine love by its love for the Divine. Once the creation is conscious, awakened, opened to love for the Divine, the Divine love pours itself without limit back into the creation. The circle of the movement turns back upon itself and the ends meet; there is the joining of the extremes, supreme Spirit and manifesting Matter, and their divine union becomes constant and complete.

Great beings have taken birth in this world who came to bring down here something of the sovereign purity and power of Divine love. The Divine love has thrown itself into a personal form in them that its realisation upon earth may be at once more easy and more perfect. Divine love, when manifested in a personal being, is easier to realise; it is more difficult when it is unmanifested or impersonal in its movement. A human being, awakened by this personal touch, with this personal intensity, to the consciousness of the Divine love, will find his work and change made more easy; the union for which he seeks becomes more natural and close. And the union, the realisation will become for him, too, more full, more perfect; for the wide uniformity of a universal and impersonal Love will be lit up and vivified with the colour and beauty of all possible relations with the Divine.

2 June 1929

CHAPTER 7

The Hostile Forces

The Hostile or Adverse Forces

The world as it is today is in its greater part under the influence of the adverse forces. We call them adverse because they do not want the divine life; they oppose the divine life. They want things to remain as they are, because it is their field and their power in the world. They know very well that they will lose all power and all influence the moment the Divine manifests. So they are fighting openly and completely against the Divine, and we have to tear away from them bit by bit, little by little, all the things they have conquered in the outer life. And so when it is torn away from them, it is so much gained.

On the other hand, if, as was done formerly, we try what is called clearing the ground, that is, if we let go all the things we consider as not capable of being transformed, then it is so much lost for the divine realisation.

All the realisations of Nature in the outer life, all that it has created — for example upon earth all this vegetable and animal kingdom, you see, and this ordinary human world which it has created — if we give up all this as an illusion incapable of expressing the Divine, then this is so much left in the hands of the adverse forces which try to keep it, no doubt, for their own ends. Whereas if we consider that all this may be at present deformed but that in its essence and origin not only does it belong to the Divine but is the Divine Himself, then we can work consciously, deliberately at the transformation and wrest all these things from the hostile influence which now governs them.

14 December 1955

*

Sweet Mother, what are the adverse powers of the subtle physical?

What are the adverse forces? There are as many of them as there are elements in the world. Only, unless they express themselves physically, we do not see them. So we are not aware of them. But I told you the other day that the atmosphere is full of countless formations which are usually made up of thoughts, desires, impulses, wills, and which are as mixed as men's thoughts. There are good ones, there are bad ones; and behind that there are all the formations of the vital world, a world *essentially* hostile to the Divine. Only the vital in man, under the psychic influence, can change and become a collaborator in the divine work. Otherwise, the vital world is essentially formed of beings *hostile* to the divine work, and those who open themselves to these forces without any control are naturally under the influence of the adverse forces.

8 September 1954

*

No, I asked whether the hostile forces were conscious of the function assigned to them. Because that would mean that the hostile forces help in the spiritual accomplishment.

There is nothing that finally does not help. If they did it deliberately, they would no longer be hostile forces, they would be collaborators. For you must take care of one thing, you must not speak of "hostile forces" when thinking of forces which are hostile to *us*. These forces are not hostile to human beings, to their quietude or happiness, they are hostile to the divine Work.

And usually I have heard many people speaking of "hostile forces" — for instance, "the hostile forces of illness which attack me". This is too personal a point of view, it may not be the result of hostile forces; you call them hostile because they attack you. But in fact, when one speaks of hostile forces it means forces hostile to the divine Work or the divine Will. So, if they collaborated with this Work, they would no longer be hostile, you see. That's quite peremptorily logical.

Therefore, one can't say that it is any kind of work for the progress of humanity or even for the progress of the universe. But there is nothing, not even the most hostile things, which can't be used for the divine Work. It depends on how it is taken. But it must be said that in their relation with human beings they take a very wicked pleasure in testing them. For example, if you are not extremely strong and extremely sincere, and you tell yourself, "Oh, I am sure of my faith" — this for instance among many other things — immediately something happens which is going to try to shake your faith completely. This is one... I suppose that's their diversion, their amusement.

How many times, you know, when someone boasts... it may be very childishly... but when someone boasts about something: "Oh, I am sure of that, I shall never make that mistake", immediately I see a hostile formation passing there, like that, and it enters by the little hole made by the boasting. It enters within, like that, and then penetrates, and so prepares everything for you to do exactly what you didn't want to. But this is an amusement, it is certainly not to help you to progress. (*Mother laughs*) But if you know how to take it, it does help you to progress. You say, "Good, another time I won't boast."

And as these forces are very conscious on the mental and vital plane, one doesn't even need to pronounce the words. If the thought... for example, if you have worked well to correct something, either a bad habit or a material weakness, anything, you have worked hard to correct this thing, and as you have worked well you have succeeded to a certain extent. Then, if simply mentally you state that you have succeeded, the next minute it begins again. It is... you see, you must not even think, it is not a question of saying, the question is simply of thinking: "Why, it was like that before, and now it is like this. Ah, it is fine!" Finished. The next minute it begins again.

And this is certain, because there are witnesses all around you who are notoriously malicious, and this amuses them terrifically. Sometimes I actually even hear them laughing when someone says something frankly. I hear a little laugh like that. Oh, it amuses them very much. And the next minute or the next day, crash! it is undone.

19 January 1955

*

Sweet Mother, does something aspire even in the most nasty people?

In the most nasty people?... yes, my child — even in the Asuras, even in the Adversaries, even in the monsters, there is something.

There is always a corner, a kind of rift, a sensitive point, which is usually called a weakness. But this actually is the strength of the being, the point by which it can be touched.

For even in the most obscure and misled beings, even in those whose conscious will is to fight against the Divine, in spite of themselves, in spite of everything, their origin is divine. And they work in vain, try in vain to cut themselves off from their origin; they cannot do it. Deliberately, consciously, they try all they can; but they know very well they cannot do it. Even the most monstrous being there is always a means to touch.

The Divine, the Divine's action in the world, always acts as a limit to the excess of evil, and at the same time gives an unlimited power to the good. And it is this unlimited power of the good which, externally, in the manifestation, serves as a limit to the spreading of evil.

Naturally, to the very limited vision of human beings it seems sometimes that evil has no limits and that it goes to its extreme. But this extreme itself is a limit. There is always a halt, because there is a point where the Divine rises up and says, "You won't go any farther." Whether it be the great destructions of Nature or men's monstrosities, there is *always* a moment when the Divine intervenes and prevents things from going farther.

28 December 1955

Possession by Hostile Beings

Have these vital beings a psychic being?

No, I said that the first thing they have to do to incarnate is to drive away the psychic being of the person whom they possess. That may happen from the very birth. There are children who are almost still-born; they are taken to be dead and suddenly they revive — this means that a vital being has incarnated in them. I have known such cases. This may happen also in the course of an illness: someone is very ill and gradually he lets go the contact with the psychic being, then, in a swoon or some other similar state, he cuts the contact entirely and the vital being rushes into the body. I have known cases of this kind also. Or it may be a slow action: the vital being enters into the atmosphere of the person, goes on influencing him and finally brings about illness, attacks, specially mental illness; then a time comes when the connection with the psychic being is entirely cut and the vital being takes possession of the body. There are cases of people falling very ill and coming out of the illness altogether different from what they were. Very often it is this that happens.

You have said that these beings of the vital world are attracted by the spiritual life. Why?

They are attracted, but this does not mean that they have decided sincerely to follow the spiritual life. The chief characteristic of these beings is falsehood: their nature is made of deceit. They have a power for illusion; they can take the appearance of divine beings or higher beings, they can appear in a dazzling light, but truly sincere people are not deceived, they immediately feel something that warns them. But if one likes the marvellous, the unexpected, if one loves fantastic things, if one likes to live a romance, one is likely to be easily deceived.

Not long ago there was a historical instance, that of Hitler, who was in contact with a being whom he considered to be the Supreme: this being came and gave him advice, told him all that he had to do. Hitler used to retire into solitude and remain there as long as it was necessary to come into contact with his "guide" and receive from him inspirations which he carried out later very faithfully. This being which Hitler took for the Supreme was quite plainly an Asura, one who is called the "Lord of Falsehood" in occultism, but who proclaimed himself the "Lord of the Nations". He had a shining appearance, he could mislead anybody except one who really had occult knowledge and could see what was there behind the appearance. He would have deceived anybody, he was truly splendid. Generally he used to appear to Hitler wearing a silver cuirass and helmet; a kind of flame came out of his head and there was an atmosphere of dazzling light around him, so dazzling that Hitler could hardly look at him. He used to tell Hitler everything that had to be done — he played with him as with a monkey or a mouse. He had decided clearly to make Hitler commit all possible extravagances till the day he would break his neck, which did happen. But cases like this are frequent, though on a smaller scale, of course.

Hitler was a very good medium, he had great mediumistic capacities, but he lacked intelligence and discrimination. This being could tell him anything whatever and he swallowed it all. It was he who pushed Hitler little by little. And he was doing this as a distraction, he did not take life seriously. For these beings men are very tiny things with whom they play, as a cat plays with a mouse, till finally they eat them up.

Are mentally deranged people possessed?

Yes, unless there is a physical lesion, a defect in the formation or an accident, a congestion. In all other cases it is always a possession. The proof of it is that if a person is brought to you who is altogether mentally deranged, if he has a lesion, he cannot be cured, while if there is no physical lesion, if it is a possession, then one can cure him. Unfortunately these things happen only to people who like them; there must be in the being much ambition, vanity, combined with much stupidity and a terrible pride — it is on such things that those beings play. I have known cases like that, of persons who were partially possessed, and I succeeded in freeing them from the beings who possessed them. Naturally they felt some relief, a kind of ease for a time, but it did not last long; almost immediately it wore off and they thought: "Now I have become quite an ordinary creature, whereas before I was an exceptional being!" They used to feel within them an exceptional power, even if it was a power to do evil, and they were satisfied with it. So what did they do? They called back with all their force the power they had lost! Of course, the being that had been destroyed could not come back, but as these beings exist in thousands it was replaced by another. I have seen this happen three times consecutively in a case, so much so that in the end I had to tell the person: "I am tired, get rid of it yourself, I am no longer interested!"

In these cases what happens to the psychic being?

Generally, it goes away.

I must tell you that the beings of the vital world are immortal — they cannot die. They can be destroyed, but it is only the pure spiritual force which can destroy them. For example, in a vital battle (there are people who have a vital fighting power), the experience is always the same: if you fight in the vital world with a vital being, you can crush it, kill it, but it will be reborn always — always they form themselves again. I think herein lies the origin of the legends of hydras or monsters with many heads.

There is only one force in the world which can destroy them categorically, that is, without any chance of return, and it is a force which belongs to the supreme creative Power. It is a force that comes from beyond the supramental world — it is not at the disposal of everybody. It is a luminous force, of a dazzling whiteness, so brilliant that if ordinary eyes looked at it, they would turn blind. A being of the vital world has just to be touched by this light to get dissolved immediately — it is liquefied, like those slugs which melt in water if a little salt is put on them.[...]

When Hitler died, did the Lord of Falsehood pass into Stalin?

It is not altogether like that that things happen, but it is something similar. This being did not wait for Hitler's death, it is there you make a mistake. These beings are not at all tied to a single physical presence. The being in question could very well possess Hitler and at the same time influence many others. Hitler was got rid of because he had behind him a whole nation and a physical power, and if he had succeeded it would have been a disaster for humanity, but there was no deluding oneself about it; it was not sufficient to get rid of him in order to get rid of the force that was behind him — that is not so easy. I must tell you that the origin of these beings is prior to that of the gods; they are the first emanations, the first individual beings of the universe; so they cannot be got rid of so easily, by winning one war.

As long as they are necessary for the universal evolution they will exist. The day they lose their utility, they will be converted or will disappear.

Besides, they know that they are nearing their last hour and that is why they are doing as much damage as they can.

There were four of them. The first one has been converted, another is dissolved into its origin. Two are still living and these two are more ferocious than the others. One is known in occultism as the "Lord of Falsehood", I have told you this, the other is the "Lord of Death". And as long as these two beings exist, there will be difficulties.

8 March 1951

Vital Incarnations

There are some human beings who are like vampires. What are they and why are they like that?

They are not human; there is only a human form or appearance. They are incarnations of beings from the world that is just next to the physical, beings who live on the plane which we call the vital world. It is a world of all the desires and impulses and passions and of movements of violence and greed and cunning and every kind of ignorance; but all the dynamisms too are there, all the life-energies and all the powers. The beings of this world have by their nature a strange grip over the material world and can exercise upon it a sinister influence. Some of them are formed out of the remains of the human being that persist after death in the vital atmosphere near to the earth-plane. His desires and hungers still float there and remain in form even after the dissolution of the body; often they are moved to go on manifesting and satisfying themselves and the birth of these creatures of the vital world is the consequence. But these are minor beings and, if they can be very troublesome, it is yet not impossible to deal with them. There are others, far more dangerous, who have never been in human form; never were they born into a human body upon earth, for most often they refuse to accept this way of birth because it is slavery to matter and they prefer to remain in their own world, powerful and mischievous, and to control earthly beings from there. For, if they do not want to be born on earth, they do want to be in contact with the physical nature, but without being bound by it. Their method is to try first to cast their influence upon a man; then they enter slowly into his atmosphere and in the end may get complete possession of him, driving out entirely the real human soul and personality. These creatures, when in possession of an earthly body, may have the human appearance but they have not a human nature. Their habit is to draw upon the life-force of human beings; they attack and capture vital power wherever they can and feed upon it. If they come into your atmosphere, you suddenly feel depressed and exhausted; if you are near them for some time you fall sick; if you live with one of them, it may kill you.

But how is one to get such creatures out of one's environment when they are once there?

The vital power incarnated in these beings is of a very material kind and it is effective only within a short distance. Ordinarily, if you do not live in the same house or if you are not in the same company with them, you do not come within their influence. But if you open some channel of connection or communication, through letters, for example, then you make possible an interchange of forces and are liable to be influenced by them even from a far distance. The wisest way with these beings is to cut off all connection and have nothing to do with them — unless indeed you have great occult knowledge and power and have learned how to cover and protect yourself — but even then it is always a dangerous thing to move about with them. To hope to transform them, as some people do, is a vain illusion; for they do not want to be transformed. They have no intention of allowing any transformation and all effort in that direction is useless.

These beings, when in the human body, are not often conscious of what they really are. Sometimes they have a vague feeling that they are not quite human in the ordinary way. But still there are cases where they are conscious and very conscious; not only do they know that they do not belong to humanity but they know what they are, act in that knowledge and deliberately pursue their ends. The beings of the vital world are powerful by their very nature; when to their power they add knowledge, they become doubly dangerous. There is nothing to be done with these creatures; you should avoid having any dealings with them unless you have the power to crush and destroy them. If you are forced into contact with them, beware of the spell they can cast. These vital beings, when they manifest on the physical plane, have always a great hypnotic power; for the centre of their consciousness is in the vital world and not in the material and they are not veiled and dwarfed by the material consciousness as human beings are.

Is it not a fact that these creatures are drawn by some peculiar fascination towards the spiritual life?

Yes, because they feel they do not belong to this earth but come from somewhere else; and they feel too that they have powers they have half lost and they are eager to win them back. So whenever they meet anyone who can give them some knowledge of the invisible world, they rush to him. But they mistake the vital for the spiritual world and in their seeking follow vital and not spiritual ends. Or perhaps they deliberately seek to corrupt spirituality and build up an imitation of it in the mould of their own nature. Even then it is a kind of homage they pay, or a sort of amends they make, in their own way, to the spiritual life. And there is too some kind of attraction that compels them; they have revolted against the Divine rule, but in spite of their revolt or perhaps because of it, they feel somehow bound and are powerfully attracted by its presence.

This is how it happens that you see them sometimes used as instruments to bring into connection with each other those who are to realise the spiritual life upon earth. They do not purposely serve this use, but are compelled to it. It is a kind of compensation that they pay. For they feel the pressure of the descending Light, they sense that the time has come or is soon coming when they must choose between conversion or dissolution, choose either to surrender to the Divine Will and take their part in the Great Plan or to sink into unconsciousness and cease to be. The contact with a seeker of Truth gives such a being his chance to change. All depends upon how he utilises his chance. Taken rightly, it may open his way to liberation from falsehood and obscurity and misery, which is the stuff out of which these vital creatures are made, and bring him to Regeneration and to Life.

Have not these beings a great control over money power?

Yes. The power of money is at present under the influence or in the hands of the forces and beings of the vital world. It is because of this influence that you never see money going in any considerable amount to the cause of Truth. Always it goes astray, because it is in the clutch of the hostile forces and is one of the principal means by which they keep their grip upon the earth. The hold of the hostile forces upon money-power is powerfully, completely and thoroughly organised and to extract anything out of this compact organisation is a most difficult task. Each time that you try to draw a little of this money away from its present custodians, you have to undertake a fierce battle.

12 May 1929

The Four Great Asuras

Would it not be better to change them [the hostile beings]?

Ah! my child, certainly it would be better, much better. But then....

It is a domain of which I have a thorough experience. After forty years of sustained effort I have found out that it is absolutely impossible to change anyone unless in truth he wants it sincerely. If he does not set himself to the task with an absolute sincerity, well — I have tried for forty years, one can try it for a hundred and forty years, it will be the same thing — he won't stir. It is the very character of these beings to be perfectly satisfied with themselves, and they do not desire, they have not the least intention to change! Even now, among the beings who are concerned with the earth, the asuric beings, the greatest of the asuras who is still busy with the earth at present, who is the asura of falsehood and calls himself the "Lord of the Nations" — he has taken a beautiful name, he is Lord of the Nations — it is he, wherever there is something going wrong, you may be sure it is he or a representative of his who is there. It is also perfectly sure that very soon his hour will come and all will be over for him, that he will have to disappear. And he absolutely refuses to change. He has no intention to do it, for immediately he will lose all his power. It is impossible. And he knows that he will disappear. But he proclaims categorically that before disappearing he will destroy all he can.... At heart, he would not consent to disappear unless everything disappeared at the same time as he. Unfortunately for him, this is not possible. But he will do all that lies in his power to destroy, demolish, ruin, corrupt as many things as he can. That is certain. Afterwards it is the downfall. He accepts the downfall on this condition. It has never crossed his mind that he might be converted. It would no longer be he, don't you see, he would no longer be himself.

There is a great difference between a human being and these beings of the vital plane. I have told you this many times, I am going to repeat it:

In a human being, there is the divine Presence and the psychic being — at the beginning embryonic, but in the end a being wholly formed, conscious, independent, individualised. That does not exist in the vital world. It is a special grace given to human beings dwelling in matter and upon earth. And because of this, there is no human being who cannot be converted, if he wants it; that is, there is a possibility of his wanting it and the moment he wants it, he can do it. He is sure to succeed the moment he wants it, whereas those beings of the vital do not have a psychic being in them, they do not have the direct divine Presence (naturally, at the Origin, they descended directly from the Divine, but that was at the Origin, that is very far away). They are not in direct contact with the Divine within them, they have no psychic being. And if they were converted, there would remain nothing of them! For they are made up entirely of the opposite movement: they are entirely made up of personal self-assertion, despotic authority, separation from the Origin, and, of a great disdain for all that is pure, beautiful and noble. They do not have within them this psychic element which in man, even in the most debased, makes him respect what is beautiful and pure; even the basest man, in spite of himself, against his own will, respects what is pure, noble and beautiful. But those beings do not have that. They are wholly on the other side, totally on the other side. It disgusts them in every way. It is for them something which should not be touched, because it destroys; it is the thing that makes them disappear. Goodwill, sincerity, purity and beauty are things which make them disappear. So they hate these things.

Now I do not know on what grounds one could convert them. What would be the point of support? I do not find it. Even in the greatest. That is, some of these beings will not disappear until hatred disappears from the earth.... One might put it the other way round. One might say that hatred will disappear from the earth when those beings disappear; but, for the reason I have just given, the power to make light spring forth in the place of darkness, beauty in the place of ugliness, goodness instead of evil, that power man possesses, the Asura does not. Therefore it is man who will do that work, it is he who will change, it is he who will transform his earth and it is he who will compel the Asura to flee into other worlds or to dissolve. After that, all will be quiet. There you are.

10 June 1953

*

If the Divine were to withdraw from the Asura, the Asura would dissolve, wouldn't he? — the Divine who is in the Asura?

I know people who have rejected their psychic being and who still continue to live; and yet, logically it would seem that a human being without a psychic being would die, still they continue to live. And perhaps it would be necessary in order finally to dissolve these asuric forces in the world — perhaps it would be necessary for the Divine to withdraw his whole creation into himself, because these are at the very origin of the creation.

Then the transformation cannot come about unless the Divine withdraws into the Divine?

That, why, that is Pralaya! It is not transformation, it is the dissolution of the earth. It is said that there were six creations, that is, six exteriorisations of the universe, and that six times the universe went back — it is recounted in the scriptures, you know — went back into the Divine. But it is said that this is the end. It is evidently one ending, but it is not the completion. It is because the creation lacked something and it was necessary to withdraw it and remake it. And it is said that our present creation is the seventh, and being the seventh it is the real one, that is, it is the final one, and it will not be withdrawn again, that it will continue being transformed and becoming more and more perfect, so as not to have to be withdrawn.

How far is what is said true?

We shall see!

But the last six times, is that what happened?

The first six, yes, it is true. Even the order is given, the order in which...
Because each creation is built on certain attributes, and the order of
these attributes is given. I know them, I have written them somewhere. But I don't have it with me. So I can't give it to you, I would
make a mistake. But one day I could bring you the paper on which it
is written. All that I know is that this time it is the creation based on
equilibrium. But a special equilibrium, for it is a progressive equilibrium. It is not a static equilibrium, the attribute of the present creation. It is *equilibrium*; that is why it is said that in this creation, if
each thing is exactly in its place, in a perfect balance, well, there is no
more evil. What is evil? — it is things not in equilibrium! There is
nothing that is bad in itself, it is only the position which is wrong,
which is not the true position.

Then what is the position of the Asuras?

To be taken back into the Divine. There were four great Asuras. Out
of the four, two are converted. They are taking part in the divine work.
The other two are holding out well. How long will they hold out? We
shall see. So, they have the choice between being converted, that is,
taking their place, poised, in the whole totality or else being dissolved,
that is, being re-absorbed by their origin.

There is one of them who has almost attempted conversion and
not succeeded. When it had to be done, it seemed to him quite unpleasant. So he has put it off till another time.

As for the other, he refuses to try. He has taken up a very, very
important position in the world, because people who don't know things
call him "Lord of the Nations". In fact, I was speaking a while ago
about the forces which govern the world and don't want to give up

their rule at all. They are perfectly satisfied with it — it is not that he does not know that his end will come one day, but still he always postpones it as long as he can.

But as they do not have human dimensions, it can go on for quite a long time, can't it? As long as they find somewhere upon earth a human consciousness ready to respond to their influence, they will remain. So you can imagine the problem! Now it is not through individuals, it is through nations that they exert their influence.[...]

Do you know what the origin of these four Asuras is?[...]

You said there were four divine forces: Love, Light, Truth and [...] Life.[...] Then these four forces separated from the Divine and changed into falsehood...

Yes, it is something like that! It is something like that!

Light or Consciousness, Ananda or Love, Life and Truth.

Then Light or Consciousness became Darkness and Inconscience. Love and Ananda became Hatred and Suffering, and Truth became Falsehood, and Life became Death. Well, it is the first two... but not exactly in the same conditions. The first is converted and works, but he has refused to take a human body, he says it is a limitation in his work; perhaps one day he will take one, but for the time being he refuses. The second is converted and has of his own will been dissolved. He has dissolved into his origin. And the last two are holding out well.

The one of Death tried to incarnate. But he could not get converted. He tried to incarnate, which is something very rare. But it was a partial, not a total incarnation. That is difficult for them, a total incarnation. Human bodies are quite small, human consciousnesses are too small.

As for the other, he has emanations which are very active in certain human bodies and have played a big role in the recent history of the earth!

Don't the Asuras quarrel among themselves?

Oh yes, oh yes! just like men who are under asuric influences. They

are the worst enemies among themselves. We must say it is a blessing, for if they had an understanding, things would be much more
difficult. Perhaps it is so just because it is a law of equilibrium that
governs the world. It is in order to lessen the strength of their influence. But still[...]

*But why is man a centre of attraction for the adverse forces? He
is so limited!*

Yes. Also they do not usually work upon one man. But they try to get
hold of the earth-atmosphere, you understand, and without getting
hold of men, they can't get hold of the earth-atmosphere, because it is
in man that the highest terrestrial force manifests. As for taking a
human body for conversion, that indeed is quite... the answer is quite
simple. It is because in man there is a psychic being and there is no
Asura who can eternally resist the influence of the psychic being,
even were he to refuse as much as he could to surrender and bind
himself closely. That's exactly the contradiction of their existence.

16 June 1954

Hostile Possession and the Psychic Being

*When a being is possessed by a hostile force, what becomes of
his psychic?*

It depends on the degree of the possession. Usually it is something
progressive. First there is an influence under which one comes, and
comes in a fragmentary way, not even totally in his being, but in certain parts and for a time. This is the first stage. The second: the influence becomes permanent and there is one part of the being which
deteriorates, which is constantly under this influence and expresses
it. After this, the being which has cast this influence tries to enter that
part. Then, usually, this produces a conflict, a kind of inner battle.
People have fits, sometimes even nervous morbid fits. In trying to
resist, the two parts of the being come constantly into conflict, and
this produces great imbalance, even physical imbalance. But if one
doesn't know how to resist and doesn't succeed in shaking off the

hold, then gradually the being that has seized upon a part of the person acts like an octopus and spreads its tentacles like that, slowly and everywhere; and finally it is a total possession. At the moment of the total possession, either the possessed person becomes completely unbalanced or he becomes a kind of monster and his psychic being leaves him.

These cases are extremely rare, fortunately. Usually, in the human being the psychic is strong enough to be able to resist, and the most frequent case is that of constant conflict between the two parts, until the psychic being, if it is strong enough and knows how to lean on a greater strength than its own, is capable of rejecting this influence and freeing itself. It is only in an extreme case of a total possession that the psychic being goes away. But these are extremely rare cases, extremely rare. It sometimes happens that a child is still-born, that is, just at the moment of birth it dies or a few minutes later, or an hour or two later, you see, just at that time. In these cases it happens that it is the psychic being which has decided not to use this body. But if, for example, the doctor who is looking after the case is a clever man or the nurse a clever person and they can bring back life into the body by artificial respiration or such means, most often it is a hostile being which gets hold of this body. There have been cases like that, children who seemed to be dead, that is, the psychic being had left the body, and before it had died completely, a vital being had entered and taken its place. Such cases have been known. And these beings are demons. In life they become veritable demons. There are not many of them.

There are beings of the vital, but of a higher kind, emanations of Asuras, for example, who have decided for one reason or another that they would try to be converted, not to be anti-divine, and manage to enter into relation with the Divine. They know that the best way is to identify themselves with a human body in order to be under the control of a psychic being. And they incarnate in human bodies, but not with the intention of driving out the psychic being, on the contrary, to try to submit to the influence of the psychic being and be converted by it. These cases also are not frequent, but still they have been known, and in these cases these human beings are gifted with very exceptional capacities, but usually they also have very exceptional difficulties, because the power which has incarnated in them is one which was, at least, if it is not still so, a hostile power; and, you see, it is difficult to get rid of all these movements of revolt immediately; sometimes it takes a whole lifetime to succeed in doing it.

Some of these asuric beings have tried to convert themselves and not succeeded. They ought to have left the body they had chosen, because they could not convert themselves. It was too difficult a task for them, it demanded too great an effort.

But all these cases about which I have just spoken to you are very rare ones, you see. We can't say that such things happen and are met with at every turn: a gentleman who is the incarnation of an adverse force or another who is possessed. Such cases are very rare, very rare.

But the case of an influence — being under an influence and expressing it — this, unfortunately, is very frequent, especially with people who undertake yoga without being sufficiently purified beforehand, or otherwise with egoistic intentions; to people who begin to do yoga for reasons of ambition or vanity it happens very often that they put themselves under the influence of certain adverse forces.

And there are also many people who are under certain influences in a way... how to put it?... one can't call it accidental, but... for example, there are psychic beings who choose a certain environment to incarnate in because they think that there they will have the experiences they want, and owing to some circumstances in this environment there is a hostile influence at work; so the body they put on is to a certain extent under this hostile influence and they have to fight against that terribly all their life. They can at a particular moment, as I said — if they know how to rely on greater forces than their own — they can conquer and gain a great victory. It is a great victory to get rid of the influence of an adverse force. It is truly a victory which goes beyond the individual's own person and has a repercussion on the whole terrestrial state. Each victory gained like this by an individual over a hostile force influencing him, is a long step forward to the day when the earth will be completely free of the presence of hostile forces. It represents a great progress for the earth.

22 December 1954

When we are afraid, is that due to the mischief of these beings?

Yes, my child. Fear is the prettiest gift these beings have given to the world. It is their first present, and the most powerful. It is through fear that they hold human beings. First of all, they create a movement of fear; the movement of fear weakens you, then hands you over little by little into their power. And it is not even a reasonable fear; it is a kind of fear which seizes you, you don't know why, something that makes you tremble, gives you anxiety. You do not know why, it has no apparent reason. It is their action.

24 June 1953

Resisting Hostile Forces

How is one to meet adverse forces — forces that are invisible and yet quite living and tangible?

A great deal depends upon the stage of development of your consciousness. At the beginning, if you have no special occult knowledge and power, the best you can do is to keep as quiet and peaceful as possible. If the attack takes the form of adverse suggestions try quietly to push them away, as you would some material object. The quieter you are, the stronger you become. The firm basis of all spiritual power is equanimity. You must not allow anything to disturb your poise: you can then resist every kind of attack. If, besides, you possess sufficient discernment and can see and catch the evil suggestions as they come to you, it becomes all the more easy for you to push them away; but sometimes they come unnoticed, and then it is more difficult to fight them. When that happens, you must sit quiet and call down peace and a deep inner quietness. Hold yourself firm and call with confidence and faith: if your aspiration is pure and steady, you are sure to receive help.

Attacks from adverse forces are inevitable: you have to take them as tests on your way and go courageously through the ordeal. The struggle may be hard, but when you come out of it, you have gained something, you have advanced a step. There is even a necessity for the existence of the hostile forces. They make your determination stronger, your aspiration clearer.

It is true, however, that they exist because you gave them reason to exist. So long as there is something in you which answers to them, their intervention is perfectly legitimate. If nothing in you responded, if they had no hold upon any part of your nature, they would retire and leave you. In any case, they need not stop or hamper your spiritual progress.

The only way to fail in your battle with the hostile forces is not to have a true confidence in the divine help. Sincerity in the aspiration always brings down the required succour. A quiet call, a conviction that in this ascension towards the realisation you are never walking all alone and a faith that whenever help is needed it is there, will lead you through, easily and securely.

Do these hostile forces generally come from outside or inside?

If you think or feel that they come from inside, you have possibly opened yourself to them and they have settled in you unnoticed. The true nature of things is one of harmony; but there is a distortion in certain worlds that brings in perversion and hostility. If you have a strong affinity for these worlds of distortion, you can become friends with the beings that are there and answer fully to them. That happens, but it is not a very happy condition. The consciousness is at once blinded and you cannot distinguish the true from the false, you cannot even tell what is a lie and what is not.

In any case, when an attack comes the wisest attitude is to consider that it comes from outside and to say, "This is not myself and I will have nothing to do with it." You have to deal in the same way with all lower impulses and desires and all doubts and questionings in the mind. If you identify yourself with them, the difficulty in fighting them becomes all the greater; for then you have the feeling that you are facing the never easy task of overcoming your own nature. But once you are able to say, "No, this is not myself, I will have nothing to do with it", it becomes much easier to disperse them.

Where can the line be drawn between the inside and the outside?

The line is very flexible; it can be as near to you and as far from you as you will. You may take everything upon yourself and feel it as a part and parcel of your real self; or you may throw it away as you would a bit of hair or nail without being touched at all.[...] Those who are capable of extending the consciousness as wide as the world, become the world; but those who are shut up in their little bodies and limited feelings stop at those limits; their bodies and their petty feelings are to them their whole self.

5 May 1929

*

Will a time come when the hostile forces will be there no longer?

When their presence in the world is no more of any use, they will disappear. Their action is used as a testing process, so that nothing may be forgotten, nothing left out in the work of transformation. They will allow no mistake. If you have overlooked in your own being even a single detail, they will come and put their touch upon that neglected spot and make it so painfully evident that you will be forced to change. When they will no longer be required for this process, their existence will become useless and they will vanish. They are suffered to exist here, because they are necessary in the Great Work; once they are no more indispensable, they will either change or go.

Will it be a long time before that happens?

All depends upon your point of view. For time is relative; you can speak of it from the ordinary external human standpoint or from the deeper viewpoint of an inner consciousness or from the outlook of the Divine.

Whether the thing to be done takes a thousand years or only a year according to the human computation, does not matter at all, if you are one with the Divine Consciousness; for then you leave outside you the things of the human nature and you enter into the infinity and eternity of the Divine Nature. Then you escape from this feeling of a great eagerness of hurry with which men are obsessed, because they want to see things done. Agitation, haste, restlessness lead nowhere. It is foam on the sea; it is a great fuss that stops with itself.

26 May 1929

CHAPTER 8

Illness and Death

Illness Is a Disequilibrium

In reality illness is only a disequilibrium; if then you are able to establish another equilibrium, this disequilibrium disappears. An illness is simply, always, in every case, even when the doctors say that there are microbes — in every case, a disequilibrium in the being: a disequilibrium among the various functions, a disequilibrium among the forces.

This is not to say that there are no microbes: there are, there are many more microbes than are known now. But it is not because of that you are ill, for they are always there. It happens that they are always there and for days they do nothing to you and then all of a sudden, one day, one of them gets hold of you and makes you ill — why? Simply because the resistance was not as it used to be habitually, because there was some disequilibrium in some part, the functioning was not normal. But if, by an inner power, you can re-establish the equilibrium, then that's the end, there is no more difficulty, the disequilibrium disappears.

There is no other way of curing people. It is simply when one sees the disequilibrium and is capable of re-establishing the equilibrium that one is cured. Only there are two very different categories you come across... Some hold on to their disequilibrium — they hold on to it, cling to it, don't want to let it go. Then you may try as hard as you will, even if you re-establish the equilibrium the next minute they get into disequilibrium once again, because they love that. They say: "Oh no! I don't want to be ill", but within them there is something which holds firmly to some disequilibrium, which does not want to let it go. There are other people, on the contrary, who sincerely love equilibrium, and directly you give them the power to get back their equilibrium, the equilibrium is re-established and in a few minutes they are cured. Their knowledge was not sufficient or their power was not sufficient to re-establish order — disequilibrium is a disorder. But if you intervene, if you have the knowledge and re-establish the equilibrium, quite naturally the illness will disappear; and those who allow you to do it get cured. Only those who do not let you do it are not cured and this is visible, they do not allow you to act, they cling to the illness. I tell them: "Ah! you are not cured? Go to the doctor then." And the funniest part of the thing is that most often they believe in the doctors, although the working remains the same! Every doctor who is something of a philosopher will tell you: "It is like that; we doctors give only the occasion, but it is the body that cures itself. When the body wants to be cured, it is cured." Well, there are bodies that do not allow equilibrium to be re-established unless they are made to absorb some medicine or something very definite which gives them the feeling that they are being truly looked after. But if you give them a very precise, very exact treatment that is sometimes very difficult to follow, they begin to be convinced that there is nothing better to do than to regain the equilibrium and they get back the equilibrium!

24 June 1953

Illness Comes from Outside

Sweet Mother, when one sees an illness coming, how can one stop it?

Ah! First of all, you must not want it, and nothing in the body must want it. You must have a very strong will not to be ill. This is the first condition.

The second condition is to call the light, a light of equilibrium, a light of peace, quietude and balance, and to push it into all the cells of the body, enjoining them not to be afraid, because that again is another condition.

First, not to want to be ill, and then not to be afraid of illness. You must neither attract it nor tremble. You must not want illness at all. But you must not because of fear not want it; you must not be afraid; you must have a calm certitude and a complete trust in the power of the Grace to shelter you from everything, and then think of something else, not be concerned about this any longer. When you have done these two things, refusing the illness with all your will and infusing a confidence which completely eliminates the fear in the cells of the body, and then busying yourself with something else, not thinking any longer about the illness, forgetting that it exists... there, if you know how to do that, you may even be in contact with people who have contagious diseases, and yet you do not catch them. But you must know how to do this.

Many people say, "Oh, yes, here I am not afraid." They don't have any fear in the mind, their mind is not afraid, it is strong, it is not afraid; but the body trembles, and one doesn't know it, because it is in the cells of the body that the trembling goes on. It trembles with a terrible anxiety and this is what attracts the illness. It is there that you must put the force and the quietude of a perfect peace and an absolute trust in the Grace. And then, sometimes you are obliged to drive away with a similar force in your thought all suggestions that after all, the physical world is full of illnesses, and these are contagious, and because one was in contact with somebody who is ill, one is sure to catch it, and then, that the inner methods are not powerful enough to act on the physical, and all kinds of stupidities of which the air is full. These are collective suggestions which are passed on from one person to another by everybody. And if by chance there are two or three doctors, then it becomes terrible. (*Laughter*)

When Sri Aurobindo says that illness comes from outside, what exactly is it that comes?

It is a kind of vibration made up of a mental suggestion, a vital force of disorder and certain physical elements which are the materialisation of the mental suggestion and the vital vibration. And these physical elements can be what we have agreed to call germs, microbes, this and that and many other things.

It may be accompanied by a sensation, may be accompanied by a taste, also by a smell, if one has very developed subtle senses. There are these formations of illness which give a special taste to the air, a special smell or a slight special sensation.

People have many senses which are asleep. They are terribly tamasic. If all the senses they possess were awake, there are many things they would perceive, which can just pass by without anyone suspecting anything.[...]

Besides, there is always a way of isolating oneself by an atmosphere of protection, if one knows how to have an extremely quiet vibration, so quiet that it makes almost a kind of wall around you. But all the time, all the time one is vibrating in response to vibrations which come from outside. If you become aware of this, all the time there is something which does this (*gestures*), like this, like this, like this (*gestures*), which responds to all the vibrations coming from outside. You are never in an absolutely quiet atmosphere which emanates from you, that is, which comes from inside outward (not something which comes from outside within), something which is like an envelope around you, very quiet, like this — and you can go anywhere at all and these vibrations which come from outside do not begin to do this (*gesture*) around your atmosphere.

If you could see that kind of dance, the dance of vibrations which is there around you all the time, you would see, would understand well what I mean. [...]

What is to be wondered at is the unconsciousness with which men go through life; they don't know how to live, there's not one in a million who knows how to live, and they live like that somehow or other, limping along, managing, not managing; and all that for them, bah! What is it? Things that happen.

They don't know how to live. All the same one should learn how to live. That's the first thing one ought to teach children: to learn how to live.

11 May 1955

*

Illnesses enter through the subtle body, don't they? How can they be stopped?

Ah! here we are.... If one is very sensitive, very sensitive — one must be very sensitive — the moment they touch the subtle body and try to pass through, one feels it. It is not like something touching the body, it is a sort of feeling. If you are able to perceive it at that moment, you have still the power to say "no", and it goes away. But for this one must be extremely sensitive. However, that develops. All these things can be developed methodically by the will. You can become quite conscious of this envelope, and if you develop it sufficiently, you don't even need to look and see, you feel that something has touched you [...] a kind of little discomfort (it is not something which is imposed with a great force), a little uneasiness coming near you from anywhere at all: front, behind, above, below. If at that moment you are sufficiently alert, you say "no", as though you were cutting off the contact with great strength, and it is finished. If you are not conscious at that moment, the next minute or a few minutes later you get a queer sick feeling inside, a cold in the back, a little uneasiness, the beginning of some disharmony; you feel a maladjustment somewhere, as though the general harmony had been disturbed. Then you must concentrate all the more and with a great strength of will keep the faith that nothing can do you harm, nothing can touch you. This suffices, you can throw off the illness at that moment. But you must do this immediately, you understand, you must not wait five minutes, it must be done at once. If you wait too long and begin to feel really an uneasiness somewhere, and something begins to get quite disturbed, then it is good to sit down, concentrate and call the Force, concentrate it on the place which is getting disturbed, that is to say, which is beginning to become ill. But if you don't do anything at all, an illness indeed gets lodged somewhere; and all this, because you were not sufficiently alert. And sometimes one is obliged to follow the entire curve to find the favourable moment again and get rid of the business. I have said somewhere that in the physical domain all is a question of method — a method is necessary for realising everything. And if the illness has succeeded in touching the physical-physical, well, you must follow the procedure needed to get rid of it. This is what medical science calls "the course of the illness". One can hasten the course with the help of spiritual forces, but all the same the procedure must be followed. There are some four different stages. The very first is instantaneous. The second can be done in some minutes, the third may take several hours and the fourth several days. And then, once the thing is lodged there, all will depend not only on the receptivity of the body but still more on the willingness of the part which is the cause of the disorder. You know, when the thing comes from outside it is in affinity

with something inside. If it manages to pass through, to enter without
one's being aware of it, it means there is some affinity somewhere,
and the part of the being which has responded must be convinced.[...]

But the condition in every case — in every case — whether one
does it oneself and depending only on oneself or whether one does it
by asking someone to do it for one, the first condition: not to fear and
to be calm. If you begin to boil and get fidgety in your body, it is
finished, you can do nothing.

For everything — to live the spiritual life, heal sickness — for
everything, one must be calm.

31 March 1951

Microbes and Illness

*"When you cut yourself off from the energy and light that sustain
you, then there is this depression, there is created what medical
science calls a 'favourable ground' and something takes advantage of it. It is doubt, gloominess, lack of confidence, a selfish
turning back upon yourself that cuts you off from the light and
divine energy and gives the attack this advantage. It is this that is
the cause of your falling ill and not microbes." (The Mother)*

One thing that is now beginning to be recognised by everyone, even
by the medical corps, is that hygienic measures, for example, are effective only to the extent that one has confidence in them. Take the
case of an epidemic. Many years ago we had a cholera epidemic here
— it was bad — but the chief medical officer of the hospital was an
energetic man: he decided to vaccinate everybody. When he discharged
the vaccinated men, he would tell them, "Now you are vaccinated
and nothing will happen to you, but if you were not vaccinated you
would be sure to die!" He told them this with great authority. Generally such an epidemic lasts a long time and it is difficult to arrest it,
but in some fifteen days, I think, this doctor succeeded in checking it;
in any case, it was done miraculously fast. But he knew very well that
the best effect of his vaccination was the confidence it gave to people.

Now, quite recently, they have found something else and I consider it wonderful. They have discovered that for every disease there

is a microbe that cures it (call it a microbe if you like, anyway, some sort of germ). But what is so extraordinary is that this "microbe" is extremely contagious, even more contagious than the microbe of the disease. And it generally develops under two conditions: in those who have a sort of natural good humour and energy and in those who have a strong will to get well! Suddenly they catch the "microbe" and are cured. And what is wonderful is that if there is one who is cured in an epidemic, three more recover immediately. And this "microbe" is found in all who are cured.

But I am going to tell you something: what people take to be a microbe is simply the materialisation of a vibration or a will from another world. When I learned of these medical discoveries, I said to myself, "Truly, science is making progress." One might almost say with greater reason, "Matter is progressing," it is becoming more and more receptive to a higher will. And what is translated in their science as "microbes" will be perceived, if one goes to the root of things, as simply a vibratory mode; and this vibratory mode is the material translation of a higher will. If you can bring this force or this will, this power, this vibration (call it what you will) into certain given circumstances, not only will it act in you, but also through contagion around you.

"Is any one of you pure and strong enough not to be affected by suggestions? If you drink unfiltered water and think, 'Now I am drinking impure water', you have every chance of falling sick. And even though such suggestions may not enter through the conscious mind, the whole of your subconscious is there, almost helplessly open to any kind of suggestion.... The normal human condition is a state filled with apprehensions and fears; if you observe your mind deeply for ten minutes, you will find that for nine out of the ten it is full of fears....

And even if by discipline and effort you have liberated your mind and your vital of apprehension and fear, it is more difficult to convince the body." (The Mother)

Why is it so difficult to convince the body, when one has succeeded in liberating oneself mentally and vitally?

Because in the large majority of men, the body receives its inspirations from the subconscient, it is under the influence of the subconscient. All the fears driven out from the active consciousness go and take refuge there and then, naturally, they have to be chased out from the subconscient and uprooted from there.

14 March 1951

Causes of Illness

Sweet Mother, if someone falls seriously ill, is this a purely physical phenomenon or is it a difficulty in his spiritual life?

That depends on the person! If it is someone who is doing yoga, it is quite obviously a difficulty in his spiritual life. If it is somebody who is not at all engaged in yoga and who lives an ordinary life in the most ordinary manner, it is an ordinary accident. It depends absolutely on the person. The outer phenomena may be similar, but the inner causes are absolutely different. No two illnesses are alike, though labels are put on diseases and attempts made to group them; but in fact every person is ill in his own way, and his way depends on what he is, on his state of consciousness and the life he leads.

We have often said that illnesses are always the result of a disturbance of equilibrium, but this disturbance can occur in completely different states of being. For the ordinary man whose consciousness is centred in the physical, outer life, it is a purely physical disturbance of equilibrium, of the functioning of the different organs. But when behind this purely superficial life, an inner life is being fashioned, the causes of illness change; they always become the expression of a disequilibrium between the different parts of the being: between the inner progress or effort and the outer resistances or conditions of one's life, one's body.

Even from the ordinary external point of view, it has been recognised for a very long time that it is a fall in the resistance of the vitality due to immediate moral causes which is always at the origin of an illness. When one is in a normal state of equilibrium and lives in a normal physical harmony, the body has a capacity of resistance, it has within it an atmosphere strong enough to resist illnesses: its most material substance emanates subtle vibrations which have the strength to resist illnesses, even diseases which are called contagious — in fact, all vibrations are contagious, but still, certain diseases are considered as especially contagious. Well, a man who, even from the purely external point of view, is in a state in which his organs function harmoniously and an adequate psychological balance prevails, has at the same time enough resistance for the contagion not to affect him. But if for some reason or other he loses this equilibrium or is weakened by depression, dissatisfaction, moral difficulties or undue fatigue, for instance, this reduces the normal resistance of the body and he is open to the disease. But if we consider someone who is doing yoga, then it is altogether different, in the sense that the causes of disequilibrium are of a different nature and the illness usually becomes the expression of an inner difficulty which has to be overcome.

So each one should find out for himself why he is ill.

From the ordinary point of view, in most cases, it is usually fear — fear, which may be mental fear, vital fear, but which is almost always physical fear, a fear in the cells — it is fear which opens the door to all contagion. Mental fear — all who have a little control over themselves or any human dignity can eliminate it; vital fear is more subtle and asks for a greater control; as for physical fear, a veritable yoga is necessary to overcome it, for the cells of the body are afraid of everything that is unpleasant, painful, and as soon as there is any unease, even if it is insignificant, the cells of the body become anxious, they don't like to be uncomfortable. And then, to overcome that, the control of a conscious will is necessary. It is usually this kind of fear that opens the door to illnesses. And I am not speaking of the first two types of fear which, as I said, any human being who wants to be human in the noblest sense of the word, must overcome, for that is cowardice. But physical fear is more difficult to overcome; without it even the most violent attacks could be repelled. If one has a minimum of control over the body, one can lessen its effects, but that is not immunity. It is this kind of trembling of material, physical fear in the cells of the body which aggravates all illnesses.[...]

Mother, how are medicines to be used for a body which is not altogether unconscious? For even when we draw on the divine

grace, we see that we need a little medicine, and if a little medi-
cine is given it has a good effect. Does this mean that only the
body needs medicine or is there something wrong with the mind
and the vital?

In most cases the use of medicines — within reasonable limits, that
is, when one doesn't poison oneself by taking medicines — is simply
to help the body to have confidence. It is the body which heals itself.
When it wants to be cured, it is cured. And this is something very
widely recognised now; even the most traditional doctors tell you,
"Yes, our medicines help, but it is not the medicines which cure, it is
the body which decides to be cured." Very well, so when the body is
told, "Take this", it says to itself, "Now I am going to get better", and
because it says "I am going to get better", well, it is cured!

In almost every case, there are things which help — a little —
provided it is done within reasonable limits. If it is no longer within
reasonable limits, you are sure to break down completely. You cure
one thing but catch another which is usually worse. But still, a little
help, in a way, a little something that gives confidence to your body:
"Now it will be all right, now that I have taken this, it is going to be all
right" — this helps it a great deal and it decides to get better and it is
cured.

There too, there is a whole range of possibilities, from the yogi
who is in so perfect a state of inner control that he could take poison
without being poisoned to the one who at the least little scratch rushes
to the doctor and needs all sorts of special drugs to get his body to
make the movement needed for its cure. There is the whole possible
range, from total, supreme mastery to an equally total bondage to all
external aids and all that you absorb from outside — a bondage and a
perfect liberation. There is the whole range. So everything is possible. It is like a great key-board, very complex and very complete, on
which one can play, and the body is the instrument.

19 June 1957

Make a Beautiful Thing of Death

[...]if one must for some reason or other leave one's body and take a new one, is it not better to make of one's death something magnificent, joyful, enthusiastic, than to make it a disgusting defeat? Those who cling on, who try by every possible means to delay the end even by a minute or two, who give you an example of frightful anguish, show that they are not conscious of their soul.... After all, it is perhaps a means, isn't it? One can change this accident into a means; if one is conscious one can make a beautiful thing of it, a very beautiful thing, as of everything. And note, those who do not fear it, who are not anxious, who can die without any sordidness are those who never think about it, who are not haunted all the time by this "horror" facing them which they must escape and which they try to push as far away from them as they can. These, when the occasion comes, can lift their head, smile and say, "Here I am."

It is they who have the will to make the best possible use of their life, it is they who say, "I shall remain here as long as it is necessary, to the last second, and I shall not lose one moment to realise my goal"; these, when the necessity comes, put up the best show. Why? — It is very simple, because they live in their ideal, the truth of their ideal; because that is the real thing for them, the very reason of their being, and in all things they can see this ideal, this reason of existence, and never do they come down into the sordidness of material life.

So, the conclusion:

One must never wish for death.

One must never will to die.

One must never be afraid to die.

And in all circumstances one must will to exceed oneself.

23 April 1951

*

There are two remedies [to overcome the fear of death]. There are many, but two at least are there. In any case, the use of a deeper consciousness is essential. One remedy consists in saying that it is something that happens to everyone (let us take it on that level), yes, it is a thing that happens to everybody, and therefore, sooner or later, it will come and there is no reason why one should be afraid, it is quite a normal thing. You may add one more idea to this, that according to experience (not yours but just the collective human experience), circumstances being the same, absolutely identical, in one case people die, in another they do not — why? And if you push the thing a little further still, you say to yourself that after all it must depend on something which is altogether outside your consciousness — and in the end one dies when one has to die. That is all. When one has to die one dies, and when one has not to die, one does not die. Even when you are in mortal danger, if it is not your hour to die, you will not die, and even if you are out of all danger, just a scratch on your foot will be enough to make you die, for there are people who have died of a pin-scratch on the foot — because the time had come. Therefore, fear has no sense. What you can do is to rise to a state of consciousness where you can say, "It is like that, we accept the fact because it seems to be recognised as an inevitable fact. But I do not need to worry, for it will come only when it must come. So I don't need to feel afraid: when it is not to come, it will not come to me, but when it must come to me, it will come. And as it will come to me inevitably, it is better I do not fear the thing; on the contrary, one must accept what is perfectly natural." This is a well-known remedy, that is to say, very much in use.

There is another, a little more difficult, but better, I believe. It lies in telling oneself: "This body is not I", and in trying to find in oneself the part which is truly one's self, until one has found one's psychic being. And when one has found one's psychic being — immediately, you understand — one has the sense of immortality. And one knows that what goes out or what comes in is just a matter of convenience: "I am not going to weep over a pair of shoes I put aside when it is full of holes! When my pair of shoes is worn out I cast it aside, and I do not weep." Well, the psychic being has taken this body because it needed to use it for its work, but when the time comes to leave the body, that is to say, when one must leave it because it is no longer of any use for some reason or other, one leaves the body and has no fear. It is quite a natural gesture — and it is done without the least regret, that's all.

And the moment you are in your psychic being, you have that feeling, spontaneously, effortlessly. You soar above the physical life and have the sense of immortality. As for me, I consider this the best remedy. The other is an intellectual, common-sense, rational remedy. This is a deep experience and you can always get it back as soon as you recover the contact with your psychic being. This is a truly interesting phenomenon, for it is automatic. The moment you are in contact with your psychic being, you have the feeling of immortality, of having always been and being always, eternally. And then what comes and goes — these are life's accidents, they have no importance. Yes, this is the best remedy. The other is like the prisoner finding good reasons for accepting his prison. This one is like a man for whom there's no longer any prison.

Now, a third thing also one must know, but for this one has to be a mighty yogi. For this means knowing that death is not an inevitable thing, it is an accident which has been occurring till now (which seems in any case to have always occurred till now), and that we have put it into our head and our will to conquer this accident and overcome it. But it is so terrible, so formidable a battle against all the laws of Nature, against all collective suggestions, all earthly habits, that unless, as I have said, you are a first-rate warrior whom nothing frightens, it is better not to begin the battle. You must be an absolutely intrepid hero, for at every step, at every second you have to fight a battle against all established things. So it is not a very easy thing. And even as an individual it is a battle against oneself, because (I think I have already told you this once), if you want your physical consciousness to be in a state which admits of physical immortality, you must be free to such an extent from everything which at present represents the physical consciousness that it becomes every second a battle. All feelings, all sensations, all thoughts, all reflexes, all attractions, all repulsions, all existing things, all that forms the fabric of our physical life must be overcome, transformed and freed from all their habits. This is a battle of every second against thousands and millions of enemies. Unless you feel you are a hero, it is better not to try. Because this solution, well... I do not know, but I believe I was asked this question once before: "Has anyone succeeded so far?" To tell you the truth I don't know, for I have not met such a person.... I do not have the feeling that anyone has succeeded till now. But it is possible. Only, he or she who has done it has not declared it, at least, not till now.

The other two solutions are safe and sure and within your reach. Now, there is a small remedy which is very very easy. For it is based on a simple personal question of one's common sense.... You must observe yourself a little and say that when you are afraid it is as though the fear was attracting the thing you are afraid of. If you are afraid of illness, it is as though you were attracting the illness. If you are afraid of an accident, it is as though you were attracting the accident. And if you look into yourself and around yourself a little, you will find it out, it is a persistent fact. So if you have just a little common sense, you say: "It is stupid to be afraid of anything, for it is precisely as though I were making a sign to that thing to come to me. If I had an enemy who wanted to kill me, I would not go and tell him: 'You know, it's me you want to kill!' " It is something like that. So since fear is bad, we won't have it. And if you say you are unable to prevent it by your reason, well, that shows you have no control over yourselves and must make a little effort to control yourselves. That is all.

14 October 1953

The Domain of Death

I was seriously ill, unconscious for two hours, and I had the impression that I had gone over to the other side, that I was in a different world. When I came back to myself, I had the impression of having made a long journey in a world quite different from the one where I normally lived.

It was a partial exteriorisation; it was not a total exteriorisation which indeed causes death. If one goes out entirely, that is, if there is a complete separation from the body and one is really dead, and then one comes back, that causes such an intense suffering that one cannot forget it. It is said that babies cry when they come into the world because the first contact with air makes them cry, but I think it is something else. The re-entry into the body causes a kind of friction, for what goes out has to be something very material if it is to bring about death, something even more material than the subtle physical, and this friction is extremely painful. Otherwise one may be externally unconscious, but one is not dead for all that. It is only when something extremely material goes out of the body and all ties are broken that there is truly "death". And that is why (I believe we are beginning to discover it) people do not die till six or seven days after their death. That is, they are not "dead" as long as the body remains intact, but only when a part of the body begins to decompose. Hence during this period, someone who has the necessary knowledge, power and capacity may "raise" a person in such a state. I believe this explains most of the cases of "miraculous" resurrection.

24 February 1951

*

What becomes of the vital being after death?

It is dissolved. Rarely does it happen otherwise. But if you have had a very strong passion, if you were divided by fixed impulses, the vital being would break up into small pieces. Instead of going off like a vapour or a liquid, it goes off by little bits. Each of these pieces of vital substance is gathered around the central impulse, the central desire, the central passion of that piece, thus creating little entities which don't have a human form but take at times an indefinite form; at times they resemble the body to which the pieces belonged, at other times they take a form expressing the desire they represent. And naturally their sole concern is to satisfy their desire or passion and they search everywhere for the means of self-satisfaction.

10 March 1951

*

Generally, "domain of death" is the name given to a certain region of the most material vital into which one is projected at the moment one leaves one's body. The part — how to put it? — of one's life that's usually the most conscious is projected there at the moment of death. Well, that region, that material vital world is very dark, it is full of adverse formations having desires at their centre or even adverse wills, and these are very, very elemental entities which have a very fragmentary life and are like vampires, in the sense that they feed on all that is thrown out from human beings. And so, at that moment, from the shock of death — for very few die without a shock, go out consciously, in full knowledge of the thing, there are not many such — usually it is an accident: a last accident; well, at that shock of death, those entities rush in upon this, upon this vitality that goes out, and feed upon it.

So long as a person is alive, they cannot touch him. For, you have all had the experience of a nightmare in which, when the situation becomes really very dangerous, suddenly you wake up — you come back into your body, for the body is your protection. In the physical they can do nothing to you but when you are completely outside the physical (and even this link I spoke about serves as a protection to a certain extent when you go out), but if the links are broken and you are entirely without a body, well, unless you take advantage of special circumstances... as for instance when a person is much loved by others who are yet alive; if at that moment these people who love him concentrate their thought and love on the departed one, he finds a refuge therein, and this protects him completely against those entities; but one who passes away without anyone's having a special attachment for him, either because he is surrounded by people he has harmed and who do not love him or by people who are in a terribly unconscious state — he is like a prey delivered to these forces. And that indeed is an experience that's difficult to bear. They cannot touch anything else except what belongs to their own domain, that is, the most material vital — the higher vital escapes them altogether, they can do nothing there. And so, this material vital goes out but the other remains; and this higher vital is attacked by other dangers, simply that. And if it also disappears, the mind remains.

But behind all this is the psychic being which nothing can touch, which is above all possible attacks, and it indeed is free to go where it wants. Usually — unless it has a special opportunity and has reached a state of complete development — it goes to rest in the psychic worlds. There it enters into a kind of beatific contemplation in which it remains, and this is an assimilation of all its experiences, and when it has finished assimilating them and resting, well, it starts preparing to come down again for a new life. That being nothing can touch. But so very few are conscious of their psychic that one can hardly say that it is such and such a person whom one has known, for people as we know them are made of what? — of all their physical experiences, all their vital reactions, all their mental formations — that is, the body, the character, the thought — and with these we have a human being! Well, all that cannot persist after death unless it is organised and centralised around the psychic being and to the extent it is perfectly unified with the psychic. Otherwise all this mixture is dissolved and the psychic being alone remains, at times just as a flame, at times as a completely conscious being.

This of course is the general law. Now there are bridges, as it were, "protected passages" which have been built in the vital world in order to cross over all these dangers. There are atmospheres which receive people leaving their body, give them shelter, give them protection. There are all kinds of other conditions; what I have told you just now is the normal state of those who die, of ordinary human beings, but as soon as we come to a little higher type of humanity, all these conditions change. The general law remains unless there is a special higher development within the being. There are people with so total a cohesion in their being that they no longer depend upon the body — not at all — whether it be there or not there.

But all this development does not come about just like that, simply by thinking about it from time to time, desiring it still less often and forgetting it most of the time — no, it is not like that that it can happen. These are disciplines, I may say, at least as arduous as the strictest spiritual disciplines.... Essentially it is for this that we are on the earth. Truly speaking, human beings were made for this purpose, to do that work, and it is perhaps because they refuse to do it that there is so much chaos in the world. If they did it truly, things would go much better.

10 March 1954

*

If at the time of death the vital being is attacked in the vital world by hostile forces or entities, does it not look for a shelter somewhere?

Yes, it is for this reason that in all countries and in all religions, it is recommended that for a period of at least seven days after someone's death, people should gather and think of him. Because when you think of him with affection (without any inner disorder, without weeping, without any of those distraught passions), if you can be calm, your atmosphere becomes a kind of beacon for him, and when he is attacked by hostile forces (I am speaking of the vital being of course, not the psychic being which goes to take rest), he may feel altogether lost, not know what to do and find himself in great distress; then he sees through affinity the light of those who are thinking of him with affection and he rushes there. It happens almost constantly that a vital formation, a part of the vital being of the dead person (or at times the whole vital if it is well organised) takes shelter in the aura, the atmosphere of the people or the person who loved him. There are people who always carry with them a part of the vital of the person who is gone. That is the real utility of these so-called ceremonies, which otherwise have no sense.

It is preferable to do this without ceremonies. Ceremonies are, if anything, rather harmful, for a very simple reason: When you are busy with a ceremony, you think more about that than about the person. When you are busy with gestures, movements, with the following of a ritual, you think much more of all that than of the person who is dead. Moreover, people perform these ceremonies most of the time for that very reason, for they are almost always in the habit of trying to forget. The fact is that one of the two principal occupations of man is to try to forget what is painful to him, and the other is to try to seek amusement in order to escape boredom. These are the two principal occupations of humanity, that is, humanity spends half of its time in doing nothing true.

12 March 1951

*

Why does one suffer when one commits suicide?

Why does one commit suicide? Because one is a coward.... When one is cowardly one always suffers.

In the next life one suffers again?

The psychic being comes with a definite purpose to go through a set of experiences and to learn and make progress. Then if you leave before its work is finished it will have to come back to do it again under much more difficult conditions. So all that you have avoided in one life you will find again in another, and more difficult. And even without leaving in this way, if you have difficulties to overcome in life, you have what we usually call a test to pass, you see; well, if you don't pass it or turn your back upon it, if you go away instead of passing it, you will have to pass it another time and it will be much more difficult than before.

Now people, you know, are extremely ignorant and they think that it is like this: there is life, and then death; life is a bunch of troubles, and then death is an eternal peace. But it is not at all like that. And usually when one goes out of life in an altogether arbitrary way and in an ignorant and obscure passion, one goes straight into a vital world made of all these passions and all this ignorance. So the troubles one wanted to avoid one finds again without even having the protection which the body gives, for — if you have ever had a nightmare, that is, a rash excursion in the vital world, well, your remedy is to wake yourself up, that is to say, to rush back immediately into your body. But when you have destroyed your body you no longer have a body to protect you. So you find yourself in a perpetual nightmare, which is not very pleasant. For, to avoid the nightmare you must be in a psychic consciousness, and when you are in a psychic consciousness you may be quite sure that things won't trouble you. It is indeed the movement of an ignorant darkness and, as I said, a great cowardice in front of the sustained effort to be made.

26 January 1955

Heaven and Hell

After death people enter the vital world, but those who do good go to paradise?

Where is your paradise? Who has taught you that? They have spoken to you of heaven and hell and purgatory?[...]

It is generally what religious priests say to the faithful to encourage them to do good. For it is a notorious fact that life is not more easy for the good than for the wicked; usually it is the contrary: the wicked succeed better than the good! So people who are not very spiritual say to themselves: "Why should I take the trouble of being good? It is better to be wicked and have an easy life." It is very difficult to make them understand that there are many kinds of good and that sometimes it is worth the trouble perhaps to make an effort to be good. So to make this intelligible to the least intelligent, they are told: "There, it is very simple. If you are quite obedient, quite nice, quite unselfish, if you always do good deeds, and if you believe in the dogmas we teach, well, when you die, God will send you to Paradise. If you have sometimes good will, sometimes bad, if, sometimes you do good, sometimes you don't and if you think very much of yourself and very little of others, then when you die, you will be sent to Purgatory for another experience. And then if you are thoroughly wicked, if you are always doing harm to others, doing all kinds of bad things and you do not care about the good of anyone and particularly if you do not believe in the dogma that we teach you, then you will go straight to Hell and for eternity."

This is one of the prettiest inventions I have ever heard of: they have invented *eternal hell*. That is to say, once you are in hell, it is for eternity.... You understand what that means, for eternity? You will be tortured and burnt (in the hot countries you are burnt, in the cold countries you are frozen), and that for eternity. That is it. So I do not know who taught you those pretty things; but they are simply inventions to make people obey, to keep them under control.

There are teachings which are not like that. There are religions which are not like that. But still one can, in a poetic, picturesque, descriptive manner speak of a paradise; because this paradise means a wonderful place where there is utmost joy and happiness and comfort.... And yet that depends upon the religion to which you belong. For there are heavens where you pass your time singing praises to God, you do nothing else — but in the end that must be somewhat wearisome; however, there you pass your time playing music and singing the praises of God. There are other heavens, on the contrary, where you enjoy all possible pleasures, all that you desired to have during your life, you have in heaven. There are heavens where you are constantly in blissful meditation — but for people who are not keen on meditating, that must be rather tiresome. However, that depends, you know: they have invented all kinds of things so that people may really want to be wise and obey the laws given to them. .

And man's imagination is so creative, such a form-maker, that there really are in the world places like these heavens. There are places also like these hells and there are places like these purgatories. Man creates out of nothing the things he imagines. If your consciousness be enlightened, then you can be pulled out of these places; otherwise you are shut up, imprisoned there by the very belief you had when alive. You will tell me that it is equal to a life, but it is an altogether illusory and extremely limited existence. It is real only for those who think like that. As soon as you think differently, it does not exist for you any longer; you can come out of it. You can pull a person out of these places, and immediately he perceives that he was imprisoned in his own formation.

Man has an extraordinary power of creation. He has created a whole set of godheads in his own image, having the same faults as himself, doing on a bigger scale, with greater power whatever he does. These beings have a relative existence, but still it is an independent existence, just like your thought. When you have a thought, a well-made mental formation which goes out of you, it becomes an independent entity and continues on its way and it does that for which it was made. It continues to act independently of you. That is why you must be on your guard. If you have made such a formation and it has gone out, it has gone out to do its work; and after a time you find out that it was perhaps not a very happy thing to have a thought like that, that this formation was not very beneficial; now that it has gone out, it is very difficult for you to get hold of it again. You must have considerable occult knowledge. It has gone out and is moving on its way....
Supposing in a moment of great anger (I do not say that you do so, but still) when you were in quite a rage against someone, you said: "Ah! couldn't some misfortune befall him?" Your formation has gone on its way. It has gone out and you have no longer any control over it; and it goes and organises some misfortune or other: it is going to do

its work. And after some time the misfortune arrives. Happily, you do not usually have sufficient knowledge to tell yourself: "Oh! It is I who am responsible", but that is the truth.

Note that this power of formation has a great advantage, if one knows how to use it. You can make good formations and if you make them properly, they will act in the same way as the others. You can do a lot of good to people just by sitting quietly in your room, perhaps even more good than by undergoing a lot of trouble externally. If you know how to think correctly, with force and intelligence and kindness, if you love someone and wish him well very sincerely, deeply, with all your heart, that does him much good, much more certainly than you think. I have said this often; for example, to those who are here, who learn that someone in their family is very ill and feel that childish impulse of wanting to rush immediately to the spot to attend to the sick person. I tell you, unless it is an exceptional case and there is nobody to attend on the sick person (and at times even in such a case), if you know how to keep the right attitude and concentrate with affection and good will upon the sick person, if you know how to pray for him and make helpful formations, you will do him much more good than if you go to nurse him, feed him, help him wash himself, indeed all that everybody can do. Anybody can nurse a person. But not everybody can make good formations and send out forces that act for healing.

In any case, to come back to our paradise, it is a childish deformation — ignorant or political — of something which is true in a sense but not quite like that.... I have told you many times and I could not repeat it too often, that one is not built up of one single piece. We have within us many states of being and each state of being has its own life. All this is put together in one single body, so long as you have a body, and acts through that single body; so that gives you the feeling that it is one single person, a single being. But there are many beings and particularly there are concentrations on different levels: just as you have a physical being, you have a vital being, you have a mental being, you have a psychic being, you have many others and all possible intermediaries. But it is a little complicated, you might not understand.

Suppose you were living a life of desire, passion and impulse:

you live with your vital being dominant in you; but if you live with spiritual effort, with great good will, the desire to do things well and an unselfishness, a will for progress, you live with the psychic being dominant in you. Then, when you are about to leave your body, all these beings start to disperse. Only if you are a very advanced yogi and have been able to unify your being around the divine centre, do these beings remain bound together. If you have not known how to unify yourself, then at the time of death all that is dispersed: each one returns to its domain. For example, with regard to the vital being, all your different desires will be separated and each one run towards its own realisation, quite independently, for the physical being will no longer be there to hold them together. But if you have united your consciousness with the psychic consciousness, when you die you remain conscious of your psychic being and the psychic being returns to the psychic world which is a world of bliss and delight and peace and tranquillity and of a growing knowledge. So, if you like to call that a paradise, it is all right; because in fact, to the extent to which you are identified with your psychic being, you remain conscious of it, you are one with it, and it is immortal and goes to its immortal domain to enjoy a perfectly happy life or rest. If you like to call that paradise, call it paradise. If you are good, if you have become conscious of your psychic and live in it, well, when your body dies, you will go with your psychic being to take rest in the psychic world, in a blissful state.

But if you have lived in your vital with all its impulses, each impulse will try to realise itself here and there... For example, a miser who is concentrated upon his money, when he dies, the part of the vital that was interested in his money will be stuck there and will continue to watch over the money so that nobody may take it. People do not see him, but he is there all the same, and is very unhappy if something happens to his precious money. I knew quite well a lady who had a good amount of money and children; she had five children who were all prodigals each one more than the other. The same amount of care she had taken in amassing the money, they seemed to take in squandering it; they spent it at random. So when the poor old lady died, she came to see me and told me: "Ah, now they are going to squander my money!" And she was extremely unhappy. I consoled her a little, but I had a good deal of difficulty in persuading her not to keep watching over her money so that it might not be wasted.

Now, if you live exclusively in your physical consciousness (it is difficult, for you have, after all, thoughts and feelings, but if you live exclusively in your physical), when the physical being disappears, you disappear at the same time, it is finished.... There is a spirit of the form: your form has a spirit which persists for seven days after your death. The doctors have declared that you are dead, but the spirit of your form lives, and not only does it live but it is conscious in most of the cases. But that lasts for seven or eight days and afterwards it is dissolved. I am not speaking of yogis; I am speaking of ordinary people. Yogis have no laws, it is quite different; for them the world is different. I am speaking to you of ordinary men living an ordinary life; for these it is like that.

So the conclusion is that if you want to preserve your consciousness, it would be better to centralise it on a part of your being that is immortal; otherwise it will vanish like a flame in the air. And it is very fortunate, for if it were otherwise, there would be perhaps gods or types of superior men who would create hells and heavens as they do in their material imagination, where they would imprison you; you would be imprisoned in heaven or in hell according as you pleased or displeased them. It would be a very critical situation and happily it is not like that.

It is said that there is a god of Death. Is it true?

Yes, I call it the spirit of Death. I know it very well. And that is an extraordinary organisation. You do not know to what an extent it is organised.

I believe there are many of these spirits of death, I believe there are hundreds. I have met at least two of them. One I met in France and the other in Japan, and they were very different; which leads one to believe that probably in accordance with the mental culture, the education, the country and beliefs there should be different spirits. But there are spirits of all the manifestations of Nature: there are spirits of fire, spirits of air, of water, of rain, of wind; and there are spirits of death.

Each spirit of death, whatever it may be, has a claim to a certain number of deaths per day. Indeed it is a fantastic organisation; it is a kind of alliance between the vital forces and the forces of Nature. For example, if the spirit of death has decided: "That is the number of people to which I am entitled", let us say four or five or six, or one or two persons, it depends on the day; it has decided that certain persons would die, it goes straight and settles down beside the person about to die. But if you happen to be conscious (not the person), if you see the spirit going to a person and you do not want him to die, then you can, if you possess a certain occult power, tell it: "No, I forbid you to take him." It is a thing that has happened, not once but several times, in Japan and here. It was not the same spirit. That is what makes me say that there must be many.

"I don't want him to die."

"But I have a right to one death!"

"Go and find someone who is ready to die."

So I have seen several cases: sometimes it is just a neighbour who dies suddenly in place of the other, sometimes it is an acquaintance and sometimes it is an enemy. Naturally, there is a relation, good or bad, of neighbourhood (or anything else) which externally looks like chance. But it is the spirit who has taken *its* dead. The spirit has a claim to one death, it will have one death. You can tell it: "I forbid you to take this one", and have the power of sending it away, and the spirit can do nothing but go away; but it does not give up its due and goes elsewhere. There is another death.[...]

Sometimes when people are dying, they know that they are about to die. Why don't they tell the spirit to go away?

Ah! well, that depends upon the people. Two things are necessary. First of all, nothing in your being, no part of your being should want to die. That does not happen often. You have always a defeatist in you somewhere: something that is tired, something that is disgusted, something that has had enough of it, something that is lazy, something that does not want to struggle and says: "Well! Ah! Let it be finished, so much the better." That is sufficient, you are dead.

But it is a fact: if nothing, absolutely nothing in you consents to die, you will not die. For someone to die, there is always a second, perhaps the hundredth part of a second when he gives his consent. If there is not this second of consent, he does not die.

I knew people who should have really died according to all physical and vital laws; and they refused. They said: "No, I will not die", and they lived. There are others who do not need at all to die, but they are of that kind and say: "Ah! Well! Yes, so much the better, it will be finished", and it is finished. Even that much, even nothing more than that: you need not have a persistent wish, you have only to say: "Well, yes, I have had enough!" and it is finished. So it is truly like that. As you say, you may have death standing by your bedside and tell him: "I do not want you, go away", and it will be obliged to go away. But usually one gives way, for one must struggle, one must be strong, one must be very courageous and enduring, must have a great faith in the necessity of life; like someone, for example, who feels very strongly that he has still something to do and he must absolutely do it. But who is sure he has not within him the least bit of a defeatist, somewhere, who just yields and says: "It is all right"?... It is here, the necessity of unifying oneself.

Whatever the way we follow, the subject we study, we always arrive at the same result. The most important thing for an individual is to unify himself around his divine centre; in that way he becomes a true individual, master of himself and his destiny. Otherwise, he is a plaything of forces that toss him about like a piece of cork on a river. He goes where he does not want to go, he is made to do things he does not want to do, and finally he loses himself in a hole without having any strength to recover. But if you are consciously organised, unified around the divine centre, ruled and directed by it, you are master of your destiny. That is worth the trouble of attempting.... In any case, I find it preferable to be the master rather than the slave. It is a rather unpleasant sensation to feel yourself pulled by the strings and made to do things whether you want to or not — that is quite irrelevant — but to be compelled to act because something pulls you by the strings, something which you do not even see — that is exasperating.

1 July 1953

CHAPTER 9

Reincarnation or Rebirth

The Process of Rebirth

To understand rightly the problem of what is popularly called reincarnation, you must perceive that there are two factors in it which require consideration. First, there is the line of divine consciousness which seeks to manifest from above and upholds a certain series of formations, peculiar to itself, in the universe which is its field of manifestation. Secondly, there is the psychic consciousness which climbs up from below, the seed of the Divine developing through time till it meets the Force from above and takes the impress of the supramental Truth. This psychic consciousness is the inner being of a man, the material from which his true soul or *jiva* can be fashioned when, in response to its aspiration, the Supramental descends to give it a consistent personality. The exterior being of man is a perishable formation out of the stuff of universal Nature — mental, vital, physical — and is due to the complex interplay of all kinds of forces. The psychic absorbs the essence, as it were, of the experiences of the various formations behind which it stands; but not being in constant contact with them it does not retain the memory of the lives in their totality to which it supplies the background. Hence by merely contacting the psychic one cannot have the recollection of all those past lives: what commonly goes by the name of such recollection is, mostly, either deliberate imposture or a fabrication out of a few spasmodic hints received from within. Many people claim to remember their animal lives as well: they say that they were such and such a monkey living in this or that part of the globe. But if anything is certain, it is that the monkey has no contact whatever with the psychic consciousness and so transmits not one jot of his experiences to it. The impressions of his exterior monkey-nature vanish with the crumbling of his animal body: to pretend to a knowledge of them is to betray the grossest ignorance of the actual facts of the problem under consideration. Even with regard to human lives, it is only when the psychic has come to the fore that it carries and preserves definite memories, but certainly not of all the details of life unless it is constantly in front and one with the exterior being. For, as a rule, the physical mind and the physical vital dissolve with the death of the organism: they disintegrate and return to the universal Nature and nothing remains of their experiences. Not until they have become united with the psychic, so that there are not two halves but a single consciousness, the whole nature unified round the central Divine Will and this centralised being is connected up with the divine line of consciousness which is above — not until this happens can one receive the knowledge belonging to that consciousness and become aware of the entire series of forms and lives which were upheld by it as its own successive means of gradual self-expression. Before this is done, it is meaningless to speak of *one's* past births and their various incidents. This precious *oneself* is just the present impermanent exterior nature which has absolutely nothing to do with the several other formations behind which, as behind the present one, the true being stands. Only the supramental consciousness holds these births as if strung on one single thread and that alone can give the real knowledge of them all.

1930-1931

*

This is what happens. Let us take a divine spark which, through attraction, through affinity and selection, gathers around it a beginning of psychic consciousness (this work is already very perceptible in animals — don't think you are exceptional beings, that you alone have a psychic being and the rest of creation hasn't. It begins in the mineral, it is a little more developed in the plant, and in the animal there is a first glimmer of the psychic presence). Then there comes a moment when this psychic being is sufficiently developed to have an independent consciousness and a personal will. And then after innumerable lives more or less individualised, it becomes conscious of itself, of its movements and of the environment it has chosen for its growth. Arriving at a certain state of perception, it decides — generally at the last minute of the life it has just finished upon earth — the conditions in which its next life will be passed.

Here I must tell you a very important thing: the psychic being can progress and form itself only in the physical life and upon earth. As soon as it leaves a body, it enters into a rest which lasts for a more or less long time according to its own choice and its degree of development — a rest for assimilation, for a passive progress so to say, a rest for passive growth which will allow this same psychic being to pass on to new experiences and make a more active progress. But after having finished one life (which usually ends only when it has done what it wanted to do), it will have chosen the environment where it will be born, the approximate place where it will be born, the conditions and the kind of life in which it will be born, and a very precise programme of the experiences through which it will have to pass to be able to make the progress it wants to make.

I am going to give you quite a concrete example. Let us take a psychic being that has decided, for some reason or other, to enter the body of a being destined to become king, because there is a whole series of experiences it can have only under those conditions. After having passed through these experiences of a king, it finds that there is a whole domain in which it cannot make a progress due to these very conditions of life where it is. So when it has finished its term upon earth and decides to go away, it decides that in its next life it will take birth in an ordinary environment and in ordinary conditions, neither high nor low, but such that the body which it will take up will be free to do what it likes. For I do not tell you anything new when I say that the life of a king is the life of a slave; a king is obliged to submit to a whole protocol and to all kinds of ceremonies to keep his prestige (it is perhaps very pleasant for vain people, but for a psychic being it is not pleasant, for this deprives it of the possibility of a large number of experiences).

So having taken this decision, it carries in itself all the memories which a royal life can give it and it takes rest for the period it considers necessary (here, I must say that I am speaking of a psychic being exclusively occupied with itself, not one consecrated to a work, because in that case it is the work which decides the future lives and their conditions; I am speaking of a psychic being at work completing its development). Hence it decides that at a certain moment it will take a body. Having already had a number of experiences, it knows that in a certain country, a certain part of the consciousness has developed; in another, another part, and so on; so it chooses the place which offers it easy possibilities of development: the country, the conditions of living, the approximate nature of the parents, and also the condition of the body itself, its physical structure and the qualities it needs for its experiences. It takes rest, then at the required moment, wakes up and projects its consciousness upon earth centralising it in the chosen domain and the chosen conditions — or almost so; there is a small margin you know, for in the psychic consciousness one is too far away from the material physical consciousness to be able to see with a clear vision; it is an approximation. It does not make a mistake about the country or the environment and it sees quite clearly the inner vibrations of the people chosen, but there may happen to be a slight indecision. But if, just at this moment, there is a couple upon earth or rather a woman who has a psychic aspiration herself and, for some reason or other, without knowing why or how, would like to have an exceptional child, answering certain exceptional conditions; if at this moment there is this aspiration upon earth, it creates a vibration, a psychic light which the psychic being sees immediately and, without hesitation it rushes towards it. Then, from that moment (which is the moment of conception), it watches over the formation of the child, so that this formation may be as favourable as possible to the plan it has; consequently its influence is there over the child even before it appears in the physical world.

    If all goes well, if there is no accident (accidents can always happen), if all goes well at the moment the child is about to be born, the psychic force (perhaps not in its totality, but a part of the psychic consciousness) rushes into the being and from its very first cry gives it a push towards the experiences it wants the child to acquire. The result is that even if the parents are not conscious, even if the child in its external consciousness is not quite conscious (a little child does not have the necessary brain for that, it forms slowly, little by little), in spite of that, it will be possible for the psychic influence to direct all the events, all the circumstances of the life of this child till the moment it becomes capable of coming into conscious contact with its psychic being (physically it is generally between the age of four and seven, sometimes sooner, sometimes almost immediately, but in such a case we deal with children who are not "children", who have "supernatural" qualities, as they say — they are not "supernatural", but simply the expression of the presence of the psychic being). But there are people who have not had the chance or rather the good fortune if one may call it that, of meeting someone, physically, who could instruct them. And yet they have the feeling that every step of their existence, every circumstance of their life is arranged by someone conscious, so that they may make the maximum progress. When they need a certain circumstance, it comes; when they need to meet certain people, they come; when they need to read certain books, they find them within their reach. Everything is arranged like that, as if someone was watching over them so that their life may have the maximum possibilities of development. These people may very well say: "But what is a psychic being?", for no one has ever used these words in speaking to them or they have not found anybody who could explain to them all that; but for them often just one meeting is sufficient, just one look, in order to wake up; one word suffices to make them remember: "But I knew all that!"

This is exactly what happens to a psychic being which has reached the last stage of its development. After that, it will no longer be bound by the necessity of coming upon earth, it will have completed its development and will be able to choose freely either to consecrate itself to the divine Work or go elsewhere, that is, in the higher worlds. But generally, having come to this stage, it remembers all that has happened to it and understands the great necessity of coming to the help of those who are yet struggling in the midst of difficulties. These psychic beings give their whole existence to the divine Work — this is not absolute, inevitable, they choose freely, but ninety times out of a hundred this is what they do.

But in ordinary lives — and by that I mean the life of a certain *élite* of sufficiently well-developed people — the contact between the external being and the psychic is quite intermittent; it is the result of certain experiences or certain inner needs. At that moment the psychic being is "in front", as Sri Aurobindo says, that is, it comes to the surface of the consciousness, it is in direct contact with material circumstances, with forms and words and sounds, etc., for a very short time; so it records all that like a photograph or a cinema, but it is just a minute, a few moments in a lifetime. These moments may repeat themselves several times, but they do not last; and it is this the psychic being remembers; and when you have real psychic memories, sincere, spontaneous, not fabricated by the mind or the vital, that is, purely psychic, exact, your memory is *intermittent*. And it is often very difficult to locate your past lives, to say: "I was this or that." It is only when the psychic experience has taken place at a very important moment of your life and a whole set of circumstances gives you, so to say, the key to the story (dresses, spoken words, customs or an environment giving you the key) that you can say: "Oh! that life, I have lived it." But if someone comes and narrates to you all his previous lives from the monkey onwards, with a mass of details, you may be sure that he is a humbug!

24 February 1951

Memory of Past Lives

When you have the psychic memory you remember a set of circumstances at one *moment* of life, particularly of the inner emotion, of the consciousness that acted at that moment. And then that passes into the consciousness along with some associations, with all that was around you, perhaps a word spoken, a phrase heard; but what was most important was the state of the soul in which you were: for that indeed remains very clearly engraved. These are the landmarks of the psychic life, things that have left a deep impression and taken part in its formation. Hence when you find your psychic being in you again constantly, continuously, clearly, it is things like these that you remember. There may be quite a few, but they are flashes in one's life, and one cannot say: "I was such and such a person, I did such and such a thing, I was called by this name and I was doing this or that." Or otherwise it would mean that at that moment (a rare one) there was a combination of circumstances good enough for one to be able to fix the date or the place, the country and the age. That can happen.

Naturally the psychic takes a greater and greater part, and the larger does the set of memories grow. And then one can retrace one's life, but not in all its details. One can say that at certain moments, "it was like this," or "I was that." Certain moments, yes, very important moments of a life.... What's necessary is a being wholly identified with the psychic, one that has organised its whole existence around it, unified its whole being — all the tiniest parts, all the elements, all the movements of the being around the psychic centre — that has made of itself a single being, solely turned to the Divine; then, if the body falls off, that remains. It is only a completely formed conscious being that can remember exactly in another life all that has happened before. It can even pass consciously from one life to another without losing anything of its consciousness. How many people upon earth have reached that state?... Not many, I believe. And usually they are not in the least inclined to narrate their adventures.

6 May 1953

*

In rebirth it is not the external being, that which is formed by parents, environment and circumstances — the mental, the vital and the physical — that is born again: it is only the psychic being that passes from body to body. Logically, then, neither the mental nor the vital being can remember past lives or recognise itself in the character or mode of life of this or that person. The psychic being alone can remember; and it is by becoming conscious of our psychic being that we can have at the same time exact impressions about our past lives.

Besides, it is much more important for us to fix our attention upon what we want to become than upon what we have been.

2 April 1935

Rebirth and Psychic Development

I have already told you many times that, for the destiny which follows after death, the last state of consciousness is usually the most important. That is, if at the moment of death one has the intense aspiration to return to continue his work, then the conditions are arranged for it to be done. But, you see, there are all the possibilities for what happens after death. There are people who return in the psychic. You see, I have told you that the outer being is very rarely preserved; so we speak only of the psychic consciousness which, indeed, always persists. And then there are people for whom the psychic returns to the psychic domain to assimilate the experience they have had and to prepare their future life. This may take centuries, it depends on the people.

The more evolved the psychic is, the nearer it is to its complete maturity, the greater the time between the births. There are beings who reincarnate only after a thousand years, two thousand years.

The closer one is to the beginning of the formation, the closer are the reincarnations; and sometimes even, altogether at the lower level, when man is quite near the animal, it goes like this (*gesture*), that is, it is not unusual for people to reincarnate in the children of their children, like that, something like that, or just in the next generation. But this is always on a very primitive level of evolution, and the psychic being is not very conscious, it is in the state of formation. And as it becomes more developed, the reincarnations, as I said, are at a greater distance from one another. When the psychic being is fully developed, when it no longer needs to return to earth for its development, when it is absolutely free, it has the choice between no longer coming back to earth if it finds that its work lies elsewhere or if it prefers to remain in the purely psychic consciousness, without reincarnating; or else it can come when it wants, as it wants, where it wants, perfectly consciously. And there are those who have united with forces of a universal order and with entities of the Overmind or elsewhere, who remain all the time in the earth atmosphere and take on bodies successively for the work. This means that the moment the psychic being is completely formed and absolutely free — when it is completely formed it becomes absolutely free — it can do anything it likes, it depends on what it chooses; therefore one can't say, "It will be like this, it will be like that"; it does exactly what it wants and it can even announce (that has happened), at the moment of the death of the body, what its next reincarnation will be and what it will do, and already choose what it is going to do. But before this state, which is not very frequent — it depends absolutely on the degree of development of the psychic and the hope formulated by the integral consciousness of the being — there is still the mental, vital and physical consciousness, united with the psychic consciousness; so at that moment, the moment of death, the moment of leaving the body, it formulates a hope or an aspiration or a will, and usually this decides the future life.

So one can't ask a question saying, "What happens and what should be done?" All possible things happen, and everything can be done.

Everyone has one thing in mind: he asks a general question but in his mind it is an altogether particular question; but this — these things one does not discuss in public.

16 March 1955

*

Mother, since in each new life the mind and vital as well as the body are new, how can the experiences of past lives be useful for them? Do we have to go through all the experiences once again?

That depends on people!

It is not the mind and vital which develop and progress from life to life — except in altogether exceptional cases and at a very advanced stage of evolution — it is the psychic. So, this is what happens: the psychic has alternate periods of activity and rest; it has a life of progress resulting from experiences of the physical life, of active life in a physical body, with all the experiences of the body, the vital and the mind; then, normally, the psychic goes into a kind of rest for assimilation where the result of the progress accomplished during its active existence is worked out, and when this assimilation is finished, when it has absorbed the progress it had prepared in its active life on earth, it comes down again in a new body bringing with it the result of all its progress and, at an advanced stage, it even chooses the environment and the kind of body and the kind of life in which it will live to complete its experience concerning one point or another. In some very advanced cases the psychic can, before leaving the body, decide what kind of life it will have in its next incarnation.

When it has become an almost completely formed and already very conscious being, it presides over the formation of the new body, and usually through an inner influence it chooses the elements and the substance which will form its body in such a way that the body is adapted to the needs of its new experience. But this is at a rather advanced stage. And later, when it is fully formed and returns to earth with the idea of service, of collective help and participation in the divine Work, then it is able to bring to the body in formation certain elements of the mind and vital from previous lives which, having been organised and impregnated with psychic forces in previous lives, could be preserved and, consequently, can participate in the general progress. But this is at a very, very advanced stage.

When the psychic is fully developed and very conscious, when it becomes a conscious instrument of the divine Will, it organises the vital and the mind in such a way that they too participate in the general harmony and can be preserved.

A high degree of development allows at least some parts of the mental and vital beings to be preserved in spite of the dissolution of the body. If, for instance, some parts — mental or vital — of the human activity have been particularly developed, these elements of the mind and vital are maintained even "in their form" — in the form of the activity which has been fully organised — as, for example, in highly intellectual people who have particularly developed their brains, the mental part of their being keeps this structure and is preserved in the form of an organised brain which has its own life and can be kept unchanged until a future life so as to participate in it with all its gains.

In artists, as for instance in certain musicians who have used their hands in a particularly conscious way, the vital and mental substance is preserved in the form of hands, and these hands remain fully conscious, they can even use the body of living people if there is a special affinity — and so on.

Otherwise, in ordinary people in whom the psychic form is not fully developed and organised, when the psychic leaves the body, the mental and vital forms may persist for a certain time if the death has been particularly peaceful and concentrated, but if a man dies suddenly and in a state of passion, with numerous attachments, well, the different parts of the being are dispersed and live for a shorter or longer time their own life in their own domain, then disappear.

The centre of organisation and transformation is always the presence of the psychic in the body. Therefore, it is a very big mistake to believe that the progress continues or even, as some believe, that it is more complete and rapid in the periods of transition between two physical lives; in general, there is no progress at all, for the psychic enters into a state of rest and the other parts, after a more or less ephemeral life in their own domain, are dissolved.

Earthly life is the place for progress. It is here, on earth, that progress is possible, during the period of earthly existence. And it is the psychic which carries the progress over from one life to another, by organising its own evolution and development itself.

12 February 1958

Emanations of Evolved Beings

After death, does the inner being continue to progress?

That depends altogether upon the person. For everyone it is different. There are people — for example, writers, musicians, artists — people who have lived on intellectual heights, who feel that they still have something further to do, that they have not finished what they had undertaken to do, have not reached the goal they had fixed for themselves, so they are ready to remain in the earth atmosphere as long as they can, with as much cohesiveness as possible and they try to manifest themselves and continue their progress in other human bodies. I have seen many such cases, I have seen the very interesting case of a musician who was a pianist (a pianist of great worth), who had hands which were a marvel of skill, exactness, precision, force, rapidity of movement, indeed, it was absolutely remarkable. This man died relatively young with the feeling that if he had continued to live he would have continued to progress in his expression of music. And such was the intensity of his aspiration that his subtle hands maintained their form without being dissolved, and each time he met anyone a little receptive and passive and a good musician, his hands would enter the hands of those who were playing — the person who was playing at the time could play well but in an ordinary way; but at that moment he became not merely a virtuoso but a wonderful artist during the time he played. It was the hands of the other that were making use of him. This is a phenomenon I know. I have seen the same thing in the case of a painter: it was also a matter of hands. The same thing with regard to some writers, and here it was the brain that kept quite a precise form and entered the brain of someone who was sufficiently receptive and suddenly made him write extraordinary things, infinitely more beautiful than anything he had written before.[...]

Do these beings who want to manifest themselves keep the same desire when they are born once again?

No, it is not the same thing. It is not the whole being, it is the special faculty which remains in the earth atmosphere, does not leave it and go away, which remains in the earth atmosphere in order to continue manifesting itself. But the psychic being can very well return to the psychic world and it is the psychic being which takes a body again. I explained to you the other day that before leaving the physical body, the psychic being decides most often what its next rebirth will be, the environment in which it will take birth and what its occupation will be, because it needs a certain field for its experience. So it may happen that very big writers and very big musicians take birth another time in somebody quite imbecile. And you say: "What! it is not possible!" Naturally it does not always happen like that, but it may. There was a case in which the contrary happened: it was a violin player, the most wonderful of the century.[...] What was his name?... Ysayë! he was a Belgian and a violinist, truly the most wonderful violinist of the epoch. Well, that man had most certainly in him a reincarnation of Beethoven. Not perhaps a reincarnation of his entire psychic being, but in any case, that of his musical capacity. He had the appearance, the head of Beethoven, I saw him, I heard him (I did not know him, I knew nothing, I was at a concert in Paris and they were giving the concerto in D major), I saw him coming on the stage to play and I said: "Strange! How much this man looks like Beethoven, he is the very portrait of Beethoven!" Then it just started with a stroke of the bow, three, four notes.... Everything changed, the atmosphere was changed. All became absolutely wonderful. Three notes started off with such power, such grandeur, so wonderful it was, nothing stirred, all waited. And he played that from one end to the other in an absolutely unique manner with an understanding I have not met with in any other executant. And then I saw that the musical genius of

Beethoven was in him.... But perhaps Beethoven's psychic being had taken body in a shoemaker or anybody else, one does not know! It wanted to have another kind of experience.

For what I saw in this man was a formation belonging to an earthly plane, it was mental-vital; and as Beethoven had disciplined his whole mental, vital and physical being around his musical capacity, that had remained in form, it was a living thing, and had incarnated in that man, just as it was, but not necessarily Beethoven's psychic being. In his first life it was the psychic being of Beethoven that had shaped all those other beings, the psychic being that had disciplined them around musical creation; but after his death, it cannot at all be said whether the psychic being remained there; it must have returned to the psychic world as is the usual rule. That however had been formed, had its own life, independent and existing in itself. It was formed for a certain manifestation and it remained to manifest itself. And as soon as it found a fit instrument, it entered there to manifest itself.

Can a psychic being take birth in two bodies?

It is not quite so simple as that.... The psychic being is the result of evolution, that is to say, evolution of the divine Consciousness which spread into Matter and slowly lifted up Matter, made it develop to return to the Divine. The psychic being was formed by this divine centre progressively through all the births. There comes a time when it reaches a kind of perfection, perfection in its growth and formation. Then, most often, as it has an aspiration for realisation, for a greater perfection to manifest yet better the Divine, it generally draws towards itself a being from the involution, that is to say, one of those entities belonging to what Sri Aurobindo calls Overmind, who comes then to incarnate in this psychic being. It can be one of those entities men generally call gods, some kind of deities. And when this fusion occurs the psychic being naturally is magnified and shares in the nature of the being incarnated in it. And then it has the power to produce emanations. These beings have the power to produce emanations, that is to say, they project out of themselves a part of themselves which becomes independent and goes into others to incarnate itself. So there can be not only two, but three, four or five emanations. That depends upon cases, it can happen thus. That is to say, one can have the same origin, psycho-divine, we might say. And generally when there are a number of emanations, the different persons feel themselves to be that being with reason, for they carry in themselves something of that godhead: it is as though a part of the godhead has flung itself out of itself and become independent in another being. It is not a redoubling but a kind of self-projection. (*To the child who put the question:*) Redoubling gives the idea that what has been redoubled has lost a part of its faculty: if you cut your body in two, only half of it will remain for you; but if you have the power to emanate something out of you, you remain quite whole, as you are, and at the same time, there is another Tara who is there in another person.... You understand? It is like that.

16 September 1953

*

Can it happen that the psychic being does not fall at the place where it wanted to take birth?

If a psychic being sees from its psychic world a light on the earth, it may rush down there without knowing exactly where it is. Everything is possible. But if the psychic being is very conscious, sufficiently conscious, it will seek the light of aspiration in a precise place, because of the culture, the education it will find there. This happens much more frequently than one believes, especially in somewhat educated circles. An intelligent woman with some artistic or philosophical culture, a beginning of conscious individuality, may aspire that the child she is going to have may be the best possible according to her idea or according to what she has read. Hence it is not so very complicated to find a place. The number of psychic beings born constantly being considerable, if each time exceptional conditions have to be found it would be difficult. Surely, there are instances where the psychic being seems to have fallen headlong and been stunned, but this is bad luck; in such a case it generally requires a long time to wake up. It is bad luck in the sense that it probably lacked a certain power of discrimination, or perhaps it had to face certain forces which thwarted its decision and won a partial victory over it. There are a thousand possibilities, you know. One cannot say that everything goes according to the same plan — every psychic being is different.

1 March 1951

The Incarnation of Evolved Souls

I may say that I have been present at innumerable incarnations of evolved souls in beings either preparing to be born or already born. As I said, the cases are quite different; it depends more on psychological conditions than on material ones, but it also depends on material conditions. It depends on the state of development of the soul which wants to reincarnate — we take the word "soul" here in the sense of the psychic being, what we call the psychic being — it depends on its state of development, on the milieu in which it is going to incarnate, on the mission it has to fulfil — that makes many different conditions.... It depends very largely on the state of consciousness of the parents. For it goes without saying that there is a stupendous difference between conceiving a child deliberately, with a conscious aspiration, a call to the invisible world and a spiritual ardour, and conceiving a child by accident and without intending to have it, and sometimes even without wanting it at all. I don't say that in the latter case there cannot also be an incarnation, but it usually takes place later, not at the conception.

For the formation of the child it makes a great difference.

If the incarnation takes place at the conception, the whole formation of the child to be born is directed and governed by the consciousness which is going to incarnate: the choice of the elements, the attraction of the substance — a choice of the forces and even the substance of the matter which is assimilated. There is already a selection. And this naturally creates altogether special conditions for the formation of the body, which may already be fairly developed, evolved, harmonised before its birth. I must say that this is quite, quite exceptional; but still it does happen.

More frequently there are cases in which, just at the moment of its birth, that is to say, of its first gesture of independence, when the child begins to develop its lungs by crying as much as it can, at that moment, very often, this sort of call from life makes the descent easier and more effective.

Sometimes days and at times months pass, and the preparation is slow and the entry takes place very gradually, in quite a subtle and almost imperceptible way.

Sometimes it comes much later, when the child itself becomes a little conscious and feels a very subtle but very real relation with something from above, far above, which is like an influence pressing upon it; and then it can begin to feel the need of being in contact with this something which it does not know, does not understand, but which it can only feel; and this aspiration draws the psychic and makes it descend into the child.

I am giving you here a few fairly common instances; there are many others; this may happen in innumerable different ways. What I have described to you are the most frequent cases I have seen.

So, the soul which wants to incarnate stays at times in a domain of the higher mind, quite close to the earth, having chosen its future home; or else it can descend further, into the vital, and from there have a more direct action; or again it can enter the subtle physical and very closely govern the development of its future body.

Now the other question — the one about departure.

That too depends on the degree of development, the conditions of death — and above all on the unification of the being and its attitude at the time of leaving the body. The question here was about fully developed beings, that is, fully developed psychic beings — and I don't know if it means a psychic being which has profited by its presence in a physical body to do yoga, for then the conditions are quite different. But in a more general way, I have often told you that, with regard to the external envelope* of the being, everything depends on its attitude at the moment of death, and that attitude necessarily depends on its inner development and its unification.

If we take the best instance, of someone who has unified his being completely around the divine Presence within him, who is now only *one* will, *one* consciousness, this person will have grouped around his central psychic being a fully developed and organised mind, an

---

* This envelope consists of the mental, vital and physical sheaths.

absolutely surrendered and collaborating vital and an obedient, docile and supple physical being. This physical being, as it is fully developed, will have a subtle body — what Sri Aurobindo calls the "true physical" — which will infinitely surpass the limits of its body and have enough suppleness, plasticity, balance to be able to adhere to the inner parts of the being and follow the movement of the soul in its... I don't want to say in its ascent, but in its peregrinations outside the body. What the soul will do, where it will go — it all depends on what it has decided before leaving the body. And this capacity to keep around itself the being that has been fully organised and unified in its physical life, will allow it to really choose what it wants to do. And this also represents a very different field of possibilities, from passing consciously from one body into another, directly — there are instances in which one of these fully conscious and fully developed beings has slowly prepared another being capable of receiving and assimilating it, and in order not to stop its material work when it leaves one body, it goes and joins another psychic being, merges with it, combines with it in another physical body; that is an extreme case, extremely rare also, but one which forms part of an altogether traditional occult knowledge — to the instance at the other extreme, where the soul having finished its bodily experience, wants to assimilate it in repose and prepare for another physical existence later, sometimes much later. And so this is what happens, among many other possibilities: it leaves in each domain — in the subtle physical, in the vital, in the mental domain — the corresponding beings; it leaves them with a sort of link between them, but each one keeps its independent existence, and it itself goes into the zone, the reality, the world of the psychic proper, and enters into a blissful repose for assimilation, until it has assimilated [...] all its good deeds, digested all its good deeds, and is ready to begin a new experience. And then, if its work has been well done and the parts or sheaths of its being which it has left in their different domains have acted as they should there, when it descends again, it will put on one after another all these parts which lived with it in a former life, and with this wealth of knowledge and experience it will prepare to enter a new body.... This may be after hundreds or thousands of years, for in those domains all that is organised is no longer necessarily subject to the decomposition which here we call "death". As soon as a vital being is fully harmonised, it becomes immortal. What dissolves it and breaks it up are all the disorders within it and all the tendencies towards destruction and decomposition; but if it is fully harmonised and organised and, so to say, divinised, it becomes immortal. It is the same thing for the mind. And even in the subtle physical, beings who are fully developed and have been impregnated with spiritual forces do not necessarily dissolve after death. They may continue to act or may take a beneficial rest in certain elements of Nature like water — generally it is in some liquid, in water or the sap of trees — or it may be, as described here (*laughing*), in the clouds. But they may also remain active and continue to act on the more material elements of physical Nature.

I have given you here a certain number of examples; I tell you, I could talk to you for hours and there would always be new examples to give! But this covers the subject broadly and opens the door to imagination.

24 October 1956

*

I must here remark in passing that there is a common misconception about rebirth. People believe that it is they who are reincarnated, yet this is a palpable error, though it is true that parts of their being are amalgamated with others and so act through new bodies. Their whole being is not reborn, because of the simple fact that what they evidently mean by their "self" is not a real individualised entity but their exterior personality, the personality composed of the outward name and form. Hence it is wrong to say that A is reborn as B: A is a personality organically distinct from B and cannot be said to have reincarnated as B. You would be right only if you said that the same line of consciousness uses both A and B as the instruments of its manifestation. For, what does remain constant is the psychic being which is not the outward personality at all, but something deep within, something which is not the exterior name and form.

1930-1931

*

Do many remember that they have passed over and are back again?

When you reach a certain state of consciousness, you remember. It is not so difficult to touch this state partially for a short time; in deep meditation, in a dream or a vision one may have the feeling or the impression that he has lived this life before, had this realisation, known these truths. But this is not a full realisation; to come to that, one must have attained to a permanent consciousness within us which is ever-lasting and holds together all our existences in past or present or future time.

28 April 1929

Families of Souls

What does "choose one's family" mean?

You have come into the world in a certain milieu, among certain people. When you are quite young, but for a few rare exceptions, what surrounds you seems altogether natural to you, because you are born in its midst and are quite used to it. But when, a little later, a spiritual aspiration wakes up in you, you may quite possibly feel yourself completely ill at ease in the environment where you have lived, if, for instance, the people who have brought you up don't have the same aspiration or if their ideas are the very opposite of what is developing in you. Instead of saying, "You see, I belong to this family, what shall I do? I have a mother, a father, brothers, sisters... ", you can set out in search (I don't mean necessarily travel), set out in search of spirits who have an affinity with yours, people who have a similar aspiration and, if you have the sincere aspiration to find those who like you are in quest of something, you will always have the occasion to meet them in one way or another, through quite unexpected circumstances; and when you have found one or more people who are in exactly the same state of mind and have the same aspiration, quite naturally there will be created bonds of closeness, intimacy, friendship and, among you, you will form a kind of brotherhood, that is to say, a true family. You are together because you are close to one another, you are together because you have the same aspiration, you are together because you want to create the same goal in life; you understand one another when you speak, you have no need to discuss anything which is said and you live in a kind of inner harmony. This is the true family, this is the family of aspiration, the family of spiritual inclinations.

									29 March 1951

								*

[...]when those born scattered over the world at great distances from one another are driven by circumstances or by an impulsion to come and gather here [in the Asham in Pondicherry], it is almost always because they have met in one life or another (not all in the same life) and because their psychic being has felt that they belonged to the same family; so they have taken an inner vow to continue to act together and collaborate. That is why even though they are born far from one another, there is something which compels them to come together; it is the psychic being, the psychic consciousness that is behind. And only to the extent the psychic consciousness is strong enough to order and organise the circumstances or the life, that is, strong enough not to allow itself to be opposed by outside forces, outside life movements, can people meet.

It is profoundly true in reality; there are large "families of beings" who work for the same cause, who have gathered in more or less large numbers and who come in groups as it were. It is as though at certain times there were awakenings in the psychic world, as though lots of little sleeping children were being called to wake up: "It is time, quick, quick, go down!" And they hurry down. And sometimes they do not drop at the same place, they are dispersed, yet there is something within which troubles them, pushes them; for one reason or another they are drawn close and that brings them together. But it is something deep in the being, something that is not at all on the surface; otherwise, even if people met they would not perhaps become aware of the bond. People meet and recognise each other only to the extent they become conscious of their psychic being, obey their psychic being, are guided by it; otherwise there is all that comes in to oppose it, all that veils, all that stupefies, all those obstacles to prevent you from finding yourself in your depths and being able to collaborate truly in the work. You are tossed about by the forces of Nature.

There is only one solution, to find your psychic being and once it is found to cling to it desperately, to let it guide you step by step whatever be the obstacle. That is the only solution.

18 March 1953

*

Why are great artists born at the same time in the same country?

That depends on the person to whom you put the question. The explanation will be different accordingly. From the point of view of evolution, I think Sri Aurobindo has explained this very clearly in *The Human Cycle*. Evolution, that is to say, culture and civilisation, describes a more or less regular spiral movement around the earth, and the results of one civilisation, it may be said, slowly go to form another; then, when the total development is harmonious, this creates simultaneously the field of action and the actors, in the sense that at the time of the great artistic periods all the conditions were favourable to the development of art, and naturally, the fact that all the circumstances were favourable, attracted the men who could use them. There have been concrete movements like that, great ages like that of the Italian Renaissance or the similar period in France, almost at the same time, when artists from all countries were gathered at the same place because the conditions were favourable to the development of their art. This is one of the reasons — a so-to-say external reason — for the formation of civilisations.

There is another, this is that from an occult point of view it is almost always the same forces and same beings which incarnate during all the ages of artistic beauty upon earth and that, according to occultists, there are cycles of rebirth: beings return, group themselves through affinity at the time of birth; so it happens that regularly, almost all come together for a similar action. Some occultists have studied this question and given very precise numbers based upon the actual facts of the development of the earth: they have said that once in a hundred years, once in a thousand years, once in five thousand years, etc., certain cycles were repeated; that certain great civilisations appeared every five thousand years, and that it was (according to their special knowledge) the same people who came back. This is not quite exact, that is why I am not going into details, but in a sense this is true: it is the same forces which are at work. It is the same forces and they are grouped according to their affinities and, for a reason which may be quite material or for a mental or cyclic reason, they reunite at a certain place, and in this place there is a new civilisation or a special progress in a civilisation or a kind of effervescence, blossoming, flowering of beauty, as in the great ages in Greece, Egypt, India, Italy, Spain.... Everywhere, in all the countries of the world, there have been more or less beautiful periods.

If you put the question to astrologers, they will explain this to you by the position of the stars; they will say that certain positions of the stars have a certain effect on the earth. But, as I have told you, all these things are "languages", a way of expression, of making oneself understood; the truth is deeper, it is more complex, more complete.

12 April 1951

*

How is it that in dreams one meets and knows people whom one meets and knows afterwards in the outer world?

It is because of the affinities that draw certain people together, affinities in the mental or the vital world. People often meet in these planes before they meet upon earth. They may join there, speak to each other and have all the relations you can have upon earth. Some know of these relationships, some do not know. Some, as are indeed most, are unconscious of the inner being and the inner intercourse, and yet it will happen that, when they meet the new face in the outer world, they find it somehow very familiar, quite well-known.

21 April 1929

*

How is it that we have met?

We have all met in previous lives. Otherwise we would not have come together in this life. We are of one family and have worked through ages for the victory of the Divine and its manifestation upon earth.

7 April 1929

*

Sweet Mother, why don't we profit as much as we should by our presence here in the Ashram?

Ah! That is very simple; it is because it is too easy!... When you have to go all round the world to find a teacher, when you have to give up everything to obtain only the first words of a teaching, then this teaching, this spiritual help becomes something very precious, like everything that is difficult to obtain, and you make a great effort to deserve it.

Most of you came here when you were very small, at an age when there can be no question of the spiritual life or spiritual teaching — it would be altogether premature. You have indeed lived in this atmosphere but without even being aware of it; you are accustomed to seeing me, hearing me; I speak to you as one does to all children, I have even played with you as one plays with children; you only have to come and sit here and you hear me speak, you only have to ask me a question and I answer you, I have never refused to say anything to anybody — it is so easy. It is enough to... live — to sleep, to eat, to do exercises and study at school. You live here as you would live anywhere else. And so, you are used to it.

If I had made strict rules, if I had said, "I shall not tell you anything until you have truly made an effort to know it", then perhaps you might have made some effort, but that's not in keeping with my idea. I believe more in the power of the atmosphere and of example than of a rigorous teaching. I count more on something awakening in the being through contagion rather than by a methodical, disciplined effort.

Perhaps, after all, something is being prepared and one day it will spring up to the surface.

That is what I hope for.

One day you will tell yourself, "Just think! I have been here so long, I could have learnt so much, realised so much and I never even thought of it! Only like that, now and then." And then, on that day... well, on that day, just imagine, you are going to wake up all of a sudden to something you never noticed but which is deep within you and *thirsts* for the truth, thirsts for transformation and is ready to make the effort required to realise it. On that day you will go very fast, you will advance with giant strides.... Perhaps, as I said [in July 1953], that day has come now after five years? I said, "I give you five years...." Now the five years have passed, so perhaps the day has come! Perhaps you will suddenly feel an *irresistible* need not to live in unconsciousness, in ignorance, in that state in which you do things without knowing why, feel things without understanding why, have contradictory wills, understand nothing about anything, live only by habit, routine, reactions — you take life easy. And one day you are no longer satisfied with that.

It depends, for each one it is different. Most often it is the need to know, to understand; for some it is the need to do what must be done as it should be done; for others it is a vague feeling that behind this life, so unconscious, so futile, so empty of meaning, there is something to find which is *worth* being lived — that there is a reality, a truth behind these falsehoods and illusions.

One suddenly feels that everything one does, everything one sees, has no meaning, no purpose, but that *there is* something which has a meaning; that essentially one is here on earth for something, that all this — all these movements, all this agitation, all this wastage of force and energy — all that must have a purpose, an aim, and that this uneasiness one feels within oneself, this lack of satisfaction, this need, this *thirst* for something must lead us somewhere else.

And one day, you ask yourself, "But then, why is one born? Why does one die? Why does one suffer? Why does one act?"

You no longer live like a little machine, hardly half-conscious. You want to feel truly, to act truly, to know truly. Then, in ordinary life one searches for books, for people who know a little more than oneself, one begins to seek somebody who can solve these questions, lift the veil of ignorance. Here it is very simple. You only have to... do the things one does every day, but to do them with a purpose.

You go to the Samadhi*, look at Sri Aurobindo's picture, you come to receive a flower from me, sit down to a lesson; you do everything you do but... with one question within you: Why?

And then, if you ask the question, you receive the answer. Why?

Because we don't want life as it is any longer, because we don't want falsehood and ignorance any longer, because we don't want suffering and unconsciousness any longer, because we do not want disorder and bad will any longer, because Sri Aurobindo has come to tell us: It is not necessary to leave the earth to find the Truth, it is not necessary to leave life to find one's soul, it is not necessary to give up the world or to have limited beliefs in order to enter into relation with the Divine. The Divine is everywhere, in everything, and if He is hidden... it is because we do not take the trouble to discover Him.

We can, simply by a sincere aspiration, open a sealed door in us and find... that Something which will change the whole significance of life, reply to all our questions, solve all our problems and lead us to the perfection we aspire for without knowing it, to that Reality which *alone* can satisfy us and give us lasting joy, equilibrium, strength, life.

13 August 1958

---

* The simple tomb in the courtyard of the main Ashram building where at the time only Sri Aurobindo's body rested. Now it also contains the body of the Mother.

CHAPTER 10

Free Will, Determinism, Karma, Grace

Freedom and Fatality

Can it be said in justification of one's past that whatever has happened in one's life had to happen?

Obviously, what has happened had to happen; it would not have been, if it had not been intended. Even the mistakes that we have committed and the adversities that fell upon us had to be, because there was some necessity in them, some utility for our lives. But in truth these things cannot be explained mentally and should not be. For all that happened was necessary, not for any mental reason, but to lead us to something beyond what the mind imagines. But is there any need to explain after all? The whole universe explains everything at every moment and a particular thing happens because the whole universe is what it is. But this does not mean that we are bound over to a blind acquiescence in Nature's inexorable law. You can accept the past as a settled fact and perceive the necessity in it, and still you can use the experience it gave you to build up the power consciously to guide and shape your present and your future.

Is the time also of an occurrence arranged in the Divine Plan of things?

All depends upon the plane from which one sees and speaks. There is a plane of divine consciousness in which all is known absolutely, and the whole plan of things foreseen and predetermined. That way of seeing lives in the highest reaches of the Supramental; it is the Supreme's own vision. But when we do not possess that consciousness, it is useless to speak in terms that hold good only in that region and are not our present effective way of seeing things. For at a lower level of consciousness nothing is realised or fixed beforehand; all is in the process of making. Here there are no settled facts, there is only the play of possibilities; out of the clash of possibilities is realised the thing that has to happen. On this plane we can choose and select; we can refuse one possibility and accept another; we can follow one path, turn away from another. And that we can do, even though what is actually happening may have been foreseen and predetermined in a higher plane.

The Supreme Consciousness knows everything beforehand, because everything is realised there in her eternity. But for the sake of her play and in order to carry out actually on the physical plane what is foreordained in her own supreme self, she moves here upon earth as if she did not know the whole story; she works as if it was a new and untried thread that she was weaving. It is this apparent forgetfulness of her own foreknowledge in the higher consciousness that gives to the individual in the active life of the world his sense of freedom and independence and initiative. These things in him are her pragmatic tools or devices, and it is through this machinery that the movements and issues planned and foreseen elsewhere are realised here.

It may help you to understand if you take the example of an actor. An actor knows the whole part he has to play; he has in his mind the exact sequence of what is to happen on the stage. But when he is on the stage, he has to appear as if he did not know anything; he has to feel and act as if he were experiencing all these things for the first time, as if it was an entirely new world with all its chance events and surprises that was unrolling before his eyes.

Is there then no real freedom? Is everything absolutely determined, even your freedom, and is fatalism the highest secret?

Freedom and fatality, liberty and determinism are truths that obtain on different levels of consciousness. It is ignorance that makes the mind put the two on the same level and pit one against the other. Consciousness is not a single uniform reality, it is complex; it is not something like a flat plain, it is multidimensional. On the highest height is the Supreme and in the lowest depth is matter; and there is an infinite gradation of levels of consciousness between this lowest depth and the highest height.

In the plane of matter and on the level of the ordinary consciousness you are bound hand and foot. A slave to the mechanism of Nature, you are tied to the chain of Karma, and there, in that chain, whatever happens is rigorously the consequence of what has been done before. There is an illusion of independent movement, but in fact you repeat what all others do, you echo Nature's world-movements, you revolve helplessly on the crushing wheel of her cosmic machine.

But it need not be so. You can shift your place if you will; instead of being below, crushed in the machinery or moved like a puppet, you can rise and look from above and by changing your consciousness you can even get hold of some handle to move apparently inevitable circumstances and change fixed conditions. Once you draw yourself up out of the whirlpool and stand high above, you see you are free. Free from all compulsions, not only you are no longer a passive instrument, but you become an active agent. You are not only not bound by the consequences of your action, but you can even change the consequences. Once you see the play of forces, once you raise yourself to a plane of consciousness where lie the origins of forces and identify yourself with these dynamic sources, you belong no longer to what is moved but to that which moves.

This precisely is the aim of Yoga, — to get out of the cycle of Karma into a divine movement. By Yoga you leave the mechanical round of Nature in which you are an ignorant slave, a helpless and miserable tool, and rise into another plane where you become a conscious participant and a dynamic agent in the working out of a Higher Destiny. This movement of the consciousness follows a double line. First of all there is an ascension; you raise yourself out of the level of material consciousness into superior ranges. But this ascension of the lower into the higher calls a descent of the higher into the lower. When you rise above the earth, you bring down too upon earth something of the above, — some light, some power that transforms or tends to transform its old nature. And then these things that were distinct, disconnected and disparate from each other — the higher in you and the lower, the inner and the outer strata of your being and consciousness — meet and are slowly joined together and gradually they fuse into one truth, one harmony.

It is in this way that what are called miracles happen. The world is made up of innumerable planes of consciousness and each has its own distinct laws; the laws of one plane do not hold good for another. A miracle is nothing but a sudden descent, a bursting forth of another consciousness and its powers — most often it is the powers of the vital — into this plane of matter. There is a precipitation, upon the material mechanism, of the mechanism of a higher plane. It is as though a lightning flash tore through the cloud of our ordinary consciousness and poured into it other forces, other movements and sequences. The result we call a miracle, because we see a sudden alteration, an abrupt interference with the natural laws of our own ordinary range, but the reason and order of it we do not know or see, because the source of the miracle lies in another plane. Such incursions of the worlds beyond into our world of matter are not very uncommon, they are even a constant phenomenon, and if we have eyes and know how to observe we can see miracles in abundance. Especially must they be constant among those who are endeavouring to bring down the higher reaches into the earth-consciousness below.

28 April 1929

*

"*Freedom and fatality, liberty and determinism are truths that obtain on different levels of consciousness.*" (The Mother)

What are these different levels of consciousness?

[...] I have already spoken to you of the different planes of consciousness. Well, on the material plane, purely material (when separated from the vital plane), it is an absolute mechanism where consequently all things are linked together; and as I was saying the other day, if you want to find the cause of one thing or what is the result of a thing, you will find another and yet another and you will make an entire tour round the universe. And it is like that, everything is absolutely mechanised. Only, in this purely material plane, there can intervene the vital plane, and it already does intervene in the vegetable kingdom. The vital plane has an altogether different determinism, its own particular determinism. But when you introduce the vital determinism into the determinism of the physical, that produces a kind of combination that changes everything. And above the vital plane there is the mental plane. The mental plane also has its own determinism where all things are linked together rigorously.

But that is the movement which could be called "horizontal". If you take a vertical movement, the mind descending into the vital and the vital descending into the physical, you have there three determinisms that intervene and naturally produce something altogether different. And where the mind has intervened the determinism will necessarily be different from the one where it does not intervene; that is, in the higher animal life there is already a mental determinism which intervenes that is altogether different from the determinism of the vegetable plane.

Above these planes there are others — above each plane there are others, following one another right up to the highest plane. The highest plane is the plane of absolute freedom. If in your consciousness you are capable of passing through all these planes, so to say in a vertical line, and reaching the highest plane and, by means of this connection, of bringing down this plane of perfect freedom into the material determinisms, you change everything. And all the intermediaries change everything. Then because of the very changes from level to level, it gives altogether the appearance of complete freedom; for the intervention or descent of one plane into another has unforeseen consequences for the other plane, the lower plane. The higher plane can foresee, but the lower ones cannot. So, as these consequences are unforeseen, that gives altogether the impression of the unexpected and of freedom. And it is only if you remain consciously and constantly on the highest level, that is, in the supreme Consciousness, that there you can see that, at the same time, all is absolutely determined but also, because of the complexity of the interlinking of these determinisms, all is absolutely free. It is the Plane where there are no more contradictions, where all things *are* and are in harmony without contradicting one another.

[...] All will be unfolded in the universe, but in what order and in what way? There are decisions that are taken up there which escape our ordinary consciousness, and so it is very difficult to foresee. But there also, if you enter consciously and if you can be present up there...

How shall I explain that to you? All is there, absolute, static, eternal: but all that will be unrolled in the material world, naturally more or less one thing after another; for in the static existence all can be there, but in the becoming all becomes in time, that is, one thing after another. Well, what path will the unrolling follow? Up there is the domain of absolute freedom.... Who tells you that a sufficiently sincere aspiration, a sufficiently intense prayer is not capable of changing the path of the unrolling?

This means that all is possible.

Now, one must have a sufficient aspiration and a prayer that's sufficiently intense. But that has been given to human nature. It is one of the marvellous gifts of grace given to human nature; only, one does not know how to make use of it.

This comes to saying that in spite of the most absolute determinisms in the horizontal line, if one knows how to cross all these horizontal lines and reach the highest Point of consciousness, one is able to make things change, things apparently absolutely determined. So you may call it by any name you like, but it is a kind of combination of an absolute determinism with an absolute freedom.[...]

I forgot to say in that book (perhaps I did not forget but just felt that it was useless to say it) that all these theories are only theories, that is, mental conceptions which are merely more or less imaged representations of the reality; but it is not the reality at all. When you say "determinism" and when you say "freedom", you say only words and all that is only a very incomplete, very approximate and very weak description of what is in reality within you, around you and everywhere; and to be able to begin to understand what the universe is, you must come out of your mental formulas, otherwise you will never understand anything.

To tell the truth, if you live only a moment, just a tiny moment, of this absolutely sincere aspiration or this sufficiently intense prayer, you will know more things than by meditating for hours.

"The Supreme Consciousness ... gives to the individual in the active life of the world his sense of freedom and independence and initiative. These things in him are Her pragmatic tools or devices and it is through this machinery that the movements and

issues planned and foreseen elsewhere are realised here."
(The Mother)

These "things in him", that is in the individual, are: the sense of freedom, independence and initiative. You know what independence is? It is precisely the freedom of choice. Independence means the freedom of choice and initiative means the fact of choosing. First of all, one feels that one is free; and then one feels that no one can prevent him from choosing; and finally one uses his freedom to choose and one decides. These are the three stages. So these three stages: the feeling that you are free, the idea that you are going to use your freedom for choosing and then the choice — these three things I call the pragmatic tools and devices.

I am sorry, my children, all this is said in a form a little too philosophical which I do not now approve of very much. I was obliged to speak a language which now appears to me a little too complicated. But what is to be done, it was like that. I was saying that these three things, the feeling of freedom, the will to choose and the choice made are the devices that Nature uses in us to make us act, otherwise we would not move.

If we did not have this illusion that we are free, this second illusion that we can use our freedom for choosing and the third illusion of choosing, well, we would not move. So Nature gives us these three illusions and makes us move, for she requires us to move.

She, with a capital S, I said it was the Supreme Consciousness, but in fact it is Nature and it is the trick of Nature; for the Supreme Consciousness has no tricks, it is Nature that has tricks. The Supreme Consciousness quite simply enters into all things with all her consciousness, because it is *the* consciousness: and with that She tries to make all this inconscience move towards consciousness, simply, without any tricks. She has no need of tricks, She is everywhere. She is at work everywhere and She puts consciousness into the inconscience. When you light a lamp in a dark room, as soon as you turn on the electricity, the room is no longer dark. As soon as you put consciousness in, there is no longer any unconsciousness. So that is what She does. Wherever She sees unconsciousness, She tries to enter. Sometimes the doors are locked, then it takes a little more time, but sometimes the doors open, then She rushes in immediately, the uncon-sciousness disappears and consciousness comes — without needing any tricks or any intermediaries. She becomes conscious. But mate-rial Nature, physical Nature is not like that, she is full of tricks; she makes you move all the time, she pulls the puppet strings; for her you are so many little dolls: she pulls the strings and makes them move. She puts all kinds of illusions in your head so that you may do the things she wants, without even your wanting it. She does not require that you should want it: she pulls the thread and you do it.

That is why we quarrel at times, but that's something we do not say.

You have said here that we are "tied to the chain of Karma", but then sometimes when the Divine Grace acts, that contradicts...

Completely, the Divine Grace completely contradicts Karma; you know, It makes it melt away like butter that's put in the sun.

That is what I was saying just now. What you have just told me is another way of speaking. I was putting myself in your place and ask-ing: There you are, if you have an aspiration that's sincere enough or a prayer that's intense enough, you can bring down in you Something that will change everything, everything — truly it changes everything. An example may be given that is extremely limited, very small, but which makes you understand things very well: a stone falls quite me-chanically; say, a tile falls; if it gets loose, it will fall, won't it? But if there comes, for example, a vital or mental determinism from some-one who passes by and does not want it to fall and puts his hand out, it will fall on his hand, but it will not fall on the ground. So he has changed the destiny of this stone or tile. It is another determinism that has come in, and instead of the stone falling on the head of some-one, it falls upon the hand and it will not kill anybody. This is an intervention from another plane, from a conscious will that enters into the more or less unconscious mechanism.

So the consequences of Karma are not rigorous?

No, not at all. In all religions there are people who have said that, who have given such absolute rules, but I believe it was in order to substitute themselves for Nature and pull the strings. There is always this kind of instinct that wants to take the place of Nature and pull the strings of people. So they are told: "There is an absolute consequence of all that you do...." It is a concept necessary at a given moment of evolution to prevent people from being in a completely unconscious egoism, in a total unconsciousness of the consequences of what they do. There is no lack of people who are still like that, I believe it is the majority; they follow their impulses and do not even ask themselves whether what they have done is going to have any consequences for them and for others. So it is good that someone tells you straight, with a severe look: "Take care, that has consequences which will last for a very long time!" And then there are others who come and tell you: "You will pay for it in another life." That, however, is one of those fantastic stories.... But it does not matter: this also can be for the good of people. There are other religions which tell you: "Oh! If you commit that sin, you will go to hell for eternity." You can imagine!... So people have such a fright that it stops them a little, it gives them just a moment for reflection before obeying an impulse — and not always; sometimes the reflection comes afterwards, a little late.

It is not absolute. These are still mental constructions, more or less sincere, which cut things into small bits like that, quite neatly cut, and tell you: "Do this or do that. If it is not this, it will be that." Oh! what a nuisance is this kind of life. And so people go mad, they are frightened! "Is it like that or rather this?" And they want it to be neither this nor that, what should they do? — They have only to climb to a higher storey. They must be given the key to open the door. There is a door to the staircase, a key is needed. The key, as I told you just now, is the sufficiently sincere aspiration or the sufficiently intense prayer. I said "or", but I do not think it is "or". There are people who like one better and others, the other. But in both there is a magical power, you must know how to make use of it.

There is something very beautiful in both, I shall speak to you about it one day, I shall tell you what there is in aspiration and what in prayer and why both of them are beautiful.... Some dislike prayer; if they entered deep into their heart, they would find it was pride — worse than that, vanity. And then there are those who have no aspiration, they try and they cannot aspire; it is because they do not have the flame of the will, it is because they do not have the flame of humility.

Both are needed. There must be a very great humility and a very great will to change one's Karma.

3 June 1953

The Journey of the Supreme

If one wants to state the problem in a way that's more easily accessible to ordinary practical thinking, one could conceive that everything exists from all eternity, and therefore simultaneously, but that this total, simultaneous, eternal existence is like the property, the possession of a Consciousness which would take pleasure in travelling through its domains, find its joy in an almost infinite or anyway indefinite journey throughout all its domains, and would go like this from discovery to discovery of things which already exist, which have always existed... but which the Supreme had never visited. And the path he follows in his discovery could be an entirely free, unexpected, unforeseen path according to his choice of the moment, so that, although his whole domain is there from all eternity, existing for ever, he could visit it in an altogether unexpected, unpredictable way, and so open the door to all relationships and possibilities.

And it is also his own self-discovery, for this domain is himself; and a discovery which could be made according to immediate decisions, without a preconceived plan such as would be mentally thought out, with all the delight of complete freedom and of the unexpectedness of every second — an eternal journey within his own being.

Everything is absolutely determined, for everything *is* from all eternity, and yet the path traversed has a freedom and unpredictability which is also absolute.

And this is how there can exist simultaneously worlds which have no apparent relationship with each other, and which nevertheless coexist, but are discovered gradually and so give the impression of a new creation.... Seeing things in this way, one could easily understand that simultaneously with this physical world as we know it with all its imperfections, all its limitations, all its ignorance, there are one or several other worlds which exist in their own zones and are so

different in nature from ours here, that for us they are as if non-existent, for we have no relation with them. But the moment the great eternal Voyage passes from this world to that, by the very fact of this passage of the eternal Consciousness, the link will necessarily be created,
and the two worlds will gradually enter into relation with each other.

Truly speaking this is what is actually happening, and we can say
with certainty that the supramental world already exists, but the time
has come for it to become the object of the journey of the supreme
Consciousness, and then, gradually, a conscious link will be formed
between this world and that, and they will have a new relation as a
result of this new orientation of the journey.

This explanation is as good as any other and perhaps it is easier
to understand for people who are not metaphysicians.... At least, I
like it!

*Mother, you said that everything was absolutely determined; then
where does personal effort come from?*

I told you just a moment ago that the Great Traveller chooses at each
instant the course of his journey, therefore it is an absolute freedom
of choice, and this is what gives the universal unfolding that unpredictable air and that possibility of change, for the Supreme is entirely
free to change his course if he wants to do so. On the contrary, this is
absolute freedom. But everything is there, and since everything is
there, everything is absolutely determined — it has always existed
but it is discovered in an altogether unforeseen way. And in this discovery lies freedom.

You are taking a walk and, suddenly, well, you feel like going
this way instead of that, so the course you take is completely new, but
in the places you are going to, the things were already there, they
existed and were therefore determined — but not your discovery.

Surely only a consciousness identified with the supreme Consciousness can have this feeling of absolute freedom. So long as you
are not one with the supreme Consciousness, you necessarily have
the impression or the feeling or idea that you are subject to the law of
a higher Will, but the moment you are identified with this Will you
are perfectly free.

This amounts to saying what Sri Aurobindo has always said: in union with the Supreme true freedom is realised.

5 February 1958

The Intervention of the Grace

If you see some catastrophe coming, can you, Mother, by your effort change it?

That depends upon the nature of the event. There are many things.... That depends also upon the level from which one sees. There is a plane where there are all the possibilities, and on that level, as there are all the possibilities, there is the possibility also of changing these possibilities. If a catastrophe is foreseen in that plane, one can have the power of preventing it also. In other cases, even though one is forewarned, one has no action upon the event. And yet there, it depends on the level from where one sees.

A case of this kind was reported to me once where the very seeing of a thing prevented it from happening. An American gentleman had arrived at one of those big American hotels where there are lifts (you do not go down a staircase, you take a lift to go up or come down); now, early in the morning just before getting up, he had a dream which he remembered well: he had seen a boy dressed as a lift-boy and making the same movement a lift-boy makes directing you to get in. He was there. And then, at the end of the movement, instead of a lift, there was a hearse! [...] And the boy was signing to him to get into the carriage. When he came out of his room, the boy was there with the lift to take him down: exactly the same boy, the same face, the same dress, the same gesture. He remembered the hearse — he did not get into the lift. He said: "No, no!" and he walked down. And before he reached the ground floor, he heard a terrible noise and the lift had crashed down to the ground and all who were in it were killed. It was because of the dream that he had not got in, for he had understood.

Therefore in such a case when you have the vision, you can avert the catastrophe.

There are other cases, as I said, when you are simply forewarned.

You are forewarned. In reality, it is to help you to prepare within for what must come, so that you may take the right inner attitude to face the event. It is like a lesson telling you: "This is what it must teach you." You cannot change the thing, but you can change your attitude and your inner reaction. Instead of having a bad reaction, a wrong attitude towards the experience that occurs, you have a good reaction, a good attitude, and you derive as much benefit as possible out of what has happened.

29 July 1953

*

People are not aware of the workings of the Grace except when there has been some danger, that is, when there has been the beginning of an accident or the accident has taken place and they have escaped it. Then they become aware. But never are they aware that if, for instance, a journey or anything whatever, passes without any accident, it is an infinitely higher Grace. That is, the harmony is established in such a way that nothing can happen. But that seems to them quite natural. When people are ill and get well quickly, they are full of gratitude; but never do they think of being grateful when they are well; and yet that is a much greater miracle!

23 December 1953

*

I have said somewhere, or maybe written, that no matter how great your faith and trust in the divine Grace, no matter how great your capacity to see it at work in all circumstances, at every moment, at every point in life, you will never succeed in understanding the marvellous immensity of Its Action, and the precision, the exactitude with which this Action is accomplished; you will never be able to grasp to what extent the Grace does everything, is behind everything, organises everything, conducts everything, so that the march forward to the divine realisation may be as swift, as complete, as total and harmonious as possible, considering the circumstances of the world.

As soon as you are in contact with It, there is not a second in

time, not a point in space, which does not show you *dazzlingly* this
perpetual work of the Grace, this constant intervention of the Grace.

And once you have seen this, you feel you are never equal to it,
for you should never forget it, never have any fears, any anguish, any
regrets, any recoils... or even suffering. If one were in union with this
Grace, if one saw It everywhere, one would begin living a life of
exultation, of all-power, of infinite happiness.

And that would be the best possible collaboration in the divine
Work.

1 August 1956

*

*"If one were in union with this Grace, if one saw It everywhere,
one would begin living a life of exultation, of all-power, of infinite happiness.*

*"And that would be the best possible collaboration in the
divine Work." (The Mother)*

The first condition is not very easy to realise. It is the result of a conscious growth, a constant observation and perpetual experience in life.

I have already told you this several times. When you are in a
particular set of circumstances and certain events take place, these
events often oppose your desire or what seems best to you, and often
you happen to regret this and say to yourself, "Ah! how good it would
have been if it were otherwise, if it had been like this or like that", for
little things and big things.... Then years pass by, events are unfolded;
you progress, become more conscious, understand better, and when
you look back, you notice — first with astonishment, then later with
a smile — that those very circumstances which seemed to you quite
disastrous or unfavourable, were exactly the best thing that could have
happened to you to make you progress as you should have. And if
you are the least bit wise you tell yourself, "Truly, the divine Grace is
infinite."

So, when this sort of thing has happened to you a number of
times, you begin to understand that in spite of the blindness of man
and deceptive appearances, the Grace is at work everywhere, so that

at every moment it is the best possible thing that happens in the state the world is at that moment. It is because our vision is limited or even because we are blinded by our own preferences that we cannot discern that things are like this.

But when one begins to see it, one enters upon a state of wonder which nothing can describe. For behind the appearances one perceives this Grace — infinite, wonderful, all-powerful — which knows all, organises all, arranges all, and leads us, whether we like it or not, whether we know it or not, towards the supreme goal, that is, union with the Divine, the awareness of the Godhead and union with Him.

Then one lives in the Action and Presence of the Grace a life full of joy, of wonder, with the feeling of a marvellous strength, and at the same time with a trust so calm, so complete, that nothing can shake it any longer.

And when one is in this state of perfect receptivity and perfect adherence, one diminishes to that extent the resistance of the world to the divine Action; consequently, this is the best collaboration one can bring to the Action of the Divine. One understands what He wants and, with all one's consciousness, adheres to His Will.

8 August 1956

The Determinism of Death

You have said: "One can neither hasten nor delay its hour." But death comes if one stops progressing. So, if one progresses, one can put off the hour. Or does this mean that from one's birth the day and the moment of death are predestined?

No. This is altogether something else and on another plane. I have written elsewhere that one dies only when one consents to die — which seems to contradict what I have said here. But this is the truth. I have told you this once already, I believe; in any case, I have written it somewhere. There are two points of view. Here I have taken quite an ordinary, material point of view, that of the physical consciousness. But I have explained somewhere that there are, as it were, different "layers of determinisms" in our being. The physical existence has a determinism; the vital existence has a determinism; the mental existence has a determinism; the higher mental, the psychic have a determinism. And then the higher existences have determinisms — the supramental existence has a determinism. And the determinism of everyone comes from the combination of all these determinisms (I am sure I have written this somewhere). If, for instance, at a given moment, when the entire physical determinism must necessarily bring death, you suddenly enter into contact with an extremely high determinism, like the supramental one, for example, and you succeed in joining the two, you change your physical determinism completely at that moment: death which had been determined by the physical determinism is abolished, and the conditions change and are pushed back.

I do not speak of this in that article ["The Fear of Death"]. I have taken a purely material point of view. I have given the example of people (and people who lived almost exclusively in their material consciousness, their physical consciousness, you understand, mental, vital and material), and who eagerly wanted to die from the time they were fifty — they lived to be eighty-seven! I have had an instance of that. I had another example the very opposite of this, of someone who ardently wanted to live very long, who felt that he had many very important things to do and that he must not die, and he took all kinds of precautions against that — and yet he died. There may be cases which seem contradictory, but that is only an appearance. There are explanations for all these things, they obey different laws. Here I have taken the purely material point of view.

If you do not make a higher determinism intervene, truly you can change nothing. That is the only way of changing your physical determinism. If you remain in your physical consciousness and want to change your determinism, you cannot... During the First War I knew a boy who had been told he would die of a shot (you know in war one dies easily), and he had even been given an approximate date. And that caused him such agony that he had succeeded in getting a long leave. He came to Paris on leave. He was an officer and had his pistol in his pocket. He jumped from a tram and fell down, the pistol went off and he was killed on the spot. He could not escape.

I could narrate any number of such examples to you. But this belongs to a single plane, the material plane — the purely material physical, mental and vital plane. It is only a higher knowledge and a contact with the higher planes and the descent of these higher planes into the physical plane, which can change circumstances. So too, if one succeeded in bringing down the supramental plane permanently into the physical life, physical life would be transformed, that is, it would change totally. But only on this condition.

10 March 1954

"The Best Will Happen"

"Absolute faith — faith that what is for the best will happen, but also that if one can make oneself a true instrument, the fruit will be that which one's will guided by the Divine Light sees as the thing to be done — kartavyam karma." (Sri Aurobindo)

Faith that always what is for the best happens. We may for the moment not consider it as the best because we are ignorant and also blind, because we do not see the consequences of things and what will happen later. But we must keep the faith that if it is like that, if we rely on the Divine, if we give Him the full charge of ourselves, if we let Him decide everything for us, well, we must know that it is always what is best for us which happens. This is an absolute fact. To the extent to which you surrender, the best happens to you. This may not be in conformity with what you would like, your preference or desire, because these things are blind: it is the best from the spiritual point of view, the best for your progress, your development, your spiritual growth, your *true* life. It is always that. And you must keep this faith, because faith is the expression of a trust in the Divine and the full self-giving you make to the Divine. And when you make it, it is something absolutely marvellous. That's a fact, these are not just words, you understand, it is a fact. When you look back, all kinds of things which you did not understand when they happened to you, you realise as *just* the thing which was necessary in order to compel you to make the needed progress. *Always*, without exception. It is our blindness which prevents us from seeing it.

6 October 1954

*

You say, "If one always had the feeling that it is the best that happens in all circumstances, one would not be afraid." Is it really the best that happens in all circumstances?

It is the best, given the state of the world — it is not an absolute best.

There are two things: in a total and absolute way, at each moment, it is the best possible for the divine Goal of the whole; and for one who is consciously connected with the divine Will, it is the most favourable for his own divine realisation.

I believe this is the correct explanation.

For the whole, it is always, at every moment, what is most favourable for the divine evolution. And for the elements consciously linked with the Divine, it is the best for the perfection of their union.

Only you must not forget that it is constantly changing, that it is not a static best; it is a best which if preserved would not be the best a moment later. And it is because the human consciousness always has the tendency to preserve statically what it finds good or considers good, that it realises that it is unseizable. It is this effort to preserve which falsifies things.

(Silence)

I saw this when I wanted to understand the position of the Buddha who blamed the Manifestation for its impermanence; for him perfection and permanence were one and the same thing. In his contact with the manifested universe he had observed a perpetual change, therefore he concluded that the manifested world was imperfect and had to disappear. And change (impermanence) does not exist in the Unmanifest, hence the Unmanifest is the true Divine. It was by considering and concentrating on this point, that in fact I saw that his finding was right: the Manifestation is absolutely impermanent, it is a perpetual transformation.

But in the Manifestation, perfection consists in having a movement of transformation or an unfolding identical with the divine Movement, the essential Movement; whereas all that belongs to the inconscient or tamasic creation seeks to preserve exactly the very same existence instead of trying to last out through constant transformation.

That is why some thinkers have postulated that the creation was the result of an error. But one finds all possible concepts: perfect creation, then a "fault" which introduced error; the creation itself as a lower movement which must have an end since it had a beginning; then the Vedic concept, as Sri Aurobindo has explained it, of an unfolding or a progressive and infinite discovery — indefinite and infinite — of the All by Himself.... Naturally, all these, these are human interpretations. For the moment, as long as you express yourself in human terms, it is a human translation. But according to the initial position of the human translator (that is to say, whether it is the position which admits "original sin" or an "accident" in the creation or a supreme conscious Will from the beginning in a progressive unfolding), in the yogic attitude, the conclusions or "descents" are different.... There are Nihilists, Nirvanists, Illusionists; there are all the religions which admit the devil's intervention under one form or another; then there is the pure Vedism which is the eternal unfolding of the Supreme in a progressive objectification. And according to taste, one places himself here, another there or elsewhere, with all the nuances between. But according to what Sri Aurobindo has felt to be the most total truth, according to this conception of a progressive universe, one is led to say that at every minute what happens is the best possible for the unfolding of the whole. It is absolutely logical. And I believe that all contradictions can arise only from a more or less pronounced tendency towards this or that, for one position or another. All who admit the intrusion of a "sin" or an "error" and the conflict resulting from it between forces which pull back and those which pull forward, may naturally contest the possibility. But one has to say that for him who is spiritually linked with the supreme Will or the supreme Truth, for him it is necessarily, at every instant, the best that happens for his personal realisation. In all instances it is like that. An unconditional best can be admitted only by one who sees the universe as an unrolling, as the Supreme's self-awareness of Himself.

(Silence)

To tell you the truth, all these things are of no importance; for that which *is*, goes in every way entirely and absolutely beyond everything that human consciousness can think about it. It is only when you are no longer human that you *know*; but as soon as this knowledge is expressed, human limits reimpose themselves and then you cease to know.

This is incontestable.

And because of this incapacity, there is a kind of futility also in wanting to reduce the problem altogether to something which human reason can understand. In this case it is very wise to say like someone I knew: "We are here, we have a work to do, and what is needed is to do it as well as we can, without worrying about the why and how." Why is the world as it is?... When we are capable of understanding, we shall understand.

From the practical point of view, this is evident.

Only, each one takes a position.... I have all the examples here. I have a sample collection of all attitudes and see very clearly their reactions. I see the same Force — the same, one Force — acting in this sample collection and producing naturally different effects; but these "different" effects, to a deeper vision, are very superficial: it is only "It pleases them to think in this way, that's all, it just pleases them to think thus." But as a matter of fact, the inner journey, the inner development, the essential vibration is not affected — not at all. One aspires with all his heart for Nirvana, another aspires with all his will for the supramental manifestation, and in both of them the vibratory result is almost the same. And it is a whole mass of vibrations which is prepared more and more to... to receive what must be.

There is a state, a state essentially pragmatic, spiritually pragmatic, in which of all human futilities, the most futile is metaphysics.

14 March 1951

CHAPTER 11

Religion and Spirituality

The Necessity of Religion

Sweet Mother, is religion a necessity in the life of the ordinary man?

In the life of societies it is a necessity, for it serves as a corrective to collective egoism which, without this control, could take on excessive proportions.

The level of collective consciousness is always lower than the individual level. It is very noticeable, for example, that when men gather in a group or collect in great numbers, the level of consciousness falls a great deal. The consciousness of crowds is much lower than individual consciousness, and the collective consciousness of society is certainly lower than the consciousness of the individuals constituting it.

There it is a necessity. In ordinary life, an individual, whether he knows it or not, always has a religion but the object of his religion is sometimes of a very inferior kind.... The god he worships may be the god of success or the god of money or the god of power, or simply a family god: the god of children, the god of the family, the god of the ancestors. There is always a religion. The quality of the religion is very different according to the individual, but it is difficult for a human being to live and to go on living, to survive in life without having something like a rudiment of an ideal which serves as the *centre* for his existence. Most of the time he doesn't know it and if he were asked what his ideal is, he would be unable to formulate it; but he has one, vaguely, something that seems to him the most precious thing in life.

For most people, it is security, for instance: living in security, being in conditions where one is sure of being able to go on existing. That is one of the great "aims", one might say, one of the great motives of human effort. There are people for whom comfort is the important thing; for others it is pleasure, amusement.

All that is very low and one would not be inclined to give it the name of an ideal, but it is truly a form of religion, something which may seem to be worth consecrating one's life to.... There are many influences which seek to impose themselves on human beings by using that as a basis. The feeling of insecurity, uncertainty, is a kind of tool, a means used by political or religious groups to influence individuals. They play on these ideas.

Every political or social idea is a sort of lower expression of an ideal which is a rudimentary religion. As soon as there is a faculty of thought, there is necessarily an aspiration for something higher than the most brutal daily existence from minute to minute, and this is what gives the energy and possibility of living.

Of course, one could say that it is the same thing for individuals as for collectivities, that their value is exactly proportionate to the value of their ideal, their religion, that is, of the thing they make the summit of their existence.

Of course, when we speak of religion, if we mean the recognised religions, truly, everyone has his own religion, whether he knows it or not, even when he belongs to the great religions that have a name and a history. It is certain that even if one learns the dogmas by heart and complies with a prescribed ritual, everybody understands and acts in his own way, and only the name of the religion is the same, but this same religion is not the same for all the individuals who think they are practising it.

We can say that without some expression of this aspiration for the Unknown and the highest, human existence would be very difficult. If there were not at the heart of every being the hope of something better — of whatever kind — he would have difficulty in finding the energy needed to go on living.

(Silence)

But as very few individuals are capable of thinking freely, it is much easier to join a religion, accept it, adopt it and become a part of that religious collectivity than to formulate one's own cult for oneself. So, apparently, one is this or that, but in fact it is only an appearance.

16 July 1958

Religion and Spiritual Life

What is exactly the nature of religion? Is it an obstacle in the way of the spiritual life?

Religion belongs to the higher mind of humanity. It is the effort of man's higher mind to approach, as far as lies in its power, something beyond it, something to which humanity gives the name God or Spirit or Truth or Faith or Knowledge or the Infinite, some kind of Absolute, which the human mind cannot reach and yet tries to reach. Religion may be divine in its ultimate origin; in its actual nature it is not divine but human. In truth we should speak rather of religions than of religion; for the religions made by man are many. These different religions, even when they had not the same origin, have most of them been made in the same way. We know how the Christian religion came into existence. It was certainly not Jesus who made what is known as Christianity, but some learned and very clever men put their heads together and built it up into the thing we see. There was nothing divine in the way in which it was formed, and there is nothing divine either in the way in which it functions. And yet the excuse or occasion for the formation was undoubtedly some revelation from what one could call a Divine Being, a Being who came from elsewhere bringing down with him from a higher plane a certain Knowledge and Truth for the earth. He came and suffered for his Truth; but very few understood what he said, few cared to find and hold to the Truth for which he suffered. Buddha retired from the world, sat down in meditation and discovered a way out of earthly suffering and misery, out of all this illness and death and desire and sin and hunger. He saw a Truth which he endeavoured to express and communicate to the disciples and followers who gathered around him. But even before he was dead, his teaching had already begun to be twisted and distorted. It was only after his disappearance that Buddhism as a full-fledged religion reared its head founded upon what the Buddha is supposed to have said and on the supposed significance of these reported sayings. But soon too, because the disciples and the disciples' disciples could not agree on what the Master had said or what he meant by his utterances, there grew up a host of sects and sub-sects in the body of the parent religion — a Southern Path, a Northern Path, a Far Eastern Path, each of them claiming to be the only, the original, the undefiled doctrine of the Buddha. The same fate overtook the teaching of the Christ; that too came to be made in the same way into a set and organised religion. It is often said that, if Jesus came back, he would not be able to recognise what he taught in the forms that have been imposed on it, and if Buddha were to come back and see what has been made of his teaching, he would immediately run back discouraged to Nirvana! All religions have each the same story to tell. The occasion for its birth is the coming of a great Teacher of the world. He comes and reveals and is the incarnation of a Divine Truth. But men seize upon it, trade upon it, make an almost political organisation out of it. The religion is equipped by them with a government and policy and laws, with its creeds and dogmas, its rules and regulations, its rites and ceremonies, all binding upon its adherents, all absolute and inviolable. Like the State, it too administers rewards to the loyal and assigns punishments for those that revolt or go astray, for the heretic and the renegade.

The first and principal article of these established and formal religions runs always, "Mine is the supreme, the only truth, all others are in falsehood or inferior." For without this fundamental dogma, established credal religions could not have existed. If you do not believe and proclaim that you alone possess the one or the highest truth, you will not be able to impress people and make them flock to you.

This attitude is natural to the religious mind; but it is just that which makes religion stand in the way of the spiritual life. The articles and dogmas of a religion are mind-made things and, if you cling to them and shut yourself up in a code of life made out for you, you do not know and cannot know the truth of the Spirit that lies beyond all codes and dogmas, wide and large and free. When you stop at a religious creed and tie yourself in it, taking it for the only truth in the world, you stop the advance and widening of your inner soul. But if you look at religion from another angle, it need not always be an obstacle to all men. If you regard it as one of the higher activities of humanity and if you can see in it the aspirations of man without ignoring the imperfection of all man-made things, it may well be a kind of help for you to approach the spiritual life. Taking it up in a serious and earnest spirit, you can try to find out what truth is there, what aspiration lies hidden in it, what divine inspiration has undergone transformation and deformation here by the human mind and a human organisation, and with an appropriate mental stand you can get religion even as it is to throw some light on your way and to lend some support to your spiritual endeavour.

In all religions we find invariably a certain number of people who possess a great emotional capacity and are full of a real and ardent aspiration, but have a very simple mind and do not feel the need of approaching the Divine through knowledge. For such natures religion has a use and it is even necessary for them; for, through external forms, like the ceremonies of the Church, it offers a kind of support and help to their inner spiritual aspiration. In every religion there are some who have evolved a high spiritual life. But it is not the religion that gave them their spirituality; it is they who have put their spirituality into the religion. Put anywhere else, born into any other cult, they would have found there and lived there the same spiritual life. It is their own capacity, it is some power of their inner being and not the religion they profess that has made them what they are. This power in their nature is such that religion to them does not become a slavery or a bondage. Only as they have not a strong, clear and active mind, they need to believe in this or that creed as absolutely true and to give themselves up to it without any disturbing question or doubt. I have met in all religions people of this kind and it would be a crime to disturb their faith. For them religion is not an obstacle. An obstacle for those who can go farther, it may be a help for those who cannot, but are yet able to travel a certain distance on the paths of the Spirit. Religion has been an impulse to the worst things and the best; if the fiercest wars have been waged and the most hideous persecutions carried on in its name, it has stimulated too supreme heroism and self-sacrifice in its cause. Along with philosophy it marks the limit the human mind has reached in its highest activities. It is an impediment and a chain if you are a slave to its outer body; if you know how to use its inner substance, it can be your jumping-board into the realm of the Spirit.

One who holds a particular faith or who has found out some truth, is disposed to think that he alone has found the Truth, whole and entire. This is human nature. A mixture of falsehood seems necessary for human beings to stand on their legs and move on their way. If the vision of the Truth were suddenly given to them they would be crushed under the weight.[...]

Things have an inner value and become real to you only when you have acquired them by the exercise of your free choice, not when they have been imposed upon you. If you want to be sure of your religion, you must choose it; if you want to be sure of your country, you must choose it; if you want to be sure of your family, even that you must choose. If you accept without question what has been given you by Chance, you can never be sure whether it is good or bad for you, whether it is the true thing for your life. Step back from all that forms your natural environment or inheritance, made up and forced upon you by Nature's blind mechanical process; draw within and look quietly and dispassionately at things. Appraise them, choose freely. Then you can say with an inner truth, "This is my family, this my country, this my religion."

If we go a little way within ourselves, we shall discover that there is in each of us a consciousness that has been living throughout the ages and manifesting in a multitude of forms. Each of us has been born in many different countries, belonged to many different nations, followed many different religions. Why must we accept the last one as the best? The experiences gathered by us in all these many lives in different countries and varying religions, are stored up in that inner continuity of our consciousness which persists through all births. There are multiple personalities there created by these past experiences, and when we become aware of this multitude within us, it becomes impossible to speak of one particular form of truth as the only truth, one country as our only country, one religion as the only true religion. There are people who have been born into one country, although the leading elements of their consciousness obviously belong to another. I have met some born in Europe who were evidently Indians; I have met others born in Indian bodies who were as evidently Europeans. In Japan I have met some who were Indian, others who were European. And if any of them goes to the country or enters into the civilisation to which he has affinity, he finds himself there perfectly at home.

If your aim is to be free, in the freedom of the Spirit, you must get rid of all the ties that are not the inner truth of your being, but come from subconscious habits. If you wish to consecrate yourself entirely, absolutely and exclusively to the Divine, you must do it in all completeness; you must not leave bits of yourself tied here and there. You may object that it is not easy to cut away altogether from one's moorings. But have you never looked back and observed the changes that have taken place in you in the course of a few years? When you do that, almost always you ask yourself how it was that you could have felt in the way you felt and acted as you did act in certain circumstances; at times, even, you can no longer recognise yourself in the person you were only ten years ago. How can you then bind yourself to what was or to what is or how can you fix beforehand what may or may not be in the future?

All your relations must be newly built upon an inner freedom of choice. The traditions in which you live or are brought up have been imposed on you by the pressure of the environment or by the general mind or by the choice of others. There is an element of compulsion in your acquiescence. Religion itself has been imposed on men; it is often supported by a suggestion of religious fear or by some spiritual or other menace. There can be no such imposition in your relation with the Divine; it must be free, your own mind's and heart's choice, taken up with enthusiasm and joy. What union can that be in which one trembles and says, "I am compelled, I cannot do otherwise"?

9 June 1929

*

Can one realise the Divine by this method [of religion]?

Those who carry within themselves a spiritual destiny and are born to realise the Divine, to become conscious in Him and live Him, will arrive, no matter what path, what way they follow. That is to say, even in religion there are people who have had the spiritual experience and found the Divine — not because of the religion, usually in spite of it, notwithstanding it — because they had the inner urge and this urge led them there despite all obstacles and through them. Everything served their purpose.

But if these very people want to express their experience, they naturally use the terms of the religion in which they were brought up, so they restrict their experience and inevitably limit it very much, they make it sectarian, so to say. But they themselves may very well have gone beyond all the forms and all the limitations and all the conventions and may have had the true experience in its pure simplicity.

23 May 1956

Mental Knowledge and Divine Truth

Sweet Mother, here it is written: "Do not be troubled by your surroundings and their opposition. These conditions are often imposed at first as a kind of ordeal." (Sri Aurobindo) Imposed by the Divine?

He has not put it that way, has he? You must take it in the way it helps you most. This is a very difficult question.

Oh, I have already explained to you very often that when you live in an ordinary consciousness, and to the extent you remain on a certain plane which is a combination of the most material mind, vital, physical, that is, the ordinary plane of life, you are subject to the determinism of this plane and it is this subjection to the determinism of this plane which puts you exactly in these conditions, for you have deep within you something which aspires for another life but doesn't yet know how to live that other life, and which pushes from inside in order to get the conditions necessary for this other life. These are inner conditions, they are not outer conditions. But this takes its support on outside obstacles in order to strengthen itself in its will to progress; and so, if you look at it from within, you can even say that it is you yourself who create the difficulties to help you to go forward.

Now, if you enter another plane and tell yourself (but this is a thing subject to many explanations and discussions), if you say that there is nothing in the universe that is not the work of the Divine, which is essentially true, though not true here, then you say, "Good. It is the Divine who organises everything; consequently it is He who has organised the difficulties also." But this is indeed a very childish way of putting things — oversimple. Only, as I said at the beginning,

"If it helps you to think in this way, think in this way." You see, thought is so approximate a thing, it is so far from *the* truth... it is only a kind of vague, incomplete, confused reflection, full of falsehood, even at its best. So, in truth, it is the moment to be practical and tell yourself, "Well, I shall adopt this thought if it helps me to progress." But if you think that it is the absolute truth, you are sure to go wrong, for there is not a single thought which is the absolute truth.[...]

Whatever your thought may be, even if it is very high, very pure, very noble, very true, it is only a very tiny microscopic aspect of the Truth, and consequently it is not entirely true. So in that field one must be practical, as I said, adopt the thought for the time being, the one which will help you to make progress when you have it. Sometimes it comes as an illumination and this helps you to progress. So long as it helps you to make progress, keep it; when it begins to crumble, not to act any longer, well, drop it, and try to get another which will lead you a little farther.

Many miseries and misfortunes in the world would disappear if people knew the relativity of knowledge, the relativity of faith, the relativity of the teachings and also the relativity of circumstances... to what extent a thing is so relatively important! For the moment it may be capital, it may lead you to life or to death — I am not speaking of physical life and death, I am speaking of the life and death of the spirit — but this is for the moment; and when you have made a certain progress, when you have grown a few years older from the spiritual point of view, and you look back on this thing, this circumstance or idea which perhaps has decided your life, it will seem so relative, so insignificant to you... and you will need something much higher to make new progress.

If one could always remember this, well, one would avoid much sectarianism, much intolerance, and annul all quarrels immediately, because a quarrel means just this, that one thinks in one way and the other in another, that one has taken one attitude and the other another, and that instead of trying to bring them together and find out how they could be harmonised, one puts them over against each other as one fights with one's fists. It is nothing else.

But if you become aware of the complete relativity of your point of view, your thought, your conviction of what is good, to what an extent it is relative in the march of the universe, then you will be less violent in your reactions and more tolerant.

6 October 1954

*

One becomes conscious of the reality only when one becomes conscious of it in oneself. All this is true. Indeed, it is true: you cannot say that it exists unless you experience it yourself. When you do not experience it, if you say, "It is like this", well... You can say, "There was a time when it was like this for me"; then that's right. But if you say, "It is like this", at a time when you don't feel it, it is quite simply a mental statement.

But everything is there! Everything is there... all the things which you can experience and infinitely more which you cannot, because a being is not absolutely complete in himself. If he were complete in himself, he could have the experience of the whole, without any exception. And in fact, potentially it is like that. Only, each one develops according to his own line. It comes to saying this: that one is conscious of the universe only to the extent to which the universe is in his consciousness. For you the universe stops at your consciousness, no matter what others may say. Everything that you read, for example, all the descriptions you are given, all the sentences you hear, you can understand only as far as they correspond to something in your consciousness; and if they are not in your consciousness, you do not understand them, and consequently they do not exist for you. But this does not mean that they do not exist outside you.

13 October 1954

*

"Each religion has helped mankind. Paganism increased in man the light of beauty, the largeness and height of his life, his aim at a many-sided perfection; Christianity gave him some vision of divine love and charity; Buddhism has shown him a noble way to be wiser, gentler, purer; Judaism and Islam how to be religiously faithful in action and zealously devoted to God; Hinduism has

opened to him the largest and profoundest spiritual possibilities. A great thing would be done if all these God-visions could embrace and cast themselves into each other; but intellectual dogma and cult-egoism stand in the way.

"All religions have saved a number of souls, but none yet has been able to spiritualise mankind. For that there is needed not cult and creed, but a sustained and all-comprehending effort at spiritual self-evolution." (Sri Aurobindo)

Mother, here Sri Aurobindo writes: "A great thing would be done if all these God-visions could embrace and cast themselves into each other; but intellectual dogma and cult-egoism stand in the way." How is it possible to fuse into one all these views?

It is not in the mental consciousness that these things can be harmonised and synthesised. For this it is necessary to rise above and find the idea behind the thought. Sri Aurobindo shows here, for example, what each of these religions represents in human effort, aspiration and realisation. Instead of taking these religions in their outward forms which are precisely dogmas and intellectual conceptions, if we take them in their spirit, in the principle they represent, there is no difficulty in unifying them. They are simply different aspects of human progress which complete each other perfectly well and should be united with many others yet to form a more total and more complete progress, a more perfect understanding of life, a more integral approach to the Divine. And even this unification which already demands a return to the Spirit behind things, is not enough; there must be added to it a vision of the future, the goal towards which humanity is moving, the future realisation of the world, that last "spiritual revolution" Sri Aurobindo speaks about, which will open a new age, that is, the supramental revolution.

In the supramental consciousness all these things are no longer contradictory or exclusive. They all become complementary. It is only the mental form which divides. What this mental form represents should be united to what all the other mental forms represent in order to make a harmonious whole. And that is the essential difference between a religion and the true spiritual life.

Religion exists almost exclusively in its forms, its cults, in a certain set of ideas, and it becomes great only through the spirituality of a few exceptional individuals, whereas true spiritual life, and above all what the supramental realisation will be, is independent of every precise, intellectual form, every limited form of life. It embraces all possibilities and manifestations and makes them the expression, the vehicle of a higher and more universal truth.

A new religion would not only be useless but very harmful. It is a new *life* which must be created; it is a new *consciousness* which must be expressed. This is something beyond intellectual limits and mental formulae. It is a living truth which must manifest.

Everything in its essence and its truth should be included in this realisation. This realisation must be an expression as total, as complete, as universal as possible of the divine reality. Only that can save humanity and the world. That is the great spiritual revolution of which Sri Aurobindo speaks. And this is what he wanted us to realise.

He has traced its broad outline in [...] *The Supramental Manifestation*.

And the first sentence I read today remains the key of the entire problem not only for the individual but also for the collectivity:

> *"All would change if man could once consent to be spiritualised; but his nature, mental and vital and physical, is rebellious to the higher law. He loves his imperfection." (Sri Aurobindo)*

3 April 1957

*

The forms of Divine Power which have incarnated in different beings, have incarnated with a specific aim, for a specific action, at a specific moment of universal development, but essentially they are only differentiated aspects of the One Being; therefore, it is in the particular purpose of the action that the difference lies. Otherwise it is always the same Truth, the same Power, the same eternal Life which manifests in these forms and creates these forms at a given moment for a specific reason and a specific aim; this is preserved in history, but eternally they are new forms which are used for new progress.

Old forms can endure as a vibration lasts, but their purpose historically, it could be said, was momentary, and one form is replaced by
another in order that a new step forward may be taken. The mistake
humanity makes is that it always hangs on to what is behind it and
wants to perpetuate the past indefinitely. These things must be used at
the time when they are useful. For there is a history of *each* individual development; you may pass through stages in which these disciplines have their momentary utility, but when you have gone beyond that moment you ought to enter into something else and see that
historically it was useful but now is so no longer. Certainly, to those
who have reached, for instance, a certain state of development and
mental control, I won't say, "Read the Dhammapada and meditate on
it"; it would be a waste of time. I give it to those who have not gone
beyond the stage where it is necessary. But always man takes upon
his shoulders an interminable burden. He does not want to drop anything of the past and he stoops more and more under the weight of a
useless accumulation.

You have a guide for a part of the way but when you have trav-
elled this part leave the road and the guide and go farther! This is
something men find difficult to do. When they get hold of something
which helps them, they cling to it, they do not want to move any
more. Those who have progressed with the help of Christianity do
not want to give it up and they carry it on their shoulders; those who
have progressed with the help of Buddhism do not want to leave it
and they carry it on their shoulders, and so this hampers the advance
and you are indefinitely delayed.

Once you have passed the stage, let it drop, let it go! Go farther.

2 October 1957

Spirituality and Active Life

*But this very attitude of wanting to become identified with the
Unmanifest and letting the world suffer, isn't this selfishness?*

Yes. And so what happens is very remarkable, the result is always the
same: those who have done that, at the last minute, have received a
sort of intimation that they had to return to the world and do their

work. It is as though they reached the door and — "Ah! no, no, not yet — go back and work. When the world is ready, then this will be all right."

Indeed this attitude of flight in the face of difficulty is a supreme selfishness. You are told, "Do this, and then, when all the others have done it, all will be well with the whole world", but it is only a very small élite among men who are ready to be able to do it. And these precisely are those who can be the most useful to the earth, for they know more about things than others, they have overcome many difficulties and can be of help to others just where those others can't. But the whole human mass, the immense human mass.... For when some have succeeded — even a few hundred — one may tend to think it is "humanity", but truly speaking it is only a kind of élite of humanity, it is a selection. The immense mass, all the people living all over the earth — merely in India, the immense population — formidable — which lives in the villages, the countryside, there is no question of their making an effort for liberation, to come out of the world in order to live the spiritual life. They don't even have the time to become aware of themselves! They are just there, attached to their work like a horse to the plough. They move in a rut from which, generally, they can't get out. So they can't be told, "Do as I do and all will be well." Because "Do as I do" means nothing at all. There are perhaps a few hundred who can do the same thing, no more!

24 February 1954

*

"... *all work must be a field of endeavour and a school of experience.*" *(Sri Aurobindo) "All work" is "a school of experience"?*

Yes, surely. You don't understand?

No, Mother.

If you don't do anything, you cannot have any experience. The whole life is a field of experience. Each movement you make, each thought you have, each work you do, can be an experience, and *must be* an experience; and naturally work in particular is a field of experience

where one must apply all the progress which one endeavours to make
inwardly.

If you remain in meditation or contemplation without working,
well, you don't know if you have progressed or not. You may live in
an illusion, the illusion of your progress; while if you begin to work,
all the circumstances of your work, the contact with others, the material occupation, all this is a field of experience in order that you may
become aware not only of the progress made but of all the progress
that remains to be made. If you live closed up in yourself, without
acting, you may live in a completely subjective illusion; the moment
you externalise your action and enter into contact with others, with
circumstances and the objects of life, you become aware absolutely
objectively of whether you have made progress or not, whether you
are more calm, more conscious, stronger, more unselfish, whether
you no longer have any desire, any preference, any weakness, any
unfaithfulness — you can become aware of all this by working. But if
you remain enclosed in a meditation that's altogether personal, you
may enter into a total illusion and never come out of it, and believe
that you have realised extraordinary things, while really you have
only the impression, the illusion that you have done so.[...]

Then, Mother, why do all the spiritual schools in India have as
their doctrine escape from action?

Yes, because all this is founded upon the teaching that life is an illusion. It began with the teaching of the Buddha who said that existence
was the fruit of desire, and that there was only one way of coming out
of misery and suffering and desire; it was to come out of existence.
And then this continued with Shankara who added that not only is it
the fruit of desire but it is a total illusion, and as long as you live in
this illusion you cannot realise the Divine. For him there was not even
the Divine, I think; for the Buddha, at least, there wasn't any.

Then did they truly have experiences?

That depends on what you call "experience". They certainly had an
inner contact with something.

The Buddha certainly had an inner contact with something which, in comparison with the external life, was a non-existence; and in this non-existence, naturally, all the results of existence disappear. There is a state like this; it is even said that if one can keep this state for twenty days, one is sure to lose one's body; if it is exclusive, I quite agree with it.

But it may be an experience which remains at the back, you see, and is conscious even while not being exclusive, and which causes the contact with the world and the outer consciousness to be supported by something that is free and independent. This indeed is a state in which one can truly make very great progress externally, because one can be detached from everything and act without attachment, without preference, with that inner freedom which is expressed outwardly.

Yet this is the real necessity: once this inner freedom has been attained and the conscious contact with what is eternal and infinite, then, without losing this consciousness one must return to action and let that influence the whole consciousness turned towards action.

This is what Sri Aurobindo calls bringing down the Force from above. In this way there is a chance of being able to change the world, because one has brought in a new Force, a new region, a new consciousness and put it into contact with the outer world. So its presence and action will produce inevitable changes and, let us hope, a total transformation in what this outer world is.

So we could say that the Buddha quite certainly had the first part of the experience, but that he never dreamt of the second, because it was contrary to his own theory. His theory was that one had to run away; but it is obvious that there is only one way of escape, to die, and yet, as he himself has said so well, you may be dead and be completely attached to life, and still be in the cycle of births and not have liberation. And in fact he has admitted the idea that it is by successive passing lives on the earth that one can manage to develop oneself to reach this liberation. But for him the ideal was that the world would not exist any longer. It was as though he accused the Divine of having made a mistake and that there was only one thing to do, to rectify the mistake by annulling it. But naturally, to be reasonable and logical, he did not admit the Divine. It was a mistake made by whom, how, in what way? — this he never explained. He simply said that it was made and that the world had begun with desire and had to end with desire. He was just on the point of saying that this world was purely subjective, that is, a collective illusion, and that if the illusion ceased the world would cease to be. But he did not come so far. It is Shankara who took over and made the thing altogether complete in his teaching.

If we go back to the teaching of the Rishis, for example, there was no idea of flight out of the world, for them the realisation had to be terrestrial. They conceived a Golden Age very well, in which the realisation would be terrestrial. But starting from a certain decline of vitality in the spiritual life of the country, perhaps, from a different orientation which came in, you see... it is certainly starting from the teaching of the Buddha that this idea of flight came, which has undermined the vitality of the country [India], because one had to make an effort to cut oneself off from life. The outer reality became an illusory falsehood, and one had no longer to have anything to do with it. So naturally one was cut off from the universal energy, and the vitality went on diminishing, and with this vitality all the possibilities of realisation also diminished.

7 September 1955

Spiritual Life and Morality

The spiritual life, the life of Yoga, has for its object to grow into the divine consciousness and for its result to purify, intensify, glorify and perfect what is in you. It makes you a power for manifesting of the Divine; it raises the character of each personality to its full value and brings it to its maximum expression; for this is part of the Divine plan. Morality proceeds by a mental construction and, with a few ideas of what is good and what is not, sets up an ideal type into which all must force themselves. This moral ideal differs in its constituents and its ensemble at different times and different places. And yet it proclaims itself as a unique type, a categoric absolute; it admits of none other outside itself; it does not even admit a variation within itself. All are to be moulded according to its single ideal pattern, everybody is to be made uniformly and faultlessly the same. It is because morality is of this rigid unreal nature that it is in its principle and its working the contrary of the spiritual life. The spiritual life reveals the one essence in all, but reveals too its infinite diversity; it works for diversity in oneness and for perfection in that diversity. Morality lifts up one artificial standard contrary to the variety of life and the freedom of the spirit. Creating something mental, fixed and limited, it asks all to conform to it. All must labour to acquire the same qualities and the same ideal nature. Morality is not divine or of the Divine; it is of man and human. Morality takes for its basic element a fixed division into the good and the bad; but this is an arbitrary notion. It takes things that are relative and tries to impose them as absolutes; for this good and this bad differ in differing climates and times, epochs and countries.

4 August 1929

*

Sweet Mother, hasn't morality helped us to increase our conscious-ness?

That depends on people. There are people who are helped by it, there are people who are not helped *at all*.

Morality is something altogether artificial and arbitrary, and in most cases, among the best, it checks the true spiritual effort by a sort of moral satisfaction that one is on the right path and a true gentle-man, that one does one's duty, fulfils all the moral requirements of life. Then one is so self-satisfied that one no longer moves or makes any progress.

It is very difficult for a virtuous man to enter the path of God; this has been said very often, but it is altogether true, for he is *most* self-satisfied, he thinks he has realised what he ought to have realised, he no longer has either the aspiration or even that elementary humility which makes one want to progress. You see, one who is known here [in India] as a sattwic man is usually very comfortably settled in his own virtue and never thinks of coming out of it. So, that puts you a million leagues away from the divine realisation.

What really helps, until one has found the inner light, is to make for oneself a certain number of rules which naturally should not be too rigid and fixed, but yet should be precise enough to prevent one from going completely out of the right path or making irreparable mistakes — mistakes the consequences of which one suffers all one's life.

To do that, it is good to set up a certain number of principles in oneself, which, however, should be for each one, in conformity with his own nature. If you adopt a social, collective rule, you immediately make yourself a slave to this social rule, and that prevents you almost radically from making any effort for transformation.

16 May 1956

Religion and Spiritual Experience

One point is very remarkable — I don't remember whether Sri Aurobindo speaks about it in what follows — but among the four activities or realisations he mentions — religion, occultism, spiritual philosophy and spiritual experience — which are necessary for the development and transformation of man, all are not equally accessible to humanity.

The one which can be practised and, one might say, "understood" — although it is certainly not an "understanding" — by the greatest number of human beings — those who live almost exclusively in the physical consciousness — is the religious method, precisely because it is based on fixed creeds and practices. Simply by an act of faith or a collective suggestion — above all a collective suggestion — many human beings who have not yet reached any considerable inner development can take up the path of religion.

For occultism we must already have come to a second stage of development and be more conscious in the vital world to be able to come into contact with the play of forces, which is indispensable in order to manipulate them.

As for spiritual philosophy, only the few who have a fairly complete mental development and are fully conscious on the intellectual plane, can usefully adopt this method; otherwise it is a dead letter for all those who don't have an ability for mental gymnastics and so cannot follow all the acrobatics of the mind.

And finally, Sri Aurobindo has told us somewhere in *The Life*

Divine that to follow the path of spiritual experience, one must have within oneself a "spiritual being", one must be "twice born" as it is said, for if one doesn't have a spiritual being within, which is at least on the point of becoming self-aware, one may try to imitate these experiences but it will only be crude imitation or hypocrisy, it won't be a reality.

Therefore, in order to follow these four paths simultaneously and to practise them with an integral benefit for the being, one must already be a complete individual, capable of having a conscious life in the four principal elements of human and spiritual nature.

Of course, this inner development is not always apparent and we may meet someone who has within him a conscious spiritual entity, ready for the most beautiful experiences, though externally he seems quite crude and incomplete.

Nor is it necessary to follow this development in the order in which it has been mentioned, but if we want our realisation to be integral and to arrive at a total transformation of our being, we must be able to use the essence of what each of these methods can bring.

The psychic or spiritual consciousness gives you the deep inner realisation, contact with the Divine, liberation from external fetters; but for this liberation to be effective, for it to have an action on the rest of the being, the mind must be open enough to be able to hold the spiritual light of Knowledge, the vital must be powerful enough to handle the forces behind appearances and dominate them, and the physical should be disciplined, organised enough to be able to *express* the deep experience, in the movements of each day and each moment, and live it integrally.

If one of these things is lacking, the result is not complete. One can make light of this thing or that under the pretext that it is not the most important, the central Thing — and to neglect outer things certainly cannot prevent you from entering into spiritual communion with the Supreme, but that is good only for a flight from life.

If we are to be total, complete beings, to have an integral realisation, we should be able to express our spiritual experience mentally, vitally and physically. And the more our expression is perfect, executed by a complete and perfect being, the more integral and perfect will our realisation be.

For someone who wants to follow the integral yoga nothing is useless and nothing must be neglected.... The main thing is to know how to put each thing in its place and to hand over the government to what truly has the right to govern.

18 June 1958

*

"Our thinking mind is concerned mainly with the statement of general spiritual truth, the logic of its absolute and the logic of its relativities, how they stand to each other or lead to each other, and what are the mental consequences of the spiritual theorem of existence...." (Sri Aurobindo)

I have a question here, but it is a verbal question, which means that it is not very interesting. It is a phrase from the beginning of the passage: What is the meaning of "the mental consequences of the spiritual theorem of existence"?

It is probably from someone who doesn't know what "theorem" means!

A theorem is the statement of a truth which has been arrived at through reasoning. The word is used quite concretely in mathematics and all the external sciences. From the philosophical point of view it is the same thing. In the present instance, the spiritual theorem of existence may be stated in this way: the Absolute in the relativities or Oneness in multiplicity. But to explain "the mental consequences", we must go into philosophy and I believe you are rather unprepared for that. And to really understand what it means, one feels that philosophy is always skirting the truth, like a tangent that draws closer and closer but never touches — that there is something that escapes. And this something is in truth everything.

To understand these things... there is only experience — *to live* this truth, not to feel it in the way the ordinary senses do but to realise within oneself the truth, the concrete existence of both states, simultaneously, existing together even while they are opposite conditions. All words can lead only to confusion; only experience gives the tangible reality of the *thing*: the simultaneous existence of the Absolute and the relativities, of Oneness and multiplicity, not as two states following each other and one resulting from the other, but as a state which can be perceived in two opposite ways depending on... the position one takes in relation to the Reality.

Words in themselves falsify the experience. To speak in words one must take not a step backwards but a step downwards, and the essential truth escapes. One must use them simply as a more or less accessible path to reach the *thing* itself which cannot be formulated. And from this point of view no formulation is better than any other; the best of all is the one that helps each one to remember, that is, the way in which the intervention of the Grace has crystallised in the thought.

Probably no two ways are identical, everyone must find his own. But one must not be mistaken, it is not "finding" by reasoning, it is "finding" by aspiration; it is not by study and analysis, but by the intensity of the aspiration and the sincerity of the inner opening.

When one is truly and exclusively turned to the spiritual Truth, whatever name may be given to it, when all the rest becomes secondary, when that alone is imperative and inevitable, then, *one single moment* of intense, absolute, total concentration is enough to receive the answer.

The experience comes first, in this case, and it is only later, as a consequence and a memory that the formulation becomes clear. In this way one is sure not to make a mistake. The formulation may be more or less exact, that is of no importance, so long as one doesn't make a dogma out of it.

It is good for you, that is all that is needed. If you want to impose it on others, whatever it may be, even if it is perfect in itself, it becomes false.

That is why religions are always mistaken — always — because they want to standardise the expression of an experience and impose it on everyone as an irrefutable truth. The experience was true, complete in itself, convincing — for the one who had it. The formulation he made of it was excellent — for himself. But to want to impose it on others is a fundamental error which has altogether disastrous consequences, always, which always leads far, very far from the Truth.

That is why all the religions, however beautiful they may be, have always led man to the worst excesses. All the crimes, the horrors perpetrated in the name of religion are among the darkest stains on human history, and simply because of this little initial error: wanting what is true for one individual to be true for the mass or collectivity.

(Silence)

The path must be shown and the doors opened but everyone must *follow* the path, pass through the doors and go towards his personal realisation.

The only help one can and should receive is that of the Grace which formulates itself in everyone according to his own need.

24 September 1958

CHAPTER 12

Science and Materialism

Understanding the World

The climax of the ordinary consciousness is Science. For Science, what is upon the earth is true, simply because it is there. What it calls Nature is for it the final reality, and its aim is to build up a theory to explain the workings of it. So it climbs as high as the physical mind can go and tries to find out the causes of what it assumes to be the true, the real world. But in fact it adapts "causes" to "effects", for it has already taken that which is for the true, the real, and seeks only to explain it mentally. For the yogic consciousness, however, this world is not the final reality. Rising above the mind into the Overmind and then into the Supermind, it enters the divine world of first truths, and looking down from there sees what has happened to those truths here. How distorted they have become, how completely falsified! So the so-called world of fact is for the Yogi a falsehood and not at all the only true reality. It is not what it ought to be, it is almost the very opposite; whereas for the scientist it is absolutely fundamental.

Our aim is to change things. The scientist says that whatever is, is natural and cannot be changed at heart. But, really speaking, the laws of which he usually speaks are of his own mental making; and because he accepts Nature as it is as the very basis, things do not and cannot change for him in any complete sense. But, according to us, all this can be changed, because we know that there is something above, a divine truth seeking manifestation. There are no fixed laws here; even Science in its undogmatic moments recognises that the laws are mere mental constructions. There are only cases, and if the mind could apply itself to all the circumstances it would find that no two cases are similar. Laws are for the mind's convenience, but the process of the supramental manifestation is different, we may even say it is the reverse of the mind. In the supramental realisation, each thing will carry in itself a truth which will manifest at each instant without being bound by what has been or what will follow. That elaborate linking of the past with the present, which gives things in Nature such an air of unchangeable determinism, is altogether the mind's way of conceiving, and is no proof that all that exists is inevitable and cannot be otherwise.

The knowledge possessed by the Yogi is also an answer to the terrible theory that all that takes place is God's direct working. For once you rise to the Supermind you immediately perceive that the world is false and distorted. The supramental truth has not at all found manifestation. How then can the world be a genuine expression of the Divine? Only when the Supermind is established and rules here, then alone the Supreme Will may be said to have authentically manifested. At the same time, we must steer clear of the dangerous exaggeration of the sense of the falsehood of the world, which comes to those who have risen to the higher consciousness. What happened with Shankara and others like him was that they had a glimpse of the true consciousness, which threw the falsehood of this world into such sharp contrast that they declared the universe to be not only false but also a really non-existent illusion which should be entirely abandoned. We, on the other hand, see its falsehood, but realise also that it has to be replaced and not abandoned as an illusion. Only, the truth has got mistranslated, something has stepped in to pervert the divine reality, but the world is in fact meant to express it. And to express it is indeed our Yoga.

1930-1931

*

I think one of the greatest difficulties in understanding things comes from an arbitrary simplification which puts spirit on one side and matter on the other. It is this foolishness that makes you incapable of understanding anything. There is spirit and matter — this is very convenient. So if one does not belong to spirit, one belongs to matter; if one does not belong to matter, one belongs to spirit. But what do you call spirit and what do you call matter? It is a countless crowd of things, an interminable ladder. The universe is a seemingly infinite gradation of worlds and states of consciousness, and in this increasingly subtle gradation, where does your matter come to an end? Where does your spirit begin? You speak of "spirit" — where does this spirit begin? With what you don't see? Is that it? So you include in "spirit" all the beings of the vital world, for instance, because you don't see them in your normal state.[...]

It is like those people who say, "When you are alive you are in matter; when you are dead, you enter the spirit. There, then! So, liberate the spirit from matter, die, and you liberate your spirit from matter." It is these stupidities which prevent you from understanding anything at all. But all this has nothing to do with the world as it really is.

For the human consciousness as it is, there are certainly infinitely more invisible things than visible things. What you know, the things which are visible to you and which you are conscious of — it's almost like the skin of an orange compared with the orange itself — and even an orange with a very thin skin, not a thick one! And so, if you know only the skin of the orange, you know nothing about the orange.

And this is more or less what happens. All that you know about the universe is just a superficial little crust — and even this you hardly know. But that is all you know about it, and all the rest escapes you.

7 March 1956

*

If one enters into a somewhat philosophical, psychological and subjective consciousness, one can very easily become aware of a sort of "objective unreality" of things; and the one thing which is real, tangible, concrete, measurable, so to speak, for the ordinary consciousness becomes so fluid, almost unsubstantial, and has a reality only in the consciousness that perceives it — an absolutely variable reality and at times quite contradictory according to the perception of the consciousness. If we put before us the different explanations that have been given about the world, the different ways in which it has been expressed, we shall have a series of notions that are sometimes absolutely contradictory, which are nevertheless perceptions of one identical thing by different consciousnesses. In fact, with this last paragraph, [in *The Life Divine*] we have an extreme point which is the affirmation that all that is, is the total and complete expression of the Divine Will — there is what could be called a certain school of thinkers who, on the basis of their personal experience, have asserted that everything is the expression of the Divine Will in a perfect way — and then, at the other extreme, the affirmation that the world is a sort of chaos without rhyme or reason, which has come into being one doesn't know how or why, which is going one doesn't know where, which has no logic, no reason, no coordination — it is just chance. It happens to be like this, one doesn't know why. Well, if you take these two extremes and put before you all that has been said, written, taught, thought about the world from one end to the other, and if you can see all that together, you will realise that, since it is all about the same world and yet the explanations are so totally different, this world exists, so to say, only in the consciousness of the one who sees it.... There must indeed be "something" there, but that something must be beyond what men think about it — far beyond, very different. And so the whole feeling is of an elusive unreality.

And in fact, the reality of the world is entirely subjective for each person's consciousness. The world has no objective reality, for in one case it can be said that it is the result of the supremely conscious, supreme Will and that all is ruled by that, and in the other case, it may be said that it is something without any reason for existence except an elusive chance — and yet, these two notions apply to one and the same thing.[...]

Everyone has his own idea which is more or less clear, more or less organised, more or less precise, and this idea he calls the world. Everyone has his own way of seeing, his own way of feeling and his particular relationship with everything else, and this he calls the world. He naturally puts himself at the centre, and then everybody is organised around him, according to the way in which he sees it, feels it, understands and desires it, according to his own reaction, but since for each consciousness, individually, it is different, this means that what we call the world — the thing in itself — escapes our perception completely. It must be something else. And we must come out of our individual consciousness to be able to understand what it is; and this is what Sri Aurobindo calls the passage from the lower to the higher hemisphere. In the lower hemisphere there are as many universes as individuals, and in the higher hemisphere there is "something" — which is what it is — in which all consciousnesses must meet. This is what he calls the "Truth-Consciousness".

As the human consciousness progresses, it has a greater and greater sense of this relativity, and at the same time a sort of feeling, it could be said, a vague impression that there is a Truth, which is not perceptible by ordinary means but must be perceptible in some way or other.

9 October 1957

*

The only really important thing modern science has discovered is that from the purely outer and physical point of view things are not what they seem to be. When you look at a body, a human being, an object, a landscape, you perceive these things with the help of your eyes, your touch, hearing and, for the details, smell and taste; well, science tells you: "All that is illusory, you don't see things at all as they are, you don't touch them as they really are, you don't smell them as they really are, you don't taste them as they really are. It is the structure of your organs which puts you in contact with these things in a particular way which is entirely superficial, external, illusory and unreal."

From the point of view of science, you are a mass of — not even of atoms — of something infinitely more imperceptible than an atom, which is in perpetual movement. There is absolutely nothing which is like a face, a nose, eyes, a mouth; it is only just an appearance. And scientists come to this conclusion — like the uncompromising spiritualists of the past — that the world is an illusion. That is a great discovery, very great.... One step more and they will enter into the Truth. So, when somebody comes and says, "But I *see* this, I *touch* it, I *feel* it, I am sure of it", from the scientific point of view it's nonsense. This could be said only by someone who has never made a scientific study of things as they are. So, by diametrically opposite roads they have come to the same result: the world as you see it is an illusion.

Now what is the truth behind this? People who have sought spiritual knowledge tell you, "We have experienced it", but of course it is a purely subjective experience; there are as yet no grounds on which one can say absolutely that the experience is beyond question for everybody. Everyone's experience is beyond question for him. And if one takes it a little further...

In fact, the value of an experience or a discovery could perhaps be proved by the power it gives, the power to change these appearances and transform things, circumstances and the world as it appears to us, in accordance with the will that manifests through that experience. It seems to me that the most universal proof of the validity of an individual or collective experience would be its power to make things — these appearances that we call the world — different from what they are. From the subjective point of view, the effect of the experience on an individual consciousness is an undeniable proof; for one who attains bliss, sovereign peace, unchanging delight, the profound knowledge of things, it is more than proved. The effects on the outer form depend on many other things besides the experience itself — depend perhaps on the first cause of these experiences — but out of all this, *one* thing seems to be a proof which is accessible to other people as well as to the one who has the experience; it is the power over other people and things — which for the ordinary consciousness is "objective". For instance, if a person who has attained the state of consciousness I am speaking about, had the power of communicating it to others, it would be partially — only partially — a proof of the reality of his experiences; but further, if the state of consciousness in which he is — for instance, a state of perfect harmony — could create this harmony in the outer world, in what apparently is not harmony, it would be, I think, the proof most readily accepted, even by the materialist scientific mind. If these illusory appearances could be changed into something more beautiful, more harmonious, happier than the world we live in now, this would perhaps be an undeniable proof. And if we take it a little farther, if, as Sri Aurobindo promises us, the supramental force, consciousness and light transform this world and create a new race, then, just as the apes and animals — if they could speak — could not deny the existence of man, so too man would not be able to deny the existence of these new beings — provided that they are different enough from the human race for this difference to be perceptible even to the deceptive organs of man.

18 December 1957

*

You have said that the world and the darkness were concomitant.
What is the cause of this concomitance?

The cause... is the light which has become the darkness and the consciousness which has become the inconscience! How to speak about
these things? You may call this an accident if you like, if that satisfies
your mind. It was perhaps, after all, the best thing that could have
happened, one can't tell. All depends upon the point of view one takes.
There must certainly be a consciousness in which this was foreseen,
and if it has not been avoided, it means that it forms part of the programme!... It is a human way of looking at the problem, for things do
not happen quite like that in those regions. One may also relate a
story which could make a subject, a magnificent drama, but it would
be only a story, a way of saying things.

A story is of value only to the extent it can help you to understand things. Ah! here is an interesting subject.... A story, that is, a
way of saying things, is of value only if it can make you understand
the thing. A language (which is a kind of story) is of value only to the
extent it is capable of putting you in contact with the Reality. Science
is a language, Art is a language — all activity is a sort of language,
that is, a way of expression. And the way of expression is of value
only in as far as it puts you in contact with what it wants to express. It
is a very interesting generalisation, for you can bring into it all the
categories you want and you will see that it is true.

It is the same for everything. The way of approaching the universe and the universal truth is also a language and all depends upon
the person who uses it, the person to whom the understanding is to be
communicated. Whatever may be the way of telling, if you understand, that is all that is necessary. If you do not understand, even if it
be the wonder of wonders, the truth of truths, it will have no value for
you. This is an essentially pragmatic point of view of the universe;
things have value only in so far as they realise that for which they
have been made, and the most beautiful philosophies of the world are
of no use to those who do not understand them. The most beautiful
works of art in the world are quite useless to those whom they do not
put on the path of the Truth. And the most perfect yoga in the world is
useless to those whom it does not lead to the Realisation. And if you

have this sense of relativity, you have finished with all dogmatism, all sectarianism, all that kind of absolutism which leads one always to think that all that has done us good is "the truth" — it is the truth for us, it is not necessarily the truth for our neighbour. And what our neighbour thinks is the truth for him, and when you say, "It is idiotic, it is quite useless", if it helps him to realise the truth, it is excellent, it is the best thing possible for him. And everything, everything on earth is like that. And if you do not want to be altogether narrow, to put on visors and not see farther than the tip of your nose, you must first of all understand this. You must understand that all things in the universe tend towards a goal and that it is to the extent they help to realise this goal that they have a value, and that this value is quite relative; and what is good for one may not be so for another, what is good at one moment may not be so at another and, consequently, every kind of dogmatism is an absurdity.

It is very easy to say, "That, that's true, now I know that it is true and I shall not think otherwise"; this is very easy, and in fact something has suddenly put you in touch with a light, you have had an experience, you have become conscious of yourself, conscious of something which transcends you and is the reality of your being, so for you it is perfect. But do not imagine that you must go from door to door, from city to city, country to country, telling people, "I proclaim the Truth", because what is true for you may not be at all good for another. What you have seen has its truth in itself — everything has its truth in itself — but the true *raison d'être* of this truth is that it has helped you to find yourself, to find the truth of your being, and it may quite possibly not help your neighbour, unless you have a considerable power of persuasion and oblige him to see things as you have seen them yourself, but this is not tremendously valuable.

When you have understood this, you will no longer say, "Why is there such a diversity in the world, why all this multiplicity, why all this confusion, why... ?" It is a confusion simply because you don't understand and things are not in their place. If things were in their place, there would be no confusion. And we come to this, that you cannot take away one atom from this world without dislocating the universe. All that is, was necessary — if it had not been necessary, it would not have been. The whole totality of things is indispensable for realising the Divine. If you took away one of these things, there would be a hole in the realisation. And I am not speaking only of material things, material points, I am speaking of all the depths. So when you say as many do, "Ah! if that were not there in the world, how fine the world would be", you are displaying your ignorance.

5 April 1951

Knowledge by Identification

Is it not possible to know the universe in its reality as it is in itself, independently of the observer or thinker?

Yes, there is a way: it is by identification. But obviously it is a means which eludes absolutely all physical methods. I think that this weakness comes solely from the method used, because one has remained in an absolutely superficial consciousness; and the phenomenon which took place the first time takes place again a second time. If you push your investigation far enough, you suddenly come to a point where your physical methods are no longer of any worth. And in fact one can know only what one is. So if you want to know the universe, you must become the universe. You cannot become the universe physically, you know; but perhaps there is a way of becoming the universe: it is in the consciousness.

If you identify your consciousness with the universal consciousness, then you know what is happening.

But that's the only way; there are no others. It is an absolute fact that one knows only what one is, and if one wants to know something, one must become that. So you see, there are many people who say, "It is impossible", but that's because they remain on a certain plane. It is obvious that if you remain only on the material plane or even on the mental plane, you cannot know the universe, because the mind is not universal; it is only a means of expression of the universe; and it is only by an essential identification that you can then know things, not from outside inwards but from inside outwards. This is not impossible. It is altogether possible. It has been done. But it can't be done with instruments, however perfected they may be. Here one must once again make something else intervene, other regions, other realities than purely material ones.[...]

One can know everything, but one must know the way. And the way is not learnt through books, it cannot be written in numbers. It is only by practising... And here then, it demands an abnegation, a consecration, a perseverance and an obstinacy — still more considerable than what the sincerest, most honest, most unselfish scientists have ever shown. But I must say that the scientific method of work is a marvellous discipline; and what is curious is that the method recommended by the Buddha for getting rid of desires and the illusion of the world is also one of the most marvellous disciplines ever known on the earth. They are at the two ends, they are both excellent; those who follow one or the other in all sincerity truly prepare themselves for yoga. A small click, somewhere, is enough to make them leave their fairly narrow point of view on one side or the other, so as to be able to enter into an integrality which will lead them to the supreme Truth and mastery.

I don't know whether ignorance is the greatest obstacle on the path of humanity... We said that it was an almost exclusively mental obstacle and that the human being is much more complex than a mental being, though he is supremely mental, for he is its new creation in the world. He represents the last possibility of Nature, and in that, naturally his mental life has taken immense proportions, because he has the pride of being the only one upon earth to have it. He does not always make a good use of it, still it is like this. But it's not here that he will find the solution. He must go beyond.

5 October 1955

Materialism and Spiritual Life

Throughout this teaching [in the Dhammapada] there is one thing to be noticed; it is this: you are never told that to live well, to think well, is the result of a struggle or of a sacrifice; on the contrary it is a delightful state which cures all suffering. At that time, the time of the Buddha, to live a spiritual life was a joy, a beatitude, the happiest state, which freed you from all the troubles of the world, all the sufferings, all the cares, making you happy, satisfied, contented.

It is the materialism of modern times that has turned spiritual effort into a hard struggle and a sacrifice, a painful renunciation of all the so-called joys of life.

This insistence on the exclusive reality of the physical world, of physical pleasures, physical joys, physical possessions, is the result of the whole materialistic tendency of human civilisation. It was unthinkable in ancient times. On the contrary, withdrawal, concentration, liberation from all material cares, consecration to the spiritual joy, that was happiness indeed.

From this point of view it is quite evident that humanity is far from having progressed; and those who were born into the world in the centres of materialistic civilisation have in their subconscient this horrible notion that only material realities are real and that to be concerned with things that are not material represents a wonderful spirit of sacrifice, an almost sublime effort. Not to be preoccupied from dawn to dusk and from dusk to dawn with all the little physical satisfactions, physical pleasures, physical sensations, physical preoccupations, is to bear evidence of a remarkable spirit. One is not aware of it, but the whole of modern civilisation is built on this conception: "Ah, what you can touch, you are sure that is true; what you can see, you are sure that is true; what you have eaten, you are sure of having eaten it; but all the rest — pooh! We are not sure whether they are not vain dreams and whether we are not giving up the real for the unreal, the substance for the shadow. After all, what are you going to gain? A few dreams! But when you have some coins in your pocket, you are sure that they are there!"

And that is everywhere, underneath everything. Scratch the appearances just a little, it is there, within your consciousness; and from time to time you hear this thing whispering within you, "Take care, don't be taken in." Indeed, it is lamentable.

We have been told that evolution is progressive and that it follows a spiral of ascending progression. I do not doubt that what one calls comfort in modern cities is a much higher degree of evolution than the comfort of the cave-man. But in ancient narratives, they always spoke of a power of foresight, of the prophetic spirit, the announcement of future events through visions, life's intimacy with something more subtle that had for the simple people of that age a more concrete reality.

Now, in those beautiful cities that are so comfortable, when one wants to condemn anything, what does one say? — "It's a dream, it is imagination."

And precisely, if a person lives in an inner perception, people look at him slightly askance and wonder whether he is altogether mentally sound. One who does not pass his time in striving for wealth or in trying to increase his comforts and well-being, to secure a good position and become an important person, a man who is not like that is mistrusted, people wonder whether he is in his right mind.

And all that is so much the stuff of the atmosphere, the content of the air you breathe, the orientation of the thoughts received from others that it seems absolutely natural. You do not feel that it is a grotesque monstrosity.

To become a little more conscious of oneself, to enter into relation with the life behind the appearances, does not seem to you to be the greatest good. When you sit in a comfortable chair, in front of a lavish meal, when you fill your stomach with delicious dishes, that certainly appears to you much more concrete and much more interesting. And if you look at the day that has passed, if you take stock of your day, if you have had some material advantage, some pleasure, a physical satisfaction, you mark it as a good day; but if you have received a good lesson from life, if it has given you a knock on your nose to tell you that you are a stupid fellow, you do not give thanks to the Grace, you say, "Oh, life is not always fun!"

When I read these ancient texts, I really have the impression that from the inner point of view, from the point of view of the true life, we have fallen back terribly and that for the acquisition of a few ingenious mechanisms, a few encouragements to physical laziness, the acquisition of instruments and gadgets that lessen the effort of living, we have renounced the reality of the inner life. It is that sense which has been lost and it needs an effort for you to think of learning the meaning of life, the purpose of existence, the goal towards which we must advance, towards which all life advances, whether you want it or not. One step towards the goal, oh! it needs so much effort to do that. And generally one thinks of it only when the outer circumstances are not pleasant.[...]

It is very unfortunate that one has to give up one thing in order to gain another. When I speak of the inner life, I am far from opposing any modern inventions, far from it, but how much these inventions have made us artificial and stupid! How much we have lost the sense of true beauty, how much we burden ourselves with useless needs!

Perhaps the time has come to continue the ascent in the curve of the spiral and now with all that this knowledge of matter has brought us, we shall be able to give to our spiritual progress a more solid basis. Strong with what we have learnt of the secrets of material Nature, we shall be able to join the two extremes and rediscover the supreme Reality in the very heart of the atom.

24 January 1958

Miracles

[Performing miracles] is a temptation that every teacher meets at each step, for the very simple reason that ordinary humanity, in a general way, not being in personal contact with the divine powers, understands nothing of what an illumined consciousness may be and asks for material proofs. It is on this demand that most religions are established and, for reasons which I may very frankly call "political", they have put at the origin of their religion a more or less considerable number of miracles as having been performed by the founders, and they have thus more or less crudely encouraged among ignorant people the taste, the necessity for seeing what they call "miracles" in order to believe in the divine power of a person. This is an extraordinary ignorance, because it is not at all necessary to have a divine power or consciousness to perform miracles. It is infinitely more easy to perform miracles with the help of small entities of the vital world who are material enough to be in touch with the physical world and act upon it, than to live in the consciousness of the higher regions and to work upon Nature only through the intermediary of all the other domains. It has been repeated over and over again to all human intellects that the proof of a being's divinity is that he can raise the dead, cure maladies, and do many other things of the same kind (except making a fool wise).* Well, I guarantee that this is not a proof; it proves only one thing, that these "Masters" are in contact with the

---

* The Mother added later: This is a Mohamedan story, I believe. As it was said that Jesus raised the dead, healed the sick, made the dumb speak, gave sight to the blind, one day an idiot was brought to him to be made intelligent, and Jesus ran away! "Why did you run away?" he was asked. "I can do everything," he answered, "except give intelligence to an idiot."

powers of the vital world and that with the help of those beings they can perform these miracles, that's all. If one relies upon that to recognise the superiority of a man, one would make a glaring mistake.

Naturally, there are other religions which are established on revelations made to their founders. These revelations are more or less happy mental transcriptions of the knowledge they received. This is already of a higher order but it is not yet a proof. And I would finally say, the human demand for proofs is not at all favourable to one's development. Because the true divine power has organised the world according to a certain plan and in this plan there was no question of things happening in an illogical way; otherwise from the very beginning the world would have been illogical and it is not so. Men imagine for the most part one of two things, either that there is a material world to which they belong, that all comes from there, all returns there and all ends there — these are the unbelievers — or, the believers, most of them, that there is something which they call "God" and then the physical world, and that this physical world is the creation of that God who knows what he is doing or does what he wants; and the confusion lies in saying that everything happens by a kind of arbitrariness, natural or supernatural.

There are very few people who know that there exists in the universe an infinite number of gradations and that each one of these gradations has its own reality, its own life, its own law, its own determinism, and that the creation did not come about "like that", by an arbitrary will, in an arbitrary way but is a deploying of consciousness and each thing has evolved as a logical result of the preceding one. I am telling you all this as simply as I can, you know, it is a very incomplete expression, but if I wanted to tell you the story exactly as it is, it would be a little difficult to make you understand. Only my conclusion I would like you to know, [...] it is this: each one of these numberless regions has its own very logical determinism — everything proceeds from cause to effect; but these worlds, although differentiated, are not separate from each other and, by numerous processes which we may study, the inner or higher worlds are in constant contact with the lower or external worlds and act upon these, so that the determinism of one changes the determinism of the other.

If you take the purely material domain, for instance, and if you notice that the material laws, the purely material laws are altered by something all of a sudden, you ought to say that it was a "miracle", because there is a rupture of the determinism of one plane through the intervention of another, but usually we do not call this a miracle. For example, when the human will intervenes and changes something, that seems to you quite natural, because you have been accustomed to it from your childhood; you remember, don't you, the example I gave you the other day: a stone falls according to the law of its own determinism, but you wish to interrupt its fall and you stretch out your hand and catch it; well you ought to call this a "miracle", but you don't because you are used to it (but a rat or a dog would perhaps call it a miracle if they could speak). And note that it is the same for what people call a "miracle"; they speak of a "miracle" because they are absolutely ignorant, unaware of the gradations between the will which wants to express itself and the plane on which it expresses itself. When they have a mental or a vital will, the thing seems quite natural to them, but when it is a question of the will of a higher world — the world of the gods or of a higher entity — which all of a sudden upsets all your little organisation, that seems to you a miracle. But it is a miracle simply because you are unable to follow the gradations by which the phenomenon took place. Therefore, the Supreme Will, that which comes from the very highest region, if you saw it in its logical action, if you were aware of it continually, it would seem to you altogether natural.

You can express this in two ways: either say, "It is quite natural, it is like this that things must happen, it is only an expression of the divine Will", or, each time you see on the material plane an intervention coming from another plane, you ought to say, "It is miraculous!" So I may say with certainty that people who want to see miracles are people who cherish their ignorance! You understand my logic, don't you? These people love their ignorance, they insist upon seeing miracles and being astounded! And that is why people who have done yoga seriously consider it altogether fatal to encourage this tendency; hence it is forbidden.

There is a "miracle" because you do not give people time to see the procedure by which you do things, you do not show them the stages.

8 February 1951

*

It is the ignorant, limited, egoistic consciousness which demands miracles. As soon as one is enlightened, one knows that everywhere and always there is miracle.

And the more faith one has in this miracle and this Grace, the more capable one becomes of seeing it, or perceiving it constantly at every place where it is. It is ignorance and lack of faith, it is blind egoism which prevents one from seeing.

23 November 1955

*

Therefore things are as one looks at them. But I have seen other things which are like this, but not very pleasant. It is from the time men have invented — not invented but discovered — and begun to play like babies with things they did not know, and have made atom bombs and other worse things still. This has truly disturbed *terribly* all these little entities* which lived indeed according to a certain rhythm which was their own, and were in the habit of commanding at least events that can be foreseen. This has disturbed them very very much, they have suffered terribly from it, and it has made them lose their heads, they no longer know what they are doing.

There was a time at the end of the War, when things had truly become *terribly* chaotic up there, they lived in a kind of absurdity; and as these unfortunate experiences continue, they have not yet come out of their panic. They are panic-stricken. Truly men play with things which they know only from outside, that is, don't know at all. They know just enough to make a wrong use of them. Anything may happen, including, alas, catastrophes which were foretold long ago. It may happen... It depends... on what will intervene.

30 November 1955

*

Mother, can physical science by its progress open to occultism?

---

* Conscious entities of the vital plane who are behind the forces of Nature and influence such things as the weather.

It does not call it "occultism", that's all. It is only a question of words.... They are making sensational discoveries which people with occult knowledge already knew thousands of years ago! They have made a long circuit and come to the same thing.

With the most recent discoveries in medicine, in the applied sciences, for instance, they are contacting in this way, with a wonder-struck interest, things which were known to certain sages a very, very long time ago. And then they present all this before you as new marvels — but indeed they are rather old, their marvels!

They will end up by practising occultism without knowing that they are doing so! For, in fact, as soon as one draws close, however slightly, to the truth of things and when one is sincere in one's search, not satisfied by mere appearances, when one really wants to find something and goes deep, penetrates behind appearances, then one begins to advance towards the truth of things; and as one comes closer to it, well, one finds again the same knowledge that others who began by going within have brought back from their inner discoveries.

Only the method and the path are different but the thing discovered will be the same, because there are not two things to be found, there is only one. It will necessarily be the same. It all depends on the path one follows; some go fast, others slowly, some go straight, others, as I said, go a long way round — and what labour! How they have laboured!... Besides, it is very respectable.

10 September 1958

"Chance"

What do we understand by the term "chance"? Chance can only be the opposite of order and harmony. There is only one true harmony and that is the supramental — the reign of Truth, the expression of the Divine Law. In the Supermind, therefore, chance has no place. But in the lower Nature the supreme Truth is obscured: hence there is an absence of that divine unity of purpose and action which alone can constitute order. Lacking this unity, the domain of lower Nature is governed by what we may call chance — that is to say, it is a field in which various conflicting forces intermix, having no single definite aim. Whatever arises out of such a rushing together of forces is a result of confusion, dissonance and falsehood — a product of chance. Chance is not merely a conception to cover our ignorance of the causes at work; it is a description of the uncertain *melée* of the lower Nature which lacks the calm one-pointedness of the divine Truth. The world has forgotten its divine origin and become an arena of egoistic energies; but it is still possible for it to open to the Truth, call it down by its aspiration and bring about a change in the whirl of chance. What men regard as a mechanical sequence of events, owing to their own mental associations, experiences and generalisations, is really manipulated by subtle agencies each of which tries to get its own will done. The world has got so subjected to these undivine agencies that the victory of the Truth cannot be won except by fighting for it. It has no right to it: it has to gain it by disowning the falsehood and the perversion, an important part of which is the facile notion that, since all things owe their final origin to the Divine, all their immediate activities also proceed directly from it. The fact is that here in the lower Nature the Divine is veiled by a cosmic Ignorance and what takes place does not proceed directly from the divine knowledge. That everything is equally the will of God is a very convenient suggestion of the hostile influences which would have the creation stick as tightly as possible to the disorder and ugliness to which it has been reduced.

1930-1931

CHAPTER 13

Occultism

The Capacity for Occultism

[Occultism] is a domain about which I have so far refrained from speaking to you, for one must be already very conscious of oneself, have a good mastery over one's reflexes and be above all fear, precisely — above all possibility of fear, in order to be able to enter upon it. It is a knowledge which in the modern world is hardly recognised as scientific, but it *is* scientific in the sense that it has exact processes and that if the circumstances are correctly reproduced, the same results are obtained. It is a progressive science and one can devote oneself to it, can make quite a regular progress, as logical as in all the sciences that are acknowledged as such in modern times. But this one concerns a reality or certain realities which do not belong to the most material domain. One needs special capacities and a special development to be conscious in that domain, for it escapes our ordinary senses.

We have subtle senses; even as we have a physical body, we have other more subtle bodies which also have senses, and much more refined senses, much more precise and much more powerful than our physical senses. But naturally, as it is not customary in modern education to work in these domains, these things generally escape our ordinary knowledge. Yet children spontaneously live a great deal in this domain. They see things which are as real for them as physical things, they speak about them — and they are usually told that they are stupid because they speak of things others don't see but which are as true for them, as tangible and real as what can be seen by everyone. Their dreams have an intensity and a capital importance in their life, and it is only with intensive mental growth that those capacities diminish. Now, there are people who have the good luck to be born with a spontaneous development, with inner senses, and nothing can prevent them from remaining awake. If these people meet in good time someone who can help them in a methodical development, they can become very interesting instruments for the study and discovery of this occult world.

In all ages there have been initiatory schools which took up these particularly talented people and educated them in this kind of science. These schools were always more or less secret or hidden, for ordinary men are quite intolerant of those capacities which are beyond them — and disturb them. But there were fine periods in human history when these schools were recognised and much appreciated and respected, as in ancient Egypt, ancient Chaldea, ancient India, and even partially in Greece and Rome. There were always schools of initiation, even in mediaeval Europe, but there they had to be very carefully hidden, for they were pursued and persecuted by the official Christian religion, and if perchance it was discovered that such and such men or women were practising these occult sciences, they were tied to the stake and burnt alive as sorcerers!... In our times this knowledge is almost lost; there are only a very few people who have it; but with mental growth the intolerance also has gone. People don't like these things very much — they are disturbed, annoyed by them — but still they are obliged to admit that these things are not crimes and people practising occultism are no longer burnt at the stake or imprisoned.

Only, there are many people who claim to know but there are very few who do know. In any case, before entering upon this study, one must have, as I told you at the beginning, a very great self-mastery, must have attained a kind of abnegation, a self-forgetfulness, an egolessness, a disinterestedness and sense of sacrifice which enables one to practise this without any danger. For, if you keep all egoistic or passionate movements, full of desires, you are sure, in the practice of this science, to meet with accidents which may have fatal consequences. As I said at the beginning, the *absolutely* indispensable condition is to have an intrepidity which does not allow any fear to enter into you. For this has been very often said, and it is quite true, that when you enter the invisible realm, the first things you meet are literally terrifying. If you have no fear, there is no danger, but the least fear puts you into danger. So, before anybody at all was allowed to practise this science, for a very long time, sometimes for years, the novice was submitted to a discipline which gave him the assurance that he could practise it without experiencing the least fear and without any danger. That is why, my children, I have never spoken to you about it.[...]

(The Mother tells the story of a Danish painter to whom she taught occultism. In an occult experience he saw a formidable tiger coming towards him. As he had no fear, the tiger "began to grow smaller and smaller and smaller and — it became a tiny little cat!")

What does the tiger represent?

It was probably... That day he had become angry with somebody, he had lost his temper and entertained bad thoughts; he had hoped that something very unpleasant would happen to this person. Now, in occultism there is the "rebound". You send out a bad thought, it returns to you as an attack. That is exactly one of the reasons why you must have a complete control over your feelings, sensations, thoughts, for if you become angry with someone or think badly of him, or if, still worse, you wish him ill, well, in your very dream you see this person coming with an extreme violence to attack you. Then, if you do not know these things, you say, "Why, I was right in having bad thoughts against him!" But in fact, it is not at all that. It is your own thought that comes back to you. And the person may be absolutely unaware of all that has happened, for — and this is one of the commonest laws in occultism — if you make a formation, for instance a mental formation that an accident or something unpleasant should happen to a certain person and you send out this formation, if it so happens that this person is in a very high state of consciousness, does not at all wish anything bad, is quite indifferent and disinterested in the affair, the formation will come up against his atmosphere and instead of entering will rebound upon the one who has made it.

3 March 1954

*

Everybody practises occultism without knowing that he does. Everybody has this power spontaneously but doesn't know he has it. It may be a very slight one, like a pin-head; it may be as vast as the Earth or even the universe. But you cannot live without practising occultism, only you don't know it.[...]

When you think — I have explained this to you I don't know how many times — when you think, you are practising occultism. Only, you don't know it. When you are thinking of someone, some part of you is automatically in contact with this person, and if to your thought is added a will that this person may be like this or like that or do this or that or understand this or that — whatever it may be — well, you are practising occultism, only you don't know it.... There are people who do this with power, and when they have a strong thought it manifests and is realised. There are people in whom it is very feeble and they do not obtain many results. It depends on the power of your thought and also on your power of concentration. But this kind of occultism everybody practises without even knowing it. So the difference from someone who really practises occultism is that he knows he is doing it and perhaps how he does it.

18 September 1957

*

Sweet Mother, Sri Aurobindo is speaking about occult endeavour here and says that those who don't have the capacity must wait till it is given to them. Can't they get it through practice?

No. That is, if it is latent in someone, it can be developed by practice. But if one doesn't have occult power, he may try for fifty years, he won't get anywhere. Everybody cannot have occult power. It is as though you were asking whether everybody could be a musician, everybody could be a painter, everybody could... Some can, some can't. It is a question of temperament.

What is the difference between occultism and mysticism?

They are not at all the same thing.

Mysticism is a more or less emotive relation with what one senses to be a divine power — that kind of highly emotional, affective, very intense relation with something invisible which is or is taken for the Divine. That is mysticism.

Occultism is exactly what he [Sri Aurobindo] has said: it is the knowledge of invisible forces and the power to handle them. It is a science. It is altogether a science. I always compare occultism with chemistry, for it is the same kind of knowledge as the knowledge of chemistry for material things. It is a knowledge of invisible forces, their different vibrations, their interrelations, the combinations which can be made by bringing them together and the power one can exercise over them. It is absolutely scientific; and it ought to be learnt like a science; that is, one cannot practise occultism as something emotional or something vague and imprecise. You must work at it as you would do at chemistry, and learn all the rules or find them if there is nobody to teach you. But it is at some risk to yourself that you can find them. There are combinations here as explosive as certain chemical combinations.

Is occultism necessary in this life?

In this life? That depends upon what one wants to do. You mean in the life of yoga? Not at all necessary. And besides, as he [Sri Aurobindo] says, there are many who are not gifted, who don't have the faculty. Lots of people, as soon as they have the least experience, the least experience, for instance when they just begin to come out of their body, are panic-stricken, and this indeed is something very difficult to cure. It can be cured if one has a strong will and a great self-mastery. But many people are not able to dissociate their states of being. If they dissociate them, something goes wrong, their body suffers; while there are others who go out, take a walk, return. For them this is quite natural. Usually, those who are interested in this — unless it is only a kind of mental curiosity — are also gifted. They may not know it but they can be taught.

But these things have to be practised with precaution. For instance — I am going to give you an example: as soon as one goes out of the body, no matter how slightly, and even just mentally, well, that part of the mind which controls the functioning goes out; and the automatic side of the mind which makes or produces movements or glandular secretions, that whole automatic side, you see, remains without the protection and control of the conscious, thinking part. Well, in the atmosphere there are always numerous little entities, very tiny, usually originating from human disintegrations, which are like physical microbes, some kind of microbes of the vital. They are more visible and have a will of their own. One can't say they are wicked but they are full of mischief. They like to have a good time and enjoy themselves at people's expense. So, as soon as they see that you are not sufficiently protected, they get hold of the automatic mind and bring upon you all sorts of quite unpleasant things — as, for example, some people swallow their tongue when in a trance; this suffocates them if they don't take care. Others bite their tongue; sometimes this hurts very badly. All sorts of things like this may happen to you — which means that normally you should never enter into a trance without having somebody nearby to watch over you, and not only watch just physically but... watch with the conscious power of preventing these little entities from getting hold of your nervous centres which are not protected by the conscious Presence. This is a general rule.

There are greater dangers than that. When one goes out of the body materially — and nothing but the contact of a link remains, you understand, it is a kind of link like a thread of light joining the being that has gone out with the one that remains behind — if this link is protected, nothing happens. But if it is not protected, there may be adverse forces, not only full of mischief but with much ill-will also, which could come and cut it. And then, once it is cut, you may try as hard as you like, but you cannot get back into the body.

One dies?

Yes, after a while. Which means that all this is not at all a joke, you understand, or just a matter of having fun or something one can do simply to amuse oneself. It must be done in the right way and in the required conditions, and with great care. And then, one thing is *absolutely* essential, absolutely: you must not touch this occult science if you have the least fear in you. For instance, if in your dreams you meet terrible things and get frightened, you should not practise occultism. If, on the other hand, the most frightful dreams you have leave you absolutely calm, and even at times amused and very much interested, if you can handle all that and know how to get out of the difficulty in every circumstance, then that means you have the ability and can do it. Some people are very brave warriors in their dreams. When they meet enemies, they know how to fight; they know not only how to defend themselves, but also to conquer; they are full of ardour, energy, courage; these indeed are the true candidates for occultism. But those who rush back into their body as fast as a rat into its hole, they should surely not touch it.

And then, you must also have an infinite patience; because just as it takes many years to learn how to handle the different chemical substances, just as you have to work for long periods without getting any visible results when you want to discover the least thing that's new, so in occultism you may try for years together and not have the least experience. And that becomes very monotonous and hardly interesting; and there is always in man that kind of physical mind, practical and positive, which keeps on telling you, "Why are you trying? You see quite well there is nothing in it, these are all stories people tell you; why are you working for nothing? You are wasting your time. There is nothing at all in it, it is all imagination." It is very difficult to keep one's conviction and faith when there is nothing upon which to found them.

30 June 1954

The Occult World

Well, the occult world is not one single region where everything is mixed, which only becomes occult because we can't see it. The occult world is a gradation of regions, one could perhaps say, of more and more ethereal or subtle regions, anyway, those farther and farther removed in their nature from the physical materiality we ordinarily see. And each one of these domains is a world in itself, having its forms and inhabited by beings with a density, one might say, analogous to that of the domain in which they live. Just as in the physical world we are of the same materiality as the physical world, so in the vital world, in the mental world, in the overmind world and in the supramental world — and in many others, infinite others — there are beings which have a form whose substance is similar to the one of that world. This means that if you are able to enter consciously into that world with the part of your being which corresponds to that domain, you can move there quite objectively, as in the material world.

And there, there are as many, and even many more things to see and observe than in our poor little material world, which belongs to only *one* zone of this infinite gradation. You meet all sorts of things in these domains, and you need to make a study as profound, perhaps still more profound than in the physical world, to be able to know what is happening there, to have relations with the beings who live there.

It is obvious that as one goes farther, as it were, from the material world, the forms and consciousness of those beings are of a purity, beauty and perfection much higher than our ordinary physical forms. It is only in the nearest vital world, the one which is, so to say, mixed with our material life — though it lies beyond it and there is a zone where the vital is no longer mixed with the material world — of that material vital one can say that in some of its aspects it is even uglier than things here, for it is filled with a bad will which is not counter-balanced by the presence of the psychic being which, in the physical world, amends, corrects, puts right, directs this bad will. But it is rather a limited zone and, as soon as one goes beyond it, one can find and meet things that are not favourable to human life, beings not on the same scale as human existence, but having their own beauty and grandeur, with whom one may establish relations which may become quite pleasant and even useful.

Only, as I have already told you, it is not very prudent to venture into these domains without a previous initiation and, above all, a purifi-cation of nature which prevents you from entering there all weighed down and deformed by your desires, your passions, egoisms, fears and weaknesses. Before undertaking these activities one needs a com-plete preparation of self-purification and widening of the conscious-ness which is absolutely indispensable.

In these invisible worlds there are also regions which are the re-sult of human mental formations. One can find there all one wants. In fact, one very often finds there exactly what one expects to find. There are hells, there are paradises, there are purgatories. There are all sorts of things in accordance with the different religions and their concep-tions. These things have only a very relative existence, but with a relativity similar to that of material things here; that is to say, for someone who finds himself there, they are entirely real and their effects quite tangible. One needs an inner liberation, a wideness of the consciousness and a contact with a deeper and higher truth to be able to escape from the illusion of their reality. But this is something almost similar to what happens here: human beings here are mostly convinced that the only reality is the physical reality — the reality of what one can touch, can see — and for them, all that cannot be seen, cannot be touched, cannot be felt, is after all, problematical; well, what happens there is an identical phenomenon. People who at the moment of death are convinced, for one reason or another, that they are going to paradise or maybe to hell, *do find* themselves there after their death; and for them it is truly a paradise or a hell. And it is extremely difficult to make them come out of it and go to a place which is more true, more real.

So it is difficult to speak of all these worlds, these innumerable worlds, in a few minutes. It is a knowledge which needs a lived experience of many years, thoroughly systematic, and which requires, as I said, an inner preparation absolutely indispensable, to make it harmless.

We all get the chance to have a little contact — very partial, very superficial — with these worlds in our dreams. And the study of dreams itself already demands much time and care, and in itself may constitute a preparation for a deeper study of the invisible worlds.

11 July 1956

*

Mother, can we go to the other planets by occult means?

Ah! Yes, one can go everywhere. What prevents us from going? One goes everywhere. Only, you see, we must know that it is not the physical body which goes; it is the most material thing... the most material vital; and this is already very difficult.

Usually it is the mental part of the vital which goes out; not the mind, the vital. For short distances one can go out from his body with the subtle physical, and in these cases one sees things materially as they are. But one can't go long distances. There are practical reasons, but above all there is the reason of safety; because if one goes too far with the subtle physical, the body is not only in a trance, it is in a cataleptic state, and then, unless it is guarded by someone who has a very profound knowledge and a great power, this can turn out badly. Therefore, for these long journeys it is usually the most subtle part of the vital (which corresponds to a kind of mental consciousness of the vital), which goes out.

So one sees everything which has a similar quality. But supposing there is something very material, one doesn't see it as it is. So one can't say with certainty, "It is like this or like that." One can say, "I saw this," that's all. But one can't recount stories like those in the papers about what is happening on the moon or Jupiter or Venus. One can have an experience and know certain things but usually they are things of a more psychological nature.

However, if it is in order to know whether there are some beings there, I don't think there's any place in the universe where there aren't beings, because that's the very principle of this universe: individual creations. Everywhere there are individual creations but they have different densities. Most of them are invisible except to those with a similar density, and only those who have the capacity of coming out of their bodies and going for a stroll can see these things. But so long as you use these eyes you can't see very much.

Such a limited field of vision! In fact, when you think of it, such an absolutely ridiculous limitation! The field of our sense experience has an absolutely ridiculous limitation; while in the mind, if you think of someone or something, a city or a place, you are there immediately, instantaneously, you see. And you are there — it is not that you are not there, you are there, and you can have so precise a mental contact that you can have a conversation, ask questions and receive answers, on condition that the other person is fairly sensitive. Why, this is something which happens constantly, constantly. Only, you must have a little knowledge, naturally, for otherwise you don't even understand what is happening.

18 May 1955

The Practice of Magic

Sweet Mother, what is white magic?

What we call "white magic" is a beneficial magic and "black magic" is a harmful magic. But in fact these are mere words, they have no meaning.

Magic?... It is a knowledge that has been reduced to purely material formulas. They are some kind of words or numbers or combinations of words and numbers, which, if they are simply pronounced or written, even by someone who has no inner power, must act. In occultism, this is what corresponds to chemical formulas in science. You see, in science you have chemical formulas for combining certain elements and producing others from them; even if you do not have any mental or vital or even physical power, if you just follow to the letter the formula you have, you obtain the required result — it is enough simply to have a memory. Well, the same thing has been tried in occultism, making combinations of sounds, letters, numbers, words, which, by their inherent qualities, have the power to obtain a certain result. In this way, any fool, if he learns this and does exactly what he is told, obtains — or believes he will obtain — the result he wants. While... let us take the mantra, for instance, which is a form of occultism; unless the mantra is given by a guru and the guru transmits his occult or spiritual power to you with the mantra, you may repeat your mantra thousands of times, it will have no effect.

That is to say, in *true* occultism, one must have the quality, the ability, the inner gift in order to use it, and that is the safeguard. True occultism cannot be practised by any fool. And this is no longer magic — neither white magic nor black nor golden — it is not magic at all, it is a spiritual power which must be acquired by long discipline; and finally, it is given to you only by a divine grace.

This means that as soon as one draws near the Truth, one is safe from all charlatanism, all pretension and falsehood. Of this I have had numerous and extremely conclusive proofs. And so someone who has the true occult power possesses at the same time, by the strength of this inner truth, the power to undo any magic, white or black or whatever colour it may be, simply by applying a drop of that truth, one might say. There is nothing that can resist that power. And this is very well known to those who practise magic, for they always take very great care, in all countries but especially in India, never to try out any of their formulas against yogis and saints, because they know that these formulas which they send out with their little mechanical, very superficial power, will go and strike, like a ball on a wall, the true power that protects one who leads a spiritual life, and quite naturally their formula will rebound and fall back on them.

The yogi or saint doesn't need to do anything, he doesn't even have to want to protect himself: it is something automatic.

He is in a state of consciousness and inner power which automatically protects him from everything that is inferior. Naturally, he can also use his power deliberately to protect others. This rebounding of the bad formation from his atmosphere automatically protects him, but if this bad formation is made against someone he is protecting or simply someone who asks for his help, then he can, by a movement of his own atmosphere, his own aura, surround the person who is exposed to the evil magic spells, and the rebounding process acts in the same way and causes the bad formation to fall back quite naturally on the one who made it. But in this case the conscious will of the yogi or saint or sage is needed. He has to be informed about what has happened and he must decide to intervene.

That is the difference between true knowledge and magic.

10 September 1958

*

Sweet Mother, I have heard that the magicians who use occult powers for their work suffer a great deal after their death. Is it true?

What sort of magicians are you speaking about? Any kind?

Those who have occult powers and use them for their personal interest? You mean these?

Yes.

I don't know whether they suffer after their death or lose their consciousness, but in any case, obviously they are not in any state of peace or happiness, that's absolutely certain. For it is a kind of absolute rule from the spiritual point of view: it is by an inner discipline and by consecration to the Divine that the powers come to you. But if with your aspiration, your discipline and consecration, an ambition is mixed up, that is, an intention to obtain powers, then if they come to you it is almost like a curse. Usually they don't come to you, but something vital which tries to imitate them comes to you with adverse influences which put you entirely under the domination of beings who give you powers simply with the intention of making use of you, using you to do all the work they have the intention of doing, and to create all the disorder they want to create. And when they find that you have served them enough and are no longer good for anything, they just destroy you. They may not be able to destroy you physically because they don't always have the power to do it, but they destroy you mentally, vitally and in your consciousness, and after that you are good for nothing, even before dying. And after death, as you are entirely under their influence, the first thing they do is to swallow you up, because this is their way of making use of people — to swallow them. So it cannot be a very pleasant experience. It is a very, very, very dangerous game.

But everywhere, in all the teachings, in all the disciplines, in all ages, the same thing has been repeated: that one must never intermingle ambition and personal interest with the sadhana, otherwise he is inviting trouble. So it is not only a particular case, it is all the instances of this kind which have fatal consequences.

Sweet Mother, are there any magicians who do not work magic for their personal interest?

You mean magical rites? Because, you see, you must not mix up magic with occultism.

Occultism is a science and it is the knowledge of invisible forces and the capacity to handle them, as one has the capacity of handling material forces if one has studied them scientifically.

Magic: these are different kinds of processes which were fixed probably by people who had a certain knowledge, and still more a certain power of vital formation. These things can be learnt without having any special capacity, that is, someone who has no inner power can learn this as he learns chemistry, for example, or mathematics. It is one of the things which are learnt like that, it is not a thing one acquires. So it doesn't itself carry any special virtues except the same kind of qualities as those one learns through chemical manipulations. You may reproduce these manipulations, but if you are an intelligent and capable being, you can by the help of these manipulations obtain an interesting and useful result, and in any case, be sheltered from all danger; whereas if you are an idiot, misfortunes may come to you. It is something similar.

With the help of magical formulas one may produce a certain result, but this result is necessarily limited and has no particular interest for those who, through their inner development, spontaneously receive powers of which they have a higher knowledge, not a mechanical one. It is not for someone who is truly a yogi; it has no interest except that of curiosity. It is interesting only for people who are precisely not yogis and who want to have certain powers which, in fact, they have in a very limited way — it is always limited.

What is special about it is that it has a direct action upon matter; while usually, apart from some rare exceptions, with people who have spiritual powers, yogic powers, it acts through the intermediary of the mental forces usually — either spiritual or mental forces — sometimes of the vital forces (more rarely), but not directly upon matter, except naturally with those who have done yoga in matter, but these are exceptional cases of which one doesn't speak. These things put into motion certain small entities which are usually the result of the decomposition of human beings and yet have a sufficient contact with the material world to be able to act there. But anyhow, if the action is of a lower order, the power is of a lower order, and it is something almost repugnant for one who is truly in relation with the higher forces.

To act in order to accomplish a work with the spontaneous powers of spiritual realisation, that is well understood. But one may say that everybody does that, because just the fact of thinking means that you are acting invisibly; and according to the power of your thought your action is more or less wide-spread. But to use small magical formulas to obtain a result is something that has no true relation with the spiritual life. From the spiritual point of view it appears even surprising that these things can always prove effective, because for each case the need is different; and how putting together certain words and making certain signs can always have an effect seems surprising.

When one wants to act spiritually and for some reason or other it is necessary, for example, to formulate words, the words come spontaneously and are exactly the words needed for the particular occasion. But things written beforehand which one repeats mechanically most of the time, without even knowing what one is saying and why one is saying it — it is difficult to see how this can always work. There is bound to be a great imprecision in the action. And one thing is certain, that this same formula cannot have exactly the same effect, and that one factor is indispensable for it to take effect: fear. The first thing is a kind of fear, a fright created in the person against whom the magic is done; for if he has no fear I am quite sure that it cannot have any effect or has so ridiculously small an effect that it's not worth speaking about it.

What opens the door to the action of these forces is fear, a kind of apprehension, the feeling that something is going to happen; and it is these vibrations of fear which put out certain forces from you, forces which give these entities the power to act.

Sweet Mother, there are people who do hypnotism. Then, when they always practise it on the same person, does that person fall ill after a while?

Not necessarily ill. It depends on the kind of hypnotism and hypnotiser. Not necessarily ill. One thing is certain, that this person loses his personal will, that the hypnotiser's will takes the place of the personal will, otherwise it would not work. But not necessarily ill, terribly dependent! It creates almost a kind of slavery.

3 August 1955

The Stone-Throwing Incident

There was a time we were living in the Guest House.* Sri Aurobindo lived on the first floor, in the room right at the end which is now the meditation-room of the children's boarding. I believe there are two rooms side by side, one used to be a bathroom but is now an ordinary room, and a room next to it which was mine — the bathroom and another room. Sri Aurobindo was on one side.

How many of us were there in that house?... Amrita was there (*turning to the disciple*), weren't you, Amrita, do you remember that day? (*Laughter*) We had a cook called Vatel. This cook was rather bad-tempered and didn't like being reproved about his work. Moreover, he was in contact with some Musulmans who had, it seems, magical powers — they had a book of magic and the ability to practise magic. One day, this cook had done something very bad and had been scolded — I don't know if any of you knew Datta, it was Datta who had scolded him — and he was furious. He had threatened us, saying, "You will see, you will be compelled to leave this house." We had taken no notice of it.

Two or three days later, I think, someone came and told me that stones had fallen in the courtyard — a few stones, three or four: bits of brick. We wondered who was throwing stones from the next house. We did exactly what we forbid children to do: we went round on the walls and roofs to see if we could find someone or the stones or something — we found nothing.

That happened, I believe, between four and five in the afternoon. As the day declined, the number of stones increased. The next day, there were still more. They started striking specially the door of the kitchen and one of them struck Datta's arm as she was going across the courtyard. The number increased very much. The interest was growing. And as the interest grew, it produced a kind of effect of multiplication! And the stones began falling in several directions at the same time, in places where there were neither doors nor windows; there was a staircase, but it had no opening in those days: there was only a small

---

* Sri Aurobindo lived in the building known as the Guest House between 1913 and September 1922. The incident related by Mother here occurred in December 1921.

bull's-eye. And the stones were falling on the staircase this way (*vertical gesture*); if they had come through the bull's-eye, they would have come like this (*slantwise movement*), but they were falling straight down. So, I think everyone began to become truly interested. I must tell you that this Vatel had informed us that he was ill and for the last two days — since the stones had started falling — he hadn't come. But he had left with us his under-cook, a young boy of about thirteen or fourteen, quite fat, somewhat lifeless and a little quiet, perhaps a little stupid. And we noticed that when this boy moved around, wherever he went the stones increased. The young men who were there* — Amrita among them — shut the boy up in a room, with all the doors and windows closed.[...] And there was the boy sitting there inside and the stones began falling, with all the doors and windows closed! And more and more fell, and finally the boy was wounded in the leg. Then they started feeling the thing was going too far.

I was with Sri Aurobindo: quietly we were working, meditating together. The boys cast a furtive glance to see what was going on and began warning us, for it was perhaps time to tell us that the thing was taking pretty serious proportions. I understood immediately what the matter was.

I must tell you that we had made an attempt earlier to exhaust all possibilities of an ordinary, physical explanation. We had called in the police, informed them that there was somebody throwing stones at us, and they wanted very much to come and see what was happening. So a policeman — who was a fine fellow — immediately told us, "Oh! you have Vatel as your cook. Yes, yes, we know what it is!" He had a loaded pistol and stood waiting there in the courtyard — not a stone! I was on the terrace with Sri Aurobindo; I said to Sri Aurobindo, "That's a bit too bad, we call the police and just then the stones stop falling! But that is very annoying, in this way he will think we haven't told the truth, for no stones are falling." Instantaneously the stones began falling again. (*Laughter*)

You should note that the stones were falling quite a long way off from the terrace and not one of them came anywhere near us.**

* Sri Aurobindo's early disciples.
** Near Sri Aurobindo and the Mother.

So the policeman said, "It's not worthwhile, my staying here, I know what it is, it is Vatel who has done this against you, I am going."

It was after this that we made the experiment of shutting up the boy, and the stones began to fall in the closed room and I was informed that the boy had been wounded. Then I said, "All right, send the boy out of the house immediately. Send him to another house, anywhere, and let him be looked after, but don't keep him here, and then, that's all. Keep quiet and don't be afraid." I was in the room with Sri Aurobindo and I thought, "We'll see what it is." I went into meditation and gave a little call. I said, "Let us see, who is throwing stones at us now? You must come and tell us who is throwing stones."... I saw three little entities of the vital, those small entities which have no strength and just enough consciousness confined to one action — it is nothing at all; but these entities are at the service of people who practise magic. When people practise magic, they order them to come and they are compelled to obey. There are signs, there are words. So, they came, they were frightened — they were terribly frightened! I said, "But why do you fling stones like that? What does it mean, this bad joke?" They replied, "We are compelled, we are compelled... (*Laughter*) It is not our fault, we have been ordered to do it, it is not our fault."

I really felt so much like laughing but still I kept a serious face and told them, "Well, you must stop this, you understand!" Then they told me, "Don't you want to keep us? We shall do all that you ask." "Ah!" I thought, "let us see, this is perhaps going to be interesting." I said to them, "But what can you do?" — "We know how to throw stones." (*Laughter*) — "That doesn't interest me at all, I don't want to throw stones at anyone... but could you perchance bring me flowers? Can you bring me some roses?" Then they looked at one another in great dismay and answered, "No, we are not made for that, we don't know how to do it." I said, "I don't need you, go away, and take care specially never to come back, for otherwise it will be disastrous!" They ran away and never came back.

There was one thing I had noticed: it was only at the level of the roof that the stones were seen — from the roof downwards, we saw the stones; just till the roof, above it there were no stones. This meant that it was like an automatic formation. In the air nothing could be seen: they materialised in the atmosphere of the house and fell.

And to complete the movement, the next morning — all this happened in the evening — the next morning I came down to pay a visit to the kitchen — there were pillars in the kitchen — and upon one of the pillars I found some signs with numbers as though made with a bit of charcoal, very roughly drawn — I don't remember the signs now — and also words in Tamil. Then I rubbed out everything carefully and made an invocation, and so it was finished, the comedy was over.

However, not quite. Vatel's daughter was the *ayah* in the house, the maid-servant. She came early in the afternoon in a state of intense fright saying, "My father is in the hospital, he is dying; this morning something happened to him; suddenly he felt very ill and he is dying, he has been taken to the hospital, I am terribly frightened." I knew what it was. I went to Sri Aurobindo and said to him, "You know, Vatel is in the hospital, he is dying." Then Sri Aurobindo looked at me, he smiled: "Oh, just for a few stones!" (*Laughter*)

That very evening Vatel was cured. But he never started anything again.

How could the stones be seen?

That's what is remarkable. There are beings that have the power of dematerialising and rematerialising objects. These were quite ordinary pieces of bricks, but these pieces materialised only in the field where the magic acted. The magic was practised for this house, especially for its courtyard, and the action of vital forces worked only there. That was why when I sent away the boy and he went to another house, not a single stone hit him any more. The magical formation was made specially for this house, and the stones materialised in the courtyard. And as it was something specially directed against Datta, she was hit on her arm.

There was yet something else.... Ah, yes! We came to know later to which magician Vatel had gone. He had gone to a magician who, it seems, is very well known here and he had said that he wanted definitely to make us leave that house — I don't know why. He was furious. And so he asked the magician to make stones fall there. The magician told him, "But that's the house Sri Aurobindo lives in!" He said, "Yes." — "Ah! no, I am not going to meddle in this business; you manage it, I am not getting involved." Then Vatel insisted very much; he even promised him a greater reward, a little more money. The magician said, "Well, look here; we are going to make a rule: in a circle of twenty-five metres around Sri Aurobindo" — I think he said twenty or twenty-five metres — "the stones will not fall. Always there will have to be twenty-five metres' distance between the stones and Sri Aurobindo." And he arranged his order of magic in this way. And that was why never did a single stone come anywhere near us, never. They fell at the other end of the courtyard.

They know how to do all that, it is written in their books. These are words and ceremonies having a certain power. Naturally, those who do that must have a vital force. A vital force is necessary — a little mental force also, not much, even very little — but quite a strong vital power to control these little entities, govern them. And these people rule them precisely through fear, for they have the power to dissolve them, so these entities fear this very much. But upon all these formations, all these entities, it is enough to put simply one drop of the true, pure light, the pure white light — the true, pure light which is the supreme light of construction — you put one drop upon them: they dissolve as though there had been nothing at all there. And yet this is not a force of destruction; it is a force of construction but it is so alien to their nature that they disappear. It is this they feared, for I had called them by showing them this white light; I had told them, "Look, here is this! Come." But their offer was touching: "Oh! we shall do everything you want." I said, "Good, what can you do?" — "Throw stones!"

10 March 1954

Twelve Senses

*What are the twelve senses?**

We are granted five, aren't we? In any case, there is one other which,

* In a previous conversation the Mother said that a fully developed physical being has not five but twelve senses.

precisely, has a relation with consciousness. I don't know if you have ever been told this, but a person who is blind, for instance, who does not see, can become aware of an object at some distance through a kind of perception which is not touch for he does not feel it, which is not vision for he does not see, but which is a contact — something that enables him to make a contact without hearing, seeing or touching. This is one of the most developed senses apart from those we habitually use. There is another sense, a sort of sense of proximity: when one comes close to a thing, one feels it as if one had contacted it. Another sense, which is also physical, puts you in touch with events at a great distance; it is a physical sense for it belongs to the physical world, it is not purely mental: there is a sensation. Some people have a sort of sensation of contact with what is happening at a very great distance. You must not forget that in the physical consciousness there are several levels; there is a physical vital and a physical mind which are not solely corporeal. Foresight on the material plane is also one of the physical senses.... We have, then, something that sees at a short distance, something that sees at a long distance and something that sees ahead; this already makes three. These are a sort of improvement of the senses we have; as for instance, hearing at a great distance — there are people who can hear noises at a great distance, who can smell at a great distance. It is a kind of perfecting of these senses.

22 March 1951

Indications from Books

Once or twice, as a game, you took one of your books or Sri Aurobindo's and opened a page at random, and read out a sentence. Can these sentences give one a sign or an indication? What should we do to get a true answer?

Everybody can do it. It is done in this way: you concentrate. Now, it depends on what you want. If you have an inner problem and want the solution, you concentrate on this problem; if you want to know the condition you are in, which you are not aware of — if you want to get some light on the state you are in, you just come forward with simplicity and ask for the light. Or else, quite simply, if you are curious to know what the invisible knowledge has to tell you, you remain silent and still for a moment and then open the book. I always used to recommend taking a paper-knife, because it is thinner; while you are concentrated you insert it in the book and with the tip indicate something. Then, if you know how to concentrate, that is to say, if you really do it with an aspiration to have an answer, it always comes.

For, in books of this kind (*Mother shows* The Synthesis of Yoga), books of revelation, there is always an accumulation of forces — at least of higher mental forces, and most often of spiritual forces of the highest knowledge. Every book, on account of the words it contains, is like a small accumulator of these forces. People don't know this, for they don't know how to make use of it, but it is so. In the same way, in every picture, photograph, there is an accumulation, a small accumulation representative of the force of the person whose picture it is, of his nature and, if he has powers, of his powers. Now, you, when you are sincere and have an aspiration, you emanate a certain vibration, the vibration of your aspiration which goes and meets the corresponding force in the book, and it is a higher consciousness which gives you the answer.

Everything is contained potentially. Each element of a whole potentially contains what is in the whole. It is a little difficult to explain, but you will understand with an example: when people want to practise magic, if they have a bit of nail or hair, it is enough for them, because within this, potentially, there is all that is in the being itself. And in a book there is potentially — not expressed, not manifest — the knowledge which is in the person who wrote the book. Thus, Sri Aurobindo represented a totality of comprehension and knowledge and power; and every one of his books is at once a symbol and a representation. Every one of his books contains symbolically, potentially, what is in him. Therefore, if you concentrate on the book, you can, through the book, go back to the source. And even, by passing through the book, you will be able to receive much more than what is just in the book.

There is always a way of reading and understanding what one reads, which gives an answer to what you want. It is not just a chance or an amusement, nor is it a kind of diversion. You may do it just "like that", and then nothing at all happens to you, you have no reply and it is not interesting. But if you do it seriously, if seriously your aspiration tries to concentrate on this instrument — it is like a battery, isn't it, which contains energies — if it tries to come into contact with the energy which is there and insists on having the answer to what it wants to know, well, naturally, the energy which is there — the union of the two forces, the force given out by you and that accumulated in the book — will guide your hand and your paper-knife or whatever you have; it will guide you exactly to the thing that expresses what you ought to know.... Obviously, if one does it without sincerity or conviction, nothing at all happens. If it is done sincerely, one gets an answer.

Certain books are like this, more powerfully charged than others; there are others where the result is less clear. But generally, books containing aphorisms and short sentences — not very long philosophical explanations, but rather things in a condensed and precise form — it is with these that one succeeds best.

Naturally, the value of the answer depends on the value of the spiritual force contained in the book. If you take a novel, it will tell you nothing at all but stupidities. But if you take a book containing a condensation of forces — of knowledge or spiritual force or teaching power — you will receive your answer.

6 June 1956

A Flu Epidemic in Japan

I was in Japan. It was at the beginning of January 1919. Anyway, it was the time when a terrible flu raged there in the whole of Japan, which killed hundreds of thousands of people.* It was one of those epidemics the like of which is rarely seen. In Tokyo, every day there were hundreds and hundreds of new cases. The disease appeared to take this turn: it lasted three days and on the third day the patient died. And people died in such large numbers that they could not even be cremated, you understand, it was impossible, there were too many of them. Or otherwise, if one did not die on the third day, at the end of

* In 1919-20, at the end of the First World War, there was a worldwide epidemic of "Spanish flu". This epidemic alone took more lives than the entire war.

seven days one was altogether cured; a little exhausted but all the same completely cured. There was a panic in the town, for epidemics are very rare in Japan. They are a very clean people, very careful and with a fine morale. Illnesses are very rare. But still this came, it came as a catastrophe. There was a terrible fear. For example, people were seen walking about in the streets with a mask on the nose, a mask to purify the air they were breathing, so that it might not be full of the microbes of the illness. It was a common fear....

Now, it so happened I was living with someone who never ceased troubling me: "But what is this disease? What is there behind this disease?" What I was doing, you know, was simply to cover myself with my force, my protection so as not to catch it and I did not think of it any more and continued doing my work. Nothing happened and I was not thinking of it. But constantly I heard: "What is this? Oh, I would like to know what is there behind this illness. But could you not tell me what this illness is, why it is there? ..." etc. One day I was called to the other end of the town by a young woman whom I knew and who wished to introduce me to some friends and show me certain things: I do not remember now what exactly was the matter, but anyway I had to cross the whole town in a tram-car. And I was in the tram and seeing these people with masks on their noses, and then there was in the atmosphere this constant fear, and so there came a suggestion to me; I began to ask myself: "Truly, what is this illness? What is there behind this illness? What are the forces that are in this illness?..." I came to the house, I passed an hour there and I returned. And I returned with a terrible fever. I had caught it. It came to you thus, without preparation, instantaneously. Illnesses, generally illnesses from germs and microbes take a few days in the system: they come, there is a little battle inside; you win or you lose, if you lose you catch the illness, it is not complicated. But there, you just receive a letter, open the envelope, hop! puff! The next minute you have the fever. Well, that evening I had a terrible fever.

The doctor was called (it was not I who called him), the doctor was called and he told me: "I must absolutely give you this medicine." It was one of the best medicines for the fever, he had just a little (all their stocks were exhausted, everyone was taking it); he said: "I have still a few packets, I shall give you some." — "I beg of you, do not give it to me, I won't take it. Keep it for someone who has faith in it and will take it." He was quite disgusted: "It was no use my coming here." So I said: "Perhaps it was no use!" And I remained in my bed, with my fever, a violent fever. All the while I was asking myself: "What is this illness? Why is it there? What is there behind it?... " At the end of the second day, as I was lying all alone, I saw clearly a being, with a part of the head cut off, in a military uniform (or the remains of a military uniform) approaching me and suddenly flinging himself upon my chest, with that half a head to suck my force. I took a good look, then realised that I was about to die. He was drawing all my life out (for I must tell you that people were dying of pneumonia in three days). I was completely nailed to the bed, without movement, in a deep trance. I could no longer stir and he was pulling. I thought: now it is the end. Then I called on my occult power, I gave a big fight and I succeeded in turning him back so that he could not stay there any longer. And I woke up.

But I had seen. And I had learnt, I had understood that the illness originated from beings who had been thrown out of their bodies. I had seen this during the First Great War, towards its end, when people used to live in trenches and were killed by bombardment. They were in perfect health, altogether healthy and in a second they were thrown out of their bodies, not conscious that they were dead. They did not know they hadn't a body any more and they tried to find in others the life they could not find in themselves. That is, they were turned into so many countless vampires. And they vampirised upon men. And then over and above that, there was a decomposition of the vital forces of people who fell ill and died. One lived in a kind of sticky and thick cloud made up of all that. And so those who took in this cloud fell ill and usually got cured, but those who were attacked by a being of that kind invariably died, they could not resist. I know how much knowledge and force were necessary for me to resist. It was irresistible. That is, if they were attacked by a being who was a centre of this whirl of bad forces, they died. And there must have been many of these, a very great number. I saw all that and I understood.

22 July 1953

CHAPTER 14

Day-to-Day Life

Make Use of Reason

Ordinary people enter life without even knowing what it is to live, and at each step they have to learn how to live. And before knowing what they want to realise, they must at least know how to walk; as we teach a tiny little child how to walk, in life one has also to learn how to live. Which people know how to live? And it is through experience, through mistakes, through all kinds of misfortunes and troubles of every sort that gradually one begins to be what is called reasonable; that is, when one has made a mistake a certain number of times and has had troublesome consequences from this mistake, one learns not to make it again. But there is a moment, when the brain is developed enough and you can use the reason, well, reason can help you to reduce the number of these mistakes, to teach you to walk the path without stumbling too often.

The immense majority of human beings are born, live and die without knowing why this has happened to them. They take it... it is like that; they are born, they live, they have what they call their joys and their sorrows, and they come to the end and go away. They came in and went out without learning anything. This indeed is the immense majority.

There is among them a small number of people called the elite, who try to know what has happened to them, why they are upon earth and why all that happens to them happens. Then among these there are some who use their reason and they find a way of walking properly on the path, much faster than the others. These are reasonable beings.

Now there is a handful — a big handful — of people who are born with the feeling that there is something else to find in life, a higher purpose to life, that there is an aim, and they strive to find it. So for these the path goes beyond reason, to regions which they have to explore either with or without help, as chance takes them, and they must then discover the higher worlds. But there are not many of this kind. I don't know how many of these there are now in the world, but I have the impression that they could still be counted. So for these it depends on when they begin.

Now there are beings, I think, who are born and whose rational period of life may begin very early, when they are very young, and it may last for a very short time; and then they are almost immediately ready to set out on new and unexplored paths towards the higher realities. But in order to set out on these paths without fear and without any danger, one must have organised his being with the help of reason around the highest centre he consciously possesses, and organised it in such a way that it is inwardly in his control and he has not to say at every moment, "Ah! I have done this, I don't know why. Ah! that's happened to me, I don't know why" — and always it is "I don't know, I don't know, I don't know", and as long as it is like that, the path is somewhat dangerous. Only when one does what he wants, knows what he wants, does what he wants and is able to direct himself with certitude, without being tossed about by the hazards of life, then one can go forward on the suprarational paths fearlessly, unhesitatingly and with the least danger. But one need not be very old for this to happen. One can begin very young; even a child of five can already make use of reason to control himself; I know it. There is enough mental organisation in the being in these little tots who look so spontaneous and irresponsible; there is enough cerebral organisation for them to organise themselves, their life, their nature, their movements, actions and thoughts with reason.[...]

Do the laws of Nature follow the law of human reason?

Oh, no!

Then how can we explain so many laws of Nature by human reason?

Because human reason is higher than Nature.

Nature is infrarational. The laws of Nature are infrarational laws. So when men come along and tell you, "But what do you want, it is the law of Nature", as for me, it makes me laugh. It is not worth being a man, it would be better for you to be a monkey or an elephant or a lion. The laws of Nature are infrarational.

This is the only superiority that man has, his having a reason, and when he doesn't make use of it he becomes absolutely an animal.

That's the last excuse to give: "What do you want, it's the law of Nature!"

25 May 1955

Attraction and Repulsion

Sweet Mother, why does one feel attracted at first sight to some people and feel a repulsion for others?

Usually this is based on vital affinities, nothing else. There are vital vibrations which harmonise and vital vibrations which don't. It is usually this, nothing else. It is vital chemistry.

One would have to be in a much deeper and more clear-sighted consciousness for it to be otherwise. There is an inner perception based on a psychic consciousness, which makes you feel which people have the same aspiration, the same aim, and can be your companions on the way; and this perception also makes you clear-sighted about those who follow a very different way or carry in them forces which are hostile to you and may harm you in your development. But to attain such a perception one must oneself be exclusively occupied with one's own spiritual progress and integral realisation. Now, that is not often the case. And usually too, when one has attained this inner clear-sightedness, it is not expressed by attraction and repulsion, but by a very "objective" knowledge, it might be said, and a kind of inner certainty which makes you act calmly and reasonably, and without attractions and repulsions.

Therefore, it may be said in a general and almost absolute way that those who have very definite and impulsive likes and dislikes live in a vital consciousness. Mixed with this, there may be mental affinities; that is, some minds like to have relationships in common activities, but here too, these are people on a much higher level intellectually, and this is also expressed even more by a comparative ease in relationships and by something much more calm and detached. One takes pleasure in speaking with certain people; for others there is no attraction, one gains nothing from it. It is a little more distant and quiet; it belongs more to the field of reason. But likes and dislikes clearly belong to the vital world. Well, there is a vital chemistry just as there is physical chemistry: there are bodies which repel each other and others which attract; there are substances which combine and others which explode, and it is like that. There are some vital vibrations which harmonise, and harmonise to such an extent that ninety-nine times out of a hundred these sympathies are taken for what men call love, and suddenly people feel, "Oh! he is the one I was waiting for", "Oh! she is the one I was seeking!" (*laughing*), and they rush towards each other, till they find out that it was something very superficial and that these things can't last. There. So the first advice given to those who want to do yoga: "Rise above likes and dislikes." This is something without any deeper reality and it can at the very least lead you into difficulties which are at times quite hard to overcome. You can ruin your life with these things. And the best thing is not to take any notice of them — to draw back a little into yourself and ask yourself why — it's nothing very mysterious — you like to meet this person, don't like to meet that one.

But, as I say, there comes a moment when one is exclusively occupied with one's sadhana, when one can feel — but both more subtly and much more quietly — that a particular contact is favourable to sadhana and another harmful. But that always takes a much more "detached" form, so to say, and often it even contradicts the so-called attractions and repulsions of the vital; very often it has nothing to do with them.

So, the best thing is to look at all that from a little distance and to lecture yourself a little on the futility of these things.

Obviously there are some natures which are almost fundamentally bad, beings who are born wicked and love to do harm; and logically, if one is quite natural, not perverted, natural as animals are — for from this point of view they are far superior to men; perversion begins with humanity — then one keeps out of the way, as one would stand aside from something fundamentally harmful. But happily these cases are not very frequent; what one meets in life are usually very mixed natures where there is a kind of balance, so to say, between the good and the bad, and one may expect to have both good and bad relations. There is no reason to feel any deep dislike, for, as one is quite mixed oneself (*laughing*), like meets like!

It is also said that some people are like vampires, and when they come near a person they spontaneously suck up his vitality and energy, and that one should beware of them as of a very serious danger. But that also... Not that it doesn't exist, but it is not very frequent, and certainly not so total that one need run away when one meets such a person.

So, essentially, if one wants to develop spiritually, the first thing to do is to overcome one's dislikes... and one's likes. Look at all that with a smile.

11 September 1957

No Two Things Are Identical

It is said that there are people who are very intelligent, and others who are foolish. Why?

Why? But, my child, there are all kinds of things in Nature! No two things are identical. All the possibilities exist in Nature: everything you can imagine and a hundred million times more. So you notice that there are intelligent people and again others who are not. And then there are others still who are unbalanced. And yet, your observations cover a very narrow field. But you can tell yourself that all this exists and hundreds of thousands of millions of other things also exist, and that no two things are alike in the world. And I don't think there is anything one can imagine which doesn't exist somewhere. This is exactly what amuses Nature most — she tries out everything, does everything, makes everything, undoes everything, and she makes all possible combinations and goes on changing them, re-handling them, remaking them, and it is a perpetual movement of all the possibilities following one another, clashing, intermingling, combining and falling apart. No two moments of terrestrial life are alike; and for how long has the earth existed?... Very well-informed people will perhaps tell you approximately. And for how long will it yet live? They will perhaps tell you that also: figures with many zeros, so many zeros that you won't be able to read them. But it won't ever be the same thing twice over nor will there be two similar moments. If you find things looking alike, that is only an appearance. There are no two things alike, and no two identical moments. And all this goes back so far that you cannot count. And it goes so far in front that you cannot count. And it will never be twice the same thing. So, you can't ask me why this exists and why that exists!...

You wanted to ask me why? Nature has much more imagination than you, you know! She imagines new things all the time. It must be so for it is changing all the time and all combinations are always new. Not two seconds in the universe are identical. She has a great deal of imagination. Have you never thought about that?... Do you ever really have two similar moments? No. You know very well that you are not today what you were yesterday and you won't be tomorrow what you are today... and that if you went back only... say, ten years, you wouldn't recognise yourself at all any longer! You don't know even what you used to think about, granting that you thought about anything!

So, there is no problem. All that you can do is to try and investigate the field of experience given to you which is extremely limited, to see all the possibilities. And you could begin noting them; you would see that it would make a huge volume immediately, simply in that tiny little field of experience which is yours!

And what are you?... One second in Eternity!

12 August 1953

*

Things come to you because they have an affinity. There is something to which they can cling, a kind of sympathy somewhere, which may not be very conscious or very open, but there is one. And if it were not there, the thing would no longer come. There is a whole set of things which never come to bother you any longer, once you have changed the essential points in your nature.

23 March 1955

Meat-Eating and Fasting

What happens if one eats meat?

Do you want me to tell you a story? I knew a lady, a young Swedish woman, who was doing sadhana; and she was by habit a vegetarian, from both choice and habit. One day she was invited by some friends who gave her chicken for dinner. She did not want to make a fuss, she ate the chicken. But afterwards, during the night suddenly she found herself in a basket with her head between two pieces of wicker-work, shaken, shaken, shaken, and feeling wretched, miserable; and then, after that she found herself head down, feet in the air, and being shaken, shaken, shaken. (*Laughter*) She felt perfectly miserable; and then all of a sudden, somebody began pulling out things from her body, and that hurt her terribly, and then someone came along with a knife and chopped off her head; and then she woke up. She told me all this; she said she had never had such a frightful nightmare, that she had not thought of anything before going to sleep, that it was just the consciousness of the poor chicken that had entered her, and that she had experienced in her dream all the anguish the poor chicken had suffered when it was carried to the market, sold, its feathers plucked and its neck cut! (*Laughter*)

That's what happens! That is to say, in a greater or lesser proportion you swallow along with the meat a little of the consciousness of the animal you eat. It is not very serious, but it is not always very pleasant. And obviously it does not help you in being on the side of man rather than of the beast! It is evident that primitive men, those who were still much closer to the beast than to the spirit, apparently used to eat raw meat, and that gives much more strength than cooked meat. They killed the animal, tore it apart and bit into it, and they were very strong. And moreover, this is why there was in their intestines that little piece, the appendix, which in those days was much bigger and served to digest the raw meat. And then man began to cook. He found out that things tasted better that way, and he ate cooked meat and gradually the appendix grew smaller and was no longer of any use at all. So now it is an encumbrance which at times brings on an illness.

This is to tell you that perhaps now it is time to change one's food and go over to something a little less bestial! It depends absolutely on each one's state of consciousness. For an ordinary man, living an ordinary life, having ordinary activities, not thinking at all of anything else except earning his living, of keeping himself fit and perhaps taking care of his family, it is good to eat meat, it is all right for him to eat anything at all, whatever agrees with him, whatever does him good.

But if one wishes to pass from this ordinary life to a higher one, the problem begins to become interesting; and if, after having come to a higher life, one tries to prepare oneself for the transformation, then it becomes very important. For there certainly are foods which help the body to become subtle and others which keep it in a state of animality. But it is only at that particular time that this becomes very important, not before; and before reaching that moment, there are many other things to do. Certainly it is better to purify one's mind and purify one's vital before thinking of purifying one's body. For even if you take all possible precautions and live physically taking care not to absorb anything except what will help to subtilise your body, if your mind and vital remain in a state of desire, inconscience, darkness, passion and all the rest, that won't be of any use at all. Only, your body will become weak, dislocated from the inner life and one fine day it will fall ill.

One must begin from inside, I have already told you this once. One must begin from above, first purify the higher and then purify the lower. I am not saying that one must indulge in all sorts of degrading things in the body. That's not what I am telling you. Don't take it as an advice not to exercise control over your desires! It isn't that at all. But what I mean is, do not try to be an angel in the body if you are not already just a little of an angel in your mind and vital; for that would dislocate you in a different way from the usual one, but not one that is better. We said the other day that what is most important is to keep the equilibrium. Well, to keep the equilibrium everything must progress at the same time. You must not leave one part of your being in darkness and try to bring the other into light. You must take great care not to leave any corner dark.

23 June 1954

*

How does fasting produce a state of receptivity?

It is because usually the vital being is very closely concentrated on the body and when the body is well fed it takes its strength from the food, its energy from the food, and it is one way — it is obviously almost the only way, not the only one, but the most important in the present conditions of life — but it is a very tamasic way of absorbing energy.

If you think about it, you see, it is the vital energy which is in either plants or animals, that is, logically it is of an inferior quality to the vital energy which should be in man, who is a slightly higher being in the gradation of the species. So if you draw from below you draw at the same time the inconscience that is below. It is impossible to eat without absorbing a considerable amount of inconscience; this makes you heavy, coarsens you; and then if you eat much, a large amount of your consciousness is absorbed in digesting and assimilating what you have eaten. So already, if you don't take food, you don't have all this inconscience to assimilate and transform inside you; it sets free the energies. And then, as there is an instinct in the being to recuperate the energies spent, if you don't take them from food, that is, from below, you instinctively make an effort to take them through union with the universal vital forces which are free, and if one knows how to assimilate them one does so directly and then there is no limit.

It is not like your stomach which can digest only a certain amount of food, and therefore you can't take in more than that; and even the food you take liberates only a little bit, a very small quantity of vital energy. And so what can remain with you after all the work of swallowing, digesting, etc.? Not much, you see. But if you learn... and this indeed is a kind of instinct, one learns instinctively to draw towards himself the universal energies which move freely in the universe and are unlimited in quantity... as much of these as you are capable of drawing towards you, you can absorb — so instinctively when there is no support from below which comes from food, you make the necessary movement to recuperate the energies from outside, and absorb as much of them as you are capable of doing, and sometimes more. So this puts you in a kind of state of excitement, and if your body is very strong and can bear being without food for a certain length of time, then you keep your balance and can use these energies for all kinds of things, as for example, to progress, to become more conscious and transform your nature.

But if your physical body doesn't have much in reserve and grows considerably weak from not eating, then this creates an imbalance between the intensity of the energies you absorb and the capacity of the body to hold them, and then this causes disturbances. You lose your balance, and all the balance of forces is destroyed, and anything at all may happen to you. In any case, you lose much control over yourself and become usually very excited, and you take this excitement for a higher state. But often it is simply an inner imbalance, nothing more. It sharpens the receptivity very much. For example, precisely when one fasts and no longer takes the energies from below, well, if you breathe in the scent of a flower it nourishes you, the perfume nourishes you, it gives you a great deal of energy; but otherwise you do not notice it.

There are certain faculties which get intensified, and so one takes that for a spiritual effect. It has very little to do with the spiritual life except that there are people who eat much, think much about their food, are very deeply absorbed in it, and then when they have eaten well — and as I say, they must digest it, and so all their energies are concentrated on their digestion — these people are dull in mind, and this pulls them down very much towards matter; so if they stop eating and stop thinking about food — because there is one thing, that if one fasts and thinks all the time that he is hungry and would like to eat, then it is ten times worse than eating — and can truly fast because they think of something else and are occupied with something else and are not interested in food — then that can help one to climb to a slightly higher degree of consciousness, to free himself from the slavery to material needs. But fasting is above all good for those who believe in it — as everything. When you have the faith that this will make you progress, is going to purify you, it does you good. If you don't believe in it, it doesn't do much, except that it makes you thin.

23 February 1955

The Need for Diversity

If you arrive at the conception of the world as the expression of the Divine in all His complexity, then the necessity for complexity and diversity has to be recognised, and it becomes impossible for you to want to make others think and feel as you do.

Each one should have his own way of thinking, feeling and reaction. Why do you want others to do as you do and be like you? And even granting that your truth is greater than theirs — though this word means nothing at all, for from a certain point of view all truths are true; they are all partial, but they are true because they are truths — but the minute you want your truth to be greater than your neighbour's, you begin to wander away from the truth.

This habit of wanting to compel others to think as you do has always seemed very strange to me; this is what I call "the propagandist spirit", and it goes very far. You can go one step further and want people to do what you do, feel as you feel, and then it becomes a frightful uniformity.

In Japan I met Tolstoy's son who was going round the world for "the good of mankind's great unity". And his solution was very simple: everybody ought to speak the same language, lead the same life, dress in the same way, eat the same things.... And I am not joking, those were his very words. I met him in Tokyo; he said: "But everybody would be happy, all would understand one another, nobody would quarrel if everyone did the same thing." There was no way of making him understand that it was not very reasonable! He had set out to travel all over the world for that, and when people asked him his name he would say "Tolstoy" — now, Tolstoy, you know... People said, "Oh!" — some people didn't know that Tolstoy was dead — and they thought: "Oh! what luck, we are going to hear something remarkable" — and then he came out with that!

Well, this is only an exaggeration of the same attitude.

Anyway, I can assure you that there comes a time when one no longer feels any necessity at all, at all, of convincing others of the truth of what one thinks.

4 April 1956

Money

You see, when one thinks of money, one thinks of bank-notes or coins or some kind of wealth, some precious things. But this is only the physical expression of a force which may be handled by the vital and which, when possessed and controlled, almost automatically brings along these more material expressions of money. And that is a kind of power. (*Silence*) It is a power of attracting certain very material vibrations, which has a capacity for utilisation that increases its strength — which is like the action of physical exercise, you see — it increases its strength through utilisation.[...]

The money-power belongs to a world which was created deformed. It is something that belongs to the vital world; and he [Sri Aurobindo] says this, doesn't he, he says that it belongs to the vital and material worlds. And so at all times, always it was under the control of the Asuric forces; and what must be done is precisely to reconquer it from the Asuric forces.

That is why in the past, all those who wanted to do Yoga or follow a discipline, used to say that one should not touch money, for it was something — they said — diabolic or Asuric or at least altogether opposed to the divine life. But the whole universe, in all its manifestation, is the Divine Himself, and so belongs entirely to Him; and it is on this ground that he says that the money-forces belong to the Divine. One must reconquer them and give them to Him. They have been under the influence of the Asuric forces: one must win them back in order to put them at the disposal of the Divine so that He may be able to use them for His work of transformation.

Sweet Mother, it is men who have created money. Then how is it a divine power?

Hm! (*laughing*) It is as though you told me: it is a man and woman who have created another person, then how can he be divine in essence? It is exactly the same thing! The whole creation is made externally by external things, but behind that there are divine forces. What men have invented — paper or coins or other objects — all these are but means of expression, nothing else but that.... I just said this a moment ago, it is not the force itself, it is its material expression as men have created it. But this is purely conventional. For example, there are countries where small shells are exchanged instead of money.[...]

It is purely conventional. What is behind is the force I am speaking about, you see, and so it manifests in all sorts of ways. For example, even gold, you know... men have given a certain value to gold, because of all metals it deteriorates the least. It is preserved almost indefinitely. And this is the reason, there's no other. But it is a mere convention. The proof is that each time a new gold-mine is found and exploited, the value of gold has fallen. These are mere conventions between human beings. But what makes money a power is not this, it is the force that's behind. As I was saying a while ago, it is a force that is able to attract and use anything whatever, all material things and...

So this is used according to a convention. Now, it is understood that wealth is represented by bits of paper which become very dirty, and on which something is printed. They are altogether disgusting, most often good only for lighting the fire. But it is considered a great fortune. Why? Because that's the convention. Yet one who is capable of attracting this and using it for something good, to increase the welfare of this world, the welfare and well-being of the world, that man has a hold on the money-power, that is to say, the force that is behind money.

28 July 1954

*

Friends from outside have often asked me this question: "When one is compelled to earn his living, should one just conform to the common code of honesty or should one be still more strict?"

This depends upon the attitude your friend has taken in life. If he wants to be a sadhak, it is indispensable that rules of ordinary morality do not have any value for him. Now, if he is an ordinary man living the ordinary life, it is a purely practical question, isn't it? He must conform to the laws of the country in which he lives to avoid all trouble! But all these things which in ordinary life have a very relative value and can be looked upon with a certain indulgence, change

totally the minute one decides to do yoga and enter the divine life.
Then, all values change completely; what is honest in ordinary life, is
no longer at all honest for you. Besides, there is such a reversal of
values that one can no longer use the same ordinary language. If one
wants to consecrate oneself to the divine life, one must do it truly,
that is, give oneself entirely, no longer do anything for one's own
interest, depend exclusively upon the divine Power to which one abandons oneself. Everything changes completely, doesn't it? — everything, everything, it is a reversal. What I have just read from this book
[by Sri Aurobindo] applies solely to those who want to do yoga; for
others it has no meaning, it is a language which makes no sense, but
for those who want to do yoga it is imperative. It is always the same
thing in all that we have recently read: one must be careful not to
have one foot on one side and the other foot on the other, not to bestride
two different boats each following its own course. This is what Sri
Aurobindo said: one must not lead a "double life". One must give up
one thing or the other — one can't follow both.

    This does not mean, however, that one is obliged to get out of the
conditions of one's life: it is the inner attitude which must be totally
changed. One may do what one is in the habit of doing, but do it with
quite a different attitude. I don't say it is necessary to give up everything in life and go away into solitude, to an ashram necessarily, to do
yoga. Now, it is true that if one does yoga in the world and in worldly
circumstances, it is more difficult, but it is also more complete. Because, every minute one must face problems which do not present
themselves to someone who has left everything and gone into solitude; for such a one these problems are reduced to a minimum —
while in life one meets all sorts of difficulties, beginning with the
incomprehension of those around you with whom you have to deal;
one must be ready for that, be armed with patience, and a great indifference. But in yoga one should no longer care for what people think
or say; it is an absolutely indispensable starting-point. You must be
absolutely immune to what the world may say or think of you and to
the way it treats you. People's understanding must be something quite
immaterial to you and should not even slightly touch you. That is
why it is generally much more difficult to remain in one's usual surroundings and do yoga than to leave everything and go into solitude;

it is much more difficult, but we are not here to do easy things — easy things we leave to those who do not think of transformation.

If someone has acquired a lot of money by dishonest means, could some of it be asked for the Divine?

Sri Aurobindo has answered this question. He says that money in itself is an impersonal force: the way in which you acquire money concerns you alone personally. It may do you great harm, it may harm others also, but it does not in any way change the nature of the money which is an altogether impersonal force: money has no colour, no taste, no psychological consciousness. It is a force. It is like saying that the air breathed out by a scoundrel is more tainted than that breathed out by an honest man — I don't think so. I think the result is the same. One may for reasons of a practical nature refuse money which has been stolen, but that is for altogether practical reasons, it is not because of divine reasons. This is a purely human idea. One may from a practical point of view say, "Ah! no, the way in which you have acquired this money is disgusting and so I don't want to offer it to the Divine", because one has a human consciousness. But if you take someone (let us suppose the worst) who has killed and acquired money by the murder; if all of a sudden he is seized by terrible scruples and remorse and tells himself, "I have only one thing to do with this money, give it where it can be utilised for the best, in the most impersonal way", it seems to me that this movement is preferable to utilising it for one's own satisfaction.

I said that the reasons which could prevent one from receiving ill-gotten money may be reasons of a purely practical kind, but there may also be more profound reasons, of a (I do not want to say moral but) spiritual nature, from the point of view of tapasya; one may tell somebody, "No, you cannot truly acquire merit with this fortune which you have obtained in such a terrible way; what you can do is to re-store it", one may feel that a restitution, for instance, will help to make more progress than simply passing the money on to any work whatever. One may see things in this way — one can't make rules. This is what I never stop telling you: it is impossible to make a rule. In every case it is different. But you must not think that the money is affected; money as a terrestrial force is not affected by the way in which it is obtained, that can in no way affect it. Money remains the same, your note remains the same, your piece of gold remains the same, and as it carries its force, its force remains there. It harms only the person who has done wrong, that is evident.

Then the question remains: in what state of mind and for what reasons does your dishonest man want to pass on his money to a work he considers divine? Is it as a measure of safety, through prudence or to lay his heart at rest? Evidently this is not a very good motive and it cannot be encouraged, but if he feels a kind of repentance and regret for what he has done and the feeling that there is but one thing to do and that is precisely to deprive himself of what he has wrongly acquired and utilise it for the general good as much as possible, then there is nothing to say against that. One cannot decide in a general way — it depends upon the instance. Only, if I understand well what you mean, if one knows that a man has acquired money by the most unnamable means, obviously, it would not be good to go and *ask* him for money for some divine work, because that would be like "rehabilitating" his way of gaining money. One cannot ask, that is not possible. If, spontaneously, for some reason, he gives it, there is no reason to refuse it. But it is quite impossible to go and ask him for it, because it is as though one legitimised his manner of acquiring money. That makes a great difference.

3 May 1951

*

The more money we have, the more we need...

The more money one has, the more one is in a state of calamity, my child. Yes, it is a calamity.

It is a catastrophe to have money. It makes you stupid, it makes you miserly, it makes you wicked. It is one of the greatest calamities in the world. Money is something one ought not to have until one no longer has desires. When one no longer has any desires, any attachments, when one has a consciousness vast as the earth, then one may have as much money as there is on the earth; it would be very good for everyone. But if one is not like that, all the money one has is like a curse upon him. This I could tell anyone at all to his face, even to the man who thinks that it is a merit to have become rich. It is a calamity and perhaps it is a disgrace, that is, it is an expression of a divine displeasure.

It is infinitely more difficult to be good, to be wise, to be intelligent and generous, to be more generous, you follow me, when one is rich than when one is poor. I have known many people in many countries, and the most generous people I have ever met in all the countries, were the poorest. And as soon as the pockets are full, one is caught by a kind of illness, which is a sordid attachment to money. I assure you it is a curse.

So the first thing to do when one has money is to give it. But as it is said that it should not be given without discernment, don't go and give it like those who practise philanthropy, because that fills them with a sense of their own goodness, their generosity and their own importance. You must act in a sattwic way, that is, make the best possible use of it. And so, each one must find in his highest consciousness what the best possible use of the money he has can be. And truly money has no value unless it circulates. For each and every one, money is valuable only when one has spent it. If one doesn't spend it... I tell you, men take care to choose things which do not deteriorate, that is, gold — which does not decompose. Otherwise, from the moral point of view it rots. And now that gold has been replaced by papers, if you keep papers for a long time without taking care of them, you will see when you open your drawer that there are small silverfish which have regaled themselves on your paper-rupees. So they will have left a lace-work which the bank will refuse.

There are countries and religions which always say that God makes those whom He loves poor. I don't know if that is true; but there is one thing which is true, that surely when someone is born rich or has become very rich, in any case when he possesses much from the point of view of material riches, it is certainly not a sign that the Divine has chosen him for His divine Grace, and he must make honourable amends if he wants to walk on the path, the true path, to the Divine.

Wealth is a force — I have already told you this once — a force of Nature; and it should be a means of circulation, a power in movement, as flowing water is a power in movement. It is something which can serve to produce, to organise. It is a convenient means, because in fact it is only a means of making things circulate fully and freely.

This force should be in the hands of those who know how to make the best possible use of it, that is, as I said at the beginning, people who have abolished in themselves or in some way or other got rid of every personal desire and every attachment. To this should be added a vision vast enough to understand the needs of the earth, a knowledge complete enough to know how to organise all these needs and use this force by these means.

If, besides this, these beings have a higher spiritual knowledge, then they can utilise this force to construct gradually upon the earth what will be capable of manifesting the divine Power, Force and Grace. And then this power of money, wealth, this financial force, of which I just said that it was like a curse, would become a supreme blessing for the good of all.

For I think that it is the best things which become the worst. Perhaps the worst also can become the best. Some people also say that it is the worst men who become the best. I hope the best don't become the worst, for that indeed would be sad.

But still, certainly, the greatest power, if badly used, can be a very great calamity; whereas this same very great power if well utilised can be a blessing. All depends on the use that's made of things. Each thing in the world has its place, its work, a real use; and if used for something else it creates a disorder, confusion, chaos. And that's because in the world as it is, very few things are utilised for their true work, very few things are really in their place, and it is because the world is in a frightful chaos that there is all this misery and suffering. If each thing was in its place, in a harmonious balance, the whole world could progress without needing to be in the state of misery and suffering in which it is. There!

So there is nothing that's bad in itself, but there are many things — almost all — which are not in their place.

Perhaps in the body also it is like that. There is nothing that's bad in itself; but many things are not in their place, and that is why one becomes ill. There is created an inner disharmony. So the result is that one is ill. And people always think that it is not their fault that they are ill, and it is always their fault, and they are very angry when they are told this. "You have no pity." And yet it is true.

16 February 1955

*

It is often said in fairy tales that a treasure is guarded by serpents. Is this true?

Yes, but it is not a physical serpent, it is a vital serpent. The key to the treasures is in the vital world and it is guarded by an immense black serpent — a tremendous serpent, ten times, fifty times larger than an ordinary one. It keeps the gates of the treasure. It is magnificent, black, always erect and awake. I happened once to be standing before it (usually these beings obey me when I give them an order), and I said to it, "Let me pass." It replied, "I would willingly let you pass, but if I do, they will kill me; so I cannot let you pass." I asked, "What must I bring you in order to gain entrance?" It said, "Oh, only one thing would oblige me to give way to you: if you could become master of the sex impulse in man, if you succeeded in conquering that in humanity, I could no longer resist, I would allow you to pass."

It has not yet allowed me to pass. I must admit that I have not fulfilled the condition, I have not been able to obtain such a mastery of it as to conquer it in all men.

That is quite difficult.

10 March 1951

Sleep and Dreams

Most people do so many things in their sleep that they wake up more tired than before. We have already spoken about this once. Naturally, if you keep yourself from sleeping, you won't sleep. I always tell those who complain of not being able to sleep, "Meditate then and you will end up by sleeping." It is better to fall asleep while concentrating than "like that", scattered and strewn without knowing even where one is.

To sleep well one must learn how to sleep.

If one is physically very tired, it is better not to go to sleep immediately, otherwise one falls into the inconscient. If one is very tired, one must stretch out on the bed, relax, loosen all the nerves one after another until one becomes like a rumpled cloth in one's bed, as though one had neither bones nor muscles. When one has done that, the same thing must be done in the mind. Relax, do not concentrate on any idea or try to solve a problem or ruminate on impressions, sensations or emotions you had during the day. All that must be allowed to drop off quietly: one gives oneself up, one is indeed like a rag. When you have succeeded in doing this, there is always a little flame, there — that flame never goes out and you become conscious of it when you have managed this relaxation. And all of a sudden this little flame rises slowly into an aspiration for the divine life, the truth, the consciousness of the Divine, the union with the inner being, it goes higher and higher, it rises, rises, like that, very gently. Then everything gathers there, and if at that moment you fall asleep, you have the best sleep you could possibly have. I guarantee that if you do this carefully, you are sure to sleep, and also sure that instead of falling into a dark hole you will sleep in light, and when you get up in the morning you will be fresh, fit, content, happy and full of energy for the day.

When one is conscious in sleep, does the brain sleep or not?

When does the brain ever sleep? When does it sleep? This is of all things the most difficult. If you succeed in making your brain sleep, it would be wonderful. How it runs on! That is vagabondage. It is this I meant when I spoke of relaxation in the brain. If you do it really well, your brain enters a silent restfulness and that is wonderful; when you attain that, five minutes of that and you are quite fresh afterwards, you can solve a heap of problems.

If the brain is always working, why don't we remember what has happened during the night?

Because you have not caught the consciousness at its work. And perhaps because if you remembered what was going on in your brain, you would be horrified! It is really like a madhouse, all these ideas which clash, all dancing a sarabande in the head! It is as if one were throwing balls in all directions at once. So, if you saw that, you would be a bit troubled.

23 April 1951

*

Sometimes, on waking up, one forgets everything, one forgets where one is. Why?

It is because you have gone into the inconscient and lost all contact with the consciousness, and this takes a little time to be re-established. Of course, it may happen that instead of going into the inconscient one goes into the superconscient, but this is not frequent. And the feeling is not the same because, instead of having this negative impression of not knowing who one is or where one is or what is what, one has a positive sensation of having risen into something other than one's ordinary life, of no longer being the same person. But when one has altogether lost contact with one's ordinary consciousness, generally it is that one has slept away and been for a long time in the inconscient. Then the being is scattered, it is absorbed by this inconscient and all the pieces have to be put together again. Naturally, this is done much more quickly than at the beginning of existence, but the conscious elements have to be gathered up again and a cohesion re-formed to begin to know once more who one is.

Sometimes in dreams one goes into houses, streets, places one has never seen. What does this mean?

There may be many reasons for this. Perhaps it is an exteriorisation: one has come out of the body and gone for a stroll. They may be memories of former lives. Perhaps one has become identified with someone else's consciousness and has the memories of this other person. Perhaps it is a premonition (this is the rarest case, but it may happen): one sees ahead what one will see later.

The other day I spoke to you about those landscapes of Japan; well, almost all — the most beautiful, the most striking ones — I had seen in vision in France; and yet I had not seen any pictures or photographs of Japan, I knew nothing of Japan. And I had seen these land-scapes without human beings, nothing but the landscape, quite pure, like that, and it had seemed to me they were visions of a world other than the physical; they seemed to me too beautiful for the physical world, too perfectly beautiful. Particularly I used to see very often those stairs rising straight up into the sky; in my vision there was the impression of climbing straight up, straight up, and as though one could go on climbing, climbing, climbing.[...]

There are always many explanations possible and it is very diffi-cult to explain for someone else. For oneself, if one has studied very carefully one's dreams and activities of the night, one can distinguish fine nuances. I was saying I thought I had a vision of another world — I knew it was something which existed, but I could not imagine there was a country where it existed; this seemed to me impossible, so very beautiful it was. It was the active mind which interfered. But I knew that what I was seeing truly existed, and it was only when I saw these landscapes physically that I realised in fact that I had seen something which existed, but I had seen it with inner eyes (it was the subtle-physical) before seeing it physically.

Everyone has certain very small indications, but for that one must be very, very methodical, very scrupulous, very careful in one's ob-servation and not neglect the least signs, and above all not give fa-vourable mental explanations to the experiences one has. For if one wants to explain to oneself (I don't even speak of explaining to oth-ers), if one wants to explain the experience to oneself advantageously, to draw satisfaction, one does not understand anything any more. That is, one may mix up the signs without even noticing that they are mixed up. For instance, when one sees somebody in a dream (I am not speak-ing of dreams in which you see somebody unknown, but of those where you see somebody you know, who comes to see you) there are all sorts of explanations possible. If it is someone living far away from you, in another country, perhaps that person has written a letter to you and the letter is on the way, so you see this person because he has put a formation of himself in his letter, a concentration; you see the person and the next morning you get the letter. This is a very frequent occurrence. If it is a person with a very strong thought-power, he may think of you from very far, from his own country and concentrate his thought, and this concentration takes the form of that person in your consciousness. Perhaps it is that this person is calling you intentionally; deliberately he comes to tell you something or give you a sign, if he is in danger, if he is sick. Suppose he has something important to tell you, he begins to concentrate (he knows how to do it, as everyone does not) and he enters your atmosphere, comes to tell you something special. Now if you are passive and attentive, you receive the message.

And then, two more instances still: someone has exteriorised himself more or less materially in his sleep and has come to see you. And you become conscious of this person because (almost by miracle) you are in a corresponding state of consciousness. And finally, a last instance, this person may be dead and may come to see you after his death (one part of him or almost the whole of his being according to the relation you have with him). Consequently, for someone who is not very, very careful it is very difficult to distinguish these nuances, very difficult. On the other hand, quite often imaginative people will tell you, "Oh! I saw this person — he is dead." I have heard that I don't know how many times. These are people whose imagination runs freely. It is possible that the person is dead, but not because he has appeared to you!... One must pay great attention to the outer forms things take. There are shades very difficult to distinguish, one must be very, very careful. For oneself, if one is in the habit of studying all this, one can become aware of the differences, but to interpret another's experiences is very difficult, unless he gives you in great detail all that surrounds the dream, the vision: the ideas he had before, the ideas he had later, the state of his health, the feelings he experienced when going to sleep, the activities of the preceding day, indeed, all sorts of things. People who tell you, "Oh! I had this vision, explain it to me!", that is childishness — unless it is someone whom you have followed very carefully, whom you yourself have taught how to recognise the planes, and whose habits, whose reactions you know; otherwise it is impossible to explain, for there are innumerable explanations for one single thing.

14 April 1951

*

Why do we forget our dreams?

Because you do not dream always at the same place. It is not always the same part of your being that dreams and it is not at the same place that you dream. If you were in conscious, direct, continuous communication with all the parts of your being, you would remember all your dreams. But very few parts of the being are in communication.

For example, you have a dream in the subtle physical, that is to say, quite close to the physical. Generally, these dreams occur in the early hours of the morning, that is between four and five o'clock, at the end of the sleep. If you do not make a sudden movement when you wake up, if you remain very quiet, very still and a little attentive — quietly attentive — and concentrated, you will remember them, for the communication between the subtle physical and the physical is established — very rarely is there no communication.

Now, dreams are mostly forgotten because you have a dream while in a certain state and then pass into another. For instance, when you sleep, your body is asleep, your vital is asleep, but your mind is still active. So your mind begins to have dreams, that is, its activity is more or less coordinated, the imagination is very active and you see all kinds of things, take part in extraordinary happenings.... After some time, all that calms down and the mind also begins to doze. The vital that was resting wakes up; it comes out of the body, walks about, goes here and there, does all kinds of things, reacts, sometimes fights, and finally eats. It does all kinds of things. The vital is very adventurous. It watches. When it is heroic it rushes to save people who are in prison or to destroy enemies or it makes wonderful discoveries. But this pushes back the whole mental dream very far behind. It is rubbed off, forgotten: naturally you cannot remember it because the vital dream takes its place. But if you wake up suddenly at that moment, you remember it. There are people who have made the experiment, who have got up at certain fixed hours of the night and when they wake up suddenly, they do remember. You must not move brusquely, but awake in the natural course, then you remember.

After a time, the vital having taken a good stroll, needs to rest also, and so it goes into repose and quietness, quite tired at the end of all kinds of adventures. Then something else wakes up. Let us suppose that it is the subtle physical that goes for a walk. It starts moving and begins wandering, seeing the rooms and... why, this thing that was there, but it has come here and that other thing which was in that room is now in this one, and so on. If you wake up without stirring, you remember. But this has pushed away far to the back of the consciousness all the stories of the vital. They are forgotten and so you cannot recollect your dreams.

But if at the time of waking up you are not in a hurry, you are not obliged to leave your bed, on the contrary you can remain there as long as you wish, you need not even open your eyes; you keep your head exactly where it was and you make yourself like a tranquil mirror within and concentrate there. You catch just a tiny end of the tail of your dream. You catch it and start pulling gently, without stirring in the least. You begin pulling quite gently, and then first one part comes, a little later another. You go backward; the last comes up first. Everything goes backward, slowly, and suddenly the whole dream reappears: "Ah, there! it was like that." Above all, do not jump up, do not stir; you repeat the dream to yourself several times — once, twice — until it becomes clear in all its details. Once that dream is settled, you continue not to stir, you try to go further in, and suddenly you catch the tail of something else. It is more distant, more vague, but you can still seize it. And here also you hang on, get hold of it and pull, and you see that everything changes and you enter another world; all of a sudden you have an extraordinary adventure — it is another dream. You follow the same process. You repeat the dream to yourself once, twice, until you are sure of it. You remain very quiet all the time. Then you begin to penetrate still more deeply into yourself, as though you were going in very far, very far; and again suddenly you see a vague form, you have a feeling, a sensation... like a current of air, a slight breeze, a little breath; and you say, "Well, well...." It takes a form, it becomes clear — and the third category comes. You must have a lot of time, a lot of patience, you must be very quiet in your mind and body, very quiet, and you can tell the story of your whole night from the end right up to the beginning.

Even without doing this exercise which is very long and difficult, in order to recollect a dream, whether it be the last one or the one in the middle that has made a violent impression on your being, you must do what I have said when you wake up: take particular care not even to move your head on the pillow, remain absolutely still and let the dream return.

Some people do not have a passage between one state and another, there is a little gap and so they leap from one to the other; there is no highway passing through all the states of being with no break of the consciousness. A small dark hole, and you do not remember. It is like a precipice across which one has to extend the consciousness. To build a bridge takes a very long time; it takes much longer than building a physical bridge.... Very few people want to and know how to do it. They may have had magnificent activities, they do not remember them or sometimes only the last, the nearest, the most physical activity, with an uncoordinated movement — dreams having no sense.

But there are as many different kinds of nights and sleep as there are different days and activities. There are not many days that are alike, each day is different. The days are not the same, the nights are not the same. (*To the child that who asked the question*) You and your friends are doing apparently the same thing, but for each one it is very different. And each one must have his own procedure.

Why are two dreams never alike?

Because all things are different. No two minutes are alike in the universe and it will be so till the end of the universe, no two minutes will ever be alike. And men obstinately want to make rules! One must do this and not that.... Well! we must let people please themselves.

                                                                    6 May 1953

                                             *

Sweet Mother, you have said that one can exercise one's conscious will and change the course of one's dreams.

Ah, yes, I have already told you that once. If you are in the middle of a dream and something happens which you don't like (for instance, somebody shouts that he wants to kill you), you say: "That won't do at all, I don't want my dream to be like that", and you can change the action or the ending. You can organise your dream as you want. One can arrange one's dreams. But for this you must be conscious that you are dreaming, you must know you are dreaming.

But these dreams are not of much importance, are they?

Yes, they are, and one must be conscious of what can happen. Suppose that you have gone for a stroll in the vital world; there you meet beings who attack you (that's what happens usually), if you know that it is a dream, you can very easily gather your vital forces and conquer. That's a true fact; you can with a certain attitude, a certain word, a certain way of being do things you would not do if you were just dreaming.

If in the dream someone kills you it doesn't matter, for it is just a dream!

I beg your pardon! Usually, the next day you are ill, or may be a little later. That's a warning. I know someone whose eye was thus hurt in a dream, and who really lost his eye a few days later. As for me, once I happened to dream about getting blows on my face. Well, when I woke up the next morning, I had a red mark in the same place, on the forehead and the cheek.... Inevitably, a wound received in the vital being is translated in the physical body.

But how does it happen? There must be some intermediary?

It was in the vital that I was beaten. It is from within that this comes. Nothing, nobody touched anything from outside. If you receive a blow in the vital, the body suffers the consequence. More than half of our illnesses are the result of blows of this kind, and this happens much more often than one believes. Only, men are not conscious of their vital, and as they are not conscious they don't know that fifty per cent of their illnesses are the result of what happens in the vital: shocks, accidents, fighting, ill-will.... Externally this is translated by an illness. If one knows how it reacts on the physical, one goes to its source and can cure oneself in a few hours.

*How is it that the symbolism of dreams varies according to tradi-
tions, races, religions?*

Because the form given to the dream is mental. If you have learnt that
such and such a form represents such and such a mythological person, you see that form and say: "It is that." In your mind there is an
association between certain ideas and certain forms, and this is continued in the dream. When you translate your dream you give it an
explanation corresponding to what you have learnt, what you have
been taught, and it is with the mental image you have in your head
that you know. Moreover, I have explained this to you a little later in
the vision of Joan of Arc (*Mother takes her book and reads*):

> *"The beings who were always appearing and speaking to Jeanne
> d'Arc would, if seen by an Indian, have quite a different appear-
> ance; for when one sees, one projects the forms of one's mind....
> You have the vision of one in India whom you call the Divine
> Mother; the Catholics say it is the Virgin Mary, and the Japanese
> call it Kwannon, the Goddess of Mercy; and others would give
> other names. It is the same force, the same power, but the images
> made of it are different in different faiths." (The Mother)*

*You say that "each person has his own world of dream-imagery
peculiar to himself."*

Each individual has his own way of expressing, thinking, speaking,
feeling, understanding. It is the combination of all these ways of being that makes the individual. That is why everyone can understand
only according to his own nature. As long as you are shut up in your
own nature, you can know only what is in your consciousness. All
depends upon the height of the nature of your consciousness. Your
world is limited to what you have in your consciousness. If you have
a very small consciousness, you will understand only a few things.
When your consciousness is very vast, universal, only then will you
understand the world. If the consciousness is limited to your little
ego, all the rest will escape you.... There are people whose brain and
consciousness are smaller than a walnut. You know that a walnut re-

sembles the brain; well, these people look at things and don't understand them. They can understand nothing else except what is in direct
contact with their senses. For them only what they taste, what they
see, hear, touch has a reality, and all the rest simply does not exist,
and they accuse us of speaking fancifully! "What I cannot touch does
not exist", they say. But the only answer to give them is: "It does not
exist *for you*, but there's no reason why it shouldn't exist for others."
You must not insist with these people, and you must not forget that
the smaller they are the greater is the audacity in their assertions.

One's cocksureness is in proportion to one's unconsciousness;
the more unconscious one is, the more is one sure of oneself. The
most foolish are always the most vain. Your stupidity is in proportion
to your vanity. The more one knows... In fact, there is a time when
one is quite convinced that one knows nothing at all. There's not a
moment in the world which does not bring something new, for the
world is perpetually growing. If one is conscious of that, one has
always something new to learn. But one can become conscious of it
only gradually. One's conviction that one knows is in direct proportion to one's ignorance and stupidity.

29 April 1953

*

*Sweet Mother, when one sees oneself dead in a dream, what does
it signify?*

Ah! I have already been asked this several times. It depends on the
context.

It can mean that one has made enough progress to get rid totally
of an old way of being which has no longer any reason for existing.
This, I think, is the most frequent case. Otherwise it depends absolutely on the context, that is, the circumstances surrounding the dream.

That is... one sees himself dead... How does he see himself dead?
Does he simply see the inert body or himself already dead, or does he
take for dead what is not dead?

You see, if you leave your body — by going out of the body as I
explained a while ago — if you have gone out materially enough, in a

very material vital, well, the body which is lying on the bed seems absolutely dead, but it is not dead for all that. But if you look at it or see it while you are outside and you don't know, it seems absolutely dead, it is in a cataleptic state. Then if you know what is necessary and what you ought to do it is very easy; but if you don't know and the imagination starts roaming, then you open the door to fear and anything may happen.

But in fact, I don't think that once in a million times it is a premonitory dream. I think it much more likely that it is a fragment of the being which has stopped being useful and so disappears; so the fragment takes the form of the whole and one sees himself dead because this fragment has stopped existing in him. This is the most frequent and the most logical instance.

Now, one may see not a death but, for example, an accident or an assassination or things like that... Then it is a very real violent dream, you know, and this may mean that one is attacked by bad forces sent by someone with a precise purpose. Then one has only to strike hard and react violently.

Sweet Mother, sometimes when one is asleep, he knows that he is asleep but he can't open his eyes. Why?

This happens when one has gone out of his body, and one must not force things, one must quite simply, slowly, concentrate his consciousness in his body and wait a while for the fusion to be made normally; one must not force things.

Sometimes the eyes are a little open and one can also see things...

And one can't move!

Yes.

It means that only a fragment of the consciousness has come back, not enough to bring back the full movement in the body. You must not shake yourself, because you risk losing a bit of yourself. You must remain quite still and concentrate slowly, slowly, on your body; it can take a minute or two at the most.

What can one lose?

Anything at all, something that has gone out, you see. It's because one part of the being has gone out; so if you shake yourself, it doesn't have the time to get back.[...]

One must never startle anyone out of his sleep because he must have time to get back into his body. It is not good, for instance, when getting up to jump out of bed — hop! You must remain quiet for a while, like this (*gesture*), as though you were bringing yourself back into yourself, like that, quietly... quietly.

27 April 1955

CHAPTER 15

Art

Art and Yoga

If one does Yoga can he rise to such heights as Shakespeare or Shelley? There has been no such instance.

Why not? The Mahabharata and Ramayana are certainly not inferior to anything created by Shakespeare or any other poet, and they are said to have been the work of men who were Rishis and had done Yogic *tapasyā*. The Gita which, like the Upanishads, ranks at once among the greatest literary and the greatest spiritual works, was not written by one who had no experience of Yoga. And where is the inferiority to your Milton and Shelley in the famous poems written whether in India or Persia or elsewhere by men known to be saints, Sufis, devotees? And, then, do you know all the Yogis and their work? Among the poets and creators can you say who were or who were not in conscious touch with the Divine? There are some who are not officially Yogis, they are not *gurus* and have no disciples; the world does not know what they do; they are not anxious for fame and do not attract to themselves the attention of men; but they have the higher consciousness, are in touch with a Divine Power, and when they create they create from there. The best paintings in India and much of the best statuary and architecture were done by Buddhist monks who passed their lives in spiritual contemplation and practice; they did supreme artistic work, but did not care to leave their names to posterity. The chief reason why Yogis are not usually known by their art is that they do not consider their art-expression as the most important part of their life and do not put so much time and energy into it as a mere artist. And what they do does not always reach the public. How many there are who have done great things and not published them to the world![...]

Art is nothing less in its fundamental truth than the aspect of beauty of the Divine manifestation. Perhaps, looking from this standpoint, there will be found very few true artists; but still there are some and these can very well be considered as Yogis. For like a Yogi an artist goes into deep contemplation to await and receive his inspiration. To create something truly beautiful, he has first to see it within, to realise it as a whole in his inner consciousness; only when so found, seen, held within, can he execute it outwardly; he creates according to this greater inner vision. This too is a kind of yogic discipline, for by it he enters into intimate communion with the inner worlds. A man like Leonardo da Vinci was a Yogi and nothing else. And he was, if not the greatest, at least one of the greatest painters, — although his art did not stop at painting alone.

Music too is an essentially spiritual art and has always been associated with religious feeling and an inner life. But, here too, we have turned it into something independent and self-sufficient, a mushroom art, such as in operatic music. Most of the artistic productions we come across are of this kind and at best interesting from the point of view of technique. I do not say that even operatic music cannot be used as a medium of a higher art expression; for whatever the form, it can be made to serve a deeper purpose. All depends on the thing itself, on how it is used, on what is behind it. There is nothing that cannot be used for the Divine purpose — just as anything can pretend to be the Divine and yet be of the mushroom species.

Among the great modern musicians there have been several whose consciousness, when they created, came into touch with a higher consciousness. César Franck played on the organ as one inspired; he had an opening into the psychic life and he was conscious of it and to a great extent expressed it. Beethoven, when he composed the Ninth Symphony, had the vision of an opening into a higher world and of the descent of a higher world into this earthly plane. Wagner had strong and powerful intimations of the occult world; he had the instinct of occultism and the sense of the occult and through it he received his greatest inspirations. But he worked mainly on the vital level and his mind came in constantly to interfere and mechanised his inspiration. His work for the greater part is too mixed, too often obscure and heavy, although powerful. But when he could cross the vital and the mental levels and reach a higher world, some of the glimpses he had were of an exceptional beauty, as in Parsifal, in some parts of Tristan and Iseult and most in its last great Act.

Look again at what the moderns have made of the dance; compare it with what the dance once was. The dance was once one of the highest expressions of the inner life; it was associated with religion and it was an important limb in sacred ceremony, in the celebration of festivals, in the adoration of the Divine. In some countries it reached a very high degree of beauty and an extraordinary perfection. In Japan they kept up the tradition of the dance as a part of the religious life and, because the strict sense of beauty and art is a natural possession of the Japanese, they did not allow it to degenerate into something of lesser significance and smaller purpose. It was the same in India. It is true that in our days there have been attempts to resuscitate the ancient Greek and other dances; but the religious sense is missing in all such resurrections and they look more like rhythmic gymnastics than dance.[...]

There is a domain far above the mind which we could call the world of Harmony and, if you can reach there, you will find the root of all harmony that has been manifested in whatever form upon earth. For instance, there is a certain line of music, consisting of a few supreme notes, that was behind the productions of two artists who came one after another — one a concerto of Bach, another a concerto of Beethoven. The two are not alike on paper and differ to the outward ear, but in their essence they are the same. One and the same vibration of consciousness, one wave of significant harmony touched both these artists. Beethoven caught a larger part, but in him it was more mixed with the inventions and interpolations of his mind; Bach received less, but what he seized of it was purer. The vibration was that of the victorious emergence of consciousness, consciousness tearing itself out of the womb of unconsciousness in a triumphant uprising and birth.

If by Yoga you are capable of reaching this source of all art, then you are master, if you will, of all the arts. Those that may have gone there before, found it perhaps happier, more pleasant or full of a rapturous ease to remain and enjoy the Beauty and the Delight that are there, not manifesting it, not embodying it upon earth. But this abstention is not all the truth nor the true truth of Yoga; it is rather a deformation, a diminution of the dynamic freedom of Yoga by the

more negative spirit of Sannyasa. The will of the Divine is to manifest, not to remain altogether withdrawn in inactivity and an absolute
silence; if the Divine Consciousness were really an inaction of unmani-
festing bliss, there would never have been any creation.

28 July 1929

Modern Art

Why is modern art so ugly?

I believe the chief reason is that people have become more and more
lazy and do not want to work. They want to produce something before having worked, they want to know before having studied and
they want to make a name before having done anything good. So, this
is the open door for all sorts of things, as we see.... Naturally, there
are exceptions.

I have known artists who were great artists, who had worked hard
and produced remarkable things, classical, that is, not ultra-modern.
But they were not in fashion because, precisely, one had not to be
classical. When a brush was put in the hands of an individual who
had never touched a brush, and when a brush was put on a palette of
colours and the man had never touched a palette before, then if this
individual had in front of him a bit of canvas on an easel and he had
never done a picture before, naturally he daubed anything at all; he
took the colours and threw them in a haphazard way; then everybody
cried out "admirable", "marvellous", "it is the expression of your soul",
"how well this reveals the truth of things", etc.! This was the fashion
and people who knew nothing were very successful. The poor men
who had worked, who knew their art well, were not asked for their
pictures any longer; people said, "Oh! this is old-fashioned, you will
never find customers for such things."

But, after all, they were hungry, you see, they had to pay their
rent and buy their colours and all the rest, and that is costly. Then
what could they do? When they had received rebuffs from the pic-
ture-dealers who all told them the same thing, "But try to be modern,
my friend; look here, you are behind the times", as they were very
hungry, what could they do?... I knew a painter, a disciple of Gustav

Moreau; he was truly a very fine artist, he knew his work quite well, and then... he was starving, he did not know how to make both ends meet and he used to lament. One day, a friend intending to help him, sent a picture-dealer to see him. When the merchant entered his studio, this poor man told himself, "At last! here's my chance", and he showed him all the best work he had done. The art-dealer made a face, looked around, turned over things and began rummaging in all the corners; and suddenly he found... Ah! I must explain this to you, you are not familiar with these things: a painter, after his day's work has at times some mixed colours left on his palette; he cannot keep them, they dry up in a day; so he always has with him some pieces of canvas which are not well prepared and which he daubs with what are called "the scrapings of palettes" (with supple knives he scrapes all the colours from the palette and applies them on the canvases) and as there are many mixed colours, this makes unexpected designs. There was in a corner a canvas like that on which he used to put his palette-scrapings. The merchant suddenly falls upon that and exclaims, "Here you are! my friend, you are a genius, this is a miracle, it is this you should show! Look at this richness of tones, this variety of forms, and what an imagination!" And this poor man who was starving said shyly, "But sir, these are my palette-scrapings!" And the art-dealer caught hold of him: "Silly fool, this is not to be told!" Then he said, "Give me this, I undertake to sell it. Give me as many of these as you like; ten, twenty, thirty a month, I shall sell them all for you and I shall make you famous." Then, as I told you, his stomach was protesting; he was not happy, but he said, "All right, take it, I shall see."

Then the landlord comes to demand his rent; the colour-man comes demanding payment of the old bill; the purse is quite empty, and what is to be done? So though he did not make pictures with palette-scrapings, he did something which gave the imagination free play, where the forms were not too precise, the colours were all mixed and brilliant, and one could not know overmuch what one was seeing; and as people did not know very much what they saw, those who understood nothing about it exclaimed, "How beautiful it is!" And he supplied this to his art-dealer. He never made a name for himself with his real painting, which was truly very fine (it was really very fine, he was a very good painter), but he won a world reputation with these horrors! And this was just at the beginning of modern painting, this goes back to the Universal Exhibition of 1900; if I were to tell you his name, you would all recognise it.... Now, of course, they have gone far beyond, they have done much better. However, he had the sense of harmony and beauty and his colours were beautiful. But at present, as soon as there is the least beauty, it won't do at all, it has to be outrageously ugly, then that, that is modern!

The story began with... the man who used to do still-life and whose plates were never round.... Cézanne! It was he who began it; he said that if plates were painted round that would not be living; that when one looks at things spontaneously, never does one see plates round: one sees them like this (*gesture*). I don't know why, but he said that it is only the mind that makes us see plates as round, because one knows they are round, otherwise one does not see them round. It is he who began.... He painted a still-life which was truly a very beautiful thing, note that; a very beautiful thing, with an impression of colour and form truly surprising.[...] But, of course, his plate was not round.[...]

What has made art what it is, do you want me to tell you this, psychologically? ... it is photography. Photographers did not know their job and gave you hideous things, frightfully ugly, it was mechanical, it had no soul, it had no art, it was horrible. All the first attempts of photography until... not very long ago, were like that. It is about fifty years ago that it became tolerable, and now with gradual improvement it has become something good; but it must be said that the process is absolutely different. In those days, when your portrait was taken, you sat in a comfortable chair, you had to sit leaning nicely and facing an enormous thing with a black cloth, which opened like this towards you. And the man ordered, "Don't move! Steady!" That, of course, was the end of the old painting. When the painter made something lifelike, a lifelike portrait, his friends said, "Why now, this is photography!"

It must be said that the art of the end of the last century, the art of the Second Empire [1852-71], was bad. It was an age of businessmen, above all an age of bankers, financiers, and taste, really, had gone very low. I don't believe that businessmen are people necessarily very competent in art, but when they wanted their portrait, they wanted a likeness! One could not leave out the least detail, it was quite comic: "But you know I have a little wrinkle there, don't forget to put it in!" and the lady who said, "You know, you must make my shoulders quite round", and so on. So the artists made portraits which indeed turned into photography. They were flat, cold, without soul and without vision. I can name a number of artists of that period, it was truly a shame for art. This lasted till about the end of the last century, till about 1875. Afterwards, there started the reaction. Then there was an entire very beautiful period (I don't say this because I myself was painting) but all the artists I then knew were truly artists, they were serious and did admirable things which have remained admirable. It was the period of the impressionists; it was the period of Manet, it was a beautiful period, they did beautiful things.

But people tire of beautiful things as they tire of bad ones. So there were those who wanted to found the "Salon d'Automne". They wanted to surpass the others, go more towards the new, towards the truly anti-photographic. And my goodness, they went a little beyond the limit (according to my taste). They began to depreciate Rembrandt — Rembrandt was a dauber, Titian was a dauber, all the great painters of the Italian Renaissance were daubers. You were not to pronounce the name of Raphael, it was a shame. And all the great period of the Italian Renaissance was "not worth very much"; even the works of Leonardo da Vinci; "You know, you must take them and leave them." Then they went a little further; they wanted something entirely new, they became extravagant. And then, from there, there was only one more step to take for the palette-scrapings and then it was finished.

This is the history of art as I knew it.

Now, to tell you the truth, we are climbing up the curve again. Truly, I think we had gone down to the depths of incoherence, absurdity, nastiness — of the taste for the sordid and ugly, the dirty, the outrageous. We had gone, I believe, to the very bottom.

Are we really going up again?

I think so. Recently I saw some pictures which truly showed something other than ugliness and indecency. It is not yet art, it is very far from being beautiful, but there are signs that we are going up again. You will see, fifty years hence we shall perhaps have beautiful things to see. I felt this some days ago, that truly we had come to the end of the descending curve — we are still very low down, but are beginning to climb up. There is a kind of anguish and there is still a complete lack of understanding of what beauty can and should be, but one finds an aspiration towards something which will not be sordidly material. For a time art had wanted to wallow in the mire, to be what they called "realistic". They had chosen as "real" what was most repulsive in the world, most ugly: all deformities, all filth, all ugliness, all the horrors, all the incoherences of colour and form; well, I believe this is behind us now. I had this feeling very strongly these last few days (not through seeing pictures, for we do not have a chance to see much here, but by "sensing the atmosphere"). And even in the reproductions we are shown, there is some aspiration towards something which would be a little higher. It will need about fifty years; then...

Unless there is another war, another catastrophe; because certainly, to a large extent, what is responsible for this taste for the sordid are the wars and the horrors of war. People were compelled to put aside all refined sensibility, the love of harmony, the need for beauty, to be able to undergo all that; otherwise, I believe, they would really have died of horror. It was so unspeakably foul that it could not be tolerated, so it perverted men's taste everywhere and when the war was over (admitting that it ever ended), they wanted only one thing, to forget, forget, forget. To seek distraction, not to think of all the horror they had suffered. Now there, one goes very low. The whole vital atmosphere is completely vitiated and the physical atmosphere is terribly obscure.

Hence, if we can escape another world war... Because war is there, it has never stopped. It has been there from almost the beginning of this century; it began with China, Turkey, Tripolitania, Morocco — you are following? — the Balkans, it has never stopped, it has become worse, but each time it has become a world war, it has assumed altogether sordid proportions. All you my children, you have been born after the war (I am speaking of the First [World] War), so you do not know much about this, and then you have been born here [in India], in a country which has been truly privileged. But the children born in Europe, latterly, these little ones, who were children of the war, carry something in them which will be very difficult to efface, a kind of horror, a fright. One could not have been mixed up with that without knowing what horror is. The first war was perhaps worse than the second. The second was so atrocious that all was lost.... But the first, oh! I don't know.... The last months I spent in Paris were truly fantastic. And it can't be told. The life in the trenches, for example, is something that cannot be told. The new generations do not know.... But, you see, the children born now will not even know if this was true, all these horrors which are related to them. What happened in the conquered countries, in Czechoslovakia, in Poland, in France — the frightful things, unbelievable, unthinkable, which took place — unless one has been very close by, has seen, one cannot believe it. It was... I was saying the other day that the vital world is a world of horrors; well, all the horrors of the vital world had descended upon earth, and upon earth they are still more horrible than in the vital world, because in the vital world, if you have an inner power, if you have the knowledge, if you have strength, you act upon them — you act, you can subdue them, you can show yourself stronger. But all your knowledge, all your power, all your strength is nothing in this material world when you are subjected to the horrors of a war. And this acts in the terrestrial atmosphere in such a way that it is very, very difficult to efface it.

Naturally, men are always very anxious to forget. There are already those who have begun to say, "Are you quite sure it was like that?" But those who have gone through that, do not want it to be forgotten; so the places of torture, massacre — hideous places which go beyond all the worst the human imagination can conceive — some of these places have been preserved. You can go and visit the torture-chambers the Germans built in Paris, and they will never be destroyed, I hope, so that those who come and say, "Oh! you know, these things have been exaggerated" (for one does not like to know that such frightful things have happened), could be taken by the hand and told, "Come and see, if you are not afraid."

This forms character. If it is taken in the right way (and I think there are people who have taken it in the right way), this may lead you straight to yoga, straight. That is, one feels such a deep detachment for all things in the world, such a great need to find something else, an imperious need to find something which is truly beautiful, truly fresh, truly good... then, quite naturally, this brings you to a spiritual aspiration. And these horrors have, as it were, divided men: there was a minority which was ready and rose very high, there was a majority which was not ready and went down very low. These wallow in the mud at present, and hence, for the moment, one does not get out of it; and if this continues, we shall go towards another war and this time it will truly be the end of this civilisation — I don't say the end of the world, because nothing can be the end of the world, but the end of this civilisation, that is to say, another will have to be built. You will perhaps tell me that this would be very well, for this civilisation is in its decline, it is on the way to perishing; but after all, there are very beautiful things in it, worthy of being preserved, and it would be a great pity if all this disappeared. But if there is another war, I can tell you that all this will disappear. For men are very intelligent creatures and they have found the means of destroying everything, and they will make use of this, for what's the good of spending billions to find certain bombs, if one might not use them? What is the use of discovering that one can destroy a city in a few minutes, if it is not for destroying it! One wants to see the fruit of one's efforts. If there is war, this is what will happen.

There we are, I am telling you things which are not very cheerful, but it is sometimes good to put a little ballast in the head to make one think.

9 April 1951

*

Why are today's painters not so good as those of the days of Leonardo da Vinci?

Because human evolution goes in spirals. I have explained this. I said that art had become altogether a mercenary affair, obscure and ignorant, from the beginning of the last century till its middle.[...] It was conventional, artificial and without any real life, so the reaction was to the very opposite, and naturally to another obscurity: "art" was no longer to express physical life but mental life or vital life. And so came all the schools, like the Cubists and others, who created from their head. But in art it is not the head that dominates, it is the feeling for beauty. And they produced absurd and ridiculous and frightful things. Now they have gone farther still, but that, that is due to the wars — with every war there descends upon earth a world in decomposition which produces a sort of chaos. And some, of course, find all this very beautiful and admire it very much.

I understand what they [modern artists] want to do, I understand it very well, but I cannot say that I find they do it well. All I can say is that they are trying.

But it is perhaps (with all its horror, from a certain point of view), it is perhaps better than what was produced in that age of extreme and practical philistinism: the Victorian age or in France the Second Empire. So, one starts from a point where there was a harmony and describes a curve, and with this curve one goes completely out of this harmony and may enter into a total darkness; and then one climbs up, and when one finds oneself in line with the old realisation of art, one becomes aware of the truth there was in this realisation, but with the necessity of expressing something more complete and more conscious. But in describing the circle one forgets that art is the expression of forms and one tries to express ideas and feelings with a minimum of forms. That gives what we have, what you may see. But if one goes a little farther still, this idea and these feelings they wish to express and express very clumsily — if one returns to the same point of the spiral (only a little higher), one will discover that it is the embryo of a new art which will be an art of beauty and will express not only material life but will also try to express its soul.

Anyway, we have not yet come to that, but let us hope we shall reach there soon.

28 October 1953

*

It is said that a synthesis of western and eastern art could be made?

Yes. One can make a synthesis of everything if one rises sufficiently high.

What will come out of it?

If it is necessary, it will be done. But fundamentally, these are things in the course of making. For, the advantage of modern times and specially of this hideous commercialism is that everything is now mixed up; that things from the East go to the West, and things from the West to the East, and they influence each other. For the moment this creates a confusion, a sort of pot-pourri. But a new expression will come out of it — it is not so far from its realisation. People cannot intermix, as men today are intermixing, without its producing a reciprocal effect. For instance, with their mania of conquest, the nations of the West which conquered all sorts of countries in the world, have undergone a very strong influence of the conquered countries. In the old days, when Rome conquered Greece it came under the influence of Greece much more than if it had not conquered it. And the Americans — all that they make now is full of Japanese things, and perhaps they are not even aware of it. But since they occupied Japan, I see that the magazines received from America are full of Japanese things. And even in certain details of objects received from America, one now feels the influence of Japan. That happens automatically. It is quite strange, there always comes about a sort of equilibrium, and he who made the material conquest is conquered by the spirit of the vanquished. It is reciprocal. He made the material conquest, he possesses materially, but it is the spirit of the conquered one who possesses the conqueror.

So, through mixing... The ways of Nature are slow, obscure and complicated. She takes a very long time to do a thing which could probably be done much more rapidly, easily and without wastage by means of the spirit. At present there is a terrible wastage in the world. But the thing is done. She has her own way of mixing people.

Is it intentional?

Not the way men understand "intentional". But it is certainly the expression of an intention and a goal towards which one is going. Only, all depends on the amount of consciousness. For a man this seems a confusion, for he can see only details, and it appears to be a terrible loss of time, because for him the idea of time is limited to the duration of his person. But Nature has eternity before her. And it is all the same to her to waste, for she is like someone who had a huge cauldron; she throws things in and makes a mixture, and if that does not succeed she throws all this out, for she knows that by taking back the same things she will make another mixture. And that is how it is. Nothing is lost, for it comes into use again all the time. Forms are broken and the substance is taken back, and it goes on constantly like that. It is made, it is unmade, it is turned inside out — what harm can it do her to try a hundred thousand times if it so pleases her! For there is nothing that is wasted, except her work. But her work is her pleasure. Without work she would not exist.

It is a pleasure for her, not for men!

No, certainly, I quite agree. I find it a little too cruel an amusement.

28 October 1953

*

Almost all man's works of art — literary, poetic, artistic — are based on the violence of contrasts in life. When one tries to pull them out of their daily dramas, they really feel that it is not artistic. If they wanted to write a book or compose a play where there would be no contrasts, where there would be no shadows in the picture, it would probably be something seemingly very dull, very monotonous, lifeless, for what man calls "life" is the drama of life, the anxiety of life, the violence of contrasts. And perhaps if there were no death, they would be terribly tired of living.

30 January 1957

Music

From what plane does music generally come?

There are different levels. There is a whole category of music that comes from the higher vital, which is very catching, somewhat (to put it roughly) vulgar, it is something that twists your nerves. This music is not necessarily unpleasant, but generally it seizes you there in the nervous centres. So there is one type of music which has a vital origin. There is music which has a psychic origin — it is altogether different. And then there is music which has a spiritual origin: it is very bright and it carries you away, captures you entirely. But if you want to execute this music correctly you must be able to make it come through the vital passage. Your music coming from above may become externally quite flat if you do not possess that intensity of vital vibration which gives it its splendour and strength. I knew people who had truly a very high inspiration and it became quite flat, because the vital did not stir. I must admit that by their spiritual practices they had put to sleep their vital completely — it was literally asleep, it did not act at all — and the music came straight into the physical, and if one were connected with the origin of that music, one could see that it was something wonderful, but externally it had no force, it was a little melody, very poor, very thin; there was none of the strength of harmony. When you can bring the vital into play, then all the strength of vibration is there. If you draw into it this higher origin, it becomes the music of a genius.

For music it is very special; it is difficult, it needs an intermediary. And it is like that for all other things, for literature also, for poetry, for painting, for everything one does. The true value of one's creation depends on the origin of one's inspiration, on the level, the height where one finds it. But the value of the execution depends on the vital strength which expresses it. To complete the genius both must be there. This is very rare. Generally it is the one or the other, more often the vital. And then there are those other kinds of music we have — the music of the *café-concert*, of the cinema — it has an extraordinary skill, and at the same time an exceptional platitude, an extraordinary vulgarity. But as it has an extraordinary skill, it seizes you in the solar plexus and it is this music that you remember; it grasps you at once and holds you and it is very difficult to free yourself from it, for it is well-made music, music very well made. It is made vitally with vital vibrations, but what is behind is frightful.

But imagine this same vital power of expression, with the inspiration coming from far above — the highest inspiration possible, when all the heavens open before us — then that becomes wonderful. There are certain passages of César Franck, certain passages of Beethoven, certain passages of Bach, there are pieces by others also which have this inspiration and power. But it is only a moment, it comes as a moment, it does not last. You cannot take the entire work of an artist as being on that level. Inspiration comes like a flash; sometimes it lasts sufficiently long, when the work is sustained; and when that is there, the *same effect* is produced, that is, if you are attentive and concentrated, suddenly that lifts you up, lifts up all your energies, it is as though someone opened out your head and you were flung into the air to tremendous heights and magnificent lights. It produces in a few seconds results that are obtained with so much difficulty through so many years of yoga. Only, in general, one may fall down afterwards, because the consciousness is not there as the basis; one has the experience and afterwards does not even know what has happened. But if you are prepared, if you have indeed prepared your consciousness by yoga and then the thing happens, it is almost definitive.

What is the cause of the great difference between European and Indian music? Is it the origin or the expression?

It is both but in an inverse sense.

This very high inspiration comes only rarely in European music; rare also is a psychic origin, very rare. Either it comes from high above or it is vital. The expression is almost always, except in a few rare cases, a vital expression — interesting, powerful. Most often, the origin is purely vital. Sometimes it comes from the very heights, then it is wonderful. Sometimes it is psychic, particularly in what has been religious music, but this is not very frequent.

Indian music, when there are good musicians, has almost always a psychic origin; for example, the ragas have a psychic origin, they come from the psychic. The inspiration does not often come from above. But Indian music is very rarely embodied in a strong vital. It has rather an inner and intimate origin. I have heard a great deal of Indian music, a great deal; I have rarely heard Indian music having vital strength, very rarely; perhaps not more than four or five times. But very often I have heard Indian music having a psychic origin, it translates itself almost directly into the physical. And truly one must then concentrate, and as it is — how to put it? — very tenuous, very subtle, as there are none of those intense vital vibrations, one can easily glide within it and climb back to the psychic origin of the music. It has that effect upon you, it is a kind of ecstatic trance, as from an intoxication. It makes you enter a little into trance. Then if you listen well and let yourself go, you move on and glide, glide into a psychic consciousness. But if you remain only in the external consciousness, the music is so tenuous that there is no response from the vital, it leaves you altogether flat. Sometimes, there was a vital force, then it became quite good.... I myself like this music very much, this kind of theme developing into a play. The theme is essentially very musical: and then it is developed with variations, innumerable variations, and it is always the same theme which is developed in one way or another.

In Europe there were musicians who were truly musicians and they too had the thing: Bach had it, he used to do the same sort of thing, Mozart had it, his music was purely musical, he had no intention of expressing any other thing, it was music for music's sake. But this manner of taking a certain number of notes in a certain relation (they are like almost infinite variations), personally I find it wonderful to put you in repose, and you enter deep within yourself. And then, if you are ready, it gives you the psychic consciousness: something that makes you withdraw from the external consciousness, which makes you enter elsewhere, enter within.

In what form does music come to the great composers? That is, is it only the melody that comes or is it what we hear?

But that depends upon the musician. This is just what I was saying. For example, here in India, the science of harmony does not exist

much, so the thing is translated by melody. As soon as the vital intervenes, there comes a kind of harmonic complexity in the music. That
gives it a richness, a plenitude which it did not have.

But is it the melody that comes?

No, it is the music, and music is not necessarily melody. It is a relation of sounds which is not necessarily melodic. Melody is a part of
this relation of sounds.

27 May 1953

*

Suffering — how does it help artistic creation?

How does it help? That depends on people. Some people are very
powerfully helped by it. I consider that man [the composer Hector
Berlioz] one of the purest expressions of music. It is almost... I could
say that he is an incarnation of music, of the spirit of music. Unfortunately his body was a little frail; that is, he did not have that solid
base which yoga gives, for instance. So this shook him up too much,
and made him too emotional, nervous, agitated, emotive. You see, it
was a serious weakness. But from the point of view of creation, I
have always felt — and the other day it was very strong — that truly
he was in contact with the spirit of music, you know, the very meaning of music, and that this entered into him with such a force that it
shook him up; but truly, truly he was like an incarnation of music.

The notion that it was suffering that made him create is purely
human; it is not true. What, on the contrary, is very remarkable is —
to turn the thing around — that there was no physical pain which was
not instantaneously translated into music in him; that is, the spirit of
music was much stronger than human pain, and each blow which he
received from life — and as he was indeed too sensitive to have the
power of resisting, he was shaken — all the same, instantly, it was
translated into music. It is something very rare.

People — all creators — usually require a little... how shall I put
it?... time and quietness to be able to begin creating again, while with

him it was spontaneous. The painful blow brought musical expression instantaneously. Truly for him his whole life began with music, finished with music. It was music and it was a... he had such a sincerity and such an exclusive intensity in his attachment to music that I feel that the spirit of music expressed itself through him. Perhaps what he has written is not the *most* beautiful music, because of that kind of weakness of what we call the "*ādhāra*" here. He was... his physical make-up was a little too weak. But from the point of view of music, it is very beautiful, very beautiful. (*Silence*) And even with his strength he had a very great simplicity. There is a kind of limpidity of line in what he has written, with a very great technical knowledge, of course. His power of orchestration was very, very remarkable. When one can orchestrate something for six hundred performers, it means a science as complicated as the most complicated mathematics. And in fact they come very close.

20 October 1954

*

Is sound particular only to the physical world or is there sound in the other domains also?

There is sound there also.

In the same way as here?

There certainly is a sound in all the manifested worlds, and when one has the appropriate organs one hears it.

There are sounds which belong to the highest regions, and in fact, the sound we have here gives the feeling of a noise in comparison with that sound.

For example, there are regions harmonious and musical in which one hears something which is the origin of the music we have here — but the sounds of material, physical music seem absolutely barbaric in comparison with that music! When one has heard that, even the most perfect instrument is inadequate. All constructed instruments, among which the violin certainly has the purest sound, are very much inferior in their expression to the music of this world of harmonies.

The human voice when absolutely pure is of all instruments the one which expresses it best; but it is still... it has a sound which seems so harsh, so gross compared with that. When one has been in that region, one truly knows what music is. And it has so perfect a clarity that at the same time as the sound one has the full understanding of what is said. That is, one has the principle of the idea, without words, simply with the sound and all the inflexions of the... one can't call it sensations, nor feelings... what seems to be closest would be some kind of soul-states or states of consciousness. All these inflexions are clearly perceptible through the nuances of the sound. And certainly, those who were great musicians, geniuses from the point of view of music, must have been more or less consciously in contact with that. The physical world as we have it today is an absolutely gross world; it looks like a caricature.

26 October 1955

CHAPTER 16

Education

Parents and Their Children

Sweet Mother, is it possible for the mother and father to give birth to... to ask for the soul they want?

To ask? For that they must have an occult knowledge which they don't usually have. But anyway, what is possible is that instead of doing the thing like an animal driven by instinct or desire and most of the time, without even wanting it, they do it at will, with an aspiration, putting themselves in a state of aspiration and almost of prayer, so that the being they are going to form may be one fit to embody a soul which they *can* call down to incarnate in that form. I knew people — not many, this does not often happen, but still I knew some — who chose special circumstances, prepared themselves through special concentration and meditation and aspiration and sought to bring down, into the body they were going to form, an exceptional being.

In many countries of old — and even now in certain countries — the woman who was going to have a child was placed in special conditions of beauty, harmony, peace and well-being, in very harmonious physical conditions, so that the child could be formed in the best possible conditions. This is obviously what ought to be done, for it is within the reach of human possibilities. Human beings are developed enough for this not to be something quite exceptional. And yet it is quite exceptional, for very few people think of it, while there are *innumerable* people who have children without even wanting to.

That was what I wanted to say.

It is possible to call a soul, but one must be at least a little conscious oneself, and must want to do what one does in the best conditions. This is very rare, but it is possible.[...]

The formation of the body depends entirely on a man and a woman, but is the soul which manifests in the child, in the body which is being formed, compelled to manifest in this body?

You mean whether it can choose between different bodies?

Yes.

Well, it is very exceptional, after all, in the great mass of humanity, that a conscious soul incarnates voluntarily. It is something very unusual. I have already told you that when a soul is conscious, fully formed, and wants to incarnate, usually from its psychic plane it looks for a corresponding psychic light at a certain place upon earth. Besides, during its previous incarnation, before going away, before leaving the earth-atmosphere, usually as a result of the experience it had in the life that is coming to an end, the soul chooses more or less — not in all details but broadly — the conditions of its future life. But these are exceptional cases. Possibly we could speak of it for ourselves here, but for the majority, the vast majority of men, even those who are educated, it is out of the question. And what comes then is a psychic being in formation, more or less formed, and there are all the stages of formation from the spark which becomes a little light to the fully formed being, and this extends over thousands of years. This ascent of the soul to become a conscious being having its own will, capable of determining the choice of its own life, takes thousands of years.

So, you are thinking of a soul which would say, "No, I refuse this body, I am going to look for another"?... I don't say it is impossible — everything is possible. It does happen, in fact, that children are still-born, which means that there was no soul to incarnate in them. But it may be for other reasons also; it may be for reasons of malformation only; one can't say. I don't say it is impossible, but generally, when a conscious and free soul chooses to take a body on earth again, even before its birth it works on this body. So it has no reason not to accept even the inconveniences which may result from the ignorance of the parents; for it has chosen the place for a reason which was not one of ignorance: it saw a light there — it might have been simply the light of a possibility, but there was a light and *that is why* it has come there. So, it is all very well to say, "Ah! no, I don't like it", but where would it go to choose another it likes?... That may happen, I don't say it is impossible, but it cannot happen very often. For, when from the psychic plane the soul looks at the earth and chooses the place for its next birth, it chooses it with sufficient discernment not to be altogether grossly mistaken.

It has also happened that souls have incarnated and then left. There are many reasons why they go away. Children who die very young, after a few days or a few weeks — this may be for a similar reason. Most often it is said that the soul needed just a little experience to complete its formation, that it had it during these few weeks and then left. Everything is possible. And as many stories would be needed to tell the story of souls as are needed to tell the story of men. That is to say, they are innumerable and the instances are as different as possible from one another.

So, to decide arbitrarily: "It is like that, not like this; this is what happens and not that", this is childishness. *Everything* can happen. There are instances which occur more frequently than others, one can generalise, but one can never say, "This is not possible and it is always like this or always like that." That is not how things happen.

But anyway — anyway — even in the best cases, even when the soul has come consciously, even when it has consciously participated in the formation of the physical body, still so long as the body is formed in the usual animal way, it will have to struggle and correct all those things which come from this human animality.

Inevitably, parents have a particular formation, they are particularly healthy or unhealthy; even taking things at their best, they have a heap of atavisms, habits, formations in the subconscious and even in the unconscious, which come from their own birth, the environment they have lived in, their own life; and even if they are remarkable people, they have a large number of things which are quite opposed to the true psychic life — even the best of them, even the most conscious. And besides, there is all that is going to happen. Even if one takes a great deal of trouble over the education of one's children, they will come in contact with all sorts of people who will have an influence over them, especially when they are very young, and these influences enter the subconscious, one has to struggle against them later on. I say: even in the best cases, because of the way in which the body is formed at present, you have to face innumerable difficulties which come more or less from the subconscious, but rise to the surface and against which you have to struggle before you can become completely free and develop normally.

27 June 1956

*

Sweet Mother, what kind of love do parents have for their children?

What kind? A human love, don't they? Like all human loves: frightfully mixed, with all sorts of things. The need of possession, a formidable egoism. At first, I must tell you that a wonderful picture has been painted... many books written, wonderful things said about a mother's love for her children. I assure you that except for the capacity of speaking about the subject in flowery phrases, the love of the higher animals like the... well, the mammals for their children is exactly of the same nature: the same devotion, the same self-forgetfulness, the same self-denial, the same care for education, the same patience, the same... I have seen absolutely marvellous things, and if they had been written down and applied to a woman instead of to a cat, superb novels would have been made, people would have said: "What a person! How marvellously devoted are these women in their maternal love!" Exactly the same thing. Only, cats could not use flowery language. That's all. They could not write books and make speeches, that is the only difference. But I have seen absolutely astonishing things. And that kind of self-giving and self-oblivion — as soon as there is the beginning of love, it comes. But men... I sincerely believe, from all that I have studied, that there is perhaps a greater purity in animals for they do not think, while human beings with their mental power, their capacity of reflecting, reasoning, analysing, studying, all that, oh! they spoil the most lovely movement. They begin to calculate, reason, doubt, organise.

Take, for instance, parents. At the risk of removing many illusions in your consciousness, I must tell you something about the source of a mother's love for her child. It is because this child is made of her very own substance, and for quite a long time, relatively long, the material link, the link of substance, between mother and child is *extremely* close — it is as though a bit of her flesh had been taken out and put apart at a distance — and it is only much later that the tie between the two is completely cut. There is a kind of tie, of subtle sensation, such that the mother feels exactly what the child feels, as she would feel it in herself. That then is the material basis of the mother's attachment for the child. It is a basis of material identity, nothing else but that. Feeling comes much later (it may come earlier, that depends on people), but I am speaking of the majority: feeling comes only long afterwards, and it is conditioned. There are all kinds of things.... I could speak to you for hours on the subject. But still this must not be mixed up with love. It is a material identification which makes the mother feel intimately, feel quite concretely and tangibly what the child is feeling: if the child receives a shock, well, the mother feels it. This lasts at least for two months.

This is the basis. The rest comes from people's nature, their state of development, their consciousness, education and capacity for feeling. This is added to the first. And then there are all the collective suggestions which go to the making of novels — for people are wonderful at constructing novels. They write novels about everything. They have used their minds to build imaginations which circulate in the atmosphere and then are caught just like that. So some catch a certain type of these, others another kind, and then, as imagination is a force of propulsion, with it one begins to act, and then finally one lives a novel in his life, if he is in the least imaginative.... This has absolutely nothing to do with the true consciousness, with the psychic being, nothing at all, but people come to speak to you in a florid style and tell you stories — all that is in wandering imaginations. If one could see, that is, if *you* could see this mental atmosphere, that of the physical mind, which is circulating everywhere, making you move, making you feel, making you think, making you act, oh, good heavens! you would lose many of your illusions about your personality. But indeed it is like that. Whether one knows it or not, it is like that.

There are many souls upon earth, human beings.... Obviously, those who have a certain culture, a certain development, a certain individualisation gather together usually: instinctively they get together, form groups. And so one can find in space and time a number

— not considerable but still sufficiently large — of cultured beings who are united, but one must not believe that this gives the exact proportion of the culture and development of human beings. It is only like a sort of foam that has been brought up and is on the surface. But even among these latter, even among these beings who are already a selection, there is hardly one in a thousand who is a truly individual being, conscious of himself, united with his psychic being, governed by his inner law and, consequently, almost if not totally free from external influences; for, being conscious, when these influences come, he sees them: those that seem to him to harmonise with his inner development and normal growth he accepts; those which are opposed he refuses. And so, instead of being a chaos — or in any case a frightful mixture — they are organised beings, individual, conscious of themselves, walking through life knowing where they want to go and how they want to.

Of these, if you like, we may say that they are men. That is, they are what Nature may produce of the best as far as men go — they are still men. But this is the summit of man. They are ready to become something else. But unless one is *that*, one is to a great extent an animal still and a very slight beginning of a man. Only *that* can be called man. So there you are, you have only to look into yourselves and know... whether you are men or not.

I am saying this in the hope that you will become that.

14 April 1954

*

Some children are wicked. Is it because their parents did not aspire for them?

It is perhaps a subconscious wickedness in the parents. It is said that people throw out their wickedness from themselves by giving it birth in their children. One has always a shadow in oneself. There are people who project this outside — that does not always free them from it, but still perhaps it comforts them! But it is the child who "profits" by it, don't you see? It is quite evident that the state of consciousness in which the parents are at that moment is of capital importance. If they have very low and vulgar ideas, the children will reflect them quite certainly. And all these children who are ill-formed, ill-bred, incomplete (specially from the point of view of intelligence: with holes, things missing), children who are only half-conscious and half-formed — this is always due to the fault of the state of consciousness in which the parents were when they conceived the child. Even as the state of consciousness of the last moments of life is of capital importance for the future of the one who is departing, so too the state of consciousness in which the parents are at the moment of conception gives a sort of stamp to the child, which it will reflect throughout its life. So, these are apparently such little things — the mood of the moment, the moment's aspiration or degradation, anything whatsoever, everything that takes place at a particular moment — it seems to be so small a thing, and it has so great a consequence: it brings into the world a child who is incomplete or wicked or finally a failure. And people are not aware of that.

Later, when the child behaves nastily, they scold it. But they should begin by scolding themselves, telling themselves: "In what a horrible state of consciousness must I have been when I brought that child into the world." For it is truly that.

30 December 1953

The Art of Living

Usually you are taught very few things — you are not taught even to sleep. People think that they have only to lie down in their bed and then they sleep. But this is not true! One must learn how to sleep as one must learn to eat, learn to do anything at all. And if one does not learn, well, one does it badly! Or one takes years and years to learn how to do it, and during all those years when it is badly done, all sorts of unpleasant things occur. And it is only after suffering much, making many mistakes, committing many stupidities, that, gradually, when one is old and has white hair, one begins to know how to do something. But if, when you were quite small, your parents or those who look after you, took the trouble to teach you how to do what you do, do it properly as it should be done, in the right way, then that would help you to avoid all — all these mistakes you make through the years. And not only do you make mistakes, but nobody tells you they are mistakes! And so you are surprised that you fall ill, are tired, don't know how to do what you want to, and that you have never been taught. Some children are not taught anything, and so they need years and years and years to learn the simplest things, even the most elementary thing: to be clean.

It is true that most of the time parents do not teach this because they do not know it themselves! For they themselves did not have anyone to teach them. So they do not know... they have groped in the dark all their life to learn how to live. And so naturally they are not in a position to teach you how to live, for they do not know it themselves. If you are left to yourself, you understand, it needs years, years of experience to learn the simplest thing, and even then you must think about it. If you don't think about it, you will never learn.

To live in the right way is a very difficult art, and unless one begins to learn it when quite young and to make an effort, one never knows it very well. Simply the art of keeping one's body in good health, one's mind quiet and goodwill in one's heart — things which are indispensable in order to live decently — I don't say in comfort, I don't say remarkably, I only say decently. Well, I don't think there are many who take care to teach this to their children.

2 June 1954

Distinguishing Good and Evil

There is another quality which must be cultivated in a child from a very young age: that is the feeling of uneasiness, of a moral disbalance which it feels when it has done certain things, not because it has been told not to do them, not because it fears punishment, but spontaneously. For example, a child who hurts its comrade through mischief, if it is in its normal, natural state, will experience uneasiness, a grief deep in its being, because what it has done is contrary to its inner truth.

For in spite of all teachings, in spite of all that thought can think, there is something in the depths which has a feeling of a perfection, a greatness, a truth, and is painfully contradicted by all the movements opposing this truth. If a child has not been spoilt by its milieu, by deplorable examples around it, that is, if it is in the normal state, spontaneously, without its being told anything, it will feel an uneasiness when it has done something against the truth of its being. And it is exactly upon this that later its effort for progress must be founded.

For, if you want to find one teaching, one doctrine upon which to base your progress, you will never find anything — or, to be more exact, you will find something else, for in accordance with the climate, the age, the civilisation, the teaching given is quite conflicting. When one person says, "This is good", another will say, "No, this is bad", and with the same logic, the same persuasive force. Consequently, it is not upon this that one can build. Religion has always tried to establish a dogma, and it will tell you that if you conform to the dogma you are in the truth and if you don't you are in the falsehood. But all this has never led to anything and has only created confusion.

There is only one true guide, that is the inner guide, who does not pass through the mental consciousness.

Naturally, if a child gets a disastrous education, it will try ever harder to extinguish within itself this little true thing, and sometimes it succeeds so well that it loses all contact with it, and also the power of distinguishing between good and evil. That is why I insist upon this, and I say that from their infancy children must be taught that there is an inner reality — within themselves, within the earth, within the universe — and that they, the earth and the universe exist only as a function of this truth, and that if it did not exist the child would not last, even the short time that it does, and that everything would dissolve even as it comes into being. And because this is the real basis of the universe, naturally it is this which will triumph; and all that opposes this cannot endure as long as this does, because it is That, the eternal thing which is at the base of the universe.

It is not a question, of course, of giving a child philosophical explanations, but he could very well be given the feeling of this kind of inner comfort, of satisfaction, and sometimes, of an intense joy when he obeys this little very silent thing within him which will prevent him from doing what is contrary to it. It is on an experience of this kind that teaching may be based. The child must be given the impression that nothing can endure if he does not have within himself this true satisfaction which alone is permanent.

Can a child become conscious of this inner truth like an adult?

For a child this is very clear, for it is a perception without any complications of word or thought — there is that which puts him at ease and that which makes him uneasy (it is not necessarily joy or sorrow which come only when the thing is very intense). And all this is much clearer in the child than in an adult, for the latter has always a mind which works and clouds his perception of the truth.

To give a child theories is absolutely useless, for as soon as his mind awakes he will find a thousand reasons for contradicting your theories, and he will be right.

This little true thing in the child is the divine presence in the psychic — it is also there in plants and animals. In plants it is not conscious, in animals it begins to be conscious, and in children it is very conscious. I have known children who were much more conscious of their psychic being at the age of five than at fourteen, and at fourteen than at twenty-five; and above all, from the moment they go to school where they undergo that kind of intensive mental training which draws their attention to the intellectual part of their being, they lose almost always and almost completely this contact with their psychic being.

If only you were an experienced observer, if you could tell what goes on in a person, simply by looking into his eyes!... It is said the eyes are the mirror of the soul; that is a popular way of speaking but if the eyes do not express to you the psychic, it is because it is very far behind, veiled by many things. Look carefully, then, into the eyes of little children, and you will see a kind of light — some describe it as frank — but so true, so true, which looks at the world with wonder. Well, this sense of wonder, it is the wonder of the psychic which sees the truth but does not understand much about the world, for it is too far from it. Children have this but as they learn more, become more intelligent, more educated, this is effaced, and you see all sorts of things in their eyes: thoughts, desires, passions, wickedness — but this kind of little flame, so pure, is no longer there. And you may be sure it is the mind that has got in there, and the psychic has gone very far behind.

Even a child who does not have a sufficiently developed brain to understand, if you simply pass on to him a vibration of protection or affection or solicitude or consolation, you will see that he responds. But if you take a boy of fourteen, for example, who is at school, who has ordinary parents and has been ill-treated, his mind is very much in the forefront; there is something hard in him, the psychic being has gone behind. Such boys do not respond to the vibration. One would say they are made of wood or plaster.

If the inner truth, the divine presence in the psychic is so conscious in the child, it could no longer be said that a child is a little animal, could it?

Why not? In animals there is sometimes a very intense psychic truth. Naturally, I believe that the psychic being is a little more formed, a little more conscious in a child than in an animal. But I have experimented with animals, just to know; well, I assure you that in human beings I have rarely come across some of the virtues which I have seen in animals, very simple, unpretentious virtues. As in cats, for example: I have studied cats a lot; if one knows them well they are marvellous creatures. I have known mother-cats which have sacrificed themselves entirely for their babies — people speak of maternal love with such admiration, as though it were purely a human privilege, but I have seen this love manifested by mother-cats to a degree far surpassing ordinary humanity. I have seen a mother-cat which would never touch her food until her babies had taken all they needed. I have seen another cat which stayed eight days beside her kittens, without satisfying any of her needs because she was afraid to leave them alone; and a cat which repeated more than fifty times the same movement to teach her young one how to jump from a wall on to a window, and I may add, with a care, an intelligence, a skill which many uneducated women do not have. And why is it thus? — because there was no mental intervention. It was altogether spontaneous instinct. But what is instinct? — it is the presence of the Divine in the genus of the species, and that, that is the psychic of animals; a collective, not an individual psychic.

I have seen in animals all the reactions, emotional, affective, sentimental, all the feelings of which men are so proud. The only differ-

ence is that animals cannot speak of them and write about them, so
we consider them inferior beings because they cannot flood us with
books on what they have felt.

> *When I was a child if I did something bad immediately I felt un-*
> *easy and I would decide never to do that again. Then my parents*
> *also used to tell me never again to do it. Why? because I had*
> *myself decided not to do it any more?*

A child should never be scolded. I am accused of speaking ill of parents! but I have seen them at work, you see, and I know that ninety
per cent of parents snub a child who comes spontaneously to confess
a mistake: "You are very naughty. Go away, I am busy" — instead of
listening to the child with patience and explaining to him where his
fault lies, how he ought to have acted. And the child, who had come
with good intentions, goes away quite hurt, with the feeling: "Why
am I treated thus?" Then the child sees his parents are not perfect —
which is obviously true of them today — he sees that they are wrong
and says to himself: "Why does he scold me, he is like me!"

8 January 1951

*

Children are not as "concretised", materialised in their physical consciousness as older people — as one grows up, it is as though one is
coagulated and becomes more and more gross in one's consciousness
unless through a willed action one develops otherwise. For instance,
the majority of children find it very difficult to distinguish their imagination, their dreams, what they see inside themselves from outer
things. The world is not as limited as when one is older and more
precise. And they are extremely sensitive within; they are much closer
to their psychic being than when they are grown up, and much more
sensitive to the forces which, later, will become invisible to them —
but at this moment are not. It is not unusual for children to have some
sort of fits of fear or even of joy in their sleep, from dreams. Children
are afraid of all sorts of things which for older people don't exist any
more. Their vision is not solely material. They have a kind of percep-

tion, more or less exact and precise, of the play of the forces behind. So, being in that state they are influenced by forces which otherwise have no hold over people who are shut up in themselves and more gross. And these forces — the forces of destruction, for example, or forces of cruelty, forces of wickedness, of ill-will — all, all these things are in the atmosphere. When one is more conscious and more well-formed within, one can see them as outside oneself and deny them any expression. But when one is very young and lives in a half-dream, these things can exercise much influence and make children do things which in their normal state they would not do. I believe it is due to that above all.

There is also the phenomenon of unconsciousness. Very often a child does harm without even being aware that it is doing harm; they are unconscious, they are shut up in their movement, and they are not aware of the effect of what they do. That happens very often.

That means that if a child is rightly educated, and if one appeals to his best feelings and explains to him that to do things in such and such a way is harmful to others (and one can make this very tangible for them with a little demonstration), they stop doing harm, very often.

It is above all a question of education. These half-conscious movements of cruelty — it is very rare for parents not to have them; well, that is enough to set its impression upon a child's consciousness. There are some — but that is a very small number — who have an adverse formation inside them. These are irretrievably wicked children. But they are very rare.

30 December 1953

Learning to Know Oneself

Essentially there is but one single true reason for living: it is to know oneself. We are here to learn — to learn what we are, why we are here, and what we have to do. And if we don't know that, our life is altogether empty — for ourselves and for others.

And so, generally, it is better to begin early, for there is much to learn. If one wants to learn about life as it is, the world as it is, and then really know the why and the how of life, one can begin when very young, from the time one is very, very tiny — before the age of five. And then, when one is a hundred, he will still be able to learn. So it is interesting. And all the time one can have surprises, always learn something one didn't know, meet with an experience one did not have before, find something one was ignorant of. It is surely very interesting. And the more one knows, the more aware does one become that one has everything to learn. Truly, I could say that only fools believe they know.

3 February 1954

*

I think it was just today or perhaps yesterday, I was pleading for the right of everyone to remain in ignorance if it pleases him — I am not speaking of ignorance from the spiritual point of view, the world of Ignorance in which we live, I am not speaking of that. I am speaking of ignorance according to the classical ideas of education. Well, I say that if there are people who don't want to learn and don't like to learn, they have the right not to learn.

The only thing it is our duty to tell them is this, "Now, you are of an age when your brain is in course of preparation. It is being formed. Each new thing you study makes one more little convolution in your brain. The more you study, the more you think, the more you reflect, the more you work, the more complex and complete does your brain become in its tiny convolutions. And as you are young, it is best done at this time. That is why it is common human practice to choose youth as the period of learning, for it is infinitely easier." And it is obvious that until the child becomes at least a little conscious of itself, it must be subjected to a certain rule, for it has not yet the capacity of choosing for itself.

That age is very variable; it depends on people, depends on each individual. But still, it is understood that in the seven-year period between the age of seven and fourteen, one begins to reach the age of reason. If one is helped, one can become a reasoning being between seven and fourteen.

Before seven there are geniuses — there are always geniuses, every-where — but as a general rule the child is not conscious of itself and doesn't know why or how to do things. That is the time to cultivate its attention, teach it to concentrate on what it does, give it a small basis sufficient for it not to be entirely like a little animal, but to belong to the human race through an elementary intellectual development.

After that, there is a period of seven years during which it must be taught to choose — to choose what it wants to be. If it chooses to have a rich, complex, well-developed brain, powerful in its functioning, well, it must be taught to work; for it is by work, by reflection, study, analysis and so on that the brain is formed. At fourteen you are ready — or ought to be ready — to know what you want to be.

And so I say: if at about that age some children declare categorically, "Intellectual growth does not interest me at all, I don't want to learn, I want to remain ignorant in the ordinary way of ignorance", I don't see by what right one could impose studies on them nor why it should be necessary to standardise them.

There are those who are at the bottom and others who are at another level. There are people who may have very remarkable capacities and yet have no taste for intellectual growth. One may warn them that if they don't work, don't study, when they are grown up, they will perhaps feel embarrassed in front of others. But if that does not matter to them and they want to live a non-intellectual life, I believe one has no right to compel them. That is my constant quarrel with the teachers of the [Ashram] school! They come and tell me: "If they don't work, when they are grown up they will be stupid and ignorant." I say: "But if it pleases them to be stupid and ignorant, what right have you to interfere?"

One can't make knowledge and intelligence compulsory. That's all.

Now, if you believe that by abstaining from all effort and all study, you will become geniuses, and supramental geniuses at that, don't have any illusions, it won't happen to you. For even if you touch a higher light, through an inner aspiration or by a divine grace, you will have nothing in there, in your brain, to be able to express it. So it will remain quite nebulous and won't in any way change your outer life. But if it pleases you to be like this, nobody has the right to compel you to be otherwise. You must wait till you are sufficiently conscious to be able to choose.

Of course, there are people who at fourteen are yet like children of five. But these — there's little hope for them. Especially those who have lived here.

Here's something then which already changes your outlook on education completely.

Essentially, the *only thing* you should do assiduously is to teach them to know themselves and choose their own destiny, the path they will follow; to teach them to look at themselves, understand themselves *and* to will what they want to be. That is infinitely more important than teaching them what happened on earth in former times, or even how the earth is built, or even... indeed, all sorts of things which are quite a necessary grounding if you want to live the ordinary life in the world, for if you don't know them, anyone will immediately put you down intellectually: "Oh, he is an idiot, he knows nothing."

But still, at any age, if you are studious and have the will to do it, you can also take up books and work; you don't need to go to school for that. There are enough books in the world to teach you things. There are even many more books than necessary.[...]

But what is very important is to know what you want. And for this a minimum of freedom is necessary. You must not be under a compulsion or an obligation. You must be able to do things whole-heartedly. If you are lazy, well, you will know what it means to be lazy.... You know, in life idlers are obliged to work ten times more than others, for what they do they do badly, so they are obliged to do it again. But these are things one must learn by experience. They can't be instilled into you.

The mind, if not controlled, is something wavering and imprecise. If one doesn't have the habit of concentrating it upon something, it goes on wandering all the time. It goes on without a stop anywhere and wanders into a *world* of vagueness. And then, when one wants to fix one's attention, it hurts! There is a little effort there, like this: "Oh! how tiring it is, it hurts!" So one does not do it. And one lives in a kind of cloud. And your head is like a cloud; it's like that, most brains are like clouds: there is no precision, no exactitude, no clarity, it is hazy — vague and hazy. You have impressions rather than a knowledge of things. You live in an approximation, and you can keep within you all sorts of contradictory ideas made up mostly of impressions, sensations, feelings, emotions — all sorts of things like that which have very little to do with thought and... which are just vague ramblings.

But if you want to succeed in having a precise, concrete, clear, definite thought on a certain subject, you must make an effort, gather yourself together, hold yourself firm, concentrate. And the first time you do it, it literally hurts, it is tiring! But if you don't make a habit of it, all your life you will be living in a state of irresolution. And when it comes to practical things, when you are faced with — for, in spite of everything, one is always faced with — a number of problems to solve, of a very practical kind, well, instead of being able to take up the elements of the problem, to put them all face to face, look at the question from every side, and rising above and seeing the solution, instead of that you will be tossed about in the swirls of something grey and uncertain, and it will be like so many spiders running around in your head — but you won't succeed in catching the thing.

I am speaking of the simplest of problems, you know; I am not speaking of deciding the fate of the world or humanity, or even of a country — nothing of the kind. I am speaking of the problems of your daily life, of every day. They become something quite woolly.

Well, it is to avoid this that you are told, when your brain is in course of being formed, "Instead of letting it be shaped by such habits and qualities, try to give it a little exactitude, precision, capacity of concentration, of choosing, deciding, putting things in order, try to use your reason."

Of course, it is well understood that reason is not the supreme capacity of man and must be surpassed, but it is quite obvious that if you don't have it, you will live an altogether incoherent life, you won't even know how to behave rationally. The least thing will upset you completely and you won't even know why, and still less how to remedy it. While someone who has established within himself a state of active, clear reasoning, can face attacks of all kinds, emotional attacks or any trials whatever; for life is entirely made up of these things — unpleasantness, vexations — which are small but proportionate to the one who feels them, and so naturally felt by him as very big because they are proportionate to him. Well, reason can stand back a little, look at all that, smile and say, "Oh! no, one must not make a fuss over such a small thing."

If you do not have reason, you will be like a cork on a stormy sea.
I don't know if the cork suffers from its condition, but it does not
seem to me a very happy one.

There, then.

Now, after having said all this — and it's not just once I have told
you this but several times I think, and I am ready to tell it to you again
as many times as you like — after having said this, I believe in leaving you entirely free to choose whether you want to be the cork on the
stormy sea or whether you want to have a clear, precise perception
and a sufficient knowledge of things to be able to walk to — well,
simply to where you want to go.

For there is a clarity that's indispensable in order to be able even
to follow the path one has chosen.

I am not at all keen on your becoming scholars, far from it! For
then one falls into the other extreme: one fills one's head with so
many things that there is no longer any room for the higher light; but
there is a minimum that is indispensable for not... well, for not being
the cork.

*Mother, some say that our general inadequacy in studies comes
from the fact that too much stress is laid on games, physical education. Is this true?*

Who said that? People who don't like physical education? Stiff old
teachers who can't do exercises any longer? These? — I am not asking for names!

Well, I don't think so.

You remember the first article Sri Aurobindo wrote in the *Bulle-
tin*?* He answers these people quite categorically.

I don't think it is that. I am quite sure it is not that, I believe,
rather — and I put all the blame on myself — that you have been
given a fantastic freedom, my children; oh! I don't think there is any
other place in the world where children are so free. And, indeed, it is
very difficult to know how to make use of a freedom like that.

* An article on the value of physical education.

However, it was worthwhile trying the experiment. You don't appreciate it because you don't know how it is when it is not like that; it seems quite natural to you. But it is very difficult to know how to organise one's own freedom oneself. Still, if you were to succeed in doing that, in giving yourself your own discipline — and for higher reasons, not in order to pass exams, to make a career, please your teachers, win many prizes, or all the ordinary reasons children have: in order not to be scolded, not to be punished, for all that; we leave out all those reasons — if you manage to impose a discipline upon yourself — each one his own, there is no need to follow someone else's — a discipline simply because you want to progress and draw the best out of yourself, then... Oh! you will be far superior to those who follow the ordinary school disciplines. That is what I wanted to try. Mind you, I don't say I have failed; I still have great hope that you will know how to profit by this unique opportunity. But all the same, there is something you must find out; it is the *necessity* of an inner discipline. Without discipline you won't be able to get anywhere, without discipline you can't even live the normal life of a normal man. But instead of having the conventional discipline of ordinary societies or ordinary institutions, I would have liked and I still want you to have the discipline you set yourselves, for the love of perfection, your own perfection, the perfection of your being.

But without that... Note that if one didn't discipline the body, one would not even be able to stand on two legs, one would continue like a child on all fours. You could do nothing. You are obliged to discipline yourself; you could not live in society, you could not live at all, except all alone in the forest; and even then, I don't quite know. It is absolutely indispensable, I have told you this I don't know how often. And because I have a very marked aversion for conventional disciplines, social and others, it does not mean that you must abstain from all discipline. I would like everyone to find his own, in the sincerity of his inner aspiration and the will to realise himself.

And so, the aim of all those who know, whether they are teachers, instructors or any others, the very purpose of those who know, is to inform you, to help you. When you are in a situation which seems difficult to you, you put your problem and, from their personal experience, they can tell you, "No, it is like this or it is like that, and you

must do this, you must try that." So, instead of forcing you to absorb
theories, principles and so-called laws, and a more or less abstract
knowledge, they would be there to give you information about things,
from the most material to the most spiritual, each one within his own
province and according to his capacity.

It is quite obvious that if you are thrown into the world without
the least technical knowledge, you may do the most dangerous things.
Take a child who knows nothing, the first thing he will do if he has
any matches, for instance, is to burn himself. So, in that field, from
the purely material point of view, it is good that there are people who
know and who can inform you; for otherwise, if each one had to learn
from his own experience, he would spend several lives learning the
most indispensable things. That is the usefulness, the *true* usefulness
of teachers and instructors. They have learnt more or less by practice
or through a special study, and they can teach you those things it is
indispensable to know. That makes you save time, a lot of time. But
that is their only usefulness: to be able to answer questions. And, in
fact, you should have a brain which is lively enough to ask questions.
I don't know, but you never have anything to ask me or it is so seldom.

13 June 1956

A Child's Dreams

When one is very young and as I say "well-born", that is, born with a
conscious psychic being within, there is always, in the dreams of the
child, a kind of aspiration, which for its child's consciousness is a
sort of ambition, for something which would be beauty without ugliness, justice without injustice, goodness without limits, and a conscious, constant success, a perpetual miracle. One dreams of miracles
when one is young, one wants all wickedness to disappear, everything to be always luminous, beautiful, happy, one likes stories which
end happily. This is what one should rely on. When the body feels its
miseries, its limitations, one must establish this dream in it — of a
strength which would have no limit, a beauty which would have no
ugliness, and of marvellous capacities: one dreams of being able to
rise into the air, of being wherever it is necessary to be, of setting

things right when they go wrong, of healing the sick; indeed, one has all sorts of dreams when one is very young.... Usually parents or teachers pass their time throwing cold water on it, telling you, "Oh! it's a dream, it is not a reality." They should do the very opposite! Children should be taught, "Yes, this is what you must try to realise and not only is it possible but it is *certain* if you come in contact with the part in you which is capable of doing this thing. This is what should guide your life, organise it, make you develop in the direction of the *true reality* which the ordinary world calls illusion."

This is what it should be, instead of making children ordinary, with that dull, vulgar common sense which becomes an inveterate habit and, when something is going well, immediately brings up in the being the idea: "Oh, that won't last!", when somebody is kind, the impression, "Oh, he will change!", when one is capable of doing something, "Oh, tomorrow I won't be able to do it so well." This is like an acid, a destructive acid in the being, which takes away hope, certitude, confidence in future possibilities.

When a child is full of enthusiasm, never throw cold water on it, never tell him, "You know, life is not like that!" You should always encourage him, tell him, "Yes, at present things are not always like that, they *seem* ugly, but behind this there is a beauty that is trying to realise itself. This is what you should love and draw towards you, this is what you should make the object of your dreams, of your ambitions."

And if you do this when you are very small, you have much less difficulty than if later on you have to undo, undo all the bad effects of a bad education, undo that kind of dull and vulgar common sense which means that you expect nothing good from life, which makes it insipid, boring, and contradicts all the hopes, all the so-called illusions of beauty. On the contrary, you must tell a child — or yourself if you are no longer quite a baby — "Everything in me that seems unreal, impossible, illusory, *that* is what is true, *that* is what I must cultivate." When you have these aspirations: "Oh, not to be always limited by some incapacity, all the time held back by some bad will!", you must cultivate within you this certitude that *that* is what is essentially true and *that* is what must be realised.

Then faith awakens in the cells of the body. And you will see that you find a response in your body itself. The body itself will feel that if its inner will helps, fortifies, directs, leads, well, all its limitations will gradually disappear.

And so, when the first experience comes, which sometimes begins when one is very young, the first contact with the inner joy, the inner beauty, the inner light, the first contact with *that*, which suddenly makes you feel, "Oh! that is what I want," you must cultivate it, never forget it, hold it constantly before you, tell yourself, "I have felt it once, so I can feel it again. This has been real for me, even for the space of a second, and that is what I am going to revive in myself".... And encourage the body to seek it — to seek it, *with the confidence* that it carries that possibility within itself and that if it calls for it, it will come back, it will be realised again.

This is what should be done when one is young. This is what should be done every time one has the opportunity to recollect oneself, commune with oneself, seek oneself.

[...] When one is normal, that is to say, unspoilt by bad teaching and bad example, when one is born and lives in a healthy and relatively balanced and normal environment, the body, spontaneously, without any need for one to intervene mentally or even vitally, has the certitude that even if something goes wrong it will be cured. The body carries within itself the certitude of cure, the certitude that the illness or disorder is sure to disappear. It is only through the false education from the environment that gradually the body is taught that there are incurable diseases, irreparable accidents, and that it can grow old, and all these stories which destroy its faith and trust. But normally, the body of a normal child — the body, I am not speaking of the thought — the body itself feels when something goes wrong that it will certainly be all right again. And if it is not like that, this means that it has already been perverted. It seems *normal* for it to be in good health, it seems quite abnormal to it if something goes wrong and it falls ill; and in its instinct, its spontaneous instinct, it is sure that everything will be all right. It is only the perversion of thought which destroys this; as one grows up the thought becomes more and more distorted, there is the whole collective suggestion, and so, little by little, the body loses its trust in itself, and naturally, losing its self-confidence, it also loses the spontaneous capacity of restoring its equilibrium when this has been disturbed.

But if when very young, from your earliest childhood, you have been taught all sorts of disappointing, depressing things — things that cause decomposition, I could say, disintegration — then this poor body does its best but it has been perverted, put out of order, and no longer has the sense of its inner strength, its inner force, its power to react.

If one takes care not to pervert it, the body carries within itself the certitude of victory. It is only the wrong use we make of thought and its influence on the body which robs it of this certitude of victory. So, the first thing to do is to cultivate this certitude instead of destroying it; and when it is there, no effort is needed to aspire, but simply a flowering, an unfolding of that inner certitude of victory.

The body carries within itself the sense of its divinity. There. This is what you must try to find again in yourself if you have lost it.

When a child tells you a beautiful dream in which he had many powers and all things were very beautiful, be very careful never to tell him, "Oh! life is not like that", for you are doing something wrong. You must on the contrary tell him, "Life *ought to be* like that, and *it will be* like that!"

31 July 1957

*

There are children who... continue their dreams. Every evening when they go to bed they return to the same place and continue their dream.

When I was a child I used to do that.

You are no longer a child, that's a pity!

Because I had no preoccupations then.

Well, become a child once more and you will know how to do it again.

Nothing is more interesting. It is a most pleasant way of passing the nights. You begin a story, then, when it is time to wake up, you put a full stop to the last sentence and come back into your body. And then the following night you start off again, re-open the page and resume your story during the whole time you are out; and then you arrange things well — they must be well arranged, it must be very beautiful. And when it is time to come back, you put a full stop once again and tell those things, "Stay very quiet till I return!" And you come back into your body. And you continue this every evening and write a book of wonderful fairy-tales — provided you remember them when you wake up.

But this depends on being in a quiet state during the day, doesn't it?

No, it depends on the candour of the child.

And on the trust he has in what happens to him, on the absence of the mind's critical sense, and a simplicity of heart, and a youthful and active energy — it depends on all that — on a kind of inner vital generosity: one must not be too egoistic, one must not be too miserly, nor too practical, too utilitarian — indeed there are all sorts of things one should not be... like children. And then, one must have a lively power of imagination, for — I seem to be telling you stupid things, but it is quite true — there is a world in which you are the supreme maker of forms: that is your own particular vital world. You are the supreme fashioner and you can make a marvel of your world if you know how to use it. If you have an artistic or poetic consciousness, if you love harmony, beauty, you will build there something marvellous which will tend to spring up into the material manifestation.

When I was small I used to call this "telling stories to oneself". It is not at all a telling with words, in one's head: it is a going away to this place which is fresh and pure, and... building up a wonderful story there. And if you know how to tell yourself a story in this way, and if it is truly beautiful, truly harmonious, truly powerful and well co-ordinated, this story will be realised in your life — perhaps not exactly in the form in which you created it, but as a more or less changed physical expression of what you made.

That may take years, perhaps, but your story will tend to organise your life.

But there are very few people who know how to tell a beautiful story; and then they always mix horrors in it, which they regret later.

If one could create a magnificent story without any horror in it, nothing but beauty, it would have a *considerable* influence on everyone's life. And this is what people don't know.

If one knew how to use this power, this creative power in the world of vital forms, if one knew how to use this while yet a child, a very small child... for it is then that one fashions his material destiny. But usually people around you, sometimes even your own little friends, but mostly parents and teachers, dabble in it and spoil everything for you, so well that very seldom does the thing succeed completely.

But otherwise, if it were done like that, with the spontaneous candour of a child, you could organise a wonderful life for yourself — I am speaking of the physical world.

The dreams of childhood are the realities of mature age.

18 April 1956

CHAPTER 17

Yoga and Meditation

Why Yoga?

Mother, here it is said: "He who chooses the Infinite has been chosen by the Infinite." (Sri Aurobindo)

It is a magnificent sentence!

And it is absolutely true. There is in *Thoughts and Glimpses* also a sentence like this where I think he [Sri Aurobindo] uses the word "God" instead of the Infinite. But the idea is the same — that it is God who has chosen you, the Divine who has chosen you. And that is why you run after Him!

And this is what gives — that's what he says, doesn't he? — this is what gives that kind of confidence, of certitude, precisely, that one is predestined; and if one is predestined, even if there are mountains of difficulties, what can that matter since one is sure to succeed! This gives you an indomitable courage to face all difficulties and a patience that stands all trials: you are sure to succeed.

And it's a fact — in fact, it is like that: the moment you thought about it, well, you thought about it because someone thought about you; you chose because you were chosen. And once you have been chosen, you are sure of the thing. Therefore, doubts, hesitations, depressions, uncertainties, all this is quite simply a waste of time and energy; it is of no use at all.

From the moment one has felt just once within himself: "Ah! *this* is the truth for me", it is finished; it is finished, it is settled. Even if you spend years cutting your way through the virgin forest, it's of no importance — it is finished, it is settled.

That is why I told you one day, "After all, you all are here because you have wanted it somewhere; and if you wanted it somewhere, it means that the Divine wanted it thus in you."

So there are some who follow a very straight path and arrive very quickly; there are others who love labyrinths, it takes longer. But the end is there, the goal is there. I know by experience that there isn't one being who, were it only once in his life, has had a great urge towards... it doesn't matter how he calls it — let us say the Divine for facility of speech, who is not sure to arrive; even if he turns his back on Him at a certain time, it's of no importance — he is sure to arrive. He will have to struggle more or less, will have more or less difficulty, but he is sure to succeed one day. It's a soul that has been chosen, it has become conscious because its hour has come — once the hour has come, well, the result will follow more or less quickly. You can do this in a few months; you can do it in some years; you can do it in some lives — but you will do it.

And what is remarkable is that this freedom of choice is left to you and that, if you decide within yourself that you will do it in this lifetime, you will do it. And I am not speaking here of a permanent and continuous decision because then you can arrive in twelve months. No, I mean: if you have suddenly been seized by this "I want this", even once, in a flash, the seal is put, there, like that.

19 October 1955

*

Sweet Mother, "The Supreme has laid his luminous hand upon a chosen human vessel of his miraculous Light and Power and Ananda." (Sri Aurobindo)

Does the Supreme choose the being who will be his instrument, or does the being choose to become his instrument?

You can take it as you like.

One can't tell who began! But the two usually take place at the same time.

If you want an order of priority, it is evident that the Divine exists before the individual, so it must be the Divine who has chosen first! But that is a choice prior to terrestrial life. In the order of the ordinary human consciousness it may be one or the other or both at the same time. In fact, it is likely that the Divine is the first to notice that this or that being is ready! But he who is ready generally does not know it to begin with, so he has the impression that it is he who has decided and is choosing. But this is more of an impression than a reality.

And once you are chosen, it is ineluctable, you can't escape even if you try.

18 January 1956

*

The fact of being born with a psychic being and upon earth which is a spiritual symbol proves that we have each one of us a great responsibility, doesn't it?

Surely. One has a big responsibility, it is to fulfil a special mission that one is born upon earth. Only, naturally, the psychic being must have reached a certain degree of development; otherwise it could be said that it is the whole earth which has the responsibility. The more conscious and individualised one becomes, the more should one have the sense of responsibility. But this is what happens at a given moment; one begins to think that one is here not without reason, without purpose. One realises suddenly that one is here because there is something to be done and this something is not anything egoistic. This seems to me the most logical way of entering upon the path — all of a sudden to realise, "Since I am here, it means that I have a mission to fulfil. Since I have been endowed with a consciousness, it is that I have something to do with that consciousness — what is it?"

Generally, it seems to me that this is the first question one should put to oneself: "Why am I here?"

I have seen this in children, even in children of five or six: "Why am I here, why do I live?" And then to search, with whatever consciousness is available, with a very little bit of consciousness: why am I here, for what reason?

This seems to me the normal starting-point.

24 March 1951

*

Well, to find out what one truly is, to find out why one is on earth, what is the purpose of physical existence, of this presence on earth, of this formation, this existence... the vast majority of people live without asking themselves this even once! Only a small elite ask themselves this question with interest, and fewer still start working to get the answer. For, unless one is fortunate enough to come across someone who knows it, it is not such an easy thing to find. Suppose, for instance, that there had never come to your hands a book of Sri Aurobindo or of any of the writers or philosophers or sages who have dedicated their lives to this quest; if you were in the ordinary world, as millions of people are in the ordinary world, who have never heard of anything, except at times — and not always nowadays, even quite rarely — of some gods and a certain form of religion which is more a habit than a faith and, which, besides, rarely tells you why you are on earth... then, one doesn't even think of thinking about it. One lives from day to day the events of each day. When one is very young, one thinks of playing, eating, and a little later of learning, and after that one thinks of all the circumstances of life. But to put this problem to oneself, to confront this problem and ask oneself: "But after all, *why* am I here?" How many do that? There are people to whom this idea comes only when they are facing a catastrophe. When they see someone whom they love die or when they find themselves in particularly painful and difficult circumstances, they turn back upon themselves, if they are sufficiently intelligent, and ask themselves: "But really, what is this tragedy we are living, and what's the use of it and what is its purpose?"

And only at that moment does one begin the search to know.

And it is only when one has found, you see, found what he [Sri Aurobindo] says, found that one has a divine Self and that consequently one must seek to know this divine Self.... This comes much later, and yet, in spite of everything, from the very moment of birth in a physical body, there is in the being, in its depths, this psychic presence which pushes the whole being towards this fulfilment. But who knows it and recognises it, this psychic being? That too comes only in special circumstances, and unfortunately, most of the time these have to be painful circumstances, otherwise one goes on living unthinkingly. And in the depths of one's being is this psychic being which seeks, seeks, seeks to awaken the consciousness and re-establish the union. One knows nothing about it.

                                                            16 January 1957

                                   *

Even a fleeting idea in a child, at a certain moment in its childhood when the psychic being is most in front, if it succeeds in penetrating through the outer consciousness and giving the child just an impression of something beautiful which must be realised, it creates a little nucleus and upon this you build your action. There is a vast mass of humanity to whom one would never say, "You must realise the Divine" or "Do yoga to find the Divine." If you observe well you will see that it is a tiny minority to whom this can be said. It means that this minority of beings is "prepared" to do yoga, it is that. It is that there has been a beginning of realisation — a beginning is enough. With others it is perhaps an old thing, an awakening which may come from past lives. But we are speaking of those who are less ready; they are those who have had at a certain moment a flash which has passed through their whole being and created a response, but that suffices. This does not happen to many people. Those ready to do yoga are not many if you compare them with the unconscious human mass. But one thing is certain, the fact that you are all here proves that at the least you have had that — there are those who are very far on the path (sometimes they have no idea about it), but at the least all of you have had that, that kind of spontaneous integral contact which is like an electric shock, a lightning-flash which goes through you and wakes you up to something: there is something to be realised. It is possible that the experience is not translated into words, only into a flame. That is enough. And it is around this nucleus that one organises oneself, slowly, slowly, progressively. And once it is there it never disappears. It is only if you have made a pact with the adverse forces and make a considerable effort to break the contact and not notice its existence, that you may believe it has disappeared. And yet a single flash suffices for it to come back.

If you have had this just once, you may tell yourself that in this life or another you are sure to realise.

26 March 1951

*

Sweet Mother, how can we find the Divine who is hidden in us?

This we have explained many, many times. But the first thing is to want it, and know precisely that this comes first, before all other things, that this is the important thing. That is the first condition; all the rest may come later, this is the *essential* condition. You see, if once in a while, from time to time, when you have nothing to do and all goes well and you are unoccupied, suddenly you tell yourself, "Ah, I would like so much to find the Divine!" — well, this — it may take a hundred thousand years, in this way.

But if it is the important thing, the only thing that matters, and if everything else comes afterwards, and you want nothing *but this*, then — this is the first condition. You must first establish this, later we may speak of what follows. First this, that all the rest does not count, that only *this* counts, that one is ready to give up everything to have this, that it is the only thing of importance in life. Then one puts oneself in the condition of being able to take a step forward.

29 September 1954

*

Anyway, happily nobody has said that he desired yoga to obtain power. There are countries and people who know vaguely that there is something called yoga, and they begin it with the idea that they will become superior to others, will get a greater power than others and consequently will be able to dominate others — this is the worst reason, the most selfish, that which brings the most harmful consequences. Others who are greatly troubled, who have a very difficult life, who have worries, sorrows, many cares, say, "Oh, I shall find something that will give me peace, tranquillity, and I shall be able to get a little rest." And they rush into yoga thinking they are going to be quite happy and satisfied. Unfortunately, it is not altogether like that. When you begin the yoga for reasons of this kind, you are sure to meet great difficulties on the way. And then there is this great virtue in men's eyes: philanthropy, love of humanity; so many people say, "I am going to do yoga to be able to serve humanity, make the unhappy happy, organise the world in the happiest way for everybody." I say this is not sufficient — I do not say that this is bad in itself, although I have heard an old occultist say wittily: "It won't be so very soon that there will be no more misery in the world, because there are too many people who are happy to live on this misery." It was a witticism but it is not altogether wrong. If there were no misery to soothe, the philanthropist would no longer have any reason for his existence — he is so satisfied with himself, he has so strong an impression that he is not selfish! I knew such people who would be very unhappy if there were no more misery upon earth! What would they do if there were no longer any misery to relieve, what would be their activity and what their glorification? How would they be able to show people "I am not selfish!", and that they are generous, full of kindness?

3 February 1951

*

What is one to do to prepare oneself for the Yoga?

To be conscious, first of all. We are conscious of only an insignificant portion of our being; for the most part we are unconscious. It is this unconsciousness that keeps us down to our unregenerate nature and prevents change and transformation in it. It is through unconsciousness that the undivine forces enter into us and make us their slaves. You are to be conscious of yourself, you must awake to your nature and movements, you must know why and how you do things or feel or think them; you must understand your motives and impulses, the forces, hidden and apparent, that move you; in fact, you must, as it were, take to pieces the entire machinery of your being. Once you are conscious, it means that you can distinguish and sift things, you can see which are the forces that pull you down and which help you on. And when you know the right from the wrong, the true from the false, the divine from the undivine, you are to act strictly up to your knowledge; that is to say, resolutely reject one and accept the other. The duality will present itself at every step and at every step you will have to make your choice. You will have to be patient and persistent and vigilant — "sleepless", as the adepts say; you must always refuse to give any chance whatever to the undivine against the divine.

7 April 1929

*

What are the dangers of Yoga? Is it especially dangerous to the
people of the West? Someone has said that Yoga may be suitable
for the East, but it has the effect of unbalancing the Western mind.

Yoga is not more dangerous to the people of the West than to those of
the East. Everything depends upon the spirit with which you approach
it. Yoga does become dangerous if you want it for your own sake, to
serve a personal end. It is not dangerous, on the contrary, it is safety
and security itself, if you go to it with a sense of its sacredness, always remembering that the aim is to find the Divine.

Dangers and difficulties come in when people take up Yoga not
for the sake of the Divine, but because they want to acquire power
and under the guise of Yoga seek to satisfy some ambition. If you
cannot get rid of ambition, do not touch the thing. It is fire that burns.

There are two paths of Yoga, one of *tapasyā* (discipline), and the
other of surrender. The path of *tapasyā* is arduous. Here you rely
solely upon yourself, you proceed by your own strength. You ascend
and achieve according to the measure of your force. There is always
the danger of falling down. And once you fall, you lie broken in the
abyss and there is hardly a remedy. The other path, the path of surrender, is safe and sure. It is here, however, that the Western people find
their difficulty. They have been taught to fear and avoid all that threatens their personal independence. They have imbibed with their mothers' milk the sense of individuality. And surrender means giving up
all that. In other words, you may follow, as Ramakrishna says, either
the path of the baby monkey or that of the baby cat. The baby monkey
holds to its mother in order to be carried about and it must hold firm,
otherwise if it loses its grip, it falls. On the other hand, the baby cat
does not hold to its mother, but is held by the mother and has no fear
nor responsibility; it has nothing to do but to let the mother hold it
and cry *ma ma*.

If you take up this path of surrender fully and sincerely, there is no
more danger or serious difficulty. The question is to be sincere. If you
are not sincere, do not begin Yoga. If you were dealing in human affairs, then you could resort to deception; but in dealing with the Divine
there is no possibility of deception anywhere. You can go on the Path
safely when you are candid and open to the core and when your only

end is to realise and attain the Divine and to be moved by the Divine.

There is another danger; it is in connection with the sex impulses. Yoga in its process of purification will lay bare and throw up all hidden impulses and desires in you. And you must learn not to hide things nor leave them aside, you have to face them and conquer and remould them. The first effect of Yoga, however, is to take away the mental control, and the hungers that lie dormant are suddenly set free, they rush up and invade the being. So long as this mental control has not been replaced by the Divine control, there is a period of transition when your sincerity and surrender will be put to the test. The strength of such impulses as those of sex lies usually in the fact that people take too much notice of them; they protest too vehemently and endeavour to control them by coercion, hold them within and sit upon them. But the more you think of a thing and say, "I don't want it, I don't want it", the more you are bound to it. What you should do is to keep the thing away from you, to dissociate from it, take as little notice of it as possible and, even if you happen to think of it, remain indifferent and unconcerned.

The impulses and desires that come up by the pressure of Yoga should be faced in a spirit of detachment and serenity, as something foreign to yourself or belonging to the outside world. They should be offered to the Divine, so that the Divine may take them up and transmute them.

If you have once opened yourself to the Divine, if the power of the Divine has once come down into you and yet you try to keep to the old forces, you prepare troubles and difficulties and dangers for yourself. You must be vigilant and see that you do not use the Divine as a cloak for the satisfaction of your desires. There are many self-appointed Masters, who do nothing but that. And then when you are off the straight path and when you have a little knowledge and not much power, it happens that you are seized by beings or entities of a certain type, you become blind instruments in their hands and are devoured by them in the end. Wherever there is pretence, there is danger; you cannot deceive God. Do you come to God saying, "I want union with you" and in your heart meaning "I want powers and enjoyments"? Beware! You are heading straight towards the brink of the precipice. And yet it is so easy to avoid all catastrophe. Become like a child, give yourself up to the Mother, let her carry you, and there is no more danger for you.

This does not mean that you have not to face other kinds of difficulties or that you have not to fight and conquer any obstacles at all. Surrender does not ensure a smooth and unruffled and continuous progression. The reason is that your being is not yet one, nor your surrender absolute and complete. Only a part of you surrenders; and today it is one part and the next day it is another. The whole purpose of the Yoga is to gather all the divergent parts together and forge them into an undivided unity. Till then you cannot hope to be without difficulties — difficulties, for example, like doubt or depression or hesitation. The whole world is full of the poison. You take it in with every breath. If you exchange a few words with an undesirable man or even if such a man merely passes by you, you may catch the contagion from him. It is sufficient for you to come near a place where there is plague in order to be infected with its poison; you need not know at all that it is there. You can lose in a few minutes what it has taken you months to gain. So long as you belong to humanity and so long as you lead the ordinary life, it does not matter much if you mix with the people of the world; but if you want the divine life, you will have to be exceedingly careful about your company and your environment.

14 April 1929

*

When can one say that one has truly entered the spiritual path?

The first sign (it is not the same for everybody) but in a chronological order, I believe, is that everything else appears to you absolutely without importance. Your entire life, all your activities, all your movements continue, if circumstances so arrange things, but they all seem to you utterly unimportant, this is no longer the meaning of your existence. I believe this is the first sign.

There may be another; for example, the feeling that everything is different, of living differently, of a light in the mind which was not there before, of a peace in the heart which was not there before. That does make a change; but the positive change usually comes later, very rarely does it come at first except in a flash at the time of conversion when one has decided to take up the spiritual life. Sometimes, it begins like a great illumination, a deep joy enters into you; but generally, afterwards this goes into the background, for there are too many imperfections still persisting in you.... It is not disgust, it is not contempt, but everything appears to you so uninteresting that it is truly not worth the trouble of attending to it. For instance, when you are in the midst of certain physical conditions, pleasant or unpleasant (the two extremes meet), you say to yourself, "It was so important to me, all that? But it has no importance at all!" You have the impression that you have truly turned over to the other side.

12 February 1951

Yoga and Life

It has been noticed that most people who live alone in the forest become friendly with all the animals and plants around them; but it is not at all the fact of being all alone that gives you the power of entering into an inner contemplation and living in communion with the Supreme Truth. Perhaps it is easier, when by force of circumstance you have nothing else to do, but I am not convinced of it. One can always invent occupations and it seems to me, according to my experience of life, that if one succeeds in subduing one's nature in the midst of difficulties, if one endeavours to be all alone within oneself with the eternal Presence, while keeping the same surroundings which the Grace has given us, the realisation which one obtains then is infinitely more true, more profound, more lasting.

To run away from difficulties in order to conquer them is not a solution. It is very attractive. In those who seek the spiritual life, there is something which says, "Oh! to sit down under a tree, all alone, to remain in meditation, not to have the temptation to speak or act, how fine it must be!" It is because there is a very strong formation in this direction, but it is very illusory.

The best meditations are those that one has all of a sudden, because they take possession of you as an imperative necessity. You have no choice but to concentrate, to meditate, to look beyond the appearances. And it is not necessarily in the solitude of the forest that it seizes you, it happens when something in you is ready, when the time has come, when the true need is there, when the Grace is with you.

It seems to me that humanity has made some progress and the true victory must be won in life itself.

You must know how to live alone with the Eternal and Infinite in the midst of all circumstances. You must know how to be free, with the Supreme as your companion, in the midst of all occupations. That is indeed the true victory.

14 July 1958

*

Some people start on the way and then, after some time, they find it heavy-going, tiring, difficult, and also that they themselves, their legs, don't walk well, their feet begin to ache, etc. You see, they say, "Oh, it is very hard to go forward." So instead of saying, "I have started, I shall go through", which is the only thing to do, they stand there, stop there, lamenting and saying, "Oh, I shall never be able to succeed", and then they leave the path. So, obviously, if they leave the path, they will never succeed. This is to lose one's faith.

To keep one's faith is to say, "Good, I have difficulties but I am going on." Despair — that's what cuts off your legs, stops you, leaves you like this: "It is over, I can't go on any longer." It is indeed finished, and that's something which should not be allowed.

When you have started, you must go to the very end. Sometimes, you see, to people who come to me with enthusiasm I say, "Think a little, it is not an easy path, you will need time, you will need patience. You will need much endurance, much perseverance and courage and an untiring goodwill. Look and see if you are capable of having all this, and then start. But once you have started, it is finished, there is no going back any more; you must go to the very end."

Sometimes I tell them, I tell them that I give them a few days or a few months. There are some to whom I have given a few years for reflection. I told them, "Look well, be quite sure." But once they come and say, "Now I have decided, I want to start", it is good. Now, one must go on to the very end, whatever the cost; even if it is very difficult, one has to go to the very end.

When one draws back from the path, one draws back for the present life or...

In this, you see, there are many different cases, and they depend on the nature of the drawing back. If it is a small set-back or a small halt, you can start again. But it is ten times more difficult than before.

Why?

Why? Because it is so. Because you have accumulated obstacles in yourself by your cowardice and weakness. All those difficulties which you must conquer are like spiritual tests which you have to pass. And if you fail in your test, well, the next one will be much more difficult. This is the general occult law. One can't escape it. If you are faced with making an effort and making progress, if you fail... And note that in the present conditions you are not warned beforehand, which makes the test much more difficult to pass. In former days, the days of old, the candidates were told, "Now, prepare yourself. You are going to undergo terrible trials: you will be enclosed in a coffin, you will have to face terrible dangers. But these are tests to find out if you have the necessary qualities." A man forewarned, you understand, is as good as ten, as we say. Once they were warned that it was a trial, they did not take it seriously and it was much easier.

But that's no longer the practice. This is no longer done. It is life itself, the circumstances of each day which are the trials through which you have to pass. Some people instinctively feel that they are facing a decision that's to be taken, a special effort that's to be made, and they make this effort within themselves and cross the step. These acquire a much greater strength to cross the next step. When one has gained a small victory over his lower being, the next time he has a much greater strength to take the next step. On the contrary, if one is blind, ignorant, stupid or ill-willed and, instead of saying "yes" to the trial that faces him, he revolts or refuses it, then, you see, this is expressed by: "One has not passed his test, one has failed in his test." But the next time, one is compelled not only to make an effort to conquer this, but to make a still greater effort to redress the wrong one has done to himself. So it is much more difficult.

But these things happen to everyone on the path, all the time, perhaps even daily. There are small things, there are things a little bigger. The small ones one can turn, you see, by chance the right way. For the big ones one must first have a kind of instinct. One must pay attention and do the right thing in the right way. But there are other things still. When one is at a critical moment of his development, and it is absolutely necessary to cross the step in order to go forward — at that moment, there are always two possibilities: that of crossing the step, and then one immediately makes a terrific progress; or else to become slack, and then this indeed is more than a halt, even more than a set-back, it can be a very serious fall into a chasm. There are abysses from which one does not come up again; and so, in this case it means a life lost.

But if one has within, besides the part that has given way and fallen, if somewhere one has a very ardent flame, if one is ready for anything, all possible suffering, all possible effort, all possible sacrifices to redress what one has done, in order to climb back from the bottom of the abyss, to find the path again, one can do it. This flame has the power to call the Grace. And with the Grace there is nothing impossible. But it must be a real flame, something very powerful, because when one is at the bottom of the hole it is not easy to come out of it. Between the first kind, which is simply a little halt on the way and which makes the next step just a little more difficult, and the last one I am speaking about, there are many degrees; and so one can't say that if one leaves the path it is for a lifetime. That would be only an extreme case.

But if one leaves the path, it is even very difficult to find it again. What is strange is that in leaving it one loses it. There are legends of this kind in all countries: of people who have left the path and then later searched for it and never found it again. It was as if it had vanished. They lost it and this truly is a very sad thing.

But when you are on the path, I said this — I was just saying it — when you are on the path, do not ever leave it. Wait a little, you can hesitate as long as you want before taking it; but the minute you set your foot on it, it is finished, don't leave it. Because this has consequences which can even extend to several lives. It is something very serious. That is why, besides, I never push anyone to take the path.

You are quite a number of children here; I have never asked anyone
— only those who came to me and told me, "I want it." And to these
also, unless I am absolutely sure of them because it is written in their
destiny that they have come for that, I always say, "Think about it,
think, be quite sure that this is what you want and nothing else." And
when they have reflected and decided, it is finished. One should no
longer move away, one should go straight to the end. I mean, one
should not leave the path any more. One should go forward at all
costs and try not to stop too often on the way, because it is easier to
continue even if it is hard, you see, than to begin all over again when
one has stopped. A much greater effort is needed to get going again
than to continue on the way.

And you see, logically I should not say it, but I have already
warned all who are here, I have told them, "Don't ever take lightly all
the circumstances of each day, all the tiny little things of life, all the
small events, you know; never take all this lightly." Never react with
your lower being. Each time you are told to do something or not to do
it — you are not told this very often, but each time you are told,
before reacting think a little, try to find in yourself the part which
reacts. Do not react just like that with what is most commonplace in
you. Enter within yourself, try to find the best in yourself and with
this you must react. *It is very important, it is very important.*

There are people who mark time for years because they haven't
done this. There are others who seem to fly, so fast do they go, because they pay attention to this. And those who don't do that throw
the blame always on the Divine. They accuse the Grace. They tell her,
"It is You who deceived me, it is You who put me into difficulty, it is
You who made me stumble, it is You who are a monster", not exactly
in these words, but their thought is like this. And so, naturally, they
make their case worse because they push away even the help they
could have had in their difficulty. There we are.

I could tell you many more things, but it will come gradually. In
any case, if you can keep within yourself a confidence, a candid trust
which does not argue, and the sense of... yes, it is truly a kind of trust
that what is done for you, in spite of all appearances, is always the
best thing to lead you in the quickest way possible out of all your
difficulties and towards the goal... if you can keep that strong in you,

well, your path will become tremendously easier.

You will tell me that it is very difficult to keep it, but children keep it very well. They must have truly come upon particularly detestable parents to lose it; but if their parents are simply good enough, they keep this very well. Well, it is this attitude; if you can tell yourself, "Good, perhaps the divine Grace deserves our confidence", simply this, nothing else, you will avoid many difficulties, many. In fact this avoids many difficulties even in ordinary life, and many worries.

22 December 1954

*

Sweet Mother, why is it said that "those who have the greatest power for Yoga ... have too, very often ... the greatest imperfections"?

Why is it like that? (*Silence*) Because one must have a very strong, very powerful nature, with great inner strength in order to have a great capacity for yoga; and very strong natures have also very strong difficulties.

People who are neutral, dull, unimportant, usually go their own little way without being disturbed very much. But they cannot do anything very much, their road is very small and very short; they reach the end very quickly. They can't do much. But people who have a strong nature have also strong difficulties. For it is absolutely impossible in this world to be without difficulties. So long as the world remains what it is and one participates in the world, one necessarily participates in its difficulties.

It is only by a very persistent effort that one can succeed in overcoming his difficulties; and yet it seems impossible to cut oneself off completely from one's solidarity with the rest of the world. Therefore a perfect purity, a perfect perfection seem impossible so long as the world has not reached at least a certain degree of perfection. Even the ascetic, the solitary, who goes and sits in a cave or under a tree or in the jungle, cannot completely free himself from solidarity with the rest of the world. The air he breathes is full of all the vibrations of the world, the food he eats, whatever it may be, even if it is reduced to the minimum, contains the vibrations of the world; and so, it is enough for him to exist to be in solidarity with the difficulties of the world.

That is why, in fact, the way is so long. Even without having any other consideration than that of what one is absorbing constantly into himself when breathing or eating, all these things one must constantly transform as one goes on absorbing them. It is a continuous alchemy in which one absorbs a particular kind of vibration containing all the possible disorders and must transmute this into something which is ready to receive the light from above. And this work is perpetual, and perpetually renewed. So it is impossible to live in this world, in the world as it is, and become perfect without the world itself making a great progress.[...]

Mother, does an individual's life depend on the experience his psychic being wants to have?

Very much!

I was speaking about just this with someone today, and I said this, that if one can become fully conscious of his psychic being, at the same time one understands, necessarily, the reason of his present existence and the experience this psychic being wants to have; and instead of having it somewhat half consciously and more than half unconsciously, one can shorten this experience and so help his psychic being to cover in a limited number of years the experiences it would perhaps take several lifetimes to go through. That is to say, the help is reciprocal. The psychic, when it has an influence on the outer life, brings to it light, order and quietude and the joy of the divine contact. But also the physical being, the body-consciousness, if it is identified with the psychic consciousness, and through that learns what kind of experience the psychic being wants to have, it can help it to have these experiences in a very brief time, and not only save time but save many lives for the psychic being. It is a mutual help.

In brief, this is what yoga means. Yoga helps you to become fully conscious of your destiny, that is, your mission in the universe, and not only at the present moment but what it was in the past and what it will be in the future. And because of this knowledge you can gather by a concentration of the consciousness all these experiences in a very short time and gain lives, do in a few years what could take a fairly considerable number of lives to achieve. The psychic being goes progressively through all these experiences towards its full maturity and complete independence, its liberation — in the sense that it no longer needs any new life. If it wants to come back to the physical world, it returns, because it has something to do there and it chooses freely to return. But till then, till this liberation, it is compelled to return to have all the experiences it needs. Well, if it happens that once the physical being is developed and conscious enough and has enough goodwill to be able to become fully aware of the psychic being, it can then and there create all the circumstances, the outer experiences necessary for the psychic being to attain its maturity in this very life.

29 December 1954

*

One must never make rules.

Every minute one must endeavour to apply the highest truth one can perceive. It is much more difficult, but it's the only solution.

Whatever you may do, don't make rules beforehand, because once you have made a rule you follow it more or less blindly, and then you are sure, ninety-nine-and-a-half times out of a hundred, to be mistaken.

There is only one way of acting truly, it is to try at each moment, each second, in each movement to express only the highest truth one can perceive, and at the same time know that this perception has to be progressive and that what seems to you the most true now will no longer be so tomorrow, and that a higher truth will have to be expressed more and more through you. This leaves no room any longer for sleeping in a comfortable tamas; one must be always awake — I am not speaking of physical sleep — one must be always awake, always conscious and always full of an enlightened receptivity and of goodwill. To want always the best, always the best, always the best, and never tell oneself, "Oh! it is tiring! Let me rest, let me relax! Ah, I am going to stop making an effort"; then one is sure to fall into a hole immediately and make a big stupid blunder!

The rest must not be one which goes down into the inconscience and tamas. The rest must be an ascent into the Light, into perfect Peace, total Silence, a rest which rises up out of the darkness. Then it is true rest, a rest which is an ascent.

31 August 1955

Difficulties and Progress

The nature of your difficulty indicates the nature of the victory you will gain, the victory you will exemplify in Yoga. Thus, if there is persistent selfishness, it points to a realisation of universality as your most prominent achievement in the future. And, when selfishness is there, you have also the power to reverse this very difficulty into its opposite, a victory of utter wideness.

When you have something to realise, you will have in you just the characteristic which is the contradiction of that something. Face to face with the defect, the difficulty, you say, "Oh, I am like that! How awful it is!" But you ought to see the truth of the situation. Say to yourself, "My difficulty shows me clearly what I have ultimately to represent. To reach the absolute negation of it, the quality at the other pole — this is my mission."

Even in ordinary life, we have sometimes the experience of contraries. He who is very timid and has no courage in front of circumstances proves capable of bearing the most!

To one who has the aspiration for the Divine, the difficulty which is always before him is the door by which he will attain God in his own individual manner: it is his particular path towards the Divine Realisation.

There is also the fact that if somebody has a hundred difficulties it means he will have a tremendous realisation — provided, of course, there are in him patience and endurance and he keeps the aspiring flame of Agni burning against those defects.

And remember: the Grace of the Divine is generally proportioned to your difficulties.

1930-1931

*

Not to be depressed means... ?

Not to be depressed — it is extremely important. Depression is a sign of weakness, of a bad will somewhere, and bad will in the sense of a refusal to receive help, and a kind of weakness that's content to be weak. One becomes slack. The bad will is obvious, because there's a part of your being which tells you at that moment, "Depression is bad." You know that you shouldn't get depressed; well, the reply of that part which is depressed is almost, "Shut up! I want my depression." Try, you will see, you can try. It is always like that. Eh, it is not true? And then later one says again, "Afterwards, afterwards I shall see... for the moment I want it, and besides I have my reasons." There you are. It is a kind of revolt, a weak revolt, the revolt of something weak in the being.

Here he [Sri Aurobindo] speaks of "the change of which this depression is a stage..."

Yes. When one comes out of the depression and one's bad will, well, then one realises that there was an attack and that some progress had to be made, and that in spite of everything something within has made progress, that one has taken a step forward. Usually, hardly consciously, it is something which needs to progress but doesn't want to, and so takes this way; like a child who sulks, becomes low-spirited, sad, unhappy, misunderstood, abandoned, helpless; and then, refusing to collaborate, and as I just said, indulging in his depression, to show that he is not happy. It is specially in order to show that one is not satisfied that one becomes depressed. One can show it to Nature, one can show it (that depends on the case, you see), one can show it to the Divine, one can show it to the people around one, but it is always a kind of way of expressing one's dissatisfaction. "I am not happy about what you demand", but this means, "I am not happy. And I shall make you too see it, that I am not happy." There you are.

But when it is over, and when for some reason or other one has made the necessary effort to come out of it, and has come out, one usually realises that something in the being has changed, because, in spite of all bad will, most often the progress was accomplished — not very swiftly, not very brilliantly, not for one's greater glory, surely, but still the progress was made. Something has changed.

12 January 1955

*

Generally, all progress made on one side is set off by an attack of the adverse forces on the other. So, the more you advance, the more vigilant must you become. And the most essential quality is perseverance, endurance, and a... what shall I call it? — a kind of inner good humour which helps you not to get discouraged, not to become sad, and to face all difficulties with a smile. There is an English word which expresses this very well — cheerfulness. If you can keep this within you, you fight much better, resist much better, in the light, these bad influences which try to hinder you from progressing.

That is the work. It is vast and complex. And one must never forget anything.

18 January 1956

*

Sweet Mother, when we make an effort to do better but don't see any progress, we feel discouraged. What is the best thing to do?

Not to be discouraged! Despondency leads nowhere.

To begin with, the first thing to tell yourself is that you are almost entirely incapable of knowing whether you are making progress or not, for very often what seems to us to be a state of stagnation is a long — sometimes long, but in any case not endless — preparation for a leap forward. We sometimes seem to be marking time for weeks or months, and then suddenly something that was being prepared makes its appearance, and we see that there is quite a considerable change and *on several points* at a time.

As with everything in yoga, the effort for progress must be made for the love of the effort for progress. The joy of effort, the aspiration for progress must be enough in themselves, quite independent of the result. Everything one does in yoga must be done for the joy of doing it, and not in view of the result one wants to obtain.... Indeed, in life, always, in all things, the result does not belong to us. And if we want to keep the right attitude, we must act, feel, think, strive spontaneously, for *that* is what we must do, and not in view of the result to be obtained.

As soon as we think of the result we begin to bargain and that takes away all sincerity from the effort. You make an effort to progress because you feel within you the need, the *imperative* need to make an effort and progress; and this effort is the gift you offer to the Divine Consciousness in you, the Divine Consciousness in the universe, it is your way of expressing your gratitude, offering your self; and whether this results in progress or not is of no importance. You will progress when it is decided that the time has come to progress and not because you desire it.

If you wish to progress, if you make an effort to control yourself for instance, to overcome certain defects, weaknesses, imperfections, and if you expect to get a more or less immediate result from your effort, your effort loses all sincerity, it becomes a bargaining. You say, "See! I am going to make an effort, but that's because I want this in exchange for my effort." You are no longer spontaneous, no longer natural.

So there are two things to remember. First, we are incapable of judging *what* the result ought to be. If we put our trust in the Divine, if we say... if we say, "Well now, I am going to give everything, everything, all I can give, effort, concentration, and *He* will judge what has to be given in exchange or even whether anything should be given in exchange, and I do not know what the result should be." Before we transform anything in ourselves, are we quite sure of the direction, the way, the form that this transformation should take? — Not at all. So, it is only our imagination and usually we greatly limit the result to be obtained and make it altogether petty, mean, superficial, relative. We do not know what the result can truly be, what it ought to be. We know it later. When it comes, when the change takes place, then if we look back, we say, "Ah! that's it, that is what I was moving towards" — but we know it only later. Before that we only have vague imaginations which are quite superficial and childish in comparison with the true progress, the true transformation.

So we say, first point: we have an aspiration but we don't really know the true result we ought to obtain. Only the Divine can know that.

And secondly, if we tell the Divine, "I am giving you my effort, but, you know, in exchange I must make progress, otherwise I won't give you anything at all!" — that is bargaining. That's all.

(Silence)

A spontaneous act, done because one cannot do otherwise, and done as an offering of goodwill, is the only one which truly has any value.

23 April 1958

*

Are illnesses tests in the Yoga?

Tests? Not at all.

You are given an illness purposely to make you progress? Surely it is not like that. That is, you may turn the thing round and say that there are people whose aspiration is so constant, whose goodwill so total that whatever happens to them they take as a trial on the path to make progress. I knew people who, whenever they fell ill, took that as a proof of the Divine Grace to help them to progress. They told themselves: it is a good sign, I am going to find out the cause of my illness and I shall make the necessary progress. I knew a few of this kind and they moved on magnificently. There are others, on the contrary, who, far from making use of the thing, let themselves fall flat on the ground. So much the worse for them. But the true attitude when one is ill, is to say: "There is something that is not all right; I am going to see what it is." You must never think that the Divine has purposely sent an illness, for that would truly be a very undesirable Divine!

22 July 1953

*

So we get started on the path. But the road is very long. Many things happen on the way. Suddenly one thinks one has overcome an obstacle; I say "thinks", because though one has overcome it, it is not totally overcome. I am going to take a very obvious instance, of a very simple observation. Someone has found that his vital is uncontrollable and uncontrolled, that it gets furious for nothing and about nothing. He starts working to teach it not to get carried away, not to flare up, to remain calm and bear the shocks of life without reacting violently. If one does this cheerfully, it goes quite quickly (note this well, it is very important: when you have to deal with your vital take care to keep your good humour, otherwise you will get into trouble). One keeps one's good humour, that is, when one sees the fury rise, one begins to laugh. Instead of being depressed and saying, "Ah! in spite of all my effort it is beginning all over again", one begins to laugh and says, "Well, well! one hasn't yet seen the end of it. Look now, aren't you ridiculous, you know quite well that you are being ridiculous! Is it worthwhile getting angry?" One gives it this lesson good-humouredly. And really, after a while it doesn't get angry again, it is quiet — and one relaxes one's attention. One thinks the difficulty has been overcome, one thinks a result has at last been reached: "My vital does not trouble me any longer, it does not get angry now, everything is going fine." And the next day, one loses one's temper. It is then one must be careful, it is then one must not say, "Here we are, it's no use, I shall never achieve anything, all my efforts are futile; all this is an illusion, it is impossible." On the contrary, one must say, "I wasn't vigilant enough." One must wait long, very long, before one can say, "Ah! it is done and finished." Sometimes one must wait for years, many years.[...]

You must arm yourself with an endless patience and endurance. You do a thing once, ten times, a hundred times, a thousand times if necessary, but you do it till it gets done. And not done only here and there, but everywhere and everywhere at the same time. This is the great problem one sets oneself. That is why, to those who come to tell me very light-heartedly, "I want to do yoga", I reply, "Think it over, one may do the yoga for a number of years without noticing the least result. But if you want to do it, you must persist and persist with such a will that you should be ready to do it for ten lifetimes, a hundred lifetimes if necessary, in order to succeed." I do not say it will be like that, but the *attitude* must be like that. Nothing must discourage you; for there are all the difficulties of ignorance of the different states of being, to which are added the endless malice and the unbounded cunning of the hostile forces in the world.... They are there, do you know why? They have been tolerated, do you know why? — simply to see how long one can last out and how great is the sincerity in one's action. For everything depends upon your sincerity. If you are truly sincere in your will, nothing will stop you, you will go right to the end, and if it is necessary for you to live a thousand years to do it, you will live a thousand years to do it.

26 March 1951

Experiences and Visions

Usually people mean by "experience" either altogether extravagant phenomena, levitation and things like that, or else sensational visions: being able to see the future or seeing at a distance or maybe ordinary things like being able to tell where a lost object can be found or all kinds of little tricks like that. This is what people call "experiences".

Well, usually people who have these faculties are not well educated, but for some reason they are born with a gift, as some are born musicians, others painters, and others scientists. These are born clairvoyants, and so it may be, when they are in need they use this faculty to earn their living, and they spoil it completely. If they happen to be in comfortable circumstances and do not need to earn their living, then they become famous among their friends. In any case, this is always an opportunity for a certain kind of commercialism. There are very few who can have these gifts without using them either to make a name for themselves or to earn money. But these gifts are not of a very high level. One can have them without having a very spiritual life. They do not depend at all on an inner spiritual height. One should not mistake them for signs of progress.

Besides, one thing is certain: those who do not have these faculties and want to acquire them, [...] then this indeed means a *formidable* work. And that is why some people attach a very great value to these things. But they have some value only when they are under one's control, done at will and the result of an inner discipline. In this case, yes, because this proves that you have entered into contact with a certain region where it is difficult to enter consciously, at will, and permanently. It is very difficult, it requires much development. And then, for you to be sure of what you have seen... because I haven't told you that with these people who make a profession of their clairvoyance, it becomes... I said "commercialism", but it is worse than that, you know, it is a fraud! When they do not see anything, they invent. When they make a profession of it, and people come to ask them something about the future, and they can see nothing at all, they are obliged to invent something, otherwise they would lose their reputation and their clientele. So this becomes a deception, you see, a falsehood, fraud or falsification.

But when one wants to have a pure, correct information, to be in contact with the truth of things, and see in advance — not according to one's petty mental construction, but how things are decreed, in the place where they are decreed and the time when they are decreed — then that requires a *very great* mental purity, a *very great* vital equilibrium, an absence of desire, of preference. One must never want anything to be of one kind or another, for this falsifies your vision immediately.

All who have visions usually deform them, *all*, almost *without exception*. I don't think there is one in a million who doesn't deform his vision, because the minute it touches the brain it touches the domain of preferences, desires, attachments, and this indeed is enough to give a colouring, a special look to what you have seen. Even if you have seen correctly, you translate it wrongly in your consciousness. This truly asks for a great perfection. But you can have perfection without the gift of vision. And the perfection can be as great without the gift as with it. If it interests you specially, you can make an effort to obtain it. But only if it interests you specially. If you lay great store by knowing certain things, you can undertake a discipline; you may undertake a discipline also in order to change the functioning of your senses. I think I have already explained to you how one can hear at a distance, see at a distance, even physically; but this means considerable effort, which perhaps is not always in proportion to the result, because these are side issues, not the central, the most important thing. These are side issues which may be interesting, but in itself this is not the spiritual life; one may have a spiritual life without this. Now, the two together can give you perhaps a greater capacity. But for this too you must tell yourself, "If I ought to have it — if I take the true attitude of surrender to the Divine and of complete consecration — if I ought to have it I shall have it. As, if I ought to have the gift of speech, I shall have it." And in fact, if one is truly surrendered, in the true way and totally, at every minute one is what he ought to be and does what he ought to do and knows what he ought to know. This... but naturally, for this one should have overcome the petty limitations of the ego, and this does not happen overnight. But it can happen.

6 October 1954

*

One can never have the same experience twice because one is never the same person twice. Between the first experience and the second, even if one hour has passed, you are no longer the same man and you can never reproduce identically the same thing. If you take care to become more conscious, more sincere, more concentrated, the experience you have will be different, but it may be deeper and more clear. But if you cling to something you have had and want to reproduce the same thing, you will have nothing at all, because you can't have the same thing and you are in a state in which you refuse to have a new experience, for you are attached to the past one. And usually when one has had an experience which was a revelation, something altogether important, one doesn't want to leave it, one is afraid of not having it any longer, and so, in this movement of clinging on to something, one prevents oneself from progressing and puts oneself in conditions in which one can't have the next experience.

Well, this has to be understood, because it is an absolute fact: one can never have the same experience twice. There may be similar experiences, very close, and particularly some which appear similar, but these experiences... if one is absolutely sincere, impartial and like a blank page, he will perceive that there is a difference, sometimes an essential one, between the two, though in appearance they seem very close. But the more ready you are to leave behind all that you have experienced, in order to be able to go towards something better and higher, the faster you will go; the more you drag the heavy weight of all the past which you don't want to get rid of, the slower is your advance.

All the past should always be simply like a stepping-stone or a ladder, something to lead you farther; it should not have any other use except to push you forward. And if you can feel this and always turn your back on what is past and look at what you want to do, then you go much faster, you don't waste time on the way. What makes you lose time is always this clinging to what has been, to what is, what seemed to you beautiful and good in what is past. This must only help you, you must not reject it, but it must help you to go forward, it must simply be something on which you lean to take a step forward.

Now, at a particular time, a set of circumstances, inner and outer, has caused one to be receptive to a certain vibration; for example, as you say, while looking at the stars or contemplating a landscape or reading a page or hearing a lecture, one has suddenly an inner revelation, an experience, something that strikes him and gives him the impression of being open to something new. But if you want to hold on to this tightly like that, you will lose everything, because one can't keep the past, one must always go forward, advance, advance. This illumination must prepare you so that you can organise your whole being on this new level, in order to be able suddenly, one day, to leap up again to a higher step.

There is a horizontal advance between abrupt ascents. It is the moment of the abrupt ascent which gives you an impression of something like a revelation, a great inner joy. But once you have climbed the step, if you want to climb it once more you would have to go down again. You must go on preparing yourself at this level in order to climb another higher step. These things which suddenly give you a great joy are always ascents. But these ascents are prepared by a slow work of horizontal progress, that is, one must become more and more conscious, establish more and more perfectly what one is, draw from it all the inner, psychological consequences, and in action also. It is a long utilisation of an abrupt leap and, as I say, there are two kinds of progress. But the horizontal progress is indispensable.

You must not stop, you must not cling in this way to your vertical progress and not want to move because it has brought you a revelation. You must know how to leave it in order to prepare for another.

*

"One must always be greater than one's experience."

(The Mother)

What I meant is this:

Whatever may be the nature, the strength and wonder of an experience, you must not be dominated by it to such an extent that it governs your entire being and you lose your balance and your contact with a reasonable and calm attitude. That is to say, when you enter in some way into contact with a force or consciousness which surpasses yours, instead of being entirely dominated by this consciousness or force, you must always be able to remind yourself that it is only *one* experience among thousands and thousands of others, and that, consequently, its nature is not absolute, it is relative. No matter how beautiful it may be, you can and ought to have better ones: however exceptional it may be, there are others still more marvellous; and however high it may be, you can always rise still higher in future. So, instead of losing one's head one places the experience in the chain of development and keeps a healthy physical balance so as not to lose the sense of relativity with ordinary life. In this way, there is no risk.

The means?... One who knows how to do this will always find it very easy, but for one who doesn't know it is perhaps a little... a little troublesome.

There is a means.

It is never to lose the idea of the total self-giving to the Grace which is the expression of the Supreme. When one gives oneself, when one surrenders, entrusts oneself entirely to That which is above, beyond all creation, and when, instead of seeking any personal advantage from the experience, one makes an offering of it to the divine Grace and knows that it is from This that the experience comes and that it is to This that the result of the experience must be given back, then one is quite safe.

In other words: no ambition, no vanity, no pride. A sincere self-giving, a sincere humility, and one is sheltered from all danger. There you are, this is what I call being greater than one's experience.

22 August 1956

The Right Attitude

Is it possible to disregard reason?... It is possible only when you have passed beyond mental activity. It is possible only when you have achieved a surrender, a total giving of yourself. It is possible only when you no longer have any desires. So long as you have desires, have an ego and a will of your own, you cannot give up reason, because, as I said just a moment ago, you would become quite unbalanced and perhaps insane. Therefore reason must be the master until one has gone beyond the state in which it is useful. And as I said, as long as there is an ego and as long as there are desires, and so long as there are impulses and so long as there are passions and preferences, and so long as there are attractions and repulsions, etc., as long as all these things are there, reason is _altogether_ useful.

I shall also add that there is another quite indispensable condition in order not to have recourse to reason any more; that is to open no door, no part of the being to the suggestions of the adverse forces. For if you are not completely liberated from the habit of responding to adverse suggestions, if you give up your reason, you also give up reason itself, that is, common sense. And you begin to act in an incoherent way which may finally become quite unbalanced. Well, to be free from suggestions and adverse influences, you must be exclusively under the influence of the Divine.

Now you see the problem; it is a little difficult. This means that unless you are in the presence of a completely illumined and transformed being, it is always better to advise people to act according to their reason. It is perhaps a limitation — it is in fact a great limitation — but it is also a control and it prevents you from becoming one of those half-idiots who are far too numerous in the world.

Reason is a very respectable person. Like all respectable people it has its limitations and prejudices, but that does not prevent it from being very useful. And it keeps _you_ from making a fool of yourself. You would do many things if you did not have reason, things which would lead you straight to your ruin and could have extremely unfortunate consequences, for your best means of discernment until you have attained higher levels is reason. When one no longer listens to reason, one can be led into all sorts of absurdities. Naturally, it is neither the ideal nor the summit, it is only a kind of control and a guide for leading a good life, it keeps you from extravagances, excesses, inordinate passions and above all from those impulsive actions which may lead you to the abyss. There you are.

One must be very sure of oneself, quite free from the ego and perfectly surrendered to the divine Will to be able to do safely without reason.

28 November 1956

*

Is it really the best that always happens?... It is clear that all that has happened had to happen: it could not be otherwise — by the universal determinism it had to happen. But we can say so only after it has happened, not before. For the problem of the very best that can happen is an individual problem, whether the individual be a nation or a single human being; and all depends upon the personal attitude. If, in the presence of circumstances that are about to take place, you can take the highest attitude possible — that is, if you put your consciousness in contact with the highest consciousness within reach, you can be absolutely sure that in that case it is the best that can happen to you. But as soon as you fall from this consciousness into a lower state, then it is evidently not the best that can happen, for the simple reason that you are not in your very best consciousness. I even go so far as to affirm that in the zone of immediate influence of each one, the right attitude not only has the power to turn every circumstance to advantage but can change the very circumstance itself. For instance, when a man comes to kill you, if you remain in the ordinary consciousness and get frightened out of your wits, he will most probably succeed in doing what he came for; if you rise a little higher and though full of fear call for the divine help, he may just miss you, doing you a slight injury; if, however, you have the right attitude and the full consciousness of the divine presence everywhere around you, he will not be able to lift even a finger against you.

This truth is just the key to the whole problem of transformation. Always keep in touch with the divine presence, try to bring it down — and the very best will always take place. Of course the world will not change at once, but it will go forward as rapidly as it possibly can. Do not forget that this is so only if you keep on the straight road of Yoga, and not if you deviate and lose your way and wander about capriciously or helplessly as though in a virgin forest.

If each of you did your utmost, then there would be the right collaboration and the result would be so much the quicker. I have had innumerable examples of the power of right attitude. I have seen crowds saved from catastrophes by one single person keeping the right attitude. But it must be an attitude that does not remain some-where very high and leaves the body to its usual reactions. If you remain high up like that, saying, "Let God's will be done", you may get killed all the same. For your body may be quite undivine, shiver-ing with fear: the thing is to hold the true consciousness in the body itself and not have the least fear and be full of the divine peace. Then indeed there is no danger. Not only can attacks of men be warded off, but beasts also and even the elements can be affected. I can give you a little example. You remember the night of the great cyclone, when there was a tremendous noise and splash of rain all about the place. I thought I would go to Sri Aurobindo's room and help him shut the windows. I just opened his door and found him sitting quietly at his desk, writing. There was such a solid peace in the room that nobody would have dreamed that a cyclone was raging outside. All the win-dows were wide open, not a drop of rain was coming inside:

1930-1931

*

Most of you live on the surface of your being, exposed to the touch of external influences. You live almost projected, as it were, outside your own body, and when you meet some unpleasant being similarly pro-jected you get upset. The whole trouble arises out of your not being accustomed to stepping back. You must always step back into your-self — learn to go deep within — step back and you will be safe. Do not lend yourself to the superficial forces which move in the outside world. Even if you are in a hurry to do something, step back for a while and you will discover to your surprise how much sooner and with what greater success your work can be done. If someone is angry with you, do not be caught in his vibrations but simply step back and his anger, finding no support or response, will vanish. Always keep your peace, resist all temptation to lose it. Never decide anything without stepping back, never speak a word without stepping back, never throw yourself into action without stepping back. All that belongs to the ordinary world is impermanent and fugitive, so there is nothing in it worth getting upset about. What is lasting, eternal, immortal and infinite — that indeed is worth having, worth conquering, worth possessing. It is Divine Light, Divine Love, Divine Life — it is also Supreme Peace, Perfect Joy and All-Mastery upon earth with the Complete Manifestation as the crowning. When you get the sense of the relativity of things, then whatever happens you can step back and look; you can remain quiet and call on the Divine Force and wait for an answer. Then you will know exactly what to do. Remember, therefore, that you cannot receive the answer before you are very peaceful. Practise that inner peace, make at least a small beginning and go on in your practice until it becomes a habit with you.

1930-1931

*

You must believe that if you take the right attitude, it is the best that will happen to you; but if you are afraid when something unpleasant happens to you, then you can do nothing. You must have this confidence within you, whatever the difficulty, whatever the obstacle. Most of the time, when something unpleasant happens, you say, "Is it going to increase? What other accident is yet going to happen!" and so on. You must tell yourself, "These things are not mine; they belong to the subconscious world; to be sure I have nothing to do with them and if they come again to seize me, I am going to give a fight." Naturally you will answer that this is easy to say but difficult to do. But if truly you take this attitude of confidence, there is no difficulty that you will not be able to conquer. Anxiety makes the difficulty greater.

Evidently there is one difficulty: in your conscious being something does not want the difficulty, wishes sincerely to overcome it, but there are numberless movements in other parts of your consciousness of which you are not conscious. You say, "I want to be cured of that"; unfortunately it is not sufficient to say "I want", there are other parts of the consciousness which hide themselves so that you may not be busy with them, and when your attention is turned away these parts try to assert themselves. That is why I say and shall always repeat, Be perfectly sincere; do not try to deceive yourself, do not say, "I have done all that I could." If you do not succeed, it means that you do not do all that you can. For, if you truly do all that you can, you will surely succeed. If you have any defect which you want to get rid of and which still persists, and you say, "I have done all that I could", you may be sure that you have not done all that you should have. If you had, you would have triumphed, for the difficulties that come to you are exactly in proportion to your strength — nothing can happen to you which does not belong to your consciousness, and all that belongs to your consciousness you are able to master. Even the things and suggestions that come from outside can touch you only in proportion to the consent of your consciousness, and you are made to be the master of your consciousness.

If you say, "I have done all that I could and in spite of everything the thing continues, so I give up", you may be already sure that you have not done what you could. When an error persists "in spite of everything" it means that something hidden in your being springs up suddenly like a Jack-in-the-box and takes the helm of your life. Hence, there is only one thing to do, it is to go hunting for all the little dark corners which lie hidden in you and, if you put just a tiny spark of goodwill on this darkness, it will yield, will vanish, and what appeared to you impossible will become not only possible, practicable, but *it will have been done*. You can in this way in one minute get rid of a difficulty which would have harassed you for years. I absolutely assure you of it. That depends only on one thing: that you truly, sincerely, want to get rid of it. And it is the same for everything, from physical illnesses up to the highest mental difficulties. One part of the consciousness says, "I don't want it", but behind there hides a heap of things which say nothing, do not show themselves, and which just want that things continue as they are — generally out of ignorance; they do not believe that it is necessary to be cured, they believe that everything is for the best in the best of worlds. As the lady with whom I had those conversations* used to say, "The trouble begins as soon as you want to change."

5 February 1951

*

If you look at yourself carefully, you will see that one always carries in oneself the opposite of the virtue one has to realise (I use "virtue" in its widest and highest sense). You have a special aim, a special mission, a special realisation which is your very own, each one individually, and you carry in yourself all the obstacles necessary to make your realisation perfect. Always you will see that within you the shadow and the light are equal: you have an ability, you have also the negation of this ability. But if you discover a very black hole, a thick shadow, be sure there is somewhere in you a great light. It is up to you to know how to use the one to realise the other.

This is a fact very little spoken about, but one of capital importance. And if you observe carefully you will see that it is always thus with everyone. This leads us to statements which are paradoxical but absolutely true; for instance, that the greatest thief can be the most honest man (this is not to encourage you to steal, of course!) and the greatest liar can be the most truthful person. So, do not despair if you find in yourself the greatest weakness, for perhaps it is the sign of the greatest divine strength. Do not say, "I am like that, I can't be otherwise." It is not true. You are "like that" because, precisely, you ought to be the opposite. And all your difficulties are there just that you may learn to transform them into the truth they are hiding.

Once you have understood this, many worries come to an end and you are very happy, very happy. If one finds one has very black holes, one says, "This shows I can rise very high", if the abyss is very deep, "I can climb very high." It is the same from the universal point of view; to use the Hindu terminology so familiar to you, it is the greatest Asuras who are the greatest beings of Light. And the day

* The conversations of 1929.

these Asuras are converted, they will be the supreme beings of the creation. This is not to encourage you to be asuric, you know, but it is like that — this will widen your minds a little and help you to free yourself from those ideas of opposing good and evil, for if you abide in that category, there is no hope.

If the world was not essentially the opposite of what it has become, there would be no hope. For the hole is so black and so deep, and the inconscience so complete, that if this were not the sign of the total consciousness, well, there would be nothing more to do but pack up one's kit and go away. Men like Shankara, who did not see much further than the end of their nose, said that the world was not worth the trouble of living in, for it was impossible, that it was better to treat it as an illusion and go away, there was nothing to be done with it. I tell you, on the contrary, that it is because the world is very bad, very dark, very ugly, very unconscious, full of misery and suffering, that it can become the supreme Beauty, the supreme Light, the supreme Consciousness and supreme Felicity.

17 February 1951

*

Mother, there are mistakes... one knows they are mistakes, but still it is as though one were pushed into making them. Then?

Pushed by what? Ah, this is exactly what happens! It is the lower nature, the instincts of the subconscient which govern you and make you do things you should not do. And so it is a choice between your will and accepting submission. There is always a moment when one can decide. It goes to the point where as I said there is even a moment when one can decide to be ill or not to be ill. It even goes so far that a moment comes when one can decide to die or not to die. But for that one must have an *extremely* awakened consciousness because this speck is infinitesimal in time and like the hundredth part of a second, and because before it one can do nothing and after it one can do nothing; but at that moment one can. And if one is absolutely awake, one can, at that moment, take the decision.

But for ordinary things, as for example, giving way before an impulse or refusing it, it is not a space, not even the space of a second; one has plenty of time before him, one certainly has several minutes. And it is a choice between weak submission and a controlling will. And if the will is clear, if it is based on truth, if truly it obeys the truth and is clear, it always has the power to refuse the wrong movement. It is an excuse you give yourself when you say, "I could not." It is not true. It is that truly you have not wanted it in the right way. For there is always the choice between saying "yes" and saying "no". But one chooses to be weak and later gives oneself this excuse, saying, "It is not my fault; it was stronger than I." It is your fault if the thing was stronger than you. Because you are not these impulses, you are a conscious soul and an intelligent will, and your duty is to see that *this* is what governs you and not the impulses from below.

29 September 1954

The Ego

Mother, here Sri Aurobindo has spoken of "the formation of ego-individuality". Ego-individuality means...?

There are individual egos and collective egos. For example, the national ego is a collective ego. A group may have a collective ego. The human race has a collective ego. It is bigger or smaller. The individual ego is the ego of a particular person; it is the smallest kind of ego. Oh, there is of course a vital ego, a mental ego and a physical ego but these are minor individual egos. But this means the ego of a particular person.

One has many egos inside oneself. One becomes aware of them when one begins to destroy them: when one has destroyed an ego, that which was most troublesome, usually it creates a kind of inner cyclone. When one comes out of the storm, one feels, "Ah, now it is over, everything is done, I have destroyed the enemy inside me, all is finished." But after a while, one notices that there is another, and another still, and yet again another, and that in fact one is made of a heap of little egos which are absolutely a nuisance and which must be overcome one after another.

Ego means what?

I think it is the ego that makes each one a separate being, in all possible ways. It is the ego which gives the sense of being a person separate from others. It is certainly the ego which gives you the sense of the "I", "I am", "I want", "I do", "I exist", even the very famous "I think therefore I am" which is... I am sorry but I think it is a stupidity — but still it is a celebrated stupidity — well, this too is the ego. What gives you the impression that you are Manoj is the ego, and that you are altogether different from this one and that one; and what prevents your body from melting away like that, dissolving in a common mass of physical vibrations, is the ego; what gives you a definite form, a definite character, a separate consciousness, the sense that you exist in yourself, independently of all others, indeed, something like that; if one does not reflect, spontaneously one has the sense that even if the world disappeared, one would be there, one would remain what one is. This of course is the super-ego.

Certainly, if one were to lose one's ego too soon, from the vital and mental point of view one would again become an amorphous mass. The ego is surely the instrument for individualisation; that is, until one is an individualised being, constituted in himself, the ego is an absolutely necessary factor. If one had the power of abolishing the ego ahead of time, one would lose one's individuality. But once the individuality has been formed, the ego becomes not only useless but harmful. And only then comes the time when it must be abolished. But naturally, as it has taken so much trouble to build you, it does not give up its work so easily, and it asks for the reward of its efforts, that is, to enjoy the individuality.

12 January 1955

*

Egoism is a relatively easy thing to correct, because everyone knows what it is. It is easy to discover, easy to correct, if one truly wants to do it and is bent on it.

But the ego is much more difficult to seize, because, in fact, to realise what the ego is one must already be out of it, otherwise one cannot find it out. You are wholly moulded from it, from head to foot, from the outermost to the innermost, from the physical to the spiritual, you are steeped in ego. It is mixed with everything and you are not aware of what it is. You must have already conquered it, come out of it, freed yourself from it, at least partially, at least in some little corner of your being somewhere, in order to realise what the ego is.

The ego is what helps us to individualise ourselves and what prevents us from becoming divine. It is like that. Put that together and you will find the ego. Without the ego, as the world is organised, there would be no individual, and with the ego the world cannot become divine.

It would be logical to conclude, "Well, let us first of all become conscious individuals and then we shall send away the ego and become divine." Only, when we have become conscious individuals, we have grown so accustomed to living with our ego that we are no longer able to discern it and much labour is needed to become aware of its presence.

On the other hand, everyone knows what egoism is. When you want to pull everything towards you and other people do not interest you, that is called egoism; when you put yourself at the centre of the universe and all things exist only in relation to you, that is egoism. But it is very obvious, one must be blind not to see that one is egoistic. Everybody is a little egoistic, more or less, and at least a certain proportion of egoism is normally acceptable; but even in ordinary life, when one is a little too egoistic, well, one receives knocks on the nose, because, since everyone is egoistic, no one much likes egoism in others.

It is taken for granted, it is part of public morality. Yes, one must be a little bit egoistic, not too much, so it is not conspicuous! On the other hand, nobody speaks of the ego, because nobody knows it. It is such an intimate companion that one does not even recognise its existence; and yet so long as it is there one will never have the divine consciousness.

The ego is what makes one conscious of being separate from others. If there were no ego, you would not perceive that you are a person separate from others. You would have the impression that you are a small part of a whole, a very small part of a very great whole.

On the other hand, every one of you is most certainly quite conscious of being a separate person. Well, it is the ego that gives you this impression. As long as you are conscious in this way, it means that you have an ego.

When you begin to be aware that everything is yourself, and that this is only a very small point in the midst of thousands and thousands of other points of the same person that you are everywhere, when you feel that you are yourself in everything and that there is no separation, then you know that you are on the way towards having no more ego.

There even comes a time when it is impossible to conceive oneself and say, "It is not I", for even to express it in this way, to say that the All is you, that you are the All or that you are the Divine or that the Divine is you, proves that something still remains.

There is a moment — this happens in a flash and can hardly stay — when it is the All that thinks, it is the All that knows, it is the All that feels, it is the All that lives. There is not even... not even the impression that... you have reached that point.

Then it is all right. But until then, there is still a little remnant of ego somewhere; usually it is the part which looks on, the witness that looks on.

So do not assert that you have no more ego. It is not accurate. Say you are on the way towards having no more ego, that is the only correct thing to say.

2 May 1958

*

There is a spiritual ego even as there is a physical, vital and mental ego. There is a spiritual ego. There are people who have made a great effort to overcome all their egoism and all their limitations, and attained a spiritual consciousness; and there, they have all the vanity and the sense of their importance and contempt for those who are not in the same condition as they. Indeed, all that is ridiculous and bad in the ego, they find there once again. There are many, many like that. They have overcome what was there in the physical or vital consciousness but the very effort they have made to master themselves and this

victory they have gained give them the sense of their extreme importance. So they become puffed up and assert their authority.

This happens so frequently that it is not even noticed.

*I didn't understand this: "The so-called forces of Nature are but
the exterior activities of beings out of proportion with man by
their size and the powers at their disposal." (The Mother)*

Didn't understand?... For instance, take the wind which blows; now
scientists will tell you: "These are manifestations of forces of Nature,
and it is the result of such and such a phenomenon", they will speak
about heat and cold, high and low, etc., and they will tell you: "That's
the cause of the wind's blowing, these are currents of air produced in
the atmosphere." But it is not this. There are entities behind, only
they are so huge that their form eludes us. It would be like your asking an ant to describe the form of a man — it couldn't, could it? It
sees at the most the tiny end of the little toe and it takes a walk on the
foot — it is a great journey, and it would not know what a man's form
would be like. Well, it is almost the same thing. These forces which
bring about wind, rain, earthquakes, etc. are manifestations of — call
them gestures, if you like — of movements of certain beings so formidably huge that we hardly see the end of their foot and don't realise
their size.

Still, the spiritual ego is better than the ordinary ego, isn't it?

It is much more dangerous than the ordinary one! For one is not aware
that it is the ego. Outwardly, when one is egoistic, not only does one
know it oneself but others make you realise it still more, and circumstances prove it to you every moment. But there, as unfortunately you
meet people who respect you highly, you are not even aware that you
are terribly egoistic.

Very dangerous. Spiritual vanity is much more serious than physical vanity.

9 December 1953

*

The most important, the most difficult thing is to renounce one's ego, for to somebody who is not ready, to renounce his ego is like dying and dying much more than a physical death, for to him the death of the ego is like a dissolution of the being — this is not correct but it begins by giving this sort of impression. To be immortal one must renounce all limitations and the ego is the greatest of limitations; hence if "I" am not immortal, what is the good of that?

3 February 1951

Organise Your Being

Sweet Mother, here it is written: "It is part of the foundation of Yoga to become conscious of the great complexity of our nature, see the different forces that move it and get over it a control of directing knowledge." (Sri Aurobindo) Are these forces different for each person?

Yes. The composition is completely different, otherwise everybody would be the same. There are not two beings with an identical combination; between the different parts of the being and the composition of these parts the proportion is different in each individual. There are people, primitive men, people like the yet undeveloped races or the degenerated ones whose combinations are fairly simple.[...] And there are people absolutely at the top of the human ladder, the elite of humanity; their combinations become so complicated that a very special discernment is needed to find the relations between all these things.

There are beings who carry in themselves thousands of different personalities, and then each one has its own rhythm and alternation, and there is a kind of combination; sometimes there are inner conflicts, and there is a play of activities which are rhythmic and with alternations of certain parts which come to the front and then go back and again come to the front. But when one takes all that, it makes such complicated combinations that some people truly find it difficult to understand what is going on in themselves; and yet these are the ones most capable of a complete, coordinated, conscious, organised action; but their organisation is infinitely more complicated than that of primitive or undeveloped men who have two or three impulses and

four or five ideas, and who can arrange all this very easily in themselves and seem to be very coordinated and logical because there is
not very much to organise.

But there are people truly like a multitude, and so that gives them
a plasticity, a fluidity of action and an extraordinary complexity of
perception, and these people are capable of understanding a considerable number of things, as though they had at their disposal a veritable army which they move according to circumstance and need; and
all this is inside them. So when these people, with the help of yoga,
the discipline of yoga, succeed in centralising all these beings around
the central light of the divine Presence, they become powerful entities, precisely because of their complexity. So long as this is not organised they often give the impression of an incoherence, they are
almost incomprehensible, one can't manage to understand why they
are like that, they are so complex. But when they have organised all
these beings, that is, put each one in its place around the divine centre, then truly they are terrific, for they have the capacity of understanding almost everything and doing almost everything because of
the multitude of entities they contain, of which they are constituted.
And the nearer one is to the summit of the ladder, the more it is like
that, and consequently the more difficult it is to organise one's being;
because when you have about a dozen elements, you can quickly
compass and organise them, but when you have thousands of them, it
is difficult.

22 June 1955

*

Is the vital distorted from the very birth?

If your birth has not been accidental, you could very well think there
was no distortion, but what you are at your birth is most of the time
almost absolutely what your mother and father have made you, and
also, through them, what your grandparents have made you. There
are certain vital traditions in families and, besides, there is the state of
consciousness in which you were formed, conceived — the moment
at which you were conceived — and that, not once in a million times

does that state conform to true aspiration; and it is only a true aspiration which could make your vital pure of all mixture, make the vital element attracted for the formation of the being a pure element, free from all contagion; I mean that if a psychic being enters there, it can gather elements favourable to its growth. In the world as it is, things are so mixed up, have been so mixed up in every way, that it is almost impossible to have elements of the vital sufficiently pure not to suffer the contagion of all other contaminated beings.

I think I have already spoken about that, I have said what kind of aspiration ought to be there in the parents before the birth; but as I said, this does not happen even once in a hundred thousand instances. The willed conception of a child is extremely rare; mostly it is an accident. Among innumerable parents it is quite a small minority that even simply bothers about what a child could be; they do not even know that what the child will be depends on what they are. It is a very small elite which knows this. Most of the time things go as they can; anything at all happens and people don't even realise what is happening. So, in these conditions how do you expect to be born with a vital being sufficiently pure to be of help to you?

One is born with a slough to clean before one begins to live. And once you have made a good start on the way to the inner transformation and you go down to the subconscient root of the being — that exactly which comes from parents, from atavism — well, you do see what it is! and all, almost all difficulties are there, there are very few things added to existence after the first years of life. This happens at any odd moment; if you keep bad company or read bad books, the poison may enter you; but there are all the imprints deep-rooted in the subconscient, the dirty habits you have and against which you struggle. For instance, there are people who can't open their mouth without telling a lie, and they don't always do this deliberately (that is the worst of it), or people who can't come in touch with others without quarrelling, all sorts of stupidities — they are there in the subconscient, deeply rooted. Now, when you have a goodwill, externally you do your best to avoid all that, to correct it if possible; you work, you fight, then become aware that this thing always keeps coming up, it comes up from some part which escapes your control. But if you enter this subconscient, if you let your consciousness infiltrate it, and look carefully, gradually you will discover all the sources, all the origins of all your difficulties; then you will begin to understand what your fathers and mothers, grandfathers and grandmothers were, and if at a certain moment you are unable to control yourself, you will understand, "I am like that because they were like that."

If you have within you a psychic being sufficiently awake to watch over you, to prepare your path, it can draw towards you things which help you, draw people, books, circumstances, all sorts of little coincidences which come to you as though brought by some benevolent will and give you an indication, a help, a support to take decisions and turn you in the right direction. But once you have taken this decision, once you have decided to find the truth of your being, once you start sincerely on the road, then everything seems to conspire to help you to advance, and if you observe carefully you see gradually the source of your difficulties: "Ah! wait a minute, this failing was in my father; oh! this habit was my mother's; oh! my grandmother was like this, my grandfather was like that" or it could well be the nurse who took care of you when you were small, or brothers and sisters who played with you, the little friends you met, and you will find that all this was there, in this person or that or the other. But if you continue to be sincere, you find you can cross all this quite calmly, and after a time you cut all the moorings with which you were born, break the chains and go freely on the path.

If you really want to transform your character, it is that you must do. It has always been said that it is impossible to change one's nature; in all books of philosophy, even of yoga, you are told the same story: "You cannot change your character, you are born like that, you are like that." This is absolutely false, I guarantee it is false; but there is something very difficult to do to change your character, because it is not your character which must be changed, it is the character of your antecedents. In them you will not change it (because they have no such intention), but it is in you that it must be changed. It is what they have given you, all the little gifts made to you at your birth — nice gifts — it is this which must be changed. But if you succeed in getting hold of the thread of these things, the true thread, since you have worked upon this with perseverance and sincerity, one fine morning you will be free; all this will fall off from you and you will be able to get a start in life without any burden. Then you will be a new man, living a new life, almost with a new nature. And if you look back you will say, "It is not possible, I was never like that!"

29 March 1951

*

First one must become a conscious, well-knit, *individualised* being, who exists in himself, by himself, independently of all his surroundings, who can hear anything, read anything, see anything without changing. He receives from outside only what he wants to receive; he automatically refuses all that is not in conformity with his plan and nothing can leave an imprint on him unless he agrees to receive the imprint. Then one begins to become an individuality! When one is an individuality, one can make an offering of it.

For, unless one possesses something, one cannot give it. First, one must be, and then afterwards one can give oneself.

So long as one does not exist, one can give nothing. And for the separative ego to disappear, as you say, one must be able to give one-self entirely, totally without reservation. And to be able to give oneself, one must first exist. And to exist one must be individualised.

If your body were not made in the rigid form it is — for it is terribly rigid, isn't it? — well, if all that were not so fixed, if you had no skin, here, like this, solid, if externally you were the reflection of what you are in the vital and mental fields, it would be worse than being a jelly-fish! Everything would fuse into everything else, like this.... Oh, what a mess it would be! That is why it was at first necessary to give a very rigid form. Afterwards we complain about it. We say, "The physical is fixed, it is a nuisance; it lacks plasticity, it lacks suppleness, it hasn't that fluidity which can enable us to merge into the Divine." But this was absolutely necessary, for without this... if you simply went out of your body (most of you can't do it because the vital being is hardly more individualised than the physical), if you came out of your body and went into the vital world, you would see that all things there intermingle, they are mixed, they divide; all kinds of vibrations, currents of forces come and go, struggle, try to destroy one another, take possession of each other, absorb each other, throw each other out... and so it goes on! But it is very difficult to find a real personality in all this. These are forces, movements, desires, vibrations.

There are individualities, there are personalities! But these are powers. People who are individualised in that world are either heroes or devils!

And now, in the mind... (*Silence*) If only you become conscious of your physical mind in itself... Some people have called it a public square, because everything comes there, goes across, passes, comes back.... All ideas go there, they enter at one place, leave by another, some are here, some there, and it is a public square, not very well organised, for usually ideas meet and knock into one another, there are accidents of all kinds. But then one becomes aware: "What can I call my mind?" or "What is my mind?"

One needs years of very attentive, very careful, very reasonable, very coherent work, organisation, selection, construction, in order to succeed simply in forming, oh, simply this little thing, *one's own way of thinking!*

One believes he has his own way of thinking. Not at all. It depends totally upon the people one speaks with or the books he has read or on the mood he is in. It depends also on whether you have a good or bad digestion, it depends on whether you are shut up in a room without proper ventilation or whether you are in the open air; it depends on whether you have a beautiful landscape before you; it depends on whether there is sunshine or rain! You are not aware of it, but you think all kinds of things, completely different according to a heap of things which have nothing to do with you!

And for this to become a coordinated, coherent, logical thought, a long thorough work is necessary. And then, the best of the business is that when you have succeeded in making a beautiful, well-formed, very strong, very powerful mental construction, the first thing you will be told is, "You must break this so that you can unite with the Divine!" But so long as you haven't made it, you cannot unite with the Divine because you have nothing to give to the Divine except a mass of things which are not yourself! *One must first exist in order to be able to give oneself.* I am repeating what I said a while ago.

Truly, in the present state of the world, the only thing one can give the Divine is one's body. But that's what one doesn't give Him. Yes, one can try to consecrate one's work! But still, here there are so many elements which are not true![...]

All this... it is not in order to swamp you that I tell you all this. It is only in order to tell you that before speaking of merging one's ego in the Divine, one must first know a little what one is. The ego is there. Its necessity is that you become conscious, independent beings, individualised — I mean in the sense of independent — that you may not be the public square where everything goes criss-cross! That you may exist in yourselves. That is why there is an ego. It is like that; that is why also there is a skin, like that... though truly, even physical forces pass through the skin. There is a vibration which goes a certain distance. But still, it's the skin that prevents us from blending into one another. But everything else must be like that too.

(*After a silence*) And then, later, one offers all this to the Divine. Years of work are needed. You must not only... (*silence*) ... become conscious of yourself, conscious in all details, but you must organise what you call "yourself" around the psychic centre, the divine centre of your being, so that it would make a single, coherent, fully conscious being. And as this divine centre is itself already consecrated (*Mother makes a gesture of offering*) entirely to the Divine, if everything is organised harmoniously around it, everything is consecrated to the Divine. And so, when the Divine thinks it proper, when the time has come, when the work of individualisation is complete, then the Divine gives you permission to let your ego merge in Him, to live henceforward only for the Divine.

But it is the Divine who takes this decision. You must first have done all this work, become a conscious being, solely and exclusively centred around the Divine and governed by Him. And after all that, there is still an ego; because it is the ego which serves to make you an individual. But once this work is perfect, fully accomplished, then, at that moment, you may tell the Divine, "Here I am, I am ready. Do you want me?" And the Divine usually says, "Yes." All is over, everything is accomplished. And you become a real instrument for the Divine's work. But first the instrument must be constructed.

28 July 1954

Purity, Aspiration, Humility

So many people doubt the effectiveness of the Protection, the safety of the Path, because others go astray. And in their egoism they tremble with fear instead of telling themselves what I have just been reading to you this evening [about the need for purification], what is the cause of all catastrophes, small or great, which threaten those who follow the path of yoga without having taken the necessary care to be sufficiently pure and sincere.

No protection, no Grace can save those who refuse the indispensable purification.

And I would add this: that fear is an impurity, one of the greatest impurities, one of those which come most directly from the anti-divine forces which want to destroy the divine action on earth; and the first duty of those who really want to do yoga is to eliminate from their consciousness, with all the might, all the sincerity, all the endurance of which they are capable, even the shadow of a fear. To walk on the path, one must be dauntless, and never indulge in that petty, small, feeble, nasty shrinking back upon oneself, which is fear.

An indomitable courage, a perfect sincerity and a sincere self-giving, so that one does not calculate or bargain, does not give with the idea of receiving, does not trust with the idea of being protected, does not have a faith which asks for proofs — it is this that is indispensable in order to walk on the path, and it is this alone which can truly shelter you from all danger.

15 August 1956

*

How to enter the [inner] room?

You take a key and open the door!
You must find the key.
Or you sit down in front of the door until you have found the word, the idea or the force which opens it — as in the *Arabian Nights* tales.
It is not a joke, it is very serious. You must sit down in front of the

door and then concentrate until you have found the key or the word or the power to open it.

If one doesn't try, it doesn't open by itself. Perhaps after thousands of years, but you want to do it immediately — so? To do it immediately, you must sit down *obstinately* before the door until you have found the means. It may be a key, it may be a word, it may be a force, it may be anything at all, and you remain there before the door until it opens.

And you do not think of anything else.

Only of the door.

Is there no key-hole through which the light can escape?

A key-hole! What do you mean? A chink through which the light can escape?... Perhaps it is escaping, but perhaps no one sees it either!

It is escaping.

But then that's another problem: you must open your eyes. You must learn to open your eyes, to look.

Very small babies do not see, even very small animals do not see, tiny baby kittens do not see. It takes them several hours or several days — they don't see.

You must learn to see.

16 May 1956

*

Sweet Mother, Sri Aurobindo writes: "A psychic fire within must be lit into which all is thrown with the Divine Name upon it." Isn't the psychic fire always lit?

It is not always lit.

Then how to light it?

By aspiration.

By the will for progress, by the urge towards perfection.

Above all, it is the will for progress and self-purification which lights the fire. The will for progress. Those who have a strong will, when they turn it towards spiritual progress and purification, automatically light the fire within themselves.

And each defect one wants to cure or each progress one wants to make — if all that is thrown into the fire, it burns with a new intensity. And this is not an image, it is a fact in the subtle physical. One can feel the warmth of the flame, one can see in the subtle physical the light of the flame. And when there is something in the nature which prevents one from advancing and one throws it into this fire, it begins to burn and the flame becomes more intense.

8 August 1956

*

There is one thing that has always been said, but always misunderstood, it is the necessity of humility. It is taken in the wrong way, wrongly understood and wrongly used. Be humble, if you can be so in the right way; above all, do not be so in the wrong way, for that leads you nowhere. But there is one thing: if you can pull out from yourself this weed called vanity, then indeed you will have done something. But if you knew how difficult it is! You cannot do a thing well, cannot have a fine idea, cannot have a right movement, cannot make a little progress without getting puffed up inside (even without being aware of it), with a self-satisfaction full of vanity. And you are obliged then to hammer it hard to break it. And still broken bits remain and these begin to germinate. One must work the whole of one's life and never forget to work in order to uproot this weed that springs up again and again and again so insidiously that you believe it is gone and you feel very modest and say: "It is not I who have done it, I feel it is the Divine, I am nothing if He is not there", and then the next minute, you are so satisfied with yourself simply for having thought that!

What is the right and the wrong way of being humble?

It is very simple, when people are told "be humble", they think immediately of "being humble before other men" and that humility is wrong. True humility is humility before the Divine, that is, a precise,

exact, *living* sense that one is nothing, one can do nothing, understand nothing without the Divine, that even if one is exceptionally
intelligent and capable, this is nothing in comparison with the divine
Consciousness, and this sense one must always keep, because then
one always has the true attitude of receptivity — a humble receptivity
that does not put personal pretensions in opposition to the Divine.

13 May 1953

The Creative Word

*Sweet Mother, there's a flower you have named "The Creative
Word".*

Yes.

What does that mean?

It is the word which creates.

There are all kinds of old traditions, old Hindu traditions, old
Chaldean traditions in which the Divine, in the form of the Creator,
that is, in His aspect as Creator, pronounces a word which has the
power to create. So it is this... And it is the origin of the mantra. The
mantra is the spoken word which has a creative power. An invocation
is made and there is an answer to the invocation; or one makes a
prayer and the prayer is granted. This is the Word, the Word which, in
its sound... it is not only the idea, it is in the sound that there's a
power of creation. It is the origin, you see, of the mantra.

In Indian mythology the creator God is Brahma, and I think that
it was precisely his power which has been symbolised by this flower,
"The Creative Word". And when one is in contact with it, the words
spoken have a power of evocation or creation or formation or transformation; the words... sound always has a power; it has much more
power than men think. It may be a good power and it may be a bad
power. It creates vibrations which have an undeniable effect. It is not
so much the idea as the sound; the idea too has its own power, but in
its own domain — whereas the sound has a power in the material
world.

I think I have explained this to you once; I told you, for example, that words spoken casually, usually without any reflection and without attaching any importance to them, can be used to do something very good. I think I spoke to you about "Bonjour", "Good Day", didn't I? When people meet and say "Bonjour", they do so mechanically and without thinking. But if you put a will into it, an aspiration to indeed wish someone a good day, well, there is a way of saying "Good Day" which is very effective, much more effective than if simply meeting someone you thought: "Ah! I hope he has a good day", without saying anything. If with this hope in your thought you say to him in a certain way, "Good Day", you make it more concrete and more effective.

It's the same thing, by the way, with curses, or when one gets angry and says bad things to people. This can do them as much harm — more harm sometimes — than if you were to give them a slap. With very sensitive people it can put their stomach out of order or give them palpitation, because you put into it an evil force which has a power of destruction.

It is not at all ineffective to speak. Naturally it depends a great deal on each one's inner power. People who have no strength and no consciousness can't do very much — unless they employ material means. But to the extent that you are strong, especially when you have a powerful vital, you must have a great control on what you say, otherwise you can do much harm. Without wanting to, without knowing it; through ignorance.

26 October 1955

Asceticism

Mother, for self-mastery are not the ascetic methods useful sometimes?

No! You cure nothing. You only give yourself the illusion that you have progressed, but you cure nothing. The proof is that if you stop your ascetic methods, the thing is even stronger than before; it comes back with a vengeance. It depends upon what you call ascetic methods. If it is not to indulge in satisfying all your desires, this indeed is not asceticism, it is common sense. It is something else. Ascetic methods are things like repeated fasting, compelling yourself to endure the cold... in fact, to torture your body a little. This indeed gives you only a spiritual pride, nothing more. It masters nothing at all. It is infinitely easier. People do it because it is very easy, it is simple. Just because the pride is quite satisfied and the vanity can get puffed up, it becomes very easy. One makes a great demonstration of his ascetic virtues, and so considers himself an extremely important personage, and that helps him to endure many things.

It is much more difficult to master one's impulses quietly, composedly, and to prevent them from showing themselves — much more! — without taking ascetic measures. It is much more difficult not to be attached to the things you possess than to possess nothing. This is something that has been known for centuries. It requires a much greater quality not to be attached to the things one possesses than to be without any possessions or to reduce one's possessions to a strict minimum. It is much more difficult. It is a much higher degree of moral worth. Simply this attitude: when a thing comes to you, to take it, use it; when for one reason or another it goes away, to let it go and not regret it. Not to refuse it when it comes, to know how to adapt yourself and not to regret it when it goes.

Even if defects come?

It is not a question of defects, I am speaking of material things. Defects are not things which come, they are things one carries in oneself. I am speaking of material things. I am speaking of asceticism, you understand.

Asceticism is an altogether material discipline. Defects — don't think they come from outside; one has enough of them inside one without needing to borrow them from elsewhere. And in fact, if one did not carry them in oneself, one could not become aware of them in others. It is because the seed of all this is in oneself that one is in contact with them. And when we say that great waves of passion pass through people, and that they are not generated in them but pass through them, it is perfectly true. But if there was someone absolutely immune from all possibility of passion, they could pass by for centuries, he wouldn't even feel them. He could see them, see them passing, as one sees a storm passing in the sky, but he would feel nothing at all. When the vibrations inside oneself answer the vibrations from outside, it means that they are there; otherwise no vibration can enter.

There are examples like this. For instance, a crowd is seized by panic. Well, it is always possible that there are one or two persons who resist the panic, who are not touched, are outside it: they can save the situation. This has happened many a time. The reason why a movement, a vibration, a forceful movement is contagious is because the ground for contagion is there.

15 December 1954

Meditation

The number of hours spent in meditation is no proof of spiritual progress. It is a proof of your progress when you no longer have to make an effort to meditate. Then you have rather to make an effort to stop meditating: it becomes difficult to stop meditation, difficult to stop thinking of the Divine, difficult to come down to the ordinary consciousness. Then you are sure of progress, then you have made real progress when concentration in the Divine is the necessity of your life, when you cannot do without it, when it continues naturally from morning to night whatever you may be engaged in doing. Whether you sit down to meditation or go about and do things and work, what is required of you is consciousness; that is the one need, — to be constantly conscious of the Divine.

But is not sitting down to meditation an indispensable discipline, and does it not give a more intense and concentrated union with the Divine?

That may be. But a discipline in itself is not what we are seeking. What we are seeking is to be concentrated on the Divine in all that we do, at all times, in all our acts and in every movement. There are some here who have been told to meditate; but also there are others who have not been asked to do any meditation at all. But it must not be thought that they are not progressing. They too follow a discipline, but it is of another nature. To work, to act with devotion and an inner consecration is also a spiritual discipline. The final aim is to be in constant union with the Divine, not only in meditation but in all circumstances and in all the active life.

There are some who, when they are sitting in meditation, get into a state which they think very fine and delightful. They sit self-complacent in it and forget the world; but if they are disturbed, they come out of it angry and restless, because their meditation was interrupted. This is not a sign of spiritual progress or discipline. There are some people who act and seem to feel as if their meditation were a debt they have to pay to the Divine; they are like men who go to church once a week and think they have paid what they owe to God.

If you need to make an effort to go into meditation, you are still very far from being able to live the spiritual life. When it takes an effort to come out of it, then indeed your meditation can be an indication that you are in the spiritual life.

21 April 1929

*

What is the difference between meditation and concentration?

Meditation is a purely mental activity, it interests only the mental being. One can concentrate while meditating but this is a mental concentration; one can get a silence but it is a purely mental silence, and the other parts of the being are kept immobile and inactive so as not to disturb the meditation. You may pass twenty hours of the day in meditation and for the remaining four hours you will be an altogether ordinary man because only the mind has been occupied — the rest of the being, the vital and the physical, is kept under pressure so that it may not disturb. In meditation nothing is directly done for the other parts of the being.

Certainly this indirect action can have an effect, but... I have known in my life people whose capacity for meditation was remarkable but who, when not in meditation, were quite ordinary men, even at times ill-natured people, who would become furious if their meditation was disturbed. For they had learnt to master only their mind, not the rest of their being.

Concentration is a more active state. You may concentrate mentally, you may concentrate vitally, psychically, physically, and you may concentrate integrally. Concentration or the capacity to gather oneself at one point is more difficult than meditation. You may gather together one portion of your being or consciousness or you may gather together the whole of your consciousness or even fragments of it; that is, the concentration may be partial, total or integral, and in each case the result will be different.

25 December 1950

*

Some imagine that the sign of spiritual life is the capacity to sit in a corner and meditate! That is a very, very common idea. I do not want to be severe, but most people who make much of their capacity for meditation — I do not think they meditate even for one minute out of one hour. Those who meditate truly never speak about it; for them it is quite a natural thing. When it has become a natural thing, without any glory about it, you may begin to tell yourself that you are making progress. Those who talk about it and think that this gives them a superiority over other human beings, you may be sure, are most of the time in a state of complete inertia.

It is very difficult to meditate. There are all kinds of meditations.... You may take an idea and follow it to arrive at a given result — this is an active meditation; people who want to solve a problem or to write, meditate in this way without knowing that they are meditating. Others sit down and try to concentrate on something without following an idea — simply to concentrate on a point in order to intensify one's power of concentration; and this brings about what usually happens when you concentrate upon a point: if you succeed in gathering your capacity for concentration sufficiently upon a point whether mental, vital or physical, at a given moment you pass through and enter into another consciousness. Others still try to drive out from their head all movements, ideas, reflexes, reactions and to arrive at a truly silent tranquillity. This is extremely difficult; there are people who have tried for twenty-five years and not succeeded, for it is somewhat like taking a bull by the horns.

There is another kind of meditation which consists in being as quiet as one can be but without trying to stop all thoughts, for there are thoughts which are purely mechanical and if you try to stop these you will need years, and into the bargain you will not be sure of the result; instead of that you gather together all your consciousness and remain as quiet and peaceful as possible, you detach yourself from external things as though they do not interest you at all, and all of a sudden, you brighten the flame of aspiration and throw into it everything that comes to you so that the flame may rise higher and higher, higher and higher; you identify yourself with it and you go up to the extreme point of your consciousness and aspiration, thinking of nothing else — simply, an aspiration which mounts, mounts, mounts, without thinking a minute of the result, of what may happen and specially of what may not, and above all without desiring that something may come — simply, the joy of an aspiration which mounts and mounts and mounts, intensifying itself more and more in a constant concentration. And there I may assure you that what happens is the best that can happen. That is, it is the maximum of your possibilities which is realised when you do this. These possibilities may be very different according to individuals. But then all these worries about trying to be silent, going behind appearances, calling a force which answers, waiting for an answer to your questions, all that vanishes like an unreal vapour. And if you succeed in living consciously in this flame, in this column of mounting aspiration, you will see that even if you do not have an immediate result, after a time something will happen.

12 February 1951

*

If while doing what you have to do — whatever it may be, whatever work it is — if you do it and while doing it are careful not to forget the Divine, to offer to Him what you do and try so to give yourself to Him that He may change all your reactions — instead of their being selfish, petty, stupid and ignorant, making them luminous, generous — then in that way you will make progress. Not only will you have made some progress but you will have helped in the general progress. I have never seen people who have left everything in order to go and sit down in a more or less empty contemplation (for it is more or less empty); I have never seen such people making any progress, or in any case their progress is very trifling. I have seen persons who had no pretensions of doing yoga, who were simply filled with enthusiasm by the idea of terrestrial transformation and of the descent of the Divine into the world and who did their little bit of work with that enthusiasm in the heart, giving themselves wholly, without reserve, without any selfish idea of a personal salvation; these I have seen making magnificent progress, truly magnificent. And sometimes they are wonderful. I have seen sannyasis, I have seen people who live in monasteries, I have seen people who professed to be yogis, well, I would not exchange one of the others for a dozen such people (I mean, from the standpoint of terrestrial transformation and world progress, that is to say, from the standpoint of what we want to do, to try that this world may no longer be what it is and may become truly the instrument of the divine Will, with the divine Consciousness). It is not by running away from the world that you will change it. It is by working there, modestly, humbly but with a fire in the heart, something that burns like an offering. *Voilà.*

So meditation is of no use?

No, and to the extent it is necessary, it will come spontaneously. All of a sudden, you will be seized by something that makes you still, makes you concentrate in the vision of an idea or of a psychological state. That captures you. You must not resist. Then you make the needed progress. At such a moment you see, you understand something; and then the next minute you start your work again with that something gained in you, but without any pretension. What I most fear are those who believe themselves very exceptional because they sit down and meditate. Of all things this is the most dangerous, because they become so vain and so full of self-satisfaction that they close up in this way all avenues of progress....

13 May 1953

*

*"The practice of this Yoga demands a constant inward remem-
brance of the one central liberating knowledge.... In all is the one
Self, the one Divine is all; all are in the Divine, all are the Divine
and there is nothing else in the universe, — this thought or this
faith is the whole background until it becomes the whole substance of the consciousness of the worker. A memory, a self-
dynamising meditation of this kind, must and does in its end turn
into profound and uninterrupted vision and a vivid and all-embracing consciousness of that which we so powerfully remember
or on which we so constantly meditate." (Sri Aurobindo)*

*Sweet Mother, what does Sri Aurobindo mean by "a self-dynami-
sing meditation"?*

It is a meditation that has the power of transforming your being. It is
a meditation which makes you progress, as opposed to static meditation which is immobile and relatively inert, and which changes nothing in your consciousness or in your way of being. A dynamic meditation is a meditation of transformation.

Generally, people don't have a dynamic meditation. When they
enter into meditation — or at least what they call meditation — they
enter into a kind of immobility where nothing stirs, and they come
out of it exactly as they went in, without any change either in their
being or in their consciousness. And the more motionless it is, the
happier they are. They could meditate in this way for eternities, it
would never change anything either in the universe or in themselves.
That is why Sri Aurobindo speaks of a dynamic meditation which is
exactly the very opposite. It is a transforming meditation.

How is it done? Is it done in a different way?

I think it is the aspiration that should be different, the attitude should
be different. "Different way" — what do you mean by "way" —
(*laughing*) the way of sitting?... Not that? The inner way?

Yes.

But for each one it is different.

I think the most important thing is to know why one meditates; this is what gives the quality of the meditation and makes it of one order or another.

You may meditate to open yourself to the divine Force, you may meditate to reject the ordinary consciousness, you may meditate to enter the depths of your being, you may meditate to learn how to give yourself integrally; you may meditate for all kinds of things. You may meditate to enter into peace and calm and silence — this is what people generally do, but without much success. But you may also meditate to receive the Force of transformation, to discover the points to be transformed, to trace out the line of progress. And then you may also meditate for very practical reasons: when you have a difficulty to clear up, a solution to find, when you want help in some action or other. You may meditate for that too.

I think everyone has his own mode of meditation. But if one wants the meditation to be dynamic, one must have an aspiration for progress and the meditation must be done to help and fulfil this aspiration for progress. Then it becomes dynamic.

14 March 1956

*

I begin to meditate and pray ardently and fervently, my aspiration is intense and my prayer full of devotion; and then, after a certain length of time — sometimes short, sometimes long — the aspiration becomes mechanical and the prayer purely verbal. What should I do?

This is not an individual case, it is extremely common. I have already said this a number of times, but still it was in passing — that people who claim to meditate for hours every day and spend their whole day praying, to me it seems that three-fourths of the time it must be absolutely mechanical; that is to say, it loses all its sincerity. For human nature is not made for that and the human mind is not built that way.

In order to concentrate and meditate one must do an exercise which I could call the "mental muscle-building" of concentration.

One must really make an effort — as one makes a muscular effort, for instance, to lift a weight — if you want the concentration to be sincere and not artificial.

The same thing for the urge of prayer: suddenly a flame is lit, you feel an enthusiastic *élan*, a great fervour, and express it in words which, to be true, must be spontaneous. This must come from the heart, directly, with ardour, without passing through the head. That is a prayer. If there are just words jostling in your head, it is no longer a prayer. Well, if you don't throw more fuel into the flame, after a time it dies out. If you do not give your muscles time to relax, if you don't slacken the movement, your muscles lose the capacity of taking strains. So it is quite natural, and even indispensable, for the intensity of the movement to cease after a certain time. Naturally, someone who is accustomed to lifting weights can do it much longer than one who has never done it before. It is the same thing; someone who is accustomed to concentration can concentrate much longer than one who is not in the habit. But for everybody there comes a time when one must let go, relax, in order to begin again. Therefore, whether immediately or after a few minutes or a few hours, if the movement becomes mechanical, it means that you have relaxed and that you need no longer pretend that you are meditating. It is better to do something useful.

If you cannot manage to do a little exercise, for instance, in order to neutralise the effect of the mental tension, you may read or try to note down what happened to you, you may express things. Then that produces a relaxation, the necessary relaxation. But the duration of the meditation is only relatively important; its length simply shows how far you are accustomed to this activity.

Of course, this may increase a great deal, but there is always a limit; and when the limit is reached one must stop, that's all. It is not an insincerity, it is an incapacity. What becomes insincere is if you pretend to meditate when you are no longer meditating or you say prayers like many people who go to the temple or to church, perform ceremonies and repeat their prayers as one repeats a more or less well-learnt lesson. Then it is no longer either prayer or meditation, it is simply a profession. It is not interesting.

18 July 1956

CHAPTER 18

The Integral Yoga

An Integral Transformation

In the integral Yoga, the integral life down even to the smallest detail has to be transformed, to be divinised. There is nothing here that is insignificant, nothing that is indifferent. You cannot say, "When I am meditating, reading philosophy or listening to these conversations I will be in this condition of an opening towards the Light and call for it, but when I go out to walk or see friends I can allow myself to forget all about it." To persist in this attitude means that you will remain untransformed and never have the true union; always you will be divided; you will have at best only glimpses of this greater life. For although certain experiences and realisations may come to you in meditation or in your inner consciousness, your body and your outer life will remain unchanged. An inner illumination that does not take any note of the body and the outer life, is of no great use, for it leaves the world as it is. This is what has continually happened till now. Even those who had a very great and powerful realisation withdrew from the world to live undisturbed in inner quiet and peace; the world was left to its ways, and misery and stupidity, Death and Ignorance continued, unaffected, their reign on this material plane of existence. For those who thus withdraw, it may be pleasant to escape from this turmoil, to run away from the difficulty and to find for themselves a happy condition elsewhere; but they leave the world and life uncorrected and untransformed; and their own outer consciousness too they leave unchanged and their bodies as unregenerate as ever. Coming back to the physical world, they are likely to be worse there than even ordinary people; for they have lost the mastery over material things, and their dealing with physical life is likely to be slovenly and helpless in its movements and at the mercy of every passing force.

An ideal of this kind may be good for those who want it, but it is not our Yoga. For we want the divine conquest of this world, the conquest of all its movements and the realisation of the Divine here. But if we want the Divine to reign here we must give all we have and are and do here to the Divine. It will not do to think that anything is unimportant or that the external life and its necessities are no part of the Divine Life. If we do, we shall remain where we have always been and there will be no conquest of the external world; nothing abiding there will have been done.

28 April 1929

*

We want an integral transformation, the transformation of the body and all its activities.

Formerly, when one spoke of transformation one meant solely the transformation of the inner consciousness. One tried to discover in oneself this deep consciousness and rejected the body and its activities like an encumbrance and a useless thing, in order to attend only to the inner movement. Sri Aurobindo declared that this was not enough; the Truth demanded that the material world should also participate in this transformation and become an expression of the deeper Truth. But when people heard this, many thought that it was possible to transform the body and its activities without bothering in the least about what was happening within — naturally this is not quite true. Before you can undertake this work of physical transformation, which of all things is the most difficult, your inner consciousness must be firmly established, solidly established in the Truth, so that this transformation may be the final expression of the Truth — "final" for the moment at least.

The starting-point of this transformation is receptivity, we have already spoken about it. That is the indispensable condition for obtaining the transformation. Then comes the change of consciousness. This change of consciousness and its preparation have often been compared with the formation of the chicken in the egg: till the very last second the egg remains the same, there is no change, and it is only when the chicken is completely formed, absolutely alive, that it itself makes with its little beak a hole in the shell and comes out. Something similar takes place at the moment of the change of consciousness. For a long time you have the impression that nothing is happening, that your consciousness is the same as usual, and, if you have an intense aspiration, you even feel a resistance, as though you were knocking against a wall which does not yield. But when you are ready within, a last effort — the pecking in the shell of the being — and everything opens and you are projected into another consciousness.

I said that it was a revolution of the basic equilibrium, that is, a total reversal of consciousness comparable with what happens to light when it passes through a prism. Or it is as though you were turning a ball inside out, which cannot be done except in the fourth dimension. One comes out of the ordinary three-dimensional consciousness to enter the higher four-dimensional consciousness, and into an infinite number of dimensions. This is the indispensable starting-point. Unless your consciousness changes its dimension, it will remain just what it is with the superficial vision of things, and all the profundities will escape you.[...] After this inner opening and this identification with the Presence in the psychic centre, you see things from within outwards, and the outer existence becomes an expression, more or less deformed, of what you see within: you are aware of the inner existence of beings and their form; their outer existence is only a more or less deformed expression of this inner truth. And it is because of this that I say that the basic equilibrium is completely changed. Instead of being outside the world and seeing it as something outside you, you are inside the world and see outer forms expressing in a more or less clumsy fashion what is within, which for you is the Truth.

4 January 1951

*

You are told: there is only one reality, and all that is, is only a multiple expression of a single reality. Therefore, all the divine manifestations, all the forms it has taken in the course of time, all the names which men have given it, are only manifestations, forms and names of one sole, unique Godhead.

As human beings are very limited, it is usually easier for them to follow one path rather than another. But that is just a tiny little beginning; and if one wants to attain the heights, one must be able to find the Divine equally through all the paths, and understand that it is the sole and same Divine, whatever the different appearances may be.

This is what Sri Aurobindo tells you: that you cannot stop, you cannot be satisfied until you have felt *absolutely concretely* that there is only one *single* Divine, there is only one *single* Reality, and that, from whatever angle It is seen or whatever path is taken to attain It, it will always be one sole and same thing which you will meet. So one who is developed enough, vast enough to be able to follow what we call the Integral Yoga, must have the capacity to approach the Divine by all possible paths. If he doesn't want to follow them himself because it takes time... though there is a certain degree of development which enables one in a few days or a few hours to follow a path which would otherwise take a whole lifetime... still, if one has no taste for this kind of gymnastics, at least one should have an understanding open enough to be aware that all this is fundamentally one sole and identical thing. And whether you give it this name or that or no name at all, you understand, or several names, you are always speaking of the same thing which is the single Divine who is all things.

Don't you catch it?

It is only the mind and the limited human consciousness which make distinctions. And through these differences you get into a confusion. You distinguish only by differences, and differences mean just the illusory outer consciousness. As soon as you really enter within, you immediately have the sense of a total identity and all these divergences seem absolutely ridiculous to you.

23 November 1955

The Individual and the Collectivity

Does an individual mastery over desire suffice or is a general, collective mastery necessary?

Ah! there we are.... Is it possible to attain a total personal transformation without there being at least a correspondence in the collectivity?... This does not seem possible to me. There is such an interdependence between the individual and the collectivity that, unless one does what the ascetics have preached, that is, escapes from the world, goes out of it completely, leaves it where it is and runs away selfishly leaving all the work to others, unless one does that... And even so I have my doubts. Is it possible to accomplish a total transformation of one's being so long as the collectivity has not reached at least a certain degree of transformation? I don't think so. Human nature remains what it is — one can attain a great change of consciousness, that yes, one can purify one's consciousness, but the total conquest, the material transformation depends definitely to a large extent, on a certain degree of progress in the collectivity. Buddha said with reason that as long as you have in you a vibration of desire, this vibration will spread in the world and all those who are ready to receive it will receive it. In the same way, if you have in you the least receptivity to a vibration of desire, you will be open to all the vibrations of desire which circulate constantly in the world. And that is why he concluded: Get out of this illusion, withdraw entirely and you will be free. I find this relatively very selfish, but after all, that was the only way he had foreseen.

There is another: to identify oneself so well with the divine Power as to be able to act constantly and consciously upon all vibrations circulating through the world. Then the undesirable vibrations no longer have any effect upon you, but you have an effect upon them, that is, instead of an undesirable vibration entering into you without being perceived and doing its work there, it is perceived and immediately on its arrival you act upon it to transform it, and it goes back into the world transformed, to do its beneficent work and prepare others for the same realisation. This is exactly what Sri Aurobindo proposes to do and, more clearly, what he asks you to do, what he intends us to do:

Instead of running away, to bring into oneself the power which can conquer.

Note that things are arranged in such a way that if the tiniest atom of ambition remained and one wanted this Power for one's personal satisfaction, one could never have it, that Power would never come. Its deformed limitations, of the kind seen in the vital and physical world, those yes, one may have them, and there are many people who have them, but the true Power, the Power Sri Aurobindo calls "supramental", unless one is absolutely free from all egoism under all its forms, one will never be able to manifest. So there is no danger of its being misused. It will not manifest except through a being who has attained the perfection of a complete inner detachment. I have told you, this is what Sri Aurobindo expects us to do — you may tell me it is difficult, but I repeat that we are not here to do easy things, we are here to do difficult ones.

3 May 1951

*

You said that to each individual is given a problem to solve. So each man upon earth has to live individually, for, in living collectively one has the difficulty of the collectivity also: it is not only one's own difficulty.

Yes, but man happens to be a social animal, and so, instinctively, he forms groups. But that also is why those who wished to go fast and did not feel themselves sufficiently strong retired into solitude. That is the reason, the justification of the ascetic who goes away into solitude, for he tries to cut himself off from the world. Only... there is an "only". One can do that physically to a certain extent, up to a point, cut oneself off from physical nature — not totally. It has been noticed, for instance, that ascetics who went away to sit under a tree in the forest, in a very short while became extraordinarily interested in all the animals living in the forest: it is the need of physical relationship with other living beings. It is possible that some do not need this, but it is a fairly general rule.

But solidarity does not stop there. There is a vital solidarity and a mental solidarity which you cannot prevent. There is, despite everything (though men are much more individualised than animals), there is a spirit of the species. There are collective suggestions which don't need to be expressed in words. There are atmospheres one cannot escape. It is certain (for this I know by experience), it is certain that there is a degree of individual perfection and transformation which cannot be realised without the whole of humanity having made a particular progress. And this happens by successive steps. There are things in Matter which cannot be transformed unless the whole of Matter has undergone transformation to a certain degree. One cannot isolate oneself completely. It is not possible. One can do the work, one can choose: there are people who have chosen to go into solitude and try to realise in themselves the ideal they saw — usually they reached a certain point, then stopped there, they could not go further. It has been thus historically.

I was saying the other day: "There are perhaps people upon earth whom I don't know who have realised extraordinary things" but exactly because they have isolated themselves from the earth, the earth does not know them. This is just to say that nothing is impossible. It seems doubtful, is all that I can say. But it is impossible, even if one isolates oneself physically, to do so vitally and mentally. There is the vast terrestrial atmosphere in which one is born, and there is a sort of spirit or genius of the human race; well, this genius must have reached a certain degree of perfection for anyone to be able to go farther. It is not that one has to wait till all have done it, no; but it is as though all had to reach a certain level for one to be able to take one's spring and go farther.... Surely the individual will always be ahead of the mass, there's no doubt about that, but there will always be a proportion and a relation.

7 October 1953

*

"Often he (the sadhak) finds that even after he has won persistently his own personal battle, he has still to win it over and over again..." (Sri Aurobindo) [...] Then does this mean that others profit by his sadhana?

You understand, it's like that for everyone.

If there was only one, it could be like this: that he alone could do it for all; but if everybody does it... you understand...

You are fifty persons doing the Integral Yoga. If it is only one of the fifty who is doing it, then he does it for all the fifty. But if each one of the fifty is doing it, each doing it for all the fifty, he does it actually for one person alone, because all do it for all.

But the work is much longer?

One must widen oneself.

The work is more complicated, it is more complete, it asks for a greater power, a greater wideness, a greater patience, a greater tolerance, a greater endurance; all these things are necessary. But in fact, if each one does perfectly what he has to do, it is no longer only one single person who does the whole thing: not one single person who does it for all, but all now form only one person who does it for the whole group.

This ought to form a kind of sufficient unity among all those who are doing it, so that they no longer feel the distinction. This is indeed the ideal way of doing it: that they now form only one single body, one single personality, working at once each for himself and for the others without any distinction.

Truly speaking, it was the first question which came up when I met Sri Aurobindo. I think I have already told you this; I don't remember now, but I spoke about it recently. Should one do one's yoga and reach the goal and then later take up the work with others or should one immediately let all those who have the same aspiration come to him and go forward all together towards the goal?

Because of my earlier work and all that I had tried, I came to Sri Aurobindo with the question very precisely formulated. For the two possibilities were there: either to do an intensive individual sadhana by withdrawing from the world, that is, by no longer having any contact with others, or else to let the group [of disciples] be formed naturally and spontaneously, not preventing it from being formed, allowing it to form, and starting all together on the path.

Well, the decision was not at all a mental choice; it came spontaneously. The circumstances were such that there was no choice; that is, quite naturally, spontaneously, the group was formed in such a way that it became an imperious necessity. And so once we have started like that, it is finished, we have to go to the end like that.

At the beginning there were five, ten, not more. There were five or six for a long time. It became ten, twelve, about twenty; then thirty, thirty-five. That remained for quite a long while. And then suddenly, you know, it started; and then here we are! The last figure was more than eleven hundred. We are growing.

Now, among these there are many who do not do the sadhana,

then the problem does not come up. But for all those who do it, it is like this, it is as Sri Aurobindo has described it here. And if one wants to do the thing in a solitary way, it is absolutely impossible to do it totally. For every physical being, however complete he may be, is only partial and limited; he represents only one law in the world; it can be a very complex law, but it is only one law; what is called in India, you know, the Dharma, one Truth, one Law.

Each individual being, even if he be of a completely higher kind, even if he is made for an absolutely special work, is only one individual being; that means, the totality of the transformation cannot take place through one single body. And that is why, spontaneously, the multiplication came about.

One can reach, alone and solitary, his own perfection. One can become in one's consciousness infinite and perfect. But when it is a question of a work, it is always limited.

I don't know if you understand me well. But personal realisation has no limits. One can become inwardly in himself perfect and infinite. But the outer realisation is necessarily limited, and if one wants to have a general action, at least a minimum number of physical beings is needed.

In a very old tradition it was said that twelve were enough; but in the complexities of modern life it doesn't seem possible. There must be a representative group. Which means that... you know nothing about it or you don't imagine it very well, but each one of you represents one of the difficulties which must be conquered for the transformation. And this makes many difficulties! (*Mother laughs*) I have written somewhere... I have said that, more than a difficulty, each one represents an impossibility to be solved. And it is the whole set of all these impossibilities which can be transformed into the Work, the Realisation. Each case is an impossibility to be solved, and it is when all these impossibilities are resolved that the Work will be accomplished.

But now I am more gentle. I take away "impossibility" and put "difficulty". Perhaps they are no longer impossibilities.

Only, from the beginning, and still more now that our group has grown so considerably, each time someone comes to tell me, "I come for *my* yoga", I say, "Oh, no! then don't come. It is much more difficult here than anywhere else." And the reason is what Sri Aurobindo has written here.

If someone comes to tell me, "I come to work, I come to make myself useful", it is all right. But if someone comes and says, "I have many difficulties outside, I can't manage to overcome these difficulties, I want to come here because it will help me", I say, "No, no, it will be *much* more difficult here; your difficulties will increase *considerably*." And that is what it means, because they are no longer isolated difficulties; they are collective difficulties.

So in addition to your own personal difficulty you have all the frictions, all the contacts, all the reactions, all the things which come from outside. As a test. Exactly on the weak point, the thing that's most difficult to solve; it is there that you will hear from someone the phrase which was just the one you did not want to hear; someone will make towards you that gesture which was exactly the one which could shock you; you find yourself facing a circumstance, a movement, a fact, an object, anything at all — just the things which... "Ah, how I should have liked this not to happen!" And it's that which will happen. And more and more. Because you do not do your yoga for yourself alone. You do the yoga for everybody — without wanting to — automatically.

So when people come and tell me, "I come here for peace, quietness, leisure, to do my yoga", I say, "No, no, no! go away immediately somewhere else, you will be much more peaceful anywhere else than here."

If someone comes and says, "Well, here I am, I feel that I should consecrate myself to the divine Work, I am ready to do any work at all that you give me", then I say, "Good, that's all right. If you have goodwill, endurance, and some capacity, it is all right. But to find the solitude necessary for your inner development it is better to go somewhere else, *anywhere else*, but not here." There we are.

I said all this just today; I had the occasion to do so. And at the same time I said, "There is an exception to this rule: that's the children." Because here the children have the advantage of living from the time when they are still unconscious, in an atmosphere which helps them to find themselves. And this one doesn't have outside. I am saying what I just said to people who are... not necessarily old but still... formed, who are past the age not only of childhood but of their first youth.

21 December 1955

*

Sri Aurobindo tells us that a true community — what he calls a gnostic or supramental community — can exist only on the basis of the inner realisation of each of its members, each one realising his real, concrete unity and identity with all the other members of the community, that is, each one should feel not like just one member united in some way with all the others, but all as one, within himself. For each one the others must be himself as much as his own body, and not mentally and artificially, but by a fact of consciousness, by an inner realisation.

(Silence)

That means that before hoping to realise this gnostic collectivity, each one should first become — or at least begin to become — a gnostic being. This is obvious; the individual work should go on ahead and the collective work should follow; but it so happens that spontaneously, without any arbitrary intervention of the will, the individual progress is controlled, so to speak, or held back by the collective state. Between the individual and the collectivity there is an interdependence from which one can't totally free oneself, granting that one tries. And even a person who tried in his yoga to liberate himself totally from the terrestrial and human state of consciousness, would be tied down, in his subconscious at least, to the state of the mass, which acts as a brake and actually *pulls* backwards. One can try to go much faster, try to drop all the weight of attachments and responsibilities, but despite everything, the realisation, even of one who is at the very summit and is the very first in the evolutionary march, is dependent on the realisation of the whole, dependent on the state of the terrestrial collectivity. And that indeed *pulls* one back, to such an extent that at times one must wait for centuries for the Earth to be ready, in order to be able to realise what is to be realised.

3 July 1957

The Spiritual Hierarchy

*Mother, when one is identified with the Divine in the higher part
of the being while neglecting the lower parts — neglecting life —
doesn't the Divine, in the part where one is identified with Him,
advise one to attend to the lower parts?*

And if before even beginning, one has decided that this must not happen, perhaps one makes it impossible for oneself to receive the advice of the Divine!

For, truly speaking, each one finds only what he wants to find of
the Divine. Sri Aurobindo has said this by turning it the other way
round; he has said — I am not quoting the exact words, only the idea:
what you expect from the Divine is what you find in the Divine; what
you want from the Divine is what you meet in the Divine. He will
have for you the aspect you expect or desire.

And His manifestation is always adapted to each one's receptivity and capacity. They may have a real, essential contact, but this
contact is limited by their own capacity for receiving and approach....
It is only if you are able to go out of all limits that you can meet the
total Divine as He totally is.

And this capacity for contact is perhaps what constitutes the true
hierarchy of beings. For everyone carries within himself the Divine,
and therefore everyone has the possibility of uniting with the Divine
— that possibility is the same in all. But according to each one's
capacity — in fact, according to his position in the divine hierarchy
— his approach will be more or less partial or total.

It could be said — although these words deform things a lot —
that the quality of the approach is the same in every being, but the
quantity, the totality is very different.... It is very difficult to explain
in words, but if one may say so, the *point* at which you are identified
with the Divine is perfect in itself, that is to say, your identification is
perfect in itself, at this point, but the number of points at which you
are identified differs immensely.

And this is very marked in the difference between the paths followed to approach the Divine. Usually people set limits; they limit
themselves by excluding everything that is not exactly the path they

have chosen, for this is much easier and they go much faster — relatively. But if, instead of following *one* road, you go forward in a sort of movement which could be called spherical, where everything is included, which takes in all the possibilities of approach to the Divine, naturally the result is much more complete — and it is this that Sri Aurobindo calls the integral yoga — but the progress is much more difficult and much slower.

One who chooses the path of knowledge — and even in the path of knowledge a special method, for everyone has his own method — and follows it, eliminating from his consciousness and life all that's not it, advances much more rapidly, for he is in search of only one aspect and this is much more direct, immediate. And so he rejects, rejects, rejects all that is not this, and limits his being just to the path he travels. And the more you want your approach to be integral, naturally the more will it become difficult, complicated, long, laborious.

But he who follows only one path, when he reaches his goal, that is, when he is identified with the Divine, his identification is perfect in itself; that is to say, it is really an identification with the Divine — but it is partial. It is perfect; it is perfect and partial at the same time.

This is very difficult to explain, but it is a fact. He is really identified with the Divine and has found the Divine; he is identified with the Divine — but at one point. And so he who is able to identify himself in his totality with the Divine is necessarily, from the point of view of the universal realisation, on a much higher level of the hierarchy than one who could realise Him only at a single point.

And that is the true meaning of the spiritual hierarchy, this is why there is a whole spiritual hierarchical organisation, otherwise it would have no basis, for from the minute you touch the Divine, you touch Him perfectly: the point at which you touch Him is perfect in itself. And, from this point of view, all who are united with the Divine are equally perfect in their union — but not equally complete, if I may say so.[...]

(*Turning to the child*) In your consciousness there is still the idea that you unite with "Something" which knows more about it than you and will make you recognise your mistake. But that no longer exists after the identification! That is just the first contact, but not the identification.

In identification there is no longer any difference between the one who is identified and what he is identified with: it is the same thing. So long as there is a difference, it is not identification.

I say that by any path whatever and by eliminating all that is not of this path, it is possible for each one to be perfectly identified with the Divine, that is to say, to become the Divine — but at only one point, the point he has chosen. But this point is perfect in itself. I don't say it contains everything, I say it is perfect in itself, that is, the identification is perfect — but it is not total.

They have the full bliss?

Perfect bliss — perfect bliss, eternity, infinity, everything.

Then what's the difference?

The difference exists only in the manifestation. By this identification, whatever it may be, one automatically goes out of the manifestation, except at the point where one is identified. And if, in the path one has followed, the aim is to go out, as for instance with those who seek Nirvana, if it is a going out of the manifestation, well, one goes out of the manifestation, it's the end. And once one goes out of the manifestation, there is no longer any difference or any hierarchy, it is finished, one has gone out of the manifestation. That is it, you understand, everything depends on the goal one pursues. If one goes out of the manifestation, one goes out of the manifestation, then there is no longer a possibility of any hierarchy at all. But as soon as one enters the manifestation, there is a hierarchy. That is to say — if we take the realisation of the supramental world — everybody will not be on the same level and made in the same pattern, and with the same capacity and possibility. It's always this illusion, isn't it, of a sort of indefinite repetition of something which always resembles itself — it is not that. In the realisation, the manifestation, there is a hierarchy of capacity and action, and of manifestation. But if the aim is to go out of the manifestation, then quite naturally, at whatever point you go out, you go out.

It all depends on the ideal one puts before oneself. And while you go out because you have chosen to do so, to enter into Pralaya, there is all the rest of the universe which continues.... But that's totally immaterial to you. As your aim was to get out of it, you get out of it. But that doesn't mean that the rest also go out! You are the only one to go out, or those who have followed the same aim and the same path as you.

(*Long silence*)

That is precisely the problem which faced Sri Aurobindo here and me in France: should one limit one's path and reach the goal first, and later take up all the rest and begin the work of integral transformation; or should one go step by step, not leaving anything aside, not eliminating anything on the path, taking in all the possibilities at the same time and progressing at all points at the same time? That is to say, should one retire from life and action until one reaches one's goal, becomes conscious of the Supermind and realises it in oneself; or should one embrace the entire creation and with this entire creation gradually go forward towards the Supermind?

(*Silence*)

One can understand that things get done by stages: you go forward, reach one stage, and so, as a consequence, take all the rest forward; and then at the same time, in a simultaneous movement, you reach another stage and again take others forward — and so on.

That gives the impression that you are not moving. But everything is on the move in this way.

1 February 1956

*

One can understand *nothing* of the spiritual life if one does not understand the true hierarchy.

Nowadays it's not in fashion. It is something which human thought doesn't favour at all. But from the spiritual point of view, it is automatic, spontaneous and indisputable. And so, if the hierarchy is true, there is a place for everybody; and for each individual in his own place, his individual truth is absolute. That is to say, each element which is truly in its place has a total and perfect relation with the Divine — in its place. And yet, on the whole, there is a hierarchy which too is quite absolute. But to understand spiritual life one must first understand that; and it isn't very easy.

Everyone can be a perfect expression of the Divine in himself, on condition that he knows his place and keeps to it.

And if they do not know the hierarchy, they cannot know this?

But they don't need to know that they form a hierarchy, it is not necessary to know it. It is only if one wants to physically organise a spiritual society — then one has to materialise the hierarchy. But generally, in the world as it is, there are so many gaps in this hierarchy that it seems a confusion.

The perfect hierarchy is a total hierarchy, and it is not concerned with time and space. But when you want to realise this physically it becomes very difficult. It's like weaving a piece of cloth with lots of holes everywhere; and the holes disturb the general harmony. Always people are missing, steps are missing, pieces are missing on the chessboard — all this is missing. So it looks like a confusion. But if everything were expressed and each thing in its place, it would be a perfect harmony and a perfect hierarchy.

There is somewhere — not in the material universe, but in the manifested universe — this perfect hierarchy; it exists. But it is not yet manifested upon earth.

Perhaps this will be one of the results of the supramental transformation: the world will be ready for a perfect, spontaneous, essentially true hierarchical manifestation — and without any kind of coercion — where everyone will become aware of his own perfection.

Mother, what does a spiritual hierarchy mean exactly? Because when we speak of hierarchy that implies something graded in a superior and inferior order, doesn't it?

Yes, and that's quite wrong. That is to say, materially it is like that. But this is not what I call a hierarchy.

Then what is a hierarchy?

It is the organisation of the functions and the manifestation in action of the particular nature of each person.

We have often tried to find comparisons, but they are worthless. For none of the things we know physically can answer to that condition. There is always the sense of superiority and inferiority as you say.... Some have compared a hierarchy to the various functions of the body, for example. But that always gives the impression that the head is at the top and the feet at the bottom, so it is a nuisance!

Each element is the whole Divine at the same time, then how can we speak of a hierarchy?

Each element has a direct and perfect relation with the Divine.

But can't they become the whole Divine?

Yes, all become the Divine; but not the totality of the Divine, for the Divine is everything. You can't take a piece of the Divine and say, "This is the Divine." And yet, in his spiritual consciousness each one has a perfect relation with the Divine, that is to say, each one is the Divine as perfectly as he can be. But to reconstruct the Divine, all the Divine is necessary. And it is precisely this that constitutes the very essence of hierarchy. But as each one is perfect in himself, there can be no feeling of inferiority or superiority.

I don't think the human mentality can understand that. I think it must be lived; once one has lived it, it is very simple, it appears luminously simple. But to understand it with the mind is not possible, it seems impossible. Above all because the mind, in order to understand anything at all, has to divide and contrast everything, otherwise it does not understand, it gets confused. By its very functioning, it becomes incapable of understanding.

18 January 1956

Realisation of the Psychic Being

Sweet Mother, where does our true spiritual life begin?

The true spiritual life begins when one is in communion with the Divine in the psychic, when one is conscious of the divine Presence in the psychic and in constant communion with the psychic. Then the spiritual life begins, not before. The *true* spiritual life.

When one is united with one's psychic being and conscious of the divine Presence, and receives the impulses for one's action from this divine Presence, and when the will has become a conscious collaborator with the divine Will — that is the starting-point.

Before that, one may be an aspirant to the spiritual life, but one doesn't have a spiritual life.

9 May 1956

*

Unless your vision is *constantly* the vision of the Divine in all things, you have not only no right but no capacity to judge the state which others are in. And to pronounce a judgment on someone without having this vision spontaneously, effortlessly, is precisely an example of the mental presumptuousness of which Sri Aurobindo always spoke.... And it so happens that one who has the vision, the consciousness, who is capable of seeing the truth in all things, never feels the need to judge anything whatever. For he understands everything and knows everything. Therefore, once and for all, you must tell yourselves that the moment you begin to judge things, people, circumstances, you are in the most total human ignorance.

In short, one could put it like this: when one understands, one no longer judges and when one judges, it means that one doesn't know.

Judging people is one of the first things which must be totally swept away from the consciousness before you can take even a step on the supramental path, because that is not a material progress or a bodily progress, it is only a very little progress of thought, mental progress. And unless you have swept your mind clean of all its ignorance, you cannot hope to take a step on the supramental path.[...]

All these ideas of good and evil, good and bad, higher, lower, all these notions belong to the ignorance of the human mind, and if one really wants to come into contact with the divine life, one must liberate oneself totally from this ignorance, one must rise to a region of consciousness where these things have *no* reality. The feeling of superiority and inferiority completely disappears, it is replaced by something else which is of a very different nature — a sort of capacity for filtering appearances, penetrating behind masks, shifting the point of view.

And these are not words, it is altogether true that *everything* changes its appearance, totally, that life and things are completely different from what they appear to be.

All this contact, this ordinary perception of the world loses its reality completely. This is what appears unreal, fantastic, illusory, non-existent. There is something — something very material, very concrete, very physical — which becomes the reality of the being, and which has nothing in common with the ordinary way of seeing. When one has this perception — the perception of the work of the divine force, of the movement being worked out behind the appearance, *in* the appearance, through the appearance — one begins to be ready to live something truer than the ordinary human falsehood. But not before.

There is no compromise, you see. It is not like a convalescence after an illness: you must change worlds. So long as your mind is real for you, your way of thinking something true for you, real, concrete, it proves that you are not there yet. You must first pass through to the other side. Afterwards you will be able to understand what I am telling you.

Pass through to the other side.

It is not true that one can understand little by little, it is not like that. This kind of progress is different. What is more true is that one is shut up in a shell, and inside it something is happening, like the chick in the egg. It is getting ready in there. It is in there. One doesn't see it. Something is happening in the shell, but outside one sees nothing. And it is only when all is ready that there comes the capacity to pierce the shell and to be born into the light of day.

It is not that one becomes more and more perceptible or visible:

one is shut in — shut in — and for sensitive people there is even that terrible sensation of being compressed, of trying to pass through and then coming up against a wall. And then one knocks and knocks and knocks, and one can't go through.

And so long as one is there, inside, one is in the falsehood. And only on the day when by the Divine Grace one can break the shell and come out into the Light, is one free.

This may happen suddenly, spontaneously, quite unexpectedly.

I don't think one can go through gradually. I don't think it is something which slowly wears and wears away until one can see through it. I haven't had an instance of this so far. There is rather a kind of accumulation of power inside, an intensification of the need, and an endurance in the effort which becomes free from all fear, all anxiety, all calculation; a need so imperative that one no longer cares for the consequences.

One is like an explosive that nothing can resist, and one bursts out from one's prison in a blaze of light.

After that one can no longer fall back again.

It is truly a new birth.

26 June 1957

*

Many people who are here forget one thing. They want to begin at the end. They think that they are ready to express in their life what they call the supramental Force or Consciousness, and they want to infuse this in their actions, their movements, their daily life. But the trouble is that they don't at all know what the supramental Force or Consciousness is and that first of all it is necessary to take the reverse path, the way of interiorisation and of withdrawal from life, in order to find within oneself this Truth which has to be expressed.

For as long as one has not found it, there is nothing to express. And by imagining that one is living an exceptional life, one lives only in the illusion of one's exceptional state. Therefore, at first not only must one find one's soul and the Divine who possesses it, but one must identify oneself with it. And then later, one may begin to come back to outward activities, and then transform them; because then one knows in what direction to turn them, into what to transform them.

One can't jump over this stage. One must first find one's soul, this is absolutely indispensable, and identify oneself with it. Later one can come to the transformation. Sri Aurobindo has written somewhere: "Our Yoga begins where the others end." Usually yoga leads precisely to this identification, this union with the Divine — that is why it is called "yoga". And when people reach this, well, they are at the end of their path and are satisfied. But Sri Aurobindo has written: we begin when they finish; you have found the Divine but instead of sitting down in contemplation and waiting for the Divine to take you out of your body which has become useless, on the contrary, with this consciousness you turn to the body and to life and begin the work of transformation — which is very hard labour. It's here that he compares it with cutting one's way through a virgin forest; because as nobody has done it before, one must make one's path where there was none. But to try to do this without having the indispensable directive of the union with the Divine within, within one's soul, is childishness. There.

I am speaking of yoga. I am not speaking of your life, of you all, you children here. That's different. You are here to develop yourselves. And when you are developed and have a precise thought of your own, a vision of your own, when you have enough knowledge to be able to choose freely what life you want to lead, then at that time you will take a decision.

But those who have already taken the decision, well for them it is first of all indispensable to find their soul and unite with their psychic being, and with the Divine who is within it. This is an absolutely indispensable beginning. One can't leap over that bridge, it is not possible. It can be done very quickly if you know how to use the help that's given to you; but it has to be done.

2 November 1955

*

Why does the divine force upset people?

Because it is too strong for them. It is as though you were in the midst of a big cyclone. It happens at times that the wind is so violent that you are not able to stand — you have to lie down and wait till it blows over. Now, the divine forces are a thousand times stronger than a cyclonic wind. If you do not have in you a very wide receptivity, an extremely solid basis of calmness, of equality of soul and inner peace, they come and carry you away like a gale and you cannot resist them. It is the same thing with light; some people get a pain in the eyes when they look at the sun and are obliged to put on dark glasses because sunlight is too strong for them. But this is merely sunlight. When you are able to look at the supramental light, it appears to you so brilliant that sunlight seems like a black stain in comparison. One must have strong eyes and a solid brain to bear that, one must be well prepared, established in something extremely calm and vast — it is as though one had such a strong basis of tranquillity that when the storm passes, when the light comes with a great intensity, one is able to remain immobile and receive what one can without being knocked over. But there is not one being in a million who can do it. Only those who have had a foretaste of inner experience can know what this means. But even if you enter consciously into the psychic, it is dazzling; and it is within your reach because it is your own psychic being, and yet it is so different from your external consciousness that the first time you enter it consciously, it seems to you truly dazzling, something infinitely more brilliant than the most brilliant sunlight.

The psychic is what may be called "the Divine within the reach of man".

12 February 1951

A Reversal of Consciousness

There is one phenomenon which obviously seems indispensable if one wants the realisation to become stable.... Experiences come, touch the consciousness, sometimes bring great illuminations, then get blurred, retreat into the background and, outwardly, in your ordinary consciousness, you don't feel that there is a great change, a great difference. And this phenomenon may occur very often, may repeat itself for many years. Suddenly you get a sort of revelation, like an illumination, you are in the true consciousness and have the feeling of having got hold of the real thing. And then, slowly or suddenly, it seems to recede behind you, and you seek but do not find that there is any great change in you.... These things seem to come as heralds or as promises: "See, it will happen", or to tell you, "Well, have faith, it *will be* like that."

And this may recur very often. There is progress, obviously, but it is very slow and hardly apparent.

But then, suddenly — perhaps because one is sufficiently prepared, perhaps simply because the time has come, and it has been so decreed — suddenly, when such an experience occurs, its result in the part of the being where it takes place is a complete reversal of consciousness. It is a very clear, very concrete phenomenon. The best way of describing it is this: a complete reversal. And then the relation of the consciousness with the other parts of the being and with the outer world is as if completely changed. Absolutely like an overturning. And that reversal no longer comes back to the same old place, the consciousness no longer returns to its former position — Sri Aurobindo would say "status". Once this has happened in any part of the being, this part of the being is stabilised.

And until that happens, it comes and goes, comes and goes, one advances and then has the impression of marking time, and one advances again and then marks time again, and sometimes one feels as though one were going backwards, and it is interminable — and indeed it is interminable. It may last for years and years and years. But when this reversal of consciousness takes place, whether in the mind or a part of the mind, whether in the vital or a part of the vital, or even in the physical consciousness itself and in the body-consciousness, once this is established, it is over; you no longer go back, you do not ever return to what you were before. And this is the true indication that you have taken a step forward definitively. And before this, there are only preparations.

Those who have experienced this reversal know what I am speaking about; but if one hasn't, one can't understand. One may have a kind of idea by analogy, people who have tried to describe yoga compare it with the reversal of a prism: when you put it at a certain angle, the light is white; when you turn it over, it is broken up. Well, this is exactly what happens, that is to say, you restore the white. In the

ordinary consciousness there is decomposition and you restore the
white. However, this is only an image. It is not really *that*, this is an
analogy. But the phenomenon is extremely concrete. It is almost as
though you were to put what is inside out, and what is outside in. And
it isn't that either! But if you could turn a ball inside-out, or a balloon
— you can't, can you? — if you could put the inside out and the
outside in, it would be something like what I mean.

And one can't say that one "experiences" this reversal — there is
no "feeling", it is almost a mechanical fact — it is extraordinarily
mechanical. (*Mother takes an object from the table beside her and
turns it upside down.*) There would be some very interesting things to
say about the difference between the moment of realisation, of *siddhi*
— like this reversal of consciousness for example — and all the work
of development, the *tapasya*; to say how it comes about.... For the
sadhana, *tapasya* is one thing and the *siddhi* another, quite a different
thing. You may do *tapasya* for centuries, and you will always go as at
a tangent — closer and closer to the realisation, nearer and nearer, but
it is only when the *siddhi* is given to you... then, everything is changed,
everything is reversed. And this is inexpressible, for as soon as it is
put in words it escapes. But there is a difference — a real difference,
essential, total — between aspiration, the mental tension, even the
tension of the highest, most luminous mind, and realisation: something which has been decided above from all time, and is absolutely
independent of all personal effort, of all gradation. Don't you see, it
is not bit by bit that one reaches it, it is not by a small, constant,
regular effort, it is not that: it is something that comes suddenly; it is
established without one's knowing how or why, but all is changed.

And it will be like that for everybody, for the whole universe: it
goes on and on, it moves forward very slowly, and then one moment,
all of a sudden, *it will be done*, finished — not finished: it's the beginning!

(*Silence*)

It is usually the first contact with the psychic being which brings
this experience, but it is only partial, only that *part* of the consciousness — or of the activity in any part of the being — that part of the

consciousness which is united with the psychic has the experience. And so, at the moment of that experience, the position of that part of the consciousness, in relation to the other parts and to the world, is completely reversed, it is different. And that is never undone. And if you have the will or take care or are able to put into contact with this part all the problems of your life and all the activities of your being, all the elements of your consciousness, then they begin to be organised in such a way that your being becomes one unity — a single multiplicity, a multiple unity — complex, but organised and centralised around a fixed point, so well that the central will or central consciousness or central truth has the power to govern *all* the parts, for they are all in order, organised around this central Presence.

It seems to me impossible to escape from this necessity if one wants to be and is to be a conscious instrument of the divine Force. You may be moved, pushed into action and used *as unconscious* instruments by the divine Force, if you have a minimum of goodwill and sincerity. But to become a conscious instrument, capable of identification and conscious, willed movements, you must have this inner organisation; otherwise you will always be running into a chaos somewhere, a confusion somewhere or an obscurity, an unconsciousness somewhere. And naturally your action, even though guided exclusively by the Divine, will not have the perfection of expression it has when one has acquired a conscious organisation around this divine Centre.

It is an assiduous task, which may be done at any time and under any circumstances, for you carry within yourself all the elements of the problem. You don't need anything from outside, no outer aid to do this work. But it requires great perseverance, a sort of tenacity, for very often it happens that there are bad "creases" in the being, habits — which come from all sorts of causes, which may come from atavistic malformation or also from education or from the environment you have lived in or from many other causes. And these bad creases you try to smooth out, but they wrinkle up again. And then you must begin the work over again, often, many, many, many a time, without getting discouraged, before the final result is obtained. But nothing and nobody can prevent you from doing it, nor any circumstance. For you carry within yourself the problem and the solution.

(Silence)

[...] And what adds to the interest of the thing is that this kind of work, this harmonisation and organisation of the being around the divine Centre can only be done in a physical body and on earth. That is truly the essential and original reason for physical life. For, as soon as you are no longer in a physical body, you can no longer do it *at all*.

And what is still more remarkable is that only human beings can do it, for only human beings have at their centre the divine Presence in the psychic being. For example, this work of self-development and organisation and becoming aware of all the elements is not within the reach of the beings of the vital and mental planes, nor even of the beings who are usually called "gods"; and when they want to do it, when they really want to organise themselves and become completely conscious, they have to take a body.

And yet, human beings come into a physical body without knowing why, most of them go through life without knowing why, they leave their body without knowing why, and they have to begin the same thing all over again, indefinitely, until one day, someone comes along and tells them, "Be careful! you know, there is a purpose to this. You are here for this work, don't miss your opportunity!"

And how many years are wasted.

6 June 1956

*

In fact, so long as there is any doubt or hesitation, so long as one asks oneself the question of whether one has or hasn't realised this eternal soul in oneself, it proves that the *true* contact has not taken place. For, when the phenomenon occurs, it brings with it an inexpressible something, so new and so definitive, that doubt and questioning are no longer possible. It is truly, in the absolute sense of the phrase, a new birth.

You become a new person, and whatever may be the path or the difficulties of the path afterwards, that feeling never leaves you. It is not even something — like many other experiences — which withdraws, passes into the background, leaving you externally with a kind of vague memory to which it is difficult to cling, whose remembrance grows faint, blurred — it is not that. You *are* a new person and definitively that, whatever happens. And even all the incapacity of the mind, all the difficulties of the vital, all the inertia of the physical are unable to change this new state — a new state which makes a *decisive* break in the life of the consciousness. The being one was before and the being one is after, are no longer the same. The position one has in the universe and in relation to it, in life and in relation to it, in understanding and in relation to it, is no longer the same: it is a true reversal which can never be undone again. That is why when people tell me, "I would like to know whether I am in contact with my soul or not", I say, "If you ask the question, that is enough to prove that you are not. You don't need an answer, you are giving it to yourself." When it is *that*, it is that, and then it is finished, it is no longer anything else.

And since we are speaking of that, I shall remind you of what Sri Aurobindo has said, repeated, written, affirmed and said over and over again, that his yoga, the integral yoga, can begin *only after* that experience, not before.

So, one must not cherish any illusions and fancy that one can begin to know what the supermind is and form any idea of it or assess it in any way, however minimal, before having had *that* experience.

Therefore, if you want to advance on the path, you must very modestly start on your way towards the new birth, first, and realise it before cherishing the illusion that you can have supramental experiences.

To console you I may tell you that by the very fact that you live on earth at this time — whether you are conscious of it or not, even whether you want it or not — you are absorbing with the air you breathe this new supramental substance which is now spreading in the earth atmosphere. And it is preparing things in you which will manifest *very suddenly*, as soon as you have taken the decisive step.

(Silence)

Whether this will help you to take the decisive step or not is another question which remains to be studied, for the experiences which are occurring and will occur more and more frequently now, being of a radically new kind, we can't know beforehand what is going to happen; we must study, and after a thorough study we shall be able to say with certainty whether this supramental substance makes the work of new birth easier or not.... I shall tell you this a little later. For the moment it is better not to rely on these things and, very simply, to start on your way to be born into the spiritual life.

When this happens to you, almost all the questions you ask yourself or ask me will be solved.

And anyway, your attitude to life will be *so* different that you will understand what is meant when one speaks of living spiritually. And at that moment you will also understand a *great* thing, a very great thing: how to live without ego.

Until then, you cannot understand it. The whole of life is so dependent on the ego that it seems absolutely impossible to live and act except with or by the ego, but after this new birth you can look at the ego with a smile and say to it, "My friend, I don't need you any more."

This is also one of the results which brings you a very decisive sense of liberation.

4 June 1958

Aspiration

Do prayers and aspirations also take a form like thoughts?

Yes. At times they take even the form of the person who has the aspiration or makes the prayer — often. That depends. Aspirations sometimes take the form of that to which one aspires, but most often, and specially prayers, clearly take the form of the one who prays.

What is the difference between prayer and aspiration?

I have written this somewhere. There are several kinds of prayers.

There is the purely mechanical, material prayer, with words which have been learnt and are mechanically repeated. That does not signify anything much. And that has usually only one single result, that of quietening the person who prays, for if a prayer is repeated several times, the words end up by making you calm.

There is a prayer which is a spontaneous formula for expressing something precise which one wants to ask for: one prays for this thing or that, one prays for one thing or another; one can pray for somebody, for a circumstance, for oneself.

There is a point where aspiration and prayer meet, for there are prayers which are the spontaneous formulation of a lived experience: these spring up all ready from within the being, like something that's the expression of a profound experience, and which offers thanksgiving for that experience or asks its continuation or asks for its explanation also; and that indeed is quite close to aspiration. But aspiration is not necessarily formulated in words; or if it is formulated in words, it is almost a movement of invocation. You aspire for a certain state; for instance, you have found something in yourself that is not in keeping with your ideal, a movement of darkness and ignorance, perhaps even of ill-will, something that's not in harmony with what you want to realise; then that is not going to be formulated in words; that will be like a springing flame and like an offering made of a living experience, asking to grow larger, be magnified and ever more and more clear and precise. All that may be put into words *later*, if one tries to remember and note down one's experience. But aspiration always springs up like a flame that rises high and carries in itself the thing one desires to be or what one desires to do or desires to have. I use the word "desire", but truly it is here that the word "aspire" should be used, for that does not have either the quality or the form of a desire.

It is truly like a great purifying flame of will, and it carries in its core the thing that asks to be realised.

For instance, if you have done something you regret having done, if that has unhappy consequences which disturb things, and several people are implicated, you do not know the reactions of the others, but you yourself wish that what has been done may take a turn for the best, and that if there is a mistake, it may be understood, and that no matter what the mistake, this may be for you an opportunity for a greater progress, a greater discipline, a new ascent towards the Divine, a door open on a future that you want to be more clear and true and intense; so all this is gathered here (*pointing to the heart*) like a force, and then it surges up and rises in a great movement of ascent, and at times without the shadow of a formulation, without words, without expression, but like a springing flame.

That indeed is true aspiration. That may happen a hundred, a thousand times daily if one is in that state in which one constantly wants to progress and be more true and more fully in harmony with what the Divine Will wants of us.

Prayer is a much more external thing, generally about a precise fact, and always formulated for it is the formula that makes the prayer. One may have an aspiration and transcribe it as a prayer, but aspiration goes beyond prayer in every way. It is much closer and much more as it were self-forgetful, living only in the thing one wants to be or do, and the offering of all that one wants to do to the Divine. You may pray in order to ask for something, you may also pray to thank the Divine for what He has given you, and that prayer is much greater: it may be called an act of thanksgiving. You may pray in gratitude for the aspect of kindness the Divine has shown to you, for what He has done for you, for what you see in Him, and the praise you want to offer Him. And all this may take the form of a prayer. It is decidedly the highest prayer, for it is not exclusively preoccupied with oneself, it is not an egoistic prayer.

Certainly, one may have an aspiration in all the domains, but the very centre of aspiration is in the psychic being, whilst one may pray in all the domains, and the prayer belongs to the domain in which one prays. One may make purely material, physical prayers, vital prayers, mental prayers, psychic prayers, spiritual prayers, and each one has its special character, its special value.

There is a kind of prayer at once spontaneous and unselfish which is like a great call, usually not for one's own self personally, but like something that may be called an intercession with the Divine. It is extremely powerful. I have had countless instances of things which have been realised almost instantaneously due to prayers of this kind. It implies a great faith, a great ardour, a great sincerity, and a great simplicity of heart also, something that does not calculate, does not plan, does not bargain, does not give with the idea of receiving in exchange. For, the majority of men give with one hand and hold out the other to get something in exchange; the largest number of prayers are of that sort. But there are others of the kind I have described, acts of thanksgiving, a kind of canticle, and these are very good.

There you are. I don't know if I have made myself clear, but this is how it is.

To be clearer, we may say that prayer is always formulated in words; but the words may have different values according to the state in which they are formulated. Prayer is a formulated thing and one may aspire. But it is difficult to pray without praying to someone. For instance, those who have a conception of the universe from which they have more or less driven out the idea of the Divine (there are many people of this kind; this idea troubles them — the idea that there is someone who knows all, can do everything and who is so formidably greater than they that there can be no comparison; that's a bit troublesome for their *amour-propre*; so they try to make a world without the Divine), these people evidently cannot pray, for to whom would they pray? Unless they pray to themselves, which is not the custom! But one can aspire for something without having any faith in the Divine. There are people who do not believe in the existence of a God, but who have faith in progress. They have the idea that the world is in constant progress and that this progress will go on indefinitely without stopping, towards an ever greater betterment. Well, these people can have a very great aspiration for progress, and they don't even need any idea of a divine existence for that. Aspiration necessarily implies a faith but not necessarily faith in a divine being; whilst prayer cannot exist if it is not addressed to a divine being. And pray to what? One does not pray to something that has no personality! One prays to someone who can hear us. If there is nobody to hear us, how could one pray? Hence, if one prays, this means that, even when one doesn't acknowledge it, one has faith in somebody infinitely higher than us, infinitely more powerful, who can change our destiny and change us also, if one prays so as to be heard. That is the essential difference.

So the more intellectual people admit aspiration and say that prayer is something inferior. The mystics tell you that aspiration is all very well but if you want to be really heard and want the Divine to listen to you, you must pray, and pray with the simplicity of a child, a perfect candour, that is, a perfect trust: "I need this or that (whether it be a moral need or a physical or material need), well, I ask You for it, give it to me." Or else: "You have given me what I asked of You, You have made me realise concretely those experiences which were un-

known to me and are now marvels I can attain at will; yes, I am infinitely grateful to You and I offer a prayer of thanksgiving to sing Your
praise and thank You for Your intervention." It is like that. To aspire it
is not necessary to direct the aspiration to someone, towards someone. One has an aspiration for a certain state of being, for knowledge,
for a realisation, a state of consciousness; one aspires for something,
but it is not necessarily a prayer; prayer is something additional.

Prayer is a personal thing, addressed to a personal being, that is,
to something — a force or a being — who can hear you and answer
you. Otherwise you can't ask for anything.

8 July 1953

*

If you are in a state of conscious aspiration and very sincere, well,
everything around you will be arranged in order to help in your aspiration, whether directly or indirectly, that is, either to make you
progress, put you in touch with something new or to eliminate from
your nature something that has to disappear. This is something quite
remarkable. If you are truly in a state of intensity of aspiration, there
is not a circumstance which does not come to help you to realise this
aspiration. Everything comes, everything, as though there were a perfect and absolute consciousness organising around you all things, and
you yourself in your outer ignorance may not recognise it and may
protest at first against the circumstances as they show themselves,
may complain, may try to change them; but after a while, when you
have become wiser, and there is a certain distance between you and
the event, well, you will realise that it was just what you needed to do
to make the necessary progress. And, you know, it is a will, a supreme
goodwill which arranges all things around you, and even when you
complain and protest instead of accepting, it is exactly at such moments that it acts most effectively.

16 June 1954

*

What are the conditions in which there is a descent of faith?

The most important condition is an almost childlike trust, the candid trust of a child who is sure that it will come, who doesn't even ask himself about it; when he needs something he is sure that it is going to come. Well, it is this, this kind of trust — this indeed is the most important condition.

To aspire is indispensable. But some people aspire with such a conflict inside them between faith and absence of faith, trust and distrust, between the optimism which is sure of victory and a pessimism which asks itself when the catastrophe will come. Now if this is in the being, you may aspire but you don't get anything. And you say, "I aspired but didn't get anything." It is because you demolish your aspiration all the time by your lack of confidence. But if you truly have trust... Children when left to themselves and not deformed by older people have such a great trust that all will be well! For example, when they have a small accident, they never think that this is going to be something serious: they are spontaneously convinced that it will soon be over, and this helps so powerfully in putting an end to it.

Well, when one aspires for the Force, when one asks the Divine for help, if one asks with the unshakable certitude that it will come, that it is impossible that it won't, then it is sure to come. It is this kind... yes, this is truly an inner opening, this trustfulness. And some people are constantly in this state. When there is something to be received, they are always there to receive it. There are others, when there is something to have, a force descends, they are always absent, they are always closed at that moment; while those who have this childlike trust are always there at the right time.

And it is strange, isn't it, outwardly there is no difference. They may have exactly the same goodwill, the same aspiration, the same wish to do good, but those who have this smiling confidence within them, do not question, do not ask themselves whether they will have it or not have it, whether the Divine will answer or not — the question does not arise, it is something understood... "What I need will be given to me; if I pray I shall have an answer; if I am in a difficulty and ask for help, the help will come — and not only will it come but it will manage everything." If the trust is there, spontaneous, candid, unquestioning, it works better than anything else, and the results are marvellous. It is with the contradictions and doubts of the mind that one spoils everything, with this kind of notion which comes when one is in difficulties: "Oh, it is impossible! I shall never manage it. And if it is going to be aggravated, if this condition I am in, which I don't want, is going to grow still worse, if I continue to slide down farther and farther, if, if, if, if..." like that, and one builds a wall between oneself and the force one wants to receive. The psychic being has this trust, has it wonderfully, without a shadow, without an argument, without a contradiction. And when it is like that, there is not a prayer which does not get an answer, no aspiration which is not realised.

17 November 1954

*

I remember that once we spoke of courage as one of the perfections; I remember having written it down once in a list. But this courage means having a taste for the supreme adventure. And this taste for supreme adventure is aspiration — an aspiration which takes hold of you completely and flings you, without calculation and without reserve and without a possibility of withdrawal, into the great adventure of the divine discovery, the great adventure of the divine meeting, the yet greater adventure of the divine Realisation; you throw yourself into the adventure without looking back and without asking for a single minute, "What's going to happen?" For if you ask what is going to happen, you never start, you always remain stuck there, rooted to the spot, afraid to lose something, to lose your balance.

That's why I speak of courage — but really it is aspiration. They go together. A real aspiration is something full of courage.

And now, surrender. In English the word is "surrender", there is no French word which gives exactly that sense. But Sri Aurobindo has said [...] that surrender is the first and absolute condition for doing the yoga. So, if we follow what he has said, this is not just one of the necessary qualities: it is the first attitude indispensable for beginning the yoga. If one has not decided to make a total surrender, one cannot begin. But for this surrender to be total, all these qualities are necessary.[...]

So here's my proposal: we put surrender first, at the top of the list; that is, we accept what Sri Aurobindo has said — that to do the integral yoga one must resolve to surrender entirely; there is no other way, this is *the* way. But after that one must have the five psychological virtues, five psychological perfections, and we say that these perfections are:

Sincerity or Transparency
Faith or Trust (Trust in the Divine, naturally)
Devotion or Gratitude
Courage or Aspiration
Endurance or Perseverance.

25 January 1956

*

Aspiration is like an arrow, like this (*gesture*). So you aspire, want *very* earnestly to understand, know, enter into the truth. Yes? And then with that aspiration you do this (*gesture*). Your aspiration rises, rises, rises, rises straight up, very strong and then it strikes against a kind of... how to put it?... lid which is there,* hard like iron and extremely thick, and it does not pass through. And then you say, "See, what's the use of aspiring? It brings nothing at all. I meet with something hard and cannot pass!" But you know about the drop of water which falls on the rock, it ends up by making a chasm: it cuts the rock from top to bottom. Your aspiration is a drop of water which, instead of falling, rises. So, by dint of rising, it beats, beats, beats, and one day it makes a hole, by dint of rising; and when it makes the hole suddenly it springs out from this lid and enters an immensity of light, and you say, "Ah, now I understand."
It's like that.

So one must be very persistent, very stubborn and have an aspiration which rises straight upwards, that is, which does not go roaming around here and there, seeking all kinds of things.

Only this: to understand, understand, understand, to learn to know, to be.

When one reaches the very top, there is nothing more to understand, nothing more to learn, one *is*, and it's when one *is* that one understands and knows.

13 July 1955

---

* A "lid" in the subtle body separating the ordinary mental consciousness from the higher levels of consciousness.

Surrender

Is not surrender the same as sacrifice?

In our Yoga there is no room for sacrifice. But everything depends on the meaning you put on the word. In its pure sense it means a consecrated giving, a making sacred to the Divine.* But in the significance that it now bears, sacrifice is something that works for destruction; it carries about it an atmosphere of negation. This kind of sacrifice is not fulfilment; it is a deprivation, a self-immolation. It is your possibilities that you sacrifice, the possibilities and realisations of your personality from the most material to the highest spiritual range. Sacrifice diminishes your being. If physically you sacrifice your life, your body, you give up all your possibilities on the material plane; you have done with the achievements of your earthly existence.

In the same way you can morally sacrifice your life; you give up the amplitude and free fulfilment of your inner existence. There is always in this idea of self-immolation a sense of forcing, a constriction, an imposed self-denial. This is an ideal that does not give room for the soul's deeper and larger spontaneities. By surrender we mean not this but a spontaneous self-giving, a giving of all your self to the Divine, to a greater Consciousness of which you are a part. Surrender will not diminish, but increase; it will not lessen or weaken or destroy your personality, it will fortify and aggrandise it. Surrender means a free total giving with all the delight of the giving; there is no sense of sacrifice in it. If you have the slightest feeling that you are making a sacrifice, then it is no longer surrender. For it means that you reserve yourself or that you are trying to give, with grudging or with pain and effort, and have not the joy of the gift, perhaps not even the feeling that you are giving. When you do anything with the sense of a compression of your being, be sure that you are doing it in the wrong way. True surrender enlarges you; it increases your capacity; it gives you a greater measure in quality and in quantity which you could not have had by yourself. This new greater measure of quality and quantity is different from anything you could attain before: you enter into an-

---

* The word *sacrifice* is derived from the Latin *sacrum facere,* to make sacred.

other world, into a wideness which you could not have entered if you did not surrender. It is as when a drop of water falls into the sea; if it still kept there its separate identity, it would remain a little drop of water and nothing more, a little drop crushed by all the immensity around, because it has not surrendered. But, surrendering, it unites with the sea and participates in the nature and power and vastness of the whole sea.

There is no ambiguity or vagueness in the movement, it is clear and strong and definite. If a small human mind stands in front of the Divine Universal Mind and clings to its separateness, it will remain what it is, a small bounded thing, incapable of knowing the nature of the higher reality or even of coming in contact with it. The two continue to stand apart and are, qualitatively as well as quantitatively, quite different from each other. But if the little human mind surrenders, it will be merged in the Divine Universal Mind; it will be one in quality and quantity with it; losing nothing but its own limitations and deformations, it will receive from it its vastness and luminous clearness. The small existence will change its nature; it will put on the nature of the greater truth to which it surrenders. But if it resists and fights, if it revolts against the Universal Mind, then a conflict and pressure are inevitable in which what is weak and small cannot fail to be drawn into that power and immensity. If it does not surrender, its only other possible fate is absorption and extinction. A human being, who comes into contact with the Divine Mind and surrenders, will find that his own mind begins at once to be purified of its obscurities and to share in the power and the knowledge of the Divine Universal Mind. If he stands in front, but separated, without any contact, he will remain what he is, a little drop of water in the measureless vastness. If he revolts, he will lose his mind; its powers will diminish and disappear. And what is true of the mind is true of all the other parts of the nature. It is as when you fight against one who is too strong for you — a broken head is all you gain. How can you fight something that is a million times stronger? Each time you revolt, you get a knock, and each blow takes away a portion of your strength, as when one who engages in a pugilistic encounter with a far superior rival receives blow after blow and each blow makes him weaker and weaker till he is knocked out. There is no necessity of a willed intervention, the action is automatic. Nothing else can happen if you dash yourself in revolt against the Immensity. As long as you remain in your corner and follow the course of the ordinary life, you are not touched or hurt; but once you come in contact with the Divine, there are only two ways open to you. You surrender and merge in it, and your surrender enlarges and glorifies you; or you revolt and all your possibilities are destroyed and your powers ebb away and are drawn from you into That which you oppose.

There are many wrong ideas current about surrender. Most people seem to look upon surrender as an abdication of the personality; but that is a grievous error. For the individual is meant to manifest one aspect of the Divine Consciousness, and the expression of its characteristic nature is what creates his personality; then, by taking the right attitude towards the Divine, this personality is purified of all the influences of the lower nature which diminish and distort it and it becomes more strongly personal, more itself, more complete. The truth and power of the personality come out with a more resplendent distinctness, its character is more precisely marked than it could possibly be when mixed with all the obscurity and ignorance, all the dirt and alloy of the lower nature. It undergoes a heightening and glorification, an aggrandisement of capacity, a realisation of the maximum of its possibilities.

4 August 1929

*

Surrender is the decision taken to hand over the responsibility of your life to the Divine. Without this decision nothing is at all possible; if you do not surrender, the Yoga is entirely out of the question. Everything else comes naturally after it, for the whole process starts with surrender. You can surrender either through knowledge or through devotion. You may have a strong intuition that the Divine alone is the truth and a luminous conviction that without the Divine you cannot manage. Or you may have a spontaneous feeling that this line is the only way of being happy, a strong psychic desire to belong exclusively to the Divine: "I do not belong to myself," you say, and give up the responsibility of your being to the Truth. Then comes self-offering: "Here I am, a creature of various qualities, good and bad, dark and enlightened. I offer myself as I am to you, take me up with all my ups and downs, conflicting impulses and tendencies — do whatever you like with me." In the course of your self-offering, you start unifying your being around what has taken the first decision — the central psychic will. All the jarring elements of your nature have to be harmonised, they have to be taken up one after another and unified with the central being. You may offer yourself to the Divine with a spontaneous movement, but it is not possible to give yourself effectively without this unification. The more you are unified, the more you are able to realise self-giving. And once the self-giving is complete, consecration follows: it is the crown of the whole process of realisation, the last step of the gradation, after which there is no more trouble and everything runs smoothly. But you must not forget that you cannot become integrally consecrated at once. You are often deluded into such a belief when, for a day or two, you have a strong movement of a particular kind. You are led to hope that everything else will automatically follow in its wake; but in fact if you become the least bit self-complacent you retard your own advance. For your being is full of innumerable tendencies at war with one another — almost different personalities, we may say. When one of them gives itself to the Divine, the others come up and refuse their allegiance. "We have not given ourselves," they cry, and start clamouring for their independence and expression. Then you bid them be quiet and show them the Truth. Patiently you have to go round your whole being, exploring each nook and corner, facing all those anarchic elements in you which are waiting for their psychological moment to come up. And it is only when you have made the entire round of your mental, vital and physical nature, persuaded everything to give itself to the Divine and thus achieved an absolute unified consecration that you put an end to your difficulties. Then indeed yours is a glorious walk towards transformation, for you no longer go from darkness to knowledge but from knowledge to knowledge, light to light, happiness to happiness.... The complete consecration is undoubtedly not an easy matter, and it might take an almost indefinitely long time if you had to do it all by yourself, by your own independent effort. But when the Divine's Grace is with you it is not exactly like that. With a little push from the Divine

now and then, a little push in this direction and in that, the work becomes comparatively quite easy. Of course the length of time depends
on each individual, but it can be very much shortened if you make a
really firm resolve. Resolution is the one thing required — resolution
is the master-key.

                                                              1930-1931

                                    *

The most important surrender is the surrender of your character, your
way of being, so that it may change. If you do not surrender your very
own nature, never will this nature change. It is this that is most important. You have certain ways of understanding, certain ways of reacting,
certain ways of feeling, almost certain ways of progressing, and above
all, a special way of looking at life and expecting from it certain things
— well, it is this you must surrender. That is, if you truly want to receive the divine Light and transform yourself, it is your whole way of
being you must offer — offer by opening it, making it as receptive as
possible so that the divine Consciousness which sees how you ought to
be, may act directly and change all these movements into movements
more true, more in keeping with your real truth. This is infinitely more
important than surrendering what one does. It is not what one does
(what one does is very important, that's evident) that is the most important thing but what one *is*. Whatever the activity, it is not quite the way
of doing it but the state of consciousness in which it is done that is
important. You may work, do disinterested work without any idea of
personal profit, work for the joy of working, but if you are not at the
same time ready to leave this work, to change the work or change the
way of working, if you cling to your own way of working, your surrender is not complete. You must come to a point when everything is done
because you feel within, very clearly, in a more and more imperious
way, that it is this which must be done and in this particular way, and
that you do it only because of that. You do not do it because of any
habit, attachment or preference, nor even any conception, even a preference for the idea that it is the best thing to do — else your surrender is
not total. As long as you cling to something, as long as there is something in you which says, "This may change, that may change, but *that*,

that will not change", as long as you say about anything at all, "That will not change" (not that it refuses to change, but because you can't think of its changing), your surrender is not complete.

28 April 1951

Sincerity

"What is the fundamental virtue to be cultivated in order to prepare for the spiritual life?"

I have said this many times, but this is an opportunity to repeat it: it is, *sincerity.*

A sincerity which must become total and absolute, for sincerity *alone* is your protection on the spiritual path. If you are not sincere, at the very next step you are sure to fall and break your head. All kinds of forces, wills, influences, entities are there, on the look-out for the least little rift in this sincerity and they immediately rush in through that rift and begin to throw you into confusion.

Therefore, before doing anything, beginning anything, trying anything, be sure *first of all* that you are not only as sincere as you can be, but have the intention of becoming still more so.

For that is your only protection.

1 August 1956

*

Fundamentally, whatever be the path one follows — whether the path of surrender, consecration, knowledge — if one wants it to be perfect, it is always equally difficult, and there is but one way, one only, I know of only one: that is perfect sincerity, but *perfect* sincerity!

Do you know what perfect sincerity is?...

Never to try to deceive oneself, never let any part of the being try to find out a way of convincing the others, never to explain favourably what one does in order to have an excuse for what one wants to do, never to close one's eyes when something is unpleasant, never to let anything pass, telling oneself, "That is not important, next time it will be better."

Oh! it is very difficult. Just try for one hour and you will see how very difficult it is. Only one hour, to be *totally, absolutely* sincere. To let nothing pass. That is, all one does, all one feels, all one thinks, all one wants, is *exclusively* the Divine.

"I want nothing but the Divine, I think of nothing but the Divine, I do nothing but what will lead me to the Divine, I love nothing but the Divine."

Try — try, just to see, try for half an hour, you will see how difficult it is! And during that time take great care that there isn't a part of the vital or a part of the mind or a part of the physical being nicely hidden there, at the back, so that you don't see it (*Mother hides her hands behind her back*) and don't notice that it is not collaborating — sitting quietly there so that you don't unearth it... it says nothing, but it does not change, it hides itself. How many such parts! How many parts hide themselves! You put them in your pocket because you don't want to see them or else they get behind your back and sit there well-hidden, right in the middle of your back, so as not to be seen. When you go there with your torch — your torch of sincerity — you ferret out all the corners, everywhere, all the small corners which do not consent, the things which say "No" or those which do not move: "I am not going to budge. I am glued to this place of mine and nothing will make me move."... You have a torch there with you, and you flash it upon the thing, upon everything. You will see there are many of them there, behind your back, well stuck.

Try, just for an hour, try!

12 May 1954

*

"The question is to be sincere. If you are not sincere, do not begin Yoga." (The Mother)

Sincerity is perhaps the most difficult of all things and perhaps it is also the most effective.

If you have perfect sincerity, you are sure of victory. It is infinitely difficult. Sincerity consists in making all the elements of the being, all the movements (whether outer or inner), all the parts of the being, all of them, have one single will to belong to the Divine, to live only for the Divine, to will only what the Divine wills, to express only the divine Will, to have no other source of energy than that of the Divine.

And you find that there is not a day, not an hour, not a minute when you do not need to intensify, rectify your sincerity — a total refusal to deceive the Divine. The first thing is not to deceive oneself. One knows one cannot deceive the Divine; even the cleverest of the Asuras cannot deceive the Divine. But even when one has understood that, one sees that quite often in one's life, in the course of the day, one tries to deceive oneself without even knowing it, spontaneously and almost automatically. One always gives favourable explanations for all that one does, for one's words, for one's acts. That is what happens first. I am not speaking of obvious things like quarrelling and saying, "It is the other one's fault", I am speaking of the very tiny things of daily life.[...]

I tell you: If you are sincere in all the elements of your being, to the very cells of your body and if your whole being integrally wants the Divine, you are sure of victory but for nothing less than that. That is what I call being sincere.

25 March 1953

*

One must be truly sincere, truly.

One must be ready, if there is something which is clinging, clinging tightly, one must be ready to tear it away completely, without its leaving any trace behind. This is why at times one makes the same mistake and repeats it, until the suffering is sufficiently great to impose a total sincerity. One must not try that method, it is bad. It is bad because it destroys many things, it wastes much energy, spreads bad vibrations. But if one can't do otherwise, well, in the intensity of suffering one can find the will for perfect sincerity.

And there is a moment — in everyone's life there is a moment — when this need for perfect sincerity comes as a definitive choice. There is a moment in one's individual life, also a moment in the collective life when one belongs to a group, a moment when the choice *must* be made, when the purification *must* be done. Sometimes this becomes very serious, it is almost a question of life and death for the group: it *must* make a decisive progress... if it wants to survive.

26 May 1954

*

What should be done?... Be sincere.

That's it; always, always, the little worm in the fruit. One tells oneself, "Oh! I can't." It is not true; if one wanted, one could.

And there are people who tell me, "I don't have the will-power." That means you are not sincere. For sincerity is an infinitely more powerful force than all the wills in the world. It can change anything whatever in the twinkling of an eye; it takes hold of it, grips it, pulls it out — and then it's over.

But you close your eyes, you find excuses for yourself.

The problem recurs all the time.

It comes back because you don't pull it out completely. What you do is, you cut the branch, so it grows again.

It takes different forms.

Yes. Well, you have to take it out every time it comes, that's all — until it doesn't come back any more.

We have spoken about it, where was it?... Oh! it was in *Lights on Yoga*, I think. You push the thing down from one part of your consciousness into another; and you push it down again and then it goes into the subconscient, and after that, if you are not vigilant, you think it is finished, and later from there it shows its face. And next, even when you push it out from the subconscient, it goes down into the inconscient; and there too, then, you must run after it to find it.

But there comes a time when it is over.

Only, one is always in too great a hurry, one wants it to be over very quickly. When one has made an effort, "Oh! well, I made an effort, now I should get the reward for my effort."

In fact, it is because there is not that joy of progress. The joy of progress imagines that even if you have realised the goal you have put before you — take the goal we have in view: if we realise the supramental life, the supramental consciousness — well, this joy of progress says, "Oh! but this will be only a stage in the eternity of time. After this there will be something else, and then after that another and yet another, and always one will have to go further." And that is what fills you with joy. While the idea, "Ah! now I can sit down, it is finished, I have realised my goal, I am going to enjoy what I have done", Oh, how dull it is! Immediately one becomes old and stunted.

The definition of youth: we can say that youth is constant growth and perpetual progress — the growth of capacities, possibilities, of the field of action and range of consciousness, and progress in the working out of details.

Naturally, someone told me, "So one is no longer young when one stops growing?" I said, "Of course, I don't imagine that one grows perpetually! But one can grow in another way than purely physically."

That is to say, in human life there are successive periods. As you go forward, something comes to an end in one form, and it changes its form.... Naturally, at present, we come to the top of the ladder and come down again; but that's really a shame, it shouldn't be like that, it's a bad habit. But when we have finished growing up, when we have reached a height we could consider as that which expresses us best, we can transform this force for growth into a force which will perfect our body, make it stronger and stronger, more and more healthy, with an ever greater power of resistance, and we shall practise physical training in order to become a model of physical beauty. And then, at the same time, we shall slowly begin and seek the perfection of character, of consciousness, knowledge, powers, and finally of the divine Realisation in its fullness of the marvellously good and true, and of His perfect Love.

There you are. And this must be continuous. And when a certain level of consciousness has been reached, when this consciousness has been realised in the material world and you have transformed the material world in the image of this consciousness, well, you will climb yet one more rung and go to another consciousness — and you will begin again. *Voilà.*

But this is not for lazy folk. It's for people who like progress. Not for those who come and say, "Oh! I have worked hard in my life, now I want to rest, will you please give me a place in the Ashram?" I tell them, "Not here. This is not a place for rest because you have worked hard, this is a place for working even harder than before." So, formerly, I used to send them to Ramana Maharshi:* "Go there, you will enter into meditation and you will get rest." Now it is not possible, so I send them to the Himalayas; I tell them,"Go and sit before the eternal snows! That will do you good."

11 January 1956

*

Is it possible for a human being to be perfectly sincere?[...]
Is there a mental sincerity, a vital sincerity, a physical sincerity?
What is the difference between these sincerities?

Naturally, the principle of sincerity is the same everywhere, but its working is different according to the states of being. As for the first question, one could simply answer: No, not if man remains what he is. But he has the possibility of transforming himself sufficiently to become perfectly sincere.

To begin with, it must be said that sincerity is progressive, and as the being progresses and develops, as the universe unfolds in the becoming, sincerity too must go on perfecting itself endlessly. Every halt in that development necessarily changes the sincerity of yesterday into the insincerity of tomorrow.

To be perfectly sincere it is indispensable not to have any preference, any desire, any attraction, any dislike, any sympathy or antipathy, any attachment, any repulsion. One must have a total, integral vision of things, in which everything is in its place and one has the same attitude towards all things: the attitude of true vision. This programme is obviously very difficult for a human being to realise. Unless he has decided to divinise himself, it seems almost impossible that he could be free from all these contraries within him. And yet, so

* The sage Ramana Maharshi had his ashram in Tiruvannamalai, about one hundred kilometers from Pondicherry. He passed away in 1950.

long as one carries them in himself, one cannot be perfectly sincere. Automatically the mental, the vital and even the physical working is falsified. I am emphasising the physical, for even the working of the senses is warped: one does not see, hear, taste, feel things as they are in reality as long as one has a preference. So long as there are things which please you and others which don't, so long as you are attracted by certain things and repulsed by others, you cannot see things in their reality; you see them through your reaction, your preference or your repulsion. The senses are instruments which get out of order, in the same way as sensations, feelings and thoughts. Therefore, to be sure of what you see, what you feel, what you experience and think, you must have a complete detachment; and this is obviously not an easy task. But until then your perception cannot be wholly true, and so it is not sincere.

Naturally, this is the maximum. There are crass insincerities which everybody understands and which, I believe, it is not necessary to dwell upon, as for example, saying one thing and thinking another, pretending that you are doing one thing and doing another, expressing a wish which is not your real wish. I am not even speaking of the absolutely glaring lie which consists in saying something different from the fact, but even that diplomatic way of acting which consists in doing things with the idea of obtaining a certain result, in saying something and expecting it to have a certain effect; every combination of this kind which naturally makes you contradict yourself, is a kind of insincerity gross enough for everybody to easily recognise.

But there are others more subtle which are difficult to discern. For instance, so long as you have sympathies and antipathies, quite naturally and as it were spontaneously you will have a favourable perception of what is sympathetic to you and an unfavourable perception of what — or whom — you dislike. And there too the lack of sincerity will be flagrant. However, you may deceive yourself and not perceive that you are being insincere. Then in that case, you have, as it were, the collaboration of mental insincerity. For it is true that there are insincerities of slightly different types according to the state of being or the parts of the being. Only, the origin of these insincerities is always a similar movement arising from desire and the seeking of personal ends — from egoism, from the combination of all the limitations arising from egoism and all the deformations arising from desire.

In fact, as long as the ego is there, one cannot say that a being is perfectly sincere, even though he is striving to become sincere. One must pass beyond the ego, give oneself up totally to the divine Will, surrender without reserve and without calculation... then one can be perfectly sincere, but not before.

That does not mean that one should not make an effort to be more sincere than one is, saying to oneself, "All right, I shall wait for my ego to disappear in order to be sincere", because one may reverse the terms and say that if you do not try sincerely your ego will never disappear. Therefore, sincerity is the basis of all true realisation, it is the means, the path — and it is also the goal. Without it you are sure to make innumerable blunders and you have constantly to redress the harm you have done to yourself and to others.

There is, besides, a marvellous joy in being sincere. Every act of sincerity carries in itself its own reward: the feeling of purification, of soaring upwards, of the liberation one gets when one has rejected even one tiny particle of falsehood.

Sincerity is the safeguard, the protection, the guide, and finally the transforming power.

19 December 1956

*

The only thing that is truly effective is the change of consciousness; it is the inner liberation through an intimate, constant union, absolute and inevitable, with the vibration of the supramental forces. The preoccupation of every second, the will of all the elements of the being, the aspiration of the entire being, including all the cells of the body, is this union with the supramental forces, the divine forces. And there is no longer any need at all to be preoccupied with what the consequences will be. What has to be in the play of the universal forces and their manifestation will be, quite naturally, spontaneously, automatically, there is no need to be preoccupied with it. The only thing that matters is the constant, total, complete contact — constant, yes, constant — with the Force, the Light, the Truth, the Power, and that ineffable delight of the supramental consciousness.

That is sincerity. All the rest is an imitation, it is almost a part one plays for oneself.

Perfect purity is *to be*, to be ever more and more, in a self-perfecting becoming. One must never pretend that one *is*: one must *be*, spontaneously.

This is sincerity.

12 June 1957

Transformation of the Body

When one wants to change something of the material life, whether the character or the functioning of the organs or habits, one must have an unfaltering perseverance, be ready to begin again a hundred times the same thing with the same intensity with which one did it the first time and as though one had never done it before.

People who are touchy cannot do this. But if one can't do it, one can't do yoga, in any case not the integral yoga, one can't change one's body.

To change one's body one must be ready to do millions of times the same thing, because the body is a creature of habits and functions by routine, and because to destroy a routine one must persevere for years.

30 March 1955

*

And that is why the work seems... interminable. And yet this is the only way it can be done. The road to be covered between the usual state of the body, the almost total inconscience to which we are accustomed because we are "like that", and the perfect awakening of consciousness, the response of all the cells, all the organs, all the functionings... between the two there seem to be centuries of labour. However, if one has learnt to open, to aspire, give oneself up, and if one can make use of these same movements in the body, teach the cells to do the same thing, then things go much faster. But much faster does not mean fast; it is still a long and slow work. And each time that an element which has not entered the movement of transformation wakes up to enter it, one feels that everything must be started again — all that one believed had been done must be done once more. But it is not true, it is not the same thing that one does again, it is something similar in a new element which was either forgotten or else left aside because it was not ready, and which, now that it is ready, awakens and wants to take its place. There are many elements like that....

The body seems to you to be something very simple, doesn't it? It is a body, it is "my" body, and after all it has a single form — but it is not like that! There are hundreds of combined entities unaware of each other, all harmonised by something deeper which they do not know, and having a perception of unity only because they are not conscious of the multiplicity of the elements and their divergence.

In fact, this multiplicity and divergence are the cause of most disorders and even illnesses. Something is going well, you have caught the guiding thread, you are following your path, you think you are going to get a result, and then, suddenly, there! — something happens quite unexpectedly, you did not know it was there: it wakes up and insists on joining the march. But it creates a terrible disorder and you must begin everything over again.

The sadhana of all the inner beings, inner domains, has been done by many people, has been explained at length, systematised by some, the stages and paths have been traced out and you go from one stage to another, knowing that it has to be like that; but as soon as you go down into the body, it is like a virgin forest.... And everything is to be done, everything is to be worked out, everything is to be built up. So you must arm yourself with *great* patience, *great* patience, and not think that you are good for nothing because it takes so much time. You must never be despondent, never tell yourself, "Oh! this is not for me!" Everyone can do it, if he puts into it the time, the courage, the endurance and the perseverance that are demanded. But all this is needed. And above all, above all, never lose heart, be ready to begin the same thing again ten times, twenty times, a hundred times — until it is really done.

And one often feels that unless *everything is* done, unless the work is finished, well, it is as if one had done nothing.

25 June 1958

*

We speak of transformation vaguely, in this way; it gives us the impression of something that is going to happen which will see to it that all is well — I think it comes to that approximately. If we have difficulties, the difficulties will disappear; those who are ill — their illness will vanish; and again, if there are physical shortcomings, these will disappear, and so on. But it is all very hazy, it's just an impression.

There is something quite remarkable: the physical consciousness, the body-consciousness, cannot know a thing with precision, in all its details, except when it is *on the point* of being realised. And this will be a sure indication when, for instance, one can understand the process: through what sequence of movements and transformations will the total transformation come about? in what order, in what way, to put it thus. What will happen first? What will happen later? — all that, in all its details. Each time you see a detail with exactitude, it means that it is on the point of being realised.

One can have the vision of the whole. For instance, it is quite certain that the transformation of the body-consciousness will take place first, that a progress in the mastery and control of all the movements of the body will come next, that this mastery will gradually change (here it becomes more vague), gradually, into a sort of transformation of the movement itself: alteration and transformation — all that is certain. But what must happen in the end, what Sri Aurobindo has spoken about in one of his last articles* in which he says that even the organs will be transformed, in the sense that they will be replaced by centres of concentration of forces (of concentration and action of forces) of different qualities and kinds which will replace all the organs of the body — that, my children, is much more distant, that is, it is something which... one cannot yet grasp the means of doing it. Take, for instance, the heart: by what means is this function of the heart which makes the blood flow through the whole body going to be replaced by a concentration of forces? By what means will the blood be replaced by a certain kind of force, and all the rest? By what means will the lungs be replaced by another concentration of forces, and what forces, and with what vibrations, and in what way?... All that will come much later. It cannot yet be realised. One can have an inkling of it, foresee it, but...

---

* "The Divine Body", written in 1949.

For the body, to know is to have the power to do. I shall give you an example that's just at hand. You do not know a gymnastic movement except when you do it. Don't you see, when you have done it well, you know it, understand it, but not before that. Physical knowledge is the power of doing. Well, that applies to everything, including transformation.

A certain number of years must pass before we can speak with knowledge of how this is going to happen, but all that I can tell you is that it has begun.

21 April 1954

*

So, if one has resolved to transform the body, well, one must wait with all the necessary patience — three hundred years, five hundred years, a thousand years, it does not matter — the time needed for the change. As for me, I see that three hundred years is a minimum. To tell you the truth, with the experience I have of things, I think it is truly a minimum.

Just imagine. You have never thought about what it means, have you? How is your body built? In a purely animal way, with all the organs and all the functions. You are absolutely dependent: if your heart stops for even the thousandth part of a second, you are gone and that's the end. The whole thing works and works automatically without your conscious will (happily for you, for if you had to supervise the functioning, it would have gone the wrong way long ago). All that is there. Everything is necessary, because it was organised in that manner. You cannot do without an organ, at least totally; there must be something in you representing it.

Transformation implies that all this purely material arrangement is replaced by an arrangement of concentrations of force having certain types of different vibrations substituting each organ by a centre of conscious energy moved by a conscious will and directed by a movement coming from above, from higher regions. No stomach, no heart any longer, no circulation, no lungs, no... All this disappears. But it is replaced by a whole set of vibrations representing what those organs are symbolically. For the organs are only the material symbols of centres of energy; they are not the essential reality; they simply give it a form or a support in certain given circumstances. The transformed body will then function through its *real* centres of energy and not any longer through their symbolic representatives such as were developed in the animal body. Therefore, first of all you must know what your heart represents in the cosmic energy and what the circulation represents and what the stomach and the brain represent. To begin with, you must first be conscious of all that. And then, you must have at your disposal the original vibrations of that which is symbolised by these organs. And you must slowly gather together all these energies in your body and change each organ into a centre of conscious energy which will replace the symbolic movement by the real one....

You believe it will take only three hundred years to do that? I believe it will take much more time to have a form with qualities which will not be exactly those we know, but will be much superior; a form that one naturally dreams to see plastic: as the expression of your face changes with your feelings, so the body will change (not the form but within the same form) in accordance with what you want to express with your body. It can become very concentrated, very developed, very luminous, very sane, with a perfect plasticity, with a perfect elasticity and a lightness as one wills... Have you never dreamt of giving a kick to the ground and then soaring into the air, flying away? You move about. You push a little with your shoulder, you go this way; you push again, you go that way; and you go wherever you like, quite easily; and finally when you have finished you come back, enter your body. Well, you must be able to do that with your body, and also certain things related to respiration — but there will no longer be lungs; there's a true movement behind, a symbolic movement which gives you this capacity of lightness; you do not belong any longer to the system of gravitation, you escape it. And so for each organ.

There is no end to imagination: to be luminous whenever one wants it, to be transparent whenever one wants it. Naturally there is no longer any need of any bones also in the system; it is not a skeleton with skin and viscera, it is another thing. It is concentrated energy obeying the will. This does not mean that there will no longer be any definite and recognisable forms; the form will be built by qualities rather than by solid particles. It will be, if one may say so, a practical or pragmatic form; it will be supple, mobile, light at will, in contrast to the fixity of the gross material form.

So, to change this into what I have just described, I believe three hundred years are truly very little. It seems many more than that are needed. Perhaps with a very, very, very concentrated work...

Three hundred years with the same body?

Well, there is change, it is no longer the same body.

But, you see, when our little humanity says three hundred years with the same body, you say: "Why! when I am fifty it already begins to decompose, so at three hundred it will be a horrible thing!" But it is not like that. If it is three hundred years with a body that goes on perfecting itself from year to year, perhaps when the three hundredth year is reached one will say: "Oh! I still need three or four hundred more to be what I want to be." If each year that passes represents a progress, a transformation, one would like to have more and more years in order to be able to transform oneself more and more. When something is not exactly as you want it to be — take, for example, simply one of the things I have just described, say, plasticity or lightness or elasticity or luminosity, and none of them is exactly as you want it, then you will still need at least two hundred years more so that it may be accomplished, but you never think: "How is it? It is still going to last two hundred years more!" On the contrary, you say: "Two hundred years more are *absolutely* necessary so that it may be truly done." And then, when all is done, when all is perfect, then there is no longer any question of years, for you are immortal.

But there are many objections that may be raised. It may be said that it would be impossible for the body to change unless something changes in the surroundings also. What would be your relation with other objects if you have changed so much? With other beings also? It seems necessary that a whole set of things changes, at least in relative proportions, so that one can exist, continue to exist. This then brings much complication, for it is no longer one individual consciousness that has to do the work, it becomes a collective consciousness. And so it is much more difficult still.

20 May 1953

*

And mark that your idea of what ought to be is so infinitely far off from what will be, that, by this very fact, even if you try to see in the most complete way possible, you will leave behind such a large portion of the universe that it will be almost a linear realisation, and in any case so small, so narrow, that the greater part of the universe will remain unchanged. And even if you have a very vast view of the whole, even if you can conceive of something more total and you go ahead on the path which is ready — for it is with paths as it is with beings, some are ready — without having the patience to wait for others, that is, if you wish to realise something very close to the true Truth in comparison with the present state of the world, what will happen? — the dislocation of a certain unity, a rupture not only of harmony but of equilibrium, for there will be an entire part of the creation which will not be able to follow. And instead of a complete realisation of the Divine, you will have a small localised realisation, infinitesimal, and nothing will be done of what finally ought to be done.

Consequently, you should not be impatient, should not be disappointed, depressed, discouraged if the truth you have seen is not immediately realised. Naturally, it is not a question of being down-hearted or grieved or in despair if you have made a mistake, for every mistake can be corrected; from the moment you have found it is a mistake, there is an opportunity to work within you, to make progress and be very happy! But the situation is much more serious and more difficult to overcome when you have seen something true, absolutely, essentially true, and the state of the universe is such that this truth is not yet ripe for realisation. I do not say this happens to many people, but perhaps it may happen to you, and it is then you have to have a great patience, a great understanding, and say to yourself, "It was true, but it was not completely true", that is, it was not a truth in keeping with all the other truths and, above all, not in keeping with the present possibilities; so we tried to realise it too quickly, and because we tried to be too quick it was belied. But do not say it was false because it was belied; say it was premature, that is all you can say — what you saw was true, but it was premature, and you must, with much patience and perseverance, keep your little truth intact for the moment when it will be possible to realise it.

The final victory is for the most patient.

17 February 1951

*

The secret is to emerge from the ego, get out of its prison, unite ourselves with the Divine, merge into Him, not to allow anything to separate us from Him. Then, once one has discovered this secret and realises it in one's being, pain loses its justification and suffering disappears. It is an all-powerful remedy, not only in the deeper parts of the
being, in the soul, in the spiritual consciousness, but also in life and
in the body.

There is no illness, no disorder which can resist the discovery of
this secret and the putting of it into practice, not only in the higher
parts of the being but in the cells of the body.

If one knows how to teach the cells the splendour that lies within
them, if one knows how to make them understand the reality which
makes them exist, gives them being, then they too enter the total harmony, and the physical disorder which causes the illness vanishes as
do all other disorders of the being.

But for that one must be neither cowardly nor fearful. When the
physical disorder comes, one must not be afraid; one must not run
away from it, must face it with courage, calmness, confidence, with
the certitude that illness is a *falsehood* and that if one turns entirely,
in full confidence, with a complete quietude to the divine Grace, It
will settle in these cells as It is established in the depths of the being,
and the cells themselves will share in the eternal Truth and Delight.

13 February 1957

*

In the very, very old traditions — there was a tradition more ancient
than the Vedic and the Chaldean which must have been the source of
both — in that ancient tradition there is already mention of a "glorious body" which would be plastic enough to be transformed at every
moment by the deeper consciousness: it would express that consciousness, it would have no fixity of form. It mentioned luminosity: the
constituent matter could become luminous at will. It mentioned a sort

of possibility of weightlessness which would allow the body to move about in the air only by the action of will-power and by certain processes of control of the inner energy, and so on. Much has been said about these things.

I don't know if there ever were beings on earth who had partially realised this, but in a very small way there have been partial instances of one thing or another, examples which go to prove that it is possible. And following up this idea, one could go so far as to conceive of the replacement of material organs and their functioning as it now is, by centres of concentration of force and energy which would be receptive to the higher forces and which, by a kind of alchemy, would use them for the necessities of life and the body. We already speak of the different "centres" in the body — this knowledge is very widespread among people who have practised yoga — but these centres could be perfected to the point where they replace the different organs by a direct action of the higher energy and vibrations on matter. Those who have practised occultism well enough, in its most integral form, it could be said, know the process of materialisation of subtle energies and can put them in contact with physical vibrations. Not only is it something that can be done, but it is something which *is* done. And all that is a science, a science which must itself be perfected, completed, and which will obviously be used for the creation and setting in action of new bodies which will be able to manifest the supramental life in the material world.

17 April 1957

CHAPTER 19

The Supramental

There are people who love adventure. It is these I call, and I tell them this: "I invite you to the great adventure."

It is not a question of repeating spiritually what others have done before us, for our adventure begins beyond that. It is a question of a new creation, entirely new, with all the unforeseen events, the risks, the hazards it entails — a *real adventure*, whose goal is certain victory, but the road to which is unknown and must be traced out step by step in the unexplored. Something that has never been in this present universe and that will *never* be again in the same way. If that interests you... well, let us embark. What will happen to you tomorrow — I have no idea.

One must put aside all that has been foreseen, all that has been devised, all that has been constructed, and then... set off walking into the unknown. And — come what may! There.

10 July 1957

Towards the Supramental

In order to know what the Supramental Realisation will be like, the first step, the first condition is to know what the supramental consciousness is. All those who have been, in one way or another, in contact with it have had some glimpse of the realisation to be. But those who have not, can yet aspire for that realisation, just as they can aspire to get the supramental knowledge. True knowledge means awareness by identity: once you get in touch with the supramental world, you can say something about its descent, but not before. What you can say before is that there will be a new creation upon earth; this you say through faith, since the exact character of it escapes you. And if you are called upon to define realisation, you may declare that, individually speaking, it means the transformation of your ordinary human consciousness into the divine and supramental.

The consciousness is like a ladder: at each great epoch there has been one great being capable of adding one more step to the ladder and reaching a place where the ordinary consciousness had never been. It is possible to attain a high level and get completely out of the material consciousness; but then one does not retain the ladder, whereas the great achievement of the great epochs of the universe has been the capacity to add one more step to the ladder without losing contact with the material, the capacity to reach the Highest and at the same time connect the top with the bottom instead of letting a kind of emptiness cut off all connection between the different planes. To go up and down and join the top to the bottom is the whole secret of realisation, and that is the work of the Avatar. Each time he adds one more step to the ladder there is a new creation upon earth.... The step which is being added now Sri Aurobindo has called the Supramental; as a result of it, the consciousness will be able to enter the supramental world and yet retain its personal form, its individualisation and then come down to establish here a new creation. Certainly this is not the last, for there are farther ranges of being; but now we are at work to bring down the supramental, to effect a reorganisation of the world, to bring the world back to the true divine order. It is essentially a creation of order, a putting of everything in its true place; and the chief spirit or force, the Shakti active at present is Mahasaraswati, the Goddess of perfect organisation.

The work of achieving a continuity which permits one to go up and down and bring into the material what is above, is done inside the consciousness. He who is meant to do it, the Avatar, even if he were shut up in a prison and saw nobody and never moved out, still would he do the work, because it is a work in the consciousness, a work of connection between the Supermind and the material being. He does not need to be recognised, he need have no outward power in order to be able to establish this conscious connection. Once, however, the connection is made, it must have its effect in the outward world in the form of a new creation, beginning with a model town and ending with a perfect world.

1930-1931

*

Mother, you have said there are many intermediary planes

between the mental and the supramental, and that if an ordinary man came in contact with one of these intermediate planes, he would be dazzled. Why then, since man is in such an undeveloped condition, do we speak of the descent of the supramental plane, instead of the descent of the intermediate planes?

For a very simple reason, because till now the whole physical, material world, the whole earth (let us take the earth) has been ruled by forces and the consciousness that come from what Sri Aurobindo calls the Overmind. Even what men call God is a force, a power coming from the Overmind and the whole universe was under the rule of the Overmind. To get there one has to pass through many intermediate planes and very few people can reach there without getting dazzled. But what Sri Aurobindo said is that now the time for the "rule" of the Overmind is coming to its end and is going to be replaced by the rule of the Supermind. All who have had spiritual experiences and have discovered the Divine and become united with him, know what it is, the Overmind. But what Sri Aurobindo says is that beyond the Overmind there is something and that it is now the turn of this something to come and rule the earth, to manifest upon earth and rule the earth. Therefore, there is no need to speak of the Overmind, for many people have spoken about it already and have had the experience of it; whereas this is something new that is going to manifest itself in a new way and nobody has been aware of it before. That is why.

The old accounts — there's no lack of people who have experienced these things or described them, or of books written on the subject. There is no need to repeat once more what others have said. Sri Aurobindo came to say something new. And it is precisely because people are unable to come out of the experiences they have known and heard being spoken of, that they try to identify this Force which Sri Aurobindo called supramental with their experience of the intermediary worlds including the Overmind. For they cannot conceive that there could be something else.... Sri Aurobindo always said that his Yoga began where the former Yogas ended, that to be able to realise his Yoga it was necessary first of all to have reached the extreme limit of what the older Yogas had realised, that is to say, the perception of the Divine, the union, the identification with the Divine. But that Divine, Sri Aurobindo says, is the Divine of the Overmind which is already something quite unthinkable, in comparison with the human consciousness, because even to reach there one must pass through several planes and in these planes one feels dazzled.

There are beings of the vital, if they appeared to men, or to say things more exactly, whenever they have appeared to men, men have taken them for the supreme God — these vital entities! If you like, we shall call that a disguise but it is a very successful disguise, because those who saw it were thoroughly convinced that they had seen the supreme Godhead. And yet, they were but beings of the vital. And these entities of the Overmind, these overmental gods are mighty entities in comparison with our humanity. When human beings come in relation with them, they become truly bewildered.

There is however a kind of Grace which makes it possible for us to profit by the experience of others. It is something similar to the way of teaching the sciences. If each scientist had to do all over again all the experiments of the past in order to arrive at a new discovery, go over all that the others had found, he would have to spend his whole life in that and there would be no time left to make his new discovery! Now one doesn't need to do all that: one opens a book and sees the results and starting from there can proceed further. Well, Sri Aurobindo wanted to do the same thing. He tells you where you can find the results of what others before him have found — the experiments they made and their results — and where you stand: historically where you stand in the spiritual history of the world. And then he takes you from there, and after the basis has been firmly laid for you, he makes you climb higher up the mountain.

30 September 1953

*

What do you mean by a "divine way of life"?

We always call "divine" all that we are not but wish to be. All that seems to us infinitely superior, not only to all that we have done, but to all that we feel we can do; all that surpasses both our conception and our present possibilities, we call "divine".

I say this not as a joke, but because I am quite convinced that if we go back some thousands of years, when men spoke of the Divine — if ever they did speak of the Divine, as I believe — they spoke perhaps of a state like that of the godheads of the Overmind; and now this mode of being of the Overmind godheads who, obviously, have governed the earth and formed many things on earth for a very long time, seems to us far inferior to what we conceive the Supermind to be. And this Supermind, which is, precisely, what we now call the Divine and try to bring down on earth, will probably strike us in the same way a few thousand or million years hence as the Overmind does today.

And I am sure that in the manifestation, that is, in His self-expression, the Divine is progressive. Outside the manifestation He is something we cannot conceive; but as soon as He manifests in this kind of perpetual becoming, well, He manifests more and more of Himself, as though He were reserving for the end the most beautiful things in His Being.

As the world progresses, what He expresses in the world becomes what we might call more and more divine.

So Sri Aurobindo has used the word Supermind to explain to those who are in the outer and evolutionary consciousness and who have some idea of the way in which the earth has developed — to explain to them that this something which is going to be beyond all this, and superior to human creation, to man, whom he always calls the mental being — this something which is going to come will be greater and better than man; and so he calls it supramental in order to make himself understood. But we could just as well say that it is something more divine than what has been manifested before.

And this he himself says, in what I read today, that it is infinite, that it has no limits.* That is to say, there will always be a growing perfection; and what now seems to us imperfect must have been the perfection for which certain ages in earth's history aspired.

There is no reason why this should stop. If it stopped, it would be finished. It would be a new Pralaya.

25 January 1956

*

* "In a certain sense it may be an error to speak of a goal anywhere in a progression which may well be infinite."

There is a state of consciousness which may be called "gnostic", in which you are able to see *at the same time* all the theories, all the beliefs, all the ideas men have expressed in their highest conscious- ness — the most contradictory notions, like the Buddhistic, the Vedan- tic, the Christian theories, all the philosophical theories, all the ex- pressions of the human mind when it has managed to catch a little corner of the Truth — and in that state, not only do you put each thing in its place, but everything appears to you marvellously true and quite indispensable in order to be able to understand anything at all about anything whatsoever. [...] Anatole France said in one of his books: "So long as men did not try to make the world progress, all went well and everybody was satisfied — no worry about perfecting oneself or perfecting the world, consequently all went well. Therefore the worst thing is to want to make others progress; let them do what they like and don't bother about anything, that will be much more wise." On the contrary, others tell you: "There is a Truth to be attained; the world is in a state of ignorance and one must at all costs, in spite of the difficulty of the way, enlighten man's consciousness and pull him out of his ignorance." But I tell you that there is a state of conscious- ness in which both the ways of seeing are absolutely equally true. Naturally, if you take only two aspects, it is difficult to see clearly; one must be able to see all the aspects of the truth glimpsed by the human intelligence and... something more. And then, in that state, nothing is absolutely false, nothing is absolutely bad. In that state one is free from all problems, all difficulties, all battles and everything appears to you wonderfully harmonious.

But if you try to imitate this condition mentally — do you under- stand? to make a mental imitation of it — you may be sure of doing stupid things; you will be one of those who have a chaos in their head and can say the most contradictory things without even being aware of it.

In that condition there is no contradiction — it is a totality and a totality in which one has the full knowledge of all the truths expressed (which are not sufficient to express the total Truth), in which one knows the respective places of all things, why and of what the uni- verse is formed. Only — I hasten to tell you this — it is not by a personal effort that one reaches this condition; it is not because one tries to obtain it that one obtains it. You *become* that, spontaneously. It is, if you like, the crowning of an absolute mental sincerity, when you no longer have any partiality, any preference, any attachment to an idea, when you do not even try any longer to know the truth.

You are simply open in the Light, that's all.

I am telling you this, this evening, because what is done, what has been realised by one can be realised by others. It is enough that one body has been able to realise that, one human body, to have the assurance that it *can* be done. You may consider it still very far off, but you can say, "Yes, the gnostic life is certain, because it has begun to be realised."

26 February 1951

*

Because until now evil has been opposed by weakness, by a spiritual force without any power for transformation in the material world, this tremendous effort of goodwill has ended only in deplorable failure and left the world in the same state of misery and corruption and falsehood. It is on the *same* plane as the one where the adverse forces are ruling that one must have a greater power than theirs, a power which can conquer them totally *in that very domain*. To put it otherwise, a spiritual force which would be capable of transforming both the consciousness and the material world. This force is the supramental force. What is necessary is to be receptive to its action on the physical plane, and not to run away into a distant Nirvana leaving the enemy with full power over what one abandons.

It is neither sacrifice nor renunciation nor weakness which can bring the victory. It is only Delight, a delight which is strength, endurance, supreme courage. The delight brought by the supramental force. It is much more difficult than giving everything up and running away, it demands an infinitely greater heroism — but that is the only way to conquer.

2 January 1957

*

Here it is written: "It is very unwise for anyone to claim prematurely to have possession of the supermind or even to have a taste of it." (Sri Aurobindo)

   What is a foretaste of the supermind?

It is still more unwise to imagine that one has it. That's it. Yes, because some people, as soon as they find a phrase in a book, in a teaching, immediately imagine that they have realised that. So, when Sri Aurobindo began speaking about the supermind — in what he was writing — everyone wrote to him: "I have seen the supramental Light, I had an experience of the supermind!" Now, it is better to keep the word "supermind" for a later time. For the moment let us not speak about it.

   Somewhere he has written a very detailed description of all the mental functions accessible to man. Well, when we read this, we say that merely to traverse the mental domain to its highest limit there are so many stages which have not yet been crossed that truly we don't need to speak about the supermind for the time being.

   When he speaks of the higher ranges of the mind, one becomes aware that one very rarely lives in these places. It is very rare for one to be in this state of consciousness. On the contrary it is in what he calls the altogether ordinary mind, the mind of the ordinary man, that we live. And to the ordinary consciousness the reason seems to belong to a very high region; and the reason for him is one of the average faculties of the human mind. There are mental regions very much higher than that, which he has described in detail. And it is quite certain that those correspondents, if they had... Suddenly they said that they were having wonderful supramental experiences, because one is rarely in these regions which lie beyond the reason, which are regions of direct perception, intuition and other faculties of intuition of the same kind, which go far beyond the reason; and these are still mental regions, they have nothing of the supramental.

Mother, you said that between the supermind and the mind there are many stages, didn't you? And it is written that the next logical stage in the evolution of Nature is the superman. Why not a race which is...

Intermediary? We shall see that later.

Does this mean that from the mind we can go to the supermind without passing through the intermediary stages?

I did not say that they were between the mind and the supermind. I said it is in the mind itself, without coming out of the mind, that there are all these regions which are almost inaccessible for most human beings. I did not say *between* the mind and supermind. [...] Before reaching the extreme limit of the mind, there are so many regions and mental activities which are not at all accessible to most human beings. And even for those who can reach them, they are not regions where they constantly live. They must make an effort of concentration to get there and they don't always arrive. There are regions which Sri Aurobindo has described which only very rare individuals can reach, and still he speaks of them as mental regions. He does not use for them the word supramental.

It can very well happen — besides, when he spoke of the supermind he said that there are many regions in the supermind itself and that it would naturally be the first ones, the lowest regions, which would manifest to begin with — it can very well happen that there are still a number of intermediary states of being, this is possible — intermediary stages.

Certainly the perfect race will not come spontaneously. Very probably not. But already, even the first attempts... in comparison with the present human being, it will make a great difference, great enough for one to feel that this is something miraculous.

It can very well happen that the first supramental manifestations will be altogether incomplete. But even to these, man as he is at present will seem something absolutely gross. There is no halt in the universal development and even the thing which would seem at a certain time absolutely perfect and finished, will still be only a stage for future manifestations. But men very much like to sit down and say, "Now I have done what I had to do."

But the universe is not like that; it does not sit down, it does not rest, it always goes on. One can never say, "Now it is over, I close the door and that's all." One may shut the door but then one cuts himself off from the universal movement. Expressions are always relative, and the first being which is no longer a human animal but begins to be a divine human, a divine man, will seem something absolutely marvellous, even if he is still very incomplete as the perfect type of this new race. One must get accustomed to living in a perpetual movement. There is something which likes very much — perhaps it is necessary for facilitating the action — to fix a goal and say, "This indeed is the end", but not at all. "This is perfection" — there is no absolute perfection. All things are always relative and constantly they are changing.

24 November 1954

*

I think that [the manifestation of the supramental] will happen the moment there is a sufficiently large number of consciousnesses which feel absolutely that it cannot be otherwise. Now, most people, the immense majority among you have to make an effort to imagine what it will be, and at best, speculate upon it and perhaps hope that this transformation will make things more pleasing, more pleasant — something like that. But your consciousness is so attached to what is, that it even finds it difficult to imagine that things can be otherwise. And until what must be becomes for a sufficiently big group of consciousnesses an inevitable necessity, and all that has been and all that still is at present appears like an absurdity which cannot last... it is at that moment that this [manifestation] can take place, not before.

There remains a problem, namely, whether it is something which can take place and will take place individually before occurring collectively. It is probable. But no individual realisation can be complete nor even approach this perfection if it is not in harmony with at least a group of consciousnesses representative of a new world. In spite of everything there is so great an interdependence of the individual and the collectivity, that the individual realisation, despite all, is limited, impoverished by the irresponsive atmosphere — if I may say so — of what surrounds it. And it is certain that the entire terrestrial life has to follow a certain curve of progress, so that a new world and a new consciousness can manifest. And that is why I said at the beginning that it depends at least partially on you.

Have you ever tried to picture what this new consciousness could be and what a new race could be like, and finally what a new world could be like?

By analogy, it is quite obvious that the arrival of man upon earth has changed the earth-condition. I cannot say that from a certain point of view this was for the greatest good of all, because there are many who have suffered terribly from it, and here it is obvious that the complications the human being has brought into life have not always been very favourable either for him or for others. But from a certain point of view this has brought about a considerable progress, even in the lower species: man meddled with the life of animals, he meddled with the life of plants, he meddled with the life of metals, of minerals; as I said, it was not always for the greatest joy of those he dealt with, but still it certainly changed their conditions of life considerably. Well, in the same way, it is probable that the supramental being, whatever it might be, will considerably change the life of the earth. In our heart and our thought we hope that all the evils the earth suffers from will be at least ameliorated if not cured, and that the general conditions will be more harmonious, and in any case more tolerable. This may happen, because it was the very nature of the mental consciousness which incarnated in man, who acted for his own satisfaction, with his own development in view, and without much consideration for the consequences of his actions. Perhaps the Supermind will act more harmoniously. In any case we hope so. That is how we conceive of it.

But I am asking you, in turn, a question: have you thought of it? Have you thought of what it could be?[...]

It is certain that for a very long time, perhaps from the very beginning (not the beginning from the evolutionary standpoint, because there were periods of intermediate beings who were much nearer the animal than the true man), when this human form was developed enough and ready to receive something from above, when the first beings of the higher worlds incarnated in human forms, from that time there were always individuals who carried in themselves this need for eternity and the absolute. But it was something individual. And it is only gradually and very progressively, through consecutive periods of light and darkness, that in the whole of humanity something has awakened to the need of a higher good.

It is quite obvious that now, through all the swirlings and all the stupidities, there is an awakening need, almost a kind of sensation of what this [the supramental manifestation] could and should be — which means that the time is near. For a very long time it has been said, "It will be, it will be", and it was promised... thousands and thousands of years ago they had already begun to promise that there would be a new consciousness, a new world, something divine which would manifest upon earth, but it was said, "It will be, it will be", like that; they spoke of ages, eons, thousands and millions of years. They did not have this sensation which we now have, that it must come, that it is very close. Of course human life is very short and there is a tendency to wish to shorten the distances so that they may be in proportion to the dimensions; but in spite of all, there will come a moment when it happens... there will be a time when it happens, there will be a time when the movement swings over into a new reality... There was a time when the mental being could manifest upon earth. The starting point might have been poor, very incomplete, very partial, but all the same there was a starting point. Why can't it be now?... That's all.

Perhaps if those who from the beginning have proclaimed that it would be, those very people say, "It is going to be...", after all, perhaps they are the best informed. I am considering how from the beginning of the earth's history (we shall not go farther back to the antecedents, you know, for we have already enough to do with the earth), from the beginning of the earth's history, in one form or another, under one name or another, Sri Aurobindo has always presided over the great terrestrial transformations; and so when he tells you, "Well, this is the right time", perhaps he knows. That's all that I can say.

So, if it is the right time, this is how the problem is put: there are people who are ready or will become ready, and these precisely will be the first to start on the new path. There are others who, perhaps, will become aware of it too late, who will have missed the opportunity; I think there will be many of this kind. But in any case, my point of view is this: even if there should be only half a chance, it would be worth the trouble of trying. For after all... I don't know... I told you just now, there is a moment when life such as it is, the human consciousness such as it is, seems something absolutely impossible to bear, it creates a kind of disgust, repugnance; one says, "No, it is not that, it is not that; it can't be that, it can't continue." Well, when one comes to this, there is only to throw in one's *all* — all one's effort, all one's strength, all one's life, all one's being — into this chance, if you like, or this exceptional opportunity that is given to cross over to the other side. What a relief to set foot on the new path, that which will lead you elsewhere! This is worth the trouble of casting behind much luggage, of getting rid of many things in order to be able to take that leap. That's how I see the problem.

In fact it is the sublimest of adventures, and if one has in him in the slightest the true spirit of adventure, it is worth risking all for all. But those who are afraid, who wonder, "Am I not going to let go the substance for the shadow?" according to the most banal proverb one can imagine, those who tell themselves, "Bah! after all it is better to profit by what one has than to risk losing everything, we don't know what is going to happen tomorrow, let us take precautions"... unfortunately this is very widespread, extremely widespread... well, about those who are in this state of mind, I can assure you of one thing: that even when the thing occurs before their very nose, they will not perceive it. They will say, "It is good, in this way I won't regret anything." It is possible. But perhaps later they will; this we do not know.

In any case what *I* call being sincere is this: if one thinks that this new realisation is the only thing which is truly worth being lived; if what is, is intolerable — not only for oneself, perhaps not so much for oneself... but still, if one is not absolutely selfish and mean, one feels that, truly, it has lasted long enough, that one has had enough of it, that it must change — well, when one feels like that, one takes everything, all that one is, all that one can, all that one has, and one throws oneself into it completely without ever looking behind, and come what may! I indeed feel that it would be preferable even to plunge into an abyss in this way than to be on the shore, trembling and wondering, "What will happen to me tomorrow if I take this rather rash step?" There we are.[...]

In fact, the only thing which is very important for the moment is the change of consciousness. And don't think that this is so easy. If you observe yourself attentively, you will perceive that you think, feel, experience and construct like a human animal, that is, like an infrarational being who is three-fourths subconscious, through almost the whole of your day. It is possible that at certain moments you escape from this; but you still need an effort to escape from it. It may happen spontaneously, as by grace, at certain moments; but most of the time you have to make an effort to be able to catch something which is not purely this.[...]

Mother, the appearance of mental man was gradual, wasn't it, from the animal to man?

That... There was all the same a time when it became a man, isn't that so? I told you that, from the standpoint of evolution it seems like that. I indeed am not very well up in all this, you see, I can't tell you how it happened, at least not what science thinks it knows about what happened. I can tell you only what I know.

Well, there was a time when what we call the human form, that is, with human capacities, was ready enough for a being with mental consciousness, entirely conscious, to be able to incarnate in it — and this indeed was truly the first man. Now, historically at what time this happened I can't tell you; but it was a very long time ago. Sometime ago I came across some numbers, which seemed to me to be absolutely reasonable and accurate — but that was extremely long ago. And for a *very* long time it was like... a kind of vast and quiet state, as when the sea has reached high-tide and spreads out and is calm. It remained calm like that for a very, very, very, very long time; and it was only after very long that what we call human activity and human civilisation began to take place, and for this, even from the beginning of this till today... we have figures, haven't we, approximately...? (*turning to Pavitra*) Pavitra, do you know them?

(Pavitra) *I don't remember them now.*

There are figures, but they are quite enormous. And this is only the period that can be called historic — though it isn't so, ordinarily reckoning — but still, they have discovered signs, documents, indications, something which can give you an idea of the time. Well, all this happened only very long after the first mental consciousness incarnated in a human form, which had become sufficiently human, you see, to become a man; and probably before this form was produced there must have been numerous trials of Nature which spread out, perhaps over thousands and thousands and millions of years. I don't know. But there was a time, as I said, when this mental consciousness was able to come and take possession of a form. After this, as I also told you, for very, very long... in order that this form could adapt itself and perfect itself sufficiently to express this consciousness completely, a very, very, very long time was necessary — that is understood. Well, it is more than probable (not more than probable, certain), that it will happen again in the same way.

There will come a time when a human consciousness is in the required state for a supramental consciousness to be able to enter this human consciousness and manifest.

But it is possible that before this becomes a new race like the human race, it may take very, very long. And it will be done progressively. But as I say, there is one thing: when it happens, it will happen. It does not happen, does not stretch out like a rubber band, you see; there is a time when it happens, when the descent takes place, the fusion occurs, the identification comes about. It can be done in a flash. There is a moment when it occurs. Later it may take very, very, very long; one must not hope that overnight one is going to see supermen springing up here and there. No, it won't be like that. Only, those who will have done what I have said, those who will have thrown themselves in entirely, risked all for all, those will know it. But they will be the only ones to know; they will know when it takes place.

The others will not be able even to see?

The others? They will not even be aware of it! They will continue their stupid life, without knowing what has happened.

But all the same, they will be able to see this superman before them. What will be the attitude of the superman towards man?

What is the attitude of man towards the animal? No, let us hope that he [the superman] is a little more kind! (*Laughter*)

But you must not delude yourself. For the supramental consciousness man is truly stupid. Yes, even with all his perfections, all his realisations, all that, even with all his accomplishments, well, he seems *terribly* stupid. Only, that's no reason for ill-treating him. But I don't think that the superman will ill-treat anyone, just because he will have a consciousness which will be able to pass behind appearances. Let us hope that he will be quite kind.

(Pavitra) *What will be man's attitude towards the superman?*

Ah! (*Laughter*) Let us hope that it is not the same attitude as the one which man has towards all his gods, because he has rather ill-treated them. His prophets and his gods, he has put them upon the cross, he has stoned them, has burnt them alive — indeed, man has behaved rather badly with all those who came to preach a new life to him. Let us hope that man becomes a little more reasonable... Now he would put them in prison.

12 October 1955

*

If there is some manifestation [of a new world], will it be purely spiritual, that is, will only those who do yoga be able to perceive it, or will there be any consequences in the world of facts?

My child, why do you put this in the future?

There have already been, for years, extraordinary, fantastic consequences in the world. But to see this, one must have a little knowledge; otherwise one takes them for quite normal and ordinary things — because one doesn't even know how they happen.

So perhaps this will be exactly the same thing; there are likely to be tremendous changes, fantastic actions, and, well, people will say, "But this — naturally, it is like that", because they don't know how it comes about.

An action in the world? — It is constant. It is something which spreads and acts everywhere, gives out everywhere new impulsions, new orientations, new ideas, new acts of will — everywhere. But still, as one does not see how it happens, one thinks it "quite natural", as they say.

It is quite natural, but with another naturalness than that of ordinary physical Nature.

Indeed, it is quite logical to say that one must be conscious of the Spirit to be able to perceive the work of the Spirit. If you are not conscious of the Spirit, how will you be able to see it at work? Because the result of what the Spirit does is necessarily material in the material world; and as it is material, you find it quite natural. What do you know of what Nature does, and what do you know of what the Spirit does? All that Nature does — I am speaking of physical Nature — we know very little about it, almost nothing, since we have to constantly learn things which upset all that we thought we knew before. And so, how to distinguish between what is purely the work of Nature and the work of the Spirit through Nature? One should know how to distinguish the one from the other. And how to distinguish them when one's consciousness is not quite limpid and sure of what the Spirit is? How to recognise It, and how to see Its Work? This seems to me very simple logic.

The world will go on. Things will happen. And perhaps there will be a handful of men who will know how they were done. That's all.

And if today one were suddenly precipitated, without any transition, into the world as it was, let us say, two or three thousand years ago; oh! even less than that perhaps — one or two thousand years ago — it would be such a suffocating contrast that probably very few people would be able to bear it. But as this came about "like that", with the amiable slowness of Nature, with all her fantasies, one finds it quite natural and doesn't even notice it.

It is not an image, it is not just fine words when it is said that if one enters the true consciousness, if one changes one's consciousness, well, the world itself changes for you. And it is not only an appearance or an impression: one sees differently than one does in the ordinary consciousness; relations are different, causes are different, effects are different. And instead of seeing only something which is not transparent — one cannot see what's behind, it is a surface, a crust; it is only this one sees and one can't even see what moves it, what makes it exist — everything is turned inside out, and it is that which appears artificial and unreal, and almost inexistent. And so, when one sees things in this way, normally, you know, without straining oneself, without having to practise meditation and concentration and make strenuous efforts to see things like this, when it is one's normal, natural vision, then one understands things in a completely different way — naturally, the world is different!

4 January 1956

*

> *"The supramental world has to be formed or created in us by the Divine Will as the result of a constant expansion and self-perfecting."* (Sri Aurobindo)

That is to say, to hope to receive, use and form in oneself a supramental being, and consequently a supramental world, there must first of all be an expansion of consciousness and a *constant* personal progress: not to have sudden flights, a little aspiration, a little effort, and then fall back into somnolence. This must be the *constant* idea of the being, the *constant* will of the being, the *constant* effort of the being, the *constant* preoccupation of the being.

If for five minutes in the day you happen to remember that there is something in the universe like the supramental Force, and that, after all, "it would be nice if it manifested in me", and then all the rest of the time you are thinking of something else and are busy with other things, there is not much chance that it would come and do any serious work in you. Sri Aurobindo says this quite clearly and precisely. He does not tell you that *you* will do it, he says it is the Divine Will. So don't come and say, "Ah! I can't." No one is asking you to do it. But there *must be* enough aspiration and adhesion in the being to make the expansion of the being, the expansion of consciousness possible. For, to tell the truth, everybody is small, small, small, so small that there is not enough room to put any supramental in! It is so small that it is already quite filled up with all the ordinary little human movements. There must be a great widening to make room for the movements of the Supermind.

And then there must also be an aspiration for progress: not to be satisfied with what one is, how one is, what one does, what one knows or thinks one knows; but to have a constant aspiration for something more, something better, for a greater light, a vaster consciousness, a truer truth and a more universal goodness. And over and above all this, a goodwill which never fails.

That can't be done in a few days.[...]

However, there is a very great difference, always, between a kind of mental curiosity which plays with words and ideas, and a true aspiration of the being which means that truly, really, it is *that* which counts, essentially, and nothing else — that aspiration, that inner will because of which nothing has any value except *that*, that realisation; nothing counts except *that*; there is no other reason for existence, for living, than *that*.

And yet it is this that's needed if one wants the Supramental to become visible to the naked eye.

And mark that I am not speaking of a physical transformation, for this everyone knows: you don't expect to become luminous and plastic overnight, to lose your weight, be able to displace yourself freely, appear in a dozen places at the same time and what not.... No, I believe you are reasonable enough not to expect this to happen right away. It will take some time.

But still, simply, the working of the consciousness, simply a certain self-mastery, a control over one's body, a direct knowledge of things, a capacity of identification and a clear vision — instead of that hazy and vague sight which sees only the mere appearances that are so deceptive, so unreal, so fossilised — a more direct perception, an inner perception, this ought to be able to come and come quickly if one has prepared oneself.

Simply to have that feeling that the air one breathes is more living, the strength one has more lasting. And instead of always groping like a blind man to know what should be done, to have a clear, precise, inner intimation: it is this — not that: *this*.

These are things one can acquire immediately if one is ready.

27 June 1956

*

Will it take long for the Supermind which is involved in material Nature to emerge into the outer consciousness and bring visible results?

That depends on the state of consciousness from which one answers, for.... For the human consciousness, obviously, I think it will take quite a long time. For another consciousness it will be relatively very fast, and for yet another consciousness, it is already accomplished. It is an accomplished fact. But in order to become aware of this, one must be able to enter into another state of consciousness than the ordinary physical consciousness.

Sri Aurobindo has spoken — I believe I have read it to you, I think it's in *The Synthesis of Yoga* — of the true mind, the true vital and the true physical or subtle physical, and he has said that they co-exist with the ordinary mind, vital and physical, and that in certain conditions one may enter into contact with them, and then one becomes aware of the difference between what really is and the appearances of things.

Well, for a developed consciousness, the Supermind is already realised somewhere in a domain of the subtle physical, it already exists there visible, concrete, and expresses itself in forms and activities. And when one is in tune with this domain, when one lives there, one has a very strong feeling that this world would only have to be condensed, so to say, for it to become visible to all. What would then be interesting would be to develop this inner perception which would put you into contact with the supramental truth which is already manifested, and is veiled for you only for want of appropriate organs to enter into relation with it.

It is possible that those who are conscious of their dreams may have dreams of a new kind which put them into contact with that world, for it is accessible to the subtle physical of all those who have the corresponding organs in themselves. And there is necessarily a subtle influence of this physical on outer matter, if one is ready to receive impressions from it and admit them into one's consciousness.

5 September 1956

The Supramental Manifestation upon Earth

(The Mother stated that the consciousness which Sri Aurobindo and she called the Supramental manifested upon earth on 29 February 1956. In April of that year she gave two messages regarding this manifestation:

"The manifestation of the Supramental upon earth is no more a promise, but a living fact, a reality.

"It is at work here, and one day will come when the most blind, the most unconscious, even the most unwilling shall be obliged to recognise it."

"Lord, Thou hast willed and I execute,
A new light breaks upon the earth,
A new world is born.
The things that were promised are fulfilled.")

Sweet Mother, you have said: The Supramental has descended upon earth. What does that mean exactly? You have also said: "The things that were promised are fulfilled." What are these things?

Ah, that's ignorance indeed! This was promised a very long time ago, this was said very long ago — not only here — since the beginning of the earth. There have been all kinds of predictions, by all kinds of prophets; it has been said, "There will be a new heaven and a new earth, a new race will be born, the world will be transformed...." Prophets have spoken about this in all the traditions.

You have said, "They are fulfilled." Where is the new race?

The new race? Wait for something like... a few thousand years, and you will see it!

When the mind descended upon earth, between the time the mind manifested in the earth-atmosphere and the time the first man appeared, nearly a million years elapsed. Now it will go faster because man expects it, he has a vague idea; he is expecting in some sense the advent of the superman, while, certainly, the apes did not expect the birth of man, they had never thought of it — for the good reason that they probably don't think much. But man has thought of it and awaits it, so it will go faster. But faster means still thousands of years probably. We shall speak about it again after a few thousand years!

(Silence)

People who are inwardly ready, who are open and in contact with higher forces, people who have had a more or less direct personal contact with the supramental Light and Consciousness are able to feel the difference in the earth-atmosphere.

But for that... Only the like can know the like, only the supramental Consciousness in an individual can perceive this Supermind acting in the earth-atmosphere. Those who, for some reason or other, have developed this perception, can see it. But those who are not even conscious of an inner being — just slightly within — and who would be quite at a loss to say what their soul is like, these certainly are not ready to perceive the difference in the earth-atmosphere. They still have a long way to go for that. Because, for those whose consciousness is more or less exclusively centred in the outer being — mental, vital and physical — things need to take on an absurd and unexpected appearance for them to be able to recognise them. Then they call them miracles.

But the constant miracle of the intervention of forces which changes circumstances and characters and has a very widespread result, this they do not call a miracle, for only the mere appearance is seen and this seems quite natural. But, truly speaking, if you were to reflect upon the least little thing that happens, you would be obliged to acknowledge that it is miraculous.

It is simply because you don't reflect upon it that you take things as they are, for what they are, without questioning; otherwise every day you would have any number of occasions to tell yourself, "Really, but this is quite astonishing! How did it happen?"

Quite simply, it is a habit of seeing things in a purely superficial way.

2 May 1956

Mother, when mind descended into the earth-atmosphere, the apes had not made any effort to change into man, had they? It was Nature which provided the effort. But here...

But it is not man who is going to change himself into superman!

No?

Just try! (*Laughter*)

That's it, you see, it is something else which is going to work.

So, we are...

Only — yes, there is an only, I don't want to be so cruel: Now MAN CAN COLLABORATE. That is to say, he can lend himself to the process, with goodwill, with aspiration, and help as best he can. And that is why I said it would go faster. I hope it will go *much* faster.

But even so, much faster is still going to take a little time!

(*Silence*)

Listen. If all of you who have heard about this, not once but perhaps hundreds of times, who have spoken about it yourselves, thought of it, hoped for it, wanted it — there are people who came here for that, with the intention of receiving the supramental Force and being transformed into supermen — that was their aim, wasn't it?... But how is it that all of you were so unfamiliar with this Force that when it came you didn't even feel it?

Can you solve this problem for me? If you have the solution to this problem, you will have the solution to the difficulty.

I am not speaking of people from outside who have never thought of this, never been concerned with it, and who don't even know that there is something like a Supermind to be received, you understand. I am speaking of those who have based their life on this aspiration — and I do not doubt their sincerity, not for a moment — who have worked, some for thirty years, some for thirty-five, some a little less, who have done everything saying,"When the Supermind comes...

When the Supermind comes... ", that was the refrain, "When the Supermind comes..." Therefore, they were truly in the best possible state, one couldn't dream of a better. How is it that the inner preparation was so — let us say simply — so incomplete, that when the Vibration came they did not immediately feel it with the impact of identity?

Individually, the aim of each one was to prepare himself, to enter into a more or less close individual relation with this Force, to help; or, if they could not help, at least to be ready when the Force would manifest, to recognise it and open to it. And instead of being an alien element in a world where what you carry within yourself is not manifested, you suddenly become *that*, you enter straight in, fully, into this very atmosphere: it is this Force that is there, surrounding you, penetrating you.

If you had had even a little inner contact, immediately you would have recognised it, wouldn't you?

Well, anyway, that is what happened to those who had a little inner contact; they recognised it, felt it; they said, "Ah! here it is, it has come." But how is it, then, that so many hundreds of people, not to speak of the small handful of those who truly wanted nothing but that, thought of nothing but that, had staked their whole life on that, how is it that they did not feel anything? What can this mean?

Of course, it is only like that knows like. That is an obvious fact.

There was a possibility of coming into contact with the Thing individually — Sri Aurobindo had even described it as the necessary process: a certain number of people who, through their inner effort and aspiration, enter into contact with this Force. That was what we used to call the ascent to the Supermind. And so, even if it were by an inner ascent — that is to say, by freeing themselves from the material consciousness — if by an inner ascent they had touched the Supermind, they should *naturally* have recognised it the moment it came. But it was indispensable to have had a previous contact: if they had not touched it, how could they have recognised it?

That is to say, the universal movement is like that — I read that to you some days ago — certain individuals, who are the pioneers, the vanguard, through inner effort and inner progress enter into communication with the new Force which is to manifest and receive it into themselves. And then, as there are calls of this kind, the thing is made possible, and the age, the time, the moment of the manifestation comes. This is how it happened — and the Manifestation took place.

But, then all those who were ready must have recognised it.

I hasten to tell you that there are some who did recognise it, but still[...]

Mother, a statement has gone round here, very recently — it says, "What has just happened, with this Victory, is not a descent but a manifestation. And it is more than an individual event: the Supermind has emerged into the universal play."

Yes, yes, yes. In fact I said all this, I acknowledge it. So?

They say, "The supramental principle is at work..."

But I have just explained all this to you at length (*Mother laughs*), this is terrible!

What I call a "descent" is this: first the consciousness rises in an ascent, you catch the Thing up there, and come down with it. That is an *individual* event.

When this individual event has happened in a way that proves sufficient to create a possibility of a general kind, it is no longer a "descent", it is a "manifestation".

What I call a descent is the individual movement, in an individual consciousness. And when it is a new world manifesting in an old world — just as, for a comparison, when mind spread upon the earth — I call that a manifestation.

You may call it whatever you like, it's all the same to me, but we should understand each other.

What I call a descent is in the individual consciousness. Just as one speaks of ascent — there is no ascent, you see: there is neither above nor below nor any direction, it is a way of speaking — you speak of ascent when you have the feeling of rising up towards something; and you call it a descent when, after having caught that thing, you bring it down into yourself.

But when the gates are open and the flood comes in, you can't

call it a descent. It is a Force which is spreading out. Understood?...
Ah!

It's all one to me, the words you use. I am not particularly attached to words, but I explain them to you, and it is better to understand each other, for otherwise there is no end to explanations.

Now, to people who ask you these insidious questions, you may
reply that the best way of receiving anything whatever is not to pull,
but to give. If they want to give themselves to the new life, well, the
new life will enter into them.

But if they want to pull the new life down into themselves, they
will close their door with their own egoism. That's all.

2 May 1956

A New World Is Born

It is quite difficult to free oneself from old habits of being and to
be able to freely conceive of a new life, a new world. And naturally,
the liberation begins on the highest planes of consciousness: it is easier
for the mind or the higher intelligence to conceive of new things than
for the vital beings, for instance, to feel things in a new way. And it is
still more difficult for the body to have a purely material perception
of what a new world will be. Yet this perception must *precede* the
material transformation; first one must *feel* very concretely the strange-
ness of the old things, their lack of relevance, if I may say so. One
must have the feeling, even a material impression, that they are outdated, that they belong to a past which no longer has any purpose. For
the old impressions one had of past things which have become historic — which have their interest from that point of view and support
the advance of the present and the future — this is still a movement
that belongs to the old world: it is the old world that is unfolding with
a past, a present, a future. But for the creation of a new world, there
is, so to speak, only a continuity of transition which gives an appearance —an impression rather — the impression of two things still in-
termingled but almost disconnected, and that the things of the past no
longer have the power or the strength to endure, with whatever modifications, in the new things. That other world is necessarily an *absolutely* new experience.

One would have to go back to the time when there was a transition from the animal to the human creation to find a similar period, and at that time the consciousness was not sufficiently mentalised to be able to observe, understand, feel intelligently — the passage must have been made in a completely obscure way. So, what I am speaking about is absolutely new, *unique* in the terrestrial creation, it is something unprecedented, truly a perception or a sensation or an impression... that is quite strange and new.

(*After a silence*) A disconnection: something which has overstayed its time and has only quite a subordinate force of existence, from something totally new, but still so young, so imperceptible, almost weak, so to say; it hasn't yet the power to impose and assert itself and to predominate, to take the place of the other. So there is a concomitance but, as I said, with a disconnection, that is, the connection between the two is missing.

It is difficult to describe, but I am speaking to you about it because this is what I felt yesterday evening. I felt it so acutely... that it made me look at certain things, and once I had seen them I felt it would be interesting to tell you about them.

(*Silence*)

It seems strange that something so new, so special and I might say so unexpected should happen during a film-show.* For people who believe that some things are important and other things are not, that there are activities which are helpful to yoga and others which are not, well, this is one more opportunity to show that they are wrong. I have always noticed that it is unexpected things which give you the most interesting experiences.

Yesterday evening, suddenly something happened which I have just described to you as best I could — I don't know if I have succeeded in making myself understood — but it was truly quite new and alto-

---

* Film-shows were often held at the Ashram Playground. The Mother attended most of them. The film described here was a Bengali movie, *Rani Rasmani,* which narrates the life of Ramakrishna Paramahansa and Rani Rasmani, the rich widow who built in 1847 the Kali temple at Dakshineshwar, near Calcutta. Sri Ramakrishna lived there for most of his life.

gether unexpected. We were shown, comparatively clumsily, a picture of the temple on the banks of the Ganges, and the statue of Kali [...] and while I was seeing that, which was a completely superficial appearance and, as I said, rather clumsy, I saw the reality it was trying to represent, what was behind, and this put me in touch with all that world of religion and worship, of aspiration, man's whole relationship with the gods, which was — I am already speaking in the past tense — which was the flower of the human spiritual effort towards something more divine than man, something which was the highest and almost the purest expression of his effort towards what is higher than he. And suddenly I had *concretely, materially*, the impression that it was another world, a world that had ceased to be real, living, an outdated world which had lost its reality, its truth, which had been transcended, surpassed by something which had taken birth and was only beginning to express itself, but whose *life* was *so intense*, so true, so sublime, that all this became false, unreal, worthless.

Then I truly understood — for I understood not with the head, the intelligence but with the body, you understand what I mean — I understood in the cells of the body — that a new world *is born* and is beginning to grow.[...]

Well, I announced to you all that this new world was born. But it has been so engulfed, as it were, in the old world that so far the difference has not been very perceptible to many people. Still, the action of the new forces has continued very regularly, very persistently, very steadily, and to a certain extent, very effectively. And one of the manifestations of this action was my experience — truly so very new — of yesterday evening. And the result of all this I have noted step by step in almost daily experiences. It could be expressed succinctly, in a rather linear way:

First, it is not only a "new conception" of spiritual life and the divine Reality. This conception was expressed by Sri Aurobindo, I have expressed it myself many a time, and it could be formulated somewhat like this: the old spirituality was an escape from life into the divine Reality, leaving the world just where it was, as it was; whereas our new vision, on the contrary, is a divinisation of life, a transformation of the material world into a divine world. This has been said, repeated, more or less understood, indeed it is the basic idea of what we want to do.

But this could be a continuation with an improvement, a widening of the old world as it was — and so long as this is a conception up there in the field of thought, in fact it is hardly more than that — but what has happened, the really new thing, is that a new world is *born, born, born.* It is not the old one transforming itself, it is a *new* world which is *born.* And we are right in the midst of this period of transition where the two are entangled — where the other still persists all-powerful and entirely dominating the ordinary consciousness, but where the new one is quietly slipping in, still very modest, unnoticed — unnoticed to the extent that outwardly it doesn't disturb anything very much, for the time being, and that in the consciousness of most people it is even altogether imperceptible. And yet it is working, growing — until it is strong enough to assert itself visibly.

In any case, to simplify things, it could be said that characteristically the old world, the creation of what Sri Aurobindo calls the Overmind, was an age of the gods, and consequently the age of religions. As I said, the flower of human effort towards what is above it gave rise to innumerable religious forms, to a religious relationship between the best souls and the invisible world. And at the very summit of all that, as an effort towards a higher realisation there has arisen the idea of the unity of religions, of this "one single thing" which is behind all these manifestations; and this idea has truly been, so to speak, the extreme limit of human aspiration. Well, that is at the frontier, it is something that still belongs *completely* to the Overmind world, the Overmind creation and which from there seems to be looking towards this "other thing" which is a new creation it cannot grasp — which it tries to reach, feels coming, but cannot grasp. To grasp it, a reversal is needed. It is necessary to leave the Overmind creation. It was necessary that the new creation, the supramental creation should take place.

And now, all these old things seem so old, so out-of-date, so arbitrary — such a travesty of the real truth.

In the supramental creation there will *no longer be any religions.* The whole life will be the expression, the flowering into forms of the divine Unity manifesting in the world. And there will no longer be what men now call gods.

These great divine beings themselves will be able to participate in the new creation; but to do so, they will have to put on what we

could call the "supramental substance" on earth. And if some of them
choose to remain in their world as they are, if they decide not to manifest physically, their relation with the beings of a supramental earth
will be a relation of friends, collaborators, equals, for the highest divine essence will be manifested in the beings of the new supramental
world on earth.

When the physical substance is supramentalised, to incarnate on
earth will no longer be a cause of inferiority, quite the contrary. It will
give a plenitude which cannot be obtained otherwise.

But all this is in the future; it is a future... which has *begun*, but
which will take some time to be realised integrally. Meanwhile we
are in a very special situation, extremely special, without precedent.
We are now witnessing the birth of a new world; it is very young,
very weak — not in its essence but in its outer manifestation — not
yet recognised, not even felt, denied by the majority. But it is here. It
is here, making an effort to grow, absolutely *sure* of the result. But the
road to it is a completely new road which has never before been traced
out — nobody has gone there, nobody has done that! It is a beginning, a *universal beginning*. So, it is an absolutely unexpected and
unpredictable adventure.

There are people who love adventure. It is these I call, and I tell
them this: "I invite you to the great adventure."

It is not a question of repeating spiritually what others have done
before us, for our adventure begins beyond that. It is a question of a
new creation, entirely new, with all the unforeseen events, the risks,
the hazards it entails — a *real adventure*, whose goal is certain victory, but the road to which is unknown and must be traced out step by
step in the unexplored. Something that has never been in this present
universe and that will *never* be again in the same way. If that interests
you... well, let us embark. What will happen to you tomorrow — I
have no idea.

One must put aside all that has been foreseen, all that has been
devised, all that has been constructed, and then... set off walking into
the unknown. And — come what may! There.

                                                              10 July 1957

*

Well, it is from this change, this sudden transformation of the universal element which quite certainly is going to bring about a kind of chaos in the perceptions, that a new knowledge will emerge. This, in the most general way, is the result of the new manifestation. [...] But it is possible, in fact, that things are happening now which we are not used to watching. But it is a question of interpretation. The only thing I am sure of is what I have just told you, that the quality, the number and the nature of the possible combinations in the universe are suddenly going to change so considerably that it will probably be quite bewildering for all those who do research.

Now, we shall see.[...]

Since no two things, two combinations, two universal manifestations are ever the same, how can anything repeat itself? It can only be an appearance but is not a fact. And to fix rigid laws in this way — not that you cut yourself off from the apparent surface laws, for the mind makes many laws, and the surface very obligingly seems to comply with these laws, but it is only an appearance — but anyway this cuts you off from the creative Power of the Spirit, it cuts you off from the true Power of the Grace, for you can understand that if by your aspiration or your attitude you introduce a higher element, a new element — what we may now call a supramental element — into the existing combinations, you can suddenly change their nature, and all these so-called necessary and ineluctable laws become absurdities. That is to say that you yourself, with your conception, with your attitude and your acceptance of certain alleged principles, you yourself close the door upon the possibility of the miracle — they are not miracles when one knows how they happen, but obviously for the outer consciousness they seem miraculous. And it is you *yourself*, saying to yourself with a logic that seems quite reasonable, "Well, if I do this, that will necessarily happen, or if I don't do that, necessarily this other thing will happen", it is you yourself who close the door — it is as though you were putting an iron curtain between yourself and the free action of the Grace.

How nice it would be to imagine that the Supreme Consciousness, essentially free, presiding at the universal Manifestation, could be full of fantasy in its choice and make things follow one another not according to a logic accessible to human thought but in accordance with another kind of logic, that of the unforeseen!

Then there would no longer be any limits to the possibilities, to the unexpected, the marvellous; and one could hope for the most splendid, the most delightful things from this sovereignly free Will, playing eternally with all the elements and creating unceasingly a new world which logically would have absolutely nothing to do with the preceding one.

Don't you think it would be charming? We have had enough of the world as it is! Why not let it become at least what we think it ought to be?

And I am telling you all this in order that each one of you may put as few barriers as you can in the way of the possibilities to come.

3 October 1956

The Evolution of Humanity

"The first obscure material movement of the evolutionary Force is marked by an aeonic graduality; the movement of life-progress proceeds slowly but still with a quicker step, it is concentrated into the figure of millenniums; mind can still further compress the tardy leisureliness of Time and make long paces of the centuries; but when the conscious spirit intervenes, a supremely concentrated pace of evolutionary swiftness becomes possible."

(Sri Aurobindo)

I am reading this to you because I have been asked about the action of the Supermind, and I had compared this manifestation of the Supermind to that of the mind which, according to all modern scientific discoveries, took nearly a million years to evolve from the animal brain, the ape-brain, to the first human brain. And I told you that, consequently, one should not expect this to take place in a few months or a few years, that it would obviously take much longer. Some people, it seems, thought that I was announcing that the superman would not come before another million years! I want to correct this impression.

Sri Aurobindo has said that as the development rises in the scale of consciousness, the movement becomes more and more rapid, and that when the Spirit or the Supermind intervenes, it can go much faster.

Therefore we may hope that in a few centuries, the first supramental race will appear.

But even that is rather disconcerting for some people, for they think it contradicts what Sri Aurobindo has always promised: that the time has come for the supramental transformation to be possible.... But we must not confuse a supramental transformation with the appearing of a new race.

What Sri Aurobindo promised and what naturally interests us, we who are here now, is that the time has come when some beings among the elite of humanity, who fulfil the conditions necessary for spiritualisation, will be able to transform their bodies with the help of the supramental Force, Consciousness and Light, so as no longer to be animal-men but become supermen.

This promise Sri Aurobindo has made and he based it on the knowledge he had that the supramental Force was on the point of manifesting on the earth. In fact it had descended in him long ago, he knew it and knew what its effects were.

And now that it has manifested universally, I could say, generally, the certainty of the possibility of transformation is of course still greater. There is no longer any doubt that those who will fulfil or who now fulfil the conditions are on the way to this transformation.

The conditions Sri Aurobindo gives in detail in *The Synthesis of Yoga* and in still greater detail in his last articles on the Supramental Manifestation.* So now it is only a question of realisation.

10 October 1956

*

Sweet Mother, now that the Supermind has descended, why can't one pass from the rational mind directly to the Supermind?

Who said that one can't?

Sri Aurobindo is describing here [in *The Life Divine*] what was to be done to enter into contact with the Supermind and prepare the

---

* These articles, written by Sri Aurobindo in 1949-50, were later published as a book entitled *The Supramental Manifestation upon Earth.*

ground for its manifestation; but now that it has entered the earth-atmosphere, I don't see why a single, precise procedure should be inflicted upon it in its manifestation. If it chooses to directly illuminate an instrument which it finds suitable or ready or adaptable, I don't see why it should not do so.

And I repeat this: who has said that it cannot be otherwise? Nobody. What Sri Aurobindo has described here is quite another thing and, indeed, this is what did happen. It was the preparation necessary for the manifestation to take place. But now I don't see why or on what basis a particular process should be imposed upon the supramental action and why it should not have the freedom to choose its own means.

I think that all possibilities are predictable and that all sincere aspiration and complete consecration will have a response, and that the processes, means, transitions, transformations will be innumerable in nature — not at all that things will happen only in a particular way and not otherwise.

In fact, anything, everything that is ready to receive even a particle or a particular aspect of the supramental consciousness and light must *automatically* receive it. And the effects of this consciousness and light will be innumerable, for they will certainly be adapted to the possibilities, the capacity of each one according to the sincerity of his aspiration.

The more total the consecration and the intenser the aspiration, the more integral and intense can be the result. But the effect of the supramental action will be countless in its manifestations — multiple, innumerable, infinitely varied, not necessarily following a precise line which is the same for all. That is impossible. For it is contrary to the very nature of the supramental consciousness.

The very quality of the atmosphere has changed.

The consequences are bound to be infinitely varied, but perceptible. That is to say, it will be possible to distinguish the consequences of ordinary movements from the consequences of the supramental action, for these will have a particular nature, a special character.

13 June 1956

*

How long it will take [for the supramental presence to be felt and perceived] is difficult to foresee. It will depend a great deal on the goodwill and the receptivity of a certain number of people, for the individual always advances faster than the collectivity, and by its very nature, humanity is destined to manifest the Supermind before the rest of creation.

At the basis of this collaboration [with the supramental] there is necessarily the will to change, no longer to be what one is, for things to be no longer what they are. There are several ways of reaching it, and all the methods are good when they succeed! One may be deeply disgusted with what exists and wish ardently to come out of all this and attain something else; one may — and this is a more positive way — one may feel within oneself the touch, the approach of something positively beautiful and true, and willingly drop all the rest so that nothing may burden the journey to this new beauty and truth.

What is indispensable in every case is the *ardent* will for progress, the willing and joyful renunciation of all that hampers the advance: to throw far away from oneself all that prevents one from going forward, and to set out into the unknown with the ardent faith that this is the truth of tomorrow, *inevitable*, which must necessarily come, which nothing, nobody, no bad will, even that of Nature, can prevent from becoming a reality — perhaps of a not too distant future — a reality which is being worked out now and which those who know how to change, how not to be weighed down by old habits, will *surely* have the good fortune not only to see but to realise.

People sleep, they forget, they take life easy — they forget, forget all the time.... But if we could remember... that we are at an exceptional hour, a *unique* time, that we have this immense good fortune, this invaluable privilege of being present at the birth of a new world, we could easily get rid of everything that impedes and hinders our progress.

So, the most important thing, it seems, is to remember this fact; even when one doesn't have the tangible experience, to have the certainty of it and faith in it; to remember always, to recall it constantly, to go to sleep with this idea, to wake up with this perception; to do all that one does with this great truth as the background, as a constant support, this great truth that we are witnessing the birth of a new world.

We can participate in it, we can become this new world. And truly, when one has such a marvellous opportunity, one should be ready to give up everything for its sake.

24 July 1957

*

"A new humanity means for us the appearance, the development of a type or race of mental beings whose principle of mentality would be no longer a mind in the Ignorance seeking for knowledge but even in its knowledge bound to the Ignorance, a seeker after Light but not its natural possessor, open to the Light but not an inhabitant of the Light, not yet a perfected instrument, truthconscious and delivered out of the Ignorance. Instead, it would be possessed already of what could be called a mind of Light, a mind capable of living in the truth, capable of being truth-conscious and manifesting in its life a direct in place of an indirect knowledge. Its mentality would be an instrument of the Light and no longer of the Ignorance. At its highest it would be capable of passing into the supermind and from the new race would be recruited the race of supramental beings who would appear as the leaders of the evolution in earth-nature." (Sri Aurobindo)

This was certainly what he [Sri Aurobindo] expected of us, what he conceived of as the superman who must be the intermediate being between humanity as it is and the supramental being *created* in the supramental way, that is, no longer belonging to animality at all and delivered from all animal needs.

As we are, we have been created in the ordinary animal way, and therefore, even if we transform ourselves, there will remain something of this animal origin. The supramental being as he conceived of it, is not formed in the ordinary animal way *at all* but directly, through a process that for the moment still seems occult to us, but is a direct handling of forces and substance in such a way that the body can be a "materialisation" and not a formation according to the ordinary animal principle.

It is quite obvious that intermediate beings are necessary, that it is these intermediate beings who must find the means of creating beings of the supermind, and, undoubtedly, when Sri Aurobindo wrote this he was convinced that this is what we must do.

I think — I know — that it is now certain that we shall realise what he expects of us. It has become no longer a hope but a certainty. Only the time necessary for this realisation will be longer or shorter according to our individual effort, our concentration, our goodwill... and the *importance* we give to this fact. For the inattentive observer things may appear very much what they were before, but for one who knows how to see and is not deceived by appearances things are going well.

Let each one do his best and perhaps not many years will have to elapse before the first visible results become apparent to all.

It is for you to know whether this interests you more than everything else in the world.... There comes a moment when the body itself finds that there is *nothing in the world* which is so worth living for as this transformation; that there is nothing which can have as great an interest as this passionate interest of transformation. It is as though all the cells of the body were athirst for that Light which wants to manifest; they cry out for it, they find an intense joy in it and are *sure* of the Victory.

This is the aspiration that I am trying to communicate to you, and you will understand that everything else in life is dull, insipid, futile, worthless in comparison with that: the transformation in the Light.

25 September 1957

*

Sweet Mother, will there not be any intermediary states between man and superman?

There will probably be many.

Man and superman? You are not speaking of the new supramental race, are you? Are you really speaking of what *we* call the superman, that is, man born in the human way and trying to transform the physical being he has received by his ordinary human birth? Are there any stages? — There will certainly be countless *partial* realisations.

According to each one's capacity, the degree of transformation will differ, and it is certain that there will be a considerable number of attempts, more or less fruitful or unfruitful, before we come to something like the superman, and even those will be more or less successful attempts.

All those who strive to overcome their ordinary nature, all those who try to realise materially the deeper experience which has brought them into contact with the divine Truth, all those who, instead of turning to the Beyond or the Highest, try to realise physically, externally, the change of consciousness they have realised within themselves — all are apprentice-supermen. And there, there are countless differences in the success of their efforts. Each time we try not to be an ordinary man, not to live the ordinary life, to express in our movements, our actions and reactions the divine Truth, when we are governed by that Truth instead of being governed by the general ignorance, we are apprentice-supermen, and according to the success of our efforts, well, we are more or less able apprentices, more or less advanced on the way.

All these are stages, so... In reality, in this race to the Transformation, the question is to know which of the two will arrive first: the one who wants to transform his body in the image of the divine Truth, or the old habit of the body to go on disintegrating until it is so deformed that it can no longer continue to live in its outer integrality. It is a race between transformation and decay. For there are only two stopping-places, two things which can indicate to what extent one has succeeded: either success, that is to say, becoming a superman — then of course one can say, "Now I have reached the goal"... or else death. Till then, normally, one is "on the way".

It is one of these two things — either attaining the goal or a sudden rupture of life — which temporarily puts an end to the advance. And on the road each one has gone more or less far, but until one reaches the end one cannot say what stage one is at. It is the final step that will count. So only the one who comes a few hundred or thousand years later and looks back, will be able to say, "There was this stage and that stage, this realisation and that realisation...." That is history, it will be a historical perception of the event. Till then all of us are in the movement and the work.

How far have we gone and how far shall we go? It is better not to think too much about that, for it cripples you and you can't run well. It is better to think only about running and nothing else. That is the only way to run well. You look at where you want to go and put all your effort in the movement to go forward. How far you have gone is not your concern. I say, "This is history", it will come later. The historians of our effort will tell us — because perhaps we shall still be there — will tell us what we did, how we did it. For the moment what is necessary is to do it; this is the only thing that matters.

8 October 1958

The Supramental Boat

(The Mother reads her comments upon an experience she had on 3 February 1958:)

Between the beings of the supramental world and men, almost the same separation exists as between men and animals. Some time ago I had the experience of identification with animal life, and it is a fact that animals do not understand us; their consciousness is so constructed that we elude them almost entirely. And yet I have known pet animals — cats and dogs, but especially cats — that used to make an almost yogic effort of consciousness to reach us. But usually, when they see us as we live and act, they do not understand, they do not *see* us as we are and they suffer because of us. We are a constant enigma to them. Only a very tiny part of their consciousness has a link with us. And it is the same thing for us when we try to look at the supramental world. Only when the link of consciousness is established shall we see it — and even then only the part of our being which has undergone transformation in this way will be able to see it as it is — otherwise the two worlds would remain apart like the animal and human worlds.

The experience I had on the third of February is a proof of this. Before that I had had an individual subjective contact with the supramental world, whereas on the third of February I moved in it concretely, as concretely as I once used to walk in Paris, in a world *that exists in itself*, outside all subjectivity.

It is like a bridge being thrown between the two worlds. Here is the experience as I dictated it immediately afterwards:

(Silence)

The supramental world exists permanently and I am there permanently in a supramental body. I had the proof of this even today when my earth-consciousness went there and remained there consciously between two and three o'clock in the afternoon. Now, I know that what is lacking for the two worlds to unite in a constant and conscious relation, is an intermediate zone between the physical world as it is and the supramental world as it is. This zone remains to be built, both in the individual consciousness and the objective world, and it is being built. When I used to speak of the new world which is being created, it was of this intermediary zone that I was speaking. And similarly, when I am on this side, that is, in the field of the physical consciousness, and I see the supramental power, the supramental light and substance constantly penetrating matter, it is the construction of this zone which I see and in which I participate.

I was on a huge boat which was a symbolic representation of the place where this work is going on. This boat, as large as a city, is fully organised, and it had certainly already been functioning for some time, for its organisation was complete. It is the place where people who are destined for the supramental life are trained. These people — or at least a part of their being — had already undergone a supramental transformation, for the boat itself and everything on board was neither material nor subtle-physical nor vital nor mental — it was a supramental substance. This substance was of the most material supramental, the supramental substance which is closest to the physical world, the first to manifest. The light was a mixture of gold and red, forming a uniform substance of a luminous orange. Everything was like that — the light was like that, the people were like that — everything had that colour, although with various shades which made it possible to distinguish things from each other. The general impression was of a world without shadows; there were shades but no shadows. The atmosphere was full of joy, calm, order; everything went on regularly and in silence. And at the same time one could see all the details of an education, a training in all fields, by which the people on board were being prepared.

This immense ship had just reached the shore of the supramental world and a first group of people who were destined to become the future inhabitants of this supramental world were to disembark. Everything had been arranged for this first landing. At the wharf several very tall beings were posted. They were not human beings, they had never been men before. Nor were they the permanent inhabitants of the supramental world. They had been delegated from above and posted there to control and supervise the landing. I was in charge of the whole thing from the beginning and all the time. I had prepared all the groups myself. I stood on the boat at the head of the gangway, calling the groups one by one and sending them down to the shore. The tall beings who were posted there were inspecting, so to say, those who were landing, authorising those who were ready and sending back those who were not and who had to continue their training on board the ship. While I was there looking at everybody, the part of my consciousness which came from here became extremely interested; it wanted to see and recognise all the people, see how they had changed and check which ones were taken immediately and which ones had to remain to continue their training. After a while, as I stood there observing, I began to feel that I was being pulled back so that my body might wake up — a consciousness or a person here — and in my consciousness I protested, "No, no, not yet, not yet! I want to see the people!" I was seeing and noting everything with intense interest.... Things continued in this way until suddenly the clock here began to strike three, and this brought me back violently. There was a sensation of suddenly falling into my body. I came back with a shock because I had been called back very suddenly, but with all my memory. I remained quiet, without moving, until I could recollect the whole experience and keep it.

On the boat the nature of objects was not the one we know on earth; for instance, clothes were not made of cloth and what looked like cloth was not manufactured: it formed a part of the body, it was made of the same substance which took different forms. It had a kind of plasticity. When a change had to be made, it took place, not by any artificial and external means but by an inner operation, an operation of consciousness which gave form or appearance to the substance.

Life created its own forms. There was *one single* substance in everything; it changed the quality of its vibration according to need and
use.

Those who were sent back for fresh training were not of a uniform colour, it was as if their body had greyish, opaque patches of a
substance resembling earthly substance; they were dull, as if they had
not been entirely permeated with light, not transformed. They were
not like that everywhere, only in places.

The tall beings on the shore were not of the same colour, at least
they did not have that orange tint; they were paler, more transparent.
Except for one part of their body, one could only see the outline of
their form. They were very tall, they seemed not to have any bones
and could take any form according to their need. Only from the waist
down had they a permanent density, which was not perceptible in the
rest of their body. Their colour was much lighter, with very little red,
it was more golden or even white. The parts of whitish light were
translucent; they were not positively transparent but less dense, more
subtle than the orange substance.

When I was called back and while I was saying "Not yet", each
time I had a brief glimpse of myself, that is, of my form in the supramental world. I was a mixture of the tall beings and the beings aboard
the ship. My upper part, particularly the head, was only a silhouette
whose contents were white with an orange fringe. Going down towards the feet, the colour became more like that of the people on the
boat, that is, orange; going upwards, it was more translucent and white
and the red grew less. The head was only a silhouette with a sun
shining within it; rays of light came from it which were the action of
the will.

As for the people I saw on board the ship, I recognised them all.
Some were from here, from the Ashram, some came from elsewhere,
but I know them too. I saw everybody but as I knew that I would not
remember them all when I returned, I decided not to give any names.
Besides, it is not necessary. Three or four faces were very clearly
visible, and when I saw them, I understood the feeling I had here on
earth when looking into their eyes: there was such an extraordinary
joy.... People were mostly young, there were very few children and
they were about fourteen or fifteen, certainly not below ten or twelve

— I did not remain long enough to see all the details. There weren't any very old people, apart from a few exceptions. Most of the people who went ashore were middle-aged, except a few. Already, before this experience, some individual cases had been examined several times at a place where people capable of being supramentalised were examined; I had a few surprises and noted them; I even told some people about it. But the ones whom I put ashore today, I saw very distinctly; they were middle-aged, neither young children nor old people, apart from a few rare exceptions, and that corresponded fairly well with what I expected. I decided not to say anything, not to give any names. As I did not remain until the end, it was not possible for me to get an exact picture; the picture was not absolutely clear or complete. I do not want to say things to some and not to others.

What I can say is that the point of view, the judgment, was based *exclusively* on the substance of which the people were made, that is, whether they belonged completely to the supramental world, whether they were made of that very special substance. The standpoint taken is neither moral nor psychological. It is probable that the substance their bodies were made of was the result of an inner law or inner movement which at that time was not in question. At least it is quite clear that the values are different.

When I came back, simultaneously with the recollection of the experience I knew that the supramental world is permanent, that my presence there is permanent, and that only a missing link was necessary for the connection to be made in the consciousness and the substance, and it is this link which is now being forged. I had the impression — an impression which remained for quite a long time, almost a whole day — of an extreme relativity — no, not exactly that: the impression that the relation between this world and the other completely changed the standpoint from which things should be evaluated or appraised. This standpoint had nothing mental about it and it gave a strange inner feeling that lots of things we consider good or bad are not really so. It was very clear that everything depended on the capacity of things, on their aptitude in expressing the supramental world or being in relation with it. It was so completely different, sometimes even altogether contrary to our ordinary appraisal. I recollect one little thing which we usually consider to be bad; how strange it was to see that in truth it was something excellent! And other things we consider to be important have in fact absolutely no importance at all: whether a thing is like this or like that is not at all important. What is very obvious is that our appraisal of what is divine or undivine is not right. I even laughed to see certain things.... Our usual feeling of what is anti-divine seems artificial, seems based on something that's not true, not living — besides, what we call life here did not seem living to me compared with that world — anyway, this feeling should be founded on our relation between the two worlds and on how things make the relation between them easier or more difficult. This would make a great difference in our appraisal of what brings us nearer to the Divine or what separates us from Him. In people too I saw that what helps them to become supramental or hinders them from it, is very different from what our usual moral notions imagine. I felt how... ridiculous we are.

19 February 1958

CHAPTER 20

The Present Situation

The Progress of Humanity

In spite of all adverse appearances, it may well be that earth has been
preparing for a certain realisation by steps and stages. There has been
a change in civilisation and a change in nature. If it is not apparent, it
is because we see from an external point of view and because matter
and its difficulties have never been seriously or thoroughly dealt with
up till now. Still internally there has been a progress; in the inner
consciousness there have been descents of the Light. But as to any
realisation in matter, it is difficult to say anything, because we do not
exactly know what might have happened there.

There have been in the distant past great and beautiful civilisations, perhaps as advanced materially as ours. Looked at from a certain standpoint the most modern might seem to be only a repetition of
the most ancient cultures, and yet one cannot say that there has been
no progress anywhere. An inner progress at least has been achieved
and a greater readiness to respond to the higher consciousness has
been born into the material parts. It has been necessary to do over and
over again the same things, because what was attempted was never
sufficiently done; but each time it has come nearer to being adequately
done. When we practise an exercise over and over again we seem to
be only repeating the same thing always, but still the accumulative
result is some effective change.

The mistake is to look at these things through the dimensions of
the human consciousness, for so seen these deep and vast movements
seem inexplicable. It is dangerous to try to explain or understand them
with the limited mental intelligence. That is the reason why philosophy has always failed to unveil the secret of things; it is because it has
tried to fit the universe into the size of the human mind.

5 May 1929

*

Mental capacity seems to have grown, mental power seems to have developed, men seem to be much more capable of playing with ideas, of having mental command over all principles, but at the same time they have lost the simple and healthy candour of people who lived closer to Nature and knew less how to play with ideas. Thus humanity as a whole seems to have reached a very dangerous turning-point. Those who are trying to find a solution to the general corruption preach a return to the simplicity of yore, but of course that is quite impossible: you cannot go back.

We must go farther on, we must advance, climb greater heights and go beyond the arid search for pleasure and personal welfare, not through fear of punishment, even punishment after death, but through the development of a new sense of beauty, a thirst for truth and light, through understanding that it is only by widening yourself, illumining yourself, setting yourself ablaze with the ardour for progress, that you can find both integral peace and enduring happiness.

One must rise up and widen — rise up... and widen.

18 April 1958

*

After all, in spite of all appearances, humanity progresses; it has progressed particularly in the mind. There are things that no longer need to be said.... Or else one must go to countries that are at a very primitive stage, and even so... ideas have spread everywhere, the mental light has spread everywhere and in the most unexpected places one finds instances of receptivity and understanding.

One really has the impression that during the last century a light came and spread upon the earth with the result that certain ideas, which were once idea-forces, new ideas with the power to stir up the consciousness in men, have lost their relevance, they are now old. A new light is at work.

In practice, the progress is not very great, even in some respects perhaps there has been a retrogression, but in the mind, in the understanding, in the intellectual vision of things, there has truly been a great change.

It seems we are marching on the way at an accelerated pace and these things which used to be of the first importance are becoming almost commonplace in the light of new discoveries. Life as it is is bad, disorder is everywhere, suffering is everywhere, confusion is everywhere, chaos is everywhere, ignorance is everywhere — we all know it, don't we? It seems so hackneyed.

But that one can emerge from it through a total realisation, a total transformation, through a new light that will establish order and harmony in things, is a message of hope that has to be given. This is the true, the dynamic message.

A new life must be built.

Then all these difficulties that seemed so unsurmountable — oh! they fall of themselves.

When you can live in light and joy, are you going to cling to shadow and suffering?

27 June 1958

The Possibility of Catastrophe

You said that if there were a third world war, it would be the end of the present civilisation. Would the terrestrial condition be affected favourably by it or adversely?

Listen. Would you ask whether a fatal illness is favourable to health or not? It is exactly that. A civilisation, whatever it may be, is the result of very long efforts to become conscious of oneself, of Nature, and to master this Nature and draw the best possible advantage from it. We were saying a while ago that the training of the physical being consists in preparing an instrument so that the Divine may manifest Himself. A civilisation prepares an instrument so that the Divine may manifest in that instrument. The more slowly, carefully, minutely the civilisation is worked out, and succeeds in conquering the laws of Nature, the more favourable is the instrument to the manifestation of the Divine. That is why we also have this idea of the prolongation of life, it is to be able to perfect the instrument so as to manifest the divine Force which wants to manifest. Otherwise, it would evidently be much easier, as soon as the body became a little ill or a little old or incapable of reacting as it did when young, to do what one does with an old torn dress — one throws it away and gets another. Unfortunately, it is not like that. All the fruit of the work, all the accumulated effort to become conscious is lost.

If, for instance, this civilisation we have built, which in a way has so considerably mastered the forces of Nature, which has succeeded in understanding laws of an altogether unique order and has accumulated so many experiences of all kinds to reach self-understanding and self-expression, if all this disappeared, it would be necessary, naturally, to begin all over again. And then, for a new-born child, how many years of slow and insipid education are needed for its brain to be ready to express even a simple general idea, for its movements to be conscious instead of being absolutely unconscious, how many years! For a civilisation, how many years would be necessary simply to get back all that is lost? There have been many civilisations on the earth, there are scientists trying to rediscover what has been, but nobody can say with certitude exactly what was there: the major part of these civilisations is completely lost (I am speaking of civilisations preceding this one which for us is historical). Well, if thousands of years are yet needed to begin another, obviously.... In any case, for our external human consciousness, it is a loss of time.

But we are told that the Work to be done, the promised Realisation is going to take place now. It is going to take place now because the framework of this civilisation seems to be favourable as a platform or a base for building up. But if this civilisation is destroyed, upon what are we going to build? First a foundation platform must be made in order to be able to build. If five or ten thousand years are still needed to make this platform, this proves that it is not now that things will be done — they will be done, that is well understood, they will be done, but... How many lives have you all had? What do you remember of your past lives? What is the good of all the efforts you have made in your past lives to perfect yourselves, to try to understand yourselves, to master yourselves a little, simply to make use of the instrument which has been given to you? What remains to you of all that? Will you tell me? Who here can tell me that he is consciously profiting by the experiences of his past lives — unconsciously there is something which remains but not much — but consciously?... No one will answer?

No, precisely, one has the impression that after having lived so long, one is only beginning to know a very little.

Yes, exactly, it is just like that. This is because the farther one goes, the more does one realise that there is everything to understand and everything to learn. And consequently, if one has behind him some sixty years, it is nothing. One would like to have hundreds and hundreds of years before one to be able to do the work. It is like that, you are all little children, you see, so the years seem to you long, because you have not lived much; but you will see, the more one advances, the more does one realise that there is a long road in front, long, very long, and one would not like to have to begin all over again, for it is so much more time lost.

17 April 1951

*

There is an idea in the earth-atmosphere — an idea which might be called preposterous, but unhappily it is much worse than preposterous, it is catastrophic — the idea that if there were a great upheaval, perhaps it would be better afterwards.... One is so jammed between prohibitions, impossibilities, interdictions, rules, the complications of every second, that one feels stifled and really gets the admirable idea that if everything were demolished perhaps it would be better afterwards!... It is in the air. And all the governments have put themselves in such impossible conditions; they have become so tied up that it seems to them they will have to break everything to be able to move forward.... (*Silence*) This is unfortunately a little more than a possibility, it is a *very* serious threat. And it is not quite certain that life will not be made still more impossible because one feels incapable of emerging from the chaos — the chaos of complications — in which humanity has put itself. It is like the shadow — but unfortunately a very active shadow — of the new hope which has sprung up in the human consciousness, a hope and a need for something more harmonious; and the need becomes so much more acute as life, as it is at present organised, becomes more and more contrary to it. The two opposites are facing each other with such intensity that one can expect something like an explosion....

(*Silence*)

This is the condition of the earth, and it is not very bright. But for us one possibility remains — I have spoken about it to you several times already — even if, outside, things are deteriorating completely and the catastrophe cannot possibly be avoided, there remains for us, I mean those for whom the supramental life is not a vain dream, those who have faith in its reality and the aspiration to realise it — I don't necessarily mean those who have gathered here in Pondicherry, in the Ashram, but those who have as a link between them the knowledge Sri Aurobindo has given and the will to live according to that knowledge — there remains for them the possibility of intensifying their aspiration, their will, their effort, to gather their energies together and shorten the time for the realisation. There remains for them the possibility of working this miracle — individually and to a small extent collectively — of conquering space, duration, the time needed for this realisation; of replacing time by intensity of effort and going fast enough and far enough in the realisation to liberate themselves from the consequences of the present condition of the world; of making such a concentration of force, strength, light, truth, that by this very realisation they can be above these consequences and secure against them, enjoy the protection bestowed by the Light and Truth, by Purity — the divine Purity through the inner transformation — and that the storm may pass over the world without being able to destroy this great hope of the near future; that the tempest may not sweep away this beginning of realisation.

Instead of falling asleep in an easy quietude and letting things happen according to their own rhythm, if one strains to the utmost one's will, ardour, aspiration and springs up into the light, then one can hold one's head higher; one can have, in a higher region of consciousness, enough room to live, to breathe, to grow and develop above the passing cyclone.

This is possible. In a very small way, this was already done during the last war, when Sri Aurobindo was here. It can be done again. But one must want it and each one must do his own work as sincerely and completely as he can.

7 August 1957

*

In present-day politics can we say in which camp [divine or anti-divine]...

Unfortunately, things become completely clear-cut in this way — to the extent that one can say these are for and these against — only when there is that frightful materialisation of a war, because at that moment it is obvious that the victory of one side is preferable to the victory of the other, not that these are better than the others — this is understood, that from the divine point of view all are equal in worth, it's the same thing — but because the consequences of the victory are such that the victory of one side is better than that of another. But this is when the thing becomes absolutely brutal, a reciprocal extermination. Otherwise, to tell the real truth, the divine Force acts for its work everywhere, in men's errors as in their goodwill, through ill-will as through favourable things. There is nothing that's not mixed; nowhere is there something which could be said to be truly a pure instrument of the Divine, and nowhere is there an absolute impossibility of the Divine's using a man or action to go forward on the path. So, as long as things are uncertain, the Divine works everywhere almost equally.

If men go in for such a great madness, then it is different. But it is truly a "great madness", in the sense that it precipitates a whole mass of individuals and wills into an activity which leads straight to destruction — their own destruction. I am not speaking of bombs and the destruction of a city or a people, I am speaking of destruction as it is spoken about in the Gita, you see, when it is said that the Asura goes to his own destruction. That's what happens, and this is a very great misfortune, because it is always better to be able to save, illumine, transform, than to have to destroy brutally. And it is this terrible choice of the war which is its true horror; it's that it materialises the conflict so brutally and totally that some elements which could have been saved during peace are, because of war, necessarily destroyed — and not only men and things but forces, the conscience of beings.

14 September 1955

*

One thing seems obvious, humanity has reached a certain state of general tension — tension in effort, in action, even in daily life —

with such an excessive hyperactivity, so widespread a trepidation, that mankind as a whole seems to have come to a point where it must either break through the resistance and emerge into a new consciousness or else fall back into an abyss of darkness and inertia.

This tension is so complete and so widespread that something obviously has to break. It cannot go on in this way. We may take it as a sure sign of the infusion into matter of a new principle of force, consciousness, power, which by its very pressure is producing this acute state. Outwardly, we could expect the old methods used by Nature when she wants to bring about an upheaval; but there is a new characteristic, which of course is only visible in an elite, but even this elite is fairly widespread — it is not localised at one point, at one place in the world; we find traces of it in all countries, all over the world: the will to find a new, higher, progressive solution, an effort to rise towards a vaster, more comprehensive perfection.

Certain ideas of a more general nature, of a wider, perhaps more "collective" kind, are being worked out and are acting in the world. And both things go together: a possibility of a greater and more total destruction, a reckless inventiveness which increases the possibility of catastrophe, a castastrophe which would be on a far greater scale than it has ever been; and, at the same time, the birth or rather the manifestation of much higher and more comprehensive ideas and acts of will which, when they are heard, will bring a wider, vaster, more complete, more perfect remedy than before.

This struggle, this conflict between the constructive forces of the ascending evolution of a more and more perfect and divine realisation, and the more and more destructive, powerfully destructive forces — forces that are mad beyond all control — is more and more obvious, marked, visible, and it is a kind of race or struggle as to which will reach the goal first. It would seem that all the adverse, anti-divine forces, the forces of the vital world, have descended on the earth, are making use of it as their field of action, and that at the same time a new, higher, more powerful spiritual force has also descended on earth to bring it a new life. This makes the struggle more acute, more violent, more visible, but it seems also more definitive, and that is why we can hope to reach an early solution.

There was a time, not so long ago, when the spiritual aspiration of man was turned towards a silent, inactive peace, detached from all worldly things, a flight from life, precisely to avoid battle, to rise above the struggle, escape all effort; it was a spiritual peace in which, along with the cessation of all tension, struggle, effort, there ceased also suffering in all its forms, and this was considered to be the true and only expression of a spiritual and divine life. It was considered to be the divine grace, the divine help, the divine intervention. And even now, in this age of anguish, tension, hypertension, this sovereign peace is the best received aid of all, the most welcome, the solace people ask and hope for. For many it is still the true sign of a divine intervention, of divine grace.

In fact, no matter what one wants to realise, one must begin by establishing this perfect and immutable peace; it is the basis from which one must work; but unless one is dreaming of an exclusive, personal and egoistic liberation, one cannot stop there. There is another aspect of the divine grace, the aspect of progress which will be victorious over all obstacles, the aspect which will propel humanity to a new realisation, which will open the doors of a new world and make it possible not only for a chosen few to benefit by the divine realisation but for their influence, their example, their power to bring to the rest of mankind new and better conditions.

This opens up roads of realisation into the future, possibilities which are already foreseen, when an entire part of humanity, the one which has opened consciously or unconsciously to the new forces, is lifted up, as it were, into a higher, more harmonious, more perfect life.... Even if individual transformation is not always permissible or possible, there will be a kind of general uplifting, a harmonisation of the whole, which will make it possible for a new order, a new harmony to be established and for the anguish of the present disorder and struggle to disappear and be replaced by an order which will allow a harmonious functioning of the whole.

There will be other consequences which will tend to eliminate in an opposite way what the intervention of the mind in life has created, the perversions, the ugliness, the whole mass of distortions which have increased suffering, misery, moral poverty, an entire area of sordid and repulsive misery which makes a whole part of human life into something so frightful. That must disappear. This is what makes humanity in so many ways infinitely worse than animal life in its simplicity and the natural spontaneity and harmony that it has in spite of everything. Suffering in animals is never so miserable and sordid as it is in an entire section of humanity which has been perverted by the use of a mentality exclusively at the service of egoistic needs.

We must rise above, spring up into Light and Harmony or fall back, down into the simplicity of a healthy unperverted animal life.

(When this talk was first published in 1958, the Mother added the following note on the lifting up of an entire part of humanity by the action of the new forces:)

But those who cannot be lifted up, those who refuse to progress, will automatically lose the use of the mental consciousness and will fall back to a sub-human level.

I shall tell you about an experience I had which will help you to understand better. It was shortly after the supramental experience of the third of February, and I was still in the state in which things of the physical world seemed so far off, so absurd. A group of visitors had asked permission to come to me and one evening they came to the Playground. They were rich people, that is, they had more money than they needed to live on. Among them there was a woman in a sari; she was very fat, her sari was arranged so as to hide her body. As she was bending down to receive my blessings, one corner of the sari came open, uncovering a part of her body, a naked belly — an enormous one. I felt a real shock.... There are corpulent people who have nothing repugnant about them, but I suddenly saw the perversion, the rottenness that this belly concealed, it was like a huge abscess, expressing greed, vice, depraved taste, sordid desire, which finds its satisfaction as no animal would, in grossness and especially in perversity. I saw the perversion of a depraved mind at the service of the lowest appetites. Then, all of a sudden, something sprang up from me, a prayer, like a Veda: "O Lord, this is what must disappear!"

One understands very well that physical misery, the unequal distribution of the goods of this world could be changed, one can imagine economic and social solutions which could remedy this, but it is that misery, the mental misery, the vital perversion, it is that which cannot change, doesn't want to change. And those who belong to this type of humanity are condemned in advance to disintegration.

That is the meaning of original sin: the perversion which began with the mind.

That part of humanity, of human consciousness, which is capable of uniting with the supermind and liberating itself, will be completely transformed — it is advancing towards a future reality which is not yet expressed in its outer form; the part which is closest to Nature, to animal simplicity, will be reabsorbed into Nature and thoroughly assimilated. But the corrupted part of human consciousness which allows perversion through its misuse of the mind will be abolished.

This type of humanity is part of an unfruitful attempt — which must be eliminated — just as there have been other abortive species which have disappeared in the course of universal history.

Certain prophets in the past have had this apocalyptic vision but, as usual, things were mixed, and they did not have together with their vision of the apocalypse the vision of the supramental world which will come to raise up the part of humanity which consents and to transform this physical world. So, to give hope to those who have been born into it, into this perverted part of human consciousness, they have taught redemption through faith: those who have faith in the sacrifice of the Divine in Matter will be automatically saved, in another world — by faith alone, without understanding, without intelligence. They have not seen the supramental world nor that the great Sacrifice of the Divine in Matter is the sacrifice of involution which must culminate in the total revelation of the Divine in Matter itself.

19 March 1958

The Possibility of Perfection

"Death is the question Nature puts continually to Life and her reminder to it that it has not yet found itself. If there were no siege of death, the creature would be bound forever in the form of an imperfect living. Pursued by death he awakes to the idea of perfect life and seeks out its means and its possibility."

(Sri Aurobindo)

There seems to be matter enough here for us not to need to go any further. This is a question which every person whose consciousness is awakened a little has asked himself at least once in his life. There is in the depths of the being such a need to perpetuate, to prolong, to develop life, that the moment one has a first contact with death, which, although it may be quite an accidental contact, is yet inevitable, there is a sort of recoil in the being.

In persons who are sensitive, it produces horror; in others, indignation. There is a tendency to ask oneself: "What is this monstrous farce in which one takes part without wanting to, without understanding it? Why are we born, if it is only to die? Why all this effort for development, progress, the flowering of the faculties, if it is to come to a diminution ending in decline and disintegration?... " Some feel a revolt in them, others less strong feel despair and always this question arises: "If there is a conscious Will behind all that, this Will seems to be monstrous."

But here Sri Aurobindo tells us that this was an indispensable means of awakening in the consciousness of matter the need for perfection, the necessity of progress, that without this catastrophe, all beings would have been satisfied with the condition they were in — perhaps.... This is not certain.

But then, we have to take things as they are and tell ourselves that we must find the way out of it all.

The fact is that everything is in a state of perpetual progressive development, that is, the whole creation, the whole universe is advancing towards a perfection which seems to recede as one goes forward towards it, for what seemed a perfection at a certain moment is no longer perfect after a time. The most subtle states of being in the consciousness follow this progression even as it is going on, and the higher up the scale one goes, the more closely does the rhythm of the advance resemble the rhythm of the universal development, and approach the rhythm of the divine development; but the material world is rigid by nature, transformation is slow, very slow, there, almost imperceptible for the measurement of time as human consciousness perceives it... and so there is a constant disequilibrium between the inner and outer movement, and this lack of balance, this incapacity of the outer forms to follow the movement of the inner progress brings about the necessity of decomposition and the change of forms. But if, into this matter, one could infuse enough consciousness to obtain the same rhythm, if matter could become plastic enough to follow the inner progression, this rupture of balance would not occur, and death would no longer be necessary.

So, according to what Sri Aurobindo tells us, Nature has found this rather radical means to awaken in the material consciousness the necessary aspiration and plasticity.

It is obvious that the most dominant characteristic of matter is inertia, and that, if there were not this violence, perhaps the individual consciousness would be so inert that rather than change it would accept to live in a perpetual imperfection.... That is possible. Anyway, this is how things are made, and for us who know a little more, there is only one thing that remains to be done, it is to change all this, as far as we have the means, by calling the Force, the Consciousness, the new Power which is capable of infusing into material substance the vibration which can transform it, make it plastic, supple, progressive.

Obviously the greatest obstacle is the attachment to things as they are; but even Nature as a whole finds that those who have the deeper knowledge want to go too fast: she likes her meanderings, she likes her successive attempts, her failures, her fresh beginnings, her new inventions; she likes the fantasy of the path, the unexpectedness of the experience; one could almost say that for her the longer it takes, the more enjoyable it is.

But even of the best games one tires. There comes a time when one needs to change them and one could dream of a game in which it would no longer be necessary to destroy in order to progress, where the zeal for progress would be enough to find new means, new expressions, where the *élan* would be ardent enough to overcome inertia, lassitude, lack of understanding, fatigue, indifference.

Why does this body, as soon as some progress has been made, feel the need to sit down? It is tired. It says, "Oh! you must wait. I must be given time to rest." This is what leads it to death. If it felt within itself that ardour to do always better, become more transparent, more beautiful, more luminous, eternally young, one could escape from this macabre joke of Nature.

For her this is of no importance. She sees the whole, she sees the totality; she sees that nothing is lost, that it is only recombining quantities, numberless minute elements, without any importance, which are put back into a pot and mixed well — and something new comes out of it. But that game is not amusing for everybody. And if in one's consciousness one could be as vast as she, more powerful than she, why shouldn't one do the same thing in a better way?

This is the problem which confronts us now. With the addition, the new help of this Force which has descended, which is manifesting, working, why shouldn't one take in hand this tremendous game and make it more beautiful, more harmonious, more true?

It only needs brains powerful enough to receive this Force and formulate the possible course of action. There must be conscious beings powerful enough to convince Nature that there are other methods than hers.... This looks like madness, but all new things have always seemed like madness before they became realities.

The hour has come for this madness to be realised. And since we are all here for reasons that are perhaps unknown to most of you, but are still very conscious reasons, we may set ourselves to fulfil that madness — at least it will be worthwhile living it.

6 February 1957

*

"*Wherefore he [God] selected or made such a material, when he had all infinite possibility to choose from? Because of his divine Idea which saw before it not only beauty and sweetness and purity, but also force and will and greatness. Despise not force, nor hate it for the ugliness of some of its faces, nor think that love only is God. All perfect perfection must have something in it of the stuff of the hero and even of the Titan. But the greatest force is born out of the greatest difficulty.*" (Sri Aurobindo)

After all, the whole problem is to know whether humanity has reached the state of pure gold or whether it still needs to be tested in the crucible.

One thing is evident, humanity has not become pure gold; that is visible and certain.

But something has happened in the world's history which allows us to hope that a selected few in humanity, a small number of beings, perhaps, are ready to be transformed into pure gold and that they will be able to manifest strength without violence, heroism without destruction and courage without catastrophe.

But in the very next paragraph Sri Aurobindo gives the answer: "If man could once consent to be spiritualised." If only the individual could *consent* to be spiritualised... could consent.*

Something in him asks for it, aspires, and all the rest refuses, wants to continue to be what it is: the mixed ore which needs to be cast into the furnace.

At the moment we are at a decisive turning-point in the history of the earth, once again. From every side I am asked, "What is going to happen?" Everywhere there is anguish, expectation, fear. "What is going to happen?..." There is only one reply: "If only man could consent to be spiritualised."

And perhaps it would be enough if some individuals became pure gold, for this would be enough to change the course of events.... We are faced with this necessity in a very urgent way.

This courage, this heroism which the Divine wants of us, why not use it to fight against one's own difficulties, one's own imperfections, one's own obscurities? Why not heroically face the furnace of inner purification so that it does not become necessary to pass once more through one of those terrible, gigantic destructions which plunge an entire civilisation into darkness?

This is the problem before us. It is for each one to solve it in his own way.

This evening I am answering the questions I have been asked, and my reply is that of Sri Aurobindo: If man could once consent to be spiritualised....

And I add: Time presses... from the human point of view.

27 March 1957

---

* "All would change if man could once consent to be spiritualised; but his nature, mental and vital and physical, is rebellious to the higher law. He loves his imperfection."

The Mother

Life-Sketch of the Mother

The Mother was born Mirra Alfassa on 21 February 1878 in Paris. A student at the Académie Julian, she became an accomplished artist. Gifted from an early age with a capacity for spiritual and occult experience, she went to Tlemçen, Algeria, in 1906 and 1907 to study occultism with the adepts Max Theon and his wife. Between 1911 and 1913 she gave a number of talks to various groups of seekers in Paris.

In 1914 the Mother voyaged to Pondicherry, South India, to meet the Indian revolutionary and mystic Sri Aurobindo. After a stay of eleven months, she was obliged by the outbreak of the First World War to return to France. A year later she went to Japan, where she remained for four years. In April 1920 the Mother rejoined Sri Aurobindo in Pondicherry. Six years later, when the Sri Aurobindo Ashram was founded, Sri Aurobindo entrusted its material and spiritual charge to her. Under her guidance the Ashram grew into a large, many-faceted spiritual community. She also established a school, the Sri Aurobindo International Centre of Education, in 1952, and an international township, Auroville, in 1968. The Mother passed away on 17 November 1973.

Sri Aurobindo

Life-Sketch of Sri Aurobindo

Sri Aurobindo was born in Kolkata on 15 August 1872. At the age of seven he was taken to England for his education. There he studied at St. Paul's School, London, and at King's College, Cambridge. Returning to India in 1893, he worked for the next thirteen years in the Princely State of Baroda (Vadodara) in the service of the Maharaja and as a professor in the State's college.

In 1906 Sri Aurobindo quit his post in Baroda and went to Kolkata, where he became one of the leaders of the Indian national movement. As editor of the newspaper *Bande Mataram*, he boldly put forward the idea of complete independence from Britain. Arrested three times for sedition or treason, he was released each time for lack of evidence.

Sri Aurobindo began the practice of Yoga in 1905. Within a few years he achieved several fundamental spiritual realisations. In 1910 he withdrew from politics and went to Pondicherry in French India in order to concentrate on his inner life and work. During his forty years there, he developed a new spiritual path, the Integral Yoga, whose ultimate aim is the transformation of life by the power of a supramental consciousness. In 1926, with the help of the Mother, he founded the Sri Aurobindo Ashram. His vision of life is presented in numerous works of prose and poetry, among which the best known are *The Life Divine*, *The Synthesis of Yoga* and *Savitri*. Sri Aurobindo passed away on 5 December 1950.

Note on the Texts

Publication History

This compilation of Georges Van Vrekhem was first brought out in 1997 in a Dutch translation entitled *Alle leven is yoga: De integral visie de Moeder*, published by Uitgeverij Ankh-Hermes bv, Deventer, Netherlands. The present English version is published by the Sri Aurobindo Ashram, Pondicherry.

Scope of Selection of Texts

The texts making up this compilation have been taken from Volumes 3 to 9 of the Collected Works of the Mother, which together comprise nearly 3,000 pages of material. The book includes selections from the Mother's early conversations (1929-31) and her conversations at the Ashram playground (1950-58). It does not include other conversations published in the Collected Works: the oral commentaries on Sri Aurobindo's *Thoughts and Aphorisms* in Volume 10, the *Agenda* conversations published during the Mother's lifetime in Volume 11, the talks on education in Volume 12, the talks on Auroville in Volume 13, and the miscellaneous talks in Volume 15.

Original Language of the Texts

The conversations from 1929 to 1931 were in English; those from 1950 to 1958 were in French. The French texts comprise about eighty-five per cent of the material. Thus most of the texts in this book are English translations of talks originally given in French.

References to the Texts

This book has been compiled from the following volumes of the Collected Works of the Mother, published by the Sri Aurobindo Ashram, Pondicherry:

Volume	Title	Year
3	*Questions and Answers [1929-31]*	1977
4	*Questions and Answers 1950-51*	1977
5	*Questions and Answers 1953*	1976
6	*Questions and Answers 1954*	1979
7	*Questions and Answers 1955*	1979
8	*Questions and Answers 1956*	1977
9	*Questions and Answers 1957-58*	1977

The references below are given in an abbreviated form. The page number of this book appears on the left; on the right come the volume and page number(s) of the Collected Works text. For example:

1   6:25-27.   This abbreviation indicates that the reference on page one of this book may be found in Collected Works Volume 6 on pages 25-27.

The references are:

Chapter 1
The Divine and
His Creation

1	6: 25-27	38	8: 231-34	67	4: 327-29
3	7: 248	40	7: 193-94	68	5: 81-82
3	7: 244	41	8: 280-81	70	7: 236-37
4	4: 370-72	42	4: 134-35	71	8: 344-46
6	8: 1-2	43	5: 40-41	73	9: 55
6	8: 75-79	44	5: 82	73	4: 240-43
8	8: 51-56	44	5: 322-23	76	5: 275-76
11	9: 429-32	45	7: 247-48	78	4: 110-12
13	4: 160-64	46	4: 243-46	79	4: 124
17	9: 175-76	48	6: 135-36		
18	9: 321-23	49	4: 392-95		

20	5: 308-13	51	5: 388-89	**Chapter 3**
25	7: 238-39	52	9: 332-34	**The Human Species**
26	5: 372-79			**in Evolution**
30	9: 205-07	**Chapter 2**		81	9: 213-17
31	5: 71-74	**The Universe**		84	7: 425-27
34	5: 147-48	55	7: 208-09	85	9: 236-38
35	5: 162-65	56	4: 217-24	87	9: 339-40
		62	7: 219-20	88	9: 303-05
		64	8: 98-99	91	9: 232-35
		65	3: 58-60	93	9: 292-94
				94	9: 245-46

Glossary

The philosophical and psychological terms in this glossary are defined almost entirely in the words of Sri Aurobindo.

Absolute, the — the supreme reality of that transcendent Being which we call God. Indian thought calls it Brahman, European thought the Absolute because it is a self-existent which is absolved of all bondage to relativities.

adhara — support, receptacle; the mental-vital-physical system as a vessel of the spiritual consciousness.

adverse forces — *see* hostile forces

Agni — the godhead of fire; the fire of aspiration, purification, transformation.

Ananda — delight, beatitude, bliss.

Ashram — a spiritual community; the house or houses of a Teacher or Master of spiritual philosophy in which he receives and lodges those who come to him for the teaching and practice.

Asura — a hostile, anti-divine being, in revolt against the Divine, against the Light and the Truth.

Avatar — a divine incarnation, one in whom the divine consciousness has descended into human birth for a great world-work. The word avatara means a descent: it is the coming down of the Divine below the line which divides the divine from the human world or status.

Brahma — the creator Deity; in the Veda the Power of the Divine which creates the worlds by the Word.

Brahman — the Reality, the Eternal, the Infinite, the Absolute, the Supreme Being, the One beside whom there is nothing else existent.

Brahmin — the priest of knowledge, the man of learning and thought and knowledge.

Chit — pure consciousness, pure awareness; the essential consciousness of the Spirit.

Conscious Force — the Power of the Divine Mother which dominates all existence and builds the worlds; the universal Energy that is the Power of the Cosmic Spirit working out the cosmic and individual truth of things.

consciousness — the self-aware force of existence. The essence of consciousness is the power to be aware of itself and its objects; but it is not only power of awareness of self and things, it is or has a dynamic and creative energy.

Cosmic Spirit — the universal aspect of the Divine, the one Self inhabiting the universe and containing everything in it.

creation, the — the manifestation; the self-projection of Brahman into the conditions of Space and Time.

dharma — the truth or law of our being; the right law of individual and social life.

Divine, the — the Supreme Being from which all comes and in which all lives. In its supreme Truth, the Divine is absolute and infinite peace, consciousness, existence, power and delight.

Divine Consciousness — the spiritual consciousness to which the Divine alone exists, because all is the Divine. Force, Light, Knowledge and Ananda together make up the higher, spiritual or Divine Consciousness.

ego — the separative sense of individuality which makes each being conceive of itself as an independent personality. Ego implies the identification of one's existence with the outer mental, vital and physical self.

evolution — the progressive unfolding of Spirit out of the density of material consciousness; the method by which the One Being and Consciousness, involved here in Matter, liberates itself from matter into life, from life into mind, from mind into the Spirit.

Force, the — the Divine Force, the one Energy that alone exists and alone makes universal or individual action possible, for this Force is the Divine itself in the body of its power. In the individual, it is a Force for purification, illumination, transformation.

Gita, the — short form of Bhagavad Gita, "the Song of the Blessed Lord", being the spiritual teachings of Sri Krishna spoken to Arjuna on the battlefield of Kurukshetra; it occurs as an episode in the Mahabharata.

gnostic — of the nature of Gnosis, a supreme totally self-aware and all-aware Intelligence having the truth-vision of things.

God — the Absolute, the Spirit, the Self spaceless and timeless, the Self manifest in the Cosmos and Lord of Nature. God is the All and that which transcends the All.

Gods, the — in origin and essence the Gods are permanent Emanations of the Divine put forth from the Supreme; in their cosmic action they are Powers and Personalities of the Divine each with its independent cosmic standing, function and work in the universe.

Grace, the — the Divine Grace, the help of a higher Divine Force other than the force of Karma, which can lift the sadhak beyond the present possibilities of his nature.

Guru — spiritual teacher; the Guide in the Yoga; one who has realised the Truth and himself possesses and is able to communicate the light, the experience.

higher consciousness — the higher spiritual or divine consciousness.

higher mind — a luminous thought-mind whose instrumentation is through an elevated thought-power and comprehensive mental sight. The higher mind is the range of spiritualised mind just above the normal mind.

higher vital — the mental vital and emotional vital parts of the vital being taken together. The mental vital gives a mental expression by thought, speech or otherwise to the emotions, desires, passions, sensations or other movements of the vital being; the emotional vital is the seat of various feelings such as love, joy, sorrow, hatred and the rest.

hostile forces — anti-divine, not merely undivine forces that are in revolt against the Divine, against the Light and Truth, and opposed to the Yoga.

Ignorance, the — the ignorance of oneness; the separative consciousness and the egoistic mind and life that flow from it and all that is natural to them.

inconscience, the — *see* inconscient, the

inconscient, the — the Supreme's state of self-involved, self-oblivious consciousness and force which is at the basis of the material world.

inner being — the inner mind, inner vital, inner physical, with the psychic behind as the inmost.

inspiration — something that comes out of the knowledge planes like a flash and opens up the mind to the Truth in a moment.

integral — of or relating to all the parts of the being, mental, vital, physical, psychic, spiritual.

Integral Yoga — a union (yoga) in all the parts of our being with the Divine and a consequent transmutation of all their now jarring elements into the harmony of a higher divine consciousness and existence; this yoga implies not only the realisation of God but the entire consecration and change of the inner and outer life till it is fit to manifest a divine consciousness and become part of a divine work.

intuition — an edge or ray or outleap of a superior light; it gets the Truth in flashes and turns these flashes of Truth-perception into intuitions — intuitive ideas.

Karma — action, work; the work or function of a man; action entailing its consequences, the chain of act and consequence.

kartavyam karma — the work to be done.

Knowledge, the — the knowledge of the One Reality, the consciousness of Unity.

Life — Being at labour in Matter to express itself in terms of Conscious Force; an energy of Spirit subordinated to action of mind and body, which fulfils itself through mentality and physicality and acts as a link between them.

Light, the — primarily a spiritual manifestation of the Divine Reality illuminative and creative. Spiritual Light is not knowledge, but the illumination that comes from above and liberates the being from obscurity and darkness.

lower nature — the universal lower Nature is a mechanism of active Force put forth for the working of the evolutionary Ignorance. The lower nature of the individual is his mind, life and body.

lower vital — the part of the vital being made up of the smaller movements of human life-desire and life-reactions. The lower vital is occupied with small desires and feelings, such as food desire, sexual desire, small likings, dislikings, vanity, quarrels, love of praise, anger at blame, little wishes of all kinds, etc.

Mahabharata — the epic poem dealing with the great war between the Pandavas and the Kauravas.

Mahasaraswati — the Divine Mother's Power of Work and her spirit of perfection and order.

manifestation, the — *see* creation, the

mantra — set words or sounds having a spiritual significance or power; sacred syllable, name or mystic formula.

material vital — the part of the lower vital plane or being turned entirely to physical things, full of desires and greeds and seekings for pleasure on the physical plane.

Matter — Being manifest as substance; substance of the one Conscious Being; a form of the force of Conscious Being.

mental, the — *see* mind

mental being — the mental conscious being, the mental self.

mind — the part of the nature which has to do with cognition and intelligence, with ideas, with mental or thought perceptions, the reactions of thought to things, with the truly mental thoughts and formations, mental vision and will etc. that are part of man's intelligence. The ordinary mind has three main parts: mind proper, vital mind and physical mind.

Mother, the — the Divine Mother, the consciousness and force of the Divine, which is the Mother of all things; the Divine in its consciousness force. The Mother is the divine Conscious Force that dominates all existence, upholding us and the universe.

Nature — the outer or executive force of the Conscious Force which forms and moves the worlds; a mechanism of active Force put out for the working of the evolutionary Ignorance.

Nirvana — nothingness; the extinction of all being as we know it.

occultism — the knowledge and right use of the hidden forces of Nature.

overmental — of or relating to the Overmind.

Overmind — the highest plane of spiritualised mind. Full of lights and powers, the Overmind sees calmly, steadily, in great masses and extensions of space and time and relation; it creates and acts in the same way. The Overmind is a delegate of the Supermind, its delegate to the cosmic Ignorance.The Supermind is the total Truth-Consciousness; the Overmind draws down the truths separately and gives them a separate identity.

physical, the — the part of the individual nature which includes the physical body and the physical consciousness.

physical being — the physical conscious being; the physical self.

physical consciousness — the physical mind and the physical vital as well as the body consciousness proper.

physical mind — the part of the mind which is concerned with physical things only; limited by the physical view and experience of things, it mentalises the experience brought by the contact of outward life and things, but does not go beyond that.

plane — a level of world-existence; a world or level in the scale of being; a settled poise or world of existence and consciousness.

Pralaya — dissolution, disintegration, destruction; the end of a cycle of aeons;

the temporary disintegration of a universal form of existence and all the individual forms which move in its rounds.

Presence, the — the Divine Presence; the sense and perception of the Divine as a Being felt as present in one's existence and consciousness or in relation with it.

psychic — of or relating to the soul (as distinguished from the mind and vital). Used in the sense of the Greek word "psyche", meaning "soul", the term "psychic" refers to all the movements and experiences of the soul, those which rise from or directly touch the psychic being; it does not refer to all the more inward and all the abnormal experiences in which the mind and vital predominate.

psychic, the — the soul; the psychic essence; the psychic being.

psychic being — the evolving of the individual, the divine portion in him which evolves from life to life, growing by its experiences until it becomes a fully conscious being. From its place behind the heart centre, the psychic being supports the mind, life and body, aiding their growth and development.

Ramayana — the life-story of Rama, a celebrated epic poem of Valmiki.

realisation — the reception in the consciousness and the establishment there of the fundamental truths of the Divine.

rebirth — the evolution and growth of the individual into a more and more developed and perfect consciousness through a succession of lives on earth.

reincarnation — *see* rebirth

revelation — the direct sight, the direct hearing or the inspired memory of the Truth.

Rishi — seer, sage.

Sachchidananda — Sat-Chit-Ananda, the One Divine Being with a triple aspect of Existence (Sat), Consciousness (Chit) and Delight (Ananda). God is Sachchidananda.

sadhak — one who practises a spiritual discipline; one who is getting or trying to get spiritual realisation.

sadhana — spiritual practice or discipline; the practice of Yoga.

Samadhi — inner or yogic trance; the sanctuary or tomb of a saint.

sannyasi — an ascetic; one who has renounced the world.

Sat — Being, Existence; pure existence.

sattwic — of the nature of Sattwa, the quality of Nature that illumines and clarifies. Sattwa is the quality of light, harmony, purity and peace.

Self — the universal Spirit, the self-existent Being, the conscious essential Existence one in all.

Shakti — Force, Power; the Divine Power; the consciousness and force of the Divine.

siddhi — perfection, accomplishment of the aims of Yoga.

soul — the psychic essence; the divine element in the individual; a spark of the Divine that comes down into the manifestation to support the evolution of the individual. In the course of the evolution, the soul grows and evolves in the form of a soul-personality, the psychic being. The term "soul" is often used as a synonym for "psychic being".

Spirit — the Consciousness above mind; the Self which is always in oneness with the Divine.

spiritual — of the Spirit. All contacts with the Self, the Higher Consciousness, the Divine above are spiritual.

spiritualised mind — the higher ranges of mind overtopping our normal mind and leading to Supermind. These successive states, levels or graded powers of being are hidden in our own superconscient parts; in ascending order they are: Higher Mind, Illumined Mind, Intuitive Mind, Intuition and Overmind.

subconscient, the — a nether diminished consciousness which lies between the Inconscient and the conscious mind, life and body; it is an automatic, obscure, incoherent, half-unconscious realm in which light and consciousness can with difficulty come. The subconscient is not to be confused with the subliminal; the subconscient is that which is below the ordinary physical consciousness, the subliminal that which is behind and supports it.

subconscious, the — *see* subconscient, the

subliminal, the — the inner being taken in its entirety of inner mind, inner vital, inner physical, with the soul or psychic entity supporting them. The subliminal in man is the largest part of his nature; it is not subconscient, but conscient and greater than the waking consciousness.

subliminal being — *see* subliminal, the

subtle body — a subtler material existence behind our outer body which provides the substance not only of our physical but of our vital and mental sheaths.

subtle physical, the — the plane of consciousness closest to the physical; it may also be considered as a sub-plane of the physical with a vital and mental character.

superconscient, the — something above our present consciousness from which the higher consciousness comes down into the body; it includes the higher planes of mental being as well as the native heights of supramental and pure spiritual being.

superman — the intermediary being between man and the supramental being; the next superior type after man, he who will consciously evolve out of man, rise above ego and mind and possess himself universalised and divinised in a divine force, a divine love and joy and a divine knowledge.

Supermind — *see* Supramental, the

Supramental, the — the Supermind, the Truth-Consciousness, the highest divine consciousness and force operative in the universe. A principle of consciousness superior to mentality, it exists, acts and proceeds in the fundamental truth and unity of things and not like the mind in their appearances and phenomenal divisions. Its fundamental character is knowledge by identity, by which the Self is known, the Divine Sachchidananda is known, but also the truth of manifestation is known because this too is that.

supramental being — the spiritual being beyond the human being, possessed of the supramental consciousness and force, who shall impose on his mental, vital, bodily workings a higher law than that of the dividing mind.

Supreme, the — the transcendent Divine Being.

Titan — an Asura.

transformation — not just a change of consciousness, but the bringing down of the higher, divine consciousness and nature into the lower nature of mind, life and body, and the replacement of the lower by the higher.

Truth-Consciousness — the Supramental, the Supermind; the consciousness of essential truth of being (satyam), of ordered truth of active being (ritam) and the vast self-awareness (brihat) in which alone this consciousness is possible.

Upanishads — a class of Hindu sacred writings, regarded as the source of the Vedanta philosophy.

Veda — a generic name for the most ancient Indian sacred literature; the term "Veda" is sometimes reserved for the mantras or metrical hymns of the Rigveda.

Vedanta — a system of philosophy and spiritual discipline based on the Upanishads and teaching the culminating knowledge of the Absolute.

vital, the — the life-nature made up of desires, sensations, feelings, passions, energies of action, will of desire, reactions of the desire-soul of man and all that play of possessive and other related instincts, anger, greed, lust, etc. that belong to this field of nature. The vital has three main parts: the higher vital, the central vital or vital proper, and the lower vital being.

vital being — the vital conscious being, the vital self.

vital plane — the plane connected with the life-world or desire-world, a plane in which life and desire find their untrammelled play and their easy self-expression and from there throw their influences and formations on our outer life.

Will, the — the Divine Will, something that has descended here into the evolutionary world of Ignorance, standing at the back of things, pressing on the Darkness with its Light, leading things presently towards the best possible in the conditions of a world of Ignorance.

Witness, the — the witness consciousness calm and detached from the outer actions of Nature.

Yoga — union (yoga) with the Divine and the conscious seeking for this union. Yoga is in essence the union of the soul with the immortal being and consciousness and bliss of the Divine, effected through the human nature with a result of development into the divine nature of being.

Yogi — one who practises Yoga, but especially one who has attained the goal of Yoga and is already established in spiritual realisation.